ISBN 978-0-331-47328-5
PIBN 11190756

This book is a reproduction of an important historical work. Forgotten Books uses state-of-the-art technology to digitally reconstruct the work, preserving the original format whilst repairing imperfections present in the aged copy. In rare cases, an imperfection in the original, such as a blemish or missing page, may be replicated in our edition. We do, however, repair the vast majority of imperfections successfully; any imperfections that remain are intentionally left to preserve the state of such historical works.

DUKE UNIVERSITY ALUMNI REGISTER

Duke Campus Beautiful in Winter as well as in Summer

The above photograph showing part of the West Campus Dormitory Section was taken during the first snow of the Winter.

January, 1931

VOLUME XVII

NUMBER 1

Duke University Alumni Register

(Member of American Alumni Council)

Published at Durham, N. C., Every Month in the Year in the Interest of the University and the Alumni

| Volume XVII | January, 1931 | Number 1 |

In This Issue

Editor and Business Manager..................:....HENRY R. DWIRE, '02

Assistant Editors............................ELIZABETH ALDRIDGE, '24
ALBERT A. WILKINSON, '26

Advertising Manager...........................CHARLES A. DUKES, '29

TWO DOLLARS A YEAR   20 CENTS A COPY

ENTERED AS SECOND-CLASS MATTER AT THE POST-OFFICE AT
DURHAM, NORTH CAROLINA

More Duke Day News

Several pages in this issue of the REGISTER are devoted to news of Duke University Day, particularly the election of new officers by the various local alumni clubs. These officers are already busily engaged in the task of formulating and carrying out a worth-while program of alumni activities. They will have the cordial support of the Alumni Office of the University in their endeavors along that line.

List of Contributors

There have been quite a number of contributors to the General Alumni Fund since the list was last published. The names will appear in the February issue. It is the intention to publish the name of every individual who contributes to the fund in any amount, though in no case will the amount of the donation appear.

Others to Follow

The series of articles about the work along various lines of members of the Duke faculty is continued in this issue. Others will appear in the February and succeeding issues of the REGISTER. It is one of the chief desires of those in charge of this publication to keep the alumni in closer touch than they have ever been before with members of the Duke faculty and their achievements.

New Director of Athletics

This issue of the REGISTER contains another article about Wallace Wade, Duke's new director of athletics, together with some snapshots taken soon after his arrival on the Duke campus. Coach Wade has received a most cordial welcome from faculty, students and alumni. The REGISTER will keep the alumni posted from month to month on doings here in the realm of athletics as they develop under the leadership of Coach Wade.

The February Issue

The February issue of the REGISTER will contain some of the most interesting photographs yet taken on the Duke campuses, together with other features. Watch for it.

THE EDITOR.

BEACH SCENE

By Jacob Märis (1837-1899)

The painting shown in the photographic reproduction above is one of two presented to Duke University last year by the late C. C. Dula, of New York. Both are by famous artists. "Beach Scene," above, being by the Dutch artist, Jacob Märis. The other painting, "Tending the Flock," by Charles Emile Jacque, famous painter of animals of the nineteenth century, was reproduced in a photograph in the REGISTER several months ago.

Jacob Maris, painter of "Beach Scene," was the eldest of three brothers, all famous artists. After some experience in France he returned to his native Holland where he spent his life chiefly at the Hague. There he studied and painted what he saw about him. The picture shown above is an admirable example of one particular group of his work called the strand pictures. The vessel is benched at low tide with sail down and anchor out; close to its right side is a cart drawn by a gray horse into which the crew are transferring the cargo.

The two paintings given by Mr. Dula, a note about whose recent death appears in this issue of the REGISTER, are hanging in the large public room of the library on the East Campus.

Duke University Alumni Register

| Volume XVII | January, 1931 | Number 1 |

Editorial Comment

"FOLLOWING UP"

Notably successful Duke University Day observances were held in thirty-six cities in North Carolina and other states on December 11.

At these meetings former students of Duke discussed the institution's past, present and future, and pledged renewed allegiance to Alma Mater.

There was in evidence a determination on the part of alumni generally to show their loyalty to Duke, not simply by talking of their love for the University but by showing that devotion in deeds as well as in words.

It would be indeed unfortunate if the enthusiasm in evidence on Duke University Day should be allowed to lag.

In every alumni club there should be a definite "follow up" campaign with the purpose in view of conserving that enthusiasm and translating it into terms of service for Alma Mater.

No alumnus should wait until another Duke Day rolls around to show his interest in things pertaining to Duke.

There are numerous things that can be done by individual alumni and local groups in the interest of Duke at this vitally important period in its history.

It is earnestly to be hoped that every such opportunity will be eagerly seized.

A GOOD SUGGESTION

Speaking of "follow up" activities, the president of one alumni club in a large city has made a request that contains an excellent suggestion for local groups generally.

He has asked for the names and addresses of Duke students in that particular area so that it may be possible for his alumni club to keep in touch with them and with their fathers and mothers, writing at intervals to the students, letting them know that the association is interested in them, watching their careers and looking forward to welcoming them into the association when they shall have completed their courses of study.

In that way the interest in the institution of all three groups will be accentuated.

Why would it not be a good idea for every alumni group to do something of this kind?

The Alumni Office will be glad to furnish information to local clubs that will enable them to keep in constant touch with Duke students and with their parents.

This is one of the best services that an alumni organization can render.

EXCELLENT EXAMPLE

The organization of the new Japan Alumni Association of Duke University, the first to be formed in a country outside the United States, is significant in a number of ways.

For one thing, it indicates very clearly that a mere matter of thousands of miles in distance is not sufficient to cause the affections of Duke alumni to grow cold.

The fact that some of those at the alumni meeting in Kobe on December 12 had to travel long distances in order to get there is worthy of note.

And that as Duke graduates are going more and more to the far corners of the earth to render service to humanity they still want to keep in touch with Alma Mater and to contribute to its alumni activities, is a cause for congratulation.

It is interesting, too, to note that at their very first meeting they outlined a definite program of work.

There is something in the example set by this alumni group in far-off Japan that should provide a suggestion for us here at home.

If they can show sufficient interest in Duke to have a meeting under difficult conditions and to make a sacrifice to help the institution though far removed from the scene of its activities, how can anyone over here justify an attitude of neglect or at least indifference?

There is something in the example of that little group in Japan that should be a constant inspiration to alumni in this country.

A DEFINITE PROGRAM

Those in the Alumni Office have been cheered very much recently by some of the letters received from the newly elected heads of local alumni groups.

A number of these letters indicate that the groups in question are planning a definite program for the year.

In addition to meeting on Duke University Day and extolling the glories of Duke, they are going to work along definite, positive lines with the constant desire to be helpful.

Every group that tries such a plan is sure to find it stimulating and beneficial.

There is nothing better calculated to keep up one's interest in a cause than to give him some work to do in behalf of that cause.

If this definite program of work idea is generally carried out by local clubs, the work of preparing for Duke Day observances on December 11 next will be greatly simplified.

THERE SHOULD BE OTHERS

"I am not able to give a great deal to the alumni work," writes one loyal alumnus of Duke, "but I am certainly going to avail myself of the privilege of having some part in what is going on there by sending the price of a subscription to the ALUMNI REGISTER. I can certainly do that much."

There are doubtless many other alumni who are sufficiently interested in the effort to make the REGISTER a constantly better alumni magazine, to do likewise.

We do not want to be continually talking about money in the REGISTER, but it cannot be out of place again to remind Duke alumni that considerable money is yet needed if there is not to be a deficit this year in the Alumni Fund.

Just the price of a $2 subscription to the ALUMNI REGISTER will help very much.

Of course, it is earnestly hoped that all who can contribute more will do so, but don't hold back for fear your small donation will not be worth sending.

Any amount will be gratefully received.

THIRTIETH YEAR

Alumni of Duke University are sure to be interested in the fact that this institution has in the *South Atlantic Quarterly,* which entered its thirtieth year with the January issue, one of the oldest publications of its kind in the South, or in the entire country for that matter.

Launched in 1902 by the late Dr. John Spencer Bassett through the agency of the 9019, the publication has given an exceptional opportunity for expression in the realms of literature, economics, history and other fields.

Many alumni already read the *South Atlantic Quarterly.*

Many others should avail themselves of the opportunity it provides to read thoughtful articles on timely subjects and at the same time to aid in perpetuating and developing to still greater importance a Southern journal devoted to scholarship and culture and the discussion of timely subjects.

WHY NOT SEVERAL MORE?

Seven new Duke University alumni clubs were organized in 1930.

There are now fifty-four local groups.

Why not make it at least sixty by Commencement, 1931, with several more to be added by Duke University Day?

Of course, there is no virtue in organizing weak alumni groups just to be able to say we have a certain number of associations.

But the alumni records show that we have former Duke students in practically every state of the Union and in twenty-one foreign countries. Why not have more local clubs?

Officers Elected at the Duke Day Meetings Already at Work

Reports From Various Alumni Groups Indicate That They Are Starting New Year With Renewed Enthusiasm—Letter From Dr. J. F. Crowell One of Features of New York Meeting—"High Spots" of Various December 11, 1930, Gatherings Recalled

THE observance on December 11 of Duke University Day, referred to briefly in the December REGISTER, was notable in various respects. First, there was in evidence in each of the thirty-six meetings held in North Carolina and other states (and one outside of the United States, in Japan), a fine spirit of enthusiasm and loyalty. Then, too, meetings were held in a number of places for the first time and at least five new alumni-groups were organized, to be added to the forty-nine already in existence, one of these being the new Japan Alumni Association. Other new alumni clubs included those formed in Los Angeles, Cal., Jacksonville, Fla., Lynchburg, Va., and Columbia, S. C., a state group being organized in the latter city to include all Duke alumni in South Carolina. There are now fifty-four local alumni clubs, seven organized during 1930.

At practically all of the thirty-six meetings officers were elected for the ensuing year, and all have started out with an enthusiasm that augurs well for the success of the work of the Alumni Association in the months ahead. Not only did the speakers at these various meetings discuss in a general way the progress of Duke University in recent years but interesting references were made to the importance of the pioneer work done by Braxton Craven and other great leaders in the cause of education who have been associated with the institution in the different periods of its history. Specific attention was called to a number of questions that are being asked from time to time by alumni and others, and definite answers were given to these. The occasion was an unusual opportunity for bringing the institution and alumni closer together on a basis of mutual understanding and interest, and from this as well as other standpoints, the observance of December 11 was notably successful.

An Ideal for Duke

As December 11, 1930, was the sixth anniversary of the signing of the Indenture of Trust making possible Duke University, naturally prominent reference was made to that document in the various meetings held on Duke University Day, and particularly to the following sentences in which Mr. James B. Duke outlined the ideal he cherished for the institution:

"I have selected Duke University as one of the principal objects of this trust because I recognize that education, when conducted along sane and practical, as opposed to dogmatic and theoretical lines, is, next to religion, the greatest civilizing influence. I request that this institution secure for its officers, trustees and faculty men of such outstanding character, ability and vision as will insure its attaining and maintaining a place of real leadership in the educational world, and that great care and discrimination be exercised in admitting as students only those whose previous record shows a character, determination and application evincing a wholesome and real ambition for life. And I advise that the courses at this institution be arranged, first, with special reference to the training of preachers, teachers, lawyers and physicians, because these are most in the public eye, and by precept and example can do most to uplift mankind; and second, to instruct in chemistry, economics and history, especially the lives of the great of earth, because I believe that such subjects will most help to develop our resources, increase our wisdom, and promote human happiness."

New York City

An address by President W. P. Few featured a largely attended meeting of Duke University alumni in the New York area, held at dinner at the Hotel Astor on December 11. Dr. Few spoke interestingly and impressively of the development of a real university and of some of the problems confronting those engaged in such an enterprise, with particular reference to the situation at Duke. (Dr. Few's address in part appears elsewhere in this issue of the REGISTER.)

Dr. George B. Pegram, of Columbia University, made a brief talk and read a letter he had received from Dr. John F. Crowell, former president of Trinity College, expressing regret that he could not accept the invitation of the dinner committee to be present. Heywood Broun, well-known newspaper writer, spoke briefly.

New officers of the New York Alumni Club were elected as follows: President, Harden F. Taylor; vice-president, E. B. McCullen; secretary, James J. Farriss; treasurer, J. Murray.

The letter from Dr. Crowell, written from his home at East Orange, N. J., follows:

"Ordinarily, it would give me extraordinary pleasure to share the hospitality of the Duke Alumni Association at the Old Astor where I have dined so often and so delightfully in the past twenty years. But I must, under doctor's orders, forego this with other winter dinners for this year, at least. It is a real sacrifice to be absent, I can but assure you. Yet, I rejoice in the magnificent outlook for that grand chain of institutional achievements extending from Brantley York's Academy to the rapidly unfolding Duke University. For the past few years I have not been idle, even though passing three score and ten. In my library portfolio lies a copy in manuscript entitled 'Personal Recollections of Trinity College, North Carolina, 1887-1894' in thirty-three chapters with one or two more to follow. This work gripped me so fully as to put me into bed for six months. Now that I am 'rebuilt' I am taking my work less intensively, upon advice of knowing and well-wishing ones. What do I do? After having spent forty years in the hardest kind of hard tasks in education, in government, in finance, etc., I confess to this truth, that I indulge myself in writing poetry. If all goes as I plan, I hope to publish before many months a collection of occasional poems numbering twenty-five or more under the title 'Twilight and Paradise.' They treat of youth, of the revival of spirituality in the life of Christendom and of man's expending outlook upon human existence and beyond. Ambitious enough, you would say. Yet, any attempt to express life in its largeness and fullness must be ambitious.

"Please give my kindest regards to the whole fellowship which may gather at your dinner on the eleventh. I cherish the bonds that bind us into cultural comradeship. For youth is dearer than ever to me, dearer because it loves and strives for the truth as the worth-while thing in life. I pray for it and that it may increasingly

"'Think less by the creed of claw and tooth
Love more in the service of the Spirit of Truth.'"

Richmond-Petersburg

The annual dinner of the Duke Alumni Club of Richmond-Petersburg was held at the Hotel Richmond on December 11. Wade H. Adams was toastmaster for the occasion.

Dr. R. L. Flowers, treasurer of Duke University, spoke most impressively of the development of the institution, particularly emphasizing the work of the liberal arts college and making it plain that in the development of the institution in its graduate and professional school work and along the lines of research and investigation, there would be no lessening of emphasis upon the work of the college, that still being regarded as the heart of the institution.

Dr. Benjamin R. Lacy, of Union Theological Seminary, and Rev. Costen J. Harrell, of the Richmond alumni group, made brief talks during the evening.

At the business meeting following the dinner officers were elected as follows: President, Costen J. Harrell; vice-president, Lillian M. Froste; secretary-treasurer, Claiborne E. Brogden.

Washington, D. C.

The meeting of the Washington club was held at the University Club at dinner. All of the alumni present told of their experiences while at Duke or Trinity. Senator Lee S. Overman had sent flowers for the dinner and had reserved a plate for the occasion, but was taken ill and passed away during the night.

New officers were elected as follows: President, Colonel Daniel C. Roper; vice-president, Richard E. Thigpen; secretary-treasurer, Miss Jane Elizabeth Newton, who served in this capacity during the past year. Hon. John H. Small, former president of the General Alumni Association, presided at the dinner.

Los Angeles, Cal.

The first meeting of Duke University alumni ever to be held in Los Angeles, Cal., was in connection with a Duke University Day dinner at 2228 West Seventh Street at 6:30 p. m. There was a good attendance and much enthusiasm.

Dr. Garland Greever presided at the dinner. Each person present gave a short account of his or her activities since leaving college. The speaker of the occasion was Dr. F. C. Baxter, of the department of English of the University of Southern California, who gave an entertaining account of his experiences as a student at Oxford, making comparisons with American institutions of learning. Attention was given during the evening to Duke University, its past achievements and present accomplishments.

An alumni club for the Los Angeles area was organized with Dr. Garland Greever, A.M., '05, president; W. Roy Shelton '16, vice-president; Myron G. Ellis, '16, secretary.

Columbia, S. C.

An organization to be known as the Duke University Alumni Association of South Carolina was perfected at a meeting of Duke alumni from various parts of that state, held at a dinner at the Jefferson Hotel on Duke University Day.

Before the organization was effected the matter was enthusiastically discussed and expressions from all the alumni present were to the effect that an organization should be formed.

The following were elected officers for the coming year and during the year will endeavor to enlist as members all of the South Carolina alumni: President, S. B. Moyle, Columbia; vice-president, Ernest J. Green, Columbia College; secretary-treasurer, Miss Gladys White, Rock Hill, S. C.

Roanoke, Va.

The first meeting of Duke alumni to be held in Roanoke, Va., was at a dinner at Hotel Roanoke, with Robert Lee Durham, president of Southern Seminary at Buena Vista, as toastmaster. Professor B. G. Childs, of the department of education, was the principal speaker and discussed "Duke University: Our Opportunity and Responsibility."

"Your alma mater has been, during her years of existence, an indomitable personality inspired by a deep sense of her debt of service to mankind," said Professor Childs.

"There are high days in the history of our country and of every institution, but December 11, 1924, was in reality a high day for the South and the nation, for on that day the great wealth of the Duke family was placed at the disposal of humanity. This was one of the most remarkable philanthropic ventures in the history of the world."

In conclusion, Professor Childs said: "Let me say that the real obligation and the real privilege which your alma mater gives you is that of service to humanity. We have builded our institution, not that she may be self-sufficient nor that she may be a thing of glory in herself; rather she has given to you the opportunity and yours is the responsibility to serve."

Jacksonville, Fla.

H. R. Mahoney, Jacksonville business man, was elected president of the Alumni Club of Duke University organized in the Florida city at the George Washington Hotel on the evening of Duke University Day. James M. Oliver was elected vice-president and Mrs. Julian W. Wallace, secretary-treasurer.

Speakers of the evening included Dr. S. H. C. Burgin, of the General Hospital Board of the Methodist Episcopal Chuch, South; Rev. Philip B. Trigg, '18; Weaver M. Marr, '10; and H. R. Mahoney, '08·

Lynchburg, Va.

Alumni of the Lynchburg area met at the Virginian Hotel for a banquet in observance of Duke University Day. Professor J. M. Ormond, of the department of sociology, represented the University and spoke of the opportunties of the institution, pointing out that its magnificent material structure lay upon it the burden of performing a great task for the country. He said the outstanding opportunity of the institution lies in the moral, social and religious development of the South, along with which opportunities comes the responsibility of producing a cultural civilization upon which all educational progress must be built.

Invited guests included Dr. D. R. Anderson, president of Randolph-Macon Woman's College, who spoke of the cordial relations existing between his school and Duke; Dr. John William Smith, pastor of Centenary Methodist Church; and Dr. A. M. Stowe, of Randolph-Macon's Woman's College, who has taught in the summer school of Duke University for several sessions.

A permanent organization was effected with the following officers: Carl H. King, president; Miss Rose Davis, vice-president; J. J. Thaxton, secretary-treasurer; Mrs. Carl H. King, representative on the alumnae council.

St. Petersburg, Fla.

The St. Petersburg, Fla., club of Duke alumni, organized last spring, observed Duke University Day in a most delightful manner with a dinner and dance at Club Brisa Del Mar. There was a good attendance and the evening was spent most delightfully in talking about Duke and the notable developments in progress there.

Officers of the St. Petersburg club are as follows: Mrs. James Bourne, president; Clifton A. Veasey, secretary-treasurer.

Atlanta, Ga.

The meeting of the Duke Alumni Club of Atlanta was held at the Atlanta Athletic Club at dinner on the evening of December 3. President W. P. Few, Dr. W. K. Greene, and Dr. Holland Holton represented the University and talked of its opportunities and responsibilities in a most effective way. A delightful spirit of good fellowship was in evidence and the meeting served effectively to pave the way for a larger meeting of the Atlanta group to be held at a later date.

Officers were elected as follows: E. Ralph Paris, president; H. A. Sigman, vice-president; Dr. N. T. Teague, secretary-treasurer.

Nashville, Tenn.

Dr. W. I. Cranford, professor of philosophy, was the speaker at the dinner meeting of the alumni in the Nashville area on the evening of Duke University Day. The second oldest man connected with Duke in point of years of service to the institution, he was able to present in a most effective way the new Duke and its development with a background of many years of experience in the life of Trinity College. A number of those in the dinner group were former students of Dr. Cranford, and the meeting had much in the nature of an old-time reunion.

The meeting was held at the Noel Hotel.

The officers for the coming year are L. W. Crawford, president; Miss Mamie L. Newman, secretary.

Those present included Dr. Bruce R. Payne, '96, Hon. LL.D., '17, president George Peabody College for Teachers; Dr. W. F. Tillett, Dean Emeritus of the Vanderbilt School of Religion, ex-'75; Dr. Edwin Mims, professor of English, Vanderbilt University, formerly professor of English at Duke; Dr. Leonidas W. Crawford, '98, professor of Religious Education, George Peabody College; Rev. J. Marvin Culbreth, '00, secretary of the Board of Christian Education; Dr. Dennis H. Cook, '25, professor of education, George Peabody College; Miss Mamie L. Newman, '12, associate professor of home economics, George Peabody College; Miss Ida Z. Carr, '96, assistant professor of home economics, George Peabody College; Dr. H. C. Sprinkle, '24, editorial department, Board of Christian Education, M. E. Church, South; John D. Freeman, Jr., A.M., '13, editor; Hoy Taylor, '06, graduate student, George Peabody College; Blanche Henry Clark, '27, teacher of history, Ward Belmont School. Wives included Mrs. L. W. Crawford, Mrs. H. C. Sprinkle, '24, Mrs. Hoy Taylor.

Raleigh

Dean W. H. Wannamaker was the speaker representing Duke University at the dinner of the alumni of Wake and Franklin counties, held in the Woman's Club building. Duke graduates and former students from these counties combined in what was one of the best meetings yet held by the two groups.

Dean Wannamaker told the alumni of the progress of the University, discussing its work in its various phases and talking especially of the student body. His long connection with the institution as a member of the faculty and as dean made his remarks of particular interest, both to Duke alumni of recent years and of an earlier period in the life of the institution as well.

Samuel W. Ruark, Raleigh attorney, was elected to succeed Alf Templeton as president of the Wake County Alumni Club. Banks Arendell was chosen vice-president, and Dr. Kemp Neal secretary-treasurer.

Albemarle

Dr. Gilbert T. Rowe, of the faculty of the Duke School of Religion, was the speaker at the annual banquet of Stanly-Anson-Montgomery alumni, held at Albemarle. He traced the history of Duke University from its beginning—Union Institute, declaring that "integrity based on faith" had carried the institution through the years.

The toastmaster was Charles A. Reap, and the speaker of the evening was introduced by J. F. Shinn, of Norwood.

John B. Harris was elected president of the club; Miss Dorothy Huneycutt, who has been secretary for the past year, was reëlected.

After speaking interestingly of the other days of the institution, Dr. Rowe discussed the present developments. "The faculty of Duke University is in mind to keep spiritual values first," declared Dr. Rowe. He added that the three things of importance, which mean most to a University and which may be found at Duke, are religious devotion, fidelity to truth and academic freedom.

Charlotte

In speaking to the Mecklenburg alumni of Duke at a banquet held at the Selwyn Hotel, Dr. J. Fred Rippy pointed out indications that Duke University of the future will lay chief emphasis on the study of man and society. "A university to be truly great," he said, "should lay emphasis on some one tihng, however intangible. There are signs on the Duke campus of some such emphasis. It may be that it will be an emphasis on the study of man and his relations to society."

Dr. Rippy declared that man had conquered his physical environment but he is yet to conquer himself. The study of man and groups of men has been neglected during this materialistic age, he said. He declared that it would be a fine thing that Duke in its march to greatness held this one dominating object in view.

Dr. Rippy presented interesting facts regarding the University and spoke in a most interesting way of its past achievements, its present activities and its future promise. He gave some interesting figures showing the reasonable cost of education at Duke.

Adopting a report to the nominating committee made by Chairman John Paul Lucas, the following officers were named: Henry Fisher, president; Mrs. Bailey T. Groome, vice-president; Marshall Pickens, secretary-treasurer; Mrs. Edwin Jones, alumnae council representative.

George Ivey was toastmaster and presented Dr. Rippy. He read a letter from Wallace Wade expressing regret at his inability to be present.

Concord

Former students of Duke now residing in Cabarrus County met at Hotel Concord, heard references to the Trinity College of the past and optimistic predictions for the Duke of the future and then named officers to head the Cabarrus club for the coming year.

A. G. Odell, retiring president, presided at the meeting, and S. Glenn Hawfield had charge of the speaking program.

After an invocation by Rev. J. A. Baldwin, a most delightful dinner was served, and the tables were decorated with handsome flowers, given for the occasion by Mrs. J. C. Query. Duke songs were sung in which those present joined with enthusiasm.

(Continued on page 23)

Japan Alumni Association First Duke Group Overseas

Organized in Kobe on December 12 at Luncheon Attended by Former Duke Students From Various Points in Japan—Program For Club Discussed—Donation Made to Alumni Fund

THE first Duke University alumni group to be formed outside the United States is the Japan Alumni Association, which was organized at Kobe on December 12, 1930, at a luncheon held at noon. (This corresponds to 10 p.m. December 11, at Duke University—on "Duke University Day.").

Nine alumni gathered at the Kobe meeting, only four of the group residing in Kobe, however. It was necessary for the others to travel long distances to attend the meeting, two coming from other islands.

The following officers were elected for the ensuing year: President, Rev. Zensuke Hinohara; secretary, Mrs. J. Doane Stott.

After election of officers, those present discussed ways and means whereby members of the association might render service to Alma Mater. Among other things discussed was the collection of documents and books for the Duke University library; the possibility of exchanging students between Duke and Kwansei Gakuin, and a contribution to the alumni fund. Before the meeting adjourned the sum of thirteen dollars was collected for the fund. The secretary was authorized to send this amount to the Alumni Secretary, and inquire through the same office if Lafcadio Hearn's set of books on Japan is in the library.

The following members were present: Rev. Zensuke Hinohara, '04, Hiroshima Girls' School, Hiroshima, Japan; Rev. Tokio Kugimiya, '03, Toyonaka, Osaka Fu; Rev. N. S. Ogburn, '05, Kwansei Gakuin, Goto Mura, Nishinomiya Shigai, Japan; Rev. I. L. Shaver, '19, Kanaya, Morino Cho, Nakatsu, Oita Ken, Japan; Mr. Tatsuo Momosake, '23, Miyagawcho, Kobe, Japan; Rev. J. W. Frank, '28, Uwajima, Japan; Rev. J. Doane Stott, '23, 24 Nakayamate Dori, 2 Chome, Kobe, Japan; Mrs. J. Doane Stott, '30, 24 Nakayamate Dori, 2 Chome, Kobe, Japan; Miss Kimiko Yamanishi, '30, 35 Nakayamate Dori, 4 Chome, Kobe, Japan.

Other members of the alumni group in Japan include the following: Prof. Kuninoshin Kodama, '20, Hiroshima Girls' School, Hiroshima, Japan; Rev. Isao Tanaka, '20, Central Methodist Church, Souel, Korea; Mr. Yasuzo Yagi, '05, Chikara Machi, Nagoya, Japan; Mr. Minosuke Uematsu, '04, Tokyo, Japan.

Standing left to right: Rev. N. S. Ogburn, Rev. Tokio Kugimiya, Rev. J. Doane Stott, Mr. Tatsuo Momosake, Rev. I. L. Shaver.
Sitting left to right: Rev. Zensuke Hinohara, Miss Kimiko Yamanishi, Mrs. J. D. Stott, Rev. J. W. Frank.

President Few Discusses Duke's Ideals at Dinner in New York

"We Are Trying to Proceed in the Light of the Best that Experience Has Taught," He Declares—Conceives of Duke as University That Is in No Sense a Copy of Any Existing Institutions But Not Out of Line With the Best Educational Traditions or Best Tendencies of Our Time

DR. W. P. FEW, President of Duke University, addressing the New York Duke Alumni at the Astor Hotel, Thursday night, December 11, spoke in part as follows:

It has been six years today since the late James B. Duke signed the Indenture of Trust by which Duke University was created. Within this period there has been a good deal of discussion (and some of it has found its way into print) as to whether there is in the southeastern section of the United States a climate of opinion that will sustain a great endowed university. Meanwhile Duke, through its construction and organization program, has steadily gone forward with the building of a university that is in no sense a copy of any existing institution but that is not out of line with the best educational traditions or the best educational tendencies of our time.

I am happy to be able to report that all this has gone on, some of it far-reaching and in its implications involving much that has been characteristic of southern civilization, without any undue interference from local public opinion and wholly uninterrupted by gusts of unwisdom that are apt to arise from time to time in any democracy. With this experience in mind and with a like experience through many years in the history of Trinity College, which is now a part of Duke University, I am ready to say that I believe Duke is no more apt to suffer from an unwholesome climate of opinion than are universities in other parts of America. On the other hand, located as it is in a part of the country that is now in the midst of its building era, this university might conceivably have an unusual chance to produce creative rather than merely critical attitudes of mind, if this distinction will pass muster, and I realize that it may be more a matter of emphasis than an essential difference in type of mind. From this standpoint, Duke University is not only an educational adventure; it is a social experiment of wide significance, and as such it is attracting and will continue to attract the attention of enlightened men throughout the country.

We have received a great deal of advice especially as to the general type of university that we should undertake to build. We have not been able to take it all, but we are grateful for it all. We are trying to proceed in the light of the best that experience has taught. Duke aspires to be not a sectional but a national university. Indeed it is already a national university in its standards and ideals and in the fact that its teachers and students come from all parts of America. But in our undertakings we cannot wholly overlook the circumstance that we are located in the South and owe it certain duties and kinds of special service. We are therefore not altogether as free as would be a new endowed university here in the East, where there are many others in the field, to make experiments involving the university as a whole. The physical sciences get a disproportionate emphasis in American civilization and American education. There ought to be here universities that place their major emphasis on the humanities, and others that stress the sciences of man as over against the sciences of nature. It has occurred to a good many thoughtful people that Duke should become a university of this specialized type. Duke should be adequately equipped for research in the human sciences, but I prefer to see this done in an institute within the university rather than undertake to develop a specialized university. The South has not yet made its due contribution towards scientific research and the scientific spirit, and so has lagged not only in its material but also in its social and political development. Duke must try to do its part at this point and at the same time strive to become a home of idealism.

Most of you are graduates of the College and will naturally be interested to know what are our plans for it. We inherited Trinity College with all its traditions and its alumni, and it is one of our major purposes to make it as strong as it can be made, and to keep it always at the heart of Duke University. Three of the ways by which we are seeking to do this are briefly (1) selective admission, (2) adequate provision for bright and ambitious students, and (3) a vigorous and persistent effort to procure or develop college teachers who have personality and teaching power as well as knowledge of their several subjects.

And what about athletics? As you know, our teams this year have been uncommonly successful. We have the most beautiful stadium I have ever seen, an abundance of playing fields, and in a campus of five thousand acres, opportunities for everybody in all forms of sports and wholesome physical living. We have as competent staff in physical training as we can procure. But let no one fear that we are going to overemphasize intercollegiate athletics. We are trying to make provision for the physical well-being of all the students, and on this wide foundation we hope to see developed reasonably successful intercollegiate sports.

It is well known that for twenty-five years our college had no football or other highly competitive games. Following the World War, we allowed football to come back and in the intervening decade we have been gradually developing a system of intercollegiate athletics. At Duke we have therefore had unusual opportunities to test in practical experience both sides of the much discussed subject of intercollegiate games. As for me I now believe we made a mistake in banning football for a quarter of a century. To be sure, American colleges have left athletics and other non-academic activities of undergraduates too much to haphazard development, and these have often gone to extremes. But organized sports have on the whole more good than bad in them; and they need guidance rather than mere repression.

It is said that if the temperature of the ocean were raised, the water would expand and rise to a new level that would flood the dry land. I believe that by improving the quality of education, we could so change the temperature of the American college campus that a rising tide of intellectual interest might lift the whole level of undergraduate life and from this new level new currents of tendency and taste would sweep the centre of student activities away from excessive devotion to athletics and other equally irrelevant undergraduate absorptions and on to the main concerns of college education. Thus we may find a surer and better way than by force of authority or even by mere repression, to rescue our colleges from a situation for which the graduates and the general public are more responsible than the undergraduates but of which the undergraduates are the victims.

Duke Alumnus Loses His Life in Effort to Save Others

CECIL CORNWELL, prominent young business man of Gastonia, member of the class of 1921 at Duke, met a tragic death in that city on December 16, 1930, as a result of asphyxiation to which he later succumbed when a gas main burst while he was supervising the installation of gas connections in a Gastonia residence.

Called to the scene of the accident from his office as manager of the Gastonia and Suburban Gas Company, Mr. Cornwell literally sacrificed his life in order that his workmen might be saved. His heroic conduct saved the lives of numbers of men, though one other associate met death in the accident.

Cecil Cornwell was born in Gaston County on January 29, 1900, a son of the late C. C. Cornwell, for many years clerk of the court in that county. He is survived by his mother, Mrs. C. C. Cornwell, of Dallas, with whom he lived, and also by two sisters, Mrs. W. S. Barfield, of Gastonia, and Mrs. Emil Merz, of Oakland, California, and two brothers, Messrs. L. C. Cornwell, of Rutherford College, and M. L. Cornwell, of Newton.

Mr. Cornwell had been manager of the gas company for the past eight years. In 1928 and 1929 he was called to the Chicago offices of his company where he was engaged in the important work of taking inventory of the company's offices and properties throughout the country.

A consistently loyal alumnus of Duke University, Cecil Cornwell with his affable personality was one of the most popular young business men in Gastonia. He was active in the affairs of the Chamber of Commerce, Lions Club, and the American Legion, and his untimely death is mourned by a host of friends.

The Gastonia *Gazette* had an editorial immediately following Mr. Cornwell's death, expressing appreciation of his many fine qualities and admiration of the heroic act which led to his death.

Duke University Pays a Tribute to Late Senator Lee S. Overman

Fitting Memorial Services In York Chapel Featured By Impressive Address By Dr. R. L.
Flowers, In Which He Emphasizes Human Qualities of the Late Duke
Alumnus and Trustee and the Idealism of His Life

THE Duke University community paid a tribute to the institution's late alumnus and trustee and one of its most devoted friends, Senator Lee S. Overman, in a memorial service held in York Chapel a few days after his death. The occasion was featured by a sympathetic and fitting tribute by Dr. R. L. Flowers, treasurer of the University, who was a close friend of Senator Overman.

A letter was read from Mrs. Overman expressing regret at the inability of herself and other members of the family to attend because of a snowstorm which began just as they were preparing to leave for Durham. An appropriate program of music preceded Dr. Flowers' address. Dean Elbert Russell, of the School of Religion, conducted the devotional service.

Dr. Flowers spoke as follows:

"It is very fitting that we should meet this morning as members of the University community to pay tribute to a distinguished graduate of our institution; to a loyal alumnus, and a diligent member of the Board of Trustees. Lee Slater Overman, United States Senator from North Carolina since 1903, died in Washington City last Thursday and was buried in Salisbury on Saturday, accompanied to his last resting place by representatives of the national and state governments and by a host of friends and admirers.

"It is not possible to evaluate a life until it is finished, and even then there must be left to future historians and students the task of estimating the permanent values. When we stand close to the grave, it is not easy to have a proper perspective. This is not the time nor the place to undertake to recount the positions of honor and responsibility Senator Overman occupied in the state and nation, nor the part he played in legislation which affected our state and nation in the last half century. All these are part of the record which he left. He was elected to the United States Senate in 1903, and remained in office until the day of his death. During the administration of President Wilson, and especially during the tragic period of the World War, he won the admiration of the President, who during the campaign of

1914 wrote as follows: 'I take it for granted that the voters of North Carolina will not deprive themselves of the distinguished services of Senator Overman in the Senate of the United States, but I want to give myself the pleasure of paying my tribute to him as a man of principle and the highest public spirit, and of expressing my sincere hope that endorsement given him by the voters at the approaching election may be of the highest kind.'

"He served well his day and generation, and in his long public career there was never in his private or official life anything that reflected on the integrity of his character or tended to besmirch his good name. "When the degree of Doctor of Laws was conferred on him in 1916, President Few said: 'Lee Slater Overman, member of the class of '74, beginning his career as private secretary to Governor Vance and continuously in the service of his people; United States Senator since 1903 and two years ago unanimously nominated and duly elected for another term; a statesman who has thought straight in a time of confusion and in the midst of all the mire and poisons of political life has kept himself singularly devoted to the public good.'

"But after all it is not on the official life of Senator Overman that I wish to dwell, but on the human qualities and the idealism of his life. He was well born and well bred and no honors that could come to him ever caused him to be anything but the lovable man that he was. He made friends with the great and the lowly, with the young and the old, with the rich and the poor. When their colleagues in the Senate last February paid a tribute to Senators Overman and Simmons on their seventy-sixth anniversary, Senator Walsh of Massachusetts said of Senator Overman: 'To me he typifies more than any other Senator the picture we are apt to have of the old Roman, toga-clad Senator—dignified, courtly, courteous. He represents by his very countenance the best type of an American Senator of our age. Visitors to the gallery point him out as a man of distinguished bearing. And he has not only looked the part, he has acted it.

Every Senator loves him and esteems him as a friend, and a good fighter, too.'

"Senator Overman's love for his Alma Mater was one of the most significant things in his life. . He was interested in everything connected with its growth and development. He never missed a meeting of the Board of Trustees unless his duties in Washington prevented him from attending. In looking over the records of the Alumni Office, the files show that he kept in close touch with the Alumni Secretary and he contributed to every enterprise undertaken by the Alumni organization.

"A few days ago an intimate friend of Senator Overman and his family for many years visited Salisbury, and afterwards sent to the University the following human interest statement which I take the liberty of reading to you this morning:

" 'It is significant that Senator Lee Slater Overman, distinguished alumnus of Duke University, died on the morning of Duke Day, when banquet meetings of alumni were held in many cities and towns throughout the state and elsewhere.

" 'Senator Overman was a loyal son of Trinity College and frequently voiced his love and admiration for the college and its larger successor, Duke University. During his career he often referred with pride to his connection with the institution.

" 'Only recently before his death, he had told relatives that he would rather be a trustee of Duke University than hold almost any other office in the country. He was enthusiastic in his compliments for the new buildings at the enlarged campus, which he visited some weeks ago.

" 'The Senator selected Duke hospital for his brother, Ed Overman, of Salisbury, during the fall, when the latter was considered desperately ill. Since the treatment there had restored the brother to health and strength, he had been even more loud in his praise of Duke.

" 'Whenever there was any news in the newspapers about Duke University, the Senator always called for a reading of the entire article, according to his beloved daughter, Mrs. Edwin G. Gregory, who read the papers to him daily during his residence in Salisbury. She says that he never wanted to miss a sentence of any article about his Alma Mater and listened intently even to all lists of names or figures connected with the institution.'

"He was a Christian gentleman. He represented the best in our Southern life. His whole career reflected credit and honor on his College. We grieve at his death, but we are proud of his life and his example. The memory and the record of these have now become a part of the permanent assets of the institution which we all love."

New Members Chosen for Alumni and Alumnae Councils

A LIST of the new members of the Alumni and Alumnae Council appears below. Members of the Alumnae Council were elected by the various local groups, the presidents of those local groups becoming members of the Alumni Council. Officers of the Alumni Association extend a most cordial welcome to the new members of the Councils, and will expect to have the benefit of their counsel from time to time.

Two meetings of the Council are held annually, the one in the fall usually being held in connection with Homecoming Day; then the Councils meet again on Monday of Commencement Week.

The list of new members of the Councils follows:

ALUMNAE COUNCIL

Maude Hurley Chadwick, '10, New Bern; Doris Christie, '27, Wilson; Isabel Hoey, '28, Shelby; Annabel Lambeth Jones, '12, Charlotte; Mary Eskridge King, '25, Lynchburg, Va.; Mamie Jenkins, '96, Greenville; Maude Moore, '01, Rockingham; Edith Parker, '28, Gastonia; Florence Bailey Pendergraph, '08, Mount Airy; Gertrude Smith, '23, Winston-Salem; Mary Wylie Stuart, '28, Monroe.

ALUMNI COUNCIL

Dr. E. C. Ashby, '10, Mount Airy; Paul Barringer, ex-'06, Sanford; Henry Belk, '23, Goldsboro; Fred Bynum, '04, Rockingham; Rev. W. A. Cade, '13, Fayetteville; Dr. L. W. Crawford, '98, Nashville, Tenn.; K. R. Curtis, G.S.-'29, Wilson; Garland B. Daniel, ex-'20, High Point; Harley B. Gaston, 14, Belmont; Dr. J. L. Gibson, ex-'00, Laurinburg; J. Horace Grigg, '16, Shelby; Rev. C. J. Harrell, '06, Richmond, Va.; Henry Fisher, '21, Charlotte, N. C.; Dr. Garland O. Greever, A.M.-'05, Los Angeles, Cal.; Rev. A. J. Hobbs, Jr., '19, New Bern; W. B. Kiker, '09, Reidsville; H. R. Mahoney, '05, Jacksonville, Fla.; Dr. S. B. Pierce, '95, Weldon; James R. Simpson, '24, Rocky Mount; S. B. Moyle, '16, Columbia, S. C.; C. W. Porter, '30, Greenville; Joseph Hampton Price, '17, Monroe; E. Ralph Paris, '14, Atlanta, Ga.; Hon. Daniel C. Roper, '88, Washington, D. C.; Sam W. Ruark, '26, Raleigh; William M. Sherrill, '15, Concord; Harden F. Taylor, '13, New York City; G. R. Wallace, '27, Morehead City; P. D. Winston, '15, Lynchburg, Va.

Some Alumni Personalities

Willis Smith, '10, recently elected Speaker of the House of Representatives of the 1931 General Assembly of North Carolina, studied law at Trinity College for two years after his graduation. He is a member of the law firm of Smith and Joyner, of Raleigh, and has been a member of the General Assembly since 1927. At the last session he was chairman of the committee on courts and judicial districts, one of the major House committees. He is one of the best known young lawyers in the state.

Mr. Smith, who is a member of the board of trustees of Duke University, is general counsel for the North Carolina Bankers' Association. He is a Kiwanian and a member of the Raleigh Community Chest Commission. He is a director of the Y. M. C. A. of Raleigh and member of several prominent clubs.

He was married in 1919 to Miss Anna Lee. They have three sons, Willis Smith, Jr., Lee Creecy Smith, and Alton Battle Smith.

Mr. Smith is deeply interested in Duke University alumni activities. He was chief marshal on Alumni Day at the 1930 Commencement.

WILLIS SMITH

Benjamin F. Few, '15, who received his A.M. degree the following year, has been with the Liggett & Myers Tobacco Company since that time except for two years in the United States Army during the World War. He is a native of South Carolina.

Beginning with the Liggett & Myers Company at Durham, he was stationed there and in Manila, Philippine Islands, from 1920 to 1930. He was transferred to the New York office, advertising department, last October.

He attended the Second Officers' Training Camp at Fort Oglethorpe, Georgia, was commissioned in the infantry and served in this country with the Twentieth Division for the duration of the war.

Mr. Few won the open and amateur golf championship of the Philippine Islands in 1930.

In 1920 he was married to Miss Caroline Weston, of Columbia, S. C.

BENJAMIN F. FEW

J. Paul Frizzelle, '04, recently elected judge of the superior court for the Fifth North Carolina District, has been holding court in Durham for the past several weeks and has been making a most excellent impression upon members of the bar and citizens generally. A very successful career on the bench seems assured for this Duke graduate.

Judge Frizzelle was a member of the first law class of Trinity College. While at Trinity he was active in college affairs and represented the institution in two intercollegiate debates with Emory University, in each instance being a colleague of the late Leslie P. Howard, '03.

Admitted to the bar in 1906, Judge Frizzelle located at Snow Hill. He was Democratic presidential elector in 1917 from the Second Congressional District; he was for several years a member of the State Democratic Executive committee; chairman of the Democratic County Executive Committee for twenty years; president of the Eastern Carolina Chamber of Commerce for two years. He married Miss Nina Warner Frizzelle, of Washington, N. C., on December 26, 1906. They have seven children.

J. PAUL FRIZZELLE

Duke Professor is One of Authors of an Important New Work

Dr. William McDougall, Professor of Psychology, Is a Contributor to the First Volume of
the History of Psychology In Biography, Along With Fourteen Other World-
Renowned Scientists—Three Other Volumes Are to Appear Later

A RECENT book of interest to psychologists everywhere and to Duke men in particular, because Dr. William McDougall has a part in it, is Volume I of the History of Psychology in Biography. The committee in charge of the publication is composed of Carl Murchison, of Clark University, chairman; Edwin G. Boring, of Harvard University; Karl Buhler, of the University of Vienna; Herbert S. Langfeld, of Princeton University; and John B. Watson, of New York City. This committee found itself confronted with the fact that it was impossible to get important facts concerning the development of psychology as a science apart from the men who have developed it. They therefore determined to secure a series of autobiographies from leaders in the field of psychology which, when published, would help to explain the development of the subject.

The following plan was used in the selection of psychologists to be invited to take part in the venture. Without consultation, each member of the committee compiled a list of a hundred names that he considered eligible for such a series. The five lists were then consolidated and a new list of a hundred and eighty-four names was prepared. Then each member of the committee voted for sixty of these. Those receiving a unanimous vote of the committee were placed on the preferred list.

Fifteen of those on the preferred list were included in the first volume. These are James Mark Baldwin, of Paris, France; Mary Whiton Calkins, of Wellesley College; Edouard Claparede, of the University of Geneva; Raymond Dodge, of Yale University; Pierre Janet, of the College of France; Joseph Jastrow, of the University of Wisconsin; F. Kiesow, of the Royal University of Turin; William McDougall, of Duke University; Carl Emil Seashore, of the University of Iowa; C. Spearman, of the University of London; William Stern, of the University of Hamburg; Carl Stumpf, of the University of Berlin; Howard C. Warren, of Princeton University; Theodor Ziehen, of the University of Halle; and H. Zwaardemaker, of the University of Utrecht.

Each of these was asked to contribute an autobiography and these biographies form the book. The committee plans to issue four volumes in the series, three of which will be out in a year's time.

DR. WILLIAM McDOUGALL

Dr. McDougall has contributed an excellent account of his parentage, his early life, and his experiences as a scientist. All of these, he believes, contributed to the making of a psychologist out of him. His grandfather was a teacher who was also greatly interested in certain types of science. Both his father and his grandfather were greatly interested in religious questions and made an extensive study of such questions. Much of his earlier education was directed toward the idea of becoming a physician.

His great interest, since his undergraduate days, has been in the human nervous system. This he felt should be studied not only from the standpoint of the psychologist, but also from that of the physician. The practice of medicine did not, however, appeal to him because of his great interest in research. An opportunity to become a member of a party of anthropologists on an expedition to the Torres Straits, he hailed with delight.

Returning to Europe, he began his definite study along the lines he has followed as a life work. In various institutions he carried on investigations in the related fields planning a new theory of social psychology. His text on this subject was published in 1907. This has become the basis of his theory of the control of human energy by the instincts.

At the outbreak of the World War, Dr. McDougall enlisted as a private in the French army, driving an ambulance on the western front. Six months later, however, he found himself a major in the Royal Army Medical Corps in charge of nervous patients. In the treatment of "shell-shock" cases, he used much of the information which he had secured in his investigations in the field of psychology. There are many scientists who believe that the work of Dr. McDougall during this period of his life has been one of his greatest contributions to science.

An offer from Harvard University of a position in its department of psychology, shortly after the war, probably is responsible for Dr. McDougall's turning definitely to the teaching of this subject.

In the opinion of many scientists, Dr. McDougall's greatest contribution to science has been his determined stand against the "behaviorist" theory of psychology. This stand of his was at first against almost the entire field of American psychologists. His effort to secure recognition for his theory has caused him to be recognized as one of the foremost of the psychologists who have protected religion from the inroads of the distinctly non-religious psychologists. Dr. McDougall, himself, very modestly declines to say much about this phase of his life.

Late C. C. Dula Was Warm Friend of Duke

THE late Caleb Conley Dula, who recently died in New York City, was a close friend of Duke University, as is abundantly evidenced by his gift of $200,000 to the institution, known as the C. C. Dula Endowment Fund, and his gift of two valuable paintings, purchased by him 20 years ago at a cost of thousands of dollars. News of his death was received with sincere regret by the University community, for he had shown in many ways his deep interest in the institution.

The income from the endowment fund is being used in assisting worthy students through the University. It is hoped that the two paintings he gave will form the nucleus of what in the years to come will be an art collection of great importance.

A dispatch from New York at the time of Mr. Dula's death said:

Caleb Conley Dula, chairman of the board of the Liggett & Myers Tobacco Co., died of pneumonia yesterday morning in his home, 31 East Seventy-ninth Street, after an illness of several months.

C. C. DULA

Mr. Dula was born in Lenoir, N. Y., Feb. 8, 1864, and first went into the tobacco business with his brother, R. B. Dula, in Wentzville, Mo. Later he went into the leaf tobacco business in Danville, Va., in his own firm, Carr & Dula, but after a few years joined the Drummond Tobacco Co. as an officer. When that company was taken over by the Continental Tobacco Co., a subsidiary of the old American Tobacco Co., Mr. Dula became an officer in Continental and later in American.

He came to New York when 34. Later he became secretary and vice-president of the Continental. With the reorganization of the American Tobacco Co. in 1911 and the formation of Liggett & Myers, Mr. Dula was elected president, serving in that capacity until 1927, when he became chairman of the board. Mr. Dula was also a director in the Guaranty Trust Co.

Mrs. Dula, formerly Miss Julia Warner, and a sister, Mrs. Laura B. English of St. Louis, survive.

Duke's Practice Court is One of the Features of the Law School

Judge T. D. Bryson, of the Faculty, Who Was for Eight Years a Superior Court Judge,
Presides Over the Court Which Is One of the Various Agencies Used at Duke for
Making Legal Education Intensely Practical—Provides Excellent Training
for Third Year Students

DUKE'S practice court is one of the outstanding features of the Law School. Presiding over the court is Judge T. D. Bryson, who for eight years was judge of the twentieth district of the North Carolina superior court. He is remembered as the presiding judge in a number of prominent cases.

Previous to his elevation to the bench, Judge Bryson was solicitor in the same court for eight years, also. Educated at the University of North Carolina, he began the practice of law early in life. He says that he is one of the few judges who just quit and returned to the practice of law.

Judge Bryson points out the fact that the practice court is not a moot court in the generally accepted sense. It is, indeed, a real court for real experience in the practice of law. The Duke court does not have student judges; it is a regularly conducted course in courtroom practice.

The courtroom has all the regular appointments.

The judge's stand has sufficient room for five judges and is frequently utilized as an appellate court, four other members of the faculty, or visiting attorneys, sitting with Judge Bryson to form the court.

The witness box and the jury box are just like those of any court. The bar is railed off from the spectators and every court facility is offered the young attorneys who are pleading the cases.

The idea of the course is to offer third year students, or special students taking the third year work, an opportunity to visualize, by actual work, the courthouse practices. Not only is the work of the courtroom required, but also the office work of a practicing attorney. The embryo attorneys must prepare contracts, draw abstracts, wills, and other legal papers.

The course features courthouse practice in both civil and criminal procedures, as well as appellate practice before the supreme court. In order to familiarize the class with the work, Judge Bryson gives frequent lectures featuring largely the code of civil and criminal procedure. One day a week the court is in session from 9 a. m. to 1 p. m., devoted exclusively to motions, demurrers, trials, and the discussion of different procedures, broken by illustrations by the court, for the benefit of the students, of any propositions which may be suggested.

In order that the work may correspond exactly to the work of the superior courts, a court stenographer is present at each session. The stenographer acts as clerk of the court, prepares

DUKE LAW SCHOOL COURTROOM

the docket and the minutes of the court, and files all papers as required by law. A very adequate filing system, for this purpose, has been provided in the office of the clerk. The records of the court are intended to be permanent, as will be the judgment roll in all the cases, which include, as a legal practitioner knows, all the papers filed in a case.

The class is divided into groups. To each group is assigned a statement of facts, each differing from the other. Some of these require cases in contracts, others in torts. Each student is required to issue summons, to make the sheriff's return, to file his complaint, prepare his issues, select a jury, introduce evidence, conduct the argument, and prepare a judgment.

JUDGE T. D. BRYSON

If the case is appealed, the young attorney must prepare his case for the appellate court. He must file his brief and argument. At the session of the appellate court, he must appear for his client and argue his case.

All members of the class are required to participate in the work of the appellate court, in drawing issues and judgments, taking notes, and joining in the discussion of legal or procedural questions raised.

The whole work of the court is designed as an effort to provide the ground work in the practical side of the profession. Judge Bryson points out that many a young attorney has had to begin his practice with practically no real knowledge of how a courtroom looks. These have had to learn how to prepare their papers and carry on their courtroom work by the system of trial and error, profiting by their mistakes. Many of them have even been unable to secure positions in the offices of older attorneys where they might get help in this work. Duke's practice court will eliminate this difficulty for the graduates of this institution.

Judge Bryson is very happy in his work at Duke. He believes that the Duke Law School has a notably promising career ahead of it. He speaks of recent additions to the law faculty as being even happier than could have been expected. He hopes to establish between himself and his students not only the relation of student to teacher, but also a personal contact which will be of real value to the student in all of his personal problems. This desire of the Judge's bids fair to be amply realized, for his "boys" speak of him with great respect and honor.

Noted Visitors From Overseas Guests at Duke University

Prof. Jules Duesberg, rector of University of Liege, Belgium, and Prof. Halvdan Koht, of University of Oslo, Norway, were dinner guests of Duke University groups recently. Speaking before a large group of physicians, medical students, and others interested in biology, Professor Duesberg, who is a distinguished investigator in the field of experimental cytology, discussed certain technical phases of cell life and functions

Professor Koht spoke at a dinner of the Duke History Club on "Beginnings of the Renaissance." His lecture covered the historical aspects of the sixteenth century awakening of interest in literature and art, and dealt with the influences leading up to the rebirth of culture in Europe.

Before the lecture by Professor Duesberg a formal dinner was held at Duke Hospital with a number of local and visiting members of the medical profession present.

Professor Koht is visiting professor of history in Harvard University, and is internationally known for his writings and researches in European and world history. He and Professor Duesberg were conducted over the new Duke unit and the woman's college campus during the day, and both expressed surprise at the exceptionally complete facilities of the University.

Among other distinguished overseas visitors heard at Duke during the present semester have been Dr. Weinberg, eminent physician of the Paris Institute, France; and Prof. R. C. Mills, of University of Sydney, Australia.

Year Just Closed was Notable One in the History of Duke

Many Important Steps Taken During 1930 In Connection With the Development of the Institution Along Various Lines—Beginnings Made In a Number of Projects That Promise to Be of Great Importance

DUKE UNIVERSITY's history will record many outstanding events in 1930, for the past 12-months period was one of many new beginnings and important accomplishments in the life of the institution.

Taking first place among the events of the year at Duke was the occupancy of the magnificent new plant of 31 stone buildings comprising a vast Gothic unit situated on a woodland campus of 5,100 acres. Removal to the new campus marked the near close of a five-year building program which still continues with the erection of the handsome new chapel.

The University quickly adjusted itself to its new surroundings and all phases of its work not only continued without a break but gained impetus, giving reasons for the belief that 1931 will bring even greater academic progress and broader service.

A review of events at Duke during the past year finds interesting happenings in many fields of activity, many of them of significance and far-reaching importance.

One of the outstanding gifts to the institution during the year was allowed by the general education board of New York in authorizing a grant of $300,000 to the school of medicine to run through a five-year period. This gift will help greatly in financing the school during the period of its first years of organization and operation.

The new university department of public relations commenced its work under the direction of Henry R. Dwire of Winston-Salem.

Appointment of Justin Miller, dean of the School of Law at University of Southern California, as dean of the Duke Law School, was the first of a series of notable law faculty additions and the general expansion of the school. Duke was admitted into membership of the American Association of Law Schools recently.

Two valuable European paintings, by Jacob Maris and Emile Jacque, were given the University by C. C. Dula, of New York. These paintings were placed in the lobby of the east campus library.

The Duke basketball team set the pace in athletics for the year, winning the first of three major sports titles by Duke teams. In the spring the baseball team won the Big Five state title, and last season the football team followed with like honors on the gridiron.

Announcement was made of Wallace Wade's coming to Duke for five years beginning 1931 as director of athletics. Coach Wade in eight years at Alabama has sent three teams to the Rose Bowl.

Work was started in the late spring on the new University chapel, to be the dominating structure of the new unit. This chapel will cost $2,000,000 and require 18 months for completion. It will be 280 feet long, 120 feet wide, and 210 feet high at the tower. Cornerstone for the edifice was laid on October 22.

The Duke Hospital opening on July 21 was preceded by visit of 20,000 persons in one day to inspect the huge plant. The 408-bed institution is the largest general hospital in this section of the country.

Secretary Ray Lyman Wilbur of Washington, Dr. Robert Russell Wicks of Princeton, and Dr. Homer J. Councilor of Washington, were the 1930 commencement speakers. Honorary degrees were awarded to Bishop Edwin D. Mouzon, Secretary Wilbur, and David Robert Coker. Degrees were conferred upon 336 graduates, the largest class in the University's annals.

George G. Allen and William R. Perkins, trustees of the Duke Endowment, and associates of the late James B. Duke, made the gift of a $70,000 carillon to be placed in the tower of the new Duke chapel.

Report of the Duke librarian revealed marked progress during the past year. The book budget reached $155,000 and 41,495 volumes were added during the period. Divided into five divisions—the medical library, the woman's college library, the general library, the law library, and the school of religion library—the libraries at Duke gave students and faculty greatly increased facilities.

Opening of the woman's college, giving it use of the fine plant on the east campus, marked the first operation of the state's newest woman's college.

With more than 70 students enrolled, selected from among 3,000 applicants, the medical school began its first quarter of work on October 1.

(Continued on page 34)

Rose Bowl Victor Comes to Duke as Director of Athletics

Wallace Wade, Football Wizard and for Eight Years Director of Athletics at University of Alabama, Assumes Duties Here—Coach Jimmy DeHart Signs Contract With Washington and Lee After Five Years at Duke

AMONG the most interested of the millions of persons who listened to the radio description and later read the newspaper accounts of the Alabama-Washington State football game in the Pasadena, California, Rose Bowl on New Year's Day were innumerable Duke alumni, students, and friends who shared with the University of Alabama and Coach Wallace Wade much of the pride in the South's victory over the West. That game marked the close of Coach Wade's brilliant coaching career at Alabama and served to turn the eyes of football fandom upon Duke University which Coach Wade is to serve in the future.

Coach Wade's success in the realm of football has been no less than phenomenal, and his fame has brought to him national recognition. Four Southern Conference championships and two victories and a tie at Rose Bowl have given his teams unquestioned supremacy in the South during the eight years he has been at Alabama.

And just as Alabama followers will continue to watch Coach Wade's work at Duke, so will Duke followers watch developments at Washington and

Lee University, to which Coach James DeHart returns in a short while after five years at Duke. Coach DeHart's renewed connections with Washington and Lee were announced several weeks ago. He will take with him to the Virginia institution the best wishes of many friends with whom he was associated and of the many students who trained and played under him during the past five years.

Coach Wade has lost no time in acquainting himself with the athletic situation at Duke and this spring will hold practices with the men who will furnish the varsity squad for next fall's schedule. While it would be unreasonable to expect him to develop immediately a team of Alabama's calibre, observers confidently expect him to have a better than average Duke team, and one that should give promise for future good things on the gridiron.

Duke's new football coach in recent years has become a dominating figure in Southern football. Beginning his gridiron career as a guard at Brown University, Wallace Wade began coaching in Tennessee. He attracted the attention of Dan.

Coach Wade "Snapped" Soon After Arrival at Duke

Wallace Wade, Jr., shown with his Dad.   A "close-up" of Duke's new athletic director.   Left to right: Dr. R. L. Flowers; Coach Wallace Wade; President W. P. Few; Dean W. H. Wannamaker.

McGugin, veteran Vanderbilt mentor, when he directed the Fitzgerald-Clark preparatory school to a Tennessee scholastic championship. The next year found Wade at Vanderbilt as line-coach, and for two seasons he worked beside the veteran McGugin. During this time the Commodores did not lose a game.

He then received a call from the University of Alabama whose teams had never proved a serious threat for Conference honors. Every football enthusiast now knows what the next eight years meant for Crimson Tide success. Few coaches have turned in so remarkable a record in their first coaching assignment. Some have reached the heights once, or twice, but none has appeared more frequently in championship class than has Wallace Wade with his Alabama elevens.

In winning or sharing four Conference titles Wade's teams have scored 1,368 points against 346 for all opposition. The percentage for eight seasons was nearly .830. The record for the years was 61 games won, 13 lost, and three tied.

A defeat by Florida in the closing game of 1923 kept Wade from a championship in his first year at Alabama. The next season his team lost to Centre, but won the Conference championship. In 1925 and 1926 the Tide swept ahead to victory and earned two invitations to the Pasadena Rose Bowl classic. The first year Wade hurled a Southern thunderbolt against the University of Washington and won 20 to 19, and the following season tied Stanford, 7 to 7.

For three years Alabama settled back to a position not so high in the Conference standings, but in 1930 a mighty machine fulfilled Wade's brightest hopes. It won nine successive games, scored 247 points and limited the opposition to 13.

While Duke University is gaining a good coach, it is likewise losing a good one. Coach DeHart has had the privilege of seeing athletics and physical education make steady progress during the five years that he has been director of athletics. Schedules have been expanded, more formidable athletic opposition taken on, new lines of sports added and developed. State championships have been won in football, baseball, basketball, wrestling, and cross-country, and Southern titles have been garnered in baseball and wrestling. Especially notable was the 1930 football record, which included one defeat, two ties, and eight victories. These five years have also seen the erection of a large stadium and a new gymnasium, with various athletic facilities in keeping with the general growth of the institution.

Duke's athletics will continue to grow, serving not only to represent the institution well in this line of activity but to stimulate student and alumni spirit, and to develop students physically by their participation in the various sports. The gymnasiums and athletic fields are well adapted for providing all facilities for physical education and intercollegiate sports.

Coach Wade has not announced the dates for his spring football practice, but he is sure to be greeted by a large squad of candidates, both letter men and others.

Coach and Mrs. Wade and their two children came to Durham on January 15.

ANNOUNCEMENT BY DR. WANNAMAKER

Soon after Coach Wade arrived in Durham the following announcement was made by Dean W. H. Wannamaker, chairman of the executive committee of the Athletic Council of Duke University:

"At the suggestion of Mr. James DeHart in order that Mr. Wade might have a free hand from the very beginning in the development of his plans, Mr. DeHart's contract as director of athletics at Duke University was terminated today rather than continued through the academic year. Mr. DeHart leaves Duke University with the best wishes of all with whom he has been associated during his five years of service here. His loyalty and ability are recognized and appreciated.

"Mr. Wallace Wade will at once assume all the duties of his position as director of athletics. His recommendations as to the staff of the department will be made from time to time after he has familiarized himself with the whole problem of physical education at Duke University.

"Mr. Wade has been cordially welcomed to the University. His sterling worth and character and his consequent great achievement as a guide and trainer of youth have won for him the respect and confidence of good people here as elsewhere. He is assured of the hearty coöperation of all those with whom his duties here will bring him in contact."

DINNER FOR TWO COACHES

A few days after Coach Wade's arrival the Athletic Association entertained Coaches Wade and DeHart at a dinner at which members of the football squad were present. Coach Wade and his predecessor both made short talks on this delightful occasion. A notably fine spirit of enthusiasm and good fellowship was in evidence.

Carl Voyles To Be Assistant Duke Director of Athletics

Coach Wallace Wade on January 23 announced the appointment of Carl Voyles, freshman coach and chief scout at University of Illinois, as assistant director of athletics and end coach at Duke University. The new member of the Duke athletic staff will begin his services at Duke this fall.

(Continued on page 22)

Duke Teams Win Seven Out of Twelve Winter Sports Contests

There Are Yet Approximately Twenty-seven Contests on Schedule—Spring Football
Practice Is Expected to Begin Next Month Under the Direction of Coach
Wallace Wade

An interesting schedule of winter sports has been begun by Duke teams, and in four sports—basketball, boxing, swimming, and wrestling—twelve events have been held, seven of them resulting in Blue Devil victories. There are yet approximately twenty-seven games and meets to be played, not including events scheduled in Conference tournaments.

In eight games the basketball quint has won five and dropped three, winning over Randolph-Macon, Wake Forest, Wofford, South Carolina and Navy, and losing to Villanova, Maryland, and Temple. The boxing team has won both meets scheduled with N. C. State and University of South Carolina. Washington and Lee defeated the Duke swimming team in the one water event staged. The wrestling team lost by a narrow score to Franklin and Marshall in the opening mat meet of the season.

February will see nine scheduled basketball games, five boxing matches, five wrestling meets, and three swimming meets. The outcome of the remaining sports events will determine whether Blue Devil teams will close with good tournament prospects and final Conference standings.

Taken as a whole Duke teams should come through the winter season with creditable records. The absence of a number of students who have worn the Blue for three years and passed into Duke athletic history has been naturally felt, but as the season wears on those who have taken their places are expected to show marked improvement and ability.

While indoor teams are concluding their winter schedules during February the first signs of spring will be revealed by the early appearance of athletes on the gridiron, diamond, and cinder track.

Coach Wade has officially taken over the destinies of Duke athletics and, providing the weather clears sufficiently, his first spring practice will be conducted early in February. Coach Jack Coombs will have an early call for his battery candidates, and Coach Buch-

heit's tracksters will be limbering up their muscles on the new stadium oval.

The new Duke track and baseball facilities will be used for the first time this spring.

Carl Voyles To Be Assistant Duke Director of Athletics
(Continued from page 21)

At the same time Coach Wade announced the personnel of his football staff for next season. Eddie Cameron, for four years assistant football coach, will become backfield coach, and E. P. Hagler, freshman coach during the past season, will be line coach. Herschell Caldwell, co-coach with Hagler of the state championship freshman team last fall, will continue as freshman coach, and later will be given assistants.

Coach Wade expressed his keen pleasure in securing Coach Voyles as his assistant, adding that he was sure the new coach would prove a valuable addition to the staff. Coach Voyles comes highly recommended, especially by Bob Zuppke, Illinois coach and a close friend of Coach Wade.

"Carl Voyles has everything that is needed in a top-notch coach and administrator," Coach Zuppke told the Duke director of athletics. "His work at Illinois has been satisfactory in every particular. He knows football and better yet, knows how to teach it to others. There never was a more popular member of our staff than Voyles. We all regret that he is leaving but are glad, of course, that he is moving up."

Paderewski Recital at Duke

Page Auditorium was filled to overflowing on the evening of Thursday, January 8, with an audience eager to hear the world-famous pianist, Paderewski. The great artist played a varied program featuring numbers by Beethoven, Chopin, Debussy and other masters. The enthusiasm of the audience caused the famous pianist to respond with a number of encores. The occasion was notably successful, drawing visitors from all parts of North Carolina.

Officers Elected at Duke Day Meetings Already at Work
(Continued from page 8)

Introductions of those present were made by themselves, it being shown that W. R. Odell was the oldest alumnus in the county, having graduated in 1875, and that Rev. Mr. Baldwin was the first graduate of Trinity College after its removal to Durham. Brief talks were made by Mr. Odell, Dr. J. Henry Highsmith, and others.

"Bells of Trinity," a composition of the late Plato Durham, was read. Officers to serve during the ensuing year were chosen as follows: S. G. Hawfield, president; Mrs. John M. Oglesby, secretary; W. M. Sherrill, member of alumni council from Cabarrus.

Fayetteville

The Cumberland County alumni met on December 11 in the social room of Hay Street Methodist Church. In addition to the Cumberland alumni a number of others from outside the county were present.

Dr. A. M. Proctor, of the department of education at Duke University, discussed the past and future of the University, giving an interesting résumé of some events of the past together with a forceful interpretation of its present activities and future promise. A number of those present made short talks following the main address of the evening.

Rev. W. A. Cade was elected president; Rev. B. T. Hurley, vice-president; Miss Leila Jeannette Hubbard, secretary-treasurer.

Gastonia

Dean Justin Miller of the Law School of Duke University delivered an inspirational address at the annual banquet of the Gaston County Alumni Club of Duke University before a large gathering of graduates and former students of the institution. He referred particularly to developments already under way and contemplated in connection with the Law School, explaining the plan to institute at Duke a legal clinic which will bear the same relation to the School of Law as does the medical clinic to the School of Medicine. He used a legal clinic plan at the University of Southern California with notable success and the Duke clinic will be operated along similar lines. Dean Miller referred to the work of other schools and departments of the University and to the general development of Duke. He outlined briefly the real purpose of the institution.

Other brief talks were made by R. Gregg Cherry, Rev. J. B. Craven, W. Grady Gaston and John E. Jankoski. L. B. Hollowell, young Gastonia attorney and graduate of the School of Law, introduced Dean Miller. The meeting is declared to have been one of the very best in the entire history of the Gaston Alumni Club.

Officers for the coming year are, president, Harley B. Gaston; vice-president, James M. Sloan; secretary-treasurer, R. H. Pinnix; alumnae representative, Edith Parker.

Goldsboro

Professor H. E. Spence, of the faculty of Duke University, spoke at the meeting of Wayne County alumni, held in the Woman's Club building in Goldsboro. He discussed "The New Duke: Its Opportunities and Responsibilities," referring to various phases of the institution's development and its great promise for the future. Professor Spence was introduced by Colonel John D. Langston, former president of the General Alumni Association.

Officers were chosen as follows: President, Henry Belk; vice-president, Thomas Griffin; secretary-treasurer, Mrs. Jonathan Jenkins.

C. B. Miller presided at the meeting. Short talks were made by Rev. C. P. Jerome, of the class of '83, Rev. W. V. McRae, Rev. W. H. Brown, R. Jack Smith, Thomas Griffin, Claude H. Martin, and E. J. Bullock.

Greensboro

Dr. Frank C. Brown, professor of English and comptroller of Duke University, addressed a largely attended meeting of the Guilford County Alumni Club held at the O. Henry Hotel. The address was preceded by a banquet and was followed by the election of officers. Garland B. Daniel was elected president; Miss Flora Meredith, vice-president; H. W. Kendall, associate editor of the Greensboro *Daily News,* was elected secretary-treasurer.

Bryce R. Holt, retiring president, was toastmaster. A musical program was a most pleasing feature of the meeting. Professor L. B. Hurley, of the North Carolina College department of English, presented the speaker.

Dr. Brown presented interesting facts and figures regarding Duke, interspersed with a pleasing bit of humor and a plea for the constant loyalty of all alumni. He referred briefly to the physical plant of Duke and then spoke of the organization of the various schools and departments, closing with an interpretation of the real spirit and purpose of the institution. "You can do much," said the speaker, "by helping us select our students, by turning the right kind of fellows our way. Above all things let us cherish an ideal. The things that count are the worthwhile ones to which we are attached."

Greenville

Dr. Bert Cunningham, professor of zoölogy, represented Duke University at the meeting of the Pitt County Alumni Club. He told something of the physical development of the University, and discussed impressively its purposes and ideals.

Officers were elected as follows: President, C. W.

Porter; vice-president, Foster Young; secretary, Kathryn Warlick; treasurer, J. L. Kilgo; alumnae representative, Mamie Jenkins.

President Carson presided at the meeting and several matters of business were discussed.

Kinston

At the meeting of the Lenoir County Alumni Club of Duke University, Dr. J. W. Carr, of the department of education, was the speaker, pointing out some of the present opportunities and responsibilities of the institution and those connected with it.

The meeting was held at Hotel Kinston, and those present talked informally of the old Trinity and the new Duke following Dr. Carr's impressive and interesting address.

Following are the officers of the Lenoir County club: R. P. Raspberry, '26, president, Kinston; Alonzo Edwards, '25, vice-president, Hookerton; A. E. Hammond, '24, second vice-president, Trenton; Larry W. Smith, '20, secretary-treasurer, Kinston.

Laurinburg

Assistant Dean H. J. Herring addressed the Scotland County Alumni Club at Laurinburg. In the course of his address he answered a number of questions that are being asked with reference to the new Duke and pointed out, among other things, the fact that expenses are exceedingly reasonable considering the facilities offered. He showed conclusively that, comparing charges at Duke with other similarly situated institutions, the cost of education here is not only reasonable but even low.

Officers for the new year were elected as follows: J. L. Gibson, president; L. M. Peele, vice-president; Edwin P. Gibson, secretary-treasurer.

Monroe

The Union County Alumni Club held its Duke University dinner at Hotel Joffre with Dr. R. S, Rankin, of the Duke department of economics, as speaker. Dr. Rankin referred to the historical background of Duke and then spoke of its spirit and purpose in the light of new developments of recent years. He pointed out effectively the non-material resources of the institution as well as its physical equipment.

New officers were chosen as follows: Joseph Hampton Price, president; Dr. Henry D. Stewart, vice-president; Oscar L. Richardson, secretary.

There is much interest in Duke University in the Monroe area and the Union Alumni Club is expected to do some effective work in accentuating that interest.

Mount Airy

The Surry County group of Duke alumni met at dinner at the Blue Ridge Inn and heard an address by Dr. W. T. Laprade, of the department of history, in which

he gave those present a new insight into the present workings of the University. He referred briefly to its past history and discussed particularly various phases of the development now in progress and its prospect for the future.

New officers elected for the coming year are as follows: President, Dr. E. C. Ashby; vice-president, E. C. Bivens; secretary, L. B. Pendergraph; Mrs. L. B. Pendergraph was elected a member of the alumnae council.

Brief remarks were made by a number of those present, deep interest in, and loyalty to, Duke University being the keynote of the meeting.

New Bern

Alumni of Duke University in Craven, Jones and Pamlico counties met at a banquet in the social room of Centenary Methodist Church and participated in a most interesting program featuring an address by Prof. R. N. Wilson, of the University department of chemistry, and the election of officers for the new year.

Rev. A. J. Hobbs, Jr., '19, was toastmaster of the occasion and was unanimously named new president of the Craven County Alumni Club. Vernon Derrickson was named vice-president; Rev. Robert M. Price, secretary-treasurer; and Mrs. W. C. Chadwick, alumnae council representative. John F. Rhodes, Jr., was chairman of the nominating committee.

Prof. Wilson traced the development of Duke University from its beginning, calling attention to the outstanding work now being done in the schools of medicine, law and religion as well as in the liberal arts colleges for men and women. He referred briefly to the various phases of the institution's development. "Carrying on its splendid old tradition," he said, "its eyes at the same time are being opened to new opportunities for service, especially in harnessing the energy of young people for developing character and building life."

During the progress of the evening a delightful musical program was rendered. In addition to the main address several others spoke, including Captain Tom C. Daniels, a football star of many years ago, who told of the first organized football in the state; A, H. Bangert, class of 1892; Vernon Derrickson, C. L. Abernethy, Jr., W. M. Whitaker of Jones County, and Mrs. W. C. Chadwick.

Newport

The Duke alumni of Cartaret County held their annual meeting on November 11. The meeting was held at the Newport high school of which W. E. Powell is principal, the dinner being served by the home economics department. N. F. Eure, president of the Carteret Association, presided, and an interesting musical and speaking program was presented.

The address of the evening was made by Professor F. S. Aldridge, of the department of mathematics at Duke, who has been associated with the institution for thirty-nine years. He sketched the growth of the University from its early days, and then discussed the new Duke founded on the high principles and ideals of Trinity College and offering opportunity to all in various spheres of life. He closed with an appeal to his hearers for their interest and zeal in the task of "carrying on" and making Duke the servant of all. He paid a deserved tribute to the benefactors of the institution.

New officers of the Carteret Alumni Club are as follows: President, G. R. Wallace; vice-president, W. E. Powell; secretary, J. C. Watts; treasurer, C. Byrd Wade.

Reidsville

The Rockingham-Caswell County alumni met at Hotel Belvidere at Reidsville with Dr. William K. Boyd, of the department of history at Duke University, as speaker of the occasion. Dr. Boyd referred to different phases of the University's development, speaking very interestingly of the library expansion, among other things. He gave something of the historical background of the institution as well as telling of its present activities and its arrangements for future expansion.

Officers elected were as follows: President, William R. Kiker, Reidsville; vice-president, Allan D. Ivie, Leakesville-Spray; vice-president, W. C. Jones, Caswell County; secretary-treasurer, Miss Annie Laurie Oliver.

The next meeting of the Rockingham-Caswell alumni group will be held December 11, next, at Yanceyville, Caswell County.

Rockingham

The Rockingham-Hamlet group met in Rockingham at dinner on December 11. The address of the occasion was delivered by Judge T. D. Bryson, of the Duke School of Law. Judge Bryson is well known in the Rockingham section and his coming for this occasion was an event of real interest and pleasure to those present.

New officers were elected as follows: Fred Bynum, president; T. P. Wood, secretary-treasurer; Maude Moore, alumnae representative.

The meeting was held in the Sunday School room of the Methodist Church. The invocation was by Rev. H. C. Smith, presiding elder of the Rockingham district. Judge Bryson answered various questions being asked about Duke and stressed particularly the aims of the institution, paying a high tribute to the late James B. Duke. A short talk was made by the president explaining the work being done by the Alumni Office at the University, and pleading for the support of the county organization. Short talks were made by a number of those present.

Rocky Mount

The Duke alumni of Nash and Edgecombe counties held a most interesting meeting at dinner in the Y. M. C. A. building. J. L. Horne, Jr., president of the Rocky Mount club, presided and an enjoyable and profitable session was spent in the discussion of various matters relating to Duke University and the part of the alumni therein.

Henry R. Dwire, director of public relations and alumni affairs, and William R. Murray, better known as "Bill" Murray, president of the student council and 1930 football star, represented the University and spoke briefly with reference to its past, present and future developments. Mr. Dwire outlined briefly the progress of the institution, particularly since the signing of the Indenture of Trust making possible Duke University. Mr. Murray spoke from the standpoint of a member of the student body and especially with reference to athletics.

A committee was named to write a letter of welcome to Wallace Wade and one of appreciation to Jimmy DeHart.

J. L. Horne, Jr., was reëlected president of the Nash-Edgecombe Alumni Club; R. M. Richardson was elected vice-president and T. E. Wagg, Jr., secretary and treasurer. J. R. Simpson is representative on the alumni council.

Sanford

An able and interesting address by Dr. W. A. Lambeth, pastor of Trinity Methodist Church, Durham, featured the meeting of the Lee County Alumni Club of Duke University, held in the Methodist Church at Sanford.

In his address, Dr. Lambeth referred to the Duke Endowment and the effect that it would have on the states of North and South Carolina, and said that generations yet unborn would feel its benefits. He spoke of the notably effective work that the institution is doing and paid a tribute to the men who are directing its destinies.

The music was in charge of the Sanford Music Club, who sang a number of hymns and anthems. Miss Eloise Bass rendered a delightful solo.

Paul J. Barringer was elected president of the Lee County club; Rev. Ivey T. Poole, Jonesboro, vice-president; J. E. Brinn, secretary-treasurer.

Shelby

The Cleveland County Duke Alumni Club held its annual meeting at the Hotel Charles at Shelby, Friday evening, December 12. The retiring president, Charles A. Burrus, presided at the dinner.

Dr. Clement Vollmer, of the department of German at Duke University, delivered an address on the plans and purposes of the institution. It was the first opportunity some of the older alumni had to hear Dr. Vollmer and his address aroused much interest. The attendance at the meeting was good and a fine spirit of enthusiasm was in evidence.

Officers were elected as follows: President, J. Horace Grigg, Shelby; vice-president, J. Roan Davis, Kings Mountain; secretary-treasurer, Miss Isabel Hoey, Shelby; representative to the alumnae council, Miss Isabel Hoey.

Weldon

The Halifax County club of Duke alumni celebrated Duke University Day at a most enjoyable dinner meeting at Weldon.

The principal feature of the evening was the address by Dr. Paul N. Garber, of the Duke University School of Religion. He covered the stages of development of Duke University under its various presidents from the time of Braxton Craven on up to the present. He especially emphasized the notable things that are being accomplished at the present time and told something of the work being made possible by the ample funds made available through the generosity of the late James B. Duke.

A short business meeting followed for the election of officers for the coming year. The following were chosen: Dr. S. B. Pierce, president; Pierce Johnson, vice-president; R. L. Towe, secretary-treasurer.

Wilson

An address by Dr. Frank S. Hickman, of the School of Religion, featured the meeting of Duke University alumni of Wilson County, held at the Briggs Hotel in Wilson. He gave a great deal of interesting information regarding the developments in progress at Duke, and closed with a fine interpretation of the real spirit and purpose of the institution. He paid a tribute to President Few and spoke most enthusiastically of the bringing into the faculty of many of the ablest men of the country in their various lines. He referred most impressively to the heart of Duke, which inherited the best of the spirit of "Old Trinity."

Rev. T. M. Grant presided as toastmaster; Colonel John F. Bruton, chairman of the Board of Trustees, referred to the high type of men and women the University is turning out and to the great responsibility resting upon them to maintain the standards and spirit of their alma mater. Mr. Kader Curtis, superintendent of schools, who teaches in the summer school of Duke, spoke interestingly of the institution. Miss Doris Christie, teacher of English in the Charles L. Coon high school, responded briefly and fittingly as did Messrs. W. A. Lucas. J. D. Gold and others

Henry R. Dwire, director of alumni affairs at Duke, who had just attended the Rocky Mount meeting, dropped in near the close of the Wilson meeting and responded briefly to the call of the toastmaster for some remarks.

New officers were elected as follows: Kader Curtis, president; Dr. C. A. Woodard, vice-president; Jessie Anderson, secretary; Mrs. T. H. Newton, treasurer; Miss Doris Christie, alumnae council representative.

Winston-Salem

Professor Malcolm McDermott, of the faculty of the Duke University Law School, was the principal speaker at the annual banquet of the Forsyth Alumni Club, held at Hotel Robert E. Lee. He declared that the greatest asset of any university lies not in material things but in spiritual values.

"The institution that possesses those priceless treasures which are spiritual values," he said, "is the worthy institution, and it has an endowment that will exceed all the millions it may receive."

The speaker was introduced by B. S. Womble, a member of the Duke board of trustees. P. Frank Hanes, retiring president, acted as toastmaster and new officers were elected as follows: M. A. Braswell, president; Clay Ring, Kernersville, vice-president; Mrs. Charles Pegram, secretary; and Miss Gertrude Smith, member of the alumnae council.

Luther Ferrell, a member of the Athletic Council, referred to the coming of Wallace Wade as director of athletics next year. He referred to athletics at Duke in a general way and urged the alumni to keep the true Duke spirit. It was voted to send a telegram to Coach DeHart, expressing appreciation of his efforts in giving Duke a winning football team.

Mr. Womble spoke briefly, as did Colonel W. A. Blair, who related some interesting humorous stories.

Duke Man Writes Weevil Bulletin

William Maughan, assistant director of Duke forest, is the author of a bulletin recently issued by the Yale University School of Forestry which describes the control of the white pine weevil on Eli Whitney forest of Yale.

Mr. Maughan, who comes to Duke from the Yale School of Forestry, spent several years in observation and experimentation getting materials for the bulletin. While the white pine weevil at present is no serious threat to North Carolina forests, weevils have been found in several sections of the state.

The author of the bulletin writes that the weevil can be successfully controlled if attacked systematically, and that trees already damaged can recover from the ravages of the pest.

What Some Duke Men Are Doing and Saying

COLONEL C. O. SHERRILL, '98, former city manager of Cincinnati, was invited recently to go to Asheville and make suggestions for solving that city's governmental problems, and in an address before a large audience in the city auditorium, he recommended very strongly the consolidation of all governmental functions of county, city and schools into a single central unit, under the council-manager form. He favored a non-partisan council with a capable executive in full charge and also suggested memorializing the state legislature to make an emergency appropriation to supplement local revenues.

While in Asheville, Colonel Sherrell was interviewed by a representative of the *Times* and talked interestingly regarding the management of American cities. He declared that the management of these cities is the biggest problem before the American people today; he outlined the problems that confronted Cincinnati when it adopted the city-manager-small council form of government in 1925 and the results that had been achieved under the new system. He was Cincinnati's first city manager, serving from January 1, 1926, to the middle of 1930 when he resigned to accept an executive position with the big Kroger Grocery and Baking Company.

Pointing to conditions in many of the larger cities of the country, Colonel Sherrill asserted that "organized disrespect for law, bootlegging, hi-jacking, racketeering, gambling, organized burglary, robbery, kidnaping, political corruption of judges and police executives—every one of these crimes perpetrated by organized gangs, with the connivance and support of unscrupulous politicians—are born, bred and thrive on the rottenness of politically dominated local governments. It is a terrible thing to admit, but the facts amply justify the statement that officials elected and controlled by professional political machines cannot be trusted to administer honestly the business of our cities."

* * * * *

One of the best of all the tributes paid Senator Lee S. Overman since his recent death was that in an article in the Asheville *Citizen-Times* by John A. Livingstone, '09, now Supreme Court Librarian, who had many opportunities as a Washington newspaper correspondent and in other ways to observe the junior North Carolina Senator and his work. Incidentally, it will be interesting to REGISTER readers to know that

Mr. Livingstone himself, who received his license to practice law in 1922, is now one of the associate editors of the Associate Law League Journal published in Chicago, having been named to that position by Judge R. H. Sykes, of Durham, President of the Commercial Law League of America. He has never given up his legal contacts, though engaged largely in newspaper and kindred work.

Speaking of Senator Overman in the article referred to above, Mr. Livingstone said in part:

"No Tar Heel was more devoted to North Carolina than he. It was near his heart always. If he were not in Washington to represent the State in the Senate, he could be found at his unpretentious home in Salisbury. He was proud of the honor of representing the state in the national capital.

"Loving his state as he did and proud of the honor of representing it as he was, it would have been tragic had he suffered defeat. No man can say what would have resulted two years hence, but there is no one who will not agree that it is better for him that he was able to die in office, even though he never achieved his ambition of being the senior North Carolina Senator.

"The veteran of many political battles, he never became cynical in his attitude toward life. His philosophy of accepting the inevitable served him well to the last. How to grow old cheerfully. Many people who did not know him well thought that he had no philosophy except that of expediency. It is true that he was not gifted with creative ideas. While in his younger days, he did manifest such qualities of leadership as to bring him to the front, he was never the bold and fearless leader, who delighted in exploring new fields.

"His leadership was exerted in the field of serving what he conceived to be the best interests of his people. He was never precipitate in arriving at conclusions. He waited until the evidence was in. Then he would make his decision. This is the essence of successful political leadership.

"Though never bold in his leadership, he could and did take advanced ground when he felt that it was to the best interests of his people. His early support of statewide prohibition was an example. Another was his early support of railroad rate regulation. In later days he consistently opposed federal centralization because he believed thoroughly in the doctrine of state

rights. While slow to take a position, he did not turn back after he had taken it. This was political wisdom of a high order."

* * * * *

The REGISTER had a reference in a recent issue to the work being done in Spain in the realm of research in political economy by Professor Earl J. Hamilton, of Duke University. *La Epoca* of Madrid published a most interesting article a few months ago regarding Professor Hamilton and his work, translation of which has been made by Professor F. E. Steinhauser, and a few extracts from the article are reprinted herewith:

"If someone asked me to explain what an intelligent countenance is, or how facial contours can symbolize quickness of perception, good sense, fine sensibility and a sharp wit, I should take the questioner by the hand and show him Professor Earl J. Hamilton of Duke University.

"Surmounting an athletic body, that countenance, lighted up by a smile of cordial optimism and youthful joviality, is the chief attraction of this famous American economist, who speaks of figures, statistics, prices and production graphs with the same simplicity with which others discuss the ordinary trivialities of light conversation.

"An agreeable simplicity, an attractive cordiality and a sincere sympathy: add all these to that intelligence which I have just mentioned and a vast culture that makes him an authority on economic questions, and you will have a picture of this Professor Hamilton who digs into Spanish archives and libraries to add new wealth to his knowledge and to develop in the laboratories of thought and scientific speculation the successful results of his investigation.

"The Rockefeller Institute has extended to Europe the investigations of five scholars who are making historic-economic studies to determine scientifically the reason for the periodicity that is evidenced in economic crises throughout the world. It is a well ascertained fact that the periods of rise and fall in the various branches of economic phenomena, if studied correlatively, show an undulatory movement that suggests the existence of certain underlying causes for this periodic recurrence of economic crises. Are these causes merely fortuitous and unpreventable? Or is there on the contrary a definite, though unknown, natural force that determines this regular oscillation of the economic pendulum? If the source of this periodicity could be determined definitely and authoritatively it would mean an important step forward in the solution of the economic problems of the world. And that marvelous Institute, which sets gold to work in the service of culture thus ennobling it, and which aids the scholar and opens up to the world new channels through which may flow universal knowledge, has seen the possibility of attaining concrete facts on this transcendental question. That is why Professor Earl J. Hamilton, professor of Political Economy, a man of wide culture, young, intelligent, understanding and cordial, is now in Spain."

* * * * *

Dr. Henry S. Curtis is not an alumnus of Duke University but he is well known to many connected with the institution because of his work as a member of the faculty of the Duke University Summer School. Writing from Milwaukee, Wisconsin, under the title "Battleships or Scholarships," he had the following in a recent issue of *School and Society*:

A short time ago as I was talking with Mr. Davis, our minister to Panama, he said that in his experience a period of study in an American university often turned a young man who was bitterly anti-American into an American sympathizer. He said many of the Spanish-American countries had a certain fear of us on account of our size and our known military strength. They suspected us of being imperialistic. But a sojourn in this country usually dispelled this idea and brought them back with quite a different mental attitude in regard to us.

Obviously our need of defense depends on the dangers that threaten us. These dangers are largely determined by the attitude toward us of surrounding countries. If they are all friendly, there is little need of powerful armaments.

I believe the naval register credits us with fifteen battleships. The most modern of these cost $45,000,000 apiece, enough to endow any but four or five of our largest universities or to build twelve hundred miles of concrete highway.

If we put this expense on an annual basis, it looks like this. Interest on $45,000,000 at 4 per cent, $1,800,000. The life of a battleship is reckoned at twenty years. Depreciation would thus be $2,250,000 a year. Our battleships have each spent several millions since the war on modern equipment, such as anti-aircraft batteries and the like. We may put this cost conservatively at $400,000 a year. Each ship carries a complement of 1,200 to 1,300 men and 70 to 80 officers. The pay-roll approximates $100,000 a month or $1,200,000 for the year. After thirty years officers and men may retire on three-quarters pay or they may be retired at any time for disability. If injured or killed, they or their dependents will draw pensions. This would represent a sum not less than $500,000 a year, in case there were no war, or a much larger sum in case there were any real fighting. The board of 1,200 men and 80 officers at fifty cents a day would amount to $220,000 a year. I have no figures as to the cost of operating a battleship for a year, but including the cost of coal, or fuel oil, electricity, ammunition and repairs, it would probably be at least $500,000.

(Continued on page 35)

News of the Alumni

Where They Are Located   **What They Are Doing**

Miss Elizabeth Aldridge, '24, Secretary of Alumnae Council, Editor

CLASS OF 1872

Millard Mial of Raleigh, class of '72, visited the University during the holidays with two of his brothers, one from Texas and the other, Dr. Mial, from New Jersey.

CLASS OF 1892

The Richmond Christian Advocate recently paid a fine tribute to the *North Carolina Christian Advocate* and to the editor and business manager. In the November 20 issue the following was said: ''North Carolina has always stood by the *Advocate*. It was never any better, if as good, as now. The Plylers who run it, Rev. A. W. being editor and assistant business manager, and M. T. (they are twins) business manager and assistant editor, have just closed a campaign in the two Conferences to add subscribers to the list. They added over five thousand and the number of subscribers sent out each week is 22,000, all of them paid.''

Rev. A. W. and M. T. Plyler are both members of the class of 1892.

CLASS OF 1894

Dr. E. C. Brooks was elected president of the North Carolina College Conference at the annual meeting in Durham, October 10, at the Washington Duke Hotel. He succeeds Dr. Robert H. Wright, of the East Carolina Teachers College.

CLASS OF 1896

Dr. J. C. Hall, a prominent physician of Albemarle, N. C., died on October 3, 1930. An editorial that appeared in the *Stanly News and Press* shows the high esteem in which he was held in his community. It said: ''When men like Dr. Hall pass on to their reward the town and county in which they live realize immediately that the vacant places will be hard to fill. This cannot be said of every man, but as one glances over the various institutions and organizations with which Dr. Hall was connected he quickly realizes that this was an unusual man who has passed away. Many men are satified to let others lead the way, but Dr. Hall was not this type of man, for of whatever organization he was a part, he was likewise one of the leaders.

''He was intensely loyal to his profession, to the fraternal and civic organizations of which he was a member, to Duke University and to his church. He always showed a deep interest in the things which would be of benefit to Albemarle and Stanly County.

''The profession to which he belonged is not an easy one to follow, for there are hardships that try men's souls, that is if they prove themselves physicians in the true sense of the word. Dr. Hall was the physician for hundreds of families of the county. They were loyal to him, and he gave them the best he had.

''Dr. Hall was a clean man, a thorough gentleman, a Christian and a good physician. Albemarle can truly say that one of her best citizens has passed on.''

Dr. Hall's only child graduated from Duke University with the class of 1926, Mrs. Evelyn Hall Turner.

CLASS OF 1899

Dr. Harry M. North, who has served four years as presiding elder of the Wilmington district, was transferred at the last Methodist Conference to Raleigh to succeed Dr. Mike Bradshaw, '78, as presiding elder of the Raleigh district. Dr. North is a former pastor of Edenton Street Methodist Church, Duke Memorial Church at Durham, First Church of Rocky Mount, and the Methodist church at Kinston, among other pastorates. He is an active member of the Board of Trustees of Duke University and served as president of the Alumni Association from 1912 to 1914.

CLASS OF 1904

Mrs. C. C. Smith (Nellie Stephenson) lives at 101 West Main Street, Greenwood, Indiana. Her husband is pastor of the Baptist church in that city.

CLASS OF 1905

Governor O. Max Gardner appointed M. Eugene Newsom as chairman of a Council on Unemployment and Relief in North Carolina. Joseph H. Separk, '96, was also named on the council. A meeting was held in Raleigh on December 2 to map out a program for administration by the State Department of Labor and the State Department of Public Welfare.

CLASS OF 1910

Dr. A. M. Proctor, Professor of School Administration in Duke University, has been recently appointed a member of the North Carolina Commission on the Enrichment of Adult Life. The appointment was made by Willis A. Sutton, president of the National Education Association. A. T. Allen, state superintendent, is chairman of the commission on which there are 37 members. Governor Gardner is vice-chairman and Jule B. Warren, '08, of the North Carolina Education Association, is secretary.

CLASS OF 1913

Henry A. Dennis makes his home in Henderson, N. C. He is president and editor of the *Henderson Daily Dispatch* and also superintendent of the Sunday School of the First M. E. Church, South, and a member of the board of stewards. He has two children, one boy and one girl.

CLASS OF 1914

Oscar H. Phillips has done an outstanding piece of work as farm agent for Stanly County. At the annual meeting of farm agents in Raleigh in December he was awarded a silver cup for the best exhibit in the farm agent's publicity contest. Last year he received honorable mention for the work that was being done in his county.

CLASS OF 1920

In the *Christian Herald* for September 20, 1930, Rev. J. Earl Gilbreath had a sermon, ''Jesus Makes a Church Survey.'' Rev. Mr. Gilbreath is pastor of the M. E. Church, South, at Cleveland, Tenn.

CLASS OF 1921

T. Aubrey Morse has recently been elected to the National Board of Directors of the Association of Boys' Work Secretaries of North America. He also holds the office of president

of the Kentucky chapter of the same organization. He is located at the Y. M. C. A. in Lexington, Kentucky.

Carl Motsinger, with Mrs. Motsinger and their two children, lives at Welcome, N. C., where he is principal of the school.

CLASS OF 1922

Kelly Elmore received his Ph.D. from Duke this past June. He recently accepted a position as head of the Chemistry Department, Arkansas Polytechnic College.

T. C. Kirkman was located in St. Augustine, Fla., for five years after graduation in the Valuation Department of the Florida East Coast Railway. He later transferred to Roanoke, Va., and this past October accepted a position with the Interstate Commerce Commission as Land Appraiser with the Bureau of Valuation. He is now located at Hotel Stewart, Bartow, Florida.

CLASS OF 1923

The wedding of Aura Holton and James M. Godard, A.M. '30, took place in the Presbyterian Church in Durham on December 21. Aura has been teaching in the Durham High School for the past few years. They will make their home at 811 Second Street, Durham. James is a graduate of Park College, Missouri, and last year received his A.M. from Duke University. He is now taking graduate work and instructing in Education at Duke.

Mr. and Mrs. Doane Stott (Flora Belle Dawson) have been sent by the Methodist Mission Board to Japan as missionaries. They are located at 24 Nakayamate Dori, 2 Chome, Kobe, Japan. They are at present studying the Japanese language before taking up their work.

CLASS OF 1924

Henry Greene holds a position with the Virginian Railway Company, Norfolk, Va.

Mrs. M. V. Koonce (Marie Davis) has moved from Roanoke, Va., to 3 B. Earle Court, Granby and Thirty-third Streets, Norfolk, Va.

CLASS OF 1925

Lemuel Lee Bridgers holds a position with the Hickory Health Department as milk and water inspector. He has a son, Lemuel Lee Bridgers, Jr., who was born on April 21, 1930.

Jasper L. Clute has been in Pensacola, Fla., for the past three years working for the Newport Company. His address is 1802 Cervantes Street.

The wedding of John Braxton Craven of Lexington, N. C., and Mrs. Margene Roha Elsner of Detroit, Mich., took place in New York City on October 27.

Lucy Glasson was married on December 20 to Harold Peyton Wheeler, A. M. '29. They were married in the Hilton Memorial Chapel, University of Chicago. They will make their home in Boonville, Missouri, where Harold is teaching in the Kemper Junior College.

Beatrice Harward, 1006 Monmouth Avenue, Durham, is teaching this year at the Aycock High School, Henderson, N. C.

Lula Mae Isley was married to Lieutenant Ralph E. Butterfield in the Little Church Around the Corner in New York City on November 15. They live at 3567—32nd. Street, San Diego, Cal.

Rosa Elizabeth King of 901 Broad Street, Durham, has a position with the Continental Life Insurance Company with offices at 506 Southern Fire Building, Durham.

Nancy Kirkman and Louise McAnally, '26, live at Apartment 1 A, 43-23 Fortieth Street, Long Island City, New York.

Mr. and Mrs. Wade Waldo Morgan and their daughter, Ethel Susan, live at 242 N. Edgeworth Street, Greensboro. Mrs. Morgan was, before her marriage, Miss Frederica Roberts.

Albert Warren Stainback is an airplane pilot in the United States Army. He is located now at Kelly Field, San Antonio, Texas. Before going to Kelly Field, he was stationed at Riverside, California.

Roy A. Swaringen, director of physical education at the North Junior High School, Winston-Salem, lives at 1816 Buena Vista Road. He formerly taught at the Oxford Orphanage.

Randleman, N. C., is the address of Robert L. Wilson. He is general manager and secretary-treasurer of the Randleman Motor Company, a Ford agency.

CLASS OF 1926

Bill Latta of Wilmington, N. C., is taking graduate work at the Protestant Episcopal Seminary, Alexandria, Va.

CLASS OF 1927

Mrs. Wilson Irby Hurt (Lois Hackney) lives at Chelsea Studios, Apartment C. 3,654 St. Mark's Avenue, Brooklyn, N. Y.

Announcement has recently been made of the marriage of Anita Riggsbee and Mr. William H. Lyle of New York City. They were married on July 28, 1930, in Richmond, Va. Mr. and Mrs. Lyle will live in New York City where he has a position with the American Telephone and Telegraph Company.

Charlie Saunders played professional baseball for several years after leaving college. He is now employed in the office of the department manager, Burlington Mills, Burlington, N. C.

James B. Taylor, assistant manager of the Bradstreet Company, North Carolina Bank Building, Greensboro, was married on September 3, 1930 to Miss Minnie Cahoon. They live at 300 Tate Street.

Frank M. Warner was one of the three young men who passed the State Personnel Committee of the Y. M. C. A. in December. They will be recommended to the National Council for ratification, which will give them rating as Y. M. C. A. secretaries. Before an employed officer of the "Y" can receive the rating of secretary he must satisfy the personnel committee as to his personal habits, ability, standing in the community, health, and preparation for his task. Candidates submit two papers, a year apart, and stand a verbal examination in addition to the written credentials presented. Frank has been in charge of boys' work at the Y. M. C. A. in Greensboro for the past several years and has made a splendid record.

CLASS OF 1928

On April 28, 1930, Thomas S. Shutt and Miss Eva Jordan Wells were married. They are making their home in Bahama, N. C., where Tom is teaching English in the Durham County schools.

Jack Caldwell, '26, and "Bohunk" Weaver, '28, live at 414 West 120th Street, New York City.

Otho Thomas Colclough, 365 Carr Street, Jackson, Michigan, is an electrical engineer and connected with Consumers' Company.

William A. Phelps lives at Fairfax Apartment, No. 1, Bessemer Avenue, Greensboro. He was married on January 2, 1928, to Miss Mary Elizabeth Thomas.

Alfred F. Hammond taught in the Durham County schools last year. He is now studying medicine at the University of North Carolina.

John Franklin Bivins, 512 Worth Drive, High Point, is salesman for the Glasgow-Stewart Company, dealers in automotive supplies.

Mrs. Galen Elliott has moved from Washington, N. C., to 13 Travis Avenue, Charlotte. She was before her marriage Marguerite Poe.

Selma Warlick has been a reporter for the *Herald-Sun, Inc.,* at Durham since graduating from college. This fall she entered the School of Journalism at Columbia University and is

(Continued on page 35)

Year Just Closed was Notable One in the History of Duke

(Continued from page 19)

Work of the Duke Press extended the number of volumes published to almost 50, comprising a varied list of scholarly and literary works.

James A. Thomas of New York, friend of the late James B. Duke, headed the Duke Memorial chapel project, for erecting a special small chapel in the large university chapel, to be dedicated to the memory of Washington Duke and his sons.

A long list of notable faculty additions was announced by President Few, bringing many outstanding scholars to the various schools and departments of the university.

Twenty-three states and several foreign countries were represented in the student body of the Duke summer school.

Dr. C. F. Korstian was chosen director of the Duke Forest and extensive development plans were begun on the University's large woodland campus.

Names of new Duke buildings were assigned. The names included those of Craven, Kilgo, Crowell, Alspaugh, Carr, Gray, York, Page, Giles, Pegram, Bassett, and Brown, all of them associated with the university history and traditions.

Alumni meetings were held in 36 cities on December 11, in observance of Duke University day.

Dr. B. Weinburg of Paris, Dr. Robert A. Milliken of California, and other distinguished scientists and scholars visited the University during the year, and were heard in special lectures.

A law school loan fund was established by the initial gift of Dean Justin Miller.

Other activities and events, too numerous to be listed, were recorded during the year, which in many ways was the fullest and most satisfactory Duke has known. Both students and faculty were exceptionally active during the year and achieved much in their various fields of study, teaching, writing, and research.

a candidate for a Master of Science degree in June. Her address is 606 West 116th Street, New York City.

John Weber says that it is easier going to school than working. He has a position in the office of the Director of Public Works, Danville, Va.

L. R. Carter, Jr., was married on February 26, 1930, to Miss Edna M. Sykes. They make their home at 216 West Trinity Avenue, Durham.

CLASS OF 1929

Grady O'Neal Cook is in the accounting department, Southern Public Utilities Company, Duke Power Building, Charlotte.

Charles E. Tuttle is now making his home in Richmond, Va., at 806 North Boulevard.

M. Grogan Beall is connected with the Citizens' Realty and Insurance Company at 102½ West Main Street, Durham.

Henry G. Ruark, Box 2185 Yale Station, New Haven, Conn., is a student in the Yale Divinity School.

Martha Gibson is teaching at the Children's Home in Winston-Salem.

John D. Hales, Jr., Temperanceville, Va., is teaching in the high school and coaching athletics.

John Sidney Shaw is a member of the high school faculty at Orlando, Fla.

Arthur Jefferson Hughes, Jr., 1126 Fairfield Avenue, Fort Wayne, Indiana, is an engineer for the General Electric Company.

Anne Piper Umstead and Evelyn Hancock are employed in the Duke University Hospital.

Mack Ivey Cline teaches in the Public Schools at Erwin, N. C.

Julian Connally is a commercial agent for the New York Telephone Company at 2177 Albemarle Road, Brooklyn.

Elizabeth Carlton lives at her home, 203 Trinity Avenue, Durham, and teaches in the Durham County Schools.

Conrad C. Cline returned to Duke to take graduate work. His address is Duke Station, Box 4791, Durham.

Vertie Moore is at Aurora, N. C.

Maxwell A. Mintz lives at 1915 Billingsby Terrace, New York City.

Frances Mason lives at her home, 608 W. Chapel Hill Street, Durham. She teaches in the city schools.

Evelyn Bell is teaching in her home town, Rocky Mount.

Milford Joseph Baum is with the Atlantic Commission Company, now stationed at 302 Prospect Avenue, Milwaukee, Wisconsin, c/o Cliff Manor.

Herbert O'Keef has located in Durham where he is a reporter for the Durham *Morning Herald*.

Fred H. Capps teaches at the Baylor School for Boys, Chattanooga, Tenn.

Thomas S. Stearnes is attending Harvard Law School. His address is 96 Winthrop Street, Cambridge, Mass.

Magruder Tuttle has been chosen captain of the Navy football team. He played on the Duke freshman team in 1926. He played in the recent Army-Navy game and one of the sports writers said: "Tuttle is a heavyweight boxing champion at Annapolis, and any Cadet player who gets in his way on Saturday will be in for a rough afternoon."

Philip Howell Crawford, Jr., Hector Paul Strickland and Emerson Thompson Sanders received LL.B. degrees from Duke in June, 1930. Philip Crawford is in newspaper work at Pinehurst, N. C. Emerson Sanders and Hector Strickland are both practicing law, the former at Dunn and the latter at Durham.

What Some Duke Men Are Doing and Saying

(Continued from page 29)

This would make a grand total of approximately $7,000,000 as the annual cost of maintaining a battleship. This is about the same as the cost of maintaining a great university like the University of Illinois, Yale or Harvard.

Seven million dollars would be sufficient for 7,000 scholarships at $1,000 each or 3,500 scholarships at $2,000 each. Two thousand dollars is the amount yielded by a Rhodes scholarship for study at Oxford and is at least twice as much as the average American student spends on a college year. Who can doubt that 3,500 international scholarships would do more to keep the peace of the world than one battleship? The Pan-American Bureau and the League of Nations should be actively interested in promoting such international study, for it means not merely peace but understanding and friendship and business and all those larger interests that a community of nations must develop along with the furling of the battle-flags.

Gray Manufacturing Co.
Flint Manufacturing Co. No. 1
Flint Manufacturing Co. No. 2
Arlington Cotton Mills
Myrtle Mills, Inc.
Arkray Mills, Inc.

Spinners and Doublers Fine Combed
and Double Carded

LONG STAPLE PEELER and EGYPTIAN YARNS

20's to 120's

Put up in all Descriptions for the Following Industries:

ELECTRICAL	WEAVERS
LACE	KNITTERS
MERCERIZERS	THREAD

MAIN OFFICE:	DIVISION OFFICES:	GENERAL SALES OFFICE:
Gastonia, N. C.	Boston	New York City
	Philadelphia	
	Chicago	
	Chattanooga	

COMPANIONSHIP

To THE cosy intimacy of the firelight hour, Camel adds a
perfect companionship. It is the smoke one might dream
of, fragrant and mellow, mild and altogether delightful.

The mildness of Camel is a natural mildness, from the
blending of choicest sun-ripened tobaccos—never over-
treated, never flat or insipid.

AMELS

DUKE UNIVERSITY ALUMNI REGISTER

February, 1931

VOLUME XVII

NUMBER 2

THE GENERAL LIBRARY OF DUKE UNIVERSITY AT NIGHT

Duke University Alum n Register

(*Member of American Alumni Council*)

Published at Durham, N. C., Every Month in the Year in the Interest of the University and the Alumni

Volume XVII   *February, 1931*   Number 2

In This Issue

Editor and Business Manager .... HENRY R. DWIRE, '02

Assistant Editors .... ELIZABETH ALDRIDGE, '24
                                 ALBERT A. WILKINSON, '26

Advertising Manager .... CHARLES A. DUKES, '29

TWO DOLLARS A YEAR   20 CENTS A COPY

ENTERED AS SECOND-CLASS MATTER AT THE POST-OFFICE AT
DURHAM, NORTH CAROLINA

Cover Page

The cover page of this issue of the REGISTER gives an idea of the beauty of the West Campus at night. The photograph shows the lighted Library tower in outline against the dark sky, the whole making one of the most impressive pictures yet taken on the new campus.

Attracting Attention

The research work being done by members of the Duke faculty is attracting wide attention. It is the desire of the REGISTER to present in every issue one or more articles showing what is being done in that line. This month the achievements in research endeavor of some of the members of the faculty are presented, and next month the series will be continued.

New Alumni Club Heads

Some more photographs are presented in this issue of new presidents of local alumni clubs, elected at the December meetings. Every newly elected president has been asked for his photograph, but quite a number are not yet in hand. It is hoped to keep on publishing them until the entire list is completed.

Organizations

In the case of many alumni who have been out of college for some time the REGISTER is naturally the most effective point of contact between the institution and the "old grad." Some things on the campus that are perfectly familiar to those who are on the scene, or who have left college in the past few years, are not so familiar to those who have been out for a considerable time. That is true of campus organizations. For that reason it is the intention of the REGISTER to publish from time to time articles relating to these organizations and their programs.

The March Issue

Unless all signs fail, the March issue of the REGISTER will be one of the very best yet issued. There will probably be some attractive new campus photographs, one or more very special feature articles, and other things of exceptional interest.

Look out for the March issue.

THE EDITOR.

ART TREASURES IN COLLECTION AT DUKE

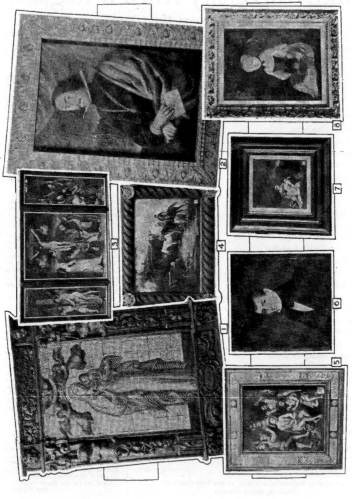

Above are pictured some of the rare paintings to be exhibited with other art objects and Americana at Duke University on Thursday, Friday, and Saturday, Feb. 26, 27 and 28. Shown in the group are: (1) A Portuguese primitive Madonna; (2) Spanish Nobleman by Pacheco; (3) Dutch primitive in triptych; (4) Smith Shop by the Road, by Jan Silbrecht; (5) A Spanish primitive; (6) Portrait by Chester Harding; (7) Pieta by Annabel Carraca; (8) Girl with Dog, by an unknown early eighteenth century artist. (A description of the art exhibit appears on another page.)

Duke University Alumni Register

| Volume XVII | February, 1931 | Number 2 |

Editorial Comment

ON THE RIGHT LINE

The Alumni Office has received recently several requests from "old grads" asking that Duke University literature be sent to prospective students.

One alumnus sent a considerable number of names of such prospective students, giving information about each one, including his scholastic attainments, personality, and so forth.

He stated that he would send another list in a few days of additional individuals who need what Duke has to offer and who are of a type to make desirable college students.

This is a way in which other alumni can render helpful service.

The idea at Duke is not to go out with a view to getting as many students as possible, but it is the purpose to see that those who do come are of a type who will be most likely to make a success of college life.

The alumni of the University, either acting as members of their local club organizations or simply acting in their capacities as individual alumni, have a real opportunity for service to Alma Mater in that connection.

DEEPLY INTERESTED

Sometimes there is a suggestion from some source that perhaps alumni of the old Trinity College days may naturally not be as much interested in the doings at Duke and the activities of the Alumni Office as those of a more recent period in the life of the institution.

And yet there is gratifying evidence from time to time that former students of all periods in the life of the institution are coming together with a common pride in Duke's achievements and a common desire to be helpful in every possible way.

The Alumni Office appeal for donations to the General Alumni Fund furnishes a case in point.

Three of the first contributors this year to that fund were the oldest alumnus in point of years, the oldest living graduate and the oldest former member of the Trinity College faculty.

The interest of these men is typical of that of many other graduates who went out from Trinity years ago.

They love the old Trinity, but they are no less loyal for that reason to the new Duke.

They realize that all are members now of one family of over six thousand alumni, representing practically every state in the Union and a number of other countries as well, and that Duke deserves and needs their support and coöperation.

ATHLETICS FOR ALL

Wallace Wade, Duke's new Director of Athletics, who recently came here after a notably successful career at the University of Alabama, has already made a deep impression upon the University community and the citizens generally of Durham and of North Carolina.

His high ideals of sportsmanship, his sincerity and his sound common sense have appealed to all.

Coach Wade has said some things that are not always emphasized by college coaches, but there is a general feeling that he is on the right line.

For one thing, he does not conceive of college athletics as intended solely for a few exceptional individuals who have the ability to shine in intercollegiate contests.

Neither does he think that the winning of victories is the only important thing in college athletics.

On the contrary, he has made it plain that one of his chief aims at Duke will be to develop a program of athletics for all the students, and that he is going to consider certain other things more vitally important than simply success in intercollegiate athletic activities.

There is no question but that athletics, including intercollegiate sports, has a legitimate place in college and university life.

But athletics are intended for more than a very small proportion of a student body, and an athletic program that does not take into account the needs of the rank and file of students is certainly defective.

It must be equally obvious that the maintenance of high ideals of sportsmanship is of decidedly more importance than the mere winning of games.

Mr. Wade does well to emphasize these points, and in reiterating and re-emphasizing them from time to time he will render the whole cause of intercollegiate athletics a needed service.

KEEP AT IT

"It's easier to be educated than to stay educated."

These words, recently attributed to President Newcomb Carlton, of the Western Union Telegraph Company, give clearly and succinctly one of the best possible arguments for adult education.

A good many people secure at college at least the fundamentals of an education.

Some stop there, seeming to imagine that in some mysterious way the educational process has been completed.

Others go ahead, continuing to study and to refresh their minds by constant contact with the best in art and literature, and in other ways.

A very few approach the ideal of the late Bishop Edward Rondthaler, of the Southern Province of the Moravian Church, who recently died in his eighty-eighth year, and whose education continued almost until the day of his death.

He was a student to the very end.

We are living in a constantly changing world.

New things are happening all the time; new inventions are changing the whole course of civilization in certain lines; new knowledge in more than one field is supplanting other, and less complete knowledge.

Certainly no man or woman in this new day can afford to stand still, content with what he or she learned years ago, and making no effort to "stay educated."

Let's try constantly, not simply to "be educated," if we may be permitted to use that expression, but to "stay educated."

WINNING AND LOSING

The newspapers told some months ago of the presentation to Sir Thomas Lipton, noted English sportsman, of a loving cup, inscribed as follows, in part: "To the World's Best Loser."

The cup was presented in New York by Mayor Walker, and the world applauded this unusual, and yet eminently sensible, tribute to good sportsmanship.

There is a lesson in this incident that college students, and alumni as well, should keep constantly in mind.

It is not necessary to win all the time in order to achieve success in sports or in other lines.

And it is quite possible to achieve victory even in the hour of defeat by maintaining high ideals of sportsmanship, such ideals as the unsuccessful challenger for the America's Cup, defeated year after year, has maintained.

To be able to win and to keep one's head in the hour of success, is important; to be able to lose and to make the very losing an element in the strengthening of character, is of equal consequence.

WHY NOT?

There are now fifty-four regularly organized local clubs of Duke alumni and three others are in process of organization.

There should be at least several more.

There are quite a few counties in this and other states that have plenty of alumni to assure successful local clubs.

The only thing needed is for one or more alumni to take the initiative and coöperate with the Alumni Office in the matter of organizing such groups.

This is a particularly good time for that type of service.

Picture of Duke Home Place Taken Many Years Ago. Late Washington Duke Sitting on the Porch.

Old Duke Home Place, Near Durham, is to be Preserved

Acquisition By Duke University of Former Home of Washington Duke, Birthplace of Benjamin N. and James B. Duke, Made Possible Through the Generosity of Mrs. Mary Duke Biddle—Grounds and Buildings are to Be Restored

THE home place of Washington Duke, where Benjamin N. Duke and James B. Duke were born, is to be restored and permanently preserved by Duke University through the generosity of Mrs. Mary Duke Biddle, of New York, daughter of Benjamin N. Duke. The old farm has just been purchased from Miss Allen, whose family has lived there for many years.

Situated three miles north of Durham, the Duke place was the cradle of the great Duke fortunes, for it was here that Washington Duke and his sons first began the manufacture of tobacco shortly after the Civil War. The original home is still standing and in a good state of preservation, and the old tobacco factory, a frame building, is likewise in good repair.

It having been the scene of their happy early years, Washington Duke and his sons were deeply attached to the old place, and visited there frequently after moving to Durham. A two-story frame structure

with a porch extending across the entire front, the house is not unlike many other country homes of its period, but has the distinction of having sheltered a family whose philanthropies over a third of a century approximated $90,000,000.

Both grounds and buildings will be restored to a likeness of their appearance half a century ago, and as far as possible original furnishings will be replaced there. More definite plans for the future of the homestead will probably be outlined soon when James A. Thomas, of New York, a close friend of the Duke family, who has been deeply interested in the matter, visits Durham and confers with Duke officials regarding the future of the old home place.

The old house was built in 1851 shortly before Washington Duke's marriage to his second wife, Artelia Roney, of Alamance County. Here were born three children, Mary Duke, Benjamin N. Duke, and

"Factory" on Old Duke Farm in Which B. N. and J. B. Duke
Worked as Boys

Original Well on the Duke Place, Near Durham.

James B. Duke. The Duke family lived here until
about 1875, moving to Durham to a newly built home
on Main Street.

Effort will be made to preserve the homestead with
its many Duke traditions, including the refurnishing
of the rooms in the style of the eighteen seventies.

There are a number of landmarks on the place that
existed at the time of the residence of the Washington
Duke family there—the old well and well house, several venerable elms and walnut trees, an old crib, and
one of the early tobacco "factories." The factory
now standing is the third built near the house by members of the family. The first two, log structures, have
long been torn down; but the third is a frame structure which, like the house, is in good state of repair.

Washington Duke and his sons visited the old place
frequently after their removal to Durham, and in the
early years of the present century he made a final trip
there and, sitting in a rocking chair, posed for a photographer on the porch of the old house.

The old home is not unlike many rural homes of
the late nineteenth century, but it has the distinction
of having been the shelter for many years for a family
whose later philanthropic gifts were to rank with the
highest in the United States.

There were three factory buildings erected on the
farm during the early days. The earliest two were log
structures, the first merely a one-story, one-room affair
with no windows. The second log factory was two
stories high and was an indication of the rising prosperity of the pioneer manufacturers. As their fortunes continued to grow and prospects for enlarged
enterprise developed, they built a third and larger factory, which still stands. Their next venture in building took them to the town of Durham.

The work in the farm factories was divided among
members of the family and a number of bound boys
who came there to live. From seedlings to the cured

and granulated smoking tobacco, the entire process of
growing and manufacture was done by hand. The
boys, including Washington Duke's sons, flailed the
cured leaves in the barn with sticks, and unpleasant
work it was in the close, ill-ventilated quarters.

There are still those in the neighborhood who recall
the activities of the Duke family on their old farm.
Several of the older men living nearby can remember
tramping over the countryside with B. N. and J. B.
Duke, and remember well their sister Mary, who
papered the parlor of the house wherein she was soon
to be married. Incidentally, that very same wallpaper
may be seen today.

The Dukes loved to return for visits to the old place,
and Washington Duke went out there in his carriage a
number of times during his last years, on one of these
occasions posing for the picture seen at the head of
this article.

Overman Books Given to Duke

The library of Duke University has received a valuable gift of books owned by the late Senator Lee S.
Overman of North Carolina. The collection, which
Senator Overman intended to go to the library of his
alma mater, numbers 450 volumes. They are the books
which he gathered in his Washington office for many
years.

The newly received collection includes 295 volumes
of the Congressional Record, 17 congressional direc-
tories, six volumes of laws relating to American charities, and reprints of the Journals of the Continental
Congress, 1776-1784.

Eight volumes of exceptional interest comprise the
set of Hind's Precedents. There are also many Senate and House documents and journals. The books
will form a serviceable addition to the volumes of a
similar nature shelved at the Duke library.

Art Objects and Americana of Great Value at Duke

First Exhibition of the Duke University Art Association Presents Several Hundred Items
Illustrative of American, European and Chinese Art and Antiques—
Valuable Collection in Confederate Wing of Exhibition

THE week-end of February 26, 27 and 28 will register a new landmark in the intellectual life of Duke University, for then the University's art association will open to the public its first exhibition. It will be held in the library on the East Campus.

Though the art association was formed only a few months past, rapid progress has been made in assembling a collection of several hundred items illustrative of European, American, and Chinese painting, English and American glassware, porcelain and pewter, early American furniture and tapestries, European and American prints; and of significance for the region in which the University is located, a novel collection of books, broadsides, manuscripts, music, and prints relating to the Confederacy.

Outstanding illustrations of early European art are a Primitive triptych of Dutch origin and a Portuguese Primitive, "Madonna and Child." Another madonna "La Belle Jardiniere," of the school of Raphael, and "Adoration of the Magi," by an unknown Spanish painter; a Pieta, by Annabel Carracha, and "Lot and His Wives" by Jordaens, round out a group of religious paintings. Of similar nature, however, are etchings of the Raphael cartoons now in Hampden Court, illustrative of the life of Christ, and a Rembrandt etching, "Descent from the Cross."

Secular subjects prior to the nineteenth century include a portrait by Pacheco, teacher of Velasquez. Two portraits by Gainsborough, a Hogarth, a Jan Silbrecht and a Dekeyser, are notable examples of English and Dutch paintings. For the more recent period are landscapes by Charles Emil Jacque and Jacob Maris. Of particular associational value is a painting "The Flight Into Egypt," by an unknown artist, dating probably from the seventeenth century, a work which was secured in Italy by a member of Mark Twain's Innocents Abroad party in 1867, and which is spoken of as an "M. A." (Michel Angelo) in "Innocents Abroad."

The illustrations of American paintings are two Sully replicas, a Chester Harding, and two unidentified portraits by unknown artists. A separate gallery is filled with 21 Chinese scrolls, landscapes and portraits, dating from the Ming dynasty to the recent past.

Further oriental pieces include six Tibetan temple banners, a similar number of temple hangings and an excellent representation of imperial embroideries.

Adjoining the Chinese collection is a large assortment of early English, Chinese, and American pewter, early American handwoven embroideries, and ceramics. A third gallery is featured by lustreware, Liverpool, Ridgeway, and Bennington pitchers, Wistarberg bowls, Bristol, Stiegal, and Sandwich glass, witchball bottles of Nilsea glass, Severs china of the Napoleonic period, and a case of early American bottles and flasks. As a wall setting for these are Louis XIV tapestries, a seventeenth century court dress, and one worn at the Court of Maximilian.

The collection of prints includes examples of the art of Breugel, Callot, Cruikshank, and Whistler. There is also a set of Audubon's "Birds of America," in four volumes, the rare elephant edition of the eighteen thirties.

Period furniture comprises a collection in a special room. Outstanding is a complete Queen Anne set, including a bed and its original lace hangings and coverings, and in this room also are early American homespuns, Sheraton tables, and a very large handmade rug. One old table, which was carried from Virginia to Missouri by ox-cart, is one of the interesting larger pieces. An assortment of old Spanish chests, large and of sturdy wood with elaborate scrolled iron bands, is an excellent illustration of European handicraft.

Finally, of peculiar local color is the Confederate wing of the exhibition. Invaluable as well as original is a manuscript Register of the Acts of the Confederate Congress in which the caption of every statute of the Congress is given, with dates of passage and approval by President Davis. Here also are unpublished manuscript statutes of the Confederate Congress, letters by Jefferson Davis and Robert E. Lee,

(Continued on page 62)

Self-Help Opportunities at Duke Aiding Many Students

Variety of Occupations on the Campus and in City Open to Those Who Need Assistance in Order to Complete Their University Courses—Some of the Ways in Which Students Help Themselves

ALUMNI and other friends of Duke University who have by inquiry or by chance learned the actual facts have been gratified to discover that self-help opportunities at Duke University have kept pace with the rapid growth of the institution in other respects.

Approximately twenty per cent of Duke students, irrespective of where they come from, do some type of work to assist in defraying their expenses. This is true not only in the undergraduate schools for men and women but also in the graduate schools.

There is a creditable percentage of students who hold graduate scholarships, assistantships, and fellowships, awarded by the University in payment for services rendered departments in the capacity of examination and quiz readers, library helpers, and research assistants.

In the undergraduate schools for men and women, it is natural that the most easily obtainable, and, in a way, the most popular, form of student help is found in dining hall service in the Student Unions. Altogether, more than a hundred students earn their board by waiting on table, and other forms of work necessary in a dining hall. Such work takes care of board, which is the largest individual item of expense that a student encounters at Duke University. This would not be true at some institutions, where tuition charges are higher than boarding costs.

Duke students, however, are by no means confined to this one type of service. Their employment on the University campus and in the city covers a wide range of work. One type of employment which has become notably successful has been the connection with the Information Office in the Union, on the West Campus. From this center, visitors are conducted by student guides over the campus; students are sought out at their rooms and elsewhere, and notified of 'phone calls; telegrams are delivered, and visitors are put in touch with their friends.

A number of students possessing clerical ability are employed around the University, and in the city, as stenographers, clerical assistants, and as file clerks. Not a small number of students secure employment

as agents for the University Laundry, collecting laundry, pressing, shoes to be repaired, and hats to be reblocked. This work is done on a commission basis, a student being assigned a certain section of a dormitory. Many of the students who have energy and enterprise build up a good and profitable personal business.

Others of the students secure jobs firing furnaces. This, of course, is seasonal work. The same students, however, usually secure employment at the same places in mowing lawns and in doing other work around the residences, in the warmer seasons.

Here and there appear individual students possessed of some special training or talent along varied lines such as insurance salesmanship; radio repairing; piano tuning; directing, or singing in, city church choirs; doing title abstracting; and other types of work. These are usually able to secure employment after a period of probation.

The above-mentioned forms of aid do not include tuition scholarships awarded to incoming undergraduates each year, nor the Angier B. Duke Memorial Student Loan Fund, which is amply endowed. Through these sources, a surprisingly large number of self-help students, and those who are not self-help students, secure assistance each year on terms seldom obtainable elsewhere.

Officials of the University say that it has always been, and will continue to be, the policy of Duke University to aid its students in securing part-time employment to assist in defraying necessary expenses. They state, however, that there is, and doubtless will continue to be, a greater demand for work than can be met in full by the self-help department. Under such conditions, the University has been forced into a policy of not definitely promising work to students prior to their enrollment. With an ever-increasing student body, it is felt that the authorities handling the self-help bureau are justified in their policy of requiring students to demonstrate their worth and need, under the observation of competent and sympathetic officials, before employment service is offered.

Thousands of Meals are Served Daily in Duke Dining Halls

Most Modern System and Equipment Characterize Boarding Department In the Two Unions—Some Interesting Facts and Figures Regarding the Food Consumed and Other Details

DUKE University's boarding department is an institution in itself. A section is operated on each campus, with the storerooms for the whole department located on the new campus in a modern setting.

J. E. Thompson, the general manager, has an office force of two, secretary and bookkeeper. He is assisted by C. N. Northcutt, in the Coffee Shop; C. H. Blanchard, in the Men's Union; Miss Nell Dooley, dietitian, in the Men's Union; and Mrs. Helen Roberson, dietitian, in the Women's Union. Miss Dooley is a graduate of the Pennsylvania School of Dietetics, and Mrs. Roberson studied at the School of Dietetics of Columbia University.

The personnel of Mr. Thompson's working force includes: Salaried employees, 43; and student waiters, 132. The student waiters are given their board for their services. Many of these students would not be able to remain in school if the dining halls were closed. The total remuneration for their work, if reckoned in terms of money, amounts to $22,000 per year.

The salaried employees include two bakers; four bakers' helpers; one butcher; two chefs and eight cooks; two janitors; four colored waiters, in the Coffee Shop; eleven "bus boys"; six dishwashers; two silver boys; four glass boys; and a number of other employees in the storeroom.

S. S. Veasey is the head baker. Mr. Veasey owned a bakery, for a number of years, in Lexington, N. C. He was head baker for Paschall's Bakery, Dur-

ham, for nine years. W. R. Miller, the head butcher, was trained in his father's butcher shop in Pennsylvania. He also owned a shop at one time. All the employees have been chosen for their ability and experience.

The buying is necessarily on a very large scale, but even the most careful buying, under annual contracts, cannot anticipate all conditions which arise in emergencies. This necessitates considerable emergency buying, which is done to the best possible advantage. Every effort is made to operate the plant on as economical a basis as possible in order that students of the University may have the benefit of securing good food, well prepared and carefully served, at as reasonable a rate of board as possible. Board rarely costs more than twenty-five dollars per month in the Union. No effort is made to show a profit in this

Student Dining Room, Woman's College Campus.

department. All money received is spent on the purchase, preparation, and service of food, and upkeep.

Food when purchased is shipped in carloads to Durham and hauled to the storerooms in the truck owned by the University; or delivered to the door of the storerooms by the shippers.

The bookkeeper keeps a record of all food purchased and placed in the storerooms. All food taken from the storerooms is charged to the department using it. In this manner it is possible to keep a very careful record of the cost of running the department. From thirty-four hundred to four thousand meals are served each day in the department, varying with the time in the week. Many students are away from the campus over week-ends. This reduces the number of meals served at that time.

An attempt is made to supply, at each meal, all the food that a student should eat. The breakfast menu usually consists of a fruit, a cereal, eggs, meat, coffee, milk, butter, sweet rolls, and either bread or toast. The other two meals include meat, three vegetables, bread, butter, a salad, drinks and dessert. With the exception of the meat, a student is not limited as to the quantity of food consumed.

Speaking of the amount of food consumed in the two Unions, here are some rather impressive figures. Duke students consume twenty-five pounds of coffee and 120 gallons of milk each day. It requires a thousand individual bags of tea for each day's consumption of hot tea. A total of 1500 sweet rolls and a thousand biscuits are eaten for breakfast. The average consumption of eggs is three and a half cases, thirty dozen to the case. When oatmeal is served for breakfast, it requires a hundred pounds to satisfy the appetites of the students. In addition, for those who do not like oatmeal, 54 eight ounce packages of corn-flakes, and seventy-two packages of bran, are usually served.

Duke students are not vegetarians. The average consumption of beef per meal is two hundred and seventy-five pounds. It takes three hundred and fifty pounds of chicken for a meal in the Union. The average weekly purchase of beef amounts to fourteen steer hinds, about a hundred and sixty-five pounds each.

Desserts are also very popular. Students consume forty-five gallons of ice-cream, or one hundred and twenty pies, at a meal. No meal is complete without its salad. This is prepared from fresh vegetables, fruits, gelatine, and salad dressings.

It is necessary to cook five cases of each kind of vegetable for each meal when they come in cans. This amounts to thirty gallons. When this is multiplied by three, one is inclined to catch his breath as he tries to imagine the vast operations necessary for cooking the food for this small army of students. At each meal, five thousand rolls, or their equivalent in bread, are used. Rolls are cooked twice a day. At other times, biscuits, or other types of bread, are provided.

Another interesting item in the operation of this institution is that of the table linen. For the two Unions and the private dining rooms two thousand linen table cloths are used each week. These are changed each day. Nine hundred linen napkins are used each week for luncheons and banquets. For ordinary use, a million paper napkins are purchased at one time. This is not sufficient to last through the school year; however,

A visit to the storerooms is an interesting experience. One finds there listed two hundred and ninety-three different items. These include, besides the staple groceries and the fresh vegetables, little items like pickles, of which thirty-six fifty gallon barrels, of various varieties, are pur-

Student Dining Room, West Campus.

chased each year. These varieties include sweet, sweet mixed, West India gherkins, dill, and fancy sliced. The storeroom is departmentalized with every item in its place. Storeroom employees are charged with the duty of keeping it in order. System reduces the amount of time required for the handling of supplies and helps with the spirit of economy.

This spirit of system operates throughout the entire department. To watch it in operation, one would never imagine it to be the outgrowth of the boarding department of an educational institution. It gives one the impression of being greater than that of most southern hotels. Every employee is in his place and the system moves like clockwork from the moment the employees punch the big time clock on entering until they punch it again on leaving.

The equipment for the whole department is the most efficient and modern that could be secured. There are five student dining halls, a coffee shop, and several private dining halls for members of the faculty, for luncheons and banquets. All the dining halls together will seat approximately 1400. A separate cafeteria is provided for serving the colored help. They have their own dishes, dishwashing machine, their own silver, coffee urn and ice water dispenser, in their own dining room.

In the bakeshop one finds the latest improved machinery for baking. The bread is mixed, and cut into rolls, or loaves, by machinery. It is shaped by machinery and placed in the raising ovens without being touched by hand. From the raising ovens, it is transferred in large pans to the baking ovens. For raising and baking four thousand rolls thirty minutes is required. The heat is provided by electricity for the baking; by live steam for raising. Great pie ovens turn these out by the score. In the bakeshop one finds also the refrigerating plant for preserving the raw materials used in the baking.

The butcher shop is just as modern as the bakeshop. The refrigerating plant, the tables, the blocks, and the butchers at work, remind one of the largest of the meat markets in the North.

The food is transferred on large platform trucks, by elevator, from the store-rooms to the kitchen. During this time it is watched carefully to protect its sanitation.

In the refrigerating plant, one finds the same modern spirit carried out. There is a special compartment provided for each of the following: the manufacture of ice; the protection of fruits; for the care of the cheese; for butter; for the storage of eggs; for fresh vegetables; for fresh meat; for cured meats; and for the protection of garbage.

The kitchens are a little world unto themselves. No finer equipment can be found anywhere. There one finds four electric ranges. Each one of these has an oven and four hot plate units, each ten by eighteen inches. Potato peelers, operated by electricity, peel two bushels in four minutes. The largest size Crescent dishwashing machinery washes about forty-eight hundred dishes per hour. There is a special machine, also, for washing glasses and silverware. Four thermotainers preserve the heat in the bread after it is brought up from the bake shop, until it is carried into the dining rooms. There are additional refrigeration provisions for preserving food, in the kitchen; dish warmers; two soup pots, which contain one hundred and twenty gallons each; two stock pots which hold sixty gallons each; two three-compartment steamers for the preparation of vegetables; and seven eight gallon coffee urns for the dispensing of coffee.

The Woman's Union is provided with the same type of equipment as the men's, with the exception that the ranges are heated with gas.

There are four private dining halls, for serving luncheons and banquets.

Coffee Shop, West Campus.

Modern Method of Treating Empyema at Duke Hospital

Tidal Irrigation and Supplementary Suction Proving Quite Successful Under Direction of Dr. Deryl Hart, Head of the Surgical Staff, who Devised the Particular System Used at the Duke Hospital

EMPYEMA, a severe infection of the pleural cavity that follows at times in the wake of pneumonia or may be occasioned by other causes, is being met effectively at Duke Hospital. And the new method of treating the disease—new in the sense that it has been employed only within the last few years and is far from receiving such wide utilization as its results would apparently justify—is more scientific than the old operation method, more practical, and happier in its aftermath.

The new method has been devised by, and is under the direction of, Dr. Deryl Hart, formerly of Johns Hopkins Hospital, and is known as tidal irrigation and supplementary suction.

Empyema of the chest is an infection of the pleural cavity caused by an organism that gains access to the cavity and grows within it, being most likely to result after pneumonia. Cases so occurring are known as acute empyema; should the lesion fail to heal chronic empyema follows the acute. Chronic empyema may also be produced by an infection with one of the organisms which more characteristically produces a chronic lesion.

In the progress of the infection pus is formed and poisons are absorbed, this condition resulting in the wasting away of the patient and loss of vitality; and, at times, of death.

The treatment of the disease by the method used at Duke Hospital, provides for the insertion of a tube about the size of an ordinary lead pencil through the chest wall and into the pleural cavity. The tube is inserted between the ribs so that these members do not sustain injury as in the case of operation by resection. Through the tube is sent a physiological salt solution, which is contained in a bottle placed above the patient's head. The solution is iso-tonic, that is, it permits diffusion into cells of the cavities without damage to the cell membrane.

And how is the fluid injected? By the patient, through natural breathing. With each inspiratory motion, he receives a portion of the solution; with each exhalation he expels a part of the solution with some of the pus with which it has been diffused. The irrigation bottle is kept replenished and the treatment goes on continually.

A further factor in the system employed is an apparatus which regulates the pressure in relation to the atmospheric pressure permitting any amount of suction desired and thus pulling the lung out. The lung thence comes in contact with the chest wall, thereby obliterating the cavity; healing begins and the patient is on the way to recovery.

It does not require a long period of time to remove the pus; a week will usually clear the cavity; the patient's temperature will drop to normal and a general improvement of his condition be noted. After that, however, the tube must be kept in the body in order to continue the work of draining and giving the lung opportunity to adhere.

In so far as is known, not a single case of chronic empyema has developed from acute cases treated by the method.

Of five patients with chronic empyema since the hospital was opened last summer, two have been discharged from the institution, apparently cured, according to Dr. Hart, and three more are on the road to recovery. One of the discharged patients was a middle-aged woman, who had undergone five operations previously; the other, a young man.

One of the patients now in the hospital, admitted during the latter part of November, the tenth month of the disease, is showing noteworthy progress. At the time of admission he was running a temperature of 105 degrees, his pulse was very rapid, and he was decidedly emaciated. Now his temperature and pulse are normal, and his weight near the average.

In the former method of treatment of chronic empyema the ribs were removed, thus allowing the chest wall to fall and close up the cavity between it and the lung. It is plainly apparent that a far more satisfactory method of treating the disease is to restore the lung through the drainage and suction method.

Another type of case more striking than any of

(Continued on page 54)

University "Y" is Accomplishing Excellent Work on the Campus

Various Features of the Program are Being Carried Out In a Notably Successful Manner
—Some Innovations In This Year's Activities Are Proving
Decidedly Popular—Review of the Work

THE Duke University Young Men's Christian Association has undertaken a real work for this school year. It has already accomplished much of the task which it set for itself in the beginning of the year. The Association is operating on a budget, about two-thirds of which has been paid in. The balance is secured by pledges due this year. All of this has come from students and members of the faculty.

The membership of the Association numbers more than a thousand. About one-fourth of this number are freshmen. Another fourth are members of the faculty. Probably half of the membership is composed of upper classmen.

The officers are W. M. Upchurch, Jr., '31, president, Charles F. Honeycutt, Jr., '31, vice-president; Henry L. Andrews, '31, secretary; and Martin K. Green, '30, treasurer. Dean H. J. Herring is chairman of the Board of Directors. J. Foster Barnes, Director of the Glee Clubs, is vice-chairman. Other members of the Board include Dr. Elbert Russell, Dean of the School of Religion; Prof. R. N. Wilson, head of the Department of Chemistry; Dr. Robert S. Rankin, Assistant Dean of the Graduate School; Judge T. D. Bryson, of the Law School faculty; and Dr. Joseph A. Speed, Medical Director of the University.

An office is maintained for the Association in the Union. The director of the Employment Bureau takes care of the office which is open every afternoon. All of the work of the Association is carried on by student officers and members, under the direction of faculty members of the board of directors. Duke is one of the few institutions of its rank which does not employ a full-time secretary for the work of the Association.

The earliest activity which the Association undertakes is caring for the in-coming freshmen. A beautiful "Duke Handbook" is published and sent away to prospective freshmen during the summer. This handbook, for 1930-31, was a work of art. It is seven by ten inches in size. It has a beautiful white cover which resembles leather. The printing is all in blue. It contains information for the new students regarding the University. There are eight divisions of this booklet which contains eighty pages. The first part contains a brief history of the University from the founding of Union Institute; greetings from officials of the University; a calendar of the University year; a brief introduction to University organizations and University traditions; and an excellent directory of all the buildings. The second part begins with greetings from Dean Wannamaker; continues with a Who's Who at Duke, giving all student officials; adds a detailed program for Freshman Week; and closes with "Tips to the New Men." The third section discusses briefly each organization for students on the men's campus. The fourth part discusses the work of the Y. M. C. A. William D. Murray, president of the Men's Student Government Association, gives a word of welcome to new students in the fifth part, and explains the work of the Association and its subsidiaries. The sixth part discusses the athletics of the University. The seventh part is devoted to the work of the College for Women, with a word of greeting from Dean Alice Baldwin. The Y. W. C. A., the Women's Student Government Association, the Student Publications, and other publications of the University, each have a section devoted to them.

The Y. M. C. A. played a large part in helping to orient the freshmen to Duke atmosphere, during Freshman Week, September 16-22, last fall. The freshmen were welcomed by Y. M. C. A. members on their arrival at the University. They were assisted in getting settled in their rooms. An informal "mixer" was provided by the Association at the Union, on the second night. The Association provided moving pictures in the auditorium, on the third night, and began a freshman tennis tournament on the fourth afternoon.

The Freshman Friendship Council, composed of freshmen working under the direction of the Y. M. C. A., continues to care for the freshmen of the institution throughout. The Council elects its own officers and carries out a program of its own which is similar to that of the Hi-Y Clubs of the city associations from which so many of the freshmen have come. It offers an opportunity for these men to continue the work which they have been doing in the Y's at home.

The Campus Service Committee provides the equipment of and looks after the reading and game rooms in the Union. These are known as the Student Club Rooms. They form the most popular social gathering place of the entire University and are filled with students from early morning until late in the evening. A new project of this committee is the music room just being opened up in the same building. This room contains a piano for the use of students, a radio-phonograph, and other means of musical entertainment. A number of new periodicals are being provided, in this room, for the musical clubs and the dramatic clubs of the campus. Plans are on foot for Sunday afternoon Victrola concerts.

The Social Committee of the Y has become a recognized institution on the campus. It has conducted a number of socials and "get-together" affairs this year which have added much to the enjoyment of the students and have helped to cement the growing student body into a real University spirit.

The Employment Bureau is not the least of the departments of the Association. This institution has placed more than fifty students in remunerative positions which are providing incomes for these men and thus making it possible for them to remain in school.

The Tuesday Recitals of the Association have also attracted much attention, even beyond the bounds of the University campus. On one Tuesday night in each month, the Y brings to Page Auditorium one or more outstanding musicians from various parts of the state. These concerts bring North Carolina talent to the attention of the students and have merited the appreciation received from the entire student body. These recitals are provided by the Association without cost to the students.

The Association has also undertaken to provide Sunday activities for the students. Each Sunday morning a Sunday School is conducted in York Chapel. Dean Herring addresses the large class of men which gathers there. Dr. Mason Crum is secretary of the organization.

Each Sunday afternoon at four o'clock vesper services are held by the Y, in York Chapel, the chapel of the School of Religion. Some of the outstanding religious speakers of the nation have already spoken there. Other speakers are brought to the campus, at other times, to speak on various subjects to the students.

The Quadrangle Pictures, another department of the Y work, operate a motion picture show in the Page Auditorium, every Wednesday and Saturday night. The pictures shown are of the highest type and the admission charged is extremely reasonable. The profits, which so far have amounted to only $125.00, help to increase the Association's funds for work on the campus.

Recently the Quadrangle Pictures celebrated its third birthday. A birthday party was given in the form of a particularly good entertainment. Coöperating in this entertainment were players from Theta Alpha Phi, National Dramatic Fraternity, under the supervision of Mr. A. T. West, Dramatic Director for Duke University; and the University Club Orchestra, under the direction of "Jelly" Leftwich. The players gave an excellent presentation of Eugene O'Neill's sea play, "Bound East for Cardiff."

This coöperation on the part of various organizations is typical of the "Duke spirit," a glorified "Trinity spirit." W. M. Upchurch, president of the Association, is particularly enthusiastic over this spirit. He speaks particularly of the Y's gratitude to Dr. R. L. Flowers for assistance in securing for the Association the picture rights from the University; to Mr. C. B. Markham and Mrs. Irwin Chesson for helping in the collection of the student pledges; and to Henry R. Dwire for coöperation regarding the student club rooms.

Welcoming a Distinguished Gentleman to the State

The arrival of Mr. Wallace Wade in Durham to take charge of the athletic fortunes of Duke University has been widely heralded in the sport sections of the papers and the former Alabama mentor has been given a cordial welcome to Tarheelia. Mr. Wade has the distinction of being perhaps the second most famous coach in the world, his fame being eclipsed only by that of Knute Rockne of Notre Dame. Followers of the great game of football are predicting that his work at Duke is certain to improve greatly North Carolina football as played at all of the state's institutions of higher learning. Whether that is to be true or not may be of little importance. Of far greater importance is the spirit that is to dominate sports in this state, and the first statement of policies from the new Duke coach leads us to believe that whatever else Mr. Wade does or fails to do he will make a contribution to good sportsmanship.

We like the modesty with which this famous coach assumes his new position. We like his record not only as a coach but also as a gentleman. We like what we read about his relationship with the student life at Alabama. We welcome him to North Carolina as a coach, as a sportsman, as a friend of youth, and as a citizen. We hope that he maintains his record of putting into the field winning teams, but whether he does or not we are glad that Wallace Wade, the man, has come to North Carolina.—*High Point Enterprise.*

Taurian Players Busily Engaged with their Spring Productions

One-Act Contest Play, "Bound East for Cardiff," Recently Presented at Page Auditorium
With Much Success—Chinese Play to Be Presented During Spring—
Successful Season Assured

THE Taurian Players are busy with their preparations for the plays which they are to present during the spring. Mr. A. T. West, the dramatic director, is very enthusiastic over the possibilities for a successful term's work.

Tryouts for the spring play were started on the twelfth of January. Mr. West reported a remarkable interest in the play on the campus. He said that enough students to occupy the time of two instructors had applied for enrollment in the course. He hopes to see the work developed to the point where some play will be in preparation all the time.

The play selected for the spring was "Loose Ankles." For this production, Mr. West planned an entirely different cast from the one which presented the fall play, "Polly With a Past." This was done, he said, in order to give as many students as possible the opportunity of appearing in the plays. That is necessary because of the remarkably ability Mr. West finds in such a large number of the players. "Loose Ankles" was given successfully on February 20.

A most successful presentation was given recently of the play which is to be presented by Duke students in the state dramatic contest, at Chapel Hill, sponsored by the Carolina Players and the Extension Department of the University of North Carolina. This is O'Neill's famous one-act sea play, "Bound East for Cardiff." It requires an all male cast. The contest play will have from one to three public presentations. The first presentation will be in the district contest. If the Taurians are fortunate enough to win in the district contest, the play will be presented in the semi-finals for the state. If they are equally fortunate there, the play will be given in the final contest. Other departments of the state contest in dramatics, such as make-up, stage lighting, costuming,

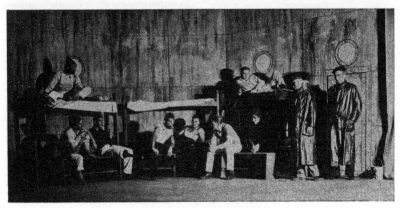

Scene from "Bound East for Cardiff."

Duke will not enter. Mr. West explained that this is due to the fact that the work of his department was just begun in the fall and the courses have not been carried to the point where Duke students could hope to compete in this work this year.

The Taurians will also present, during the spring, a Chinese play, "The Gooseberry Mandarin." This is also one of the larger productions. In addition, there will be the Mayday Play. For this, Mr. West has under consideration Shakespeare's "Taming of the Shrew." If this play is given, it will be in modern costumes.

Among the short plays planned by the class are: "Moonshine," a Carolina folk play, by Arthur Hopkins; and "Tomorrow at Ten," and "Catesby," two charming little interludes by Percival Wilde. The interludes are to be used for semi-public performances on University programs.

Mr. West said that he was not planning a road trip this year. He looks forward to a very successful trip next year, however.

Graduate Fellowships for 1931-32 Are Announced

DEAN W. H. Glasson, of the Graduate School of Arts and Sciences, has made announcement of graduate fellowships, scholarships and assistantships for the year 1931-1932. The announcement in full is as follows:

FELLOWSHIPS

"One Angier Duke Memorial Fellowship of one thousand dollars. Two University Fellowships of eight hundred dollars each. Seven University Fellowships of seven hundred fifty dollars each. Eighteen University Fellowships of six hundred fifty dollars each. In appointing fellows, preference is usually given to applicants who have completed at least one year of successful graduate work.

"Fellows will be required to give a limited amount of assistance in reading papers, in laboratories, or in other departmental duties. Both fellows and scholars carry a full program of graduate work.

"When it seems advisable, a fellowship may be divided between two applicants; or a fellowship and a scholarship may be combined and the total amount divided between two applicants.

GRADUATE SCHOLARSHIPS

"Twenty scholarships of the value of three hundred fifty dollars each are open to graduate students. Scholars may be asked to give a limited amount of assistance in departmental work.

APPOINTMENTS AS GRADUATE ASSISTANTS

"A considerable number of appointments as teaching assistants or readers will be available for graduate students. The compensation will usually range from $350 to $800, depending upon the nature and amount of the work assigned. Assistants receiving $500 or more will not be able to carry a full program of graduate studies.

"All holders of fellowships and scholarships, and such graduate assistants as carry a full program of studies, will be expected to pay the same tuition, matriculation, and minor fees as are paid by other graduate students. The tuition fee of graduate assistants not carrying a full program will be adjusted with due regard to the program of studies followed. Information regarding tuition, fees, room rent and other expenses can be found in the bulletin of the Graduate School of Arts and Sciences.

"Applications should be received on or before March 15, 1931. Address requests for information and application blanks, applications, and testimonials to William H. Glasson, Dean of the Graduate School of Arts and Sciences, Duke University, Durham North Carolina."

Five Periodicals are Now Issued by the Duke University Press

South Atlantic Quarterly, Hispanic American Historical Review, American Literature,
Ecological Monographs and Papers of Trinity College Historical Society
Making Real Contribution In Their Various Fields

DUKE University Press now publishes five periodicals. The oldest of these, with one exception, is the *South Atlantic Quarterly*. This magazine, now in its thirtieth year, was founded in 1902 by the 9019 Scholarship Society of Trinity College. It is a literary review which has gained an excellent reputation throughout the entire nation.

SOUTH ATLANTIC QUARTERLY

Until recently, it was edited by Dr. William H. Wannamaker and Dr. W. K. Boyd. During the past summer, a reorganization was effected because of the pressure of Dr. Boyd's duties as director of libraries. Since then the policies of the magazine have been under the control of an editorial board composed of Dr. William H. Wannamaker, vice-president of Duke University, and Professors William T. Laprade, Newman I. White, and Calvin B. Hoover. Henry R. Dwire is managing editor.

The January issue contains an article on "Recent Political Crises in Great Britain," by William Thomas Morgan; one on "The South Examines Itself," by J. Fred Rippy; a discussion of "The Political Philosophy of William Blake," by Margaret Louise Plunkett; Alban B. Widgery's discussion of "The Motives of the Nationalist Movement in India"; Paul Fatout's account of the life and work of Fitz-James O'Brien, which he has called "An Enchanted Titan"; a discussion of "Unemployment and the Alien," by Harold Fields; "The Shakesperian Serenity," by Harry T. Baker; and Judge Robert W. Winston's excellent account of the strange career of Colonel Tazewell Lee Hargrove. This latter article was reprinted in part by the Boston *Transcript*. The New York *Times* and other newspapers have reviewed articles in the January issue.

The *Quarterly* was established primarily as a medium of opinion concerning southern questions, historical, economic, and literary. It is still seeking to serve this purpose but it now welcomes articles on national and international questions also. Its articles are frequently cited in works dealing with the history and problems of the past thirty years.

HISPANIC AMERICAN REVIEW

One of the most valuable of the publications of the Duke Press is *The Hispanic American Historical Review*. The *Review* is edited by Arthur Scott Aiton, Clarence H. Haring, J. Lloyd Meacham, W. W. Pierson, Jr., J. Fred Rippy, James A. Robertson, Arthur Preston Whitaker, and Mary W. Williams. Its advisory editors include Herbert E. Bolton, Charles E. Chapman, William Spence Robertson, and William R. Shepherd.

The *Hispanic American Historical Review* was founded in 1918. At the end of 1922 it suspended publication because of lack of financial support. It was revived, however, in 1926, Duke University Press assuming responsibility for its publication. Professor James A. Robertson is the managing editor. Associated with him is Professor J. Fred Rippy, of Duke University, a recognized authority on Pan-American political and economic conditions.

The purpose of the *Review* is the publication of historical articles concerning the growth of the two Americas, in the effort to promote a mutual understanding and goodwill between the two. That it is succeeding in this purpose is evidenced by the fact that its articles are being quoted by leaders of the New World in their discussions of economic and political questions.

AMERICAN LITERATURE

American Literature, "A Journal of Literary History, Criticism, and Bibliography," is published by the Duke University Press, with the coöperation of the American Literature Group of the Modern Language Association of America. Dr. Jay B. Hubbell, of Duke University, is chairman of the Board of Editors. Dr. Hubbell said of the magazine when it was founded: "Within the last few years American scholars have awakened to the fact that our literary history supplies a rich and comparatively unworked field. For those who wish to discuss the work of living authors, there are many periodicals available; but *American Literature* is the only scholarly journal devoted solely to research in the field as a whole. *Ameri-*

can Literature was founded to meet a distinct need."
That it is meeting this need the financial receipts are
showing as well as the appreciation which it is receiving from scholars and the literary public.

Having just completed its third year of existence,
this quarterly is well on its way toward success. The
November issue featured several articles in research
concerning the work of Edgar Allan Poe. One of
these discusses Poe's ideas concerning phrenology. It
was written by Edward Hungerford, of Northwestern
University. Another was on the source of Poe's
"Three Sundays in a Week," by Fanny N. Cherry, of
Edinburg College.

The Board of Editors of *American Literature* includes, besides Dr. Hubbell, W. B. Cairns, of the University of Wisconsin; Kenneth Murdock, of Harvard
University; Fred Lewis Pattee, of Rollins College;
and Ralph Lewis Rusk, of Columbia University.

ECOLOGICAL MONOGRAPHS

The youngest member of the family of Duke publications is *Ecological Monographs*, a quarterly. The
January, 1931, issue was its "Volume I, Number 1."
It is the official publication of the Ecological Society
of America. "Ecological" means the adaptation of
Life to Environment. The quarterly is concerned
with the publication of articles which are purely scientific. In addition, the Society is interested in assisting
in the development and conservation of natural resources.

Ecological Monographs will work in close coöperation with its older contemporary *Ecology*, although
the *Monographs* will publish much longer articles.
Dr. A. S. Pearse, of Duke University, is the editor of
the new publication. Associated with him are Bar-
rington Moore, editor of *Ecology*, Washington, D. C.;
H. A. Gleason, of the Brooklyn Botanical Garden;
J. E. Weaver, of the University of Nebraska; R. N.
Chapman, of the University of Hawaii; E. N. Transou,
of Ohio State University; R. E. Coker, of the University of North Carolina; and Chancey Juday, of
the University of Wisconsin.

The first issue of *Ecological Monographs* contained
two articles: "The Rôle of the Sense Organs in Ag-
gregations of Ameiurus Melas," by Edith S. Bowen;
and "Experimental Study of the Water Relations of
Seedling Conifers with Special Reference to Wilting,"
by Robert Marshall.

OLDEST OF PRESS PUBLICATIONS

The oldest of the Duke University Press publications are the *Historical Papers of the Trinity College
Historical Society*. These papers are published from
time to time as material may be secured for them.
Series I was published in 1897. It contained articles

by Robert L. Flowers, Sanders Dent, Edward Graham Daves, John S. Bassett, W. H. Pegram, C. C.
Weaver, and W. K. Boyd. This series is now out of
print.

The work began as an effort on the part of the
Trinity College Historical Society to publish the work
of its members on local history. Succeeding years
have reduced the number of members of the society.
The Duke Press has assumed the publication of the
papers and has accepted a number from outside
sources dealing also with local history.

But for such a medium as this bits of local history,
which have already become valuable, and which will
increase in value as time goes on, could not have been
preserved. It is the purpose of the press to continue
the publication of these papers from time to time as
such material can be secured.

As an evidence of the opinion of the leaders of the
Historical Society as to the value of local history,
there appear, in the list of the papers published, a
number of bits of history of North Carolina individuals and localities. Side by side with "James Robert Brent Hathaway—A Gleaner in North Carolina
History," by Willis Smith, there appears "The Rose
of Sharon Baptist Church," by R. T. Howerton, Jr.
Edgar R. Franklin's paper on "Henry Clay's Visit
to Raleigh," appeared with "Some Social Traits of
the Quakers of Rich Square," by W. A. Bryan.

Through the years of publication run the names of
such authors as Edward Graham Daves, John S. Bassett, W. K. Boyd, R. L. Flowers, John C. Kilgo, N. H.
D. Wilson, W. L. Grissom, M. T. Plyler, P. M. Sherrill, John W. Carr, and James K. Turner, all well-
known in North Carolina.

The latest issue of the *Historical Papers* contains
the "Letters of Richard D. Arnold," edited by Professor Richard H. Shryock, of Duke University.

Modern Method of Treating Empyema at Duke Hospital

(Continued from page 48)

those hereinbefore referred to is being treated at the
hospital—perhaps the first of its type to be thus
treated in the history of medicine. The patient, an
eight-year-old girl, has an infection of the pleural
cavity with a fungus, actinomycosis. The disease has
been, in so far as medical records show, fatal.

Duke Hospital authorities do not know what will
result in the case. But the tidal drainage treatment
is providing free drainage, the temperature of the
child is lower, she is gaining weight and showing general improvement in health.

Number of Books Published by Duke University Men

Members of Faculty and Alumni Issue Volumes that Are Meeting With a Hearty Response From Readers In Several Different Fields—Brief Mention of Some Recent Volumes

[The ALUMNI REGISTER is noting, from month to month, books issued by Duke University men and women in various fields of study and research. Last month and the month before mention was made of several noteworthy volumes. There will be other similar references in the March issue.—EDITOR.]

MUCH attention has been attracted by the book recently issued by the Macmillan publishing firm from the pen of Dr. Calvin B. Hoover, of the Duke Department of Economics. The title of the volume is "The Economic Life of Soviet Russia," a subject which Dr. Hoover is in an exceptional position to discuss in an authoritative manner after a residence of more than a year in Soviet Russia, during which time he made a careful study of economic and other problems.

From prominent newspapers and magazines and from other sources have come many fine commendations of Dr. Hoover's work. One critic has referred to it as "the best thing yet written on this subject."

BOOK BY DUKE ALUMNUS

Recent Duke graduates, as well as older alumni and professors in the institution, are gaining attention in the publishing field, an indication being the publication of "The White Superintendent and the Negro Schools of North Carolina," by Dr. Dennis H. Cooke.

Dr. Cooke received his B.A. degree in 1925 and three years later obtained his master's degree in education. His thesis was a study of the age-grade group distribution at Oxford Orphanage school. He was connected with the orphanage at the time of his study for the master's degree. His Ph.D. degree was recently obtained from George Peabody College for Teachers at Nashville.

Dr. Cooke's book, a copy of which has been received at the general library, reveals a rather thoroughgoing study of the relation of superintendents to negro education in this state, and makes certain recommendations looking to the betterment of conditions. Topics treated include a short history, setting of problem, administration of negro schools, their supervision, and some opinions.

None of the superintendents has received special training in negro problems, the survey brought out, a fact due, it was explained by county and city superintendents, to the absence of training offered in such matters.

"HANDBOOK OF THE LAW OF EVIDENCE"

Another recent publication, which has been placed in the Law Library, is the second edition of "The Handbook of the Law of Evidence," by Walter S. Lockhart of the Durham bar, and formerly of the Duke law department.

The second edition is a revision and enlargement of the first, in which Mr. Lockhart has the assistance of Richmond Rucker of the Winston-Salem bar. A new chapter concerning rules for trial of causes has been added, as well as other material.

"THE WORLD'S RAW SILK INDUSTRY"

In the January issue of the Bulletin of the Geographical Society of Philadelphia, Dr. Charles E. Landon, assistant professor of economics and economic geography, has an article on "The World's Raw Silk Industry."

The culture of the silk worm in Europe and the Orient and sources of the American supply of silk are discussed in the article.

BOOK BY REV. A. W. PLYLER

"The Iron Duke of the Methodist Itinerancy" is a book recently issued by the Methodist Board of Publication, the author being Rev. A. W. Plyler, editor of the North Carolina *Christian Advocate* and a well-known Duke alumnus. It is an appreciation of John Tillett, father of Dr. Wilbur F. Tillett, of Vanderbilt University. Regarding the work President W. P. Few said: "This volume holds one's attention from the first page to the last and is a fascinating book."

The author's brother, Rev. M. T. Plyler, business manager and associate editor of the North Carolina *Christian Advocate*, published some time since a book, "Thomas Neal Ivey: Golden-Hearted Gentleman," which attracted much favorable notice. The two brothers have published other books of merit.

Some Alumni Personalities

E. RALPH PARIS

E. Ralph Paris, '14, was recently elected president of the Duke University Alumni Club of Atlanta. He is well known in business circles there, being treasurer and business manager of the Atlanta Casket Company. He is a very active Rotarian, chairman of the third division of the Boy Scouts court of honor, member of the Capital City Club and Piedmont Driving Club, of Atlanta, and the Florida Yacht Club, of Jacksonville.

MARION A. BRASWELL

Marion A. Braswell, '20, is the new president of the Winston-Salem Alumni Club. He is a member of the legal staff of the R. J. Reynolds Tobacco Company. After graduating from Trinity College, Mr. Braswell received the LL.B. degree from Harvard University in 1923. He was formerly president of the Junior Chamber of Commerce of Winston-Salem. He is a member of the American Legion and Twin City Country Club.

RALPH E. PARKER

Ralph E. Parker, '17, who received his A.M. degree in 1919, is the new president of the Birmingham, Ala., Alumni Club. He has been for some time assistant city attorney in Birmingham. Before beginning the practice of law he taught history and political science at the University of Alabama and Birmingham-Southern College. He has been president of the Cosmopolitan Club and Commander of the Marine Corps League.

Vienna Seems to Have Found Solution of Housing Problem

Has Perhaps Most Efficient Plan In Europe, Says Duke Professor—Berlin Ultra-Modern
—Switzerland Making Strides In Technical Education—
Other Observations In Europe

Dr. Charles Albert Krummel, Professor of German in Duke University, spent the second semester of the last school year on leave of absence, in Europe. In discussing his visit to Europe, Dr. Krummel said that his purpose was to investigate and to collect first-hand information in the Gottfried Keller Archives in the University of Zurich, in Switzerland. He is now preparing the manuscript for a paper which will be known as "Keller's Activities as a Literary Critic." He wished, also, he said, to study the present changed conditions in German speaking countries, especially in Germany.

Dr. Krummel had not been there since 1910. He said that he found Germany, especially, in a very uncertain state, industrially and politically. These conditions, Dr. Krummel said, are growing largely out of the unemployment situation, with the reparation indemnities to raise. The situation is especially acute, he said, because Germany has government support for the unemployed. This unemployment insurance must be provided for in the taxes.

Dr. Krummel, however, pointed out the fact that one would not know from mere observation that the Germans are facing financial depression. The people, he said, look prosperous. They have a way of husbanding their resources and keeping up essentials with very little income. But the margin on which they live is a very, very, narrow one. A slight decrease causes considerable disaster.

Dr. Krummel found the German people still manifesting a fine appreciation for culture, art, the theatre, the opera and music. To a very large class, he said, this has become one of the essentials of life. They make sacrifices in other directions in order to participate in these activities.

Dr. Krummel spent the most of the time of his German visit in Berlin, the center of all modern Germany. Berlin, he pointed out, is a very unique city and is getting to be a very cosmopolitan one. Very complicated situations arise there and varied currents and counter-currents are constantly clashing. In aesthetics, Berlin represents the ultra-modernists. It seems, he said, to be the ambition of the people of that city to appear modern. He has never seen a place so frantically anxious to be up-to-date.

In business matters, he pointed out, the Germans seem to be looking primarily to England and America for ideas and they would like to rival them in new, progressive enterprises.

Dr. Krummel saw a very marked increase of development in sports and athletics. "The Germans," he remarked, "are getting about as wild as we are over sports." They have caught the great American craze for "breaking records." They are using the word "record" all the time.

The housing situation in Berlin he found going through a markedly changing condition. Suburban sections are growing where the houses are all separate. The people want everything in these houses to be thoroughly modern. The rent is very high. Dr. Krummel was told that a rental contract often cost a thousand marks, in addition to the monthly rental.

Vienna, he found somewhat reduced in size. This city has also been modernized. It is clean and beautiful. But it still has the old charm of the pleasure loving resort. There is, however, a strong modern element which is coming into prominence in the city. This is evidenced, especially in the architectural and the housing fields. The Viennese claim that they have solved the housing problem better than any metropolis in Europe. This seems to be true, Dr. Krummel said.

The Viennese solution of the housing problem is the building of municipal apartment houses, four or five stories high, and renting them at very low rates. In some instances, Dr. Krummel found three small rooms and bath, equipped with all modern apartment house conveniences, renting as low as $3.00 a week, American money.

Anyone, he said, will always fall in love with the place. It is still a most hospitable city. It is still the home of music and of the waltz. There is still a Strauss composing. The younger Strauss is a member of the third generation of this famous family.

The nature of Dr. Krummel's work kept him in

Switzerland longer than in any other country of Europe. He found that little country less affected by the financial depression, although there, too, it is keenly felt. He thinks, however, that the Swiss, more so than the Germans, can manage with very little to maintain respectability. In their civilization, they are stressing more technical education-engineering. Dr. Krummel believes that they are really leading in this field.

Turning back to a discussion of Germany, Dr. Krummel said that he found their attitude toward America and American people quite different from that of 1910, when he was last there. They seem to know more about us than they did before the war. This increase of knowledge has brought a higher regard for us. To many of them, before the war, we were more or less out of the world. Their attitude is somewhat divided among the various classes. But all of them are exceedingly anxious to stay on peaceful and coöperative terms with Americans. He found that very apparent.

The official class, he said, perhaps more or less resent our political isolation and commercial ambitions. They rather have the notion that we have sprung into prominence lately through profits gained in the war.

But he found the greatest difference in the masses—the great middle class. They are intensely interested in America and things American. They have the great interest in democracy. They rather look to us as a sort of model in government and civilization. The slogan "Made in America" has about the same effect in Germany, today, that "Made in Germany" used to have in America. They seemed, Dr. Krummel said, to be greatly delighted even with our American "movie." The grotesquely comic ones please even the middle aged. They seem to think that we Americans can do anything we want to. They believe that Americans "just play with life," as one German expressed it in Professor Krummel's hearing.

Dr. Krummel said that, of course, there is an extreme unrest in Germany. Such a field is usually open to new movements. But he does not anticipate the coming of either Fascism or Communism to Germany, in the near future. Those who consider Germany the next most fertile soil for these movements, he said, fail to take into account the deep seated love for peace and order in the German temperament. "The German's strong individualism," he insisted, "is a pretty safe screen against any blanket dictatorship being firmly established there."

Good Progress in Landscape Program on the West Campus

GOOD progress has been made in recent weeks in the landscape program of the West campus, attention having been directed to the quadrangle, with the Medical building at one extremity and the dormitory quarters at the others.

Trees, shrubs and grass have been planted, the work being done by the Duke Construction Company under the immediate direction of R. M. Torrence, landscape engineer.

Most of the trees set out are willow oak or American elm, species found in the Duke Forest of which the campus is a part. The difficult task of removing a good-sized tree from one site to another has been under way. Those being transplanted to the quadrangle are about four or five inches in diameter and around ten years old. In removing trees of this sort, a larger specimen is obtained that will sooner reach its growth, but the tree may not survive the removal. Some of the campus soil—that near the Men's Union for example—is of such nature, Mr. Torrence explained, that water will hardly leave it. In this impervious soil section pipes are being placed for drainage purposes, so that the newly-planted trees will not be destroyed by the dampness.

An unusual tree for Southern climes, the Japanese flowering cherry, has been ordered for the campus. Two or three of the specimens, whose buds have given such distinction to the tree, are to be set out. A good many magnolias will also be placed, according to Mr. Torrence. Already around two hundred red cedars have been planted about the campus.

Shrubs there will be in great number, there being two hundred and ten varieties called for in the landscape scheme prepared by Olmstead Brothers, landscape architects, of Brookline, Mass.

These will include golden bell, spirea, rhododendron, mountain laurel, azalea and hydrangea. There will be various flowering shrubs, so chosen as to provide blooms in the different seasons of the year. A fairly uniform distribution of the shrubs about the campus is planned.

A mixture of grasses is being placed on the north side of the quadrangle, with the expectancy of a stand during the spring. In the tree and shrub crew and the grass-planting force together about thirty men are being employed, Mr. Torrence said.

And the Boston ivy or companion climbers, as the trumpet creeper and yellow jasmine, are to be placed on every building on the campus.

Duke Has Unique System for Housing Its Fraternities

Members of Various Greek Letter Organizations Have Their Own Quarters in Separate
Sections of Dormitory Groups on the West Campus—Brief Explanation
of Duke's Fraternity Housing System

DUKE University has a system for housing its fraternities which seems to be operating very successfully. In building the dormitories, one quadrangle was designated as Fraternity Court. Late in the spring of 1930, the Pan-Hellenic Council held a meeting for the purpose of assigning quarters to the various fraternities. The assignment was made by choosing lots.

Eight of the national fraternities are housed in this court. These are: Delta Sigma Phi, Pi Kappa Phi, Phi Delta Theta, Phi Sigma Delta, Delta Tau Delta, Pi Kappa Alpha, Lambda Chi Alpha, and Sigma Phi Epsilon.

In the large court to the rear of this two fraternities, Kappa Sigma and Sigma Chi, are located. On the third floor in the tower facade, is domiciled Pi Epsilon, a local fraternity which is petitioning Phi Gamma Delta national. Directly above and running into the clock tower is Alpha Tau Omega. Kappa Alpha occupies the top floor and part of the tower in Kilgo House. In the court of Kilgo House is located Sigma Delta, a local fraternity with aspirations for Zeta Psi national.

A number of local fraternities are located in Craven House. Among these are Sigma Tau Alpha, which has been actively petitioning Delta Upsilon, national; Sigma Alpha Omega, and Phi Kappa Delta. Psi Delta Sigma, whose petition to Sigma Alpha Epsilon, national, was recently granted, has been living in section E of this dormitory. The Sigma Alpha Epsilon chapter was installed last week.

Thus, the fraternities are housed in the same type of dormitories as other students and on the same campus. Each fraternity has its own section in which its members live. Each has its own common room, a living room provided with furniture and equipment which is the property of the fraternity. On the top floor of each section a chapter room is provided for the meetings of the fraternity. Dr. Frank C. Brown has called this the "goat room." The name has become the popular designation for the room.

The common rooms have a very homey atmosphere.

The color harmonies of the rugs, draperies, and upholstery, as worked out by the college men, are beautiful. Each of these common rooms has its own radio, and many of them have pianos, in addition. The reading tables are furnished with the fraternity magazines and other periodicals. Here the fraternity members entertain their friends.

Each fraternity section is visited each day by a staff of maids. The fraternity dormitories are subject to the same daily inspection which all the other dormitories have. The men take a great deal of pride in the conduct and quality of the living conditions of their quarters. One interesting phase of the fraternity life is that the fraternities have agreed on the hours of quiet each evening for study. The individual as well as the group conduct is looked after very carefully.

The rushing season occupied the first two weeks of college last fall. After that time bids were extended to freshmen and each of them might accept the invitation which pleased him. In order to be initiated, a freshman must pass four out of his five subjects. Fraternity members are much interested in the scholastic success of "their" freshmen and help them in every way possible to "make the grade."

The fraternity members pay the same rent for their rooms as other students and have the same furnishings and equipment furnished by the University. In addition, the fraternities pay to the University rent on their common rooms and their chapter rooms. This rent, University officials say, added to the costs which arise from the purchase and depreciation of furniture, and incidental expenses for social and routine functions, does not exceed the ordinary cost of operating a fraternity house off the campus.

Professor D. M. Arnold, dean of freshmen, has expressed his great satisfaction with the Duke system. He says that while the fraternity men have the privacy of their own sections, the fraternity sections are sufficiently close to each other and to the other dormitories to create a democratic relationship among themselves and between them and the men who are not members of any fraternity. Duke's fraternities have no excessive exclusiveness or distinctions attached to them. Non-fraternity men are welcome in the fraternity sections at any time.

Many universities, says Dean Arnold, allow their fraternities to build and maintain their own houses because they are not able to provide sufficient dormitory facilities for all students on the campus. Duke is not handicapped in this manner.

Dr. R. L. Flowers, vice-president of the University, has said that should the experiment of housing the fraternities in this manner work out satisfactorily, in the early future it may be possible to build fraternity courts in which even more comfortable provisions would be offered.

Fraternity members and University authorities are well pleased with the harmony and coöperation which exists between the two.

"Tambo and Bones" a Worth-While History of Minstrelsy

Dr. CARL WITTKE, Professor of History in the Ohio State University, has written a delightful book on the history of the American minstrel stage, which he has called "Tambo and Bones." It was issued recently by the Duke University Press.

In his introduction to the book, which he wrote last summer while getting the book ready for the press, Dr. Wittke says that the minstrel show was a distinctively American institution, a purely native form of entertainment. He has written the account of the development of the minstrel as a serious contribution to American social history and to the history of the stage in the United States.

Dr. Wittke was inspired by more than a professional interest in social history, in writing this account of the development of the burnt cork circle. "Happy memories," he says, "of the burnt cork semi-circle, gathered during barn-storming student days, are responsible for an abiding interest and a real love for the old-time minstrel show."

In preparing his little book, Dr. Wittke began with a splendid piece of historical research. He gives us in his first chapter the results of his efforts to discover the origins of negro minstrelsy. With keen insight into the values of subject, he speaks of the value of the negro spirituals and the negro plantation songs which have become the basis of American folkmusic. These are the songs, he says, which voice the joys and the sorrows, the longing, the fatalism, the aspirations and the sufferings of one of the most musically-gifted peoples of the earth.

He sketches rapidly the development of the minstrel, beginning with the entertainment on board ship as the African negroes were being brought to this country as slaves, through the plantation entertainment at the "Great House," to the imitation of these on the part of American white actors. He admits, however, that the negro of the minstrel show was a creation of the white actors. The plantation negro had little of the minstrel trouper in him. The stage "negro," created by the white minstrels, was distinguished by a large mouth; he dressed in gaudy colors; he loved chickens so well that he could scarcely get past a chicken coop without taking away some of the chickens; and he was very skillful in the use of a razor. His love for the grand manner made him use long words which constantly twisted his tongue and produced merriment for the audience.

Dr. Wittke says that nobody really knows when the negro was first depicted on the American stage. He has, however, found a definite reference to a part of this nature taken by Lewis Hallam in Isaac Bickerstaff's opera, "The Padlock," in New York, in 1769. In 1799, a German immigrant named Gottlieb Graupner sang a negro song, in a negro make-up, in Boston. Graupner, says Dr. Wittke, appeared in the Federal Theatre, a famous old theatre, which at that time had been open five years. It was built of brick, lighted by candle-light or whale oil lamps. The ushers wore large wigs, powdered heavily. The "guests" were shown to their seats after having passed through a very pretentious "saloon." The building also included a dancing pavilion, card and tea rooms, and a kitchen.

Many of the first minstrels, Dr. Wittke points out, were circus clowns, graduating first to the vaudeville and then to the legitimate stage. George Washington Dixon, who was the first to organize a blackface company, came up through this route. The title of "father of American Minstrelsy" is given by Dr. Wittke to Thomas Dartmouth Rice, popularly known as "Daddy" Rice, and "Jim Crow" Rice. Rice introduced to America an entirely new negro dance which was an imitation of an old rheumatic negro trying to dance. With this he sang an original descriptive negro song. Rice is said to have been equally successful in his portrayal of a plantation darkey and of a "dandy" negro. Dr. Wittke says that Rice preferred to perform his act alone between the acts of a serious drama. Few minstrels were able to count him as a member of their troupe.

(Continued on page 65)

Wallace Wade Gives Views on Athletics in Assembly Talk

New Director and Head Football Coach Expresses Himself as Delighted With Situation
at Duke—Development of Athletics for all Students Is to Be the Goal—Little
Danger of "Over-Emphasis" of Athletics By Students Themselves

WALLACE WADE, Duke's new director of athletics and head football coach, recently spoke on the subject of athletics at the University assembly. He was heard with real interest and pleasure, this being his first public appearance before the University community, and his remarks made a decidedly favorable impression.

Mr. Wade said in part:

I hope you appreciate the fact that I am not accustomed to this sort of occasion and will be as charitable with me as you can. Football coaches ordinarily do not appear before groups like this.

In the first place, I am certainly delighted with the situation which I have found at Duke University. It seems to me, as I have gone about the campus during the past two and one-half weeks, that there is a very fine atmosphere here. I believe that the students are very serious about the business that they seem to be here for—getting an education. I want to congratulate you on the attitude and the bearing which I have observed since I have been here. I think you are also very fortunate in your situation in that there are very few institutions in the country, if any, that have the wonderful equipment, the beautiful campus, that you have here. No doubt this background is a great inspiration to you in your work. I am certain that you also realize the privilege that you have in following the leadership of the great men who compose the faculty of Duke University. I am looking forward myself to the privilege and pleasure of associating with these men.

The only excuse or reason why young men should leave their homes and spend four years on a college campus is to develop themselves mentally, morally, and physically. We realize that the main business of a student is his classroom activities. We hope that we can organize and carry on our athletic department in such a way that it will make a contribution towards this development. We hope you will develop in such a way that you will leave here as better men and better citizens than you were when you came.

You can find on a college campus certain mental, physical, and moral training that you cannot get elsewhere and you can find also on a college campus certain experiences that will develop you that you cannot get elsewhere; that is why you are here. You should keep that in the foreground of your mind all the time. You can find other activities which are pleasant and enjoyable, but they are side issues; and do not mistake the side issues for the real purpose.

Your purpose here is, as we sometimes say, to get an education. But when we say get an education we mean to participate in the training and experiences that are going to turn you out bigger men and better citizens, and we want our athletic program to participate helpfully in this course of training, and we want the experiences that you enjoy on the athletic field to be such that they will be helpful experiences.

We realize that athletics can give to you a certain kind of training that you cannot get in the classroom or in any other place on the campus. You benefit from your competitive experience on the athletic field in a way that you are not allowed to benefit in your other scholastic activities.

We want to carry on our athletic program as a part of the curriculum. I think the real solution of whatever problems there are connected with over-emphasis of athletics is to organize the athletic department as a part of the curriculum of the University. I believe college credit should be given for athletic activity just as it is given for activity in other lines and I believe that athletics should be supervised and controlled by the college administration just as the other departments in the institution are.

I think that when we say there is an over-emphasis on athletics we make a mistake. I believe there can be no over-emphasis on athletics. I think today in the general field of athletic activity there is a tremendous over-emphasis on the importance of winning in athletics. The mistake we make is in believing that it is so important to win. It is not a mistake for boys to work hard, put in a lot of thought and time, and give much attention to football, baseball, or any other sport. As a matter of fact, gentlemen, it would not be worth your time if you did not take it seriously. I believe it is worth almost any amount of effort to be a good football player. I think the experience and the satisfaction that comes to a man who is a good football player is worth the effort. But I believe the man who is an indifferent football player is harmed rather than benefited by his experience. I think a boy who is going to be an indifferent athlete, an indifferent trainer, or an indifferent competitor would be much better off at the picture show than he would be on the athletic field. There is no place in athletics for the man who does not take his work seriously.

There can be no harm in emphasizing the importance, while you are at football or baseball, of giving it your best, but the mistake comes in when these outside followers feel like you must win and feel like you have made a great mistake or committed some serious crime when you lose a game. As I come in contact with college people it seems to me that whatever overemphasis there is on winning is largely not with the students, nor with the players, nor with the faculty, but it is with people who should have very little connection with the game. It is with the followers. Many of the people who are talking about football today and criticizing it for its over-emphasis are not particularly interested in the good of the game.

College boys today are taking football very seriously. Just as good students in mathematics take their work seriously, so the good football players are taking it seriously. I think myself that football should have a place along somewhere in the same line as mathematics and the other courses in college.

When we speak of athletics here and what we want to do in athletics, we are not referring to football, baseball, track, or any of the major teams. We are just as much interested and believe that just as much good can come from the minor sports as from the major sports, and we also think there is a great opportunity in the American college for the development of intramural athletics. I hope the time will come soon here when we can offer to every student the privilege of competing on some kind of athletic team. I hope that we can have intramural athletics so developed and organized that the man who has not the time and the ability to make one of the varsity teams can compete on a team against his own college mates. Of course we realize that such a development is going to take time and will require a certain amount of money. But that is what we have in mind and that is what we want to do in order to round out an athletic program that will have its place in the curriculum.

Magnificent Organ Will Be Installed in New Duke Chapel

One of the outstanding organs possessed by American universities is being built by the Aeolian Company for the new Duke University chapel and will be installed for the chapel opening next year. It will be a four-manual instrument with many resources and a wide range of stops and fine tonal qualities.

Order for the instrument has already been placed. It will be equipped with scores of stops and thousands of pipes, representing the highest type of organ construction. The pipes will be both exposed and concealed and will measure from several feet to 32 feet in length.

The selected great organ will have a range of 73 pipes, and the other divisions of the large instrument will have an equally versatile range. Organists and other musical experts state that the Duke organ's stop list is one of the most complete ever to be provided in an instrument of this type.

Art Objects and Americana of Great Value at Duke

(Continued from page 43)

the latter being a selection from 37 Lee letters recently secured by the University.

Among the broadsides and prints is the rare one of the Charleston *Mercury*, entitled "The Union is Dissolved," announcing the secession of South Carolina, and the rare anti-Union cartoons by Dr. A. J. Volk, of Baltimore. Journals of the secession conventions of the various states, textbooks, novels, poetry and a large collection of sheet music are also to be seen.

The climax of the Confederate collection, however, is a table used by Generals Sherman and Johnston in drawing up the Sherman-Johnston convention at the Bennett House near Durham, in April, 1865. Along with the table is a bottle which contained refreshments for the occasion, an etching of the Bennett House from a contemporary portrait, and also muster rolls of companies enlisted in the Confederate service from Durham County.

The art association has been able to assemble this large exhibition through the coöperation of Mrs. Margaret Barber, of Missouri, a lifelong collector, and Prof. W. K. Boyd of the department of history of Duke University. Membership in the art association is not limited to members of the University community, but is open to all persons interested in the promotion of art.

Duke Again Wins the State Basketball Championship

FOR the second consecutive year the Duke basketball team clinched the state championship in winding up its February campaign in a dazzling burst of speed, defeating Carolina and Davidson in rapid order to clinch top position in the final standings column. Thus the basketeers will go to the Atlanta tournament again with a Big Five title in their possession.

Duke teams as a whole came through their February schedules in a creditable fashion to bring the winter sports season to a pleasing close.

The basketball team through February 21 had played eight games, winning six of them—from Davidson twice, from Virginia, Wake Forest, Carolina, and Vanderbilt once each—and losing to Tennessee and N. C. State.

Less success was met by the boxing team, but in four meets made a good showing each time. Three defeats were encountered, against L. S. U., Tulane, and North Carolina, but one victory was won over Virginia. All of the scores were close.

Three wrestling meets were held, Duke winning over N. C. State and Davidson, and losing by a two-point margin to V. P. I.

The one swimming meet went to Virginia.

Spring sports actively got well under way early in February. Coach Buchheit lined up his track men and so long as fair weather continues, the cinder track men will be training for the spring schedule. Coach Jack Coombs opens early with some preliminary workouts for his baseball battery men. Meanwhile, on the practice fields in the stadium, Coach Wade has been leading his first spring football practice.

Freddie Sington, All-American Star, is to Join Duke Staff

COACH Wallace Wade has rounded out his football coaching staff for 1931, announcing early in February that Freddie Sington, Alabama grid star for three years and an All-American and All-Southern guard during the past season, would become a member of the staff this fall.

Sington will coach the freshman line, working with Herschell Caldwell, another Alabama football light, who will coach the backs.

For the varsity staff Coach Wade will have Carl Voyles, head Illinois frosh mentor, as end coach and assistant director of athletics; Eddie Cameron, for the past five years a member of the Duke staff, as backfield coach; and Ellis Hagler, another Alabama star, as line coach.

Sington's record has been a brilliant one. In addition to winning highest American athletic honors last year he won highest honors in scholarship, winning the coveted key of the Phi Beta Kappa scholarship society.

Between Sington, Caldwell, and Hagler, every great Alabama team in recent years is represented. They have been on every Alabama title team and have played in the three Rose Bowl games participated in by Alabama.

For three years of varsity playing Sington was outstanding. He made his first mythical position in 1929 as an all-Southern selection, and repeated last fall while taking national honors as well. His positions were guard and tackle.

FREDDIE SINGTON

The Editor's Mail Bag

A Suggestion

Editor of ALUMNI REGISTER:

What procrastinators we sometimes be!

When I received my copy of the March, 1930, issue of the ALUMNI REGISTER I read it through with a thrill and then started a letter to you. Now I am going to finish it for two reasons: First, the March issue and those that have followed have come near to being all that I have long felt that an alumni magazine should be. I wanted to tell you that! Second, that article by Dr. Blomquist, in this same issue, on "Botanizing in Western North Carolina," fanned into flame the glowing coals of a fire kindled in my mind several years ago. I want to tell all thinking North Carolinians about that and incite them to action.

A book listing and picturing in natural colors all North Carolina's native wild flowers would be a beautiful and worth while thing to build. It can be done—it should be done!

"But how?" is asked.

By application of young and native talent of the State now sleeping.

"What would be the good of it?"

What would be the value of guiding youthful souls along pleasant and healthful paths of growth? What would be the value of revealing but limitless mines of cultural and economic wealth?

Let there be put on a five-year program (not a Soviet five-year program!) that will reach each student, each youth, each child in every single university, college, high school, and elementary school in the State. Let there be given prizes for the best pictures, for the best descriptions, for the most complete lists, for the best maps of distribution of all wild flowers common to each locality.

Let such prizes be given each year for the five-year period. There should be prizes for each school, there should be county prizes, and then prizes for the best work for the whole State for each year. Then there can be the Grand Prize announcements at the end of the five-year period of those which are to be honored by being selected to go into the volume, or volumes, of wild flowers to be published.

"All students will not have the talent to lead active participation," some may say.

That is easily solved, for there should be prizes for the best and most complete descriptions of all wild flowers to be found in each township; for the best single water color or oil painting of a flower; for the best pencil sketch of any single flower; and for the best single camera picture of any single flower. There may be prizes for groups of pictures.

The main thing to strive for would be to get every student in each school, advanced or elementary, at least interested. Out of this should come as complete as possible pictorial and descriptive lists of all wild flowers in their natural habitat. Another point worth striving for would be to obtain the best possible information relative to the present abundance of each flower in comparison with that existing in the past.

"What would be the good of it all?"

No one knows—no one can fathom all the good that would result. But some of the good things would be: Development of healthful hobbies; development of character and initiative; teaching the citizenship of the state to appreciate a wealth few now notice; get youth interested in the worth-while things of the open fields; accumulation of economic information of unlimited value in the future growth of the state; and of most importance, there would be training in coöperation and healthful competition which leads to healthful self-discipline, the greatest need of civilization today.

"How can such an undertaking be achieved?"

Easily.

A large part of North Carolina's womanhood is already organized through the women's clubs. Much of the state's better manhood is organized through its various civic clubs. There are the Parent-Teacher associations, and other organizations.

Here would be a youth movement to glorify the state! Its adulthood would be rejuvenated through encouraging and supporting the movement. Young men and women would find recreation and interests in the open fields they never suspected of existing. Ask Dr. Blomquist. The boys and girls would find pleasing tasks for idle hands. Some would find lifelong hobbies. With our growing national wealth there must come more careful education in proper use of spare time; there must be a greater appreciation of hobbies. Some will find permanent friends in the open fields. Who knows how many embryo Burbanks the childhood of the state enfolds? Awakening of interest leads to effort and achievement.

All organized women and men's clubs could do no better than to adopt this movement as THEIR hobby for a period of five years. The teachers of the state would lend their aid with joyful willingness.

Out of it all would come hobbies for many, gathered data one one of the state's neglected sources of revenue, lessons in coöperation, lessons in art, and exhibits to which those of all ages would be drawn because of the wide interest that would be awakened throughout the length and breadth of the whole state. Such interest would not be confined within North Carolina's borders. Before the program could be finished, educators all over the world would be watching.

What women's club would not take pride in mothering exhibits of art centering around their state's wild flower life? There would be exhibits at county fairs, at other community affairs, and at the annual state fairs. Think of the points of interest. Here would be such a wealth of material to work with and all so close to home, so personal, so full of possibilities for lifting all whom the movement would touch to the higher planes of spiritual growth. Who will take the lead—alumnae and alumni members of our civic clubs?

With the five-year program completed the wealth of material, pictorial and descriptive, could automatically go to some university or college library. Here then would be material to draw upon for years to come. Its building into the North Carolina Book of Wild Flowers would prove a labor of love with the interests of the whole state spurring the workers on.

In addition to the main Book of Wild Flowers there could be built up a number of booklets from this same source of material. Graduate students would find here in all the collected material varied approaches to the problem of commonwealth enrichment.

Who will lead?

O. A. PICKETT.

Kenvil, New Jersey,
February, 1931.

From Japan

The editor of the REGISTER recently received a personal letter, written just before Christmas, from Rev. Z. Hinohara, Duke alumnus at Hiroshima, Japan, in which he gave the following interesting information:

"Hiroshima has at present 639 students and children at her college, high school, primary school and kindergarten, with 69 teachers and workers. Christian education through and through and from the very bottom to the top is what my little school (Hiroshima Girls' School) is for. I am exceedingly busy with this new duty, but I cannot let a single Sunday pass by without preaching the gospel. I am not too busy to say good things of my Master. Next Sunday is our Christmas Sunday and I am going to preach at the Central Church here, at which occasion I am to baptize eight of our school girls."

"Tambo and Bones" a Worth-While History of Minstrelsy

(Continued from page 60)

In his second chapter, Dr. Wittke discusses some of the early minstrel shows. He says that probably the first public presentation of a real minstrel show was given in the old Bowery Amphitheatre, in New York, in 1843. The minstrel show grew out of desire of some of the best performers of negro imitations to put on a combined program. Among those taking part were Whitlock, Brower, Pelham, and the afterward famous Dan Emmett. The Virginia Minstrels and Christy's Minstrels disputed each other's right to be called the original American Minstrel Troupe.

Minstrel troupes toured Europe during the heyday of that type of entertainment. Even Hindu theatres, in India, were said to have offered performances of American minstrels. But nowhere, says Dr. Wittke, did they succeed as they did in America. This he believes to have been true because the American people understood them better.

The third chapter discusses, in an interesting manner, the prosperity and the decline of the American minstrel show. The fourth discusses the technique of the minstrel show in detail.

The fifth, the concluding, chapter discusses in a very entertaining manner the careers of the famous American minstrel men. Among these were Dan Emmett, Al G. Fields, Billy Whitlock, Dick Pelham, Frank Brower, Edwin P. Christy, Dan Bryant, Billy Emerson, Nat Goodwin, George M. Cohan, Lew Dockstader, and even Al Jolson, of the present day.

Through Dr. Wittke's book runs an undercurrent of sympathetic understanding which makes it more than the facts of history. It is more of an interpretation of the hearts and of the feelings of these men who have made history, in that they have taught Americans how to laugh in times of adversity and depression.

Duke Carillon to Have Great Unit of Bells

The carillon to be installed in the new chapel of Duke University will comprise 48 bells now being cast in Loughborough, England. Largest of the bells will be the lowest G natural, weighing 11,200 pounds and having a diameter of six feet nine inches.

This carillon is being given to the University by George G. Allen and William R. Perkins, of New York, close friends of the late James B. Duke, and will cost approximately $70,000.

| Where They Are Located | # News of the Alumni | What They Are Doing |

Miss Elizabeth Aldridge, '24, Secretary of Alumnae Council, Editor

CLASS OF 1878

Dr. M. Bradshaw has returned to Durham to make his home. He served here as pastor and presiding elder for thirteen years. At a recent meeting of the board of stewards of Duke Memorial Church he was named pastor emeritus. He served this church for nine years as pastor. He is one of Durham's most beloved and highly respected ministers and has been prominently identified with local, civic and church affairs for many years. Dr. Bradshaw entered the ministry in 1891 and has retired after nearly forty years of active service.

CLASS OF 1883

Bosworth C. Beckwith has been in the active practice of law since 1883. He was secretary of the State Democratic Executive Committee for a number of years. He married Iola Bledsoe on February 3, 1892, and they have two children. His office is located at the Durham Life Insurance Building, Raleigh.

CLASS OF 1884

Henry L. Coble makes his home at Pleasant Garden, N. C. He is a salesman for the Davis Drug Company of Greensboro.

CLASS OF 1888

Theodore Earl McCrary, postmaster and lawyer at Lexington, N. C., sent his only daughter, Helen, to Trinity. She graduated in 1921 and married Banks Arendell, '17, of Raleigh.

CLASS OF 1891

Duke University Y. M. C. A. has been sponsoring a series of monthly recitals. On January 20, they presented the Raleigh Male Chorus, assisted by Mrs. Margaret Highsmith Brown. The director of this group for the past ten years has been William H. Jones, '91, who has had a varied musical career. During his college days he directed the Glee Club. After being graduated from Trinity, he continued his study of the organ and piano in the United States and in Austria and Germany. In the last named countries he studied four years, and has frequently returned there. At present he is director of music at St. Mary's College, Raleigh, and has pupils in organ and piano in addition to his choral work. In recognition of his knowledge of organ music and his ability on that instrument, Mr. Jones has been made dean of the North Carolina Chapter of the Organists Guild.

CLASS OF 1900

Mr. and Mrs. Richard Webb (Minnie Wilson, '24) live at 147 Walnut Street, Baldwin Park, California. Mr. Webb is a rancher and also agent for the Los Angeles *Times*.

Julian P. Moorman has a daughter, Mary, in the senior class this year. He is secretary, treasurer and manager of the Kings Mountain Memorial Hospital, Bristol, Virginia. There are two other children, Frances Louise and Julian P. Moorman, Jr.

Linville L. Hendren has been teaching at the University of Georgia since 1908. He is professor of physics and astronomy.

Rev. R. R. Grant joined the North Carolina Conference of the M. E. Church, South, in 1899 and has been in regular pastoral work since that time. He has three daughters, Etta Beale, Elizabeth and Minnie, who have received their A.B. degrees from Duke. He is located at Seaboard, N. C.

CLASS OF 1901

Otis Brantley Lackey is temporarily located at Georgetown, Kentucky. He is a civil engineer for the Southern Railway System. He married Miss Mary Martha Crawley on December 1, 1904.

CLASS OF 1903

William A. Lucas has been practicing law in Wilson, N. C., for a number of years. He was married on October 15, 1913, to Miss Mamie Doss Jennings of Nashville, Tennessee.

Edward Wright Spencer is manager for the Virginia Insurance Rating Bureau with offices in the American Bank Building, Richmond, Va. He has one daughter, Louise.

Rev. Frank B. Noblitt is located at Lumberton, N. C., where he is pastor of the Methodist churches on the Lumberton circuit.

CLASS OF 1905

Haynes R. Mahoney, president of the Mahoney Lumber Company of Jacksonville, Florida, and a prominent lumberman of the state, was elected president of the Jacksonville chapter of the Duke Alumni Association at their meeting on December 11.

Charles W. Bagby is a member of the law firm of Self, Bagby, Council, Aiken and Patrick at Hickory, N. C. He married Frankie Self on April 17, 1913, and they have three children, Mary, Frankie and Charles.

Dr. Charles R. McAdams received an M.D. degree from North Carolina Medical College in 1912. Since that time he has practiced medicine at Belmont, N. C.

CLASS OF 1911

Rev. George Reid Andrews has announced the change of his address from Brooklyn, New York, to Park Street Congregational Church at Bridgeport, Conn.

CLASS OF 1912

John N. Aiken, formerly with the *Virginian Pilot*, Norfolk, Va., is now with the Baltimore *Sun* and has his office at the National Press Building, Washington, D. C.

CLASS OF 1916

Atha S. Baugh is manager of the Royal Typewriter Company at Louisville, Kentucky. His home address is 2045 Douglas Boulevard.

CLASS OF 1919

Ethel M. Murray has been librarian at Louisburg College, Louisburg, N. C., for the past two years. She is now instructing classes in library science at Louisiana State Normal College, Natchitoches, La.

CLASS OF 1920

Robert L. Thornton has been in Japan for several years, but recently returned to America and is now located at 37-52 Eighty-ninth Street, Jackson Heights, New York.

The announcement has been made of the birth of James Earl Ramsey, Jr., on December 26. He is the son of Mr. and Mrs. J. E. Ramsey of Denver, N. C.

Walter J. Rothensies of Red Lion, Pennsylvania, has been appointed by Congressman Harry L. Haines as his private secretary.

CLASS OF 1921

James Scott Burch, Jr., married Miss Mary St. Clair Carrington of Sanford, N. C., on June 9, 1928, and they live at 2301 Cathedral Avenue, Washington, D. C. James is assistant engineer for the American Road Builders Association.

CLASS OF 1922

Mr. and Mrs. R. E. Thigpen (Dorothy Dotger, '23) of 4616 Norwood Place, Chevy Chase, Maryland, announce the arrival of Richard Elton Thigpen, Jr., on December 29.

CLASS OF 1923

Classmates and friends of Florence Harris, Washington, N. C., will be grieved to hear of the death of her mother on January 25. Mrs. Harris has been in declining health for the past two years.

Kenneth W. Litaker is an architect with the well-known firm of architects, Coolidge, Shepley, Balfinch and Abbott, 122 Ames Building, Boston, Mass. Since his graduation he has spent three years in the office of Louis H. Asbury, '00, in Charlotte. He then attended Massachusetts Institute of Technology for two years and went with the above firm. He has been engaged for the past two years in the design and planning of the new group of buildings for Harvard University, and the new medical center for New York Hospital and Cornell Medical School in New York City.

Bryce R. Holt, Jr., was four months old on Christmas Day. His father is a lawyer in Greensboro, N. C. His mother was Miss Grace Marion Knaur of Denison, Texas.

CLASS OF 1924

: Dr. John Tate Lanning has been appointed by Dr. Few as a delegate to the Montevideo Congress in Uruguay as a representative from Duke University. This educational congress will attract educators from all parts of the Western Hemisphere. The Duke professor is now in South America on a Guggenheim Traveling Fellowship and has lectured at a number of national universities on the subject of Hispanic-American Universities, a line of research in which he is now engaged. Two of his most recent lecture engagements have been with the National Universities of Chile and Argentina. According to John Tate, South American educators are showing an exceptionally keen interest in the development of Duke University and have questioned him closely on various phases of the University's work.

Mr. ('96) and Mrs. Harvey B. Craven of Lakeland, Florida, recently announced the marriage of their daughter, Alice, and Mr. Steven R. Mohr. They were married in Clearwater, Florida, on September 13.

Nell Brock's address is 416 Tennis Apartments, Forest Hills, Long Island, New York.

Mr. and Mrs. William Hix Cherry have a daughter, Julia Pamela, who was born on November 26, 1930. Hix is principal of the Willie P. Mangum High School, Bahama, N. C.

Orlin Flowe Barnhardt has been teaching in the high school at Wilkesboro, N. C., for the past six years. He is head coach and also teaches history and civics. A daughter, Mary Jane Barnhardt, was born on April 25, 1930.

CLASS OF 1925

On Sunday, December 28, Willis J. Liles and Miss Louise Griffin were married at the bride's home in Greensboro. Mr. and Mrs. Liles make their home in Greensboro where he holds a position with the Western Union Telegraph Company.

Mr. and Mrs. J. Raymond Shute, Jr. (Sarah Mason), live at Monroe, N. C., where Ray is in the real estate and rental business. They have two children, J. Raymond Shute III, and Sarah Mason Shute.

CLASS OF 1926

Robert T. Johnson and Miss Mabel Gertrude Coble were married in Burlington, N. C., on December 27. Robert has held a position with the May Hosiery Mills in Burlington, but will be transferred to New York in the near future.

The wedding of Shelley A. Mabry and Miss Lillian Irene Meyer took place in St. Peter's Lutheran Church at Bethlehem, Pa., on January 1. They will make their future home in Norwood, N. C.

Dr. Van M. Ellis is on the staff of the Wisconsin General Hospital, Madison. After leaving Trinity he attended Wake Forest College and University of Virginia, receiving an M.D. degree from the latter institution in 1930.

Ethel M. Davis returned a card asking her whereabouts with the following comments: "In answer to the enclosed card and its inquiry all I can say is that I didn't know that I was lost, but here I am. This is my second year as head of the English Department in Kosciusko High School, Mississippi. I love the work but sometimes get lonesome for a sight of the Duke campus and friends there. My home address is 1005 Eighth Street, Durham, to which the ALUMNI REGISTER finds its way. When I do see an issue of the REGISTER, I enjoy it very thoroughly. Since I left Duke after taking an A.M. in 1928, I have just taught and done library work and last summer did some work on a Ph.D., though I doubt if that ever materializes."

CLASS OF 1927

Alma Swindell lives at 306 C. Street, N. W., Washington, D. C. She is clerk in the Department of Commerce, Bureau of Census.

J. Murray Atkins in writing about the Duke University Day dinner in New York City said: "I want to express my pleasure that we could get together for so enjoyable an evening and have the pleasure of hearing a splendid and inspiring talk by Dr. Few who brought a welcome message from the University." Murray is located at 250 West 78th Street.

C. A. Waggoner, better known as "Firpo," sailed on the *Rotterdam* from New York, February 5, returning to Turkey. He has been on several months vacation in this country, returning to Duke for a short while during his sojourn. He is connected with the American Express Company and will be located at Constantinople.

CLASS OF 1928

Announcement has been made of the marriage of David Primrose Cannon and Miss Margaret Lee Fultz on January 7 at Washington, D. C. Mrs. Cannon is the daughter of Rev. and Mrs. R. L. Fultz of Front Royal, Virginia. They live at 2115 F. Street, N. W., Washington, D. C.

William Hays Simpson was married during the Christmas holidays to Miss Mary Lucille McNab of Trenton, New Jersey. She is the daughter of Rev. and Mrs. John McNab. Both Mr. and Mrs. Simpson are graduates of Tusculum College, Greenville, Tennessee. He received his Master's degree from Duke

in 1928 and is now teaching and taking graduate work at Duke in the Political Science Department.

John Troy and Hazel Ferguson were married at Trinity Methodist Church in Durham on December 22. John is a young attorney in Durham. Hazel returned to Waynesville to complete the school year as teacher in the public schools.

Otho Thomas Colclough of 365 Carr Street, Jackson, Mich., is an electrical engineer with the Allied Engineers, Inc., in the Consumers Power Building, Jackson.

CLASS OF 1929

The arrival of Mary Carolyn Merritt on November 26 has been announced by her parents, Mr. and Mrs. Walter Davis Merritt, of Tudor Hall Apartments, Englewood, New Jersey.

Thomas Edward Martin is a salesman for the Jerome B. Rice Seed Company, Cambridge, New York.

Charles Nelson Swan, Law '29, is practicing law with the firm of Sells, Simmonds and Bowman at Johnson City, Tenn.

Mercer Wall Guthrie has been practicing law with his father in Durham since January, 1930. His address is Box 426.

CLASS OF 1930

Esther Morris, 606 West 116th Street, New York City, is in the Anthropology Department of the American Museum of Natural History.

Henry C. Ferrell is a representative of the Liggett and Myers Tobacco Company with headquarters at Gastonia, N. C.

Robert Bruce Billings, Robert R. Pearson, Claude S. Scurry, all of Durham, and Emile Saint Amand, of Wilmington, received license to practice law in North Carolina by successfully passing the examination before the Supreme Court in Raleigh in January. They will continue their law studies at Duke until June, working toward an LL.B. degree.

Ruth Elizabeth Martin teaches at Holladay, Virginia.

Edna Kilgo Elias of Charlotte, N. C., is secretary in the Department of Anatomy, Duke Medical School.

Voris Glenn Brookshire was married on April 10, 1930, to Miss Helen McMichael. He is an industrial sales engineer for Cothran-Bayles Company, Charlotte.

CLASS OF 1932

The engagement of Iola Slator Boult, daughter of the Rev. William T. Boult, Treasurer of the National Council of the Congregations Churches, and Mrs. Boult, to Lieutenant Chester Odlin French, Jr., of New Rochelle, N. Y., was announced at a tea dance given by the parents of Miss Boult on Saturday afternoon, December 27, 1930. A number of guests enjoyed the affair at the Davenport Shore Club, New Rochelle. The bride-elect graduated at Drew Seminary before attending Duke. Mr. French is a graduate of the Guggenheim School of Aeronautics, New York University, and is a lieutenant in the U. S. Army Reserve Flying Corps. He is connected with the Standard Oil Company of New York.

"LET'S GO!"

DUKE UNIVERSITY ALUMNI REGISTER

Beautifully Carved Gateway to the West Duke Campus

Duke University Alumni Register

(Member of American Alumni Council)

Published at Durham, N. C., Every Month in the Year in the Interest of the University and the Alumni

| Volume XVII | March, 1931 | Number 3 |

In This Issue

Editor and Business Manager .... HENRY R. DWIRE, '02

Assistant Editors .... ELIZABETH ALDRIDGE, '24
ALBERT A. WILKINSON, '26

Advertising Manager .... CHARLES A. DUKES, '29

TWO DOLLARS A YEAR   20 CENTS A COPY

ENTERED AS SECOND-CLASS MATTER AT THE POST-OFFICE AT
DURHAM, NORTH CAROLINA

Cover Page

The cover page in this issue of the REGISTER shows the new gateway to the West Campus, the home just inside the gate to the right, partly shown in the photograph, being that of Dean W. H. Wannamaker.

Last month's cover page, showing the General Library at night, attracted much favorable attention. The cover for next month is already being prepared and is sure to prove one of the most attractive of all.

From Japan

Many exceedingly kind letters regarding the ALUMNI REGISTER have been received in recent months. One of the most appreciative of all came from far-off Japan. The writer spoke of the eagerness with which each issue of the alumni publication is awaited. Another such letter came recently from South America.

Important Point of Emphasis

"I am delighted," says one alumnus, writing the editor, "to note the attention you are paying to things other than the building program—to the faculty, the new fields of development at Duke, the libraries, the spirit of the student body, the outstanding work being done by professors and students and the other things that mean so much more than mere stone and mortar.

"I am not discounting the handsome new buildings. On the contrary, I am very proud of them. But I do want people to know more of what Duke is doing in other lines than the construction of buildings, and I am grateful to the REGISTER for publishing so much information of that kind."

And the intention is to publish in the various issues of the REGISTER more and more matter relating to the serious work being done at Duke along different lines.

The Libraries

Many alumni doubtless fail to realize just the asset that Duke has in its five libraries. The article in this issue gives much information on that point. Another article, with further facts about Duke's great library developments, will be published next month. Don't fail to read it.

THE EDITOR.

A MARCH SCENE IN THE DUKE FOREST OF 5000 ACRES

Many of the trees in this part of the Duke Forest are ready for cutting. Nearby is the so-called "Cornwallis Road," over which the British Commander-in-Chief went during the Revolutionary War. It is a portion of the Duke University Campus.
(Article on Page 77)

Duke University Alumni Register

Volume XVII   *March, 1931*   Number 3

Editorial Comment

FORESTRY AT DUKE

Considerable attention is devoted in this issue of the ALUMNI REGISTER to the Duke Forest and plans for its development.

It is felt that this emphasis is particularly timely just now because of the rapidly increasing interest in forestry all over the country, and because there are certain unique features of the Duke project that make it outstanding.

The proposition, too, is a new one for Duke University, and it is the purpose of the REGISTER to keep its readers informed from time to time of new developments along any line.

What is being done here in forestry already is attracting considerable attention on the outside. Just recently the *American Journal of Forestry* had an interesting article on the significance of the Duke development in connection with announcement of the appointment of an Assistant Director of the Forest and Assistant Professor of Forestry. Extracts from the article follow:

"That Duke University intends to go forward with its plan to develop its forest property as a laboratory before it announces formal courses of instruction is evidenced by its appointment, effective January 1, 1931, of William Maughan as Assistant Director of Duke Forest and Assistant Professor of Forestry.

"In Maughan, Duke Forest obtains a man already well-trained to assist in the development and management of a demonstration forest area. Under Professor R. C. Hawley of the Yale Forest School, whom he assisted in reorganizing the Eli Whitney Forest as a demonstration area, he learned the problems of applied forestry from an able and experienced teacher.

"Mr. Maughan's first work at Duke University will be to organize the Duke Forest as an operating demonstration, research and school forest in coöperation with Dr. C. F. Korstian, Director of the Forest and Professor of Silvi-

culture. Plans are being formulated to develop a program of research which will be followed eventually by the organization of forestry educational work. This will probably be graduate work, largely of a research nature, leading to the higher degree in forestry.

"Demonstration forests are sadly needed in every forest region of this country. It is not enough to know the basic sciences controlling tree growth and the silvicultural systems developed in Europe; the American forester needs more urgently, actual experience in applying his classroom knowledge.

"When Duke University is ready to receive students it will be in a far better position to train forestry practitioners because of its own forest laboratory and activities than if it had to resort to lectures and books alone. Furthermore, remembering that 'forest extension' is sorely needed and that it is a type of education directed to adult timberland owners, the availability of a demonstration forest makes it possible for the extension specialist to remove forestry from the realm of conjecture and imagination and to translate it into actual woods practice which the woodsman can understand.

"American forestry schools, with several notable exceptions, are deplorably weak in forest laboratories. While some have acquired forests after their organization, others still evade the burden of an expensive demonstration area. Duke is unique in starting with a forest before it develops classrooms."

What is said above of Duke's start in the field of forestry is true of the institution's development in other lines.

The purpose of Duke University is not to go into new fields of study and research without first making preparation, through the provision of laboratory facilities and in other ways, for that development.

This plan of procedure may not seem so fast at times, but it is one that assures far better results in the end.

A NOTABLE CAREER

In the recent retirement from the United States Senate of Hon. F. M. Simmons, after a long and distinguished service in that body, North Carolina and the nation lose the services in public life of a Duke alumnus whose career has been indeed a notable one.

Mr. Simmons entered the Senate in 1901 and has the honor of serving in that body longer than any other North Carolinian, except Thomas H. Benton, native of this state, who represented Missouri in the Senate at one time.

Before his election as Senator, Mr. Simmons had represented the Second District in the House of Representatives, having been elected in 1886.

For many years he was prominent in the deliberations of the Senate, particularly in the World War period, when he was chairman of the vitally important Finance Committee.

As a student of the tariff, Senator Simmons made a record which will live long in the annals of the upper branch of Congress.

As chairman of the Finance Committee, he was leader some years ago of the fight for what the Raleigh *News and Observer* refers to as "the best tariff measure Congress ever enacted since the Walker tariff. . . . Since that time when tariff and fiscal questions were at the fore in the Senate the Democrats without question followed Mr. Simmons."

During the Wilson administration Senator Simmons was a strong supporter of the war president, and since that time, though a member of the minority in the Senate, he has rendered worthy service.

Senator Simmons has always been recognized as a man of convictions and with the courage to express them.

In the campaign of 1928 his uncompromising stand caused many former supporters to disagree with him but nobody has been found to question his absolute sincerity and his confident belief that he was pursuing the right course.

In his retirement from public life to a well earned rest, at his New Bern home and on his Jones County farm, he carries with him the best wishes of a host of members of both political parties, not only in North Carolina but throughout the nation, for he has been indeed for many years a national figure.

The REGISTER, speaking in behalf of his fellow alumni of Duke University, joins his many other friends in the expression of good wishes for Mr. Simmons in his retirement after a public career that has reflected so much credit upon his State, upon his Alma Mater and upon himself.

A GOOD EXAMPLE

Alumni of Duke University are showing from time to time their continued interest in the institution through donations of various kinds as well as in other ways.

Recently several of them have made contributions of collections of books or individual volumes to the Duke Library. Others have signified an intention to do the same at an early date.

Among others, the recently organized Japan Alumni Association has taken up the matter of presenting books to the University.

This is one of the best ways for an alumnus or group of alumni to demonstrate a desire to be helpful to this institution.

The building up of the Library is one of the major projects of Duke University and deserves the support of every former student who can help.

Of course, large sums of money are being expended out of the University budgets to increase the number of volumes in Duke's five libraries, but that source alone will not be sufficient to make the Library what it should be.

For one thing, there are many books, particularly of a historical type, which may be available to alumni but which cannot be readily purchased, and volumes of that kind are particularly welcomed.

It must be a source of real satisfaction to Duke alumni to know that the library of this institution stood fifth among the universities of America last year in the accession of books.

Certainly there is enough in this record to inspire all former students with a desire to do something to the end that this record may be made better and better from year to year.

Trip Through Duke Forest a Decidedly Interesting Experience

Plans Now in Process for Remaking of Old Forest Will Only Enhance Its Beauty and Value—Work of Reforestration Being Carried Out on an Impressive Scale—Complete Inventory Being Made

A TRIP through the Duke forest is one never to be forgotten. The beauty of the forest is not to be surpassed in its section of the state. Sights and scenes in the depths of the more than five thousand acres speak of memories for the old forest of events of human interest which are stamped indelibly on its life. Plans for the remaking of the forest, by the University, will only enhance its beauty and value.

A representative of the ALUMNI REGISTER enjoyed just such a trip, recently, in company with the Director of the Duke Forest, Dr. C. F. Korstian; his assistant, Mr. William Maughan; a photographer, and his assistant. The trip was made along North Carolina State Highway 751, which runs through the heart of the forest. This highway, which is soon to be hard-surfaced, connects Highway 75 with Highway 10. Two cars carried the members of the party and the photographic equipment. Stops were made at various places along the highway, from which points the party penetrated the forest on either side, studying the timber and the soil, enjoying the scenery, and securing photographs for this article and for the annual report of the Forestry Department of the University.

"We'll stop here, first," said Dr. Korstian, suddenly. "I want you to see some of our work of reforestration." There before the party lay what had been an abandoned tobacco field. The soil was worn out and useless for farm land. In the clearing stood a cabin, empty and forlorn, and rapidly falling into ruins.

"We have planted this field with loblolly, or old field pine," said Dr. Korstian. "It will grow here in rows, just as the tobacco which used to be here. In a few years it will be too thick. It will then be necessary for us to come in and cut out a certain number of the trees to leave room for the others. The trees cut out will be too small for timber but they can be sent to the pulp mill. These seedlings we obtained from the State Nursery at Clayton, east of Raleigh. In all, we have forty-five acres of this reforestration

going forward, at this time. We are only planting trees where they are not coming back naturally.

"The reforestration includes longleaf, shortleaf, slash, Norway, and white pines; white ash; white oak; and black locust. The white pine we secured from the Champion Fibre Company at Canton, N. C., beyond Asheville. The cost, this year, has averaged $5.84 an acre. We expect this cost to be relatively cheaper next year."

As the cars were left, at the next stop, Dr. Korstian continued the conversation. "This young pine through which we are going now is probably eleven to twenty years old. It is growing in an old field which was abandoned years ago. The seed for these trees were blown over the abandoned field from pines in the forest surrounding it. Some of these pines are a hundred and fifty years old."

Suddenly there was a remarkable scene. There in the heart of the forest was what had been a tobacco and cotton farm, at one time. The furrows could still be seen in the fields. The "broom sedge" which had first covered the field was more than waist high. All over the field was the bright green of the young pine trees growing everywhere.

"How old would you say these young pines are?" was asked Dr. Korstian. "Just guessing, I should say about ten years," he replied. Then he called Mr. Maughan and asked him. Mr. Maughan said that he would say about seven since he had examined them carefully only recently. To be sure, Dr. Korstian cut one of the trees and showed how to count the little rings and tell the age of the tree. It was six years old.

"How about these little fellows?" was asked. "Aren't they much younger?"

"No," he replied, "they would all be about the same age. These are loblolly pines. That little one is a shortleaf pine, which grows much slower. You see it pays better to plant loblolly pines as they produce timber much quicker."

"How about red cedar?" was asked.

"There is much red cedar in the forest. It comes as an under-story to the pine.. It is very much more valuable than pine. But its growth is slower than that of the pine so that a forester might realize more from the pine timber while he is waiting for the cedar to grow." It does offer some value, however, as Christmas trees."

Then the party turned toward the center of the clearing. There they were surrounded by pines on one side from twenty to thirty years old, on another side by trees as old as fifty-five. In the dim distant background rose an old-timer whose age Dr. Korstian said would be at least 150 years. Just about were the shrubbery and the flowers of a human habitation to which some young man may have brought his bride years ago. All that is left of the house, now, is an occasional beam covered with moss, and the ruins of the old chimney.

Mr. Maughan called attention to a large tree near the ruins.

"This," he said, "is an 'ailanthus' or 'tree of heaven,' imported from China for decorative purposes. For us, as foresters, it is an exotic. We must cut it down and get it out of the way of the new forest which is to come."

He is right. But one thinks of the hands which planted that tree for the young bride; of the little feet which pattered from there to the "honey locusts" planted just in front of the old house, to the peach trees nearby, and back again to the old stone doorway.

Back again on the highway, some beautiful pictures were made of the hardwood trees which line the highway. Some of these old trees are from eighty to a hundred years old. Many of them, Dr. Korstian said, must be cut soon. Some of them are slowing up in their growth now and are ripe for the saw mill. Others are so old that they are beginning to decay. Room must be made for the younger timber which will rapidly increase in value.

As the party plunged deep into the forest, at the next stop, Dr.

Korstian began to tell of the University's plans for the forest and for the new department of forestry.

- "First of all," he said, "we have had to make an inventory of the forest. Mr. Maughan has charge of that and I'll let him tell you about it. We plan to develop the forest for three major purposes. First, we shall use it for demonstration of forestry practices, in connection with our forestry courses in the University. Second, we shall conduct our own research work in the forest in order to augment our knowledge in properly caring for the property. Third, we shall offer research opportunity for students wishing to secure higher degrees in forestry.

"The phases of forestry that probably will be taught at Duke, will be those of silviculture, forest management, and forest soils. Silviculture is tree farming. Students will be taught how to raise trees for timber for the market. Forest management includes not only a knowledge of planting and cultivating the trees, but the management of a large forest in a way in which it will bring in a profit to the owner or owners. This includes a knowledge of when to cut timber and for what reasons. The study of forest soils provides knowledge not only as to what soil is best used for particular purposes, but also a knowledge of how to rebuild dead soil for further use in farming operations, and also how to protect the forest soil.

"Why," Dr. Korstian interrupted himself, "look at this." He stooped and began scraping away the leaves under the feet. "This top soil is much more animal and vegetable than it is mineral. Most people believe that the roots of trees feed far down in the earth. See these tiny little roots. The big roots of the trees go far down in the soil to give them strength, but they turn up again and end in these tiny little roots which feed here just on the surface. This fine fungus growth appears on these little roots almost everywhere throughout the forest.

"Much of this top layer is composed of decayed leaves and other

SOME PHOTOGRAPHS RECENTLY TAKEN IN THE DUKE FOREST

vegetable matter. But it is fairly alive with animal life. See here—this little salamander, picking his way through the leaves. Here's the runway of a rodent. That's a field mouse or a shrew. If we sat down quietly here for a while, on a hot day, the whole place would be alive with sounds of the animal life—the spiders, the worms, the bugs, the rodents.

"Most people do not understand just what this life means not only to the trees of the forest but also in rebuilding the soil for further use as farming land. It must be protected by all means. A forest fire means the death of all animal and vegetable life in this top soil which is so valuable."

"Some people," someone interrupted him," call this 'leaf mold'.

"Yes," he said, "that's a good name for it, if we leave out all the animal life which is a very little world of itself in it."

Dr. Korstian went on to say that the University plans a cultural elective course in forestry for upperclassmen in the undergraduate school. This course will be just about what is offered in a farm forestry course at a state agricultural college. The emphasis will be placed, probably, however, on graduate courses in research for masters' and doctors' degrees in forestry. This emphasis will be possible because of the exceptional opportunities for research in the University's own forest.

Mr. Maughan told of his work in making the inventory of the forest. This he said first required that he should make an inventory of the resources of the forest. Then he has been engaged in type-mapping. He explained that this is mapping the boundaries of certain types of timber and showing the condition of the timber within these boundaries. The map also shows the area in the stand and the volume per acre, the age of the stand and its origin.

He is also endeavoring to determine the density of each stand. This will determine whether it must be thinned or not. Some of it is stagnant—slow growing—and some of it is thrifty.

The map also will show what treatment each stand needs in order to "step up" the growth to as near the maximum as can be reached.

The inventory will show whether an old clearing is reseeding itself, naturally, or whether it needs reforesting.

Mr. Maughan is also determining the actual state of growth of each stand and tabulating these data so that he may have a clear knowledge of the entire forest. He is studying the property as a whole for the preparation of a scheme for fire protection. He must ascertain what roads should be kept open and what others should be built so as to provide access quickly to any part of the forest in case of fire. He must know what equipment will be needed for this purpose.

The members of the exploring party turned away from the forest, which is so old, and yet so new, whose life is young, old, and middle-aged, with a feeling that perhaps they had been close to the heart of one of the greatest parts of this great institution.

Honorary Degrees Conferred on Presidents Few and Graham by Alabama Institution

Dr. William P. Few, president of Duke University, returned a few days ago from Birmingham, Ala., where he delivered an address at the celebration of the seventy-fifth anniversary of Birmingham-Southern College. In his address Dr. Few praised the small college, asserting that it had a rare opportunity to serve American civilization.

The Duke University president said he believed the time is at hand when every good American college should use the utmost care to admit as students only those whose previous record demonstrates conclusively a serious purpose in life. He described such a step as necessary "in improving the quality of education."

Honorary degrees were conferred upon Dr. Few and Frank P. Graham, president of the University of North Carolina.

While in Birmingham Dr. Few was guest of honor at a dinner given by Duke alumni.

Legal Aid Clinic Will be a Part of The Duke Law School

Will Be Under Direct Supervision of Professor John S. Bradway, Who Comes to Duke
Next Fall from the University of Southern California, Where
He Has Been Conducting Legal Aid Clinic

PROFESSOR John S. Bradway, who comes to the Duke Law School, in September, as Professor of Law, is recognized as a national authority on what is known as legal aid work and the work of the legal clinic. He is secretary of the National Association of Legal Aid Organizations.

Mr. Bradway is now Professor of Law and Director of the Legal Clinic at the University of Southern California, which he established in 1929. He was graduated from Haverford College in 1911, and received his Master's degree from that institution in 1915. He received the degree of Bachelor of Laws from the University of Pennsylvania, in 1914, and was admitted to the bar that year.

Mr. Bradway began his law practice with Taylor and Robey of Philadelphia, with whom he continued until 1920. Two of these years, during the World War, he spent in the United States Navy. In 1920, he began private practice in Philadelphia, and continued this until 1929, when he was appointed to the position which he now holds. During these years of private practice, Mr. Bradway was busy with a number of activities. He was instructor in Political Science in the University of Pennsylvania from 1920 to 1925, and instructor at Haverford College from 1921 to 1923. He was also instructor, during a part of that time, in the Pennsylvania School of Social and Health Work. Probably his main interest, however, lay in the work which he did as Chief Counsel for the Philadelphia Legal Aid Bureau. Much of his time in recent years has been spent in writing and editorial work in this same field.

Mr. Bradway, in a recent article on Legal Aid work, has this to say:

"The Legal Aid Society is the poor man's law office. In a given community it is the largest law office in number of clients. The idea of legal aid work is based on the theory that under our form of government all men before the law must be equal." Legal aid, Mr. Bradway says, helps to lift the man without money over the three obstacles in his way to secure justice. These obstacles, he says, are court costs, de-

lay, and the expense of counsel. When the legal aid society is joined to the law school the result is a legal clinic. This clinic corresponds to the clinic operated in connection with the medical school. It provides practice for the third year classmen in the law school, who sit beside the attorney in the real court and hear the trial, watching to see how the case is handled. It provides expert assistance for the poor man who cannot employ counsel.

The clinic differs from other law offices in that it charges no fee and accepts cases only when neither the client nor the case has sufficient in funds to warrant an attorney charging a fee. The clinic seldom takes a divorce case or a personal injury case. Mr. Bradway says that perhaps only about five per cent of the clinic's cases go to court.

He lists five objectives of the legal aid clinic course in the law school. The first of these is a practical practice course. The second is a course which will help to synthesize the material the student learns in his other courses but has no particular opportunity elsewhere to gather together into one focus. He lists as the third objective, an opportunity to see the law and his clients not as isolated facts but as parts of the social and economic life that is going on in the community. The fourth objective, he says, is a practical course in legal ethics where amenities between one lawyer and another and between lawyers and clients are discussed so that the student comes to think of himself as a citizen with civic responsibilities to his clients. Fifth, is a practical course in initiating the students into the vast field of legal strategy.

Mr. Bradway continues: "The legal profession of today is under fire of public criticism. Through the legal aid movement, the idealism of the profession is made apparent to the public at large in a very practical way. Through the legal aid movement, the two branches of the legal profession—the law professors and the practicing lawyers—are brought closer together because each may work out his relations with the other so that the professional element is strengthened and the bar is better prepared to meet its responsibilities toward the court, the client, and the community.''

Legal clinics are now in operation in connection with the law schools at Harvard, Northwestern, Minnesota, Cincinnati, and Southern California Universities. Yale coöperates with the New Haven Legal Aid Bureau; Pennsylvania, with the Philadelphia Legal Aid Bureau; Pittsburgh with the Pittsburgh Legal Aid Society; Wisconsin, with the Madison Legal Aid Committee; the University of Memphis, with the Memphis Legal Aid Society; and the University of California, with the Alameda County Legal Aid Society. A number of other law schools have carried on somewhat the same activity.

There are three types of legal aid clinics. The Harvard Legal Aid Bureau is an organization composed of second and third year honor men, who are entirely responsible for the operation of the Bureau. There is no faculty supervision, although faculty members are available for consultation. The work is carried on in an office provided by a social agency.

The Northwestern and the Minnesota clinics are operated in connection with courses in practice and pleading in the law school. At Northwestern, the law professor handles part of the work. The law students spend a part of their time in the afternoons at the offices of the local aid society.

The Southern California Clinic has already been described in this article. The offices of the clinic are housed in the law school building. The entire operation of the clinic is under the responsible supervision of the director who is a professor in the law school. Mr. Bradway is to establish and direct a legal aid clinic at Duke similar to the one he is now directing in the University of Southern California.

Mr. Bradway believes that much experimentation must still be made before legal clinics may be said to have reached a standardized basis. But in the legal aid field, he concludes, in the field of legal education, and in the ethical field of the bar, the clinic has a place.

Three Distinguished Visitors at Duke

DR. EDWIN S. CORWIN   DR. GEORGE GRAFTON WILSON   PIERRE LANUX

Among the distinguished speakers at the recent Student Conference on International Relations, held at Duke University, were Pierre Lanux, head of the Paris Information Office of the League of Nations; Dr. George Grafton Wilson, Professor of International Law at Harvard University, and Dr. Edwin S. Corwin, Professor of Jurisprudence at Princeton University.

A Far Reaching Program of Honors Courses is Planned

Significant Step at Duke University in Answer to Demand that American Institutions of Learning Get Away from Mass Education and Give Exceptional Student Opportunities to Go Forward as Rapidly as His Ability and Industry Justify

BEGINNING with the 1931-32 session a far-reaching program of Honors courses is to be inaugurated at Duke University—a program that may prove highly significant in new educational developments in America.

The purpose of the system, as outlined by the special committee appointed to submit a program, is "to provide students with the opportunity for broad, independent and intensive study in particular branches of knowledge that they may secure a higher type of general culture, or more adequate preparation for later work in teaching, research or professional study than the regular program of work affords."

Honors courses are a comparatively recent development among American schools and colleges, it was pointed out by Dr. W. K. Greene, chairman of the committee to investigate and also of the Honors Council, created in answer to the demand that schools get away from the system of mass education, and give the exceptional student the opportunity to go forward as his industry and ability will carry him.

The Honors courses are being introduced for the benefit of those specially gifted in intellectual matters; but it does not mean of course any neglect of other students. There, too, constant effort will be made, Dr. Greene averred, to raise the general level.

"The genius of the Honors course," said he, "consists in the supervision of the student in independent reading and study. The student, therefore, is given a great amount of freedom in the pursuit of knowledge in the particular field in which his interests happen to be."

The history, economics, and chemistry Honors courses have already been approved; and some time during the spring it is expected a general bulletin will be issued by the University containing the general program of the Honors courses together with all syllabi of various departments, giving in outline the plan of Honors work in each department.

Briefly the Honors course plan as presented by the special Committee and adopted by the Duke faculty is:

Before the end of the freshman year a student wishing to read for honors makes application to the University council on a form provided for that purpose, counter-signature of the Honors committee for the department concerned being required. General excellence in all courses or special excellence in the course or courses concerned is required of the applicant.

Upon acceptance of the student by the Honors council, he is assigned to the qualifying work by the departmental committee on Honors. Should a student desire to continue through the sophomore class without choosing a particular Honors course he may do so on condition he meets the qualification requirements.

At the close of the sophomore year each group committee presents to the council the names and qualifications of those candidates who are adjudged qualified to proceed with the Honors course of the junior year.

The Honors course in each group shall consist of work entirely superseding the regular program save general required work. Each department will be the judge—subject to the approval of the Council—of work to be done, tests, etc., in its program.

Special advisers are to be appointed in each department—to work with students taking Honors; at the end of each semester the advisers report to the dean's office as to whether or not the work of the student taking Honors is satisfactory.

Syllabi are to be prepared from various departments, setting forth requirements for Honors, including what is expected on the final examinations, plan for the conduct of the course, fields to be covered, outline of required and suggested readings, and, in the cases of sciences, laboratory work. The syllabus of each group is to be submitted to the council and thence to the faculty for approval.

Comprehensive examinations—written, oral or both —are to be given at the end of the senior year. Upon the completion of the Honors course the student shall be graduated with honors, and this distinction shall be printed on the program at commencement.

Requirements for graduation under "The Honors group," a new division in the curriculum, for the present, will be: English, 12 semester hours; foreign languages, 18 semester hours; science, 16; Bible, mathematics, economics and history, 6 each.

Students who seem ill-fitted for honors work may receive credit for courses taken and completed in case sanction is given by group committee. Removal of a student from the list, or inclusion of students coming from other institutions after the freshman or sophomore years, is also provided.

The committee making the report consisted of Dr. Greene, Dean of Undergraduate Instruction, and Professor of English; Miss A. M. Baldwin, Dean of the Woman's College and Professor of History; H. J. Herring, Assistant Dean of the college; F. K. Mitchell, Associate Professor of English; and R. N. Wilson, Professor of Chemistry.

The Duke University Council on Honors is composed of 15 members, each of whom is ex-officio chairman of the Honors committee for his department. These, by departments are: W. K. Greene, chairman; mathematics, W. W. Elliott; psychology, C. E. Zener; religion, H. E. Myers; education, Holland Holton; chemistry, W. C. Vosburgh; history, W. D. Laprade; economics, C. B. Hoover; Greek, C. W. Peppler; zoölogy, G. T. Hargitt; English, Paull F. Baum; physics, W. M. Neilsen; German, Clement Vollmer; philosophy, Alban Widgery; and Romance languages, A. M. Webb.

A committee has been named by the Council to work on specific requirements for graduates in the Honors group, Dr. Hoover being at the head, with Professors Holton, Hargitt, and Baum as the other members.

This committee is now working on the requirements for graduation which will likely be quite different from the general requirements of graduates in the other groups.

Portrait of Chinese Friend of James B. Duke in East Campus Library

AN INTERESTING and greatly appreciated new feature of the East Campus Library of Duke University is the portrait of Mr. Cheang Park Chew, of Shanghai, China, recently sent here as a part of Mr. Chew's donation to the Duke Memorial. It is noteworthy, in this connection, that Mr. Chew was the first contributor to the Duke Memorial, his donation of $2,500 being made immediately upon receipt of cable advices of the death of James B. Duke.

It was about 1895 that Mr. Cheang Park Chew had business transactions with Mr. Duke's concern. As time went on he became acquainted with Mr. Duke. In 1907 he came over to America and met him and the two became friends. From that time on Mr. Chew and Mr. Duke worked together with perfect confidence. Mr. Chew, incidentally, has been tremendously successful in his mercantile pursuits in China. He has two daughters now at St. Mary's School, Raleigh. After completing their studies there, they will come to Duke.

That the widely known Chinese business man is still deeply interested in the Duke Memorial is emphasized by his now sending his portrait, painted by a Chinese artist, in accordance with the Chinese custom, which impels an individual who puts his heart deeply into a subject first to give something, then to follow the gift with a portrait or photograph of the donor. The portrait is an excellent likeness of Mr. Chew.

What Help Can Sociology Be To Religion?*

By PROFESSOR CHARLES A. ELLWOOD
Professor of Sociology, Duke University

IF THE more philosophical and critical-minded sociologists are taken as representative of the sociological movement, the trend is distinctly favorable not only to religion but to Christianity. The trend is not toward emphasizing the incompatibility of science and religion but rather toward discovering the bridges or connections which exist between these two human interests. This is particularly seen in what is known as the cultural approach to sociological problems. Both science and religion are now recognized by all sociologists as phases of human culture; and most sociologists would acknowledge that they are both equally necessary phases. Now culture has been built up in human groups by a process of learning. The process of culture is a process of discovery, appreciation, utilization, and diffusion. This is as true in that phase of culture which we call religion as in the phase which we call science. Just as science has been a search for the truth regarding concrete processes, so religion has been a search for the truth regarding the values which transcend individual experience. It follows, of course, that there has been a learning process going on through the centuries in religion just as much as in the concrete arts of life, and consequently that there has been real evolution of religious concepts and values. Sociology forbids one to believe that all religions are equally developed or that the categories of high and low when applied to religious concepts and systems have no meaning. On the contrary, if all human culture has been built up by learning, then it follows that the religious evolution of mankind has been a search after rational and socially useful religions, quite as much as the political evolution of mankind has been a search after rational and socially useful forms of government. There is accordingly no warrant in social evolution for believing that the existing vagaries of religion will survive; that the lower forms of superstition will survive along side of the highest forms of Christianity. As for the belief in God, there can be hardly any doubt that the trend in human history has been toward ethical

* Excerpt from a paper read at the Conference of Church Workers in Universities and Colleges, Chicago, Jan. 1, 1931.

monotheism. The very nature of the learning process, moreover, forbids us to believe that mankind will be content with such negations in the world of religious values as are implied in agnosticism and atheism. The concepts and values of religion are not unchecked by social experience but are continually refined by the experience and thinking of the best minds of the race.

Moreover, mankind has been seeking not simply a rational religion but a social religion; a religion which will reconcile men not only to God but to one another, which will teach men to coöperate as brothers and to minimize their conflicts. To some extent, religion has doubtless always done this within narrow groups, but it has only been within the last two thousand years that it has attempted to do this between strange groups and on a world-wide scale. Perhaps Christianity may claim that it has attempted to teach men sympathy, coöperation, and mutual service more than any other religion. Now the study of the social problems of our world shows increasingly the need of maximizing harmony and coöperation among men and of minimizing hostility and conflict. The scientific study of culture shows that it has come not so much through the learning of individuals as through the coöperative efforts of groups. All the civilization that our human world has achieved has been built up through coöperation. Moreover, an increasing number of social thinkers are acknowledging that coöperation cannot be long and successfully maintained in human groups without sympathy and understanding. Something like the universal love which Christianity has tried to teach to mankind is therefore acknowledged by the students of society to be necessary for the upbuilding of the human world.

At this point, the study of society can be very useful to religion, because such study shows that human nature is not fixed in its expressions, but is one of the most variable things which we know. Religion has long emphasized that the natural man must be transformed, that his selfish impulses must be replaced by altruistic ones. The social sciences find that this is entirely possible if the individual is surrounded by a culture which stimulates the development of the nobler, more altruistic impulses and emotions. Nothing is clearer in the social sciences than that the same individual may, according to the culture in which he is brought up, be either a savage or a civilized man, a criminal or a saint. The social sciences accordingly find human character not only to be indefinitely modifiable through group culture, but indefinitely modifiable in the direction of the attainment of the higher social values.

Finally, the social sciences show that we have not yet begun to fathom the possibilities of collective human life through the molding power of tradition, morale, and group spirit. Examples in history of the transformation of whole peoples through the power of group tradition and morale are numerous. We can even see the same result in many smaller groups around us, which often take ordinary individuals and mold them into something extraordinary in their behavior, through the power of their tradition or morale. Here comes in, of course, the whole significance

of the church as an ideal social group. Just as the individual is low or high in his social and ethical development according to the culture of his group, so the group itself in its inner organization, harmony, and unity, is low or high according to the morale or discipline which prevails among its members. Accordingly the possibilities of human social life in the way of the creation of ideal groups are only beginning to be explored by the social sciences; but the explorations already made indicate that human societies can attain to a much higher degree of unity, harmony, and social justice than they now generally exhibit, and that this is true even of the world as a whole.

If the task of religion is to save the world from evil, then it would seem that religion must seek the aid of the social sciences for the accomplishment of its task. Religion cannot work successfully in the modern world without the guidance of social science, without knowledge of the forces which make and mar the lives of men. That these forces are social no longer admits of any doubt.

Seventy-Sixth Birthday of Duke Trustee

WILLIAM R. ODELL, well-known alumnus and trustee of Duke University, who has been associated in various ways with the life of the institution since the days of Dr. Braxton Craven, celebrated his seventy-sixth birthday recently at his home in Concord. In honor of the occasion his son, Arthur G. Odell, gave a dinner, at which members of the family and a few close friends were guests, and the following day the Concord Rotary Club devoted its regular weekly meeting to a celebration of the occasion, Mr. Odell being a prominent member and past president of the club.

President W. P. Few and Henry R. Dwire represented Duke University at the meeting in Concord. Dr. Few briefly sketched the life of Mr. Odell and told of his valuable service as a member of the Duke University Board of Trustees.

"Your fellow clubman has gone through all the changes from the old to the new order and has made a wonderful record," said Dr. Few. "His life from early manhood has shown those qualities of character

and fineness that have made him loved by all who know him, and he is setting a marvelous example for members of the younger generation to follow. x x x

"W. R. Odell is a friend and neighbor to everyone. Thinking of him as seventy-six years young rather than seventy-six years old is far more natural.

"Concord is very fortunate to have two such men as W. R. Odell and D. B. Coltrane—men who simply refuse to grow old. The best citizens after all are the young ones and those who refuse to allow themselves to grow old through the mere passage of time.

"North Carolina needs more citizens of Mr. Odell's type, a man with foresight, ability and the desire to serve."

Mr. D. B. Coltrane, lifelong friend and associate of Mr. Odell, spoke feelingly in eulogy of his friend. Henry R. Dwire referred briefly to him as a loyal alumnus of Duke. The beloved Concord citizen responded to the various expressions of the speakers in an appropriate way.

Duke Faculty Member Head of National Organization

Dr. Frank C. Brown Elected President of Omicron Delta Kappa, Honorary Fraternity
Which Has Had Notably Successful Career Since Its Inception in
1914—Ninth National Convention This Month

AT THE recent biennial convention in Lexington, Kentucky, of Omicron Delta Kappa, national honorary fraternity, Dr. Frank C. Brown, Comptroller of Duke University and Professor of English, was elected president for the next two years. Other officers were elected as follows: Dr. George Lang, of the University of Alabama, vice-president; Dr. William Moseley Brown, of Atlantic University, executive secretary.

The first official duty of the newly elected president was to install, on Saturday after the convention, the Alpha Theta circle of the University of Cincinnati.

HISTORY OF ORGANIZATION

Omicron Delta Kappa was founded in 1914 with two chief purposes in mind, that of encouraging leadership in five different fields of activity and that of effecting an organization that would serve as a link between students and those representing the administrative policies. A charter will not be granted for the establishment of a circle in any institution unless the president or ranking administrative officer is among the petitioners as a charter member.

The five fields of academic life in which students may attain such leadership as to receive recognition by the fraternity are scholarship, forensic activities, journalism, social usefulness, and athletics. No man can be considered for membership unless he has attained a high count of points in the various fields and unless he is a man of fine character and personality; then he must be approved by the members of the individual circles.

Membership in a circle of Omicron Delta Kappa means the opportunity and the obligation for effective work in the causes of the institution at which

DR. FRANK C. BROWN

the circle is situated, and some of the most worthwhile accomplishments by student organizations in American institutions have been effected by circles of this fraternity. The truth held uppermost by members of this organization is that virtue is its own reward and that there can be no higher satisfaction that can come to any man than the accomplishment of good for his Alma Mater.

Membership in Omicron Delta Kappa includes, in addition to the undergraduate members, outstanding leaders in the various faculties where circles have existence, distinguished alumni, and a very few men who have deserved recognition by outstanding service to state or nation; men in the last group may be initiated as honorary members.

The fraternity has expanded until there are now thirty-two active circles with a total membership of approximately four thousand; during the last year the number of initiates numbered almost one thousand. Omicron Delta Kappa is one of the eight honorary fraternities constituting the Association of College Honor Societies.

The ninth national biennial convention met as the guest of Kentucky Nu Circle at the University of Kentucky, Lexington, Kentucky, March, 5, 6, and 7. Besides the routine business, there were addresses by Dr. Frank LeRond McVey, President of the University of Kentucky, by Dr. Frank C. Brown, National Vice-President of Omicron Delta Kappa, and by Dr. William Moseley Brown, Executive Secretary; President and Mrs. McVey gave a reception to the delegates and friends Friday afternoon; on Friday night the Kentucky Nu Circle as host gave the delegates a formal dinner dance in the Gold Room of the Lafayette Hotel.

Summer School Sessions Have Been Showing Rapid Growth

First Summer School Was Held at Trinity in 1919 With 88 Students, While Enrollment
Last Summer Was 1,212—Next Summer Session Begins June 12 on
the West Campus—Many Inquiries Are Already Being Received

PROSPECTS now indicate the most successful sessions of summer school yet held at Duke University, judging by the number of preliminary inquiries received. These had reached between 1,500 and 2,000 by March 15, according to Dr. Holland Holton, director of the school.

Due to this indication of a heavy demand for summer school courses the school will be held on the West campus, which provides greater facilities and more dormitory space.

The first session of the school extends from June 12 to July 22; and the second, July 23 to August 31.

Growth is being manifested, however, in other respects than mere numbers. Instead of five branches in which graduate students may obtain their Master's after five years of summer study, eight such divisions are being offered. The new graduate cycles are: Economy and government, Latin, and psychology. The other five are: Education, English, French, history, and mathematics.

There has been notable expansion in the economics department; Latin and psychology courses are for the first time being offered during both sessions; and Greek and sociology are newcomers to the summer schedule.

One course of note in the education field is that of American College Problems, a study under Dr. A. R. M. Stowe of the Randolph-Macon Woman's College, for graduate students who are either teaching in college or preparing to do so.

Several visiting professors who have taught in previous Duke summer sessions are returning. These include: Luther Mason Dimmitt, of the Presbyterian Church Board of Education, in education; Dr. Oscar Berry Douglas, University of Texas, Austin, Texas, education; William Daniel Ellis, principal of the Richmond Normal School, Richmond, Va., education; Dr. John Thomas Lister, College of Wooster, Spanish; Dr. Dennis C. Troth, Pennsylvania State College, education; and Dr. Stowe.

Other visiting members of the faculty are: Dr. Wilfrid H. Callcott, the University of South Carolina, Columbia, S. C., history; Dr. M. Slade Kendrick, Cornell University, economics; Dr. John Lord, dean of the graduate school, Texas Christian University, Fort Worth, Texas, government; Dr. Joseph C. McElhannon, dean, Sam Houston State Teachers' College, in Texas, education; Dr. Douglas E. Scates, director of research and statistics, Cincinnati, Ohio, public schools, education; and Walter Prescott Webb, University of Texas, history.

Dr. Kendrick is reckoned as an authority on state finance; Dr. Scates is accounted high among those versed in scales and measurements; and Professor Webb is recognized for his knowledge in Western American history, particularly that of the southwestern part of the country.

The first summer school at Trinity College was held in 1919, there being 88 students, of whom 65 were teachers. Steady growth has been shown since that time, with an enrollment last year of 1,212 students for the two sessions, exclusive of duplications.

Dedication of Medical School and Hospital April 20

AN OUTSTANDING event in the career of Duke University and of American medical education and hospitalization generally will be the dedication on April 20 of the Duke Medical School and Hospital. Members of the medical profession and others from various sections of the country will be present as guests on that occasion. Distinguished members of the profession will speak and in various ways the event will be a notable one.

"HONORING SOUTHERN SCIENTISTS"

Among other features of the Hospital that have been attracting attention in the press and otherwise is the naming of wards in honor of distinguished Southern physicians and surgeons. Referring to this the Richmond *News-Leader* said editorially recently in part, under the caption, "Honoring Southern Scientists":

(Continued on page 98)

Some Alumni Personalities

EDGAR S. BOWLING

Edgar S. Bowling, of New York, '99, is vice president of the Duke University Alumni Association. From the time of his leaving college until 1906 he was factory manager for the American Tobacco Company; from 1906 to 1917 he was southern manager of factories for the British-American Tobacco Company; 1917-19 director British-American Tobacco Company. He is officially connected with a number of important business organizations, being president and director of Bowmac Investment Corporation, treasurer and director of Selected Industries, Inc., vice president and director of Reynolds Metals Company, Inc., of United States Foil Company, Eskimo Pie Corporation, Stonewall Corporation, Inc., and Thomas Young's Nurseries. For two years he was president of the North Carolina Society of New York. He established the $25,000 Bowling Scholarship and Loan Fund in memory of his sister, May Bowling Bennett, '12.

Leonidas W. Crawford, '98, received his M.A. degree from Columbia University in 1903 and his Ph.D. from Northwestern University in 1922. He is president of the Nashville, Tenn., Alumni Club of Duke University, and is an alumni member of the Phi Beta Kappa chapter of Duke. He is professor of religious education in the George Peabody College for Teachers, Nashville; member of the faculty of the summer session of Columbia University, New York; director of religious education of the West End Methodist Church, Nashville; contributing editor of the General Sunday School Board of the M. E. Church, South; instructor in the standard training schools of the M. E. Church, South. He has done considerable writing of a high order in the field of religious education.

LEONIDAS W. CRAWFORD

ARTHUR M. PROCTOR

Arthur M. Proctor, '10, who has been professor of education at Duke University since 1923, was recently elected to membership in the local chapter of Phi Beta Kappa on account of his outstanding work in the field of education. He was also recently appointed a member of the North Carolina Commission on the Enrichment of Adult Life, the appointment being made by Willis A. Sutton, president of the National Education Association. Since he has been at Duke, Dr. Proctor was granted a year's leave at the request of the State Department of Education in order that he might make educational surveys in various counties of the state. He received his A.M. degree from Columbia University in 1922 and his Ph.D. in 1930. He had wide experience in teaching before becoming a member of the Duke faculty.

Tribute By One Duke Alumnus to Another in U. S. Senate

At Recent Memorial Service to the Late Lee S. Overman, His Colleague of Many Years, Hon. F. M. Simmons, Tells of His Many Fine Qualities of Mind and Heart and His Long Record of Successful Service in State and Nation

ONE Duke alumnus, member of the United States Senate, recently paid tribute at a memorial session of that body to another Duke alumnus who died in December last while serving as a member of the Senate. The occasion was the memorial service to the late Senator Lee S. Overman by his colleague of many years, Senator F. M. Simmons. The latter was ill at his home at New Bern at the time, his eulogy being read to the Senate by Hon. Cameron Morrison, Senator Overman's successor. Fitting tributes were paid by other members of the Senate. Members of Senator Overman's family attended the memorial service.

North Carolina's senior senator retired on March 4, two weeks after the memorial service to Senator Overman, following a long and distinguished career as a member of the Senate. Elected many years ago to that body, he rendered his state and nation conspicuous service, particularly as a member of the all-important Senate finance committee. During the Wilson administration he was one of the dominant figures in American public life. His recent retirement brought forth many expressions from students of public life in this and other states relative to the great value to state and nation of his public career.

Senator Simmons' address on Senator Overman follows in part:

"Mr. President, it is a far cry back to March 4, 1903, when I walked down the middle aisle of this chamber escorting Lee S. Overman to the vice-president's chair, where he then took for the first time the oath of office of a senator of the United States. Looking over all the members of the present senate, I see only one senator, the distinguished senior senator from Utah, Mr. Smoot, besides myself, who was here on that day in 1903, and the senator from Utah was just then taking his oath of office for the first time as a member of this body. At that time I had been a senator for two years, having entered this body on March 4, 1901.

"I can see yet in my mind, the picture presented by my old friend and colleague when he first appeared at the bar of the senate; handsome, courtly, stalwart, and of distinguished bearing, just in the prime of life, 49 years old. One needed only a glance to know that here was indeed a man fitted by nature to be a senator. Surely upon that day Lee Overman seemed a fortunate man. He had health, strength, great ability, personal charm, and he had at last attained his life's ambition in the way of public office. The years stretched bright and promising before him. He was equally fortunate in his private and family life. He was a happy man.

"And it is worthy of remark, Mr. President, that at least in this one instance, fulfillment came in ample measure. In the years that followed, Senator Overman had a great career. He served his state and his country with usefulness and distinction. He was a statesman and a true patriot. He was happy in the senate, for the senate was his place. He was happy in the discharge of his duties and in the obligations of his position as well as in its privileges. He won high rank here, and no man in my day has been better loved by his associates in this chamber. He was worthy of our respect and affection. Senator Overman loved all humanity and the desire of his heart was to help everybody who needed help or asked it of him. If he ever had any unhappiness in his senatorial life, it grew out of the fact that it was not possible for him to do for everybody everything that was requested. He died in the fulness of years and honors, still enthroned in the hearts of his friends and the people of his state. He was fortunate never to have suffered the unhappiness of seeing his people and his friends turn against him; they supported him to the end, and his death caused sincere and widespread sorrow throughout North Carolina and affected, alike, all classes of our people.

WAS REAL LEADER

"I will not undertake to name, Mr. President, the numerous great causes in which Senator Overman either led or was highly useful in this chamber in the interest of the people of the United States. It is sufficient to say that his desire always was to serve his country and the American people. His handling of legislation was skillful and successful, and his devotion to duty as a member of this body was with him a veritable religion. The great traditions of the senate and its rules and reputation were all sacred in his sight. Nothing would so quickly arouse him to indignation as the proposal of any measure which in his opinion would impair in the slightest degree the power, dignity or reputation of the senate. He had great reverence for the constitution of the United States and was always on guard against any movement that might tend to weaken, impair, or in any way, disregard it. His feeling of indignation or resentment was, however, never against individuals: it was entirely impersonal, and grew out of his deep reverence for the constitution, the senate and the free institutions set up by our fathers. He was sure the fathers had builded well; and, generally, any proposals of change or innovation, met with little favor at his hands.

"My late colleague's feeling for our own state, North Carolina, was that of the most devoted of sons for the best of mothers. To speak the name of North Carolina except with pride, or to refer to our state in any other terms than of praise, would bring him instantly to his feet, his body erect, and his voice vibrant with anger and indignation.

TOGETHER 30 YEARS

"Mr. President, it is no light matter, this severance of the ties forged by the fires of half a century. My colleague and I had been in the senate together for almost 30 years, but our friendship and association dated back much farther than the beginning of our senatorial service. We were both native North Carolinians and were both born in the same month of the same year, my colleague being just 13 days my senior. We were college mates at old Trinity college (now Duke University) in the early 70's, Senator Overman graduating in 1874 and I one class earlier. When I came to the lower house of Congress in the 80's, Senator Overman was actively associated with me and our contemporaries in North Carolina politics, and he was at that time a member of the state legislature, attaining before the end of his legislative services in North Carolina, the post of speaker of the House of Representatives. In the important campaigns of the early 90's, when I was for the first time Democratic state chairman, we fought side by side. In the late 90's, when I was again chairman of the Democratic state committee, in the campaigns that redeemed our state from the control of the fusionists (a combination of Republicans, populists and negroes), Lee Overman and I were still shoulder to shoulder in battle, as we were also, later, in the great movements for the moral and material upbuilding and development of North Carolina which was launched in those eventful years. I was so fortunate as to be chosen in 1900 to fill the first seat belonging to North Carolina that became vacant in the United States senate, following the restoration of the Democratic party to control in our state; and I entered the senate, as I have already stated, on March 4, 1901. Two years later, when the term of the remaining Republican senator from North Carolina ex-

pired, Senator Overman was elected as his successor. My colleague came on here and was sworn in as I have pictured on March 4, 1903. And, again, we were together.

"Our association in the senate was always a joy to me, and I am happy to believe that my deceased colleague's feeling about it was the same as my own. In all our service here, we never had a serious personal difference. Often we had differences of opinion and voted differently, as men of independent thought and action necessarily must do, but these differences of opinion were never permitted to cast a shadow across the genuine friendship which we felt for each other.

SERVED JOINTLY

"Together, thus, for more than a quarter of a century, Lee Overman and I sat here and jointly served our beloved state and country as best we could according to our lights. We have been concerned with some great events, and have seen some great days. There was the great war, when thrones and nations tottered and fell, with liberty itself in the balance, at last to emerge triumphant. We have seen the tide of political conflict in the nation rise and fall and change. The personnel of the actors upon the stage has been constantly changing, not only here, but, of course, also in the other branches of the government. Beginning with the gentle and lovable Major McKinley, who was President when I entered the senate, we have, during our service here, seen presidents come and go—the dynamic Roosevelt, the learned, kindly and honest Taft, the great Wilson, the kindly and friendly Harding, the calm and efficient Coolidge, and recently, still together, we saw enter the White House the able engineer and administrator who is now our chief executive. We have seen hundreds of America's ablest and best enter this chamber, serve well their day, and pass out. Even the Supreme Court of the United States, which fortunately changes its personnel but slowly, has been entirely reconstituted in its personnel since I entered the senate, and, with the exception of the beloved Associate Justice Holmes, it has been remade entirely since my colleague entered the senate in 1903. When Overman and I first came here, the honored and revered Fuller was chief justice and had still nearly 10 years to serve before passing away on the Independence Day of his country, July 4, 1910. Then came the great Louisianian, Edward Douglas White, a Democrat and a gallant ex-Confederate soldier, who was appointed Chief Justice of the United States by a Republican President, Mr. Taft, whose heart was big enough to embrace every section of his country and the members of all political parties. We saw Chief Justice White add immeasurably to his own fame and enrich the judicial history of his country and then pass to the Master, to be succeeded as chief justice by the illustrious ex-President from whom the great southern lawyer and judge had received his own appointment as head of the judicial branch of the government. It was given to us then to see Chief Justice

SIMMONS LEFT BEHIND

"The Lord has been kind to us—to Overman and me. He has given us length of days and reasonably good health. Of late years, particularly when illness laid its hand rather heavily on me, I had perhaps little right to expect that I would still be here for a brief period after the shadows had closed on my colleague and friend of 50 years. But it was so ordered, by Him who holds us as in the hollow of His hand.

"The senate is not the same to me without Overman. His seat in this chamber, as all of us know, has been for many years just in front of mine, and whenever I addressed the chair or cast my glance toward the presiding officer, I looked across the good, gray head of my friend. He sits there no longer. He is with the Lord, and his mother State has taken his body whom I love—men on both sides of the aisle that bosom. And I feel a deep sense of loneliness in the senate without him. There are many men in this body I love—men on both sides of the aisle that divides us politically who know that I love them—but this man is gone, this comrade whose life was entwined with mine even back in the days of our youth when the beckoning smile of the future seemed so sweet to both of us.

"To my old friend and colleague, I say 'Good-by; until we meet again'; and upon his bereaved wife and family, I pray the blessings of God, who gave them this gallant gentleman and who took him away from them only in the ripeness of age and accomplishment."

Senator Morrison, before taking the position of the presiding officer, and while still at the Simmons desk, expressed briefly his deep reverence for the memory of Senator Overman, and his deep regret that illness had detained Senator Simmons at his home.

Senator Morrison was followed by Senator Robinson, minority leader, who told how Senator Overman had entered upon his professional and public career at a trying time, when social and political conditions in his state were far from settled, and how he had been obliged to learn the worth while things of life in the hard school of experience. But he had learned, and had learned so well that few men had entered the senate better fitted for a service that was destined to extend over a period of 27 years, during which time his name was associated with legislation of the utmost importance in times of peace, and in times of war, when President Wilson had reposed the greatest confidence in his fidelity and judgment. Senator Robinson described the late senator from the state as the best beloved member of the body, a man devoted to his country, his family and his friends.

OTHERS PAY TRIBUTES

Similar testimony was given by Senator Swanson, of Virginia, who said that North Carolina had sent some great men to Congress, but none had excelled in fineness of character the man whom the senate was then engaged in honoring. Senator Borah thought Mr. Overman a man not alone gentle and kind, with friendliness that embraced people in all walks of life, but he attributed to him, as altogether characteristic, an unswerving devotion to the constitution. This fidelity to the organic law, said Mr. Borah, was in Senator Overman a natural instinct, believing as he did that the constitution comprised a charter that should be preserved in the form in which it had been given to the American people.

Senator Smith, of South Carolina, joined Messrs. Borah and Smoot in paying tribute to Senator Overman's devotion to the constitution, recording the belief that the North Carolina senator had always listened to the voice of conscience in his private and public life, and kept principle rather than expediency in mind. Senator Overman, he recalled, had upon one occasion faced considerable criticism, when he declined to vote against the admission of a senator-elect who came to Washington bearing the certificate of election from a sovereign state.

Other speakers during the afternoon were Senators Jones, Sheppard, Moses, McKellar, Goff, Harris, Davis and Walsh, of Massachusetts. The next day in the house, there were memorial services for Major Stedman, and Representative Hammer, among other members who have died of late months.

Annual Dinner of Durham Alumni Club a Notable Success; 160 at Delightful Event

The annual dinner of the Durham Alumni Club of Duke University was held on the evening of Monday, March 9, in the West Campus Union with an attendance of 160 alumni and guests. It was regarded the most successful meeting in the history of the local alumni club.

Dr. W. B. McCutcheon, president of the Durham Alumni Club, presided. Henry R. Dwire, Director of Public Relations and Alumni Affairs, spoke briefly, after which the main addresses of the evening were delivered by Coach Wallace Wade, Professor Malcolm McDermott, of the School of Law, and Dr. R. L. Flowers.

The election of officers resulted as follows:

President—H. G. Hedrick.
Vice President—Miss Ruby Markham.
Secretary-Treasurer—W. M. Speed.
Representative on Alumnae Council—Miss Mary Louise Cole.

During the evening musical selections were rendered by the Glee Club Quartet and the University Club Orchestra. The dining room was attractively decorated for this occasion.

Many Treasures Are Stored in Duke University Library

Collection of Newspapers One of Most Valuable to Be Found Anywhere—Many Rare Books—Various Departments of General Library Equipped in Most Modern Manner—all Duke Libraries Have Over 233,000 Volumes

DUKE UNIVERSITY'S new General Library is a genuinely modern university library. The building which houses the library is four stories high, exclusive of the basement. This includes the top story in the tower.

In the basement one first finds the newspaper work room and stacks for more than six thousand volumes of newspapers. This room is in charge of one member of the staff who has one or more assistants. Here the newspapers are gathered, put in order, sent away to the binders, and returned to the stacks. The Duke collection of newspapers is a very valuable one. Mr. J. P. Breedlove, the Librarian, says that, in his opinion, there is not another collection so valuable anywhere south of the Congressional Library, in Washington.

In the basement, also, there is a large and airy work room which is used for pasting, marking, and accessioning the books, and getting them ready for the cataloguers. From this work room there is an entrance to the lowest floor of the stacks.

On this floor also are the offices of the order department. There are three of these offices. One of them is for the chief of the order department, one for the cashier, and one large receiving office. The rear entrance to the building provides access to these offices from the mail and express trucks bringing new books and periodicals ordered. The large door of this entrance opens into a small hallway connected with the receiving office and also with a small stairway hall. This stairway hall contains a stairway which goes to the top of the building. It also contains an elevator which provides access for heavy loads of books to three floors.

In the elbow, at the front, is a beautiful vestibule. The vestibule, of Gothic architecture, has a domed ceiling reaching for three stories. In the center of the dome hangs a beautiful chandelier which lights the vestibule. On either side of the vestibule is a stairway which leads to the second floor. The interior of the vestibule is in limestone, beautifully carved.

Opening from the vestibule, first, is the periodical room. Here one finds tables and chairs accommodating one hundred and two students. Against the north wall of the periodical room are pigeonholes with doors. These pigeonholes accommodate nearly a thousand different periodicals. On the doors to the pigeonholes are fastened cards having the name of the periodical printed in bold letters.

The electric lighting in this room is indirect and is very efficient. The room has a southern exposure, with a beautiful view from the windows, which furnish excellent ventilation and light during the day.

At the end of a short hall opening off the vestibule toward the north, on this floor, is the reserve book room. This room has windows opening on the east-

A Vault in Manuscript Room of the General Library

ern, northern, and western sides. It has tables and chairs to seat one hundred and eighty students. Along the walls where there are no windows, doors or delivery shelves, are shelves sufficient to accommodate 10,000 books. An attendant has charge of this room and the books on reserve back of the delivery counter. From this room there is an entrance to the stacks, also. Two book lifts and a telephone help in the service given to students in this room. These book lifts reach the general delivery room and every floor of the stacks. The telephone connects with every department of the Duke University plant.

At the end of a long hall, running parallel to the periodical room, is the Manuscript Room. This room is equipped with metal cabinets, with glass doors, in which are kept 1,710 metal boxes to hold the manuscripts. Here also one finds a metal cabinet with steel doors in which are kept valuable books in manuscript form.

At the rear of the library building, on this floor, is a study for the director of libraries, and an office for the custodian of the manuscripts.

The two stairways in the front vestibule lead to a landing in the center on the second floor. This landing provides an entrance to the Public Catalogue Room. This room has an indirect system of electric lighting, also, and seven Gothic windows for lighting and ventilation, during the day. It is equipped with three large double faced card catalogue cabinets. These cabinets provide space for cataloguing more than a million and a half volumes. There is space also in the room for another double faced cabinet and a single faced one.

A short flight of stairs leading from the landing in the vestibule, toward the north, brings one to a small landing. To the left, on this landing, one enters the general delivery room. There is also an entrance to this room from the public card catalogue room. The general delivery room is 19 by 65 feet. It is divided by a counter extending the full length of the room. The office of the Reference Librarian is at the south end of this counter, glassed in. The counter itself is used by the attendants for checking out books to students from the circulation division. The Reference Librarian is also Chief of the Circulation Division.

The delivery desk in this room is equipped with pneumatic tubes running through each of the seven floors of the stacks, to the Law School Library, and to the School of Religion Library. It also has two book lifts operated by electricity to bring books from any of the seven floors of the stacks. These book lifts also serve the Reserve Book Room below and the Graduate Reading Room above.

On the outside of the counter there are thirty shelves on which are displayed new books received at the Library, to which students may go and make their own selection for unassigned and recreational reading. These books may be taken out of the library after they have been signed for at the desk.

Adjoining the general delivery room is the reference reading room. This is a large room which has tables and chairs to seat one hundred and seventy-six students. It is finished in mission oak and has an arched ceiling extending to the roof. The walls are adorned with various shields carved in white limestone. The room has Gothic windows opening on the entire east and north sides and part of the west side. The windows are high above the floor and all around the room except where the doors interfere there are shelves for the reference books. These shelves will accommodate more than 12,000 books.

At the rear end of the public catalogue room, running toward the west, is a hallway leading to the rear of the building. On this hallway are four offices for the Librarian and the Staff. At the end of the hall is a large Cataloguing Room. This room is equipped with fourteen desks occupied by fourteen cataloguers and assistant cataloguers. It also houses the accession books and the official catalogue of the library.

Leading away from the front entrance to the general delivery room there is a stairway to the third floor. From the hallway on this third floor is a doorway opening into the graduate reading room. This room is equipped with tables and chairs to seat fifty-eight graduate students. It also has a delivery counter behind which an attendant cares for the books on reserve. Back of this counter, also, are the two book lifts which serve this room from any level of the stacks, from the reserve book room, and from the general delivery room. It has telephone connection, also, with all parts of the University plant. Along the walls of this room are shelves sufficient to accommodate 5,000 volumes. In this room are kept the books reserved for graduate students and those working in seminars. This feature has been found very satisfactory by University authorities in that it relieves the library administration from putting books in Seminar rooms where they are restricted in their use to a small group and where they are frequently lost.

On the same floor with the graduate reading room are seven studies for faculty members and seven seminar rooms. From the vestibule on the third floor is a stairway leading to the fourth and fifth floors which are in the tower. Each of these floors has four rooms, two for studies and two for seminars.

The stack room is also in the shape of an L and has seven levels. It has on each level a pneumatic tube station, a book lift station, and a telephone. Stack attendants care for these stations, securing books called for and sending on the lifts to the floor asking for them. The shelves are of steel. The capacity of the stacks is 400,000 volumes.

On the first and second levels of the stacks are lock rooms. The one on the second level is called the Treasure Room. In it are stored theses and dissertations offered in partial fulfillment of requirements for degrees in Trinity College, and Duke University; valuable reports connected with the history of the institution; catalogues of Union Institute, Normal College, Trinity College, and Duke University; and other valuable papers.

On the third, fourth, fifth, sixth, and seventh, levels of the stacks are one hundred and eight carrels for graduate students writing theses and dissertations. In each carrel is a table and chair and two shelves to accommodate the needed books.

There is also, in the stacks, a passenger elevator connecting with each of the seven levels and each of the three reading rooms. This elevator is used only by members of the staff.

In the front of the basement, reached by a stairway down from the entrance vestibule, is a smoking room for men. Students are requested not to smoke in any of the reading rooms or in the stacks. Just to the left of the entrance to the reserve book room, on the first floor is a well equipped ladies' retiring room. The entire building is well equipped with rest rooms, cloak rooms, and lockers for the members of the staff.

The libraries of the School of Religion and of the Law School are in the buildings occupied by these institutions, but are connected by hallways with the General Library. The entrance to the Law Library is used only by members of the staff, who also have a private entrance into the stacks of the Library of the School of Religion. The Medical School, also, has its own library, as has the Woman's College. The buildings of these institutions are too far away to afford physical connections. The Woman's College Library is the old Trinity College Library so well known to all alumni.

The furnishings and equipment of the entire General Library Building are the best of their kind on the market. They were chosen with great care by the officials and are giving excellent service.

The floors of the reading rooms, the general delivery room, and the public card catalogue room are of rubber tiling. This helps to insure quiet for those working in the library. The stack floors are marble, except the first one which is of cement. The entire building is the last word in fireproof construction.

The building is heated from the University's central heating plant. The radiators are controlled by thermostats which makes the heating almost automatic.

All of the libraries of the University contained 233-665 volumes, on March 1, 1931.

Dr. William K. Boyd is the director of libraries for the University. Mr. J. P. Breedlove is the librarian; Miss Eva E. Malone is assistant librarian, in charge of cataloguing; Mr. Ben E. Powell is chief of the circulation and reference divisions; Mr. Eric Morrell is chief of the order division. There are thirty-five full time and forty-two part time members of the Library Staff.

North Carolina Division, A. A. U. W., Will Hold Annual Conference at Duke

THE North Carolina Division of the American Association of University Women will hold its fourth annual conference in Durham on Friday and Saturday, April 24 and 25, 1931. Headquarters for the conference will be at the Washington Duke Hotel. All meetings, with the exception of luncheon on Saturday at the hotel, will be held in the Woman's College Union, East Campus, Duke University.

The following is a tentative program of the conference:

FRIDAY, APRIL 24, 1931

1:30- 6:00	Registration, Washington Duke Hotel.
2:00- 4:00	Drives around the city.
4:00- 6:00	Tea. Durham Branch A.A.U.W. hostess.
7:00-	Banquet for delegates and guests. Duke University host. Speaker: Dr. Kathryn McHale, Executive and Education Secretary of the A. A. U. W.

SATURDAY, APRIL 25, 1931

9:00-	Registration. The Union, Woman's College, Duke University.
9:30-12:00	Business meetings and discussions.
12:30-	Luncheon—Washington Duke Hotel. Speaker: Professor Winifred Cullis, President of the International Federation of University Women. Professor Cullis is head of the Department of Physiology at the Women's Medical College, University of London.

The State Association feels that it has been particularly fortunate in securing for its principal speakers Dr. McHale, who is well known to all university women, and Professor Cullis who is coming to America to attend a meeting of the International Council of University Women at Wellesley College earlier in April. Professor Cullis is Professor of Physiology at the Women's Medical College, London University. She is a brilliant woman and an interesting speaker. It is hoped that many alumnæ will attend the meetings and the luncheon on Saturday, when Professor Cullis will speak. Anyone who wishes to reserve a plate at the luncheon will please send her name to Miss Elizabeth Anderson, Duke University, on or before April 23, 1931.

Eleven Nations Represented in Graduate Applications

Avalanche of Requests for Fellowships and Scholarships at Duke on Last Day Designated for Such Applications—Total of 595 Candidates, Increase of 216 Over Last Year

THE last date for receiving applications for fellowships and scholarships in the Graduate School of Arts and Sciences brought an avalanche of applications from all parts of the United States and from many foreign countries. When the total was ascertained it was found that 595 candidates for appointments have applied this year as compared with 379 last year, an increase of 216. Among the distant parts of the world represented in the applications were Germany, Austria, Czechoslovakia, England, Egypt, Syria, India, Hawaiian Islands, China and Japan. There are 48 fellowships and scholarships. The fellowships range in value from $650 to $1,000, the amount of the Angier Duke Memorial Fellowship.

The 20 graduate scholarships have a value of $350 each. There is in addition a considerable number of graduate assistantships in the various departments. These assistants in most cases give part of their time to graduate work and part of their time to supervision in laboratory courses, reading themes and similar duties. Probably it will not be possible to award graduate appointments to more than one from each seven or eight of the candidates. It is noteworthy that many of those applying have already had one or two years of graduate work in other universities. Among the applicants are many faculty members of other colleges and universities. The fellowships which are available will be awarded to graduate students of advanced standing, but there will be opportunity to appoint to graduate scholarships some of the more promising students who are beginning graduate work next fall.

It is interesting to note that 16 departments of the University were represented in the list of applicants. More than 100 of the applicants are in the single department of English. Other departments in which 25 or more candidates applied are History, Chemistry, Economics, Biology, Mathematics, Education, Psychology and Physics. During the past week the applications in each department have been receiving the consideration of the faculty of the department. After each department has concluded its study of the applications the candidates are rated and recommendations are sent to the Committee on Fellowships, Scholarships and Graduate Assistantships appointed by President Few. In view of the very largely increased number of applications to be considered the task of making the awards will be more difficult than ever this year. It is expected that the work of the departments and of the Committee on Fellowships will be concluded and the appointments announced early in April.

Duke Alumnus and Trustee is Named Member of District of Columbia Board of Education

HON. Daniel C. Roper, of Washington, D. C., prominent Duke alumnus and member of the board of trustees of the institution, was again honored recently by appointment to membership on the District of Columbia Board of Education in succession to Dr. Charles F. Carusi, former president of the board, who died early in February. The selection was made by the justices of the District Supreme Court.

In a front page article in its issue of March 11, accompanied by a photograph of Mr. Roper, the *Washington Post* said regarding his appointment:

"Appointment of Daniel C. Roper, local attorney and former Commissioner of Internal Revenue, as a member of the District Board of Education to fill the unexpired term of Dr. Charles F. Carusi, former president of the board, who died early in February, was announced yesterday by the justices of the District Supreme Court, who made the selection.

"The term to which Mr. Roper is appointed ends June 30, 1932. After that time he will be eligible for reappointment. Dr. H. Barrett Learned, vice-president of the board, is now acting president. The board may call an election at its next meeting Wednesday, March 18, to elect a permanent president and

(Continued on page 98)

Athletic Interest Turns Now To Baseball, Tennis, Track

Winter Sports Give Duke Teams Reasonably Satisfactory Results in Four Sports—
Grantland Rice to Star Duke Football Squad in Special Motion
Picture Feature—Baseball Practice in Progress

WITH the basketball season a memory, wrestling, boxing and swimming a matter of record, and the first period of football training under Coach Wallace Wade closed, Duke athletes and their followers have turned their attention to baseball, tennis, and track.

Winter sports gave Blue Devil teams reasonably satisfactory results in four sports, though few particular brilliant highlights were registered except the State basketball championship registered by the basketeers. An outstanding indoor track record was made by Henry Fulmer, sophomore broad-jumper, who set a new Southern leap mark at Chapel Hill.

Football practice closed with a great thrill for the Blue Devils, when Grantland Rice, famed sports editor and sports reel producer, sent a staff of cameramen to Durham to star the entire squad in a special feature depicting the fundamentals of the game as taught by Coach Wade, in a full-length talking picture. Several days were spent in getting the picture, part of which was taken in "slow moving pictures" to reveal usually unseen technical details of a player's actions.

Coach Coombs has been with his baseball aspirants for several weeks, and faces a hard task of building a new team from a squad virtually depleted of veterans. A new team will use a new diamond this spring, for the new baseball park, one of the most beautiful to be found anywhere, is about completed. Eighteen games are on the schedule, beginning April 1 with Cornell at Durham. Coach Coombs has not simmered down a large number of candidates to his final squad, but it looks as though seven to nine sophomores will take the field on the opening day.

Robertshaw at short and Kersey at second seem to be the best bets for these berths. The best-looking pitchers are Duffey, McKeithan, and Coombs. Werner has been receiving well, but has keen competition in Voorhees and Howell. Hot fights are still on for other positions. Shore and Colley are looking to the third base post, alternating with Klare at first. Bost, Bostic, Harrington, Bennett, Rochelle, Umstead, and several others are scrapping for the outfield positions.

Coach Buchheit has fair to middling prospects in track, with the burden of the optimism falling on several promising sophomores. If they come through, Duke may have the best track season in several years. John Brownlee and Fulmer are all-around stars, doing sprints and jumps, as well as clearing the hurdles. Lemons, Doughty, and Sharpe are also hurdlers. Captain Simons leads in the middle and long distance running events, working with Heizer, Hicks, Howard, Massengill, Flinton, and Wood. Bradsher and Lewis, sophomores, are also bidding for starting positions.

The field events have attracted Turner and Ripley, Smith, Leonard, Brewer, Bryan, Keegan, Mullen, Menaker, McLarty, and others. Seven track meets are slated.

Tennis will find two veterans, Captain Jack Meyers and George Rogers. John Shaw, Garber, Peake, Stewart Clark, Powers, and Fulp are working hard for a place on the net team. The new courts near the gymnasium are filled daily, and the racquet swingers are working hard to be in shape for the opening of the season.

Outdoor sports at Duke this spring will be in a beautiful setting, as were winter sports in the new gymnasium. New tennis courts, a new cinder track, and the new baseball diamond will be used.

The baseball schedule finds most of the games in April, only five games coming in May. The list follows:

April 1—Cornell at Durham.
April 2—Cornell at Durham.
April 3—Penn State at Durham.
April 4—University of Pennsylvania at Durham.
April 6—Princeton and Univ. of Pennsylvania.
April 10—Wake Forest at Wake Forest.
April 11—N. C. State at Durham.
April 17—Wake Forest at Durham.
April 22—Davidson at Davidson.
April 25—North Carolina at Durham.
April 27—Univ. of Pennsylvania at Philadelphia.
April 29—Princeton at Princeton.

April 30—Fordham at New York.
May 1—N. Y. U. at New York.
May 2—Navy at Annapolis, Md.
May 9—N. C. State at Raleigh
May 13—Davidson at Durham.
May 16—Carolina at Chapel Hill.

TRACK'S SCHEDULE FOLLOWS:

March 28—Washington and Lee at Durham.
March 31—Wake Forest at Durham.
April 13—Davidson at Davidson.
April 18—N. C. State at Raleigh.
April 22—North Carolina at Chapel Hill.
May 2—N. C. Intercollegiate Meet at Greensboro.
May 15-16—S. I. C. Meet at Birmingham, Ala.

Dedication of Medical School and Hospital April 20

(Continued from page 87)

Duke University's unique service to medical history in naming the fourteen wards of its new hospital after distinguished physicians associated with the South is doubly interesting because of the sound judgment displayed in selecting the names. Naturally, the Johns Hopkins group is prominent. Wards are named after three of the "big four" that Sargent put on his famous canvas of the "four doctors"—Osler, Welsh and Halstead. x x x John Howland, the pediatrician, gives his name to the children's ward. Walter Reed is remembered in one of the medical wards, and Josiah Nott, who partially anticipated Reed's theory of the insect transmission of yellow fever, is also commemorated. Crawford Long, of Georgia, discoverer of ether, is memorialized in one of the surgical wards, and another is intended to keep in grateful remembrance the fame of Edmund Strudwick, of North Carolina, a pioneer surgeon of an heroic mould. Virginia naturally feels honored that the distinguished James L. Cabell, long professor of anatomy, physiology and surgery at the University of Virginia, is among the fourteen, as he deserves to be. One of the three obstetrical wards is to be styled Sims, after the great Alabama scientist, James Marion Sims; a second is to be called Campbell, as a tribute to the Georgia gynecologist, Henry F. Campbell; and the other will be a memorial to Dr. Francois Marie Prevost, of Louisiana, credited with performing the first successful Caesarian section in the United States. It is an inspiring list, and if great Duke hospital grows, it may well be lengthened, for in no field are Southern men contributing more to human progress than in the medical sciences. This generation will present as many great names as the last.

Duke Alumnus and Trustee is Named Member of District of Columbia Board of Education

(Continued from page 95)

vice-president. Dr. Learned is understood to be favored for the place of president.

"Mr. Roper is a member of the law firm of Roper, Hagerman, Hurrey & Dudley. He has six children, all of whom are in public schools here. He served as First Assistant Postmaster General from March, 1914, until August, 1916. He was vice-president of the United States Tariff Commission from March 22 until September 25, 1917. He was then appointed Commissioner of Internal Revenue, serving until 1920.

"From 1892 until 1894 Mr. Roper was a member of the South Carolina House of Representatives. He was clerk of the United States Senate committee on interstate commerce from 1894 to 1897. From 1900 until 1910 he served as expert special agent of the United States Census Bureau and clerk of the ways and means committee of the House from 1910 until 1913.

Mr. Roper was born in Marlboro County, S. C., April 1, 1867. He took the A.B. degree at Duke University, North Carolina, in 1888, LL.B. at National University in Washington in 1901 and LL.D. at Tusculum College in 1927. Mr. Roper is a Democrat. He is a member of the Chevy Chase Club, University Club and New York Club. His home is at 3001 Woodland Drive Northwest.

Where They Are Located	News of the Alumni	What They Are Doing

Miss Elizabeth Aldridge, '24, Secretary of Alumnae Council, Editor

CLASS OF 1902

George Markham March of Route No. 2, Mobile, Alabama, is sales manager for the Adams Motor Company. He is also president of his local county Chamber of Commerce and a member of the school board.

The Motte Business College has been opened in Lumberton, N. C., by Leon L. Motte of Wilmington. Mr. Motte has been teaching business courses more than thirty years and has successfully operated a college in Wilmington for the past eighteen years. He plans to open a school in New Bern at an early date. After leaving Trinity, he read law in Spartanburg, S. C., and taught business courses to students at Wofford. He was later admitted to the North and South Carolina bars. For twenty-one years he served as court reporter and in that capacity has been to the Robeson County court in Lumberton. He has also served as deputy recorder in Wilmington.

Elizabeth Caldwell of Monroe has been elected May Queen at Duke University for 1931. She is the daughter of Mr. ('02) and Mrs. G. B. Caldwell (Annie Whitaker, '05). This is one of the most coveted honors among the women students at Duke University. Other daughters of alumni who have been chosen in the May court follow: Courtney Sharpe of Lumberton, daughter of J. A. Sharpe, '98; Carlotta Satterfield of Durham, daughter of Mr. ('04) and Mrs. H. C. Satterfield (Carlotta Angier, '05); Mary Bradsher of Petersburg, Va., daughter of Mr. ('04) and Mrs. A. B. Bradsher (Elizabeth Muse, '05), and Cornelia Yarbrough, daughter of E. S. Yarbrough, '02, of Durham.

George A. Hoyle is in the general insurance business at Shelby, N. C.

CLASS OF 1903

Fletcher W. Fink is general manager of the Christian-Todd Telephone Company, Hopkinsville, Kentucky. His oldest daughter, Dorothy, attended Duke in 1926-27.

Dr. Mark T. Frizzelle has been a successful physician in Ayden since graduating from the University College of Medicine, Richmond, Va., in 1907. He is vice-president of the First National Bank of Ayden and chairman, Board of Stewards, of the local Methodist Church.

CLASS OF 1904

Arthur G. Elliott is general superintendent and part owner of the F. T. McQuire Company, paving contractors, at Washington, N. C. He served as mayor of Washington for one year and has always taken an active part in the Elks Club and Rotary.

Zachery P. Beachboard is superintendent of the schools at Blountsville, Tennessee.

CLASS OF 1905

Lloyd K. Wooten of Kinston, is manager of the Kinston Auto Parts Company. He married Miss Anna Spencer Jones on May 1, 1909. They have four sons.

CLASS OF 1907

Mr. and Mrs. J. T. Jerome and their three children have moved to 107 Chamberlain Street, Raleigh. Mr. Jerome was for a number of years superintendent of the Wayne County schools and resigned to take a position with Rand-McNally Company.

CLASS OF 1909

Mrs. Evelyn Jones Hawkes was one of the two alumni elected to membership in Phi Beta Kappa Fraternity by the local chapter. She is associate professor of education at New Jersey State College for Women, New Brunswick, N. J., and has done outstanding work in her field.

CLASS OF 1912

Mr. and Mrs. Edwin L. Jones (Annabel Lambeth) of Charlotte, N. C., are located at Ancon, Panama, Canal Zone. Mr. Jones is one of the officers of the J. A. Jones Company which is carrying on a two million dollar job at the Pacific end of the Panama Canal. They are building the second largest airport of the U. S. Army, the largest being in San Antonio, Texas. This project was started the first of the year and is already two months ahead of the schedule, having had advantage of the dry season. Mr. and Mrs. Jones and Edwin, Jr., are planning to be in Panama about two years.

CLASS OF 1915

S. Glenn Hawfield, president of the Cabarrus County Alumni Association, is popular in the civic and social life of his community. He is a member of the Board of Stewards of Central Methodist Church and superintendent of the Sunday School; secretary-treasurer, Concord Rotary Club and prominently identified with the Masonic Order. He is a member of the Board of Directors of the Y. M. C. A., Council of Associated Charities, and the Cabarrus County Industrial Board. He has been in school work continuously since leaving college, having spent four years as superintendent of the Monroe Schools and since that time as superintendent of the Cabarrus County Schools. Under his supervision, the county school system has grown to be one of the most up-to-date and progressive in the state.

S. GLENN HAWFIELD

Mr. Hawfield was married in 1916 to Miss Kate Clark of Union County and they have three sons, Glenn, Jr., William Dallas and Harold Houston.

Mr. and Mrs. Sanford S. Jenkins are receiving congratulations on the birth of a son, Sanford S. Jenkins, Jr., on February 8, in Baltimore, Maryland.

CLASS OF 1917

John B. Holloway, ex-'17, and Miss Lila Compton of Greenwood, S. C., and Newport, N. C., were married Sunday, February 15, at the parsonage of Centenary Methodist Church, New Bern, N. C. Rev. A. J. Hobbs, '19, performed the ceremony. Miss Compton has been teaching music in the Newport Schools for several years. Mr. Holloway is with his father on his farm about ten miles from Durham.

Edwin Burge operates his own shoe store at 39 Battery Park Avenue, Grove Arcade, Asheville.

CLASS OF 1918

Hallie Baldwin was married last summer in Washington, D. C., to Mr. R. L. Perry at the Mount Vernon Church. They are now living at 838 Park Avenue, Bridgeport, Conn. Mr. Perry is with the National Register Company.

CLASS OF 1919

Mrs. Clarence L. Ausbon (Imogene Hix) has moved her address from Elizabeth City, N. C., to 914 W. South Street, Raleigh. Mr. Ausbon is connected with the Raleigh *Times*.

Wesley Williams Bouterse is a Salvation Army Officer and also a member of the faculty of the Salvation Army Training College at 339 Luckie Street, Atlanta, Ga. Mr. and Mrs. Bouterse have one daughter, Doris, who was born on October 22, 1928.

CLASS OF 1920

Dr. LeRoy Warren Saunders is chief physician of the Consolidated Gas, Electric Light and Power Company of Baltimore, Maryland. Dr. and Mrs. Saunders, who was Dorothy L. Perkins before her marriage on November 8, 1930, live at 6 East 30th Street.

CLASS OF 1921

Hugh T. Lefler received his Ph.D. degree from the University of Pennsylvania in February, 1931. He teaches history at North Carolina State College, Raleigh.

CLASS OF 1922

William Allen Tyree was married on February 28 to Miss Helen Davis Long of Catawba, N. C. They make their home in the Powe Apartments, Buchanan Boulevard, Durham. Allen is director in the business division, Duke University. Mrs. Tyree is a graduate of Greensboro College.

Houck and Thomas, advertising agency of High Point, has received national recognition from two authoritative sources. The agency has just received a letter from the Associated Business Papers, Inc., of New York City, with the information that the agency is placed on its recognized list. A few days ago a letter extending recognition was received by the agency from the Southern Newspaper Publishers Association, Chattanooga, Tenn. Houck and Thomas Agency has been in operation little more than two years, and has made unusual progress. C. B. Houck, one of the members of the firm, taught in Greensboro for a few years after leaving Trinity, before going to High Point.

Joe Edward Caviness practiced law for several years after leaving Trinity. He also served as judge of Harnett County recorder's court. He is now agent for The Texas Company, Henderson, N. C. Mr. and Mrs. Caviness have two children, Joseph Edward and Edith Ann.

CLASS OF 1923

Robert Lee Davis, Jr., was born on March 5, at 1510 Paris Avenue, Nashville, Tennessee. Mrs. Davis, before her marriage, was Miss Martha A. Stewart of Nashville. Lee is secretary-treasurer, Shares in the South, Inc. He received his A.M. degree from Vanderbilt in 1925.

CLASS OF 1924

Mr. and Mrs. W. J. Rudge, Jr., have announced the birth of W. J. Rudge, III, who was born on December 31 at Pittsfield, Mass. Bill has a position with the General Electric Company in Pittsfield.

Mrs. Jack Hinton (Lou Davis Lyon) has recently moved to Goldsboro and her address is the Goldwayne Apartments.

Carrie Hearn lives at 809 Grove Street, Delmar, Delaware. She received an M.D. degree from London University and plans to take up her internship right away.

Robert Hoyle Smathers, of Canton, N. C., is principal of the Long Creek High School, Route No. 1, Huntersville, N. C.

CLASS OF 1925

Alene McCall teaches science in the Bethany Consolidated School, Summerfield, N. C. She has written a number of articles on scientific subjects which have been printed in the *Popular Science Monthly* and the *Progressive Teacher.*

An attractive announcement was received in the Alumni Office from Mr. and Mrs. J. Rhyne Killian announcing the birth of Carolyn Makepeace Killian on February 26. Rhyne is editor, *Technology Review*, an outstanding alumni publication. His offices are located at 202 D-Holden Green, Cambridge, Mass.

Alfred T. Withrow is employed by Swift and Company, Chicago, as a salesman. His residence is 587 Webford Avenue, Des Plaines, Illinois.

CLASS OF 1926

Mr. and Mrs. Albert R. Weaver, of Corinth, Mississippi, announce the birth of Olivia Ann on February 11.

CLASS OF 1927

Lester C. Butler has opened law offices in the Trust building, Durham, for the general practice of law.

Courtney Bright is located at 1152 W. Hilton Street, Philadelphia, Pa.

Antoinette Burr recently married Harry C. Knight. They make their home at 2023 Milan Street, New Orleans, La.

Paul N. Carmichael is sales manager for the Cyclone Fence Company, Hartford, Conn. His home address is 410 Asylum Street.

Ethel Leigh Glover is a registered nurse and does private nursing in Durham. Her home address is 117 South Driver Avenue, East Durham.

CLASS OF 1928

Mr. and Mrs. C. C. Swaringen (Anita Scarboro) have moved from Goldsboro to Greensboro. Swaringen was formerly manager of the Montgomery-Ward store in Goldsboro, but has been transferred to the office of the company in Greensboro.

Haskelle M. Bivens has moved from Concord, N. C., to Monroe.

William A. Palmer lives at 255 West 97th Street, New York City. He is in the advertising department of the *New York Times*.

Maurice W. Turnipseed attended Alabama Polytechnic Institute, receiving a B.S. degree in 1929. He is engaged in farming with his father at Fitzpatrick, Alabama.

CLASS OF 1929

Marion P. Bolich and Miss Julia Prather, of Mount Airy, were married in Winston-Salem on January 3. They make their home at 1748 Virginia Road, Winston-Salem.

W. Burke Mewborne is assistant traffic superintendent of the New Jersey Bell Telephone Company at 2 Maple Avenue, Morristown, N. J.

Richard Caswell Horne of Winston-Salem is connected with the Standard Oil Company of New Jersey. He has recently been assigned to the West India Oil Company as foreign marketing assistant in San Juan, Porto Rico.

Norman Bright Kelley, 1306 Carroll Street, Durham, is timekeeper for the Golden Belt Manufacturing Company.

CLASS OF 1930

Sarah Alice Harris and Mr. Robert Glenn Sewell were married on November 1, 1930, at Seaboard, N. C. They now make their home at Murfreesboro.

Charles Walter Porter, better known as "Soup," is in Springfield, Mass., this year working toward his M.A. degree in physical education.

Ola Simpson teaches the sixth grade at Bethesda school near Durham. She lives at her home, 1801 Vale Street.

Théron B. Brock teaches this year at Mamers, N. C. His home address is Bunnlevel.

William H. Rousseau, Jr., is assistant to the treasurer, Duke University.

News has just reached the Alumni Office reporting the death of John Jay Sterner of New Bethlehem, Pa. He was killed when struck by a car at Dushore, Pa., on October 13, 1930. While he was a student at Duke, he received the Carnegie Hero Medal and award for saving Bernard C. Cook from drowning at New Bethlehem, Pa.

CLASS OF 1931

Mrs. Joseph E. Peele, née Catherine Groves, is managing editor and half owner of the *Edenton Daily News*, Edenton, N. C. She received her A.B. degree from the University of North Carolina in 1929.

Sarah Anderson of Wilson, N. C., daughter of Dr. ('98) and Mrs. Wade H. Anderson, was married on March 3, to Mr. Raphael Smith, Jr., of Owensboro, Kentucky. Sarah attended Goucher College before coming to Duke and for the past year she has been attending Peabody College, Nashville, Tennessee. Mr. Smith was graduated from Vanderbilt University in 1926. He has been engaged in construction work in Tennessee since receiving his degree.

Alice Elizabeth Holmes was married on November 5, 1930, to Dr. Edwin H. Douglas, Jr., of 217 East 27th Street, New York City. She is head hostess in one of Alice Foote McDougal's Tea Shops.

SWING ALONG!

THERE'S a thrilling freshness in the smoke of a Camel—a delicately blended fragrance, sunny and mild—that's never even been approached by any other cigarette. Swing along with the modern crowd! They've graduated to Camels and real smoke-enjoyment.

CAMELS

DUKE UNIVERSITY
ALUMNI REGISTER

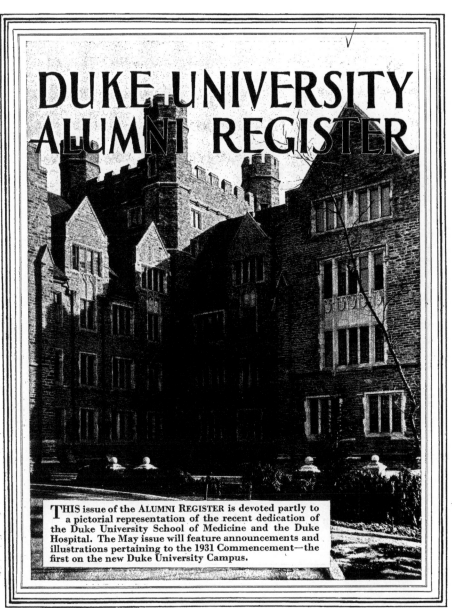

THIS issue of the ALUMNI REGISTER is devoted partly to
a pictorial representation of the recent dedication of
the Duke University School of Medicine and the Duke
Hospital. The May issue will feature announcements and
illustrations pertaining to the 1931 Commencement—the
first on the new Duke University Campus.

VOLUME XVII   NUMBER 4

Duke University Alu n n Register

(*Member of American Alumni Council*)

Published at Durham, N. C. Every Month in the Year in the Interest of the University and the Alumni

| Volume XVII | April, 1931 | Number 4 |

In This Issue

Editor and Business Manager......................HENRY R. DWIRE, '02

Assistant Editors............................ELIZABETH ALDRIDGE, '24
ALBERT A. WILKINSON, '26

Advertising Manager..........................CHARLES A. DUKES, '29

TWO DOLLARS A YEAR   20 CENTS A COPY

ENTERED AS SECOND-CLASS MATTER AT THE POST-OFFICE AT
DURHAM, NORTH CAROLINA

This Issue

This, the April number of the ALUMNI REGISTER, appears just a few days after one of the most notable events in the history of Duke University—the dedication of the Medical School and Hospital. Naturally considerable space is devoted to that event. Next month it is hoped to publish some of the addresses, in part at least.

The May Register

The greater proportion of the matter in the May issue will naturally have reference to the 1931 Commencement. There will be messages to, and from, different reunion classes. The complete Commencement program will be published, and there will be illustrations and reading matter bearing upon various features of the event.

In the Alumni News this month the reunion classes are being featured. That will be the case again next month. These notes will be of interest, of course, to alumni generally, but especially to those whose classes have reunions this year.

Departments Featured

During the past few months the REGISTER has made it a point to feature from time to time various schools and departments of Duke University. This month the School of Religion and the Department of Education are both given attention. Next month it is hoped to present an interesting feature article on the Department of Engineering. Other similar features will follow from time to time.

Covers

"The REGISTER cover pages for the past few months have been superb," said an alumnus the other day. "I look forward eagerly to each issue of the REGISTER for that as well as other features."

Speaking of covers, the one for May will be especially unique. Watch for it.   THE EDITOR.

(1) *Left to right:* President W. P. Few, Chairman J. F. Bruton, of Board of Trustees; Chairman G. G. Allen, of Duke Endowment Trustees.

(2) Academic procession forming in front of Medical School Building.

(3) *Left to right:* Dr. Welch, Dr. Edsall, Dr. Weed, Dr. Davison, Dr. Russell, President Few, Dr. Kitchin.

(4) *Left to right:* Mrs. E. C. Marshall, Charlotte; Miss Doris Duke; Mrs. W. P. Few.

(5) Academic procession in front of School of Law.

(6) Academic procession passing the Library.

(7) Another view of the procession.

Duke University Alumni Register

Volume XVII · · · · April, 1931 · · · · Number 4

Editorial Comment

HEARD AT THE DEDICATION

We wish more of the alumni could have been here on April 20, at the dedication of the Medical School and Hospital, and heard the many fine comments on Duke's rapid development and wonderful prospects in medical as well as in other lines.

Some of the leading men of the medical profession from all parts of the country voiced on that occasion sentiments of amazement at what has already been done and brilliant prophecies regarding the future.

"I wonder if the people generally even of your own state realize just what is being done here," remarked one visitor.

We wonder if Duke alumni themselves actually realize it.

It would be a fine thing indeed if more of them could come here, at Commencement or some other time, and see just what is being done.

It is impossible to tell it in the printed page in such a way as to "put over" the message adequately.

Frequently these days, when an alumnus comes back to the campus, he marvels at the changes that just a few years have wrought, not simply in physical equipment but in other lines.

Which indicates that more frequent visits "back home" to Alma Mater would be an excellent thing, both for the institution and for the alumni themselves.

"NOT CASES, BUT PERSONALITIES"

President T. D. Kitchin, of Wake Forest College, delivered a timely address at the dedication of the Duke Medical School and Hospital on April 20.

He set forth one of the tasks ahead of Duke University.

This is the making of the Hospital and Medical School a "House of Mercy" in which "patients shall be treated not as cases, but as personalities."

"In this way," he said, "the austerity of science could be blended with the sympathetic art of medicine, with no compromise of either."

Dr. Kitchin has set a high standard for the greatness of Duke University.

But it is not a standard higher than that which she has set for herself.

And it is a standard which is to be applied, not only to the Medical School and Hospital but to the institution as a whole—this policy of handling those who come within the scope of its influence, "not as cases, but as personalities."

Several steps are already being taken along that line.

For one thing, the personnel work has as its aim the recognition of each individual as a separate personality, and his treatment as such. The intensive work that is carried out with Freshmen, for instance, is based on a realization of the fact that a man entering college for the first time is particularly in need of personal direction and guidance.

But this work does not stop with the Freshman year, by any means.

The system of honors courses is another movement in the same direction. The idea here again is to emphasize personality and to get away from excessive standardization.

We have every reason to believe that Mr. James B. Duke himself, when providing for Duke University, had in mind an ideal, not of so-called "mass education," but of a careful selective process that would magnify personality.

And to make effective that ideal is to be the constant aim, we feel sure, of administration; faculty and student body.

COMMENCEMENT

The thoughts of Duke alumni are naturally turning now to the 1931 Commencement.

The first Commencement on the new campus, it will be remembered by historians with the first Commencement of Trinity College in Randolph County, the last Commencement before the death of Dr. Braxton Craven, Trinity's first president, and the first Commencement after the removal of Trinity College to Durham.

It will witness a great "gathering of the clans" similar in importance to those of the old days when alumni and friends of the college went a day's journey on foot, or horseback, or in buggies, to the great occasion of the year.

Movements started this year will have much to do with the shaping of the future of Duke.

It is an excellent time for those who have not been here in some years, as well as those who have, to come again and have a part in the inauguration of a new era in the life of the institution.

Many events in the future life of the University will be dated as "before" or "after" the "first Commencement on the new campus."

It is hoped and believed that the attendance of alumni will establish a new record.

It may seem a little early to be talking about Commencement.

But the last five or six weeks before that event will pass rapidly.

It will come "almost before you know it."

Make your plans now to attend.

JUST A REMINDER

The REGISTER has not had much to say about money this year.

Perhaps we should have brought more forcefully to the attention of alumni the matter of increased support of the work of the Alumni Office, but the idea has been to avoid that if possible.

However, the fiscal year is nearing its end, and there are one or two things that should be said.

And they will be said briefly.

First, the donations by alumni to the Alumni Fund this year are still considerably short of the amount needed for the alumni work.

We do not believe the alumni want this condition to continue, but in the rush of other matters many who otherwise would have responded to the call for funds have simply neglected it.

There is still time to correct that deficiency before a new fiscal year starts July 1.

THEY REFUSE TO GROW OLD

In speaking recently at a Rotary meeting in Concord in celebration of the seventy-sixth birthday of William R. Odell, of that city, Duke alumnus and trustee, President W. P. Few referred to W. R. Odell, and D. B. Coltrane, his lifelong friend, aged 86, as men who simply refuse to grow old.

In that expression, Dr. Few pointed out a vital difference to be seen as between various individuals when they approach what is commonly referred to as old age.

Some individuals become old at fifty, some at sixty, and so on, and there are some who, like Mr. Odell and Mr. Coltrane, never become old in spirit, though advanced in years.

Real education, the education that is of the right type, makes for the kind of disposition that does not measure age in terms of years.

That kind of education causes individuals to continue to read and study and to be a part of the life about them.

This, after all, is one of the prime secrets possessed by those who never grow old—knowing the companionship of books and of people with experience and knowledge along various lines, and the companionship of other elements that give zest to life and keep the spirit young even in age.

WHY NOT EXTEND IT?

At its spring meeting on Saturday evening, May 2, the Washington, D. C., Alumni Association of Duke University is going to have as its guests parents of students in the Washington area who are now at Duke.

In this way alumni, parents, students and institution will be brought closer together.

Why should this idea not be adopted by other alumni groups?

Dedication of the Medical School and Hospital a Notable Success

Representatives of Outstanding Institutions in All Parts of United States and Some
from Canada Participate in Ceremonies—Dr. William H. Welch Is
Guest of Honor and a Speaker at the Dedication

THE DEDICATION of the Duke Medical School and the Duke Hospital on April 20 was a great event in the history of the institution. Not since the inauguration of President William P. Few, in 1910, has so elaborate a program been planned for any occasion.

Crowds thronged the entire institution throughout the day. More than eight hundred out-of-town guests were present. These included representatives from hospitals and medical schools, colleges and universities, and funds and foundations, throughout the United States and Canada. Hundreds of physicians were present from all over North Carolina and from other states. The North Carolina Medical Society, meeting in Durham, at the same time, attended in a body. Members of the boards of trustees of the Duke Endowment and of Duke University were present. Miss Doris Duke, of New York, daughter of the late James B. Duke, was an honored guest.

Ten o'clock was set as the hour to begin the enrollment of guests and delegates at the office of the Dean of the Medical School. Long before that hour, however, the halls of the twin institutions were thronged with enthusiastic, eager visitors.

At ten-forty-five the academic procession was formed. This was one of the most striking and colorful events of the day. Hundreds of delegates, physicians, speakers and members of the Duke faculty, robed in academic costume, marched in the line. The procession, led by

JAMES B. DUKE
His generosity made possible the School of Medicine and Hospital

the University Chorus, extended from the Medical School, down the quadrangle, past the Law School, and the Library to Page Auditorium, in which the morning exercises were held.

President Few presided at the session which was opened with prayer by Dean Elbert Russell of the Duke School of Religion. George Garland Allen, of New York, long an associate and close friend of Mr. James B. Duke, presented the buildings of the Medical School and Hospital, for the board of trustees of the Duke Endowment, of which he is chairman. Mr. Allen spoke feelingly of Mr. Duke's purpose to provide not only a part of a great university, in these institutions, but also a great healing center for the surrounding territory. He said that Mr. Duke was present in spirit. "Unquestionably," he said, "his spirit pervades this hall, today, for did I not hear him say that he expected to be looking down upon this work one thousand years hence?"

The buildings were accepted by Colonel John Fletcher Bruton, chairman of the board of trustees of Duke University. Colonel Bruton assured the trustees of the endowment that their work would not, could not, be forgotten. He praised them as men who have demonstrated the unerring judgment of Mr. Duke in selecting them as men who can do big things. High tribute to Mr. Duke was paid by Colonel Bruton. He said, "Mr. Duke stepped outside the ranks of ordinary men in establishing the Endowment. It is eminently fitting," he continued, "that the school of medicine and the hospital should have this first recognition, serving as the most practical human expression of Mr. Duke's interest in his fellow man."

Dr. Thurman Delna Kitchin, President of Wake Forest College, brought greetings from the medical professor of North Carolina. Himself the president of an institution which offers the first two years of a medical course, Dr. Kitchin was sure that both types of institution would endure. He said that Duke Medical School and Hospital should become a "house of mercy," from which angels of mercy should go forth to all the surrounding country.

The address of the morning was delivered by Dr. David Linn Edsall, Dean of the Harvard Medical School. Dr. Edsall spoke on the changes in medicine and surgery which have developed during the past generation. He said these changes had been brought about through coöperation with other sciences. Medical laboratories have contributed much to the success of modern medicine, using the methods of chemistry and physics. The future development of medicine, he said, will also be aided by coöperation with sociological and economic forces.

Dr. Wilburt Cornell Davison, Dean of the Duke School of Medicine, presented the honorable delegates, and Dean Russell pronounced the benediction. Music was interspersed throughout the program by the University Club Orchestra.

At half past one o'clock, the delegates and invited guests, more than a thousand, were entertained at a luncheon in the Men's Union. The spacious student dining halls were used for this purpose. Opening into each other, the dining halls made an ideal place for the luncheon.

President Few presided again and introduced as the speakers Dr. Lewis Hill Weed, Director of the Johns Hopkins School of Medicine, and Dr. Watson Smith Rankin, Director of the Division of Hospitals of the Duke Endowment.

Doctor Weed spoke on "Experimentation in Medical Education." He called attention to the fact that educators everywhere are expressing themselves as dissatisfied with educational methods in use at the present time. In the elementary and secondary schools, he said, there is a search for methods of instruction which shall arouse and hold the child's interest; in the colleges, similar efforts are being made to widen the intellectual horizon of the students; and, in the graduate schools, there is a movement to develop students as individuals rather than as stereotyped products. In the medical schools, he continued, the change appears in the tendency to swing toward the greater freedom of instructional methods and a decrease in obligatory teaching. That the Duke University Medical School is being established at this time of change he believed augurs well for its success.

Dr. Rankin spoke on "Hospitalization." He told of the increase of the quantity and of the quality of medical service which comes to a community which has a hospital and of the great boon which a hospital proves for the poor. He spoke of the Duke Hospital

Four Speakers on the Dedication Program

DR. LEWIS HILL WEED   DR. W. S. RANKIN   DR. DAVID LINN EDSALL   DR. WILLIAM H. WELCH

as being the great central hospital of the Duke Endowment system which owes its hearty coöperation to the district hospitals and to the smaller hospitals participating in the Duke program.

The portrait of Dr. William Stewart Halsted at three o'clock was unveiled, in the amphitheatre of the hospital. Doctor Halsted was for many years surgeon-in-chief of Johns Hopkins Hospital, and is known as one of America's greatest medical men. A number of his relatives were present for the occasion as guests of the university.

For an hour, delegates and guests continued their inspection of the Medical School and Hospital buildings. These buildings and their equipment were provided for in the bequest of Mr. James B. Duke. The cost has exceeded $4,000,000, leaving an endowment of $6,000,000 for maintenance. Medical men say that the plant is comparable with the best anywhere.

The important social event of the day was the reception given by President and Mrs. Few, in honor of the delegates, and invited guests, and members of their families. This reception was held in the University Union Reception Room from 4:30 to 5:30 o'clock.

Dinner was served at seven o'clock, for the delegates and invited guests, in the Union of the Coördinate Woman's College on the East Campus. The luncheon and dinner gave opportunity for the University's culinary department to demonstrate its possibilities. Right well did it do so, to the credit of the university, its own officials and its humblest subordinate.

The evening session was held in the Auditorium of the Woman's College. Doctor Few presided again and Dean Russell led the prayer. The speaker of the evening was Doctor William Henry Welch, Professor of the History of Medicine, Johns Hopkins University School of Medicine. Doctor Welch spoke on "Medical Education and Research," his address bringing to his hearers many observations based on a long experience.

Dr. Wilburt C. Davison, Dean of the Duke Medical School, announced the names of the wards of the Duke Hospital. These wards, he said, have been named for distinguished physicians and surgeons, as follows: William H. Welch, the only living physician for whom a ward is named, and who attended the dedication exercises; Sir William Osler, noted physician who made his home in Maryland for many years; Josiah Clark Nott, of South Carolina; Daniel Drake, of Kentucky; Walter Reed, of Virginia; William Stewart Halsted, of Maryland; Edmund Charles Fox Strudwick, of North Carolina; Crawford Williamson Long, of Georgia; Ephraim McDowell, of Kentucky; James L. Cabell, of Virginia; J. Marion Sims, of South Carolina; Francois Prevost, of Louisiana; and Henry Fraser Campbell, of Georgia. Many relatives of these

great men were present and were introduced by Dean Davidson.

After the benediction by Dean Russell, the great throng filed out of the auditorium. Another of the notable events in the life of Duke University had become history.

Arrangements for the dedication ceremonies were handled by a committee composed of Dr. Frank C. Brown, chairman; Dr. R. L. Flowers and Dr. W. C. Davison.

The construction and announcement of the Medical School and Hospital were greatly admired by visitors from all parts of the country, tribute being paid to the architect, Horace Trumbauer, of Philadelphia, and the W. S. Lee Engineering Corporation, of Charlotte and New York, which was in charge of the engineering and construction under the immediate supervision of Mr. A. C. Lee.

Duke University Professor Awarded Guggenheim Fellowship

Dr. B. Harvie Branscomb, Professor of New Testament in the Duke School of Religion, has been awarded a Guggenheim fellowship. This fellowship provides for a year in Europe, Asia, and Africa, studying and

lecturing. Professor Branscomb's new work, for which he has been granted a year's leave of absence, will begin in June. He plans to take his family with him.

Doctor Branscomb will begin his work in Berlin, Germany. Until January 15, he will work in Berlin and in Munich. Two months will be spent in Jerusalem, using the library of the American School of Oriental Studies. Professor Branscomb will also go to the American University at Cairo, Egypt, to deliver a course of lectures.

DR. B. HARVIE BRANSCOMB

After the stay in Cairo, Professor Branscomb will return to Europe in the spring of 1932 for special study in Paris and London. He is engaged at the present time in a comparative study of early Christian and Hebrew (?) Ethics. It is this work which he will pursue during the coming year.

May Day and Alumuae Home-Coming on Saturday, May 2

Miss Elizabeth Caldwell, Chosen May Queen at Recent Election, Selects Miss Hettie
English as Maid of Honor—Attendants Chosen—Number
of May Day Features Announced

THE MAY Day Home-Coming of the Alumnae this year will feature the crowning of the Woman's College May Queen, in the new stadium, and a play by the Taurian Players, in the theatre of Page Auditorium. An elaborate pageant has been arranged for the crowning ceremony which will take place at 5 p. m., Saturday, May 2. This is to be an original pageant selected from among a number written by Duke students.

Miss Elizabeth Caldwell, of Monroe, a senior, was chosen May Queen of the college, at a recent election. Miss Caldwell has selected Miss Hettie English, of Mt. Olive, as her maid of honor. Twelve attendants for the queen were chosen in the election in which five hundred students of the Woman's College voted. These attendants are: Misses Courtney Sharpe, Lumberton; Elizabeth Williams, Charlotte; May Purdy, Oriental; Cornelia Yarbrough, Carlotta Satterfield, and Eleanor Peek, of Durham; Charlotte Crews, Dabney, Mary Brown, Raleigh; Mary Bradsher, Petersburg, Va.; Nellie Graw Wilson, Oxford; Iva Pitt, Roanoke Rapids; and Elizabeth Rucker, Rutherfordton.

The Taurian Players, at 8:30 p. m., will present a modern version of Shakespeare's "Taming of the Shrew." The play is being given under the direction of Mr. A. T. West, Duke University's Director of Dramatics. Mr. West was elected president of the North

ELIZABETH CALDWELL
May Queen

Carolina Dramatic Association at its recent convention at Chapel Hill. The Taurian Players, this year, won first place in the Dramatic Contest for Class A colleges and universities of the state. Their work has been well received throughout the entire year.

The program for the day begins, at 10:30 a. m., with a meeting of the Executive Committee of the Alumnae Council. Mrs. Estelle Flowers Spears is chairman of this committee. Arrangements will be made at this time for the Commencement Luncheon.

A tea, for all visiting alumnae, will be given at 3 p. m. in the Alumnae Room, 108 Faculty Apartments. Members of the Alumnae Council will be hostesses at this tea, and a number of the wives of faculty members will be present as invited guests. Alumnae may feel free to attend the tea and not hurry away. Buses will be waiting after the tea on the East Campus to take them to the pageant on the West Campus. The pageant will begin at five o'clock.

The program lists "Tea Gardens," at 6 p. m., in the Stadium. Alumnae will find the Stadium a delightful place to visit and to talk over the old days and the new experiences. The sun will have dropped below the great tiers of seats and will be casting long shadows over the soft green velvet of the Stadium's carpet of grass. The famous echo of the Stadium, which has added so much to the cheering at the football games, this year, will be in full swing with the chatter of voices and the hurrying to and fro of Duke men and women, old and new. Colorful costumes will add to the scene a charm all their own. The pageant will serve as the setting for a beautiful scene.

Then will come the treat of the evening in Duke's attractive new theatre. Hardly any theatre anywhere has a better equipment. The stage settings and the scenery for each play are made by the players. They have developed considerable skill at this work, under Mr. West's direction.

Altogether, it will be a red letter day, one long to be remembered by Duke Alumnae. A message from the Alumnae Council to Alumnae has gone out. It says:

"Of course you are coming back for May Day!

"It's hard for those who have not been on the campus this year to realize that the women have an auditorium, an administration building, and even West Duke, all their own. The May Day Pageant will be held in the Stadium on the West Campus. In this way, we will see both the Men's Campus, and our own, where the Alumnae Tea will take place. The only thing to do is to plan right now to meet all your old 'pals' here on Saturday, May 2. There is no place like the Alumnae Tea for seeing all the familiar faces of your college days.

"A room will be prepared for you on the campus, if you will make your reservation in the Alumni Office by April 29.

"If you have a position, tell your boss right now that you will have to be off on May 2. If you have a husband and family, make plans to have someone else to look after them that week end. If you teach school, there is no excuse for your not being with us. We are looking forward to your Home-Coming. Don't disappoint us."

The message is signed, "Sincerely yours, Anne Garrard, Chairman, Alumnae Council.

A table on the lawn at East Duke, marked "Alumnae Headquarters," will broadcast a welcome to visitors, and will give any information necessary.

Portrait of Dr. James J. Wolfe in Biology Building

THE BIOLOGY Department of Duke University has recently placed a portrait of Dr. James J. Wolfe, late head of the department, in the lobby of the new Biology Building. Dr. Wolfe will be remembered by alumni of Trinity College because of his excellent record as a teacher and as a scientist. He is known, however, among his colleagues on the faculty, and his associates in the scientific world as a gentleman of the old school and as a painstaking research worker.

Dr. Wolfe, born in South Carolina, educated at Wofford College, received the Ph.D. degree from Harvard University, in 1904. He was married immediately after receiving his doctor's degree and brought Mrs. Wolfe to Trinity to take up his new work as head of the biology department, that fall. His reputation as a builder of the department has lasted through the years. His sudden death on the morning of Commencement, in 1920, came as a great shock to the college community and to the scientific world.

Dr. Bert Cunningham, long his associate, and his immediate successor, said, in the *Journal of the Elisha Mitchell Scientific Society*, early that fall:

"He was a frank, straightforward man, always avoiding, if possible, the hurting of another; kind, patient, considering the other man more than himself, and never seeking retaliation for wrongs done him; interested in civic welfare, and especially devoted to the relief of suffering.

"As a teacher, he was exceptionally well-grounded by knowledge much broader than his field; accurate and exacting in the classroom and laboratory; a leader and stimulator of thought on the part of his students; a personal friend and adviser to them.

"As an investigator he was exceedingly accurate and painstaking, endeavoring to get the 'last word' of a subject before laying it down; keen in seeking methods for the attack of problems and in recognizing the relations of a problem to the whole problem of life; and exceptionally careful in his writing that there might be no ambiguity.

"I am incompetent to write a eulogy for this splendid man. Words fail when I try to express my appreciation. To have lived with him and worked with him has been a great opportunity that I shall ever appreciate. To be without his judgment, guidance and friendly counsel is an irreparable loss."

The placing of Dr. Wolfe's portrait in the Biology Building is but the beginning of a movement to secure the portraits of other men of science who have served Trinity College. It is hoped that a number of others may be secured.

"Treasure Room" Is an Interesting Section of the General Library

Almost Every Type of Literature Is Represented in Collection—Catalogues, Theses, Early Southern Documents of Various Kinds, Volumes of Poetry Now Out of Print and Other Valuable Matter Included

ONE OF the most interesting sections of the Duke University Library is the "Treasure Room." This room is separated from the remaining group of stacks on the fourth level by fireproof steel walls. It contains the most valuable and the rarest of the treasures of the library. It is kept locked to prevent the contents being lost or mutilated. While the material is available for research work, it is kept under very careful supervision.

Almost every type of literature is represented in the entire collection. What is probably the most valuable to Duke University is a collection of catalogues of York Institute, Normal College, Trinity College, and Duke University, the succession of titles which have been used for the institution in its years of growth and development. Catalogues of Trinity Park School are also listed in the catalogue of the Treasure Room. This collection is not complete but it is the most complete of any within the knowledge of the librarians. To it are being added the bulletins and records of Duke University, as fast as they are issued.

The thesis collection of the institution is kept in manuscript form, in the Treasure Room. These represent the work of the men and women who have received degrees from the college and the university. In one section of the Treasure Room. These collection of early documents of North Carolina and other southern states. These include debates, accounts of trials famous in history, proceedings of legislatures and conventions, and early codes of laws, many of them in their original editions. States represented among others are Texas, Alabama, North Carolina, South Carolina, and Virginia. It has not been possible always to secure the originals of these records. Some of them are photostatic copies of the originals in the Library of Congress, and in the Libraries of Harvard, and other universities. These photostatic copies include the correspondence on Nullification between John C. Calhoun, of South Carolina, and Governor Hamilton, of New York; the speeches of Chancellor Harper, of Columbia, South Carolina, on States' Rights; and many others of that eventful period in America's history.

Many volumes of early southern poetry, now out of print, appear on the shelves. Among these is "Virginia Wreath," a collection of the poems of John Wharton, published in Winchester, Virginia, in 1814. There are volumes, also of extinct southern periodicals. One of these is "The Southern Rose," which was published in Charleston, South Carolina, during the second quarter of the nineteenth century.

Early southern history also forms a part of the collection. One of these volumes is "The History of the First Discovery and Settlement of Virginia." It was written by "William Stith, A.M., Rector of Henrico Parish, and one of the Governors of William and Mary College." It was published in Williamsburg, Virginia, in 1747.

Among the early southern text-books appears "Outlines of the Lectures on Chemistry, Mineralogy, and Geology, Delivered at the University of North Carolina; for the use of students." It was printed in Raleigh, by J. Gates, but does not give the name of the author. On the torn fly-leaf, in pencil, appears the inscription, "George Tarry's."

There are many volumes which would be of interest to students of the Revolutionary period of America's history. Among these appears "Military Instructions for Officers," by "Roger Stevenson, Esq.," dedicated to George Washington. This book is evidently a first edition. It was published in Philadelphia in 1775. Across the top of the title page, in small letters in ink appears the following inscription, "Gift of G. S. to L. Edwards, April 10, 1793." On the same shelf stands "Clinton's Observations on the Earl of Cornwallis's Answer." This book was written by Lieutenant-General Sir Henry Clinton, K. B., and was published in London in 1783.

Of equal interest are two volumes each with the same title, "Monuments of Washington's Patriotism." They are from the first and second editions of a book which was issued to secure funds for the founding of a "male orphanage, as a memorial to George Washington." They contain a collection of Washington's public documents, issued during the Revolution, together with facsimiles of his record of accounts with the United States, for the same period. They were collected and printed by Thomas Franklin, near 1800. On the fly leaves of one of the volumes appear letters of endorsement from a number of members of the United States Senate. These include among others, Thomas W. Gilmer, Dan'l Webster, H. Clay, T. Ewing, Levi Woodberry, J. J. Crittendon, John Sergeant, Geo. Evarts, John Henderson, and Richard M. Young. Efforts to discover whether these endorsements were written or were printed facsimiles failed because of the age of the paper.

A large collection of books of interest to students of English literature have also been secured and placed in the Treasure Room. Ten volumes on "The English Stage," printed in Bath, and issued in London, in 1832, were procured at a cost of approximately a hundred dollars. There is also a volume of the fifth edition of the "Plays of Beaumont and Fletcher, Gentlemen, complete in one volume," which was published in 1679. Nearby is a set of the sermons and religious essays of Isaac Barrow, D.D., of Trinity College, Cambridge University, published in 1716, in three volumes.

Among the collection of the early editions of the works of John Milton appear a number of titles. One of these is a "History of that part of Britain called England," published in London in 1677. Another is the "Doctrine and Discipline of Divorce," published in 1645, for the benefit of parliament. Two others of his works appear in Latin. One of these is the "Art of Logic," published in 1672. The other is "Literae Psuedo-Senatus Cromwelli," published in 1676.

One of rarest of the entire collection is "The Life of our Learned English Poet, Geoffrey Chaucer." The book is in early English, appears to have been made from wood cuts, and seems to have been a long time in the making. It contains not only the life of Chaucer, but also his "Canterbury Tales." The portrait on the title page, the publisher says, was made by "Thomas Occleu, a scholar of Chaucer, wherefore we know it to be genuine." The publication was begun in 1597 and concluded in 1599. An interesting history of the book appears on the fly leaf, in pen, signed "J. W. C. 20 May 1791." This is probably the John Wilson Croker, whose name is also written on the title page, as is that of "Arthur Marks Edinburgh 1889."

In the collection of English History is "Londinopolis, an Historical Discourse or Perlustration of the City of London," by "Jam Howell, Esq.," published in London, in 1657.

There is a large collection of early French books, as well as one of German literature. One of these, written by Pierre d'Avity, was published in 1625. It contains an account of the systems of governments of all the nations of the world, at that day, as well as the "institutions of religion." The French collection also

contains eleven volumes of "Portraits of Chateaux of Ancient France."

The Paul Hamilton Hayne Library, in its entirety, has been placed in the Treasure. It is interesting to note that this is the only intact library of any antebellum literary man of the south. Many of these books contain the original of much of Hayne's work in manuscript form on their fly leaves. His signature, the date, and the place of purchase, is written in many of them.

There is also in the Treasure Room quite a collection of Peruvian literature in the native language.

Wake County Alumni Group and the Teachers Have Annual Dinner April 24

Under the auspices of the Wake County Alumni Association of Duke University, the annual alumni dinner in connection with the meeting of the North Carolina Education Association was held at Edenton Street Methodist Church on Friday evening, April 24.

Dr. K. P. Neal, Secretary of the Raleigh group, presided. Dr. J. Fred Rippy, Professor of History at Duke, delivered the principal address, speaking forcefully of Duke's development and of the institution's relation to the teaching profession.

Washington, D. C. Alumni Are to Have Spring Dinner on Saturday, May 2

A decidedly interesting and important event in Duke alumni circles will be the spring dinner of the Washington, D. C., Alumni Association on Saturday evening, May 2, at the National Press Club in the Capital City. Coach Coombs and the baseball team will be guests at the dinner. The team plays Navy at Annapolis that day.

Parents of Duke students in the Washington area will be specially invited guests. The Duke "Movie" will be shown and there will be other features.

Hon. Daniel C. Roper is president of the Washington Association; R. E. Thigpen, vice-president; Miss Jane Elizabeth Newton, secretary.

Phi Beta Kappa Anniversary

Phi Beta Kappa celebrated its eleventh year at Duke University on March 28. Dr. Edgar J. Goodspeed, noted translator of the New Testament, delivered the address on that occasion, his subject being "The Faith of Humanism."

The initiation of members pledged this year was a feature of the celebration.

Some Alumni Personalities

CECIL B. ARTHUR

Cecil B. Arthur, '06, started with the American Tobacco Company soon ·after his graduation, taking a position with Mr. W. W. Flowers and remaining with the company until its dissolution; then he went with the Liggett & Myers Tobacco Company, with which concern he has been associated since that time. He lived in China from 1921 to 1929. He is now with the New York Office of his company, 212 Fifth Avenue. He belongs to the twenty-fifth year anniversary class.

H. G. Hedrick, of the Class of 1911, is a member of the law firm of McLendon and Hedrick, Durham, N. C. He was the second man to receive the Bachelor of Laws degree from Trinity College, this being in 1915. From 1914 to 1920 he was Professor of Law in Trinity College. He is chairman of the Duke University Athletic Council and president of the Durham County Alumni Association, having been elected to the latter position at the annual meeting recently held by the Durham-County Alumni.

H. G. HEDRICK

R. T. HARDAWAY

R. T. Hardaway, who received his A.B. degree from Duke in 1925 and his A.M. degree in 1928, has accepted an instructorship in German in the University of Rochester, at Rochester, New York, for the coming year. Mr. Hardaway is now in the Graduate School of the University of Chicago, as a student of Germanic Languages and Literature. He holds one of the best scholarships in that institution, and the appointment he has just received furnishes increased evidence of his high standing in his field of study.

Significant Facts Concerning Duke School of Religion

Sixteen States and One Foreign Country are Represented in Its Student Body—
Enrollment Shows Representation from Seven Different Denominations—
School Has Grown from 18 Students in 1926 to 143 This Year

A STATISTICAL study concerning the student body of the School of Religion of Duke University, recently issued from the office of the Registrar, exhibits some interesting facts. The report shows a total registration of 143 students. Of this number a hundred and thirty-three are men and ten are women. The senior class enrolls forty-two students, the middle class thirty-seven, the junior class sixty-two. There are two special students enrolled in the school. Thirty-five colleges and universities are represented in the student body of the school. Of these Duke University, naturally has the largest number, sixty. Wofford College is represented with eight students, Emory and Henry College with seven, Birmingham-Southern College, Hendrix-Henderson College, and Lambuth College, each have six. High Point College has contributed five students, Asbury and Southern Colleges each four. Three colleges, Elon, Kentucky-Wesleyan, and Millsaps, are each represented by three students, while Randolph-Macon, Southwestern, University of Florida, University of North Carolina, and Wake Forest, each have two students, in the enrollment of the school. Other colleges have only one each.

Sixteen states and one foreign country are represented, as follows: North Carolina 83, Tennessee 10, Virginia 9, South Carolina 8, Arkansas 7, Florida 5, Alabama 3, Kentucky 3, Mississippi 3, Texas 3, Louisiana 2, Oklahoma 2, Maryland, Minnesota, New Mexico, and Washington each one. One student is registered from Japan. The enrollment also shows representation from seven different denominations. The Methodist Episcopal Church, South, has 130 students in the school; the Methodist Protestant Church, 5; the Christian Church, 3; the Baptist Church, 2; the Methodist Episcopal Church, 1; the Disciples of Christ, 1; and the Jewish, 1.

Twenty-four conferences of the Methodist Episcopal Church, South, are represented, as follows: Western North Carolina, 37; North Carolina, 31; Holston, 6; Memphis, 6; North Arkansas, 5; Virginia, 5; Baltimore, 4; Florida, 4; North Alabama, 4; South Carolina, 4; Upper South Carolina, 4; Kentucky, 3; North Mississippi, 3; Cuba, 2; Louisville, 2; Oklahoma, 2; Alabama, 1; Central Texas, 1; Little Rock, 1; Louisiana, 1; Missouri, 1; New Mexico, 1; Tennessee, 1; Texas, 1.

The figures which show the growth of the institution from the time of its founding in 1926, until the present time, are also interesting. At the opening of the school in the fall of 1926, eighteen students registered for the courses. This number was increased to twenty-five in the spring of 1927. The next year saw a continued increase, thirty-eight registering in the fall and fifty in the spring. A large increase was noted in the fall of 1928. Seventy-one students registered at that time, and in the spring of the same scholastic year there were eighty-six. This number increased to ninety-eight in the fall of 1929, and to one hundred and twelve in the spring of last year. At the opening of school last fall the registration had mounted to a hundred and thirty-five, eight having been added since that time. This enrollment, of course, does not include the large number of undergraduate students at Duke who are preparing themselves for the ministry.

Since the opening of the School of Religion, thirty-one students have been granted the Bachelor of Divinity degree. Two of these were in the class of 1927, one in 1928, ten in 1929, and eighteen last year. The entire thirty-one are actively engaged in Christian service. Nineteen are serving as traveling preachers in the Methodist Episcopal Church, South; two are pastors of Baptist churches; two are serving as instructors in religion in a denominational school; three are continuing their theological education, two at Union Theological Seminary, and one at Duke University; one is a preacher in the church of the Disciples of Christ; one is holding a pastorate in the Christian Church; one is a Director of Religious Education in a local church; one is a missionary to Japan; and one is a minister in the Methodist Episcopal Church.

In a brief résumé of the extra-curricular work of the students of the school, the report shows considerable activity on the part of the student body in the religious life of the city of Durham and neighboring territory. Fifty-one of the students are now serving as pastors in student charges, near Durham. Four are serving as part-time assistant pastors. "Of the remaining number of students in the School of Religion," the report continues, "it can safely be estimated that two-thirds of them are giving their services gratis to the churches of and near the city of Durham. These students serve as members of choirs, Sunday School officers and teachers, and supply preachers.

"During the summer vacations a large number of the students in the School of Religion serve under the Duke plan for aiding rural Methodist churches, that is, they render ten weeks of service to the rural churches of North Carolina. The following statistics show the increasing popularity of this plan: During the summer of 1927, 6 students served under the plan; in 1928, twenty-one; in 1929, thirty-nine; in 1930, fifty-seven; and in 1931, sixty-seven have promised their services."

The Booklover's Room of the Woman's College Library

An attractive feature of the Woman's College Library of Duke University is the Booklover's Room which has been opened since February, 1931. This room is intended as a place in which to read for pure enjoyment.

The room selected for booklovers is on the main floor of the library. It is a large room with windows facing the main quadrangle. A handsome marble fireplace opposite the door forms a center of interest. The furnishings are incomplete, as yet, but consist of several comfortable chairs, tables, rugs, pictures, and vases selected from college supplies. Flowers and posters lend color to the room.

After making the Booklover's Room attractive in appearance, several hundred books, selected from the stacks of the library and selected, in the main, for their readability, were placed in the bookcases. Since the opening of the room in February, members of the library staff and faculty have been making lists of books to be added to the collection. Various lists from other colleges, compiled for similar purposes, were used as a basis for selection. Drama, poetry, humorous books, essays, and books on art and music, intermingled with standard works on all subjects, form the present collection.

Poetry readings and book talks supplement the pleasure derived from personal reading. These entertainments are given on Thursday evenings and in a very informal manner. Books mentioned are later placed on tables in the room. A victrola concert of symphony orchestra music, given by one professor, aroused interest in a collection of books on music appreciation. Thus, an interest is stimulated for cultural and recreational reading.

The atmosphere of the Booklover's Room is very informal and free. There is no library attendant to give unwanted advice on reading and a disciplinarian is unnecessary. The books, within easy reach, and the attractiveness of the surroundings make an inviting place for reading. It is possible that students will feel that hours spent in the Booklover's Room were among the most pleasurable and valuable of their college life.

Booklover's Room of the Woman's College Library

Vocational Addresses for the Freshman a Feature at Duke

First of Series of Saturday Morning Class Meeting Events Featured by Dean Justin Miller Who Spoke on "Choosing Law as a Vocation"—Disposes of Some Common Fallacies Regarding Practice of Law

DUKE freshmen are being given an opportunity to become acquainted with the different vocations, in order that they may make choices wisely. Professor D. M. Arnold, dean of freshmen, has announced that each Saturday morning during the spring semester, at the freshman class meeting, an address on some vocation will be delivered by a man who is an outstanding leader in his field.

The first of these addresses was delivered by Dean Justin Miller, of the Duke Law School, on "Choosing Law as a Vocation." Dr. W. C. Davison, dean of the Duke Medical School, was announced as the next speaker, on "Choosing a Career in the Field of Medicine and Surgery." Dean Arnold says that he is having notes on these addresses mimeographed to be distributed among the freshmen. He intends to make the course a serious one and one which will be helpful to the students.

In introducing his subject, Dean Miller said that he wished to remove some illusions concerning the practice of law which seemed to be common. The first of these, he said, is that a lawyer has to be a spellbinder, that he spends his time making impassioned speeches to a jury. History has given us many lawyers of this type, but the leaders in the profession do not come from this group, now. Another illusion which is common, Dean Miller said, is that lawyers make a lot of money. The dean said that the truth is that the average lawyer makes less than a thousand dollars a year. He asserted that the profession has too many of that type, however—the type that reads law, independently, and just manages to pass the bar and to eke out an existence as a shyster, afterward. Leaders in the profession, he said, are successful, financially, as a rule.

Two of the standards which Dean Miller insisted that lawyers must reach in order to become leaders are to be honored and respected in society.

In discussing what lawyers do, the dean mentioned first the general practitioner. Much of the work of this type of lawyer is meeting clients in his office and settling petty disputes. This type of client does not consult a lawyer unless he has gotten into trouble out of which he cannot get himself. A general practitioner must be able to meet such people sympathetically and help them. The general practitioner tries cases in court. He is considered a successful trial lawyer if he has as many as one case a month in the Superior Court. If, however, the only qualification a young man has for this work is that he was able to make himself a general nuisance in high school, always opposing everybody, he has little to recommend him to the vocation. Sweet patience is worth much more.

The second type of lawyer mentioned, by the dean, is the solicitor—the attorney who appears as the prosecutor. The most of this work is done by the public prosecutor chosen by the people. Such a lawyer must educate all the people of the county that his office is, or is not, a place where free legal advice may be secured. He must make his own choice in such a decision. It is expected, by the politicians, also, that the solicitor shall be able to put on a dramatic show in court.

Another field for the lawyer, said the dean, is that of legislation. Some people feel that we have too many lawyers in our legislatures, now. But we need more good lawyers there. Lawyers always play an important part in the work of the legislative committees, where most of the legislative work is done.

The judicial field, the dean said, is a distinct one in the work of the law. A young man may well look forward to such a career and plan for it in his Law School course.

A group of specialists in the field of the law provides many leaders in the profession, in the opinion of Dean Miller. A lawyer, he said, may specialize in one field and practice for himself. On the other hand, he may associate himself in a law firm, with specialists in other fields. Such firms usually employ, on salary, trial lawyers for the work of the courts. Virtually all of their own work is done in the quiet of their offices, working up opinions on certain problems in the law. For the chief duty of a lawyer is to keep his clients out of court.

"A great business leader of America," said the dean, "recently made the remark that he preferred for an executive position a man who had been trained in the law." More and more men who plan business careers for themselves are taking degrees in law schools. Many executives of railroads, officers of banks, and other large commercial institutions, are men who have gone through college taking courses in economics or engineering and "then topped it off with a law school course."

Success as a lawyer, the dean pointed out, requires first of all real intelligence. A pleasing personality is necessary. A lawyer must meet people who are in trouble. He helps them straighten out their difficulties. The conferences of business men, about which we have heard so many facetious stories, may have three-fourths of the time taken up with funny stories. There are times when it is necessary for a man to be able to tell a funny story to relieve the tension of such conferences in which the strain is so great that men are ready to fly at each others' throats. The lawyer in the group must be able to ease the tension with his pleasing personality. But this pleasing personality can never take the place of real intelligence. The lawyer must be able to see the whole situation. He must know it as it relates to the business organization and to the law, also.

A successful lawyer, Dean Miller said, must also have initiative. He must have power to take hold of a proposition and drive it through. Without this initiative he may only be a law clerk. Of course there are many men who are satisfied with a comfortable living wage; who like living quietly and contentedly. These men may become detail men in the offices of the large law firms. They may be trusted and honored as faithful employees. But they never make much money and they never become famous, as such.

Patience he had already spoken of but he stopped a moment to emphasize it. Patience has untangled many a tangled situation which haste would only have tangled more.

Finally, he said, a successful lawyer must have emotional stability. He must be able, on occasion, to make a fine emotional speech as an actor. But the man who allows his emotions to carry him will soon find himself lost in them. A lawyer must learn to carry his emotions under control.

The dean concluded his address with the statement that in the vocation of the law there is opportunity to take leadership in the direction of world affairs.

Dean Miller, in speaking to students, couches his address in a language which makes a real appeal. His personality is very pleasing to young men and interest shown in his address was keen.

Large Attendance is Expected for the Pastors' School

THE 1931 Pastors' School, to be held at Duke University, June 15-26, promises to be very strong, both in the faculty secured for the coming session, and in the student body. The attendance this year is expected to exceed that of any previous session. The Board of Managers met recently with Professor J. M. Ormond, dean of the school, to formulate plans for the session.

At this meeting the following officers were elected: Rev. M. T. Plyler, Durham, President; Rev. E. K. McLarty, Charlotte, Vice-President; Rev. H. G. Hardin, Greensboro, Secretary; and Dr. H. M. North, Raleigh, Treasurer.

Dean Ormond has announced the appointment and acceptance of the following faculty: Dr. James Moffatt, translator of the modern Bible; Dr. Henry H. Tweedy, of the Yale Divinity School; Dr. W. P. King, editor of the *Methodist Quarterly Review*; Dr. Elbert Russell, Dr. F. S. Hickman, and Dr. G. T. Rowe, of the Duke School of Religion; Bishop Edwin D. Mouzon, of Charlotte; and Bishop Paul Kern, now in the Orient.

Fourteen graduate courses will be offered, in the following fields: Bible, Old and New Testaments; religious education; the country church; the industrial church; church worship and homiletics; social teachings of the gospel; Christian beliefs; and the Spirit and Genius of Methodism.

The undergraduate courses, previously offered in the school, have been eliminated from the course. This has been done for two reasons. These courses may now be secured by correspondence, and many of the young men entering the two conferences in North Carolina are already B. D. graduates.

In addition to the courses, there will be two platform addresses each day, open to the public. Dinner discussions will be held each evening at which members of the conferences and the faculty will take part.

Rhodes Scholarship Applicants in State to Meet Here

Dean W. C. Davison, of Duke Medical School, Is Secretary for North Carolina—State
Committee to Assemble at Duke on December 5 to Determine Winners
from This State—Some of the Requirements

ANNOUNCEMENT of annual competition for the Rhodes scholarship has been made by Dean W. C. Davison of the Duke University Medical School, who has charge of applications for North Carolina.

The scholarship entitles the successful students to three years' study at Oxford University, England; as most scholars receive their degree in two years, however, the appointments are made for such time, and if the student wishes to continue his studies there he must present a satisfactory plan as to work to be done. Should he desire to pursue his studies elsewhere he may be sent to some other institution.

A stipend of $400 a year is allowed the Rhodes scholar. Applications for the scholarship are to be made prior to October 17, the endorsement of the president of the institution as to the suitability of the applicant being required. Age limit requirement for candidates to be elected this year to enter Oxford in 1932 are: birth date between October 1, 1907 and October 1, 1913; and preparation, at least two years' work in a degree-conferring American college.

Assigned to the United States each year are 32 scholarships. The country is divided into eight districts of six states each; each state committee selects two candidates; and from the 12 in each district (two from each state) four are selected as Rhodes scholars. State committees are to meet December 5, the North Carolina committee assembling at Duke, and district committees shortly thereafter.

North Carolina is in the third district, the other states in the district being Virginia, South Carolina, Georgia, Florida, and Tennessee.

There are four groups of qualities in the basis of selection, the two chief being: (1) literary and scholastic ability and attainments; and (2) qualities of manhood, truth, courage, devotion to duty, sympathy, kindliness, unselfishness and fellowship. The other qualities are: (3) exhibition of moral force of character and of instincts to lead and to take interest in his schoolmates; (4) physical vigor as shown by interest in outdoor sports or in other ways.

"Distinction both in character and personality and in intellect is the most important requirement for a Rhodes scholarship and it is upon this the committees will insist," the announcement points out. "Success in being elected to office in student organizations may or may not be evidence of leadership in the true sense of the word. Mr. Rhodes evidently regarded leadership as consisting of moral courage and in interest in one's fellow men quite as much as in the more aggressive qualities. Physical vigor is an essential qualification for a Rhodes scholarship, but athletic skill is of less importance than moral qualities developed in playing outdoor games."

Requirements for applicants other than those previously stated include: male citizen of the United States of at least five years' residence, and unmarried.

Exemption from examinations except the Final Honour Schools is provided for students who have approved degrees from approved universities. These students obtain senior standing.

Those receiving scholarship awards with less preparation are given a junior standing at the English institution. The prior study of two foreign languages, at least one of which is to be Latin or Greek, and the other to be selected, if needs be, from French, German, Spanish or Italian, is provided. Passing of responsions is required for students who cannot meet requirements stated.

There are no restrictions in the scholar's choice of studies. He may prepare for the Oxford B.A. in any of the Final Honours school: Literæ Humaniores, mathematics, physics, chemistry, animal psychology, zoölogy, botany, geology, astronomy, engineering science, jurisprudence, modern history, theology, Oriental subjects, English language and literature, philosophy, politics and economy, or modern languages. Or he may seek diplomas courses in certain subjects or do work toward an advanced degree.

A candidate is to submit with the application for the scholarship a birth certificate, statement of the president as to selection of the student to represent his institution, two copies of a personal photograph,

two copies of course of study certified by school official, certificate from a physician as to candidate's being in good health, and two copies of connected statement as to interests in college and plans for study at
Oxford.

Not more than five students should be selected to
represent a given institution, the memorandum ad-
vises. Students who are unable to meet with the
state committee December 5 are advised to make arrangements through Dr. Davison for interviews with
members of the committee.

Railroad fare of those selected from the state will
be paid to the district committee meeting. Candidates
may apply either from their home state, or from
the state where they have received college training: a
Pennsylvania student in Duke University, for example, can apply either to the Pennsylvania secretary
or to the North Carolina.

Two Presidents Named by Duke Student Groups

William Farthing, of Durham, and Martin Green,
of Raleigh, will head the two most important student
groups at Duke University next year. In recent elections the Durham student was named president of the
Y. M. C. A. and Green was chosen president of the
men's student government association.

Other officers of the student government association
elected are: Marcus Hobbs, of Wilmington, vice-president; and Wendell Horne, of Vienna, Ga., secretary-
treasurer.

James R. Peake, of Norfolk, Va., was chosen vice-
president of the student "Y"; Edwin C. Kellam, of
Princess Anne Court, Va., was named secretary; and
Rawlins Coffman, of Drexel Hill, Pa., was elected
treasurer.

Ralph Howland, of Henderson, and Edgar Hocutt,
of Enfield, were made representatives on the publications board.

The newly elected officers will be inaugurated during the next several weeks.

Green is retiring treasurer of the Y. M. C. A., manager of the tennis team, and a member of Pi Kappa
Alpha fraternity. Farthing during the past year has
been secretary of the Y. M. C. A., a member of the
swimming team, and a member of Sigma Chi- fraternity.

Duke Alumnus Receives a Valuable Fellowship

CLYDE OLIN FISHER

Clyde Olin Fisher, of the Class of 1911, was recently
awarded a greatly prized fellowship by the Social Science Research Council, this being in the form of a grant-in-aid to
assist in the financing of an intensive study of the regulation
of public utilities in Connecticut. He anticipates doing this
work next summer and in spare time during the coming
academic year.

Dr. Fisher is Professor of Economics and Social Science at
Wesleyan University, Middletown, Conn. He has written a
number of articles for the *American Economic Review* and
other publications. An article by him will be published in an
early issue of the *South Atlantic Quarterly*.

Dr. Fisher was a Fellow in economics at Cornell, 1916-17;
Professor White Fellow in social science at Cornell, 1917-18;
he was instructor there, 1917-19; Assistant Professor of Economics in Clark College and lecturer in economics, Clark University, 1919-20, going from there to Wesleyan.

He is a member of Phi Beta Kappa and of the American
Economic Association. He is author of "The Use of Federal
Power in the Settlement of Railway Labor Disputes."

Members of the Science Faculty Engaged in Research Projects

Number of Duke Professors Taking Part in Experiments that Promise to Be of Far-Reaching Importance—Series of Investigations Cover a Wide Range But All Promise Definite Benefit to Humanity Along Some Line

VIRTUALLY every man on the staff of the science departments of Duke is doing special research work, officials of the departments report. The lines of investigation cover a wide range but all of them are eventually to benefit mankind.

Dr. Bert Cunningham, professor of biology, is very enthusiastic over the type of men selected for the faculty of the departments and over the equipment provided for the work of research. Each man in this department, he says, is interested in some particular field. This makes it possible for the university to conduct research in so many more fields than would be possible if several of the instructors were working together in one field.

Just now, Dr. Cunningham is conducting experiments in an effort to establish the relation between endocrines and embryological processes. He has, in the laboratory, a considerable set-up of experiments with nearly five hundred rats. Professor Cunningham says that one hundred and fifty-one rats were born in the laboratory in one week.

These experiments are being carried on in connection with the Endocrine Foundation at the Harvard Medical School. A number of the rats were recently shipped to Boston for the continuation of the experiments in the Harvard laboratories.

Dr. Cunningham, who is a member of the editorial staff of Endocrinology, the bulletin of the association for the study of internal secretions, expects to publish the results of the experiments.

The physics department is working along four different lines of research. One of these is being undertaken in coöperation with the Medical School.

Prof. Charles W. Edwards is conducting experiments in the general field of spectroscopy in connection with the raman effect in water vapors. This is an effort to determine the molecular and atomic structure of compounds. Professor Edwards expects to find out, he says, a good deal of how molecules are built into structures. He is himself directing the work of the experiments. He has been assisted by Dr. C. C. Hatley and by Miss Isabel Hanson, graduate assistant. Miss Hanson is from the University of

Georgia. Dr. Hatley is now away for the second semester on leave of absence.

Professor Edwards and Dr. Hatley have also undertaken research work in the field of ultra-violet rays. This is a coöperative study with Dr. Harold L. Amoss, of the Medical School. It is a study of the reaction of ultra-violet rays on the skin of persons who are in the very early stages of pellagra. Dr. Amoss describes it as the beginning of a coöperative study on the part of a number of specialists in the field of pellagra.

Dr. Frank W. Constant and Mr. F. E. Lowance, graduate assistant, are conducting experiments in the nature of the sensitive structure of certain magnetic materials, including iron.

The fourth project is being conducted by Mr. David Carpenter. This is an attempt to determine magneto-electric effect. Mr. Carpenter will use a thermo couple for this experiment. One junction of the couple will be put in a strong magnetic field, the other in a zero magnetic field. The attempt will be made to measure the electric product. It has been predicted that this lies within the limits of experimental technique.

Other members of the science faculty are doing research work of importance, and the REGISTER will refer to their activities later.

Duke has a chapter of the national physics honor fraternity. Dr. C. C. Hatley, professor of physics at Duke, is the national president. Mr. Russell Ranson, a senior, and Mr. David Carpenter are local president and secretary, respectively. Eight new members have been elected at Duke. This brings the total membership for Duke up to twenty-two.

Brazilian Collection

More than 600 volumes have been added to the Brazilian collection of the Duke University Library within the last two years, historical and geographical works and literary productions being included, according to the *Hispanic American Historical Review.*

Real Problems of Education Taken Up by Duke Students

Work Done in Preparation of Theses for Degrees in Education May Prove of Much Value in Connection With Educational Developments in State and South—Wide Variety of Topics Discussed By More Than 50 Students

THAT much work is being done by Duke University students in the preparation of theses for higher degrees in education—efforts that may prove quite valuable in the educational developments in the state and southeast as well as to the students themselves—is shown in a list of such students prepared by the office of Dr. Holland Holton, director of the department of education.

The theses enumerated have been recently completed or are in process of completion under the supervision of the department of education, it was stated. A wide variety of topics is taken by the more than 50 students—some in the University doing graduate work, teachers, superintendents—engaged in activities.

Those working on theses, their subjects and present occupation or pursuit follow:

Mrs. Hazel Stewart Alberson: "A Project in Curriculum Building in French, Buncombe County." Mrs. Alberson is teaching French and Latin in the Black Mountain high school.

Miss Lila McLin Bell: "An Activity Curriculum at Work." Miss Bell is teacher in the Raleigh city schools.

Miss Ikie Brock: "An Analysis of American Text Books in Plane Geometry Published Since 1800, with Indications of Changes and Trends in Emphasis." Miss Brock is teaching mathematics in the Louisburg high school.

Mr. J. J. Brothers, Jr.: "The Status of the Elementary School Principalship in North Carolina." Mr. Brothers is principal of Kitty Hawk high school.

Miss Blanche Burke: "A Course of Study in Civics for the Elementary Grades." Miss Burke is teacher of civics in the Durham city schools.

Chas. F. Carroll, Jr.: "Taxation Supplementary to State Support of Schools in North Carolina Since 1868." Mr. Carroll is superintendent of the Bryson City schools.

Cecil E. Cooke: "Aims, Methods, and Materials in High School Algebra as Set Forth in State Department Courses of Study." Mr. Cooke is acting principal of the Central Junior high school, Durham.

Dennis H. Cooke: "A Study of Age-Grade Distribution in the Oxford Orphanage School." Dr. Cooke is Associate Professor of Education, George Peabody College for Teachers.

C. T. Davies: "A Study of the Methods of Transporting School Children in Certain Consolidated School Districts of Florida." Mr. Davies is principal of the Ancilla high school, Ancilla, Fla.

Miss Ione H. Dunn: "Some Contributions of Private Schools to the Education of the Mountaineers in Buncombe and Madison Counties." Miss Dunn is dean of the Asheville Normal and Associate schools.

Roland Otis Edgerton: "A System of Cumulative Records for Elementary Schools." Mr. Edgerton is principal of the Thomas Jefferson and Fifth Street schools, Portsmouth, Va.

Miss Eleanor Brynberg Forman: "A Study of Teacher-Training in four Non-State Colleges of North Carolina." Miss Forman is Professor of Education in Salem College.

Roy Charles Garrison: "Studies in the Development of Standardization and Uniformity in the Public Schools of North Carolina from the Civil War to 1927." Mr. Garrison is principal of Helena high school.

Claud Grigg: "State Support of Public Elementary and High Schools in North Carolina Since 1868." Mr. Grigg is superintendent of the Kings Mountain schools.

I. F. Grigg: "The Organization and Administration of County Systems of Transportation of School Children in North Carolina." Mr. Grigg is principal of the Berea school, Granville County.

Richard Abraham Haddock: "The Support of Public Education in Sampson County." Mr. Haddock is principal of the Rose Hill high school, Sampson County.

R. S. Haltiwanger: "Pupil Participation in the Government of the Richard J. Reynolds High School, Winston-Salem, N. C." Mr. Haltiwanger is Boys' adviser, Richard J. Reynolds high school.

Benjamin Love Harton, Jr.: "The Development

of Public Education in South Carolina, as Revealed by Legislative Action and Supreme Court Decisions." Mr. Harton is superintendent of Whitton schools, Tyronza, Arkansas.

Miss Lucy Hazlewood: "The Development of High School Text Books in Algebra During the Nineteenth Century." Miss Hazlewood is teacher of mathematics, Thomasville high school.

Miss Sibyl Henry: "A Study of Second Grade Reading: Suggestions for Curriculum Essentials and Activities." Miss Henry is primary teacher in Durham city schools.

Ray W. House: "A Study of High School Bands in North Carolina." Mr. House is Director of Band, in the Statesville schools.

Daniel S. Johnson: "Religious Education in the Public Schools." Mr. Johnson is principal of Oxford Orphanage high school.

William Porter Kellam: "Development of Public Education in Guilford County." Mr. Kellam is at present in the School of Library, Emory University.

Mrs. Mary Knight Buell: "The Teaching of Health Habits Through Coöperation Between the Home and the School." Mrs. Buell is primary supervisor, Buncombe County schools.

Albert E. Lee: "School Room Beautification and Its Influence on Pupil Morale." Mr. Lee is principal at Polkton, N. C.

Lawrence Calvin Little: "Religious Education in the Methodist Protestant Church." Mr. Little is Educational Secretary, Methodist Protestant Church. Present address Yale University, New Haven, Conn.

Leslie Emory Logan: "An Experiment in Teaching Normal School Students How to Study." Mr. Logan is principal of the practice school at Lincoln Memorial University, Harrogate, Tenn.

A. C. Lovelace: "The Work of the Supervising Principals." Mr. Lovelace is superintendent of Henrietta-Caroleen schools.

John Walker McCain: "Legislative Development of Higher Education in South Carolina." Mr. McCain is Professor of English, Winthrop College, S. C.

Noble R. McEwen: "The Legal Development of Education in Alabama as Revealed Through the Statutes and Supreme Court Decisions of the State." Mr. McEwen is a graduate fellow, Duke University.

L. C. McKee: "A Trade School Curriculum in Automobile Mechanics and Related Subjects." Mr. McKee is head of Vocational Arts division, Norristown high school, Pennsylvania.

M. E. Milner: "The City School Principal as a Supervisor." Mr. Milner is assistant principal of the New Hanover high school, Wilmington, N. C.

Mrs. Lillian Nunn Wynne: "Preliminary Testing and Orientation Courses at Duke University, 1924-28,

in Relation to the Academic Record of Freshmen." Mrs. Wynne is teacher in Central Junior high school, Durham.

Mrs. Lorraine Pridgen: "A Study of the Evolution of the Geography Textbooks 1784-1930." Mrs. Pridgen is a teacher of geography and science, Geo. Watts school, Durham.

H. N. Rath: "Student Hand-Books for Junior High Schools." Mr. Rath is a Junior High School principal, Miami, Fla.

B. B. Robinson: "Programs of Study Possible for a Three-Teacher High School." Mr. Robinson is a Union school principal in Cleveland County.

Miss Bessie Alice Rooker: "Development of Public Education in Warren County." Miss Rooker is a teacher in West Durham high school.

Mrs. Roxie J. Sasser: "Critical Analysis of Supervisory Plans with Special Emphasis of Evaluating Rural Supervision in N. C." Mrs. Sasser is a primary teacher, Durham city schools.

Miss Sarah Olive Smith: "A Study of Intelligence Quotient and High School Grades as Means of Predicting Success and Stay in College." Miss Smith is teacher of mathematics, Richard J. Reynolds high school, Winston-Salem.

L. E. Spikes: "Tying Up the Work of the School With the Community." Mr. Spikes is superintendent of the Rutherfordton-Spindale schools.

E. C. Staton: "The Status of Public Secondary Education in Davie County, North Carolina." Mr. Staton is superintendent of the Mocksville schools.

Miss Elizabeth Davis Tyree: "The Development of Public Secondary Education in North Carolina." Miss Tyree is grammar grade teacher in the Durham city schools.

Miss Elizabeth Wannamaker: "An Activity Curriculum in the Third Grade." Miss Wannamaker is a primary teacher, High Point, N. C.

Edward Warrick: "Adult Elementary Education in Buncombe County, N. C." Mr. Warrick is principal of Candler high school, Buncombe County.

Otis Whaley: "A Survey of State Support of County Elementary School and High School Education in Tennessee." Mr. Whaley is a graduate assistant, Duke University.

J. B. White: "Study of Pupil Retardation in High Schools." Mr. White is superintendent of Brunson, S. C., schools.

Fred Greene: "The High School Principal as a Supervisor of Instruction." Mr. Greene is principal of the Wilson High School, N. C.

J. B. Page: "Causes of Elimination from an Elementary School in a Cotton Mill Village." Mr. Page is principal of elementary school, Belmont, N. C.

(Continued on page 128)

Rhodes Scholar From Duke Writes of Life at Oxford

Grady C. Frank Finds Both Oxford and England Very Much as Described by Former
Rhodes Scholars—Points Out Some Differences Between English and
American University Training—Discusses Tutorial System

WHEN Grady C. Frank went to Oxford University some months ago as a Rhodes scholar, the editor of the ALUMNI REGISTER asked him to write a letter at his convenience giving some of his impressions of student life at the great English university, and kindred topics. The letter came recently and is sure to be of interest to REGISTER readers. Writing from St. John's College, Oxford, Mr. Frank says:

"It has been several months now since I last saw Duke, and my days as a student there seem very distant. I have kept in close touch, however, with what is happening at Duke through the medium of the REGISTER and the *Chronicle.* I would like to congratulate all on the great development that has taken place, and especially I would like to congratulate the football team and the coaches on their wonderful showing last season. I was able only to see the South Carolina game before leaving for Oxford, so I was not very optimistic at the time.

"I have found both Oxford and England very much as they were described to me by former Rhodes Scholars—the country, the city, the colleges, the river Thames, the athletics, the climate, and last but not least, Brussels sprouts, which is practically the only vegetable served at meals.

"The country is very beautiful, with its quaint little old-fashioned villages, green meadows, and narrow winding roads. Oxford, the city, which rambles all over the countryside, with its spires and domes, is indeed an inspiring sight. I never will forget my first view of the city from a hill not far from the outskirts. The bus-driver obligingly stopped to give us a view of the city below us, in a sort of hollow.

"Oxford University, as you all know, consists of a number of colleges, with separate buildings, and separate athletic fields. All the colleges have in common the fact that they are members of the same University, and must conform to the University regulations, and share with other colleges their lecturers and tutors. In addition to the Varsity athletic teams,

each college has its own teams, and there is keen inter-collegiate rivalry.

"The Oxford system of education is far different from that of Duke University. Each student is assigned to a tutor, whom he sees one hour each week as a rule, and who outlines the work for the next week, and helps smooth out difficulties. There are lectures which the student is free to attend if he thinks they will help him in any way. This system is undoubtedly very effective in many courses, especially in the more cultural courses such as philosophy, and history, but in my course, mathematics, I find I need more supervision, and more assistance than I receive under the tutorial system. In my opinion, mathematics is a study which requires a thorough understanding of every point as one goes along, and frequent supervision and "quizzes" are quite essential. I must confess that it adds greatly to my happiness not to have to worry about quizzes, but the prospect of final examinations is very alarming. A lecture on mathematics is of very little help; it is just like listening to a text-book read aloud. Thus practically the entire burden is placed on the shoulders of the student. On the other hand, under the tutorial system the student is left entirely to himself; under the guidance of his tutor an ambitious student can advance as fast as he likes, and is unhampered by those who prefer to go more slowly.

"It is not hard to get a degree at Oxford. A pass degree means little more than the fact that a man has been in residence at Oxford four years. The important question asked of every Oxford graduate is not, 'Do you have a degree?' but, 'What honors did you receive?'

"Another thing which stamps Oxford as different from the American college is the vacation; it is long, as one is in residence at college only six months of the year. But the vacation is the time when the student really gets down to work. During the term he is too busy with sports and social activities to be bothered with much study. Usually the foreign stu-

(Continued on page 128)

Phi Beta Kappa Celebrates its Eleventh Year at Duke

Dr. Goodspeed, Famed Translator of a Modern Version of New Testament, the Speaker at Observance of Phi Beta Kappa Day Here—National Publication to Have a Study of Duke

PHI BETA KAPPA, national honor fraternity, which came into being the year that the American colonies declared their independence, marked its eleventh year in Duke University with the celebration March 28 of the establishment of the local chapter.

Various exercises featured the anniversary of the fraternity at Duke, including the initiation of members pledged this year, and an address by Dr. Edgar J. Goodspeed, famed translator of a modern version of the New Testament.

Phi Beta Kappa has flourished at Duke, having drawn into its local organization during the eleven years of its existence around 300 students and alumni of old Trinity and the new institution that replaced it.

The program of celebration was held in Page Auditorium at 11:30 o'clock Saturday, March 28. Dr. Goodspeed, who is a member of the faculty of the University of Chicago, spoke on "The Faith of Humanism." The initiation was at 3 o'clock; and a dinner was given at the Washington Duke hotel Saturday night.

Members of the organization in course are: On junior standing—J. Gaither Pratt, Herman Walker, Jr., Charles H. Livengood, Jr., Gladys M. Higgins, Edgar J. Hocutt, Helen Jenkins, Whitfield H. Marshall, Allen O. Gamble, Morris A. Jones, Lila M. Woodward, Anna K. Moses, and Elizabeth F. Mulholland; on senior standing—Argyle Glenn, Frances E. Rowe, Carl F. Bretholl, Richard J. Bisson, Clarice Margaret Bowman and Willie A. Gee.

Added to the membership of the chapter during 1931 from the alumni association were: A. M. Proctor, '10, of the education department of Duke, and Dr. Evelyn Jones Hawkes, of the New Jersey College for Women. Honorary choices were: Dr. Elbert Russell, dean of the School of Religion of Duke; and Dr. C. B. Hoover, of the Duke economics department.

There are 56 members among the Duke faculty and 24 members among graduate students.

Officers of the local chapter are: H. E. Spence, president; Jay B. Hubbell, vice-president; James Cannon III, secretary-treasurer.

A SPECIAL STUDY OF DUKE

A special study of Duke University is soon to be made by a representative of the quarterly publication of the organization, *The Phi Beta Kappa Key*, Oscar M. Voorhees. In a former article in the publication in regard to the earning power of men of high rank in college, Dr. Voorhees, secretary of the national organization, takes issue with the measurement of accomplishment on the money basis.

After referring to tests that have been made to show that scholarship is not conducive to high earning power, he explains in the article, "Culture and the Commercial Yarkstick," that the time taken, ten years, is not a sufficient period; if a longer period is taken greater earning power among Phi Beta Kappa members, who are uniformly selected from among the high-ranking students, would be, he suggests, revealed.

Although Phi Beta Kappa makes no claim to having all the leaders of thought and action, it is confirmed in its "purpose to recognize outstanding scholarly endeavor." From high-grade students will come, it believes, high-grade men and women, who will lead in political, social and religious thought. Forty-four per cent of the men and women honored by inclusion in the American Hall of Fame were among its members, Mr. Voorhees points out.

Since this is true, since forty per cent of the United States Supreme Court justices and a similar ratio of secretaries of state were Phi Beta Kappas, and "since so many great teachers, great college presidents, great religious leaders, and workers in every line of altruistic endeavor, have come from the ranks of high-grade students who sought broad knowledge and wide culture as the chief gift of the college, the society looks with confidence to the future, being well assured that its influence and power will not grow less. It insists, however, that the commercial yardstick is inadequate and unreliable, and should be disregarded when estimating the contribution of its members to the life of their times."

Real Problems of Education Taken Up by Duke Students

(Continued from page 125)

A. H. Best, Jr.: "Retardation in a Given Elementary School District: Causes and Remedies." Mr. Best is an assistant principal, Durham County schools.

Robert Edwin Boyd: "The Constants, Sequentials, and Free Electives in the High School Curriculum." Mr. Boyd is superintendent of the Farmville schools.

K. R. Curtis: "A Measure of the Efficiency of County School Systems." Mr. Curtis is superintendent of Wilson county and city schools.

George H. Enfield: "Development of the Junior College in North Carolina." Mr. Enfield is a graduate student, Duke University.

Miss Juanita Hufstettler: "The Amount of Emphasis in Social Studies in the Junior High School." Miss Hufstettler is a teacher of social studies in a junior high school, Miami, Fla.

R. E. Gooch: "Social Aspects of the Junior College." Mr. Gooch is a graduate student, Duke University.

D. W. Kanoy: "Study of the Principalship in Union Schools, North Carolina." Mr. Kanoy is principal of the McLeansville, N. C., school.

Miss Elida Lohr: "A Study of the Development of High School Text-Books in Algebra." Miss Lohr is teacher of mathematics at Valdese, N. C.

Rhodes Scholar From Duke Writes of Life at Oxford

(Continued from page 126)

dent settles down in some quiet spot in England or the Continent, where he can study as well as see life in Europe. I spent my Christmas vacation in the Basque region of Southern France, near the Spanish border.

"At Oxford very nearly everyone plays some form of sport. There are no paid coaches, and only members of the boat clubs go in seriously for training and practice; the other teams get most of their practice by playing games. Rugby is a game which is as strenuous as football, yet the varsity and college teams play two, sometimes three, games a week during the season.

"I am enclosing an editorial from the *Isis*, the most important of Oxford magazines, which shows the attitude of some of the Oxford men to the 'co-eds.' Most of the men, however, are quite tolerant, and in fact are almost unaware of the presence of the co-eds.

"The Englishmen, I find, are very reserved, but very friendly once the ice is broken. They are anxious to learn about America and American ways, and are very much interested in the activities of Al

Capone, et al., which are painted in glowing colors by the British press.

"Oxford is a very cosmopolitan place—men of every race, and from every continent mingle freely with each other. One is led to realize strongly the importance and influence of the British Empire in all corners of the earth."

Notable Records So Far for Four Duke Athletic Teams

Varsity and Freshman Baseball Teams, Track Squad and Golf Aggregation. Make an Exceptionally Good Showing—Many More Dates Are to Be Filled, However, Before the Season Is Over

PLUNGING early into a brilliant season, four Duke teams have turned in notable records up to the time of this writing and virtually assure the best spring sports summary of several years. The freshman and varsity baseball teams have been undefeated in college circles, the track squad has won all its meets but one, and the golf team has yet to meet defeat.

Coach Coombs' lads have defeated Cornell, Penn State, Wake Forest twice, and N. C. State, losing only to the Durham Bulls in two exhibition games. The nine has undergone strenuous polishing, and Coach Coombs has a better club of sophomores than anyone would have predicted two months ago. Four games have been rained out, depriving the youngsters of valuable competitive playing, but there are ten more games scheduled. The new baseball park is being used this spring, and there is a possibility that a state championship may be brought to it with the first season.

Baseball results thus far:
Duke 7; Cornell 0.
Duke 6; Penn State 5
Duke 3; Wake Forest 0.
Duke 5; N. C. State 3.
Duke 1; Durham 11.
Duke 7; Wake Forest 2.
Duke 6; Durham 7.

The frosh nine's record:
Duke 5; Oak Ridge 4.
Duke 13; N. C. State 9.
Duke 20; Carolina 7.

Coach Buchheit's track team has been a sensation of the season, defeating four dual-meet opponents in a row: Washington and Lee 74 to 52; Wake Forest 94 to 32; Davidson 64 to 62; and N. C. State 75 to 51. John Brownlee in the sprints, Bill Simon in the distance runs, Fulmer in the broad jumps, and Brewer in the high jumps have been principal point-getters.

In their first dual meet of the season, the Carolina team defeated Duke, 68 to 58. Good records were made in all events.

Tennis has given Duke three wins and a loss. The Devil net men have won over Wake Forest 8 to 1, State 9 to 0, Davidson 6 to 3, and lost to Carolina's crack outfit 9 to 0.

Washington and Lee was first to lose to the Duke golf team, 9½ to 8½, and Georgia Tech was next, losing to the Duke link men 12 to 6. Carolina's strong team came back strong in the second division of play to tie up the count 9 all.

There is still a long way to go in each sport. Eight more dates are to be filled by the golfers. ten more games for the baseball team, nine more freshman baseball games, three more track dates, another frosh track engagement, and ten more tennis engagements.

"BOBBY" COOMBS, *Pitcher*

The Editor's Mail Bag

LETTER FROM AN ALUMNUS

W. M. Sherrill, associate editor of the *Concord Daily Tribune*, an alumnus of the Class of 1915, was recently a visitor on the campus for a few days, at which time he was a patient at the Duke Hospital. On his return home he wrote a member of the faculty a letter which is so full of the real Duke spirit, and which brings out so clearly certain considerations that all Duke alumni should keep in mind, that the editor of THE REGISTER is taking the liberty of reprinting certain extracts from it:

"I have derived unusual gratification from my visit to Duke University: first, because of the results of my examinations at the hospital which showed negative reactions; and second, because of the fine spirit I found manifested among students and faculty; and third, because of the gracious manner in which I was welcomed by you and other members of the faculty who have been able to see Trinity College grow into a major university without losing that fine touch of personal interest which seems to me to be essential to the success of any enterprise in which personalities are at stake.

"When I first knew that my alma mater was to become only an integral part in a larger, and I hoped a more useful institution because of its enlargement, I confess to a feeling of doubt as to what the change would mean to me and other graduates and former students at Trinity College. This question was not the result of doubt as to the ability of the guiding heads to meet their new duties successfully, but rather was created from natural sources, knowing full well that the greater the task the greater the amount of time and talent required, and I have experienced no deeper sense of pleasure than came to me on this visit when you and others who are taxed with the full responsibility of maintaining a gigantic enterprise found time to tie the old with the new by the same graciousness which characterized your dealings with me when a student on the old campus.

"I found doubt in my mind at one time, too, as to what my feelings would be toward the new university, and you can understand, I am sure, the gratification which has come to me with the realization that I am as deeply interested in and feel as much a part of Duke University as I did of Trinity College. I find it just as easy to sing of the Duke that is, as of the Trinity that was, and certainly this would not have been pos-

sible, for me, at least, had there not been that manifested interest in me on the part of you and others who knew me first as a Trinity student and who now greet me as an alumnus of Duke. The change to the new order of things has been made without interrupting the cordial relations which existed between Trinity and her sons and daughters, and surely we who boast of having served under the college have you and others who have labored for the two institutions to thank for the metamorphosis which has moved so smoothly as to cause no discord.

"My contact with Coach Wade only served to strengthen my faith in him as the man needed more than any other at Duke. He has made a profound impression over the entire State, not merely or primarily as a coach, but as a man fully conscious of his duties and fully able to fulfill them. I feel confident that football at Duke will take on new meaning under his guidance and that you, and I and those countless others who want to see the Duke standard held high will find in Coach Wade and his system a source of much gratification. I hope some time in the near future that he can visit Concord and talk informally not only to Duke alumni but to our scores of football fans who feel as we do, that his coming to North Carolina marks the beginning of a new era in Tar Heel football."

The letter closes with a most appreciative reference to Dean W. H. Wannamaker, based on the writer's contact with him while a student at Trinity, particularly in connection with the way in which he "sensed the needs and requirements of the students." The writer stated that when he was at Trinity the students felt that in Dr. Wannamaker they had a friend who was always deeply interested in their problems, and he added that his visit to the new campus had convinced him that this fine attitude had been transferred to the new surroundings. He referred to the way in which the Dean made him feel entirely at home though he had been out of college for many years.

Concluding, the writer said: "If I can serve Duke in any fashion, it will be a pleasure to do so."

It is needless to say that the recipient of the letter and the University community generally appreciates its notably fine spirit. Not only is Mr. Sherrill a loyal Duke alumnus who has a fine conception of alumni coöperation with the institution, but his father, J. B. Sherrill, who has been for years one of the best known newspaper publishers in the state, is a trustee of the institution who is deeply interested in its affairs.

Where They Are Located	News of the Alumni	What They Are Doing

Miss Elizabeth Aldridge, '24, Secretary of Alumnae Council, Editor

(Most of the alumni notes in this issue of the REGISTER relate to the members of various classes which will hold reunions in connection with Commencement this year. In the next issue there will be notes about members of other reunion classes.—EDITOR.)

1871

SIXTIETH ANNIVERSARY CLASS

The class of 1871 has the distinction of having for one of its members the oldest living graduate of the University, Henry W. Norris of Holly Springs. After graduation Mr. Norris' experience was varied, but he was successful in every venture. He served in the state senate, and was later superintendent of public instruction for Wake County. He is now president of the Bank of Holly Springs.

The only other surviving member of the class of 1871 is Wesley B. Owen of Liberty, N. C. He came to college for only one year. He has lived in Liberty for a number of years, where he has been a prominent member of the community.

1876

FIFTY-FIFTH YEAR

Four graduates of the class of '76 are located in the office records. They are, Shubal G. Coltrane, Route No. 1, Randleman; T. M. Cross of Sanford; Peter J. Kernodle, 1012 Marshall Street, Richmond, Va.; and W. D. Turner of Statesville. Other members of the class who did not graduate follow: W. B. Bobbitt, Odd Fellows Home, Goldsboro; E. D. Hardesty, Newport; James N. Leake, 112 West Washington Street, Greensboro; Isaac N. Petty, Hillsboro; R. L. White, Glenola; J. C. Wilborn, York, South Carolina.

1881

GOLDEN ANNIVERSARY

Byron N. Boddie is a successful merchant at Leesville, S. C. He also owns a large farm.

Rev. Robert H. Broome, a minister in the M. E. Church, South, is located at Southport, N. C. He has been a member of the N. C. Conference of the M. E. Church, South, for forty-two years.

W. J. Adams has diligently pursued success. In 1893, he became a member of the N. C. Legislature, later the State Senate. He also served as a member of the North Carolina Board of Internal Improvements. In 1908 he became judge of the Superior Court of N. C. He is now Associate Justice, N. C. Supreme Court.

Dr. R. B. Beckwith practices medicine at Fayetteville.

James C. Fink's son and granddaughter have both attended Duke University. He is an accountant with the Southern Cotton Oil Company at Concord.

E. S. Gray, farmer and dairyman, lives at 403-4th Street, Winston-Salem.

M. R. Harris lives on his farm at Route No. 3, Thomasville.

L. J. Huntley is in the mercantile business at Wadesboro.

Rev. J. M. Lowder has been in the pastorate of the M. E. Church, South, since 1887. He now lives at Connelly Springs.

Rev. W. H. Townsend, minister in the Methodist Church, is located at High Point.

1886

FORTY-FIVE YEARS OUT

James A. Bell is a member of the well-known firm of Pharr, Bell & Pharr, attorneys at law, 418 Law Building, Charlotte. He exercises a wholesome type of leadership in his community, being a staunch layman and advocate of higher social order. He is a member of the Board of Trustes, Duke University, and is a loyal son of Alma Mater.

Lee J. Best had a son to graduate at Trinity in the class of 1918. They both practice law at Dunn, N. C.

Jesse A. Carpenter, an alumnus who always has the interest of Alma Mater at heart, lives at Wadesboro, N. C.

Dr. Charles L. Jenkins has his office in the Professional Building, Raleigh.

J. C. Pinnix lives in Murfreesboro, Arkansas.

Lola P. Skeen of Decatur, Georgia, has retired from the regular practice of law.

Lee Andrews and Stokes M. Clark are both farmers. The former lives at Archdale and the latter at R. F. D. No. 1, Ansonville.

Rev. Robert W. Bailey, a retired Methodist minister, makes his home in the Bailey Apartments, Raleigh.

William A. Brame makes his home at the Ricks Hotel in Rocky Mount. He travels for a firm in Baltimore, Maryland.

James C. Brooks is engaged in the practice of law at Elizabeth City.

William N. Reynolds is a prominent tobacco manufacturer at Winston-Salem. He is also a member of the board of trustees of Duke University.

CLASS OF 1889

Rev. Zadok Paris and Mrs. Paris celebrated the forty-second anniversary of their marriage in Charlotte on January 29, and from there they went to Orlando, Florida, to spend the rest of the winter.

1891

FORTIETH ANNIVERSARY

Dr. William I. Cranford has been a member of the faculty of Trinity College since 1890. He has won a place in the hearts of all students who have come under his teaching.

Thomas Cowper Daniels is manager of the Elks Club, New Bern, N. C.

Robert Lee Durham, president of Southern Seminary, Buena Vista, Va., has given a large part of his time to civic and public enterprises. He is a director and active member of the local Chamber of Commerce, and his name is synonymous with the campaign for good roads in his county and state. He has been a delegate several times from the local Rotary Club to conventions of Rotary International and his name has been presented this year as a candidate for District Governor. He is the lay leader of his church and chairman of the official board. He is a lawyer, educator, and writer. One of his books, "The Call of the South" proved to be very popular and was said by some critics to be a clear and unanswerable defense of the South's attitude toward the negro race.

Fred Harper practices law in Lynchburg, Va. He has taken an active interest in Alumni affairs, having served as president of the Alumni Association in 1917. He was elected mayor of Lynchburg in 1921 and also served as Grand Exalted Ruler of Elks.

David A. Houston is connected with the Carolina Mortgage Company at Raleigh.

Rev. William B. Lee has engaged in educational work for a number of years in Brazil. Being at such a great distance has not lessened his interest and loyalty to his Alma Mater. He has sent a number of publications to the Library in the past years. He may be reached at 123 Liberdade, Sao Paulo, Brazil.

Charles E. McCandless has been teaching for a number of years in Pennsylvania. He is at present located at Springboro.

John R. McCrary has enjoyed a long and successful career as a lawyer in his native county. His home is Lexington, N. C. His daughter, Virginia, is now a member of the Sophomore Class at Duke.

Since leaving college, Rev. L. S. Massey has served as pastor of Methodist churches in the North Carolina Conference, except for a few years that he spent as editor, *Raleigh Christian Advocate* and as president of Louisburg College. He has retired from active service and makes his home at Route No. 7, Durham.

Dr. Luther R. Christie is pastor of the Ponce de León Baptist Church in Atlanta, Georgia.

John Walter Lambeth makes his home in Thomasville where he is president and general manager of the Lambeth Furniture Company. He, at one time, served as mayor of Thomasville, and as treasurer, Davidson County Road Commission. He is a director, First National Bank and a member of both the city and county school board. His son, J. Walter Lambeth, Jr., congressman-elect, graduated from Trinity in 1916.

Frank Lee McCoy teaches in Emory University Academy, Oxford, Georgia.

Clifton B. Cheatham, president of the C. B. Cheatham Company, Inc., at Farmville, N. C., is a leaf tobacco dealer. He makes his home in Raleigh.

1896

THIRTY-FIFTH YEAR

The three women graduates of the class of 1896 are teaching in colleges. Ida Z. Carr at George Peabody College, Nashville. Tenn.; Mamie E. Jenkins at East Carolina Teachers College, Greenville, N. C.; and Annie M. Pegram at Greensboro College, Greensboro.

Harvey B. Craven sent three of his daughters to Duke. Mary Elizabeth is in college now. Alice (Mrs. S. R. Mohr) graduated in 1924; and Irene (Mrs. W. N. Covington) is a member of the class of 1928. He is a bond broker with offices in the Van Huss Building, Lakeland, Fla.

Ernest J. Green teaches English at Columbia College, Columbia, South Carolina.

Robert A. Mayer is with the Travelers Insurance Company, His office is located in the Johnston Building, Charlotte. He has served as a member of the Board of Trustees of Duke University since 1898. His only child, Walter B. Mayer graduated at Trinity in the class of 1925.

Joseph Smith Maytubby's address is Wapanucka, Oklahoma.

Samuel W. Sparger is general agent for the Mutual Life Insurance Company at Durham.

Charles R. Thomas operates a drug business at Thomasville.

Rev. J. A. Dailey of Pittsboro, N. C., has a daughter, Alma, in Duke this year.

B. Winston Rogers is connected with the Durham Loan and Trust Company, Durham.

1901

THIRTY YEAR CLASS

For nineteen years after leaving college, Henry B. Asbury, was connected with the British American Tobacco Company, spending most of that time in foreign countries. He is now secretary, treasurer and partner, Charles Moody Company in Charlotte.

Mabel Chadwick married Dr. R. P. Stephens, Dean of the Graduate School, University of Georgia. Her home address is 230 Woodlawn Avenue, Athens.

Mrs. Z. B. Vance (nee Mary L. Hendren) teaches English in the Woman's College, Duke University.

Rev. William A. Lambeth served as pastor of Mount Vernon Place Methodist Church, Washington, D. C., before coming this past year to Trinity M. E. Church, Durham.

Arthur S. Daniels has a son, Royden E. Daniels, in the junior class at Duke this year. Mr. Daniels is secretary, treasurer, and manager, Globe Fish Company, at Elizabeth City, N. C.

Stephen W. Anderson is a member of the firm, P. L. Woodard and Company, general merchants, at Wilson, N. C. He married Miss Maude Shamburger on October 11, 1918.

Mrs. William H. Busing, Jr., who was before her marriage, Ethel Lewis, lives at 37 Prospect Street, White Plains, New York.

Maude Moore is a popular teacher in Rockingham, N. C.

David D. Peele is a member of the faculty of Columbia College. Columbia, South Carolina.

Lloyd A. Rone has been engaged in mining enterprises in Torreon, Mexico, for a number of years. His address is Apt. 333, Coahuila, Torreon.

Mrs. C. L. Hornaday (Bess Jones) is with her husband, who is teaching at Williams College, Williamstown, Mass.

Junius C. Wren is engaged in furniture manufacturing at Siler City, N. C. He takes an active interest in church work and has served on some very important committees in the North Carolina Conference.

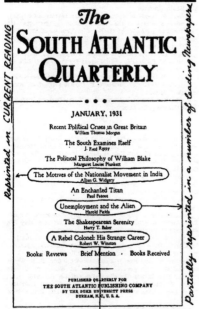

Reprinted on CURRENT READING

Partially reprinted in a number of leading Newspapers

The
SOUTH ATLANTIC
QUARTERLY

• • •

JANUARY, 1931

Recent Political Crises in Great Britain
William Thomas Morgan

The South Examines Itself
J. Fred Rippy

The Political Philosophy of William Blake
Margaret Louise Plunkett

The Motives of the Nationalist Movement in India
Alban G. Widgery

An Enchanted Titan
Paul Fatout

Unemployment and the Alien
Harold Fields

The Shakespearean Serenity
Harry T. Baker

A Rebel Colonel: His Strange Career
Robert W. Winston

Books Reviews   Brief Mention   Books Received

PUBLISHED QUARTERLY FOR
THE SOUTH ATLANTIC PUBLISHING COMPANY
BY THE DUKE UNIVERSITY PRESS
DURHAM, N. C., U. S. A.

THIRTIETH YEAR
Reprinted in BOSTON TRANSCRIPT

Recent articles in the SOUTH ATLANTIC QUARTERLY have received editorial comment from many of the outstanding newspapers of the country. Among prominent publications which have given such recognition from time to time to the QUARTERLY, may be mentioned: *New York Times, New York Herald-Tribune, Boston Transcript, Collier's, Baltimore Sun, Springfield Republican, Review of Reviews,* and *Current Reading.*

The SOUTH ATLANTIC QUARTERLY is published in January, April, July and October. Subscription rates: $3.00 one year; $5.00 two years. Enter your subscription now. Use coupon below.

DUKE UNIVERSITY PRESS
Durham, North Carolina

Gentlemen:

Please enter my subscription to the SOUTH ATLANTIC QUARTERLY. Begin with the current issue and continue until further notice.

NAME ....

ADDRESS ....

1906
SILVER ANNIVERSARY

President—T. G. Stem.

Secretary-Treasurer—Bessie Whitted Spence.

Rev. John W. Autry, a minister in the M. E. Church, South, is pastor at Timberlake, N. C.

R. Guy Baldwin is a member of the firm, Baldwin & Prince, Cotton Brokers, at 517 Bank of Commerce Building, Norfolk, Va.

Eva Hughes Branch lives at 2913 Brook Road, Richmond, Va. She is a member of the John Marshall High School faculty.

Mrs. E. R. Stamps (Eliza Brown) lives on Milledgeville Road, Macon, Georgia.

Emma B. Foushee married Robert B. Hicks. They make their home at 961 Washington Avenue, Brooklyn, N. Y.

Mrs. C. L. Read (Nan Goodson) has two daughters in college, Mary Anna and Margaret Howard. She lives at Franklinton, N. C.

Rev. C. J. Harrell, pastor of Monument M. E. Church, Richmond, Va., was formerly pastor of Epworth M. E. Church, Norfolk, Va.

Thomas Alfred Holton has been engaged in educational work for a number of years. He is located at Perrine, Florida. His oldest daughter, Mildred, graduated from Duke with the class of 1929.

J. Allen Morgan recently moved from New York to Greensboro where he accepted a position as trust officer in the N. C. Bank and Trust Company.

Mr. and Mrs. Fred W. Obarr (Mattie Oldham, '08) and their four year old son are living at 15045 Altata Drive, Pacific Palisades, Cal.

Mr. and Mrs. George F. Cochran (Emeth Tuttle) live at Lakeland, Florida. Mr. Cochran is connected with the *Lakeland Ledger.*

Charles B. Arthur started working for the American Tobacco Company after leaving college and later went with Liggett & Myers where he has remained. He spent a number of years in China in interest of Liggett & Myers. He has recently been transferred to the New York Office, 212 Fifth Avenue.

TO CLASS OF 1926

To members of the class of 1926:

This is to notify you that the Class of 1926 will celebrate the fifth anniversary of graduation on Tuesday, June 9, 1931. Let me urge each member of the class to reserve this entire day for our class reunion. Make your plans now to be in Durham for the celebration and don't let anything keep you away. It will be a long time before we have another reunion, and we will be more widely separated in 1936 than in 1931.

In a few days you will receive a letter to which I hope that all will reply. Each member of the class should do his part to make our fifth anniversary a success; and as renewing our friendships, talking old times and being together again constitute a successful reunion, your presence is essential.

Please do not ignore the letter that you will receive in a few days, as it will be important and much will depend upon your reply. But, above all, remember you have a date with the class on June 9, and don't break it.

Sincerely,
EDWARD L. CANNON,
401 23rd Street N. W., Washington, D. C.

P.S. If your address is not on file at the Alumni office please write to them at once and if you have changed your address do the same or notify me.

CAMEL-LIGHTING TIME

SOFT LIGHTS and friendly shadows, intimate, alluring — and the mellow contentment of a Camel!

The pleasure of *any* moment is heightened by Camel's fresh, cool fragrance, tingling with the delicate aromas of the world's choicest tobaccos—sun-ripened—naturally mild.

CAMELS

DUKE UNIVERSITY ALUMNI REGISTER

Some Features of This Pre-Commencement Issue

PROGRAM OF FIRST COMMENCEMENT ON
NEW CAMPUS

PHOTOGRAPH OF FORTIETH YEAR
REUNION CLASS

LIST OF THE MEMBERS OF REUNION
CLASSES

MAY DAY PHOTOGRAPHS

DUKE'S ENGINEERING DEPARTMENTS
(with photographs)

A RARE MANUSCRIPT DISCOVERY
(illustrated)

BIRDS OF THE DUKE FOREST

Other Articles Relating to Commencement and
Other Subjects.

SOME TALL TREES IN THE DUKE FOREST

VII   *May, 1931*   NUMBER 5

Duke University Alumni Register

(*Member of American Alumni Council*)

Published at Durham, N. C. Every Month in the Year in the Interest of the University and the Alumni

Volume XVII   *May 1931*   Number 5

In This Issue

Editor and Business Manager ....Henry R. Dwire, '02

Assistant Editors ....Elizabeth Aldridge, '24
                               Albert A. Wilkerson, '26

Advertising Manager ....Charles A. Dukes, '29

Two Dollars a Year   20 Cents a Copy

Entered as Second-Class Matter at the Post-Office at Durham, North Carolina

THE CURRENT ISSUE

The present issue of the Alumni Register is devoted, to a considerable extent, to matters relating to the 1931 Commencement. Of particular interest to many alumni will be the names of members of the Reunion Classes. If there are any inaccuracies in this list a note to that effect to the Alumni Office will be greatly appreciated. If you observe that any names of living alumni are omitted, please do not hesitate to call attention to that fact, as this will help in making the alumni records as nearly correct as possible.

JUNE

The June issue of the Alumni Register, which will appear soon after Commencement, will have much news and comment of interest relating to that event. The addresses of Commencement speakers will appear; there will be some exceptional photographs showing Commencement scenes, and in addition to this there will be a variety of other matter that is sure to be interesting to alumni and other readers of the Register as well. There will be some unusually interesting photographs in the June Register.

THE EDITOR.

THE FORTIETH YEAR CLASS TO HAVE REUNION AT 1931 COMMENCEMENT

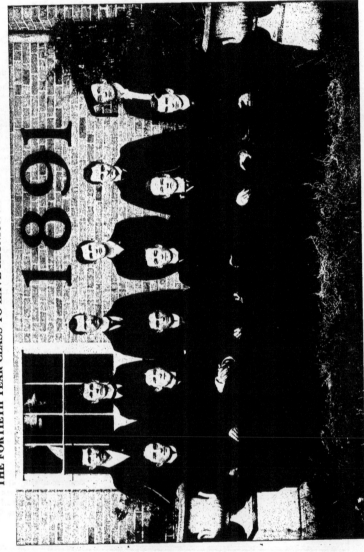

Front Row.—T. C. Daniels; Fred Harper; J. R. McCrary; D. A. Houston; W. H. Jones; D. R. Davis (Deceased)
Back Row.—W. I. Cranford; Charles E. McCandless; L. S. Massey; R. L. Durham; W. B. McDowell; W. B. Lee.

Duke University Alumni Register

Volume XVII   *May, 1931*   Number 5

Editorial Comment

WRITE TO THEM

Alumni and alumnae of Duke University are in a position to render a specific service of real value in connection with the Commencement June 7-10—the first on the new campus.

This is especially true of the members of the fourteen Reunion Classes.

In this issue of THE REGISTER are published the names of living members of Reunion Classes whose addresses are in the Alumni Office files. (Of course, there may be errors, and it will be greatly appreciated if those detecting such errors will call attention to them).

It would be fine if members of each Reunion Class would go over the list and communicate with the other members of the class, as far as possible, urging them to "come home" for the first Commencement on the new campus.

Just a few words to another member of your class, urging him or her to come to the reunion on June 9, might be effective in increasing the attendance.

Certainly we feel sure that alumni generally will be glad to help along this line.

WOULD NOT MISS IT

Some interesting letters are being received at the Alumni Office from former students who contemplate coming back for the first Commencement on the new campus.

One is from an alumnus of some years back who lives hundreds of miles away. He says:

"I realize that I have a considerable distance to travel and also that times are not as good as they might be, but I am just simply not going to miss the 1931 Commencement if it is possible for me to get there.

"I was at the first Commencement held after Trinity College was moved to Durham, and I want to be a participant in the latest phase of the institution's growth and progress."

There are doubtless others who attended that first Commencement at Durham who will also make a particular effort to take part in the first similar occasion on the new campus.

It might be a good idea for the group to get together during the 1931 event, and indulge in reminiscences of that other Commencement held back in the "gay nineties," and of the events that have intervened between the two.

Speaking of reunions, what about a reunion of this kind?

THE OLD IN A NEW SETTING

The editor received a letter a few days ago from an alumnus in response to one sent out from the Alumni Office recently with reference to the 1931 Commencement.

"I like that expression at the bottom of your letter," he said—"'come back to Alma Mater—the same Alma Mater in a new setting.'

"It seems to me that this expresses the idea exactly."

There have doubtless been some alumni who have felt a bit strange at first on coming back to the new Duke and finding things in some respects so different.

Yet they only have to be here a short while before they realize that certain things that they knew here in the old days are still present in a very gratifying degree—the spirit of devotion to an ideal, the passion for service, the friendliness and kindliness of an earlier day, the fine traditions.

True, there is a New Duke, so to speak, but a mere change in setting, due to the demands of expansion and growth, has not changed, and will not change, those fundamental characteristics of the Old Trinity to which we have referred.

To be sure, there is a new location and new equipment and a new situation in various respects, but it is the same institution in essentials that mean so much.

WHY NOT DO LIKEWISE?

One local alumni group has just taken a step that will be of real value to Duke, not only now but in the years ahead.

A special scholarship has been set up, to be awarded from year to year to a worthy student of the institution.

There is no better service that an alumni group can render than to do something of this kind.

With an entire group participating, the expense does not fall heavily upon anyone, and the possibilities of good results are far out of proportion to the amount of the investment.

One scholarship of this kind, carefully administered, can mean the difference between success and failure in some life in the years ahead. It is indeed difficult to estimate, even in a general way, the chances for good offered by such a proposition.

Perhaps other alumni groups desirous of finding some definite, specific plan for the service of Alma Mater may be interested in some similar project.

There are fifty-six local alumni groups now, and if even a few of them become interested in something of this kind the ultimate result in terms of effective service can be readily imagined.

"DE-EDUCATED"

In reading an article in the *Chautauqua Quarterly* recently on the subject of adult education, the above word was discovered.

It expresses, in ten letters of the alphabet, a world of meaning.

It might be used more generally than it is.

The meaning of "de-educated" is simply this:

There is such a thing as an individual getting it into his head that a College Commencement, despite the meaning of the word "Commencement" itself, is an end in the realm of education rather than a beginning.

A good many college graduates unfortunately seem to have this idea.

They go on in that way a while, and then seem to lose their taste for education; they are not interested in keeping themselves educated.

Having imagined that a college course gave them an "education," the matter of acquiring education after college days never seems to occur to them.

And thus they become "de-educated" through neglect, in the end having less education than many alert individuals who have never had the advantage of a college course, and who in spite of that go ahead, learning something new all the while.

To enable the individual to escape the "de-educating process" is one of the purposes of adult education, to which the REGISTER has frequently referred.

Fortunately, more and more college graduates are realizing that there is a real place for this adult education in the lives of those who have already been through college.

The Alumni Office of Duke University is working now on plans to be of service to alumni in that direction through the suggestion of reading courses and in other ways.

PROGRESS IN ANOTHER FIELD

We feel sure that readers of the REGISTER will be interested in an article in this issue on the development of the Engineering Departments at Duke.

Not so much has been said about this phase of the institution's development, but the field of work described in the article is one in which substantial and steady progress is being shown.

The Engineering Departments are being expanded, both in enrollment and instructional facilities, in the three lines of civil, electrical and mechanical engineering, and there is good reason to believe that this development will continue.

The article on Duke's work in engineering is simply another of the series that the REGISTER is printing from time to time, dealing with facts about the institution's growth and development with which alumni are not always as familiar as they should be.

First Commencement on New Campus of Duke University June 7-10

Dr. Robert Norwood, Pastor of St. Bartholomew's Episcopal Church, New York, to Deliver Sermon Tuesday, June 9, and Hon. Huston Thompson, Washington, D. C., to Be Heard in Address Wednesday, June 10— Other Notable Features

WITH THE beautiful new campus as its setting, the seventy-ninth commencement of Duke University will be held June 7 to June 10 and promises to be one of the most significant finals exercises in its history as a degree-conferring institution. Aside from the fact that this commencement will be the first held on the new campus, the program is one which will attract a host of alumni, friends and relatives of the graduates, and patrons of the University.

Dr. Huston Thompson, of Washington, D. C., attorney and former Chairman of the Federal Trade Commission, will deliver the commencement address on Wednesday, June 10; and Dr. Robert Norwood, pastor of St. Bartholomew's Church, New York City, will preach the commencement sermon on Tuesday, June 9. President W. P. Few will deliver the baccalaureate address unless he follows a custom of recent years in inviting a guest speaker to take his place.

Fourteen reunion classes are expected to be well represented. Beginning with the class of '71, the fifth-year classes will reunite through the class of 1926, and the classes of '28 and '30 will also gather. Tuesday will again be Alumni Day, and class headquarters will be established at the West Campus Union. John Allen Morgan, '06, of Greensboro, has been invited to extend greetings from the twenty-fifth year class at the Alumni luncheon, and similar brief greetings

HON. HUSTON THOMPSON   DR. ROBERT NORWOOD

will be brought from the alumnae members of the class by Mrs. Emeth Tuttle Cochrane, of Daytona Beach, Fla., at the alumnae luncheon.

Commencement this year will feature many novelties for returned alumni and other visitors. In an entirely new setting there will be much of new interest for all those who attend. Truly it may be said that the Seventy-ninth will be unlike any commencement Duke University or Trinity College has ever known.

Dr. Thompson is a graduate of Princeton, and a former student of the New York Law School. He began his practice in 1899 in Denver, Col., and later was lecturer in law at University of Denver Law School. He also served as assistant attorney general of Colorado.

In 1913 he was appointed assistant United States Attorney General by President Woodrow Wilson, and served in that capacity until 1918. In 1918 he was appointed Federal Trade Commissioner for a term of seven years, two years of which he was chairman. In 1922 the degree of Doctor of Laws was conferred upon him by George Washington University.

Dr. Norwood's distinguished career in the ministry began in 1897 in his native Nova Scotia, and during the next score years took him to many sections of Canada where he held the pastorates of several of the largest churches in Ontario. He has been

(Continued on page 153)

Many Members of the Reunion Classes Expected to Return

Large Attendance at 1931 Commencement From These Groups Is Assured—List of Living Members of the Fourteen Reunion Classes, Beginning With Class of 1876 and Ending With the 1928 Class

THE CLASS reunions are always a conspicuous feature of a Duke University Commencement. This year will be no exception, from present indications. Already class officers are arranging dinners and other "get-together" occasions and a time of good fellowship and of pleasant and profitable renewal of old friendships is assured.

Fourteen classes are to hold reunions in June in connection with the 1931 Commencement—'76, '81, '86, '91, '96, '01, '06, '11, '16, '21, '26, and '28. The following list of names of reunion class members contains living members of the various reunion classes, whether they graduated or not. There may be some errors or omissions, and if so, the editor of the REGISTER will be glad to have attention called to the same. Unless a class member is living and his definite address is contained in the Alumni Office files his name does not appear in this list. If a name is omitted, notify the REGISTER, giving the person's address.

CLASS OF 1871

Everett, J. F., ex'71.....Bennettsville, S. C.
Norris, Henry W.............Holly Springs

CLASS OF 1876

Bobbitt, W. A....................Goldsboro
Coltrane, Shubal G.............Randleman
Cross, T. M...........,.............Sanford
Hardesty, E. D...................Newport
Kernodle, Peter J.........Richmond, Va.
Leak, James N..................Greensboro
Petty, Isaac N....................Hillsboro
Turner, W. D....................Statesville
White, R. L......................Glenola
Wilborn, J. C...................York, S. C.

CLASS OF 1881

Adams, Judge W. J................Raleigh
Beckwith, Roburton B., Dr.......Fayetteville
Boddie, Byron N............Leesville, S. C.
Broom, Rev. Robert H............Southport
Edwards, B. W..................Snow Hill
Fink, James C....................Concord
Gray, E. S...........,.............Winston
Harris, Melanchon R..........Thomasville
Huntley, L. J....................Wadesboro
Lowder, Rev. J. M........Connelly Springs
Robertson, J-................Williamston
Townsend, Rev. W. H...........High Point

CLASS OF 1886

Andrews, Lee ....Archdale
Bailey, Rev. Robert W............Raleigh
Bell, James A....................Charlotte
Best, Lee J., Sr...................Dunn
Brne, William A...........Rocky Mount
Brooks, James C............Elizabeth City
Carpenter, Jesse A..............Wadesboro
Clark, Stokes M..................Ansonville
Hester, James W...........Waco, Texas
Hudson, William J...............Monroe
Jenkins, Dr. Charles L............Raleigh
Lippard, A. J....................Concord
Pinnix, J. C..............Murfreesboro, Ark.
Reynolds, William N........Winston-Salem
Rogers, Rev. J. Marion..Heath Springs, S. C.
Skeen, Lola P...............Decatur, Ga.
Thompson, W. M...............Richlands

CLASS OF 1891

Barbee, Alonzo L................Durham
Barker, Rev. J. J.................Ahoskie
Boyles, Franklin C..............Greensboro
Cheatham, Clifton B.............Farmville

Christie, Dr. Luther R....:.........Atlanta, Ga.
Cranford, Dr. W. I................Durham
Daniels, Thomas C...............New Bern
Deans, Ernest....................Wilson
Durham, Robert Lee........Buena Vista, Va.
Harper, Fred ....Lynchburg, Va.
Houston, David A.................Raleigh
Hudson, Thomas ....Waxhaw
Jones, William H..................Raleigh
Lambeth, John W.............Thomasville
Lee, Rev. W. B..........Soa paulo, Brazil
Lindsey, Joseph H...............Reidsville
March, Alfred H...........Fayetteville, Tenn.
Massey, Rev. Lucius Saunders........Durham
McCandless, Charles Enoch...Springboro, Pa.
McCoy, Frank Lee.............Oxford, Ga.
McCrary, John R................Lexington
Newsom, Larry E..................Lucama
Nichols, Dr. R. E.................Durham
Pierce, Ovid W...................Weldon
Remfry, L. A. V............Jackson, Miss.
Steed, John Daniel...............Maxton
Thorne, William H..................Airlie
Watkins, Jesse C..............Greensboro
Weeks, William ....Southport
Williford, Benjamin B..........Rocky Mount

CLASS OF 1896

Aldridge, Fred S..................Durham
Banger, Albert H.................New Bern
Bolton, Harvey..............Richmond, Va.
Brock, Furnifold ...:..............Trenton
Brooks, Fletcher Hastings..:...Baltimore, Md.
Carr, Edward Parrish........Thermal, Cal.
Carr, Ida Z................Nashville, Tenn.
Champion, John D.........Fuquay Springs
Christian, V. Seymour............Durham
Craven, Harvey B.............Lakeland, Fla.
Curtis, Zebulon F................Asheville
Dalley, Rev. John A,.............Pittsboro
Daniels, John William...........Gloucester
Davis, William Iverson.........Morganton
Debnam, Louis B...................Raleigh
Dowless, Rev. David E........Tebbetts, Mo.
Fuller, Jones M...................Durham
Giddens, James F...........Morehead City
Grant, Leroy C....................Jackson
Grantham, E. J.....................Wilson
Green, Ernest J............Columbia, S. C.
Harrison, Dr. Edwin M........Chicago, Ill.
Howerton, Thomas J.......Washington, D. C.
Hayden, Jesse F................High Point
Jenkins, Mamie C...............Greenville
Kerley, Robert P...:.:......West Durham
Lane, Guy S.....................Greensboro
Lindsey, William C................Durham

Mayer, Robert Andrew.............Charlotte
Maytubby, Joseph Smith....Wapanucka, Okla.
Miller, Frank W.................Waynesville
Payne, Dr. Bruce R.........Nashville, Tenn.
Pegram, Annie M...............Greensboro
Perry, J. Sidney..................Durham
Raper, Rev. Albert S.............Stoneville
Riddick, Charles R................Ayden
Rogers, Benjamin Winston........Durham
Separk, Joseph H.................Gastonia
Sherrill, Frank C................Cornelius
Smith, Herbert Lee...............Durham
Sparger, Samuel W...............Durham
Taylor, Charles W.............Mount Airy
Thomas, Charles R.............Thomasville
Troy, Dr. T. S.........Tokoma Park, Md.
Webb, Albert S...................Concord
Woodward, George J............Greenville

CLASS OF 1901

Anderson, Stephen W.............Wilson
Asbell, John N..................Belvidere
Asbury, Henry B.................Charlotte
Barbee, Daisy B.................Gastonia
   (Mrs. M. D. Herndon)
Barnett, Blanche H...............Clinton
   (Mrs. H. H. McKeown)
Blakeney, Carl T................Charlotte
Blanchard, Joseph C.............Hertford
Brown, William E.................Durham
Carden, Frank Stamper....Chattanooga, Tenn.
Carmichael, William D....New York, N. Y.
Chadwick, Mabel.................Athens, Ga.
Crawford, Wade H.................Wilson
Daniel, Arthur S..........Elizabeth City
Davis, Marion Stuart............Louisburg
Dickinson, Charles L...........Wilmington
Ellington, Richard L............Reidsville
Green, William B.................Graham
Hammond, Dr. Alfred F........Pollocksville
Hanes, John L.................Pine Hall
Hendren, Mary L..................Durham
   (Mrs. Z. B. Vance)
Jones, Kenneth R................New Bern
Jones, Myra B...........Williamstown, Mass.
   (Mrs. C. L. Hornaday)
Lackey, Otis Brantley........Cowpens, S. C.
Lambeth, Rev. W. A.............Durham
Langston, William H. B..........Goldsboro
Lewis, Ethel Maye.......White Plains, N. Y.
   (Mrs. William H. Busing, Jr.)
Lunsford, Annie J.............Four Oaks
   (Mrs. N. C. Yearby)
Malone, Jones Fuller............Louisburg
Mayer, Hazel G..................Charlotte
Moore, Elizabeth Maude....:....Rockingham

Pelle, David D..............Columbia, S. C.
Reade, Rev. C. L................Franklinton
Robey, Dr. Wesley M................Charlotte
Rone, Lloyd A..............Torreon, Mexico
Sessoms, William A.............Bonifay, Fla.
Tucker, Rev. Paul W..............Lincolnton
Umstead, Joseph Martin...............Durham
Vaughan, Leo B.............Lynchburg, Va.
Vestal, R. M..............Washington, D. C.
Ware, James A.....................Asheville
Watson, James C....................Fairfield
Williams, Leon F....................Raleigh
Windley, Dr. Richard E..........Washington
Winstead, Samuel G.................Roxboro
Womble, Samuel W...................Moncure
Wood, John K......................Asheboro
Wren, Junius S....................Siler City
Wannamaker, William H.............Durham

CLASS OF 1906

Anderson, Mary S....................Charlotte
(Mrs. Paul H. Allen)
Arthur, Cecil B..............New York, N. Y.
Autry, Rev. John W..............Timberlake
Baldwin, R. Guy................Norfolk, Va.
Barringer, Paul J....................Sanford
Bassett, Lucy ....Pelham, Ga.
(Mrs. John O'Neal)
Bethea, Charles L..................Wilmington
Bostian, John C....................Albemarle
Branch, Eva Hughes..........Richmond, Va.
Brown, Eliza R....................Macon, Ga.
(Mrs. E. R. Stamps)
Brown, Robert Anderson...............Raleigh
Browning, Rev. Raymond.....Columbus, Ohio
Burton, Anna B..............Blacksburg, Va.
Carter, Henry C...................Washington
Clement, John H...................Walkertown
Cochran, George F..............Lakeland, Fla.
Crook, William M..................Macon, Ga.
Ellis, Mary E.......................Southmont
(Mrs. Emmett C. Willis)
Foard, Osborne G..................Wilmington
Foushee, Emma B.............Brooklyn, N. Y.
(Mrs. Robert B. Hicks)
Goodson, Nannie ....Franklinton
(Mrs. C. L. Read)
Gibson, Francis D......................Gibson
Gibson, Leroy B........................Gibson
Harrell, Rev. Costen J.........Richmond, Va.
Herrine, Kate M........................Raleigh
(Mrs. J. Henry Highsmith)
Hobgood, Alton S.............Baltimore, Md.
Holton, Thomas Alfred..........Perrine, Fla.
Horton, Daniel W......................Durham
Justus, William J....................Belhaven
Lambeth, James E.................Thomasville
Lister, Marvin W...................Weeksville
Markham, Charles B...................Durham
Marten, William Samuel
Morgan, John Allen................Greensboro
Neal, Henry A.........................Durham
Obarr, Fred W.........Pacific Palisades, Cal.
Odell, Arthur G........................Concord
Owen, Annie ....Rockville, Md.
(Mrs. B. T. Wilson)
Pegram, William H., Jr........Houston, Texas
Phillips, Dr. D. B..........Youngstown, Ohio
Pitts, Joel A., Jr....................Creedmoor
Proctor, Robert T...........Arkadelphia, Ark.
Pugh, C. R.....................Reno, Nevada
Rochelle, Zalpheus A..................Durham
Roper, Robert R.........................Roper
Shotwell, Mary G............New York, N. Y.
Sidbury, Kirby Cleveland.........Wilmington
Singleton, Rev. L. T.....................Selma
Stallings, Cleve ....Littleton
Starr, George H................Turlock, Cal.
Steele, Dr. Fleete S...........San Diego, Cal.
Stem, Thaddeus G.......................Oxford
Taylor, Hoy ....Nashville, Tenn.
Thomas, Mary Reamey...............Durham
(Mrs. W. P. Few)
Thomas, William Archer ....Charlotte
Thompson, Bennie Oscar.............Charlotte
Tillett, Mary Belle.................Greenville
Tillett, Wilbur F..........Newport News, Va.
Tuttle, Emeth....................Lakeland, Fla.
(Mrs. George F. Cochran)
Walker, Herman C..........Bradentown, Fla.
Warren, Charles R..............Chatham, Va.
Webb, Paul ....Cameron, Texas
Whitmore, Sudie C....................Durham
Whitted, Bessie O.....................Durham
(Mrs. H. E. Spence)
Wilkerson, Maude ....Durham
(Mrs. W. B. Dunn)
Woodard, John R..................Tulsa, Okla.

CLASS OF 1911

Adams, Hugh B....................Atlanta, Ga.
Andrews, Rev. George Reid..Bridgeport, Conn.
Angier, Samuel J......................Durham
Babbitt, Emma ....Bayboro
(Mrs. Blount Whitesides)
Beavers, Dr. John Thomas..Newport News, Va.
Bell, William R..............New York, N. Y.
Benson, Rev. Walter C..............Tarboro
Blalock, Rev. John E..................Parkton
Brinn, Joseph E.......................Sanford
Bruce, Mabel.................New York, N. Y.
Cockerham, Effie Grace...............Durham
Cooper, John D., Jr..................Henderson
Cooper, Lewis G....................Greenville
Courtney, Jefferson B..........Winston-Salem
Daniels, Maynard Preston..........Wanchese
Dunn, William B.......................Durham
Elder, Dr. Jeffrey N............Hopewell, Va.
Elliott, Thomas G..................High Point
Evans, Dennis E.......................Manteo
Ferguson, Robert L..............Dallas, Texas
Fisher, Dr. Clyde O.........Middletown, Conn.
Folger, Rev. Julius S...................Stanley
Gaston, Woodfin Grady...............Gastonia
Gladstein, Fannie B............Baltimore, Md.
Gray, Charles D......................Gastonia
Gray, Julia E..........................Gastonia
Gregg, Benjamin S., Jr..........Wilmington
Hanes, P. Frank..............Winston-Salem
Harris, Theo B......................Asheville
Hedrick, Henry G.....................Durham
Hundley, Kate Lee......................Durham
(Mrs. Arthur Harris)
Hunter, Henry Reid......Stone Mountain, Ga.
Hurley, Bolivar Stedman..................Troy
Hurley, Rev. B. T.................Fayetteville
Hutchings, Chesley M........Cincinnati, Ohio
Ingram, Henry B................Mount Gilead
Isley, Cary T.........................Asheville
Isley, Mabel B................Beaumont, Cal.
(Mrs. S. J. Gantt)
Jaffe, Louise I....................Norfolk, Va.
Korner, Russell De..................Charlotte
Kiker, Paul Jones..................Wadesboro
Kilgo, Rev. B. L..............Ridge Springs
Laten, James T............Fayetteville, Tenn.
Lyda, Minnie Y....................Weaverville
(Mrs. Allen D. Closson)
Lyon, Osborne Henry...............Plymouth
Mahoney, Wilbur Alexander..Lake Wales, Fla.
Matton, William George...Mexico City, Mexico
McIntosh, Christine A..............Asheboro
(Mrs. Fred Page)
McLean, A. A., Jr...........New York, N. Y.
Miller, Rev. J. Herbert..................Biscoe
Moore, John Craven.................Elm City
New, Rebecca J.........................Durham
(Mrs. E. Burke Hobgood)
Nicholson, Blanche B.............Washington
(Mrs. J. D. Webb)
Page, Frederick C....................Asheboro
Parkin, Elizabeth S.................Thomasville
(Mrs. T. J. Covington)
Payne, Abner C....................Taylorsville
Perkins, Willis Marion, Jr..........Littleton
Pinnix, Hugh ....Gastonia
Proctor, Baxter G.......................Durham
Richardson, Robert M...........Rocky Mount
Ross, Mark C.........................Bonnerton
Royal, John A., Jr...............Mount Olive
Sheetz, Silas..........................Wilmington
Shields, Lester H...........Fort Wayne, Ind.
Smith, Thomas P..........Florence Villa, Fla.
Snader, Prof. David L..........Hoboken, N. J.
Stikeleather, Mary ....Asheville
(Mrs. N. W. Beadles)
Taylor, George Frederick...Schenectady, N. Y.
Taylor, John Leonard.........Boscobell, Wis.
Turrentine, Samuel B., Jr.....Nashville, Tenn.
Tuttle, Herndon Wescott...........Goldsboro
Tuttle, Mattie Lou Ola...............Ashboro
(Mrs. I. C. Moser)
Vick, Rev. Giles W...........Winston-Salem
Vickers, Rev. T. G...............Rocky Mount
Warbutton, James H...........Marietta, Ohio
White, Moses A....................Greensboro
Whitley, Theophilus C................Edward
Wilson, James Christopher.........Chapanoke
Worley, Harry ....Little Rock, Ark.

CLASS OF 1916

Abel, Hugh.........................Waynesville
Abernethy, Charles Everett.....Pulaski, Tenn
Adams, Robey E....................Four Oaks
Adams, Luther Wiley............Tupelo, Miss.
Allen, Louis Carr......................Graham
Austin, Eugene B................Elkton, Tenn.
Baird, William A.....................Asheville
Baldwin, Lucille E.............Shreveport, La.
(Mrs. George S. Sexton, Jr.)
Baucom, Henry M..................Unionville
Baugh, Atha Shepard..........Louisville, Ky.
Belvin, Mary A.........................Durham
(Mrs. W. I. Pickett)
Bender, Paul Vermont.........Cleveland, Ohio
Bennett, William Henderson.............Cary
Bivins, Laura Mae...........Greenville, S. C.
(Mrs. J. H. Britt)
Brady, Sophie................New York, N. Y.
Brandon, Lillian E.....................Durham
(Mrs. Lloyd E. Brown)
Britt, George W. H..........New York, N. Y.
Brooks, Harry E.......................Clayton
Brown, Rev. Adrian E..........Robersonville
Buckman, Edmund Taylor........Washington
Bunting, Carl F......................New Bern
Bullard, Lucille M..................Goldsboro
(Mrs. Henry Belk)
Cannon, Dr. Wallace Bennett.....Stonega, Va.
Carrington, Dr. George Lunsford..Burlington
Chaffin, Leonidas M., Jr............Lillington
Chappelle, Iris Odelle.....................Dunn
(Mrs. H. C. Turlington)
Cheek, Mamie G..............Fuquay Springs
(Mrs. J. B. Johnson)
Cobbs, Robert R...............Pulaski, Tenn.
Ooman, James H.......................Durham
Cook, Henry L., Jr., Dr...........Greensboro
Cooper, Marius ....Statesville
Council, Arthur R..............Richmond, Va.
Cox, Dr. Ella B..............New York, N. Y.
(Dr. E. B. Cox, Brazil)
Craig, Carrie B..............Irvington, N. J.
(Mrs. Ed. T. Campbell)
Crabtree, Lida May...................Durham
(Mrs. W. E. Wells)
Crompton, Ethel M....................Durham
Culler, Dr. Oscar E...........Baltimore, Md.
Cunningham, Bert ....Durham
Curtis, Albert B. ....Canton
Dalton, Harry L......................Charlotte
Dalton, Rufus W..............Winston-Salem
Davis, Rose M..................Lynchburg, Va.
Dixon, Laurence Fitche...............Durham
Duncan, John Nelson..................Raleigh
Edmiston, William C........Petersburg, Tenn.
Egerton, Walter D..............Richmond, Va.
Ellis, Myron G............Santa Monica, Cal.
Erwin, John Ira......................Charlotte
Eubanks, Virgil M..........Brussels, Belgium
Eudy, Banks E...................Euproa, Miss.
Farrar, Rev. Walter G...............Nashville
Ferrell, Wesley Luther........Winston-Salem
Fields, Robert Lindsay.................Bonlee
Fitzgerald, Dr. Joseph H..........Smithfield
Gaither, Jasper Clyde..........Richmond, Va.
Gardner, Simon M...................Warrenton
Garrette, Virginia Bera..............Charlotte
Gibbs, Frank H.......................Warrenton
Gibbs, Richard Stevens.......Portsmouth, Va.
Gibson, John Kilgo..........Straatsburg, N. Y.
Giles, W. Everett........New Kensington, Pa.
Gill, Emmet Fitzgerald ....Laurinburg
Glass, Edward W., Rev................Durham
Glauss, Harvey Andrew......Belle Haven, Va.
Glaze, John William.............Elkton, Tenn.
Grigg, Jasper Horace...................Shelby
Hambrick, John J.....................Roxboro
Hardee, Parrotte B....................Durham
Harley, George W........Libena, West Africa
Harris, Jethro J......................Seaboard
Hathcock, Bernard D.......Washington, D. C.
Hawfield, Dr. James.......Washington, D. C.
Hearn, Francis H..................Augusta, Ga.
Hightower, Gurney I.......Washington, D. C.
Holmes, Russell Irwin...............Louisburg
Holloway, Marion E............West Durham
Hopkins, Gordon C....................Durham
Holton, Florence E......O.klahoma City, Okla.
Horton, Marye Thomas..........Rocky Mount
(Mrs. John T. Usher)
Houser, Rev. J. B....................Jefferson
Howie, Herbert B....................Charlotte
Hoyle, John W., Jr., Rev.......Rutherfordton
Hudson, Hilary Thomas, Jr............Shelby
Ingram, Hal B..........................Hamlet
Irby, Dr. Henry C.............Blackstone, Va.
Jenkins, Richard Harold...Long Island, N. Y.
Johnson, Kent B..............Portsmouth, Va.
Johnson, Pierce ....Weldon
Johnson, Susie M.....................Fountain
(Mrs. H. F. Owen)
Johnston, Cyrus C...................Mooresville
Johnston, Robert M..............Chicago, Ill.
Jones, B. Braxton......................Kinston
Jones, Ida F............................Durham
Kearns, Walter Clark..........Winston-Salem
Kimball, W. W...................West Durham
Kluttz, Gill Wyley........................Lenoir
Knight, Kinchen Coffield...........Whitakers
Knight, Madeline ....Durham
Lackey, Dr. Marvin A.............Mooresville
Lambeth, J. Walter, Jr...........Thomasville

Lee, Heath E. .... Columbus, Ga.
Lilley, John J. .... Waverly, Va.
Lindsey, Isaac A. .... Durham
Litchfield, Charles A. .... Aurora
Lowder, James P. .... Norwood
Loy, Rev. W. L. .... Creedmoor
Markham, Allan B. .... Durham
Matton, Charles F. .... Winston-Salem
McCauley, Sadie M. .... Elm City
(Mrs. Thomas E. Braswell)
McKay, James A. .... Asheville
McNeely, Roy K. .... Mooresville
Moss, Thomas E. .... Creedmore
Moyle, Samuel Boddie .... Columbia, S. C.
Moyle, William W. .... Ridgefield Park, N. J.
Newman, Lela C. .... Charlotte
Newton, Giles Y. .... Kansas City, Miss.
Nichols, Frank M. .... Durham
Nichols, Rev. Hugh L. .... Durham
O'Neal, Augustus P. .... Baltimore, Md.
Osborne, Joe .... Bristol, Tenn.
Palmer, Nathan Milam, Jr. .... Lynchburg, Va.
Parker, Franklin N. .... Emory University, Ga.
Parker, Julius Franklin .... East Marion
Patton, Frank C. .... Morganton
Patterson, Dr. Fred Marion .... Greensboro
Pearce, Frederic Thorn .... Greensboro
Peele, Raymond .... Clinton
Pickens, Wiley Miller .... Lincolnton
Pickett, Bianca .... Winston-Salem
(Mrs. Ed. Fowler)
Pope, Charlton A. .... Wilmington
Pridgen, Wilbur Linton .... Durham
Purnell, Burkett .... Rockingham
Reeves, Fred C. .... New London
Rhyne, Walter N. .... Leland
Richardson, Rev. James C. .... Connelly Springs
Rigsbee, Bernice O. .... Durham
Ring, Clay V. .... Kernersville
Rogers, Orpie C. .... Fuquay Springs
Rone, J. Ralph .... Charlotte
Ross, Clarence .... Graham
Sasser, Frank M. .... Durham
Secrest, Vann V. .... Monroe
Sledge, John B. .... New York, N. Y.
Shelton, Rev. William R. .... Los Angeles, Cal.
Smith, Benjamin L. .... Shelby
Smith, Dr. Franklin C. .... Charlotte
Smith, James H. .... Cornelius
Smith, Robert K. .... Richmond, Va.
Snow, Lt. Beverly C. .... Fort Humphreys, Va.
Sprinkle, Thomas W. .... High Point
Stack, Amos M., Jr. .... Bules
Stallings, Kindle E. .... Durham
Stevenson, Walter H. .... Kendall Grove, Va.
Stone, William S. .... Kernersville
Storey, Walter E. .... Burlington
Stroud, William C. .... Reidsville
Swain, Thomas J. .... Plymouth
Taylor, J. H. .... Fayetteville
Teeter, Horace Brevard .... Charlotte
Thomas, Preston P. .... Asheville
Troutman, Roy W. .... Mooresville
Tucker, Charles Arden .... Warrenton
Tuttle, Ella Worth .... New Rochelle, N. Y.
(Mrs. Walter P. Hedden)
Wallace, Jack W. .... Statesville
Waller, Tula N. .... Mount Airy
(Mrs. G. K. Snow)
Wheeler, Dr. J. H. .... Henderson
White, Sidney B. .... Denver, Colo.
Williams, Curtis Clarkson .... Lillington
Williams, Odies B. .... Hillsboro
Wilson, Austin Willis .... Nashville, Tenn.
Woodward, John A. .... Washington, D. C.
Wyatt, Lucy S. .... Durham
(Mrs. Vernon Andrews)
Young, Theodore C. .... Wilson
Zagier, Coleman .... Asheville
Zuckerman, William .... New York, N. Y.

GLASS OF 1921

Adams, Rev. G. G. .... Gold Hill
Agner, Edgar Jennings .... Durham
Aiken, Ernest Marvin .... Bethesda, Md.
Alexander, William L. .... Columbia, Tenn.
Allen, Robert P. .... Weldon
Ashe, Alex E. .... Durham
Ashe, James E. .... Asheville
Avera, Charlotte F. .... Richmond, Va.
Bamberg, J. McGee .... Charleston, S. C.
Barnhardt, Luther W. .... Raleigh
Barrow, Beverly Hunter, Jr. .... Dinwiddie, Va.
Beavers, Ella May .... Durham
(Mrs. Hubert B. Belvin)
Benson, Chase H. .... Greensboro
Blalock, Tom C. .... Norwood
Boone, Alberta .... Durham
(Mrs. Stanley C. Harrell)
Brady, Joseph W. .... New York, N. Y.
Braudwell, Dr. Leslie J. .... Chicago, Ill.
Britt, Mary Verna .... Charlotte
(Mrs. J. M. Roberts, Jr.)
Brothers, Rev. Lloyd C. .... Spring Hope
Brown, Caviness H. .... Lillington
Bruton, Earl D. .... Candor
Bryan, Junius Harvey .... Durham
Buckner, Caney E. .... Durham
Bundy, Charles W. .... Charlotte
Burch, James Scott, Jr. .... Washington, D. C.
Cameron, Marcellus S. .... Southern Pines
Carroll, Charles Fisher, Jr. .... Bryson City
Carver, Willie Sidney .... Rougemont
Cavenaugh, Ernest D. .... Washington, D. C.
Cashion, Shelley Walker .... Cornelius
Chaffin, Emma LeGrand .... High Point
Chapin, John R. .... Aurora
Chapman, John S. .... Grifton
Chandler, Washington Lee .... Jacksonville, Fla.
Chesson, Eugene .... Rio Grande De Sul, Brazil
Clark, Nancy Lewis .... Durham
(Mrs. B. N. Goodwin)
Cole, Henry P. .... New York, N. Y.
Cole, Mary Louise .... Durham
Cooper, Mildred B. .... Greenville, S. C.
(Mrs. J. C. Cosby)
Cox, Dr. Clinton C. .... Durham
Davenport, Dr. Carlton A. .... Hertford
Davis, Emma E. .... Durham
(Mrs. R. H. Holden)
Davis, Rev. Harvey L. .... Wilmington
Douglas, Jay B. .... Washington, D. C.
Draper, Dr. L. M. .... Borger, Texas
Dunstan, Robert T. .... Greensboro
Durham, Lee Ballinger .... Detroit, Mich.
Edgerton, Claude G. .... Roanoke Rapids
Edgerton, Norman E., Jr. .... Raleigh
Fallon, Margaret .... Washington, D. C.
Farrington, Dr. R. Kirby .... Thomasville
Ferrell, D. Thomas .... Richmond, Ky.
Ferrell, George W. .... Durham
Few, William P., Jr. .... Greer, S. C.
Fisher, Henry E. .... Charlotte
Flythe, Arthur P. .... Jackson
Foy, Mary Josie .... Rio Grande De Sul, Brazil
(Mrs. Eugene Chesson)
Fulp, Willard W. .... Kernersville
Fussell, Tina .... Mebane
(Mrs. L. A. Wilson)
Geddie, Hendrix C. .... Four Oaks
Giles, Roy Williams .... Savage, Md.
Giles, Robert Theodore .... Hillsboro
Glass, William Paul .... Kannapolis
Grady, Leonidas V. .... Raleigh
Graham, Thomas N. .... Durham
Griffin, Dockery C. .... Richmond, Va.
Griffin, Pearl L. .... Rowland
(Mrs. D. A. Petty)
Griffin, William M. .... Raleigh
Grigg, Claud .... King's Mountain
Hall, John H. .... Elizabeth City
Harmon, George D. .... Bethlehem, Pa.
Harris, Charles A. .... Roxboro
Hathaway, Lloyd B. .... Winston-Salem
Hathcock, Joseph W. .... New York, N. Y.
Higgins, Howard B., Dr. .... Spartanburg, S. C.
Holt, Allen Bascom .... Greensboro
Holton, Emelyn G. .... Oxford
(Mrs. Nathaniel V. Daniel)
Hooker, Dr. John Samuel .... Farmville
Humble, Lelia .... Farmville, Va.
Humble, Lelia .... Wilmington
Humphrey, Wm. Harrell, Jr. .... Lumberton
Hunter, Berry Burnett .... Charlottesville, Va.
Jeffreys, Richard T. .... Rocky Mount
Jones, Barnie P. .... Durham
Jones, Joseph S. .... Mebane
Jones, Merritt H. .... Charlotte
Kanoy, Donald Wesley .... McLeansville
Kingsley, Paul Martin .... Kalamazoo, Mich.
Knox, Edward Montgomery .... High Point
Leake, Dr. Everett M. .... Norfolk, Va.
Lefler, Hugh T. .... Raleigh
Levy, Israel David .... Charlottesville, Va.
Lewis, Julian D. .... Whiteville
Lilley, Eulis M. .... Orlando, Fla.
Long, Rev. J. O. .... Rocky Mount
Lynn, Lollie T. .... E. Durham
(Mrs. A. P. Wiggins)
Mabry, Carl Edward .... Norwood
Macon, Mary Litchfield .... Norfolk, Va.
Mann, William Marion .... Enfield
Mason, Lily Nelson .... High Point
(Mrs. James R. Reitzel)
McArthur, Glenn T. .... Durham
McCrary, Helen .... Raleigh
(Mrs. Banks Arendell)
McGranahan, Fred N. .... Durham
McLean, Earl D. .... Mobile, Ala.
Merritt, Woodley C. .... Knoxville, Tenn.
Morse, T. Aubrey .... Lexington, Ky.
Morris, Cecil O. .... Atlantic
Morris, Derwood .... Atlantic
Moser, Rev. Claude H. .... Spencer
Motsinger, Carl .... Welcome
Mumford, Grover S. .... Greensboro
Murphy, W. F., Jr. .... Wallace
Nicholson, Maude L. .... Statesville
Nicholson, William T. .... Statesville
Oliver, Claude B. .... Durham
Oswald, Hubert L. .... San Francisco, Cal.
Page, Frank M., Jr. .... Aberdeen
Parham, Robert A. .... Southern Rhodesia, Africa
Parker, Agnes Lucille .... Bladenboro
Parker, Colon C. .... Tampa, Fla.
Parker, Wixie E. .... Durham
Parrish, Charles V. .... Durham
Peterson, Prof. Jesse L. .... New York, N. Y.
Pierce, Blackwell .... Weldon
Pitts, Martha Irene .... Fremont
Richardson, Henry D. .... Dover
Richardson, Dr. George A. .... Philadelphia, Pa.
Richardson, Oscar L. .... Monroe
Richmond, Dr. Lewis C., Jr. .... Russell, Ky.
Rogers, Maude F. .... Durham
Rosenstein, Abraham .... Durham
Rosenstein, Eva .... Asheville
(Mrs. Joe Dave)
Russell, Marguerite M. .... Shanghai, China
(Mrs. W. H. Hollings)
Sandford, Francke Warren .... Asheville
Sasser, Louis L. .... Durham
Shinn, James H. .... New York, N. Y.
Singer, Beulah M. .... New Rochelle, N. Y.
(Mrs. Lincoln C. Ramsdell)
Skidmore, Lloyd James .... Albemarle
Skinner, Oliver Lee .... Montgomery, Ala.
Smathers, E. Pauline .... Asheville
Smith, James Francis .... Bellows Falls, Vt.
Tanaka, Isawo .... Seoul, Korea
Taylor, James W. .... Richlands
Teeter, Marvin Frank .... Asheville
Thomas, James Oscar .... Spray
Thomas, Margaret K. .... Gastonia
(Mrs. Erskine Boyce)
Thorne, Maynard G. .... Farmville
Towe, William Thompson .... Durham
Townsend, Robert Edgar .... Wilson
Tucker, Dr. William Arnold .... Auburn, N. Y.
Tysor, Ray J. .... Greensboro
Umstead, William B. .... Durham
Vaughan, Rev. William N. .... Vanceboro
Vise, James K. .... Decaturville, Tenn.
Waddell, Rosa .... Indianapolis, Ind.
(Mrs. N. J. Horner)
Waller, May B. .... New York, N. Y.
(Mrs. W. D. Carmichael)
Walton, Beulah E. .... Ithaca, N. Y.
Ward, Marie A. .... Crisfield, Md.
Warren, Rosa M. .... Durham
(Mrs. H. E. Myers)
Watson, Penn T. .... Wilson
White, Robert S. .... Durham
Wiggins, Aubrey P. .... E. Durham
Wiggins, Martha E. .... Gastonia
(Mrs. Charles Hill Ross)
Wilkerson, Numa F. .... Jackson, Miss.
Wilkins, Alexander B. .... Sanford
Wilson, Jessie M. .... Weeksville
Woltz, Howard O. .... Mt. Airy
Woodard, Chas. F., Dr. .... Black Mountain
Wooten, James Taylor .... Rocky Mount
Worthington, Thelbert G. .... Ayden
Young, Mabel R. .... Durham

CLASS OF 1926

Abram, William Amos .... Tarboro
Adams, Rowena Darden .... Goldsboro
(Mrs. Charles McNairy, Jr.)
Ader, Olin B. .... Brevard
D'Affonseca, J. C. .... Mirias Sereas, Brazil, S. A.
Airheart, John Milton .... Durham
Aldridge, Thomas A. .... Araraquara, Brazil, S. A.
Allen, Gay W. .... Painesville, Ohio
Allen, Ivey .... Oxford
Alston, Nancy R. .... Jacksonville, Fla.
(Mrs. Julian Howard Wallace)
Anders, Annie Blair .... Concord
Anderson, Jack Epps .... Weldon
Andrews, Clinton Toms .... Hickory
Arnold, Dean M. .... Durham
Ashby, Charles G. .... Mt. Airy
Ashmore, Hubert R. .... Stedman
Atwater, Warren E. .... Newport News, Va.
Babington, Robert B., Jr. .... Gastonia
Barnard, Fred E. .... Asheville
Baugh, Robert .... Elkton, Tenn.
Baynes, Aubrey H. .... Hurdle Mills
Baynes, Jubal B. .... Hurdle Mills
Beaty, Brooks, L. .... Mt. Holly
Beaver, James A. .... Salisbury
Bernhardt, James Douglas .... Lenoir
Biggerstaff, Foye E. .... New York, N. Y.
Biggerstaff, Ralph L. .... Fall River, Mass.

(Continued on page 169)

Annual May Day Pageant Proves a Brilliant Event

Home-Coming in Connection With the Celebration Attracts Many Alumnae—Presentation in the Evening of Modernized Version of "Taming of the Shrew" by the Taurian Players is Notably Successful

WEATHER conditions, sometimes accounted disastrous for the staging of an outdoor event, were utilized to give a distinctive touch to the annual May Day pageant of the Woman's College of Duke University. The pageant was to have been held at the new Stadium on the West Campus, but rain earlier in the day of May 2 made the grounds unsuitable for such an event, and the entertainment was transferred to the auditorium of the East Campus.

Lighting effects here contributed to the staging that would not have been available in the open space; and the fantasy was such as to make happy the use of the lights. The production, "The Dance of the Day", gave a history of the progress of the hours from before dawn until sunset and after. It was the work of Duke women students, contributors in the main being Misses Jeanne Manget and Betty Burch.

The other chief event of the afternoon program was the crowning of Miss Elizabeth Caldwell, '31, as May queen. Taking part in the coronation ceremonies with Miss Caldwell were Miss Hettie English, of Mt. Olive, '31, her maid-of-honor, and 12 attendants.

Other chief events of the May Day celebration were a tea, given during the afternoon in the Alumnae Room in the Faculty Apartments, and the presentation Saturday night of a modernized version of Shakespeare's "Taming of the Shrew" in Page auditorium. Rewriting and rearranging of scenes was done under the direction of Prof. A. T. West and members of his classes.

The May Day program was attended by many out-of-town visitors, alumnae returning for the Alumnae Homecoming being, of course, well represented.

The pageant and coronation of the May queen was executed to the accompaniment of music by the orchestra of George E. Leftwich, Jr. Miss Caldwell was attired in a lace dress of striking design with long satin train.

"The Dance of the Day" gave a graphic and interesting picture of the coming of day, a storm, and sunset, there being ten dances in all. While limited somewhat as to space, the 60 young women performing were adept in execution; and scenic effects and music, which was contributed by Miss Mildred Murrell,

The Crowning of the Queen

Scene from Modernized Version of "Taming of the Shrew"

pianist, and A. J. Tannenbaum, and H. E. Holtz, violinists, combined to make the fantasy a delightful event.

The contribution of small children,—crown bearer, train carriers and flower girls—added much to the entertainment.

The presentation of the Shakespearean play brought to a close the dramatic season of the Taurians, who have established quite a reputation on the Duke campus and its environs.

The revision was aimed at a modernization of language, costumes, scenery, and atmosphere so as to make the play more intelligible to the ordinary theater-goer. The Taurians received praise for their successful presentation.

The leads were taken by Frank Menaker, of Reading, Pa., as Petrach; and Miss Gloria Sieger, a freshman, also a Pennsylvanian, who was in the role of Katerina. They were supported by a large and able cast.

Another Honor For Member of Duke University Faculty

Another honor has come to a member of the Duke University faculty. Dr. Frederick A. Wolf, professor of botany, was recently elected president of the winter meeting of the North Carolina Academy of Science in the annual session held at Raleigh.

Before coming to Duke, Dr. Wolf already had wide teaching and laboratory experience. He was instructor in the University of Texas, 1908-10; Fellow Cornell University, 1910-11; plant pathologist Alabama

Polytechnic Institute, 1911-15; botanist North Carolina Experiment Station, 1915-25; pathologist United States Department of Agriculture, 1925-27.

Dr. Wolf's various researches in his chosen line of work have been published in technical journals and bulletins from experiment stations and the United States Department of Agriculture. About 90 technical papers by him have been published.

Dr. Wolf received his Ph.D degree from Cornell University in 1911. Before that he had received his A.B. and A.M. from the University of Nebraska.

Washington Alumni Dinner is Notably Successful; Will Make Student Award

The dinner of the Washington, D. C., alumni club of Duke University, held at the University Club in that city, on May 2, was a notably successful occasion in every way. Coach Coombs and the members of the Duke baseball team and members of the families of Duke students in the Washington area were special guests. Coach Coombs made a brief talk that was most enthusiastically received.

At the meeting the alumni authorized the establishment of an award of $200 to be known as the Washington Bicentennial Award of the Duke University Alumni of Washington, D. C. The plan is to make all Duke students from that vicinity who have completed at least one full academic year of residence study at the University eligible for the award. Final details will be worked out later and a definite announcement made.

A Rare Document Is Acquired In Germany by Duke University

Provides Institution With Only Complete Manuscript New Testament in United States— Only 46 Greek Manuscript New Testaments in Existence—Important Discovery Made by Dr. Branscomb, of School of Religion Faculty

RECENT acquirement of a medieval Greek manuscript New Testament gives Duke University one of the rarest and most important documents to be found in any library in the United States. Announcement of this accession to the University collection was made a short time ago by library officials.

According to authorities in this field the manuscript dates from the thirteenth century, with southern Italy as its probable place of origin. It is the only complete manuscript New Testament in the United States, containing as it does all the books of the canon, including the Apocalypse. Something of the volume's importance may be seen from the fact that there are only forty-six Greek manuscript New Testaments in the world, practically all of which are in the libraries of the great European universities and most of which are incomplete.

Dr. Harvie Branscomb, Professor of New Testament in the School of Religion, is responsible for the discovery and acquisition of this unusual treasure. While traveling in South Germany in 1929 Professor Branscomb stopped in an antiquarian shop to make some minor purchases and as he was leaving asked the dealer if he possessed any Greek manuscripts. The dealer showed him several which were of no special value, and finally remarked that he knew where there was a manuscript of the Greek New Testament. Professor Branscomb followed up the remark with the result.

(Continued on page 163)

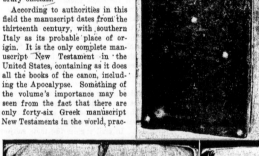

Top—Front cover of the complete Greek New Testament recently acquired by Duke University. The heavy hand-made nail studs are shown, as well as the intricate foliage tooling. The binding is apparently of monastic origin, probably made in South Italy several hundred years after the original manuscript was completed. The leather and heavy board back are in a remarkable state of preservation.

Left—Architectural decorations in red, blue, and gold feature the Greek New Testament's pages of Table of Contents and references. The intricate penmanship obviously required a long period for execution and is one of the features of the volume, which contains 199 folios dating from the twelfth century.

Right—The painstaking care with which the Testament was copied is clearly shown in this illustration of the first page of a new chapter. Uniform script throughout will facilitate the translation of the volume, which contains many slight variations from others of the 46 known complete Greek New Testaments.

Engineering Departments at Duke Are Showing Steady Progress

Are Forging Ahead in Number of Students, Equipment and Calibre of Work—Extensive Courses in Civil, Electrical and Mechanical Engineering Being Offered—Sixteen States Represented in Enrollment of Departments

FAR FROM the newness and activity of the West Campus of Duke University and somewhat removed likewise from the Woman's Campus rectangle is the Engineering Group—occupying buildings that once served as the Trinity Park School but exhibiting new spirit as it forges ahead in number of students, equipment and calibre of work.

The course of the Engineering Departments has not always been entirely smooth. Once, the school flourished; but later it came upon lean days, and it was discontinued for some time.

With the creation of Duke University on the firm foundation of old Trinity College in 1926, however, the Engineering Departments took on new life and during the régime of Prof. Harold C. Bird, and Prof. S. R. Schealer, the present heads of the division, have been making steady progress.

MECHANICAL ENGINEERING ADDED

To the engineering courses of civil and electrical, which have been maintained for several years, mechanical engineering is being added, so that degrees will be given in these three fields. The Engineering Departments were the agencies which effected the reinstatement of the Bachelor of Science degree at Duke, reoffering of which began in 1928.

Requirements for entrance to the engineering studies are being made more rigid, with examinations in physics or chemistry being included in the compulsory list of freshman requirements beginning with the 1931-32 session.

A large enrollment is assured, however, and another class similar in size to the present class, which began with a total of 73, is expected. The cosmopolitan quality of the present first year group is a notable feature, there being 15 states and the District of Columbia represented, aside from North Carolina. The list includes all the New England States save Vermont, and New Jersey, Pennsylvania, Ohio, Illinois, Kentucky, West Virginia, Maryland, Virginia, South Carolina, and Alabama.

CURRICULA REVISED

Curricula of both the civil and electrical engineering schools have been recently revised and correspond closely to standards set up by the Society for the Promotion of Engineering Education. About 40 semester hours are given to the major engineering group, and 138 hours—12 more than the requirement in arts—are required for graduation. Engineering students are required to take some of their electives in the economics department, this order prevailing because of the recognition of the importance of training for administrative posts in engineering and business.

Uniform courses are given engineering students during the freshman year with some divergence in the sophomore year. During the first two years the young engineer is drilled in the fundamentals of all engineering, such as mathematics, science, drawing, mechanics, strength of materials and hydraulics. During the last two years the more professional subject matter is provided. In civil engineering these subjects include railroads, highways, steel and reinforced concrete structures, sanitary and hydraulic engineering and some geodesy; in the electrical engineering group are found differential equations, electrical measurements, principles of electrical engineering, direct currents, alternating currents, electric power transmission, high frequency currents, electrical machinery, electric power stations, and electric railways; details of the courses in mechanical engineering are shown in the new catalogue but students will be admitted at present only to the freshman and sophomore years.

AN ABLE FACULTY

Members of the engineering staff "hold graduate degrees from leading universities," one of the University bulletins states, "and were chosen particularly for their ability to teach." Members of the staff in addition to Professor Bird, who is head of the department of civil and mechanical engineering, are Prof. S. R. Schealer, head of the department of electrical engineering; Prof. William H. Hall, professor of engineering; and Walter James Seeley, professor of electrical engineering. Ralph B. Matthews has been added this year as instructor in mechanical engineering.

HOUSING OF ENGINEERING GROUP

The Engineering Group is housed in two buildings, Asbury, the larger and more imposing structure, and Bivins, situated to the west of the Woman's Campus group. The prin-

PROF. HAROLD C. BIRD

PROF. S. R. SCHEALER

Duke engineering department, equipped with Maihak indicators, Cochrane steam separator, receiver, Brown electric flow-meter, and prony-brake.

Other items in the laboratory include a small Worthington reciprocating pump, a 112 gallon centrifugal pump, steam syphon, pressure gauges, thermometers, barometer,

cipal laboratories, all classrooms, most of the offices and the library are found in Asbury; Bivins contains laboratories and offices.

Engineering students are housed, since the beginning of the 1930-31 semester, in the James H. Southgate Memorial building, occupying a prominent position on the East Campus. The building is of white pressed brick and is three stories in height. In addition to providing good living quarters for the students, it has been a telling factor in the development of the morale of the engineering department members.

ADDITIONS TO LABORATORIES.

Important additions have thus made possible the performing of more thoroughgoing and accurate work. Equipment of the civil engineering laboratory, which is situated in the main in the Asbury building, includes a 50,000 universal testing machine, a 100 ton hydraulic press, abrasion machine, and impact machine, diamond core drill and diamond saw and lap used in testing strength of materials and highway testing; a large size Beggs deformeter, the first in North Carolina; apparatus for steam flow measurements; plenty of new surveying instruments; full equipment for testing of cements and bituminous materials; and—recently installed—complete apparatus for the testing of water and sewage. There are three well-lighted drawing rooms in the Asbury building for the preparation of plans and like features of engineering work.

During the past year a steam laboratory has been started in the basement of the Asbury building. At present installation consists of a seven by eight horizontal Troy steam engine built especially for the

psychrometer, apparatus for the testing of oils and gases, welding equipment, and a cut-open Ford motor. Close-coöperation with the two new University heating plants affords exceptional opportunities to the student in mechanical engineering, it is said.

A Gnome airplane motor has recently arrived and has been placed on exhibition.

OPPORTUNITY TO SPECIALIZE

Electrical engineering students are given opportunity to specialize in power machinery, communication or electric railways. In the basement of the Asbury building there is a power machinery laboratory, measuring about 45 by 40 feet; while a radio laboratory is provided on the second floor.

EXTENSIVE EQUIPMENT

Machinery in the electric power laboratory is available for illustrating practically every commercial use for direct and alternating electric currents. Equipment includes a $17\frac{1}{2}$ kilowatt, alternating current to direct current motor-generator set for supplying the laboratory with direct current, three direct connected direct current to direct current motor-generator sets, two direct current to alternating current belted sets, a sine wave motor-generator set, a synchronous converter, for one, two, three or six phase operation, a self-starting single-phase battery, charging converter, single phase constant potential transformers, a three-phase transformer, a constant current transformer equipped with a typical load of series street lamps, a three-phase induction regulator, electrical and mechanical loading devices, miscellaneous motors and generators, and measuring instruments for general

Southgate Building

Asbury Building

testing purposes, and oscillographs for viewing and photographing wave forms.

Extensive experiments in both audio and radio frequencies may be carried on by means of the high frequency laboratory, oscillators provide for generating alternating currents in 60 to 75,000 cycle frequency a second.

Recent acquisitions to this communication laboratory include: a 200 mile open wire artificial telephone line, an amplifier-milliammeter vacuum-tube volt merer for making measurements on amplifiers, etc., a beat-frequency oscillator for studies of frequency characteristics of loud speakers, etc., a fading recorder to make records of the fading of broadcast signals, which was donated by Dr. G. W. Pickard of the Radio Corporation of America, a resistance-coupled amplifier, a short wave radio receiver, a 75 watt short-wave transmitter, and special phonograph records for study of sound problems as they affect communication apparatus.

ENGINEERING LIBRARY

The engineering library is situated on the second floor of the Asbury building. There are about 1,000 volumes, including some French and German texts, and a considerable number of periodicals.

Greater space for the engineering departments, and better arrangement has been afforded through the removal of physics classes to the new building on the West Campus. Appearance of Asbury building has been improved through some renovation and through the addition of pictures relating to engineering subjects.

Moving pictures of various manufacturing processes are afforded students in the school several times each semester, the films being provided by the United States Department of Commerce.

UNUSUAL OPPORTUNITY

The Duke University building program has offered unusual opportunity for direct study of engineering problems; and the large area of land owned by the university provides suitable space for survey work during summer months.

Eventually the engineering division, which is included in the terms of the Duke Indenture, intends to join other schools and departments on the West Campus. Meanwhile, it is making good use of its present quarters—training youth of many states in a broad and comprehensive knowledge of engineering subjects and trying to aid in the upbuilding of a profession long renowned for the scholarship of its adherents.

Greetings '28!

It's hard to realize that we have been separated for three years. On the other hand, it does seem an awfully long time since we've seen each other; so let's drop everything else and give Durham another break, if only for a few days. This new campus is worth seeing, too, and I'll give you my word that it will be worth the trip from anywhere to be here then. And, being the A-1 class, we should have, and will have, the best crowd here for commencement. Besides all that, it will be open season for swapping stories, old and new, and that's enough for me. So here's hoping to see each and every one of you at our headquarters in the Union on the West Campus from the seventh till the tenth of June.

JOHNNIE BURWELL,
President Class of '28·

Seventy-Ninth Commencement Program 1931

Reunion Classes 1931 Commencement—'71, '76, '81, '86, '91, '96, '01, '06, '11, '16, '21, '26, '28, '30—Alumni Day, Tuesday, June 9th

SUNDAY, JUNE 7

8:30 P.M. Baccalaureate Address. Page Auditorium.

MONDAY, JUNE 8

10:30 A.M. Meeting of the Alumni Council. Alumnae Room, Woman's College campus.
Meeting of the Alumni Council. Room 206, University Union.

1:00 P.M. Luncheon for Members of Board of Trustees, the Alumnae Council and Alumni Council. University Union.

3:00 P.M. Meeting of Board of Trustees. Administration Building.

8:30 P.M. Wiley Gray Contest—Graduating Orations. Page Auditorium.

TUESDAY, JUNE 9

9:00 A.M. Registration of Returning Alumni and Alumnae Begins at Alumni Headquarters, University Union. Members of Reunion Classes—'71, '76, '81, '86, '91, '96, '01, '06, '11, '16, '21, '26, '28, '30—assemble at Class Headquarters in the Union.

11:00 A.M. Commencement Sermon by the Reverend Robert Norwood, Pastor of Saint Bartholomew's Episcopal Church, New York City. Page Auditorium.

1:00 P.M. Alumni and Alumnae Luncheons.—Tickets $1.50. Greetings from Twenty-fifth Anniversary Class.

6:00 P.M. Alumni Class Dinners.

9:00 P.M. Reception in Honor of the Class of 1931 and Returning Alumni and Alumnae.

WEDNESDAY, JUNE 10

10:45 A.M. Academic Procession: Members of Board of Trustees and Faculty, Persons Receiving Honorary Degrees, Members of Graduating Class, Graduate Students, form line.

11:00 A.M. Commencement Address by Doctor Huston Thompson, Former Chairman of the Federal Trade Commission, Washington, D. C.

5:45 P.M. Reception by the Faculties in Honor of Parents and Candidates for Degrees. Woodland Stage, Woman's College campus.

7:25 P.M. Sunset. Lowering of the Class Flag.

Some Commencement Information For Alumni

Alumni and Alumnae, whether members of reunion classes or not, are expected to attend the 1931 Commencement and participate in the Alumni Program.

The Alumni Office, University Union, will maintain an Information Bureau at all times for your convenience.

Tickets for the Alumni and Alumnae Luncheons may be purchased in advance through the Alumni Office.

Alumnae returning for these reunions may secure accommodations on the Woman's College campus, but reservations must be made by June 1, as the rooms available for alumnae are limited.

An effort will be made to provide rooms on the campus for alumni who desire such accommodations, provided notice is given the Alumni Office by June 1. No definite assurance of any particular number of reservations can be made. An advance notice will be absolutely necessary.

All reservations for men will be on the University campus and those for women on the Woman's College campus.

Bird Life In the Duke Forest Provides An Interesting Study

A Natural Sanctuary for Bird Life Exists Here as Effectively as If It Had Been Specifically Set Apart for That Purpose—Five Classes and 125 Different Birds
Found in the Forest

THE Duke Forest provides an interesting study, not only from the standpoint of tree life but of bird life as well. Feeling that readers of the REGISTER would like to read something of the bird life in the forest, the editor requested Mr. Ernest Seeman, manager of the Duke University Press and a man who has made a study of birds for many years during his spare time, to write something on the subject. The result is the following informative and entertaining article.—EDITOR.

* * * *

WITH THE exception of game birds and a few of the larger waterfowl, there are probably almost as many varieties of feathered inhabitants occurring today in the Duke Forest as when young Daniel Boone passed along its northern boundary en route from Pennsylvania to the Yadkin Valley. For as its generous acres include a diversity of dense timberlands, pine barrens, swamps, meadows, and several miles of New Hope Creek's meandering length, a natural sanctuary for bird life exists here as effectively as if it had been set apart for the purpose.

Five classes of birds occur in those portions of Durham and Orange counties embraced in the Duke domain, viz.: all-the-year-'round residents, or non-migratory species; migrants from the south that arrive in spring to summer here; migrants from the north that arrive in autumn to winter here; transients that pass through in spring or autumn, tarrying but a few hours or a few days; and lastly, stragglers that rove outside their natural range, or are blown off their course by storms.

The migration of birds is one of those marvelous phenomena of Nature which offer perpetual challenge and romance to her devotees. And as our own Forest is an important stop-over for the great throng of aerial travelers, that more surely than the exodus of human migrants to Palm Beach or Maine sweeps twice annually from the Arctic Circle to the Argentine, it offers a double interest to Duke nature-lovers.

In their migrations birds travel almost wholly by night; flying usually at a height of from two to three miles, and oftentimes plainly discernible through a telescope as they cross the face of the moon. In foggy weather, however, the feathered ranks are forced to descend very low in order to follow the topography of the route; and on any such night in April or October the sharp-eared observer may distinguish, from dark to dawn, the distinctive piping calls by which the travelers keep together.

In that portion of the Durham County countryside now known as the Duke Forest one hundred and eleven species of birds have, during the past thirty years, been identified by the writer. Approximately a dozen additional species were recorded (between 1889 and 1899) by Drs. Pearson and Atkinson from in and around the Orange County end of the tract. Within the past two years, Mr. P. M. Jenness, a Duke Construction Company engineer with naturalistic leanings, discovered within the environs of the Forest two more species hitherto unknown to this section, viz.: the Pine Siskin and the Cowbird.

One of the Birds Found in the Duke Forest

The total list of birds thus far known to occur in the Duke Forest is given below. But this should be taken only as an indication of the richness of its ornithological life; for certainly we may expect many other varieties to be found there in the course of time by enterprising observers. The list follows:

pied-billed grebe	vesper sparrow
brown pelican	grasshopper sparrow
wood duck	Savannah sparrow
green-winged teal	white-throated sparrow
pintail duck	chipping sparrow
lesser scaup duck	field sparrow
bittern	slate-colored junco
great blue heron	song sparrow
little blue heron	swamp sparrow
green heron	fox sparrow
American coot	pine siskin
woodcock	towhee
solitary sandpiper	cardinal
spotted sandpiper	blue grosbeak
lesser yellowlegs	indigo bunting
killdeer	scarlet tanager
bob-white	summer tanager
wild turkey	cowbird
mourning dove	purple martin
turkey vulture	tree swallow
black vulture	rough-winged swallow
marsh hawk	cedar waxwing
sharp-shinned hawk	migrant shrike
cooper's hawk	red-eyed vireo
red-tailed hawk	yellow-throated vireo
red-shouldered hawk	white-eyed vireo
sparrow hawk	blue-headed vireo
American osprey	black-and-white creeping warbler
barred owl	parula warbler
screech owl	yellow warbler
great horned owl	black-throated blue warbler
yellow-billed cuckoo	myrtle warbler
belted kingfisher	chestnut-sided warbler
southern downy woodpecker	blackpoll warbler
southern hairy woodpecker	blackburnian warbler
red-headed woodpecker	yellow-throated warbler
pileated woodpecker	pine warbler
yellow-bellied sapsucker	yellow palm warbler
flicker	prairie warbler
whip-poor-will	oven bird
nighthawk	water thrush
chimney swift	Louisiana water thrush
ruby-throated hummingbird	Maryland yellow-throat
kingbird	Kentucky warbler
crested flycatcher	yellow-breasted chat
phoebe	hooded warbler
wood pewee	redstart*
acadian flycatcher	mockingbird
blue jay	catbird
crow	brown thrasher
red-winged blackbird	Carolina wren
meadowlark	house wren
orchard oriole	winter wren
rusty blackbird	brown creeper
purple grackle	white-breasted nuthatch
starling	brown-headed nuthatch
purple finch	red-breasted nuthatch
English sparrow	tufted titmouse
goldfinch	

* This is the species portrayed by the illustration on page 152.

Carolina chickadee	wood thrush
golden-crowned kinglet	hermit thrush
ruby-crowned kinglet	robin
blue-gray gnatcatcher	bluebird

First Commencement on New Campus of Duke University

(Continued from page 141)

pastor of St. Bartholomew's since 1925.

Dr. Norwood is a graduate of University of King's College, Windsor, N. S., did post-graduate work at Columbia University, and the S. T. D. degree was conferred on him by University of Pennsylvania. His literary attainments were recognized by Acadia University when it conferred upon him the Litt. D. degree. He is a member of the Poetry Society of America, and other literary organizations.

Duke University Editors Elected

Editors and managers of three student publications of Duke University have just been elected to head the journals for the new academic year beginning in September.

Elections were made by the publications board, which is composed of student, faculty, and administration representatives.

Edward Thomas, of Greenville, S. C., will edit *The Chronicle*, weekly newspaper, and John Minter, of Laurens, S. C., will serve as business manager.

Ovid W. Pierce, of Weldon, is the new editor of *The Archive*, literary monthly; and Alfred Williams, of Hertford, was elected business manager.

The *Chanticleer*, yearbook, will be edited by Paul Garner, of Winston-Salem, and managed by Martin Green, of Raleigh.

Duke Senior Class Names '32 Officers

James E. Mullen, of Dothan, Ala., has been named president of the senior class of Duke University. For the women's division of the class Miss Louise Moses, of Norfolk, Va., will serve as president.

Mullen is quarterback on the football team. Other officers elected are: Philip Bolich, of Winston-Salem, vice-president; James Wellons, of Smithfield, secretary; John Gamble, of Birmingham, Ala., treasurer; and Pierce O. Brewer, of Winston-Salem, representative on the athletic council.

Miss Margaret Bledsoe, of Baltimore, Md., is vice-president of the women's division of the class; Miss Florence Moss, of Mobile, Ala., the secretary; and Miss Mary Jane Tate, of South Bend., Ind., treasurer.

Some Alumni Personalities

CARL H. KING

Carl H. King, '24, of Lynchburg, Va., received his B.D. degree from Yale in 1927, also doing further graduate work at Yale and having completed his preliminary examinations for the Ph.D. degree. He is director of religious education of Court Street M. E. Church, South, at Lynchburg, being the first full time director of religious education employed by any church in the Virginia Conference. He is president of the Lynchburg Club of Duke University.

William H. Jones, '91, is director of music at St. Mary's School in Raleigh, and organist for Christ Church in that city. He is director of the Raleigh Male Chorus. Mr. Jones studied in Germany and Austria. He is a lecturer on musical subjects and is Dean of the North Carolina Chapter of the American Guild of Organists. While living in Norfolk he was Dean of the Virginia Chapter. His class will hold its fortieth reunion at the 1931 Commencement.

WILLIAM H. JONES

KADER R. CURTIS

Kader R. Curtis, Wilson, N. C., who did graduate work at Duke in 1927-28, has been superintendent of the Wilson county and city schools since 1928. For a number of years he has been a member of the Commission on Higher Education of the Southern Association of Colleges and Preparatory Schools. For the past five summers he has been a member of the staff of the Duke University summer schools. He is president of the Wilson County Alumni Club.

A Message From the Medical Profession
of the State

Was Delivered in an Inspiring Manner by Dr. Thurman D. Kitchin, President of Wake
Forest College, at the Dedication on April 20 of the Duke University School
of Medicine and the Duke Hospital

ONE OF the many "high spots" in the exercises incident to the dedication on April 20 of the Duke University Medical School and the Duke Hospital was the address delivered in behalf of the medical profession of North Carolina by Dr. Thurman D. Kitchin, president of Wake Forest College. At the request of a number of those who heard it the address is reprinted herewith:

President Few, Ladies and Gentlemen:

As the representative of the medical profession of North Carolina I have the honor and happiness to bring to you on this occasion an expression of their greeting, good will, and Godspeed in this noble enterprise. Doctors are humanitarians, and as such we welcome an institution that has for its purpose the amelioration, cure, and prevention of the ills that affect humanity. As North Carolinians, we are proud to have in our midst such a school of medicine, so strategically located, as scientifically constructed, and so ably manned. We not only welcome its coming, but we also pledge in advance our professional sympathy and coöperation to the end that the dream of its benefactor may be fulfilled and the hopes of its executives realized.

North Carolina has great pride and joy in remembering that one of her own sons founded this institution. It is a new development and expression of our own vitality and intelligence. While the whole State and all its agencies of enlightenment rejoice in this fresh flowering of our life, the devotees of our science of medicine may be allowed some distinction in the general happiness of this occasion. For what these agencies have already accomplished makes most opportune this important addition to our resources of training and service, and supplies a promising soil for the highest development of this great ministry.

In a remote corner of the State a friend has built a cabin which is all his own. It is sentineled by long leaf pines and giant oaks, and when spring comes the dogwood and redbud make a garden spot of his retreat. For it is a retreat; there it is he goes when he is burdened by care, when, as an old negro servant expressed it, "his mind is overstocked." He can lie on the ground and feel the kind and understanding earth drawing his worries and grievances out of him. He goes there for inspiration also, for he can do his best planning and thinking there. And he comes away from his woodland haunt renewed in body and spirit, with a new vision of tomorrow's tasks.

You must forgive this seeming digression and the humble analogy of the cabin in the woods to Duke University's wonderful plant and broad acres. The truth is, I never come on this campus without being impressed by the wisdom and prophetic genius of those who selected this site for this great institution. They knew that this majestic wooded expanse would have its effect on those persons whose days would be spent here—whether the man at the fountainhead of knowledge, the student, the patient in the hospital, or the stranger who makes a reverent pilgrimage to these gates. The founders of Duke University knew that in a place like this nerves would be soothed and abilities quickened. On this campus, so recently borrowed from the unbroken forest, the mystery and magic of the woodland lingers and will linger. Here indeed the spirit can ask and receive.

It may seem trite to say that the age of miracles is not past, but these words will rise to my lips when I remember that a few years ago this place was a pine forest, and the beautiful stone which speaks so eloquently from these buildings was silent in a quarry. Yes, a miracle has been wrought—yesterday a forest, today a city set on a hill; yesterday a place of silence, unbroken save by the wind in the pines and the songs of the birds, today the Mecca of leaders in medical thought. Again I say we have seen a miracle.

We have waited for the coming of the Duke Medical School, but we have not waited in idleness. We find this day the culmination of a dream, the fitting and joyous climax of years of endeavour. We have sought to create an intellectual and scientific atmosphere in North Carolina in which such an institution as this may thrive and it is our pride that we are ready to fall into step and march forward with this great new enterprise. And if we all work together, is there any limit to what we can achieve? During past generations we have been—so to speak—cracking the great mother of the sciences—Medicine—into smithereens (like petroleum in order to learn more about its component parts) making specialty after specialty. This was absolutely necessary in order to search out the inner secrets to the last remote hiding place. But we hope and believe that in this place, unfettered by tradition, unhampered by lack of resources, and with provision made in the most ideal way for intellectual and physical contacts—all under one roof—we may witness a reassembling of these now-understood parts into the original organism, medicine. In other words, we hope that analysis may be followed by synthesis. Have we not seen in the field of medicine the disjointing of the mythical jointed snake and is it not time now for us to view the spectacle of re-jointing?

There is another task before us—a task and a privilege. We hope that in this mild Southern climate the ice-bound quality, the rigidity, of the science of medicine may thaw a little, so that the patient himself who is afflicted may be considered as well as his disease. In other words, that the patients admitted to this hospital will be regarded as personalities and not merely as cases. In this way the austerity of science could be blended with the sympathetic art of medicine, with no compromise of either. Surely the heart is just as necessary as the mind in the great business of healing. And if ever a neighborhood were suited in all its phases for this dual task, this seems to be the chosen one.

You will pardon me if I lay special stress here on the greetings from the two-year medical schools of the state. In speaking for these institutions (which give the pre-medical courses and only the first two years of the medical course) allow me to say that we in no way consider that we are in competition with you. The roads we travel lie side by side, with many pleasant and mutually helpful convergences. All these roads lead ultimately to the same great and important destination—the well-being of humanity. Your road goes further than ours and climbs higher, but we are ready to cheer you on to the last mile. With such coöperation we feel that nothing but mutual good can result. We think the two-year medical school is sound theoretically and will continue indefinitely for two reasons:

1. The high standards required for medical students re-acts on the academic work most favorably. The premedical students set a high standard for other students because they have to do so. Moreover, the presence of medical students who are serious, hard workers, of maturer age, and who have frequently already obtained academic degrees, does much to stimulate academic undergraduates and give dignity and tone to campus life.

2. It is commonly recognized that the drill work of the first two years of medicine can best be done where the group of students is small and the individuals brought into personal contact with the instructors. The fact that these instructors are selected for their capacity for this fundamental teaching makes for additional satisfaction to the extent that the great centers are relieved of this burden, they are the better able to occupy their most important field of clinical research.

Upon reading Lord Macaulay's address upon his installation as Rector of Glasgow University in 1849, I am struck with the appropriateness to this occasion of one paragraph, which I shall read with necessary paraphrasing:

"There is no lack of alarmists, who will tell you that you are commencing under evil auspices. But from us—, the medical profession of North Carolina—you must expect so much gloomy prognostications. We are too much used to them to be scared by them. Ever since we began to make observations on the state of our country we have seen nothing but growth and we have been hearing of nothing but decay. The more we contemplate our noble institutions, the more convinced we are that they are sound at heart, that they have nothing of age but its dignity and that their strength is still the strength of youth. The hurricane that has recently overthrown so much that was great and that seemed durable has only proved their solidity. (Might not this refer to our own financial depression!) They still stand, august and immovable. . . . I see no reason to doubt that, by the blessing of God on a wise and temperate policy, on a policy of which the principle is to preserve what is good by reforming in time what is evil, our civil institutions may be preserved unimpaired to a late posterity, and that under the shade of our civil institutions, our academical institutions may long continue to flourish. I trust, therefore, that when a hundred years have run out, this university will still continue to deserve well of our country and of mankind. I trust that after another century we may find the spirit of the institution the same, that the one who stands here in my place may boast that the hundred years have been glorious years, that he may be able to vindicate that boast by citing a long list of eminent men, great masters of experimental science, of ancient learning. He will, I hope, mention with high honor some of the young men who are now present; and he will, I also hope, be able to add that their talents and learning were not wasted on selfish or ignoble objects, but were employed to promote the physical and moral good of their species."

May I, in closing, remind you that there was in Jerusalem in the days of the Great Physician a pool, meaning in the Hebrew "House of Mercy." It was a place of focalized pain, the five porches being crowded with the blind, the halt, and the withered. According to tradition an angel came at certain intervals and "troubled the waters," impregnating them with curative power. This, of course, may only refer to intermittent springs whose waters were supposed to have medicinal value. I mention this traditional "Fountain of Miracles" because it may be said to have its modern counterpart in the Duke University Medical School. But this does not depend on magic or supernatural cures; it goes deeper than that. A God-given science furnishes the means, and science is indeed the well-spring by which the diseased body may be cleansed and made whole. From this school hundreds of angels of mercy will go forth to heal and prevent diseases that afflict the bodies and minds of men. These humane and philanthropic souls will help the Psalmist to fulfill his words: "For with Thee is the fountain of life; and in thy light shall we see light."

Professor-Elect at Duke Scores In Recent Address

DR. HOWARD E. JENSEN, of the University of Missouri, who comes to Duke next session as professor of Sociology, delivered an address recently at the Texas Conference of Social Welfare, which has attracted much attention. Many newspapers have given wide publicity to Dr. Jensen's views as expressed on that occasion.

The following is from an article which appeared in the *Dallas News* of April 25:

"In a stirring address in which he declared that the increasing burden of philanthropy is one of the prices of human progress, Dr. Howard E. Jensen, now professor of sociology at the University of Missouri and professor-elect of sociology at Duke University, scored the high point of Friday's sessions of the Texas Conference of Social Welfare, meeting in the Baker Hotel.

"Dr. Jensen spoke at the night session, presided over by Elmer Scott of Dallas, who was introduced to the conference by Dr. W. E. Gettys of the University of Texas, conference president.

"In a penetrating analysis, Dr. Jensen declared that despite philanthropic millions, agencies and beneficiaries, a vast amount of social work remains undone. He answered the challenge that this increase in philanthropy is a symbol of social decay, of the destruction of rugged individualism and independence with the statement that increasing philanthropy is making available to the less fortunate citizens the same service that the more fortunate demand, and hence is a sign of progress.

"Just as education was once the privilege of the few and is now the right of all, Dr. Jensen pointed out,

health is now being considered the right of each member of society as the safeguard of all. This is an increased burden on society, he pointed out, but one evidencing progress.

"Dr. Jensen pointed out that the same thing is true of providing recreational facilities in crowded cities, an increased philanthropic burden that safeguards society against future burdens of delinquency. Legal aid work and public defenders, he went on, indicate society's recognition that there is a minimum right to justice as much as to health and education.

"There can be no intelligent opposition to such a program, Dr. Jensen declared, any more than there can be to paying more for better roads.

"Dr. Jensen demanded for every child the right to as good a birth as is biologically possible, and deplored the setback given the work done by the Sheppard-Towner maternity bill by Congress' failure to appropriate money for it last session."

Dean Justin Miller Talks on Topic, "Preventive Justice"

Director of the Duke Law School Declares It Is More Difficult to Interest Individuals in
Prevention Than in the Emergency Measures Involved in Law Enforcement
—Real Leadership Needed in Problem of Preventing Crime

IN A RECENT address Dean Justin Miller, of the Duke Law School, reiterated some views on "Preventive Justice," which he had expressed before the National Probation Association in annual session in San Francisco.

Dean Miller prefaced his address with the statement that this is an age of changing concepts and rapidly changing ideas. By way of illustration, he recounted an incident which occurred in the State of California in 1905. The legislature had passed a law prohibiting the use of automobiles between sunset and sunrise. The Supreme Court of California held that the law was constitutional. Since that time, he said, automobiles have become things of common usage and most people travel in them.

The probation movement, the juvenile court, probation officers, and juvenile court judges, have all come into existence within the past twenty-five years. We take for granted their propriety where they were not even thought of by most people twenty-five or thirty years ago.

The dean pointed out that the best popular definition of "preventive justice" is that it is the idea held by a particular individual of what should be done under particular circumstances which will best serve his own interest. This probably accounts for the disparaging contrast so frequently made between law and justice. He said that it was his purpose to emphasize the idea of "prevention" rather than the word "justice," in discussing his subject. This he compared to the fact that in "preventive medicine," prevention is emphasized to almost the exclusion of medicine. For this reason, "justice" is a better word for the subject than "law."

It is more difficult, said the dean, to interest individuals in prevention than it is in the emergency measures involved in law enforcement. You can turn out a good crowd at any time of the night by putting in a fire alarm. But if you announce the demonstration of a method of fire prevention only a few experts and insurance people will appear. So it is with preventive justice or with preventive medicine.

The difference, however, between preventive medicine or fire prevention, on the one hand, and the work of preventive justice, on the other hand, is that the development and successful operation of preventive methods in other fields require the interest of small groups of people, while preventive work in the field of justice is a matter which requires the intelligence, the education and the coöperation of large groups of people. Its successful operation awaits the education of the large mass of the people. Let us recognize that this may be a long process. For this reason it is all the more necessary that there should be real leadership and that that leadership should be an assertive one.

Very definite standards should be established and the importance of reaching these standards should be demonstrated to the world. In accomplishing these results, said Dean Miller, there is needed, in the first place, a real fact basis. Adequate statistics concerning the causes out of which crime arises are important. To secure these statistics will require the coöperation, guidance, and sponsorship, of all national organizations interested in any way in the subject. It cannot be done by a few enthusiastic individuals. It cannot be accomplished by a number of organizations in conflict with each other. One of the serious difficulties which confronts us is the inability of participants in different lines of work to coöperate. This has been particularly true of those working in the preventing, prosecuting, or retaliatory fields. The person who states that the way to solve the crime problem is by capturing all the criminals and putting them in jail for life has a mistaken view of the purpose of the criminal law.

What is the real purpose of the criminal law? he asked. Then he proceeded to point that there are several answers to this question. Some people say that the criminal law provides for the capture and confinement of criminals. Police and prosecutors with some fortunate exceptions, seem to hold this view. The lawyer group will tell you the purpose of criminal law is to provide a definition of crime. It may be possible to unite all the groups on a com-

mon definition of the fundamental purpose of the criminal as a provision for protecting certain interests or institutions of society, which we value. We value human life, so we have a crime defining murder, in an effort to protect human life. Whatever society values as a fundamental primary interest it will protect with criminal law.

A great many of our present-day offenses were formerly controlled by the home, the family, the church, and by social custom. We have grown to have less confidence in these institutions as controllers of human actions. The great national pastime, at present, is passing laws. Prohibition, said the dean, is one which is disturbing us very much, at the present time, but it is only one of many which have been passed during recent years.

Dean Miller stated that in his opinion the largest problem in preventive justice is the elimination of the potential criminal. He said that he realized that this statement would bring various reactions from several groups. There are those who will say that the potential criminal is a natural criminal and that it is impossible to eliminate. Then there is another group which will say that all persons are potential criminals. The solution of this problem is one for a smaller group to undertake. It must be prepared to go ahead on its own, establish facts, set up hypotheses and educate the others. But the real problem lies in eliminating the potential criminal. We must discover the potential criminals by scientific, psychological methods. Having done this we can trace the causes out of which their potentiality grew.

Among the groups of potential criminals, Dean Miller listed first the juvenile delinquents. This group he said represented a cross section of human society since we have juvenile criminals from every group of society. He believes that this group is an easily studied one, and substantial progress has been made in determining the causes of juvenile delinquency. He believes also that to the extent that the causes of juvenile delinquency are established the causes of adult delinquency may be established "because much of it comes out of and is a secondary phase of juvenile delinquency."

Then there is the group of the unemployed. There is no doubt, the dean said, that unemployment is one of the causes of crime. There are many explanations for the existence of this group. Sometimes they are physically or mentally incapacitated. This, the dean said, suggest the importance of investigating the argument of the eugenists in an effort to see whether we should attempt to eliminate hereditary incapacity. Then again they may be both physically and mentally qualified but be without the proper training. Per-

haps they may be ill adjusted because they have not been properly selected and placed.

Proceeding the dean asked the question as to what remedies should be used to cope with the unemployment situation. He said that the favorite method in America is to pick up these people, throw them in jail, overnight, fine them whatever amount of money they may happen to have, and give them a warning to be out of our county within twenty-four hours. Of course, he pointed out, the result of this policy is to make them a little more "potential."

We have an educational system designed, the dean said, in a measure to cope with the vagrancy problem. We are training children in vocations, to a limited extent. But we have discovered that about 25 per cent of all the students in the first year classes in our larger universities are failures. When these are sent home the stamp of failure is placed upon them and their courage broken at the most dangerous point in life. Obviously, there is something wrong with school methods which permit this sort of treatment, the dean said. He believed, he said, that this situation might possibly be remedied if schools were established for students who are being failed in the first year of other colleges at the present time.

In the dean's opinion, the educational system itself has contributed to our crime problem. He pointed out the fact that we have been educating our young people for more effective and intelligent participation in government and then we've allowed them to vote once in a while. Voting, he said, is a very unsatisfactory method of expressing the desire to become president —a possibility which has been offered to every one of them. When a boy goes out and holds up a filling station to get money to entertain his girl friend in a way in which she is accustomed to being entertained, he averred, all he is doing is attempting to find some romance in life. He may be a normal person, otherwise.

"Indeed," said the dean, "I doubt very much whether there is anyone in this audience who has not at some time or other committed an act which would now be defined as a crime. If this is true, you can see how futile it is to attempt to think in terms of criminals, or in terms of a method of administration which talks about putting all people in jail when they commit crimes, and keeping them there. It just doesn't work. As a matter of public economy, we could not put all the criminals in jail, anyway, the jails and penitentiaries are already full."

The dean pointed out that the church is among the forces formerly used to prevent crime. He said, however, that we have apparently largely abandoned the church. "Have we anything to substitute for the church?" he inquired.

Public opinion in the community, the dean said,

used to be a powerful deterrent of crime. Nowadays, people leave the small communities, where everybody knows what his neighbor is doing and go to the large city where they can "get away with murder." He did not know whether we shall ever reëstablish this old time social control. "This age doesn't want it," he said.

The dean thought that perhaps this means that we should overhaul our laws. It might be of great benefit, he said, to reclassify our criminal law. He felt that it would increase the respect of the people for major offenses if we eliminated from the body of criminal law the larger number of minor offenses which have been written into it during the past few years.

The dean said that he considered the motion picture to be one of the various contributing causes of crime at the present time. He did not suggest that this is true because the motion pictures teach methods of committing crime. They are giving us increased standards of living. The poor child or the underprivileged adult sees things in the pictures which he wants and cannot have. This produces a state of mind which contributes to delinquency. The dean did not suggest that motion pictures be eliminated. He said that about the only thing he could suggest was the establishing of better methods for giving people an opportunity to get the things they want.

The dean's solution for the situation, he said, comes from David Starr Jordan's definition of success—doing the thing you most want to do and doing it well enough so some one else will pay you for it. "If everyone," said the dean, "in his range of activity was able to achieve that sort of success, we should not have a crime problem."

He called attention to the fact that there would still be mental and moral defectives who would have to be taken care of by society. He does not expect a millennium, nor does he expect any substantial change in the present situation, except over a long period of time. The accomplishment of any of it calls for a group of real leaders with real vision.

A Rare Document Is Acquired In Germany by Duke University

(Continued from page 147)

that the manuscript has finally become the permanent possession of the University.

The manuscript is of a high grade vellum, written in black ink, with red and blue uncial headings for the various books, and is so exceptionally well preserved that all of the writing can be deciphered by a student

of Greek. Much of the lettering of the marginal comments is exceedingly fine and must be read with the aid of a glass but the handwriting is quite legible. The book has a monastic binding of wooden boards, with a covering of heavy black leather, and with an added protection of hand-made metal studs to keep the leather from wearing out from contact with the reading desk or pulpit. Experts date this binding as sixteenth century, or three hundred years later than the volume itself.

Inside the back cover and written on the exposed portion of the wooden board is the name of an archbishop to whom the testament seems to have belonged. It was thought at first that this might throw some light on the origin of the manuscript but the name is so illegible that it has not yet been deciphered, only the title "Archbishop" being clear enough to read. This of course is written in Greek characters. This name on the cover of the book suggests the practice by which the most famous of the Greek texts have received the names they now bear. "Codex Beza," "Codex Ferrar," and other manuscripts are named in honor of the donors who presented them to the libraries which now own them. The practice of naming manuscripts for donors is still followed.

One of the remarkable features of the manuscript is its decorative treatment. The titles of the various books are in illuminated lettering of red, blue, and gold, and are embellished with scrolls and symbolic designs, quite evidently the work of a monk who was more than a mere copyist. An example of the decorative treatment may be seen on one of the pages in which a body of reading is arranged in the shape of a patriarchal cross. Other interesting examples may be seen in the illustrations which accompany this article.

Another feature of equal interest is in the unusual order of the books. Instead of the order followed in the English Bible, James is placed between Acts and Romans, though the rest of the General Epistles are in the usual location. The text of the manuscript for the most part is that of the type which has come to be known as the "Received Text," but a number of quite different readings are to be found. These will be studied and published by Professor Branscomb.

The value of the manuscript to Duke University however, will be more than the possession of a relic It will provide an original source of research and study for students which can be found in no other library in America, and in the years to come will greatly stimulate work in this field. The University is to be congratulated on the acquisition of such a treasure, as is Dr. Branscomb upon its discovery and its bringing to this country.

Rapid Development of the Law School of Duke University

Has Been Approved By Council of Legal Education of the American Bar Association—
Previously Recognized By Association of American Law Schools—Some
Significant Facts

NOTIFICATION has been given the Duke University School of Law of its approval by the council on legal education of the American Bar Association. Action of this body makes Duke the seventy-sixth approved school of law in the United States.

Duke was previously accepted into membership of the Association of American Law Schools, and is now recognized by the two outstanding legal organizations in this country. There are 71 members of the law schools' organization.

Will Shafroth, of Denver, Colo., recently visited the Duke Law School as a representative of the council of legal education and admission to the bar, and was enthusiastic in his praise of the law school facilities here.

The development of the Duke law school in recent months has been remarkable. Its staff consists of eleven full-time professors, a lecturer, two librarians, and an assistant dean, all of whom are lawyers. Occupying an entire new building of its own, the school has every facility for the conduct of its work. Its library has a collection of 30,000 volumes treating of every phase of law and allied subjects.

Members of the law school faculty are prominently identified with the work of national legal bodies. Dean Justin Miller is chairman of the committee on survey of crime, criminal law, and criminal procedure of the American Association of Law Schools; is a member of the committee of the association delegated to coöperate with the American Law Institute; is a member of the committee on briefs and records of the Supreme Court; and is chairman of the joint committee of the American Judicature Society and the National Municipal League to make a study of judicial selection and tenure. He is a member of the round table council on wrongs of the law schools association.

Professor Marion R. Kirkwood, Professor Douglas B. Maggs, and other members of the faculty hold important posts with committees of the national association of law schools. Prof. John S. Bradway is secretary of the National Association of Legal Aid Organizations, and Prof. Alexander H. Frey is a special adviser of the American Law Institute on the subject of business associations.

Now that all the members of the Law School faculty for next session have been announced, some facts regarding the wide spread of experience which these men bring to the Duke University Law School faculty are significant.

In the first place, the list of law schools in which they received their training is an imposing one, including as it does Harvard, Yale, Stanford, California, Iowa, Oxford, Pennsylvania, Montana, and the University of Southern California. An even wider spread is represented in the law schools in which these men have taught before coming to Duke. That list includes Harvard, Yale, Columbia, Pennsylvania, West Virginia, Illinois, Oregon, Minnesota, California, Iowa, Stanford, Southern California, Cornell, Chicago, Wisconsin, Tennessee. There is no section of the country; there is no type of law school training or experience with which these men have not had contact. Moreover, included in the faculty are men, two of whom have been deans of other law schools before coming here, two of whom have been presidents of state bar associations, one president of the Association of American Law Schools, and practically all of the others have had official contacts with local, state and national associations of various kinds.

There will be eleven full-time men in the faculty, commencing with the school year in September, in addition to one lecturer, a librarian, a research librarian and an assistant to the Dean, all of whom are themselves lawyers.

Graduated In 1876

It was stated in the course of some alumni news in the April issue of the ALUMNI REGISTER that J. C. Wilborn, of York, S. C., did not graduate with the Class of 1876. This was an error, as Mr. Wilborn did graduate on June 8, 1876. The REGISTER is glad to make this correction.

Messages From Heads of General Alumni Groups

THE LAST FIRST

To the Alumni of Duke University:

The history of Alma Mater may be definitely divided into periods set off by first and last commencements. There were the first and last commencements of Normal College, the first and last commencements of Trinity College before the progressive move from Randolph County, the first and last commencements on the East Campus at Durham, and now we are upon the threshold of the last first commencement—June 7 to 10. This commencement is the first to be held on the new and permanent campus, its natural beauty enhanced by gems of Gothic architecture. Our benefactors envisioned the future and provided well for Duke's place in the educational world.

Alumni and alumnae of all eras, particularly those of the several reunion classes, are urged and expected to attend this last first commencement. The opportunity to inspect the physical plant of Duke University in its new setting is well worth the trip to Durham. The association with our classmates and friends of college days will turn back memory's pages to the "good old days" under Craven, Crowell, Kilgo, or Few. The buoyant optimism of college youth may be ours again, if only for a day, if we will return to Alma Mater's shrine during commencement and partake of the events of Alumni Day, Tuesday, June 9th. The Alumni Dinner will bring us together on that day and I invite you to join the happy throng of Alma Mater's sons on that occasion.

In future years it will be something to remember with pride—that you were at the first commencement at the new Duke University.

J. G. KORNER, JR.,
President of the General Alumni Association.

Washington, D. C.,
May 20, 1931.

THE CALL OF ALMA MATER

To the Alumnae of Duke University:

The call of Alma Mater to her daughters this year is one of peculiar interest in that the year marks the definite establishment of the Coördinate College for Women. Since the time when through the generosity of Mr. Washington Duke the institution was opened to women their opportunities have continually increased. Grateful for the past, we rejoice that in the marvelous expansion with which the university has been blessed the status of women has been given such large consideration. With equipment comparable to none other distinctly for women and no scholastic door closed to us, we can not escape a greater sense of responsibility and duty to exemplify the best in ourselves in our relationships to the institution.

As alumnae, it is most fitting and needful that we return this year to acquaint ourselves with the new physical readjustment, to revive our spiritual interests for the mutual benefit of all concerned and to think on our course for the future.

With this in view, it is to be hoped that every Duke alumna will make a special effort to attend the 1931 alumnae meeting. Our university has been most generous with us; let us assure her of our everlasting loyalty.

FANNIE KILGO GROOME,
President of General Alumnae Association.

Charlotte, N. C.,
May 21, 1931.

Duke's Baseball Team Is Again State Championship Winner

This Is the Third Consecutive Year that Duke Diamond Aggregation Has "Copped" First Honors In North Carolina—Victory Over U. N. C. Saturday, May 16, Clinches Championship—Brownlee Makes New Track Record

FOR THE third consecutive year Duke's baseball team has taken the North Carolina collegiate championship, the trick being neatly turned on May 16 when the Carolina Tar Heels were defeated 8 to 4 on the Blue Devils' home diamond. The game marked their eighth straight baseball win over the Tar Heels. Duke lost the last game of the season to U. N. C., however, by a 6-2 score.

The title-taking baseball team followed in the example of two other major sports teams for 1930-1931. In the fall the football team clinched its first state championship, and in the winter the basketball team likewise proved itself superior to competition in this state. Baseball and basketball were likewise championship sports at Duke during 1929-1930.

To round out matters, the freshman baseball team registered an additional diamond title. In track Duke attracted wide attention this spring, and the tennis team has marked up the best record a Blue Devil net outfit has shown in recent years.

Two track stars represented Duke well in the Conference meet in Birmingham, during the week-end of May 16. Brownlee, dash star, broke a 220-yard low hurdles record of long standing in his 24 seconds mark. Fulmer, another sophomore flash, placed third in the broad jump.

During the season, through May 16, the varsity baseball team lost but three games, winning eleven. Navy, Fordham, and Pennsylvania were the teams winning over the Blue Devils, all in one week during the annual trip into the east.

The tennis team has won all its matches except three with Carolina, Georgetown, and Virginia. Victories were won over State, Wake Forest, Davidson, Sewanee, Richmond University, and the Country Club of Virginia.

ROBERTSHAW, *Duke Shortstop*

Summer School For Athletic Coaches at Duke

Coach Wallace Wade will lead a summer school for athletic coaches at Duke University from July 22 to July 25, it was announced recently. All phases of sports will be taught, and high school coaches in the section are especially invited to participate. There will be no charges for registration fees, the only expense to be incurred by those enrolling being room and board at a nominal rate. Coaches on the Duke staff will teach classes and conduct the field drills, in baseball, basketball, football, track, and other sports.

Many Members of the Reunion Classes Expected to Return

(Continued from page 144)

Billings, Robert Bruce..............Durham
Bishop, Willie R..................Washington
Black, Martin L., Jr..................Durham
Blakeney, Whitford S., Jr...........Charlotte
Blackwell, Rev. H. Conrad.....Jackson, Miss.
Boswell, Thomas J...............Atlanta, Ga.
Boyer, Hugh C......................Charlotte
Bradsher, Ruth Pearl..............Unionville
(Mrs. Paul E. Griffin)
Bragg, Fredda H.......................Durham
Brewer, Henry E., Jr............Red Springs
Britt, Edgar W......................Milwaukee
Brothers, Joe J...................Kitty Hawk
Brown, William Hinton.............Charlotte
Brown, Wyatt L.................New York, N. Y.
Brown, George C....................Kannapolis
Brown, Grace E.........................Durham
(Mrs. Joseph E. Kennedy)
Burroughs, Robert Eli.......Rochester, N. Y.
Bryan, Thomas Conn.................Asheville
Buffaloe, Margaret Lois......New York, N. Y.
Buffaloe, Norman B....................Raleigh
Bullington, Louise P...................Durham
(Mrs. Max L. Barnhardt)
Bullock, Ed. J......................Goldsboro
Burgess, Claudia M....................Old Trap
Butler, Marion E.................Thomasville
(Mrs. W. R. Hinkle)
Butler, William Earl..............Glen Alpine
Bynum, Mary P......................Germanton
(Mrs. Marshall Matthews)
Caldwell, Garah B., Jr.......New York, N. Y.
Cannon, Edward Lee.......Washington, D. C.
Carter, Barney Adrian.....St. Augustine, Fla.
Carter, Fred Orr..........Sweetwater, Tenn.
Casey, Dewey W..............Southern Pines
Cassida, Janette Ella..............Burnsville
Chandler, Thelma Arline................Durham
Chappell, John Herbert................Durham
Chase, Millard Burke........Cleveland, Tenn.
Christenbury, Sadie Belle.........Mount Airy
(Mrs. William H. Foy)
Clarke, Clarence Irwin, Jr..........Reidsville
Clarkson, John Montgomery......Ithaca, N. Y.
Clegg, Charles Stevens............Thomasville
Clendenin, John P............Richmond, Va.
Coble, Ernest Frank..............Rockingham
Coker, Marvin W...........Turbeville, S. C.
Collins, John W........................Waxhaw
Coltrane, James E.............Albany, N. Y.
Cothran, Lizzie Loyde......................Efland
Covington, Helen ....Lexington
Cozart, Virginia R......................Durham
(Mrs. Herbert J. Herring)
Craven, Wesley Frank..............New York
Crowder, Nannie O.................Mayo, Va.
Crumley, Edward C.........Washington, D. C.
Crumpton, Dallas Hunter............Roxboro
Culbreth, Carl C........................Durham
Cunningham, Ernest L., Jr.....Richmond, Va.
Currie, Lum Balton.................Wadesboro
Davis, Ethel M...............Kosciusko, Miss.
Davis, John Candler..........Greenville, S. C.
Davis, Merle Holland...................Durham
Davis, William Joe......................Wilson
Deal, Harry Alexander.................Waxhaw
Deyton, Ora Texanna..........Green Mountain
Douglas, Thos. S., Jr...........Winston-Salem
Dowling, Minnie Carolina......Swansea, S. C.
Dulin, Rev. Grady N......................Canton
Duncan, Edward Ernest ....Raleigh
Elliott, Belle ....Shelby
Elliott, Vivian Augusta.......Roanoke Rapids
Ellis, Louis O., Jr..................Wilmington
Ellis, Van M.....................Madison, Wis.
Elmore, Hubert Lynwood.........Rocky Mount
Elmore, William S..................Wilmington
Epps, Will Hasford..........Lake City, S. C.
Eury, Leonard E............................Boone
Evans, Kathryn ....Durham
Everett, John M. C...................Laurinburg
Fairey, Franklin ....Durham
Faucette, Olive C..........................Durham
Featherstone, Robert B................Roxboro
Few, Frances ....Charleston, S. C.
(Mrs. F. B. Edwards)
Field, Joseph Ingram ......Washington, D. C.
Fink, Ethel Mae........................Mooresville
(Mrs. Harry Kerr Hethcox)
Frank, John P.............................Mt. Airy
Freedman, Israel ....Durham
Freeman, Ethel W..........................Ether
Frye, John O.........................Franklinton
Garrett, Glenn T.....................Rockingham
Gaskill, David W...................New Holland
Gibson, Alton B......................Laurel Hill

Gibson, Arthie Paterson ....Laurinburg
Giles, Noah Yates..................Glen Alpine
Glass, Helen Chaplin..........Savannah, Ga.
Goebel, Wallace B............Gainesville, Fla.
Graham, Annie Leo.........Washington, D. C.
Gray, Annie V.......................Henderson
(Mrs. D. L. McCallum)
Gray, Frances Macrae..........West Durham
(Mrs. Lewis Patton)
Green, Garland O........................Raleigh
Green, Virginia Lee.....................Durham
(Mrs. W. N. Cox)
Grigg, Ivey Franklin..................Lawndale
Hadley, George F....................Greenville
Hall, Evelyn ....Albemarle
(Mrs. Dent Turner)
Hall, James Prentice..................Roseboro
Hargrove, Augustus Ray...............Durham
Harshaw, Moses Richard................Lenoir
Harrington, Charlie Dew..............Marietta
Harris, Edgar Hunter..................Pinetown
Harris, George P......................Charlotte
Harriss, Robert Preston.........Paris, France
Harton, Roman ....
Hassell, Thomas Raymond, Jr.....Norfolk, Va.
Hathcock, Fannie M.......................Tabor
Hays, Hubert H........................Asheville
Heffner, Leonard T.....................Roxboro
Herbert, Chesley C., Rev.......Winston-Salem
Herring, Carl A............Birmingham, Ala.
Hester, Mary Etta............................Sims
Hicks, Gypsy Helen.......................Weldon
(Mrs. B. W. Israel)
High, Johnny Augustus.................Durham
Hill, Millard D.........................Smithfield
Hinkle, William Ralph...............Thomasville
Hodge, Marvin S.................Stonegar, Va.
Hollowell, Linwood Branton....Winston-Salem
Holmes, Frances............New York, N. Y.
Holmes, George W..............Richmond, Va.
Holt, James Thomas..................Rural Hall
Holt, William S......................Greensboro
Howell, John Hoke..................Cherryville
Howell, John Iver...................Stantonburg
Hunter, Lillian Maude........Roanoke Rapids
Hunter, Willie N..........................Durham
Hurst, Annie ....Columbus
(Mrs. Charles B. Trammel)
Hurst, Irene.........................East Durham
(Mrs. Lawyer J. Rainey)
Ivey, Leon S...............................Hickory
Jackson, William F...........Roanoke Rapids
Jarrett, Louis E............... Cherryville
Jerome, Rev. Robert L...... New York, N. Y.
Johnson, Edna Y..........................Durham
Johnson, George B........Newport News, Va.
Johnson, Harvey B......................Charlotte
Johnson, Robert T....................Burlington
Jones, Dewey ....Gum Neck
Jones, Lillian J..........................Pink Hill
(Mrs. R. J. Smith)
Jones, Sarah W...................Holland, Va.
Jones, Terrell A...........................Polkton
Judd, Edith Lucille.........................Varina
(Mrs. Harold Edwin Parker)
Kale, James E.............................Waxhaw
Keistler, Kemmett Lee. ....Cornelius
Kellam, William Porter...........Emory, Ga.
Knight, Alton J.............................Durham
Kodama, Kuninoshin........Hiroshima, Japan
Kyles, Alpheus A.....................Morganton
Land, Augusta C............................Hamlet
Land, Virginia L............................Hamlet
Lathan, Samuel H.........................Monroe
Latta, William M...............Alexandria, Va.
Leach, George T., Jr..................Washington
Lee, Fulton, A...................................Dunn
Lewis, Harriet P.............Cleveland, Ohio
(Mrs. John Harry Sikes)
Lim, Chang Choon..........Hongkong, China
Little, Frank M...................Winston-Salem
Liu, Chester ....Hankow, China
Long, Mary Willie............................Bostic
(Mrs. S. C. Gettys)
Love, Roderick Milnor....................Durham
Lunsford, Mildred Edna Ruth........Durham
Lynn, Clarence L................East Durham
Lyon, Margaret ....Creedmoor
Mabry, Shelly Adams...................Norwood
Mangum, Euva ....Chadbourne
(Mrs. Paul H. Brown)
Martin, Thomas Leon.........Roanoke Rapids
Mason, Sara Catherine..................Monroe
(Mrs. J. Ray Shute)
Masten, Irvin Fleatwood..............Charlotte
Maultsby, William DeVance.........Maysville

Maxwell, William C......................Durham
May, William Henry......Fredericksburg, Va.
Mayer, Walter Brem....................Charlotte
McAnally, Louise R........Long Island, N. Y.
McArthur, Elbert Roy..................Greenville
McCanless, Frank H.............Stoney Point
McCutchen, Ernest P.....................Durham
McDaris, Earl C.................New York, N. Y.
McFee, Earl Puette..........New York, N. Y.
McKee, Lynn C................Norristown, Pa.
McLaurin, Raymond Kelly........Fayetteville
McLean, John Silas.......................Raleigh
McLellan, Mack H........................Concord
McNairy, N. Dalton....................Greensboro
McSwain, Annie Ruth.........Winston-Salem
Mecum, Cora Elizabeth..................Durham
Meehan, Joseph Lee..................Lumberton
Mehaffey, Joseph Hawley...............Newton
Midgett, John B..........................Hillsboro
Miller, Osborne H.........................Concord
Millner, Evelyn Lyman..............Senoia, Ga.
(Mrs. Louis C. Nolan)
Mock, Jacob P.............................Pfafftown
Moore, Harold P..........................Asheboro
Moore, Henry L..............................Wilson
Morris, Clara Elizabeth..................Oxford
Morris, Pattie C............................Matthews
Morse, Thomas D., Dr..........Winston-Salem
Moss, Charles Otey.........................Wilson
Moss, Paul E..........................Forest City
Mulholland, Vester M....................Durham
Murdock, William H......................Durham
Murray, Anna Ruth........................Durham
(Mrs. Anna Murray McCarson)
Myers, Ford M........................Thomasville
Neal, Joseph W., Jr.................Walnut Cove
Newton, Harriet Louise....Washington, D. C.
Norris, Henry T..........Framingham, Mass.
Oakley, Kenneth H........................Roxboro
O'Brien, Asa W...........................Goldsboro
O'Kelley, James F..........................Durham
Owings, Louis J....................Owings, S. C.
Owens, Charles F................Baltimore, Md.
Owens, Fredrick C..........................Durham
Parker, Harold E..............................Varina
Parker, Thomas Wiley................Laurinburg
Patterson, James Alton, Jr.........Mount Holly
Peeler, Olin C...............East Orange, N. J.
Pegram, Charles H..............Winston-Salem
Perry, Haywood Arnold.......Willow Springs
Perryman, Franklin Columbus......Lexington
Petrea, James Farrell......................Concord
Phifer, William Bates........................Raleigh
Phillips, June Alton......................Asheboro
Pickens, Stanton W.................Atlanta, Ga.
Pierce, Frank Grainger....................Weldon
Plyler, Leroy ....Durham
Poe, Bertha Mae.............................Durham
Porter, Eloise ....Washington, D. C.
Potts, Julia ....Greensboro
(Mrs. E. H. Strickland)
Powell, Benjamin E........................Durham
Raiford, Ralph P............................Kinston
Rainey, Lawyer J.....................East Durham
Raper, Hugh Maxton........................Gilkey
Raper, S. Eugene.........................Lexington
Rasberry, Robert P..........................Kinston
Ratliff, Evelyn Pauline.......Hartsville, S. C.
(Mrs. W. Dorse Bryant, Jr.)
Ray, Taylor ....New York, N. Y.
Reade, Ethel G...............................Durham
Reel, Mabel ....Bayboro
Renfro, Carl B................................Durham
Ricks, Thomas Nelson....................Florence
Rich, Millard Rowland...............Chadbourn
Rigsbee, Edith L.............................Durham
Roane, Samuel R............................Whittier
Robbins, John W........................Greensboro
Roberts, Elizabeth H.......Washington, D. C.
(Mrs. Edward Lee Cannon)
Roberts, Ivon L., Rev........................Hickory
Rock, Lester E................................Durham
Rose, Estelle C........................Hot Springs
(Mrs. Russell H. Caudill)
Rowe, Sara Louise..................................
Rowland, Claude Roger........Richmond, Va.
Rowland, William Burns..................Durham
Royal, Adelaide E...........................Durham
(Mrs. Algernon Noell)
Royal, Samuel B..................St. Louis, Mo.
Ruark, Sam W..............................Raleigh
Salmon, Sarah Evelyn.........Winston-Salem
Sawyer, Chas. F..............................Durham
Sawyer, Henry Curtis..........................Eure
Sawyer, Lucy Ermine........................Tabor
Schoen, Charles Carroll, Jr...New York, N. Y.

Scott, Hugh A.......Guatamala City, C. A.
Scott, Samuel Harrison.......Durham
Scruggs, Lewis.......Hickory
Sechriest, Walter S.......Ensley, Ala.
Sessoms, Louise Elizabeth.......Durham
Sharpe, Ivey Lawrence.......West Hickory
Sharpe, William G.......Elm City
Sharpe, William N.......Salisbury
Shaw, Thetus Alonzo.......Lafayette, La.
Shipp, Fred H., Jr.......New Bern
Shooter, Sara Carolyne.......Morganton
(Mrs. A. A. Kyles)
Shuster, Chas. W.......Newton, Pa.
Sink, Robert F.......Savannah, Ga.
Skidmore, Mary I.......Albemarle
Slaughter, Frank Gill, Dr.......Roanoke, Va.
Smaw, Louise A.......Raleigh
Smith, Earle.......Arcadia, Fla.
Smith, H. Preston.......Wake Forest
Smith, William H.......Durham
Smith, William Harley.......Cary
Smith, Wm. Hall, Jr.......Durham
Snipes, R. E.......Snow Hill
So, Fung Hui.......Canton, China
Spann, Herbert Alva.......Anderson, S. C.
Spence, Mattie G.......Rocky Mount
(Mrs. James R. Simpson)
Spencer, Sarah.......Atlanta, Ga.
(Mrs. Banks Otis Godfrey)
Stott, William E.......Wendell
Straughan, Isaac W.......Walkertown
Strawbridge, Rev. Ishmael J.......Manns Harbor
Strother, Eura V.......Durham
Sullivan, Raymond E.......Ellaville, Ga.
Sumrell, Charlotte R.......Ayden
Suther, Leonard B.......Chile, S. A.
Taylor, Howard Foard.......Alma
Thompson, Loy Frank.......Shelby
Thompson, Lillian.......Wadesboro
(Mrs. Alfred A. Johnson)
Thornburg, J. Lewis, Rev.......Statesville
Tiller, Hiram B.......Cleveland, Va.
Timberlake, Casper Hill.......Lexington
Tippett, Augustus Crawford, Rev.......Ramseur
Trammel, Charles Buford, Rev.......Columbus
Townsend, Folger L.......Lenoir
Tucker, Thomas Lionel.......Madison
Turner, Dorcas Tomlinson.......Auburn, N. Y.
(Mrs. W. A. Tucker)
Twaddell, William Freeman.......Madison, Wis.
Underwood, Carl H.......Gastonia
Umstead, Carrie Moyle.......West Durham
Underwood, William A., Jr.......Asheboro
Usry, Sterling Thomas.......Kershaw
Vest, Samuel A., Jr.......Baltimore, Md.
Vickers, Lina Ruth.......Durham
(Mrs. Sidney Webster)
Vincent, Chas. P.......Weldon
Wallace, Mary.......Star
Walston, Robert Edward.......West Durham
Ward, Edith Mary.......Durham
(Mrs. Robert G. Deyton)
Warlick, Joe S.......Newton
Watts, Hessie.......Winston-Salem
Watts, Mary G.......Williamston
Weaver, Albert R.......Corinth, Miss.
Weaver, A. Kenneth, Jr.......Corinth, Miss.
Weaver, Edward Cicero.......Emory, Va.
Weaver, Wade.......Emory, Va.
Westmoreland, Larry E.......Canton
White, Margaret W.......Franklinton
Whitesides, John Edward, Jr.......Caroleen
Wilkinson, Albert Alexander.......Durham
Wilson, Lillian Thomas.......Durham
Williams, Lina Elizabeth.......Elizabeth, N. J.
(Mrs. Roland M. Stoneback)
Williams, Madge.......Portsmouth, Va.
(Mrs. Joe Ewton)
Winters, John E.......Springfield, Mass.
Wolf, Dora.......Oxford
Woolf, Hyman, A.......Mebane
Wright, Samuel Ernest, Rev.......Warrenton
Wyche, John Ira, Jr.......Weldon
Zachary, Ralph H., Jr.......Brevard
Zimmerman, Helen B.......Lexington

CLASS OF 1928

Abernethy, L. Ethel.......Durham
Adams, Edna Gertrude.......West Durham
Adams, Sam H., Jr.......Winston-Salem
Alberson, Hazel Stewart.......Black Mountain
Alexander, Welborne Excell.......Connelly Springs
Apperson, Juanita Irvyn.......Durham
(Mrs. H. E. Cratch)
Anderson, Kathleen L.......Raleigh
Atwood, Theodore Winslow.......Boston, Mass.
Austin, William Edwin.......Durham
Avera, Jane Kennon.......Smithfield
Avera, Nicholas Allen.......Smithfield
Avett, Margie Louise.......Norwood
Aycock, George Williams.......Pantego
Bailey, James Allen.......Greer, S. C.
Bailey, Margaret Anne.......Mt. Airy
(Mrs. Owen A. Cheatham)
Barfield, Marion Lee.......Clarks
Barrow, Seth Tyson.......Farmville
Baucom, Frances Irene.......Durham
(Mrs. J. Bryant Hinnant)
Beall, Lawrence Lincoln.......Richmond, Va.
Beasley, Wilbur Morris.......Apex
Beavers, Edward Parker.......West Durham
Bethea, William Carlisle.......Lumberton
Biggerstaff, Frank Malcolm.......Forest City
Biscoe, Alvin B.......Charlottesville, Va.
Bishop, Lyman Henry.......New Jersey
Bivens, Harry Lee.......Charlotte
Bivens, Haskelle March.......Monroe
Bivins, John Franklin.......High Point
Blackwell, Margaret.......Durham
(Mrs. James William Michaels)
Blades, Lemuel Showell, Jr.......Elizabeth City
Blalock, Verona.......Hickory
Boggs, Pearl.......Cherryville
Boring, William Neal.......Gibsonville
Boses, Erven.......Charlotte
Bowles, Charles Phillips.......Guilford College
Bowling, Jackson Murrell.......Richmond, Va.
Boyd, James Emory.......Athens, Ga.
Bracey, H. G.......San Luis Potosi, S. Lp. Mexico
Bradsher, Kenneth Arthur.......Hurdle Mills
Brantley, Bishop Lee.......Raleigh
Brawley, Pressley.......Mooresville
Bridgers, Mamie.......Durham
Brinkley, Hiram E.......Elk Park
Browning, Alan, Jr.......Hillsboro
Brock, Miss Ikie.......Berea
Brock, Yetta Deane.......Winterville
Brogden, Fannie Elizabeth.......Kinston
Brothers, John Able.......New Orleans, La.
Bunn, Robert E.......Hertford
Burch, James Charlie Horton.......Durham
Burgess, Dorothy.......Old Trap
Burnett, James Grady.......McCullers
Burnette, Hilda Long.......Tarboro
Burt, Lucy Perry.......Louisburg
Burwell, John Cole, Jr.......Warrenton
Bush, Mrs. L. E.......Columbus, Ohio
Butler, Algernon Lee.......Clinton
Bryan, William Homer.......Durham
Cable, James Erwin.......West Durham
Cale, John Carter.......Philadelphia, Pa.
Cannon, David Primrose.......Washington, D. C.
Carlton, Eugene W.......Durham
Carpenter, Virginia Magnolia.......Gibsonville
Carpenter, C. Ray.......Stanford University, Calif.
Carson, Thomas Coleman.......Johnson City, Tenn.
Carstarphen, Bryant Bennett.......Austin, Texas
Carter, James Lois.......Charlotte
Cash, Leon.......Winston-Salem
Cartwright, Ella Zona.......Roxboro
Chappell, Joseph Marvin.......Hertford
Chandler, Helen Deane.......Gastonia
Chandler, Lillian Alice.......Raleigh
Chandler, Minnie Elizabeth.......Dobson
Chesson, Rosagray.......Forest City
(Mrs. B. T. Jones)
Chrisco, Edwin.......Badin
Christian, Nell Elizabeth.......Durham
Coke, Cecil Edward.......Durham
Clapp, Clarence, Jr.......Newton
Clapp, John Garland.......Greensboro
Cliff, Jack Bernard.......Durham
Colclough, Otho Thomas.......Grand Rapids, Mich.
Cole, Cary Colgate.......Durham
Cole, Hazel Lewis.......West Durham
Coleman, T. Rupert.......Durham
Conrad, Thomas Edward, Jr.......Salisbury
Copeland, Mary Rhodes.......Powersville
Couch, Georgia Anne.......Durham
Couch, Leon V.......Walstonburg
Covington, George Emerson.......Rockingham
Covington, Hugh Buie.......Lawndale
Cox, Alma Clarice.......Durham
Cox, Grace Winnifred.......Durham
Cranford, Evolyn Herman.......Ashboro
Cranford, Robert Joshua.......Charlotte
Craven, Irene.......Lakeland, Fla.
(Mrs. W. N. Covington)
Craven, Margaret Elizabeth.......Candler
Crews, John Madison.......Walkertown
Cross, Alice Roane.......Durham
(Mrs. John H. Tyler)
Cross, Lethia Elizabeth.......Durham
Crowder, Myrtle Catherine.......Buie's Creek
Crowder, Willie E.......Zebulon
Culp, Harry R.......Spencer
Davenport, Harry Lefler.......Horse Shoe
Davidson, Ruth B.......North Birmingham, Ala.
Davis, Emma J.......Roanoke Rapids
Davis, James Hunter.......Smithfield
Deaton, Laura Bell.......Durham
Dickerson, Norma.......Hurdle Mills
Dill, Sara Meadows.......New Bern
Dillon, Willard Julius.......Greensboro
Dimmette, Joel Walter, Rev.......Swepsonville
Doub, Isabel Bryan.......Concord
Drake, William Caswell.......Norfolk, Va.
Dulin, Albert L.......Charlotte
Dunlap, Tyler Bennett.......Wadesboro
Dunn, M. Charles.......Bahama
Durham, Wade Hadley.......Siler City
Eads, Joseph Albright.......Mount Airy
Eanes, Tom Shell, Jr.......Lexington
Eatman, Edward Laughton.......Bailey
Edmonson, Irma Iris.......Charlotte
Edwards, Christine Dixon.......Hookerton
Edwards, Earl Bowling.......Elk Park
Edward, Eugene Wahab.......Spartanburg
Elliott, Lalin.......Stedman
Elmore, George Roy.......Gastonia
Enos, Alvin Bush.......Rosman
Ervin, Paul R.......Durham
Ervin, William Howard.......Durham
Erwin, John Wesley.......Troutman
Farmer, Mollie Arnold.......Newman, Ga.
Faucette, Viola Winfield.......Franklinton
Ferguson, Hazel Elizabeth.......Waynesville
(Mrs. John C. Troy)
File, Laura Faye.......Shelbyville, Mo.
(Mrs. Lawrence E. Hauser)
Fincher, Orville Taylor.......Derita
Finley, Frank Alfred.......Upper Montclair, N. J.
Fischer, Debryda.......Hazelwood
(Mrs. Hubert Liner)
Floyd, William Carlton.......Fairmont
Flythe, Simon S.......Jackson
Forrest, Robert Oswin.......Hillsboro
Forest, Vincent M.......Hillsboro
Foscue, Kathleen.......High Point
(Mrs. R. W. Slate)
Fulford, William Edward.......Farmville
Fulgham, Monroe Glenn.......Kenly
Fulp, George Vance, Jr.......Kernersville
Fulton, Fred Bryant.......Independence, Va.
Fulton, Kenetta.......Independence, Va.
Fuquay, Mary Evelyn.......McCullers
Gaines, Dr. Francis P.......Lexington, Va.
Gambill, Robert Mack.......Crumpler
Gamble, Richard Lee.......Summerfield
Garrand, Nellie Combs.......Durham
Garren, Martin Thompson.......Hendersonville
Gasque, Boyd Randolph.......Rockingham
Gibbons, Guy A.......Colfax
Gilbert, Lorena Mary.......Minneapolis, Minn.
Glasson, Mary Embry.......Hertford
Glenn, Charles Edward, Jr.......Durham
Goldberg, Harold Leon.......Hickory
Goldwin, Richard H.......Chicago, Ill.
Grady, Nancy Ida.......Asheville
Grant, Elizabeth Carter.......Seaboard
Grant, Minnie Spencer.......Jackson
Graves, John Wendell.......Danville, Va.
Gray, Jarome Christopher.......Gray Court, S. C.
Greene, James Dewitt.......High Point
Greene, Zula Mae.......Roxboro
(Mrs. Cooper Lawson)
Greer, George W.......Chase City, Va.
Griffin, Mabel Jeanette.......West Durham
Grigg, Benjamin Fred.......Gastonia
Grisgalsky, Phillip I.......New York, N. Y.
Grose, James Chalmus.......Belmont
Guffy, Edith.......Durham
Gwyn, Henry W.......Norfolk, Va.
Hale, William Robert.......Rocky Mount
Hamilton, Charles Everette.......Gastonia
Hamlin, William Thomas.......Charlotte
Hanchey, James LaFayette.......Rocky Point
Hardaway, Elizabeth Annie.......Newton Grove
Hardin, Lawrence Legare, Jr.......Camden, N. J.
Harris, Arthur Parker, Jr.......Albemarle
Harris, Frank.......Henderson
Harrison, Edith.......Dallas, Texas
Hart, William Albert.......Weaverville
Hatcher, Robert Lee, Jr.......Winston-Salem
Hatchett, Edward Wallace.......Durham
Hayes, Walter Harold.......Roanoke, Va.
Haywood, Ernest Lee.......Parkton
Helms, Rufus Marshall.......Goldsboro
Hendricks, Dr. Burton J.......Garden City, N. Y.
Herman, Alice Palmer.......Asheville
Hester, Hanselle Lindsey.......Durham
Hodges, John Kennedy.......Columbia, S. C.
Hoey, Isabel Young.......Shelby
Holton, Alfred Jesse.......Philadelphia, Pa.
Holton, Clarence Spencer.......Bahama
Hood, George Franklin.......Durham
Holl, Dr. Frederick John.......Buffalo, N. Y.
Holloway, Nellie Ward.......Durham
Houck, George Fielder, Rev.......Marion
House, Robert Lee.......Durham
House, Ray Weldon.......Statesville
Howell, Hugh Johnson.......New York, N. Y.

Hubbard, Leila Jeannette.........Fayetteville
(Mrs. H. R. Ashmore)
Huckabee, Ellen Harris..............Durham
Hudson, Thomas B.........Washington, D. C.
Hughes, Eugene Anderson, Jr.........Durham
Huneycutt, Dorothy Louise.........Albemarle
Hunter, James Magrauder, Jr.........Kittrell
Hunt, Joseph Marvin, Jr..........Greensboro
Isenhour, Lewis D.......................Colon
Israel, Kate Ola.....................Durham
Ivie, Allan D., Jr..................Leaksville
Jacobs, William Ralph................Wilson
James, Clarence Henry......New York, N. Y.
Jarvis, Mariana E..............Swan Quarter
Jenkins, Wilbert A..............Ithaca, N. Y.
Jennett, John Robert...............Goldsboro
Johnson, Avery Bennette...........Morganton
Johnson, Dr. Charles B............New Bern
Johnson, Charlie Benjamin.........New Bern
Johnson, Horace ....Ahoskie
Johnson, Robert Glenn...............Kipling
Johnston, Robert Meredith...........Durham
Jones, Beryl ....Durham
Jones, Dr. E. Stanley........New York, N. Y.
Jones, Faylene ....Durham
Jones; Garland ....Sylva
Jones, Linwood Thomas..............Nashville
Jones, Marvin..........................Statesville
Jones, Nely Grogan............Ridgeway, Va.
Jones, Otho Jerone, Jr..............Charlotte
Jones, Wilford G.............Winston-Salem
Jourdan, Charles Herbert............Durham
Judd, Glenn B...............Nashville, Tenn.
Kelley, Douglas Leffingwell.........Wilmington
Kelley, Rhoda A.................South Mills
Kellner, Abe Nathan Hugh....Greenville, Miss
Kelsey, Mary Alida.............Chicago, Ill.
Kennedy, Joseph Everette.............Durham
Kidd, John Grydon............Baltimore, Md.
Kiker, Rev. Frank Wade.............Webster
Kirkpatrick, Charles A...A. & M. College, Miss.
Kirkpatrick, Rebecca......New Haven, Conn.
(Mrs. W. V. Sprinkle)
Koonce, Thelma ....Wilmington
Kramer, Willis Krebs..............Norfolk, Va.
Kumro, Donald M..............Buffalo, N. Y.
Kornegay, George Cobb.............Goldsboro
Lagerstadt, Kenneth R........Maryville, Tenn.
Lambeth, Benjamin Green..........Greensboro
Laws, Thelma ....Oxford
Leathers, Jessie Lewis...............Durham
Lee, Virginia J........................Kingston
(Mrs. Errol P. Dixon)
Leight, Edwin Milton.............Walkertown
Lemmond, Harry ....Lawndale
Leonard, Elmo Lee..................Lexington
Lewis, Bruce Gordon................Whiteville
Lilley, Catherine Celia..............Gatesville
Litaker, Charles Hart......Charleston, W. Va.
Little, Mary Evelyn..................Salemburg
Lively, Roy Hamilton........Portsmouth, Va.
Logan, Leslie E............Morristown, Tenn.
Lohr, Elida Emmeline ....Vale
Lotspeich, Jane Inman......Harrogate, Tenn.
Lotz, John Henry, Jr.........Red Hook, N. Y.
Love, William S., Jr............................Troy
Lumpkin, Donald Richard ....Durham
Lyon, Annie Hazel.....................Durham
Lyon, John Fleming..................Durham
Lyon, Theodore W.............Newton, Iowa
Lyon, W. Thomas.....................Northside
Malick, Clay P...............New York, N. Y.
Malone, Eva Candler..................Durham
Maness, Madison Ward..............Shallotte
Martin, Lucille ....Mocksville
Massey, Clara Odessa...........Wilson's Mills
Matheson, Joe K.......................Troutman
Matheson, Malcolm Randle...Hightstown, N. J.
Matthews, Claude Bonson...Jamestown, N. Y.
McAnnally, Mary Duncan.........High Point
McCain, John Walker.........Rock Hill, S. C.
McConnell, Kathleen ....
McDougle, Edwin Andrew....Black Mountain
McDowell, Gladstone Wadley.........Durham
McKeel, Columbus A...............Greensboro
McKenzie, Elizabeth C.....Timmonsville, S. C.
McKenzie, Willie Nelson, Jr.............Gibson
McKnight, James Earl............Mooresville
McLaurin, Ausby Martin...........Fayetteville
McLean, Jack Harold................Asheville
McLendon, Evander, Jr..................Ashton
McNair, Roderick Evander............Maxton
McNeill, Ruth Leslie..........................Bass
Mercer, Rev. Seymour Esmond, Jr....Elm City
Midgette, Mildred ....Rich Square
Milburn, Kennedy Abbott..San Antonio, Texas
Miller, Clyde, Jr..........................Old Fort
Miller, Charles Hinson............Greensboro
Mills, Catherine ....Henderson
(Mrs. Thomas Skinner Kittrell)
Mitchell, Charles Greyson.............Ahoskie
Mitchell, Irene Swindell.............Old Trap
Mitchell, John Howard..........Ardmore, Pa.
Moffitt, Walter V............New York, N. Y.
Mott, Ralph H.................Mahaffey, Pa.
Morgan, John Wesley..................Wilson
Morgan, William Roney, Jr...Philadelphia, Pa.
Morphew, Glenn Gilbert.............Jefferson
Morris, William Edward, Jr.......Tulsa, Okla.
Mullen, John Chaiborne............Drum Hill
Myers, Fred Weaver...................Lenoir
Myrick, Annie Lou.....................Durham
(Mrs. Eugene M. Oakley)
Nance, Annie Jenannette............Asheville
Nanny, Cecil Charles.........Black Mountain
Nelson, Richard Alonzo...............Grifton
Newbold, William Bradsher...........Raleigh
Newman, Sallie Banks...............Leesburg
Newsom, Dallas Walton, Jr....Montclair, N. J.
Nichols, Henry Archie............Chicago, Ill.
Old, Logan Edwards, Jr.........Richmond, Va.
Oliver, Annie Laurie..............Greensboro
Orfield, Lester Bernhardt.......Lincoln, Neb.
Palmer, William Anderson....New York, N. Y.
Parker, Edith Gibbons..............Gastonia
Parker, Louise Pierce.................Wilson
Parrish, Julia Paschall..........Summerfield
Pegram, Allen Wooseley........Winston-Salem
Pennington, James Claiborn.......Thomasville
Peterson, James Galloway.........Greensboro
Petty, Clara Octavia...................Durham
Phelps, William Augusta..........Greensboro
Phillips, Cynthia Celene....Independence, Va.
Phillips, Fletcher O..............Saint Charles
Pierce, Sterling Blackwell............Weldon
Pigford, James Marvin...............Wallace
Pitts, Otis Hampton..............Glen Alpine
Poe, Marguerite ....Charlotte
(Mrs. Galen Elliott)
Pope, George Edward.................Durham
Pope, Samuel Allen...................Farmville
Potter, Robert D...............New York, N. Y.
Priest, Thomas Allen...................Durham
Purdy, Lewis William.................Oriental
Quern, Noreen M. (Miss)...........Charlotte
Rabinowitz, Selma ....Durham
Randall, Eunice Annette........West Durham
Reed, Minthorne Woolsey...Mt. Clemens, Mich.
Regan, Rev. James Robert......Stumpy Point
Rogers, William Stewart.....Cambridge, Mass.
Register, James Harmon...............Clinton
Rhine, Mrs. J. B.........................Durham
Rhine, Joseph Banks ....Durham
Rigsbee, Daphne C.......................Zebulon
(Mrs. Ector P. Hayes)
Ross, Claiborne Carl....................Durham
Rogers, Harvey Daniel.......Lake View, S. C.
Rosser, Mary Hazel.........................Erwin
Rogers, Roy Reuben ....Richfield
Ross, Lottie Dail ....Wilson
(Mrs. W. J. Davis, Jr.)
Rowland, Ronie ....Henderson
Royster, Marvin Everett............Lincolnton
Ruark, Robert James........Philadelphia, Pa.
Rudasill, Dwight Armstrong...Baltimore, Md.
Rumbold, Dean Warren.......Richmond, Ky.
Russell, Marcia Rachel.....New Haven, Conn.
(Mrs. L. L. Gobbel)
Satterwhite, Alonzo Vance.....Memphis, Tenn.
Saunders, Carl E.................Augusta, Ga.
Saunders, Harry Ivory..............Beaufort
Saylor, John H..........................Durham
Sawyer, Roma Elizabeth.............Durham
Scanlon, Mary Cuyler ....Erwin
Scarboro, Anita ....Greensboro
(Mrs. C. C. Swaringen)
Schallert, Dorothy Amaryllys...Winston-Salem
Schurman, Louise Ann.....Washington, D. C.
Scoggins, Nellie W.......................Durham
(Mrs. Dante Germino)
Sellers, Earl S....................Danville, Va.
Sigman, Hartwell Alonzo, Jr......Atlanta, Ga.
Simpson, Guy H., Jr..........................Vass
Simpson, William Hays...............Durham
Shaw, Thomas J., Jr..................Greensboro
Shaw, William Henry....................Durham
Sherrill, Edith ....Cornelius
Sherrill, Mildred ....Cornelius
Shuford, Norris V....................Gastonia
Shumaker, Ralph B................Chapel Hill
Shutt, Thomas Samuel.................Bahama
Sloan, Louise Withers...............Davidson
Smith, Emma Lee......................Salisbury
Smith, Juanita ....Concord
(Mrs. Dewey L. Maness)
Smithwick, Ollie Macon.......Greenville, S. C.
Smithwick, O. S..............Greenville, S. C.
Smithwick, Rena M................Burlington
(Mrs. E. G. Overton)
Snuggs, Henry Lawrence............Durham
Snyder, Charles Walter, Jr......Winston-Salem
Solomon, Elizabeth ....Durham
(Mrs. Winfrey Bramham)
Southerland, John Sprunt.............Faison
Spears, Virginia ....Beaver Creek
Speed, William Moore, Jr......Baltimore, Md.
Sronce, John Alexander.............Asheville
Stables, Frederick Kenneth ....Durham
Stallings, Robert Archibald......Stantonsburg
Stevens, Frederick Albert.....Brockton, Mass.
Stone, Elsie L............................Durham
(Mrs. Otho L. Barbee)
Stott, James Henry ....Wendell
Stamey, Eunice ....Baltimore, Md.
(Mrs. W. M. Nicholson)
Stanfield, William Wesley......Richmond, Va.
Stevens, Edith Virginia........Richmond, Va.
Strother, Melissa Adela..............Durham
Stuart, Mary Wylie......................Monroe
Sugden, Herbert W.....................Durham
Sullivan, Jordan James...........Chipley, Ga.
Swain, Louis Hall.......................Maxton
Swofford, Thomas Hoyle, Rev.........Gastonia
Tabor, Mary Louise....................Spencer
Tandy, Mrs. G. W.......................Durham
(Eloise Lloyd)
Taylor, Ethel May.......................Kinston
Taylor, Homer Paxton ....Siloam
Taylor, John Ivor........Salt Lake City, Utah
Teague, Marvin D. Russell..........Siler City
Thomas, Phillip Langston.........Chapel Hill
Thomas, Ralph Newton.......Portsmouth, Va.
Thompson, Bessie Virginia.........Bellarthur
Thompson, Emerson M...................Garner
Thompson, Wilbur Carlisle ....Greensboro
Thompson, Heywood C.......New Orleans, La.
Thompson, Lily Frances............Pittsboro
(Mrs. William L. London)
Tilley, Ernest Clarence...............Durham
Tilley, Umstead D..............West Durham
Towe, Fannie ....Rocky Mount
Tower, Ralph Burnett...........Ithaca, N. Y.
Townsend, Mary G........................Lenoir
Truesdale, James Nandin............Durham
Turnipseed, Marie ....Charlotte
Turnipseed, Maurice W.......Fitzpatrick, Ala.
Tuttle, Frederick B............Columbus, Ohio
Tuttle, Robert Gregory......Port Deposit, Md.
Tyler, Marie ....Durham
Tyson, Henry G.............................Wilson
Underwood, Clarence Edward........Gastonia
Umstead, Dan Holloway..............Durham
Vann, Norbert Lynwood........Newton Grove
Varner, John Wesley.............Thomasville
Vaughan, Alma Lee...........Winston-Salem
Vause, Rubie Jackson............Rocky Mount
Walston, Forrest Davenport..........Conetoe
Walters, Murray Moses..................Wilson
Walters, Sam W.......................Siler City
Warlick, Annie Selma.......New York, N. Y.
Warlick, Katherine Rebecca........Greenville
Waters, Audley Alexander...Milledgeville, Ga.
Watson, Harriett Durham............Durham
(Mrs. Jack Newton)
Weaver, Charles Clinton, Jr...New York, N. Y.
Weber, John M.................Danville, Va.
Webster, Clarence Davis.............Madison
Wescott, Mabel Isabelle..................Shiloh
Wesley, Lucy ....Macon, Ga.
Weston, Neila Elaine...........Swan Quarter
Wheeler, Thomas Peace..................Hamlet
Wheeler, William Felix........Columbia, S. C.
White, Gladys Ruth.................Rock Hill
Whitley, Melvin Preston............Goldsboro
Whitener, Annie Elizabeth.........High Point
Wilkerson, Maxine ....Durham
Wilkerson, Oscar Floyd................Durham
Williams, Charles Alexander.......Warrenton
Williams, Rachel Kramer.......Elizabeth City
Winstead, Leylah Opal..........Augusta, Ga.
Woody, Robert Hilliard................Durham
Wright, Samuel David...................Gibson
Yates, Selvia Alton.................Greensboro
Yearby, Norman Lunsford............Durham
Young, Edwin Tyler..................Henderson
Zachary, Margaret Elizabeth....Sanford, Fla.
Zigler, Benjamin H.................Greensboro
Zimmerman, Herman W............Lexington

CLASS OF 1930

Abbott, Charles Francis......New York, N. Y.
Acey, Rev. A. E.................Chatham, Va.
Albright, Clara ....Henderson
Alexander, Luther Leon.............Charlotte
Allen, Thomas E., Jr....................Durham
Allison, Clyde C..........................Parkton
Andrews, Chester James.............Durham
Andrews, Robert Skeen.........Mount Gilead
Arons, Edward Maurice......New York, N. Y.
Ashburn, Karl Everett.....Fort Worth, Texas
Ashworth, Rufus Charles..San Antonio, Texas
Balch, Clifford Perry...........Mansfield, Pa.
Barker, Ralph ....Durham

Barnes, Joshua Chesyer........Hampton, Va.
Barnes, Roger Lewis.............Black Creek
Barnette, Texie Elizabeth...............Roper
Basler, Roy P.......................Durham
Bashaw, James Alfred............Greensboro
Baucom, William Mathew...........Durham
Baughman, Burr Hastings.....Hendersonville
Baum, Milford Joseph........Milwaukee, Wis.
Beall, Edward Leyburn........Richmond, Va.
Beall. M. Grogan....................Durham
Bell, Florence Evelyn...........Rocky Mount
Bell, Lila Mae.........................Raleigh
Bell, Lucille Frances....................Dunn
(Mrs. R. A. Haddock)
Belue, Jean Shelton...............Charlotte
Bennett, Margaret Virginia....Blackstone, Va.
Best, Farquhard Smith.......New York, N. Y.
Best, Charles Graham.........Lexington, Ky.
Biggs, Charles Grayson..........Norfolk, Va.
Biggs, William Campbell............Goldston
Bidwell, A. McLean, Jr....Middletown, Conn.
Blalock, Claiborne C.................Durham
Book, Abraham B....................Asheville
Boothe, Elther Louise................Durham
Bolles, Charles P., Jr...............Wilmington
Boren, Allen Cook..................Greensboro
Brawley, Jeter B.....................Durham
Bridgers, Arthur D.....................Raleigh
Brintle, Joe Howard.............White Plains
Brock, Theron B......................Memers
Brooks, Lena T.........................Durham
(Mrs. Jack Dowling)
Brinegar, Earl Cleveland......Lewistown, Pa.
Brown, Robert Lloyd.................Cullowhee
Brecker, Gerhard Karl Odolf Otto....Germany
Budd, William Pritchett...............Durham
Burch, Donald Harden..................Durham
Burns, Roy Herman..........Harrisburg, Pa.
Bynum, Vivian.......................Chapel Hill
(Mrs. Kermit Perkins)
Caldwell. Todd R....................Lawndale
Campbell. Marshall A..................Durham
Capps. Fred H............Chattanooga, Tenn.
Carruthers, Archie B...............Greensboro
Carson, Frank Eugene................Asheville
Carter, David L....................Fayetteville
Carlton, Elizabeth....................Durham
Carroll, James Ellwood...............Durham
Cash. Tom, Jr..................Winston-Salem
Caudle, Mack Ivey........................Erwin
Caudle, James N.................Greensboro
Cheek, Vernon Roy....................Durham
Clutz, Garland William................Durham
Coker, Dr. D. R..................Hartsell, S. C.
Coleman, Frances Rebecca...........Durham
Conner, Charles Arthur..............Charlotte
Colvard, Virginia.....................Champion
Conley, Mabel..........................Monroe
Connally, Julian...............Brooklyn, N. Y.
Copeland. Bessie......................Parkton
Cotton. Albert Henry...................Durham
Councilor. Harry A.....................Durham
Cousins, Reba Thurston...............Durham
Cox, Louisa.............................Harmony
Crawford, Phillip Howell, Jr.........Pinehurst
Crabtree. Catherine Brown............Durham
Crosier, Vernon Earl.........Zanesville, Ohio
Cummings, Ellen Isabel.........Trinidad. Colo.
Cunningham, Bertha....................Willard
Currin, Frances Lelia........Fuquay Springs
Davis, Mrs. Harvey L...................Durham
Davis. Thomas J. J., Jr........Richmond, Va.
Dawson, Flora Belle.............Kobe, Japan
(Mrs. J. D. Stott)
Dean, Dayton...........................Durham
Doob. Leonard William......New York, N. Y.
Dowd, Rozzelle............................Dunn
Dry. Verne Ritchie....................Richfield
Dunn. Osborne Eugene...............Clinton
Dunn. William Lyman, Jr............Pinetops
Dunkle. Margaret Robert...Brookhaven, Miss.
Edwards. Montgomery Roger....Rutherfordton
Essey, Eugene Kinsmon............Greenville
Elias. Edna Kilgo......................Durham
Exum, Janie Herring.................Snow Hill
Fawcett, Fernley Goddard..Washington, D. C.
Farriss, Carter Wood...............High Point
Ferrell, Henry C......................Gastonia
Felmet, Lucian Holt....................Asheville
Ferrell. Clara Mae......................Durham
Fearing, Robert...................Toledo, Ohio
Fearing. William Lumsden........Chapel Hill
Finch, William Atlas, Jr.................Wilson
Fink, Dorothy R............Hopkinsville, Ky.
Finley. Robert C.......Upper Montclair, N. J.
Fly, James Garrette............Summer, Miss.
Ford, Grover Mancil...........Mt. Berry, Ga.
Forbes, Bannett........................Durham
Fortescue. William Nicholas..........Durham
Foushee, Frances Leake......Philadelphia, Pa.
Fowler, Horace W......................Durham

Frick, Harvey Lee......................Durham
Fussell, Elizabeth.....................Stedman
Funk, Rev. Sherwood W....Charleston, W. Va.
Garner, George Lee...................Durham
Gathings, James Anderson........Chicago, Ill.
Garrard, Hubert Lee..................Durham
Gibbons, John P., Jr....................Hamlet
Gibson. Martha...................Winston-Salem
Giles, Douglas C...................Detroit, Mich.
Gillikin, Paul Edward.........Richmond, Va.
Gibson, William Marion.......Baltimore, Md.
Gillock, Emmie May..........Lula, Mississippi
Glover, Bettie Annie....................Raleigh
Godard, James McFate...............Durham
Gordon, Ella Margaret..........Winston-Salem
Goode, Hal Kelly..........Rutherford College
Grimes, Hal Alma......................Lexington
Groom, Wilbur.......................Creedmoor
Grady, Paul........................Chicago. Ill.
Graupner, Ernest Arnold......New York. N. Y.
Groce, William Harolds...............Durham
Green, Margie Holden..............Warrenton
Gunnin, Carroll Edgar..........Chicago, Ill.
Gudger. Harry F........................Candler
Guice, Rev. John A.....................Edenton
Hackney. James F....................Lexington
Harris, Sarah Alice.............Murfreesboro
(Mrs. Robert Glenn Sewell)
Harvey, Charles Wesley.............Greenville
Hassell, John Linwood, Jr..........Greenville
Hales. John D............Temperanceville, Va.
Hampton, Patsy Catherine............Durham
Hampton, William Beams, Jr......Rougemont
Hancock. Evelyn.......................Durham
Hanes, J. Chrisman.........Cambridge, Mass.
Harbison. Annie C. Elizabeth..........Drexel
Harris, James Wesley.................Durham
Hathaway, Offie Lemuel............Middlesex
Hatley, Raymon C....................Oakboro
Hauss, William Cecil................Lincolnton
Haynes, S. E...White Sulphur Springs, W. Va.
Hepler, Joseph Madison.....Philadelphia. Pa.
Herman, Benjamin......Mount Vernon, N. Y.
Henry. Sibyl............................Durham
Hill, Thomas Spencer............Indian Trail
Hix. Mary Elizabeth..................Durham
Hicks, Charles Glenn, Jr..............Raleigh
Hippert, G. W., White Sulphur Springs, W. Va.
Holler, Rev. A. C................Union, S. C.
Hough, Mrs. Marie Craig.......Jackson. Miss.
Holcomb, Hugh Lindsay..........Mount Airy
Holland. Mary Gattis...............Smithfield
Hobgood, Virginia Lucille............Oxford
Holt, Gladys............................Durham
Holt, Isaac Terry.........................Erwin
Horton, Dan W., Jr....................Durham
Hostetler. Lynn. Williamson.........Troutman
Howie, Henry Gilmer.................Charlotte
Huffman, Norman Ara.................Durham
Hughes, Arthur J., Jr......Schenectady, N. Y.
Hughes, Mary Sue...........Roanoke Rapids
Hull, Oscar Coleman...................Norlina
Huneycutt. Francis Ruth...........Albemarle
Jennette, Dorothy......................Tarboro
Jennings, William H...............Rocky Mount
Johnson. Theron Ruffin.............Smithfield
Jonas, Charles M.......................Lenoir
Johnson. Rev. Hugh H.........Virgilina, Va.
Jones, John Bunyan...................Durham
Johnson, Delacy.....................Thomasville
Johnson, Hazel..........................Ingold
Judd, Violette C.........................Garner
Keever, Nancy.......................Lewisville
Kent. Alfred A., Jr......................Lenoir
King, George Benjamin, Jr...Philadelphia, Pa.
Kistler, Henry A.......................Charlotte
Knight, Thomas Baker......Birmingham, Ala.
Kramer, Joseph Perry..........Elizabeth City
Lake. Charles E..........Mount Vernon, Ohio
Lassiter, William C.....................Durham
Lavinder, Peggy....................Hurley, Va.
Laws, Ross..............................Oxford
LeGette, Melva Iris...................Salisbury
Leggett, Julia............................Erwin
Lewis, William..........................Durham
Lewis, William W........................Roper
Lee, Margaret B.......................Lincolnton
Leonard, Reuben L..............Coalinga, Calif.
Lewis, Essie........................Manns Harbor
(Mrs. Ishmael J. Strawbridge)
Lipnard, Homer Luther........Philadelphia, Pa.
Lindroth. Dr. Eric...................Atlanta, Ga.
Little, Thomas Marshall.............Wadesboro
Long, Harry Glenn....................Gastonia
Long, John Henry............Unionville, S. C.
Long, Mrs. J. O...................Rocky Mount
Lucas, John Paul, Jr...................Raleigh
Luquire, Claude Rufus...............Durham
Lyon, Frederick M...........Charlottesville, Va.
Lynch, Haywood Eugene...........Goldsboro
Markham, Katherine.........Fuquay Springs

Martin, Bessie Mary...................Durham
Martin, Ruth Elizabeth........Richmond, Va.
Mason, Frances.........................Durham
Mattox, Alvah Stone...........Glade Hill, Va.
Max, Charles......................Newark, N. J.
Matney, William Lee, Jr..........Waynesville
Mazza, Peter A......................Rome, Italy
Matheson, John Lewis..Riverhead, L. I., N. Y.
Matthews, Charles Eden...............Jackson
McCaslin, B. H....................Stanton, Tenn.
McCracken, Frank Webb..............Sanford
McCracken, Maude....................Durham
McCurdy, Harold Grier................Durham
McDonald, Florence Isabel.........Lillington
McFayden, Elizabeth Anne............Durham
McGary, George Nelson..............Durham
McKay, Patsy..........................Durham
McIntire, William Calhoun............Raleigh
McDuffie, Duncan Cameron.........Asheville
McGlaughon, William Pleasant....Wilmington
McEwen, Noble Ralph.................Durham
Mebane, William Carter, Jr........Chapel Hill
Melton, Claude Hood......St. Petersburg, Fla.
Melton, Harold Sumner.......Granite Quarry
Miller, Hugh H..................Winston-Salem
Miller, Mabel Watson...........Wythville, Va.
Miles, James Gaylord.............Bristol, Va.
Mintz, Max..........................L. I., N. Y.
Mouzon, Dr. Edwin D.................Charlotte
Moore, Susie Pearl.....................Durham
Montgomery, Elizabeth..............Four Oaks
Moore, Margaret M................Forest City
Moore, Vertie N........................Aurora
Morgan, Katherine....................Durham
Morris, Esther Jane.........New York, N. Y.
Mullen, Edith Kells....................Durham
Nelson, Rev. W. Fletcher..........Greensboro
Neagle, Margaret Louise..............Durham
Neal, Joseph William............Walnut Cove
Nichols, Charles Eugene.............Asheville
Norris. Jesse Allen.....................Raleigh
Noland, James Hugh................Waynesville
Ogden, Warren Cox...............Mobile, Ala.
O'Keef, Herbert Edward, Jr...........Durham
Pappalardo, William Vito..East Orange, N. J.
Parker, James Saunders......Brooklyn, N. Y.
Paschal, Lawrence Hughes.............Glendon
Patterson. John Clarke..............Fulton, Mo.
Peeler, Melvin A...................Washington
Peoples, Marjorie.....................Durham
Pearce, Lucille Dowell................Durham
Pegram, William Allen..................Hamlet
Pettigrew. Richard Campbell..........Salisbury
Phillips, Katherine M...........West Durham
Pickett, William Clifton. Jr...........Lexington
Pierce, William Alexander, Jr...........Weldon
Pitts, Ralph Simpson................Glen Alpine
Porter, Thomas William, Jr.............Franklin
Poole, Mrs. Rob Lem..................Durham
Porter, Charles W....................Greenville
Priepke, Rudolph Julius...............Durham
Presson, Irene..........................Monroe
Pritchett, William Kendrick...........Durham
Rae, Lily Thomas......................Hillsboro
Ragan, Doris Lee..................East Durham
Rawlings. Sleby Moore.........Emporia, Va.
Reade, Helen...........................Durham
Reams. James Monroe.......Kingsport. Tenn.
Reynolds. Rufus Wiley................Durham
Ritter, William Johnson.......Winston-Salem
Riddle, Floyd Lacy..................Fayetteville
Robertson. Archibald Thomas, Jr....Pinehurst
Ross, Oscar Eugene, Jr................Durham
Robertson. Emma Laura..............Princeton
Robbins, Paul Nelson.................Siler City
Roberts, Frank C...................Buffalo, N. Y.
Robertson. Samuel Berry.....Greenville, S. C.
Rodwell, Mary Frances.............Warrenton
Rousseau, William Hamilton, Jr.......Durham
Rowe, James B......................Chapel Hill
Royster, Mary Elizabeth........Bessemer City
Royall, Margaret Louise.................Dover
Royster. Fred Stovall...............Henderson
Rubinstein, Nathan..........New York, N. Y.
Ruark. Henry Gibbons.....New Haven, Conn.
Ruddick, Ronald...................Ardmore, Pa.
Russell, Rev. Leon.....................Hatteras
Runion, Fred Cole.....................Asheville
Sanders, Emerson Thompson..........Durham
Sadler, Alton Guy.................Rocky Mount
Safrit, Robert W., Jr...............Mount Gilead
Savage, Joe A., Jr......................Durham
Salyer, Bryce Floyd..........Jersey City, N. J.
Sample, Richard L..............Fort Pierce, Fla.
Seagrove, Ann.................Washington, D. C.
(Mrs. Arnold W. Hurt)
Separk, Joseph Gray..................Gastonia
Sechriest, Vernon Franklin......Rocky Mount
Self, Lela................................Durham
Shaw, John Sidney................Orlando, Fla.
Shull, Horatio S., Jr.................Easton, Pa.

Simpson, Ola ....Durham
Sink, John Moyer, Jr....................
Sink, John Moyer, Jr................Greensboro
Sloan, Virginia.................Hopewell, Va.
Smith, Charles Moody...............Durham
Smith, Kathleen ....
Smith, Robert Sidney........Madrid, Spain
Smith, Paul Wesley................Charlotte
Smith, Leroy Richards........Portland, Conn.
Smith, Sarah Olive..........Winston-Salem
Snidow, James F........Princeton, W. Va.
Snyder, Clyde William.........Winston-Salem
Spence, Mary Elizabeth............Goldsboro
Spivey, Nell ....Norfolk, Va.
Stanley, James Savage, Jr............Charlotte
Stearns, Richard ....Maywood, Ill.
Stearns, Thomas Suddard....Cambridge, Mass.
Stacy, Oliver Hicks................Wilson
Stine, Will Arthur, Jr......Rock Hill, S. C.
Stone, William Alexander...........Charlotte
Strader, Chester Virgil.............Greensboro
Stuckey, Alan Patterson........Tampa, Fla.
Starling, Mary Lee................Durham
Strickland, Hector Paul................Dunn
Strickland, Gladys Mae..............Durham
Suther, Mary Irene................Concord

Suitt, Viola Elizabeth................Durham
Sutton, Joseph Sam.............Fayetteville
Swaringen, Johnson Harold.......Albemarle
Taylor, Henry Wallace..........Greensboro
Teague, Everett Reid............Atlanta, Ga.
Thompson, Lucie Elizabeth.........Creedmoor
Thorpe, David H............Haverford, Pa.
Thorpe, Robert Patterson.............Airlie
Thrift, Charles T., Jr................Durham
Tilley, Pauline ....Erwin
Trueblood, Paul Graham.............Durham
Turner, James Moody.........Brooklyn, N. Y.
Tuttle, Magruda Hill.........Annapolis, Md.
Tyson, Thomas David........Baltimore, Md.
Umberger, Anita ....Mount Pleasant
Umstead, Annie Piper..............Durham
Underwood, Verna Mary..........Mt. Holly
Upchurch, Mrs. Otho Carlton.........Durham
Varner, Robert Milton............Concord
Vaughn, Leo Bernard, Jr....Lynchburg, Va.
Vaughan, William Thomas......Virgilina, Va.
Wade, Alice Lee..................Henderson
Warren, Allen Linwood..............Durham
Waters, William Edison.............Plymouth
Walston, Fred Ivan...................Johns
Ward, William Thomas.............Coleridge

Washam, Conrad Cline................Durham
Weatherby, Carlton E............Waynesville
Weatherspoon, Everett ....Durham
Webster, James H................Stokesdale
Welton, Mabel L....................Durham
  (Mrs. Oscar Eugene Ross)
White, W. A................Patterson, N. J.
Whitener, Katherine ....Hickory
Wilson, Max Clyde........Washington, D. C.
Wilbur, Dr. Ray Lyman...Washington, D. C.
Weingarten, Harold Charles.. Brooklyn, N. Y.
Werber, William Murray..Takoma Park, Md.
Widenhouse, Arthur Lee............Concord
Widenhouse, Edna ....Durham
  (Mrs. David W. Carpenter)
Williams, Calvin U.................Jackson
Wingate, William James, Jr.......Lincolnton
Womack, Rev. C. P................Scotts Hill
Womack, John Gamble.............Durham
Womble, Susan ....Raleigh
Wright, John Monroe............Mount Olive
Wyche, Alma Virginia.............Durham
Wynne, Walter, Jr................Durham
Yaminishi, Kimiko..............Kobe, Japan
Yarbrough, Edward Pass.............King
Yokeley, Hayes Hampton......Richmond, Va.

Gray Manufacturing Co.
Flint Manufacturing Co. No. 1
Flint Manufacturing Co. No. 2
Arlington Cotton Mills
Myrtle Mills, Inc.
Arkray Mills, Inc.

Spinners and Doublers Fine Combed
and Double Carded

LONG STAPLE PEELER and EGYPTIAN YARNS

20's to 120's

Put up in all Descriptions for the Following Industries:

ELECTRICAL	WEAVERS
LACE	KNITTERS
MERCERIZERS	THREAD

MAIN OFFICE:	DIVISION OFFICES:	GENERAL SALES OFFICE:
Gastonia, N. C.	Boston	New York City
	Philadelphia	
	Chicago	
	Chattanooga	

It keeps them so
MILD and FRESH!

THERE'S more real mildness in a Camel, *sealed fresh* in the new package, than in any cigarette you ever smoked!

CAMELS

TIGHT-SEALED IN MOISTURE-PROOF CELLOPHANE

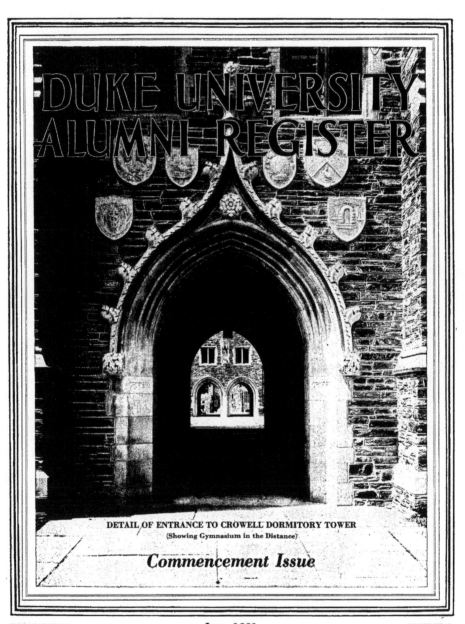

DETAIL OF ENTRANCE TO CROWELL DORMITORY TOWER
(Showing Gymnasium in the Distance)

Commencement Issue

VOLUME XVII   *June, 1931*   **NUMBER 6**

Duke University Alumni Register

(*Member of American Alumni Council*)

Published at Durham, N. C. Every Month in the Year in the Interest of the University and the Alumni

Volume XVII   *June, 1931*   Number 6

In This Issue

Editor and Business Manager .... HENRY R. DWIRE, '02

Assistant Editors .... ELIZABETH ALDRIDGE, '24
ALBERT A. WILKINSON, '26

Advertising Manager .... CHARLES A. DUKES, '29

TWO DOLLARS A YEAR   20 CENTS A COPY

ENTERED AS SECOND-CLASS MATTER AT THE POST-OFFICE AT
DURHAM, NORTH CAROLINA

COMMENCEMENT ISSUE

The present issue of the ALUMNI REGISTER is devoted to Commencement matters. Most of the Commencement addresses are given either in full or in part, and various features of the occasion are reported in as much detail as possible. Alumni are sure to want to preserve this 1931 Commencement Issue for future reference. It makes interesting reading now, but it will be valuable from the standpoint of historical information in the years to come.

THE JULY ISSUE

The July issue of the REGISTER will contain a number of special features. Duke University developments along various lines will be treated in this issue and in addition to the articles there will be some photographs of unusual interest. The cover design, incidentally, is expected to be especially attractive.

Don't fail to read the July REGISTER.

THE EDITOR.

SCENES AT SEVENTY-NINTH COMMENCEMENT

(1) Parents of graduates entertained at reception given by University faculties at Woodland Stage. (2) Dean Wannamaker and Dr. Huston Thompson. (3) Academic procession. (4) Dr. W. A. Lambeth, Dr. R. L. Flowers, and Dr. Daniel Poling. (5) Nine candidates for the Doctor of Philosophy degree. (6) Graduates of the School of Law. (7) The commencement chorus leading the procession. (8) A few of the 230 new Bachelors of Art. (9) Class presidents Yarbrough and Pratt present flag to Dean Wannamaker following traditional lowering exercises.

Duke University Alumni Register

Volume XVII   *June, 1931*   Number 6

Editorial Comment

A COMMENCEMENT TO BE REMEMBERED

Never before have Duke alumni and alumnae registered in such numbers as this year for a Commencement occasion.

A total of 720 were present at the Alumni-Alumnae Luncheon.

And alumni representation at all features incident to the Seventy-Ninth Commencement established a new record.

The absence of President Few because of illness was deeply regretted but there were many commendatory remarks concerning the constructive work of the administration, work that was apparent to every Commencement visitor.

One of the best things about the whole Commencement was the fine spirit in evidence on every hand.

Members of many of the older classes were present and these joined loyally with the alumni of a later day in devotion to Alma Mater—"the same Alma Mater in a new setting."

Everybody was talking, not simply about the past, but about the great era of constructive service ahead of the new Duke University.

And all were showing a commendable willingness to coöperate in the task of increasing and intensifying that service.

UNUSUAL ADDRESSES

It is not often that Commencement addresses are of such a timely and compelling nature that they are quoted and re-quoted in publications of various kinds.

As a matter of fact, very often such addresses are simply looked upon as a necessary part of a Commencement occasion without a great deal of attention being directed to them.

Certainly this was not true of the Duke Commencement addresses of 1931.

Dr. Daniel A. Poling's masterful sermon on "Three Imperatives of Faith," and Honorable

Huston Thompson's discussion of present-day problems, particularly his advocacy of a World Trade Tribunal, and Professor McDermott's treatment of the subject, "Enduring Values," have been productive in a very unusual degree of newspaper comment.

These addresses were immediately recognized, not as simple platitudes like many that are delivered from time to time on Commencement occasions, but as real messages of vital importance at a time when real messages are needed.

A few more Commencement deliverances of the Poling-Thompson-McDermott type would cause such utterances to be taken more seriously than they often have been in the past.

KEEP THEM

The little alumni programs and booklets of alumni information distributed at the Alumni-Alumnae luncheon have been sent to the entire list of those whose names appear in the office files as souvenirs of the occasion.

They should be preserved as condensed handbooks of alumni information.

If you have lost or misplaced yours, other copies may be had from the Alumni Office as long as they last.

SEND IN THE ADDRESSES

A particularly interesting feature of the Alumni-Alumnae Luncheon at Commencement was the induction into the General Association of the members of the 1931 Senior Class.

They are welcomed most cordially into the Alumni Association of Duke University.

Just one request of these new members:

Will you not send in your permanent addresses just as soon as you know what they will be?

If you do not know yet what the permanent address is to be, kindly give the address you have, and the change can be made later when the additional information is available.

ONE OF THE BEST OF ALL

Information is being published from time to time of gifts to the Duke University Library, some of them by alumni.

This provides one of the best possible answers to the question that former students often ask themselves:

"What can I do for Duke University that will be a permanent contribution to the institution at this vitally important period in its career?"

Books of the right type are a permanent asset of the very best kind for any institution.

They will go on performing their service of usefulness to future generations.

They will make real contributions to the lives of those who read them in a variety of ways.

We read some time ago of an institution whose graduates were being asked to give as soon after graduation as possible at least one book of permanent value as part of a class collection, the various classes participating in friendly rivalry to see which could provide the most valuable collection.

There is an idea in that plan that might be adopted to advantage by other institutions.

NOT TOO EARLY TO BEGIN

It is not too early for officers of local alumni groups to be thinking of ways in which they will observe "Duke University Day" on December 11, 1931.

The actual plans need not be made yet, of course, but serious thought on ways and means of making the best possible use of the occasion can well be indulged at this time.

And please remember this:

The Alumni Office is anxious to assist you in making the best possible use of your dinner meeting on "Duke University Day."

Do not hesitate to communicate with us early, and as often as necessary, about the plans and purposes for the day of your local group.

AN INNOVATION

The Coaching School to be conducted by Coach Wallace Wade at Duke University from July 22 to 25 inclusive will be an interesting innovation.

And the ability of Coach Wade and his assistants in this line of work gives every reason to believe this summer school for high school coaches will be a permanent feature of the summer activities at Duke from now on.

This is another Duke University enterprise in which the alumni may render valuable assistance.

Just simply bring the matter of the coaching school to the attention of some high school coach of your acquaintance who might be interested.

And remember that no tuition or registration fees are being charged.

A GOOD EXAMPLE TO FOLLOW

An alumnus of Duke recently sent to the REGISTER a whole typewritten page full of interesting information about other alumni.

Who will be the first to follow this very excellent example?

It is needless to say that this would provide many alumni a simple and effective way of aiding Alma Mater through the REGISTER.

THE DUKE PRESS

One Duke University institution about which many alumni know entirely too little is the Duke University Press.

It is the intention of the REGISTER to give them information from time to time regarding this useful agency.

The Press is preparing to issue during the next few months at least six new books that are sure to attract much attention.

Nearly 50 volumes have already been issued.

Four scholarly periodicals in different lines are regularly published, some of these being circulated in European countries as well as in the United States.

If you are interested in knowing more about the Press, just address the REGISTER or the Press a request for information on the subject.

First Commencement on New Duke Campus is Outstanding

Large Attendance, Exceptionally Good Addresses, Fine Spirit in Evidence Everywhere
Combine to Make Occasion One Long to Be Remembered—
Closing Features on Woman's College Campus

TO THE series of academic successes, formal openings and house-warmings that have marked Duke University's first year on its new campus, the seventy-ninth commencement, June 7-10, proved a crowning event, judged not merely by its novel setting and the unprecedented size of the graduating class, but by the enthusiasm and interest manifest by the hundreds of "old grads" who joined the trek "back home."

One thing the 1931 finals clearly indicated: Wherever Alma Mater moves will be "home sweet home" to her host of sons and daughters. Pride in the University's growth and achievements and a desire to keep pace with the rapid strides she is making to the forefront of American education brought alumni and alumnae to the new campus in record numbers.

While there was much for which to be gratified in connection with the graduation program, there was one regret felt by all who participated in the signally successful series of events, the inability of President W. P. Few to take part in the exercises which he had not only anticipated but in the planning for which he had such a large part. It was not until two days before the finals were to begin with the baccalaureate address that President Few definitely found that illness would prevent him from opening the first commencement on the new campus. He has almost completely recovered now.

Speaking for President Few, Prof. Malcolm McDermott, of the Duke School of Law, addressed the graduates on Sunday evening on "Enduring Values,"

President Few and Commencement Speakers

PRESIDENT WILLIAM PRESTON FEW   DR. DANIEL A. POLING   HON. HUSTON THOMPSON

making an impression upon a large audience that will last. Here, for the first time, Page Auditorium was the scene of a Duke commencement exercise. The soft folds of the stage curtains and the deep blue sky-cyclorama made a beautiful background for the brilliance of the academic hoods of the speakers and other principals on the programs, and for the large vested chorus rendering the musical numbers.

Scores of relatives and friends of the graduates were on hand for the first event of commencement, but Monday brought the first suggestion of the throng that was to pour through the Gothic doors of the university on Tuesday and Wednesday. On Monday morning highly successful meetings were held by the Alumni and Alumnae Councils, in which interesting reports were read and worth-while business transacted.

Miss Anne Garrard, of Durham, presided over the meeting of the alumnae officers, and Vice Chairman Charles H. Livengood, of Durham, presided at the alumni council session. The annual report of Henry R. Dwire, director of public relations and alumni affairs, was read at the meetings, in which he cited the active interest throughout the year by alumni in the affairs of the University and their own organizations. At noon the two councils met with the Board of Trustees at a luncheon in the Union. The annual commencement session of the trustees was held in the afternoon.

WILEY GRAY ORATIONS

Speaking on "The Outlook for Peace," Joseph Gaither Pratt of Winston-Salem, won the Wiley Gray medal on Monday evening, competing with three other senior orators in Page Auditorium. Three alumni and trustees served as judges: Dr. Dred Peacock, High Point; Don S. Elias, Asheville; and Dr. W. W. Peele, Charlotte. Other speakers and their subjects were: Charles H. Livengood, Jr., of Durham, "Our Great Inconsistency: Democracy and the New Order"; John Irvin Morgan, Jr., of Farmville, "The Builder's Call to Youth"; and Charles Daniel Rosen, of New York City, "The Younger Generation Versus the Old." All of the orations were excellent, and the extended consultation of the judges indicated their difficulty in determining their choice.

And did they come back on Alumni Day!

MANY ALUMNI IN ATTENDANCE

Making some allowances for the "repression," but on the other hand expecting stimulated interest in the new campus to balance an expected decline in attendance, alumni leaders were expecting not a great deal more than an average in-pouring of Trinity's and Duke's far-flung family on Tuesday. One class wit

observed that either the present economic disturbance has left a large part of Duke alumni untouched, or else has thrown so many of them into the ranks of the unemployed that they took their first opportunity to attend commencement. For they did come back, and with bells on!

ALUMNI DAY TUESDAY

Stealing the spotlight from the graduates, the Old Grads made a memorable day of Tuesday. Like an invading army they swarmed through Duke's wide-open doors, eager to see and to conquer, and they did both. The Union was headquarters for the fourteen reunion classes, but the whole campus proved the stamping-ground for the alumni rampant upon inspecting the University's new home. A strange home-coming for a group of alumni who could not go to a dormitory room and point to their carved initials on the door; but they liked it all the more in knowing that their sons attending Duke have better rooms. For Duke alumni, pride in new and better University facilities has taken the place of other sentiments but without the slightest depreciation of the distinctive and noble contributions made by the men and the things of the past.

To many of those, however, who have followed the development of the new campus in frequent visits there during the past several years, the scenes were not new. During the four days of commencement every building was given a thorough "once-over" by the out-of-town visitors.

COMMENCEMENT SERMON

The commencement sermon by Dr. Daniel A. Poling, distinguished New York church leader, editor of *The Christian Herald,* and president of the International Society of Christian Endeavor, was an inspiring and challenging feature of the Alumni Day program.

Dr. Poling spoke of "The Three Imperatives of Faith," which are, he pointed out, faith in oneself, faith in one's fellowmen, and faith in God. It was the first of two moving messages commencement attendants were to hear from Dr. Poling that day. The second came as one of the inspiring moments of the most successful alumni luncheon ever held at a Duke commencement.

ALUMNI-ALUMNAE LUNCHEON

The 720 persons who gathered at the notable luncheon on Alumni Day will serve as a committee to account for its success and the lasting impression it made on all who shared in the fellowship of the occasion. One feature, however, was unique—it was the first time the alumni and alumnae lunched together at commencement—and that may account for something of its success!

More than 100 extra plates had to be set in an adjoining dining hall when all the ticket-holders came into the Union for the fellowship feast. It was the largest assemblage of Duke alumni ever gathered at one time.

Members of the various classes sat together in rows of tables, and the special guests of the day were members of the graduating class, the youngest alumni of the University. The associations extended two-fold congratulations to members of the class, first upon their formally joining the ranks of graduated alumni and also upon being the first class to be graduated on the new campus.

OFFICERS FOR THE ENSUING YEAR WERE ELECTED

The filling of a vacancy on the University Board of Trustees was confirmed with the approval by the alumni of the election of Henry R. Dwire to membership on the board, succeeding the late Senator Lee S. Overman. Mr. Dwire is a member of the class of 1902, and for a year and a half has been an officer of the University administration.

The entire assemblage greeted Henry W. Norris, '71, oldest living graduate of Trinity College, when the sole representative of the sixtieth year class was introduced. Likewise members of the fiftieth year class were extended congratulatory applause.

DINNER GATHERINGS

During the evening dinner gatherings were held by a number of classes, in which both business and pleasure played a part. The final event of Alumni Day was the colorful reception in honor of the graduating class and returned alumni.

GRADUATION DAY

Graduation day continued the successes of Alumni Day. Following a brilliant address by Dr. Huston Thompson, of Washington, D. C., degrees were conferred upon 348 candidates. Many alumni remained over for the exercises, and not a few saw their sons and daughters among the first to receive their degrees from their newly domiciled Alma Mater.

ON WOMAN'S COLLEGE CAMPUS

The scene shifted back to the Woman's College campus for the closing events of the successful four days. Following an informal reception at the Woodland Stage, given by the faculties in honor of the parents of graduates, the traditional flag-lowering exercises were held at sunset around a new steel shaft recently placed for the occasion.

The seventy-ninth commencement will not be soon forgotten, and in many ways it established precedents which should make the future commencements on the new campus increasingly successful.

Sons and Daughters of Alumni In '31 Class

It is interesting to note the sons and daughters of former students who graduated in the 1931 Class. The institution has such a firm hold upon the affections of its graduates that many of them have sent sons and daughters to keep alive the family traditions on the campus. The list follows:

Student	Home Address	Parents	Class
Margaret Boddie	Durham	N. J. Boddie,	'08
Mary Elizabeth Bradsher	Petersburg, Va.	Elizabeth Muse Bradsher,	'05
		Arthur B. Bradsher,	'04
Elizabeth Caldwell	Monroe	Garah B. Caldwell,	'02
		Annie Whitaker Caldwell,	'05
William G. Coltrane, Jr.	Greensboro	W. G. Coltrane, '00, A.M.,	'27
		Mrs. W. G. Coltrane, A.M.,	'27
Mary Anna Howard	Franklinton	Nan Goodson Howard Read,	'06
		Rev. L. P. Howard, '03 (Deceased)	
Bain Johnson	Winston-Salem	Rev. T. B. Johnson,	'95
Charles H. Livengood, Jr.	Durham	Mary Johnson Livengood,	'04
		C. H. Livengood,	'04
Emmett K. McLarty, Jr.	Charlotte	Rev. E. K. McLarty,	'95
Inez Pearce	Richmond, Va.	Hubert E. Pearce,	'09
Carlotta Satterfield	Durham	Carlotta Angier Satterfield,	'05
		H. C. Satterfield,	'04
Courtney Sharpe	Lumberton	J. A. Sharpe,	'98
Walter A. Stanbury, Jr.	Durham	Rev. W. A. Stanbury,	'08
Samuel Underwood, Jr.	Greenville	Samuel J. Underwood, '06 (deceased)	
Isabel Wannamaker	Durham	W. H. Wannamaker, A.M.,	'01
Cornelia Yarbrough	Durham	E. S. Yarbrough,	'02
William Southgate Martin	Wilmington	Rev. W. C. Martin,	'07

52 Classes Represented at Seventy-Ninth Commencement

Nearly 500 Alumni, from '71 to '30, Gather at the First Finals on the New Duke University
Campus and "Talk Over" the Old College Days—List of Those
Registered on Alumni Day, With Their Classes

THE 1931 Commencement of Duke University was notably successful in a number of ways. It was outstanding from the standpoint of alumni participation, over 400 alumni representing fifty-two different classes registering at the Alumni Headquarters in the University Union. Quite a number who were here at some time during Commencement are not included in the registration, so it is safe to conclude that at least 475 graduates and former students were here for the alumni and other activities in connection with Commencement.

The oldest class represented was that of 1871. Its representative, Henry W. Norris, of Holly Springs, is the oldest alumnus of Duke University. The class of 1872 had as its representative Millard Mial, of Raleigh; class of 1875, W. R. Odell, of Concord; 1876, former Lieutenant Governor W. D. Turner, of Statesville. Other classes with one representative each included 1882, with D. N. Farnell, of Suffolk, Virginia;

1884, George W. Sparger, of Baltimore, Maryland; 1886, J. A. Bell, Charlotte; 1889, G. T. Adams, of Sanford. The other classes included had from two to 45 representatives each.

Most of the fourteen reunion classes were particularly well represented. The golden anniversary class of 1881 had four members present, these being R. H. Broom, of Southport; B. N. Bodie, of Leesville, S. C.; W. H. Townsend, High Point; R. B. Beckwith, Fayetteville. The twenty-fifth year class of 1906 was represented by 16 members, an unusually good attendance for a class a quarter century out of college.

The reunion classes were '71, '76, '81, '86, '91, '96, '01, '06, '11, '16, '21, '26, '28, '30.

Following is a list by classes of alumni registered for the 1931 Commencement. If there are any omissions from the list, or if any alumni who were present were not registered, the ALUMNI REGISTER will greatly appreciate information regarding them:

1871
Henry W. Norris.........Holly Springs

1872
Millard Mial...................Raleigh

1875
W. R. Odell....................Concord

1876
W. D. Turner ....Statesville

1878
M. Bradshaw..................Durham
James F. Brower...............Clemons

1880
Goodwin D. Ellsworth, Washington, D. C.
G. T. Sikes...............Youngsville

1881
R. H. Broom................Southport
B. N. Bodie...........Leesville, S. C.
W. H. Townsend...........High Point
R. B. Beckwith..........Fayetteville

1882
D. N. Parnell............Suffolk, Va.

1883
Albert Anderson..............Raleigh
B. C. Beckwith................Raleigh
W. H. Nicholson............Henderson

J. B. Hurley.................Lexington
C. P. Jerome..................Goldsboro

1884
George W. Sparger......Baltimore, Md.

1886
J. A. Bell....................Charlotte

1887
Dred Peacock..............High Point
B. B. Adams................Four Oaks

1889
G. T. Adams..................Sanford

1891
L. S. Massey..................Durham
Ray McCrary.................Lexington
John W. Lambeth..........Thomasville
Robert Lee Durham....Buena Vista, Va.
W. I. Cranford...............Durham
W. H. Jones...................Raleigh

1892
M. T. Plyler..................Durham
H. D. Stewart.................Monroe
C. A. Barbee...............High Point

1893
W. C. Merritt............Murfreesboro

1894
C. W. Edwards................Durham

1895
C. C. Weaver...........Winston-Salem
H. E. Gibbons................Hamlet

1896
R. A. Mayer.................Charlotte
H. B. Craven...........Lakeland, Fla.
J. H. Separk................Gastonia
F. S. Aldridge.................Durham
Mamie Jenkins..............Greenville
Guy S. Lane...............Greensboro
Annie M. Pegram..........Greensboro
J. A. Dailey.................Pittsboro
A. S. Raper.................Stoneville
B. Winston Rogers...........Durham
Ernest J. Green........Columbia, S. C.
W. C. Lindsey................Durham
J. P. Gibbons.................Hamlet

1897
W. W. Graves.................Wilson
John F. Kirk...............Greensboro

1898
J. A. Sharpe...............Lumberton
W. F. Howland..............Henderson
N. C. Newbold................Raleigh
R. T. Poole.....................Troy

1899

Harry M. North...............Raleigh
J. H. Barnhardt............Salisbury

1900

J. Ed. Pegram................Durham
M. B. Clegg................Albemarle
G. B. Cladwell ....Monroe

1901

Frank S. Carden...........Chattanooga
W. E. Brown...................Durham
W. A. Lambeth.................Durham
Maude E. Moore............Rockingham
J. C. Blanchard...............Hertford
L. F. Williams................Raleigh
D. D. Peele............Columbia, S. C.
O. L. Read...............Franklinton
Steve W. Anderson.............Wilson
Junius W. Wren............Siler City
W. J. Turner................Statesville
J. Martin Umstead.............Durham
S. G. Winstead................Roxboro

1902

Marjie Jordan Biggs...........Raleigh
E. S. Yarbrough...............Durham
Lila Markham Brogden........Durham

1903

Florence Egerton Underhill, Anderson,
   South Carolina.
Rosa Langston Elmore.....Rocky Mount
C. M. Lance.............Swan Quarter
Irene Pegram..................Durham
W. W. Peele...............Charlotte
Bruce Craven.................Trinity
Edna Kilgo Elias............Charlotte

1904

A. B. Bradsher...........Petersburg, Va.
R. E. Sessions, A.M., Birmingham, Ala.
Charles Scarlett...............Durham

1905

O. I. Hinson..................Durham
A. V. Cole...................Durham
Elizabeth Muse Bradsher, Petersburg, Va.
Annie Whitaker Caldwell........Monroe

1906

Maude Wilkerson Dunn........Durham
C. B. Markham...............Durham
J. A. Morgan...............Greensboro
Kate Herring Highsmith.......Raleigh
Paul Barringer................Sanford
Mary Thomas Few............Durham
Emeth Tuttle Cochran, Daytona Beach,
   Florida
Z. A. Rochelle................Durham
L. T. Singleton................Selma
J. W. Autry................Timberlake
Eure Strother.................Durham
T. G. Stem...................Oxford
C. R. Warren............Chatham, Va.
J. E. Lambeth..............Thomasville
Nan Goodson Read........Franklinton
Bessie Whitted Spence........Durham

1907

Josiah W. Bailey......Washington, D. C.
J. R. McPhail, Jr............Fayetteville
Kemp B. Nixon............Lincolnton

1908

Elise Mims Walker............Raleigh
Jule B. Warren...............Durham
Bertha Leckey Rochelle.......Durham
R. T. Howerton...............Durham

K. W. Parham................Raleigh
Mary Wrenn Morgan.......Greensboro
J. Gilmer Korner.....Washington, D. C.
C. K. Proctor.................Oxford
Don S. Elias..................Asheville

1909

Frances Markham Briggs......Durham
L. E. Blanchard..............Raleigh
Homer H. Winecoff...........Charlotte
Herbert E. Pearce.......Richmond, Va.
W. W. Watson.........Lake Landing
John A. Livingston...........Raleigh

1910

Mary Tapp Jenkins...........Kinston
Willis Smith.................Raleigh

1911

L. I. Jaffe...............Norfolk, Va.
P. Frank Hanes........Winston-Salem
W. Grady Gaston..............Gastonia
Paul Kiker.................Wadesboro
J. E. Brinn..................Sanford
T. G. Vickers............Rocky Mount
J. Herbert Miller.............Biscoe
Emma Babbitt Whitesides.....Bayboro
G. W. Vick............Winston-Salem
Lou Ola Tuttle Moser........Asheboro
Christine McIntosh Page......Asheboro
T. G. Vickers............Rocky Mount
H. G. Hedrick...............Durham

1912

Florence-Green Lockhart.......Durham
Polly Heitman Ivey...........Raleigh
L. M. Epps...................Newton
Leon M. Jones...............Raleigh
Emma McCullen Covington..Rockingham
Ruby Markham...............Durham
Ethel Thompson Ray...........Durham

1913

Fannie Kilgo Groome........Charlotte
W. A. Cade................Fayetteville
Thomas P. Pace.........Purcell, Okla.
L. D. Hayman..............Burlington
Bess Widenhouse Hayman....Burlington

1914

Estelle Flowers Spears........Durham
E. C. Durham.................Raleigh
H. B. Gaston................Belmont
H. O. Lineberger.............Raleigh
A. S. Parker...................Troy
Mrs. A. S. Parker...............Troy
J. O. Renfro.................Wendell

1915

Fannie Vann.................Clinton
F. R. Richardson..............Marion
J. Glen McAdams.........Burlington
Ellen Constable Watson...Lake Landing
Annie H. Swindell.............Durham
Ivey T. Poole...............Jonesboro
John Wesley Bennett.......Cherryville
B. W. Evans.................Edenton
L. L. Ivey...................Raleigh

1916

B. B. Jones..................Kinston
W. Luther Ferrell.......Winston-Salem
E. W. Glass..................Durham
J. H. Taylor...............Fayetteville
Laura Mae Bivins Britt, Greenville, S. C.
V. V. Secrest................Monroe
W. L. Loy.................Creedmoor
B. L. Smith.................Shelby
Hugh L. Nichols............Durham

Wiley M. Pickens...........Lincolnton
J. Walter Lambeth........Thomasville
L. C. Allen..................Graham
A. E. Brown...........Robersonville
Bernard D. Hathcock..Washington, D. C.
W. G. Farrer...............Nashville
John N. Duncan..............Raleigh
J. H. Coman..................Durham
Rufus W. Dalton............Charlotte
Harry L. Dalton............Charlotte
Lucile Bullard Belk..........Goldsboro
Ina Young.............Chapel Hill

1917

Annie T. Smith..............Durham
Joe H. Britt.........Greenville, S. C.
Sally May Tuttle Woodall....Smithfield
M. B. Woosley................Newton
John Cline................Troutman
Banks Arendell...............Raleigh
Edna Taylor Poindexter.....Greensboro
J. Watson Smoot.............Gastonia
Edwin Burge................Asheville

1918

L. L. Gobbel.................Durham
J. S. DeLapp...............Lexington
Kathleen Watkins............Durham
Madge Nichols...............Durham
Jane Elizabeth Newton, Washington, D. C.

1919

Sallie Tuttle Woodall........Smithfield
H. L. Caviness...............Raleigh
A. J. Hobbs, Jr.............New Bern
L. H. McNeely..............Wendell
Ethel Murray..............High Point
Reginald Turner ....Wilmington
Frank McNeill.............Lumberton
C. A. Woodard...............Wilson

1920

Jesse T. Carpenter......New York City
Claire Nichols...............Durham
Margaret C. Tyson...........Durham
Elizabeth Floyd..............Oxford
Glenn T. McArthur..........Durham
W. A. Rollins..............Charlotte
Garland Daniel.............High Point

1921

Robert Dunstan............Greensboro
C. E. Buckner...............Durham
George W. Ferrell...........Durham
L. C. Brothers...........Spring Hope
M. F. Teeter................Asheville
J. O. Long..............Rocky Mount
L. W. Barnhardt..............Raleigh
A. B. Wilkins................Sanford
Helen McCrary Arendell.......Raleigh
Mary Louise Cole.............Durham
Charles W. Bundy..........Charlotte
A. Rosenstein...............Durham
G. G. Adams...............Gold Hill
W. H. Humphrey, Jr......Lumberton
Ella Mae Beavers Belvin.......Durham

1922

Coma Cola Willard.........Helena, Ark.
Lyda Bishop................Durham
Lucille Allen................Durham

1923

Lizzie Gray Chandler........Durham
Catherine Dowdee Penny.......Garner
Lucille Howell Parris.......Hillsboro
Homer M. Keever.........Southmont
Tom G. Neal.............Laurinburg
Charles E. Jordan...........Durham

1924
Inez Newsom Fonville......Wilmington
Harry E. Sheetz............Fayetteville
Fred W. Greene................Wilson
Frances Ledbetter.............Princeton
Agnes Doub Jones................Garner
Elizabeth Newcomb Harden.....Graham
Myrtise Washburn Martin, New York City
Ethel Merritt...........Murfreesboro
Carl H. King..........Lynchburg, Va.

1925
Anne Garrard....................Durham
Joseph C. Whisnant...............Shelby
John F. Rhodes.................New Bern
Alice Thomas Robards.........Henderson
Mrs. Alex Summers.........Statesville
S. B. Crews....................Oxford
R. B. Martin...........New York City
Belle Gholson..................Durham
C. C. Jernigan.................Durham
Louise Seabolt.................Durham
Mary Eskridge King.......Lynchburg
M. Simon Rose.................Durham
Marshall Pickens..............Charlotte
W. A. Kale..................Greensboro
Edgar H. Nease............China Grove

1926
Eure Strother.................Durham
R. E. Walston.................Durham
Frank B. Jordan.............Burlington
Elizabeth Roberts Cannon,
                      Washington, D. C.
Linwood Hollowell.............Gastonia
Adelaide Royal Noell...........Durham
Clara Becton..................Henderson
L. J. Rainey..................Durham
Mrs. L. J. Rainey..............Durham
Vivian Elliott.................Milbrook
Alton J. Knight...............Durham
Hugh M. Raper...............Lexington
Isaac Wade Straughn......Walkertown
George P. Harris.............Charlotte
C. S. Clegg................Thomasville
L. S. Ivey......................Hickory
A. B. Gibson................Laurel Hill
W. D. Maultsby...............Maysville
M. L. Black, Jr................Durham
E. L. Cannon........Washington, D. C.
S. W. Ruark...................Raleigh
C. H. Timberlake..........Lexington
Ben Powell....................Durham
Fulton A. Lee..................Raleigh
Olive Faucette.................Durham

1927
Lillian Zachary Jankoski......Gastonia
D. D. Holt..................Albemarle

Frank Warner.............Greensboro
W. E. Whitford..............Durham
Charles Farriss..............Durham
Mrs. Wade Straughn......Walkertown
S. N. Wrenn.........Charleston, S. C.
Jesse G. Wilkinson.....Sherrill's Ford
Ermine Peek..................Durham
Ruth Roney Dailey............Durham
R. H. Ross............Montelair, N. J.
Mary Stewart................Charlotte

1928
John Burwell..................Durham
Lewis W. Purdy...............Oriental
Marcia Russell Gobbel........Durham
R. W. House...............Statesville
Pearl Boggs..............Statesville
Louise Parker...........Rocky Mount
Lethia Cross.................Durham
Melissa Strother.............Concord
J. C. Horton Burch...........Durham
C. C. Weaver, Jr........New York City
Charles Miller.............Greensboro
Mary Wylie Stuart...........Monroe
Harry Lemmond.............Lawndale
T. Rupert Coleman............Durham
J. R. Regan...............Elizabethtown
Minnie Chandler..............Durham
R. B. Shumaker...........Chapel Hill
Elizabeth Craven.........Rocky Mount
J. W. Dimmette...............Graham
E. W. Hatchett..............Durham
Verona Blalock..........Willow Springs
W. H. Hayes............Roanoke, Va.
R. H. Goldwin..........Brooklyn, N. Y.
Earl B. Edwards............Elk Park
Laura Beaton................Durham
Mary Glasson................Durham
Nellie Garrard...............Durham
C. C. Weaver, Jr........New York City
Tom Shaw, Jr.............Greensboro
E. Clarence Tilley............Durham
Paul R. Erwin.................Durham
Ellen Huckabee..............Albemarle
W. H. Erwin..................Durham
H. L. Hester.................Durham
R. H. Goldwin............Chicago, Ill.
Cary C. Cole.................Durham
Marie Tyler..................Durham
Beryl Jones..................Durham
Eva Malone...................Durham
Jim McLarty.................Lincolnton
Furman McLarty....New Haven, Conn.
Faylene Jones................Durham

1929
Sara Stewart................Charlotte
Mrs. W. L. Loy............Creedmoor

Rosa Long Thomas..........Henderson
Helen Knapton................Durham
Chester Andrews..............Durham
Henry L. Kendall, Jr.........Kipling
Catherine Crews..............Durham
Lucille Hayes................Durham
Pauline Cross................Durham
Annie Louise Caldwell........Durham
Sara Powers Waggoner........Eldorado
LeRoy Harris...............Pink Hill
Anna Keever.................Southmont
Lawrence Little, A. M., '29,
                      New Haven, Conn.

1930
Katherine Markham..........Durham
C. F. Thrift..................Durham
Edna Kilgo Elias............Charlotte
Maude McCracken.............Durham
Carlos P. Womack.........Scotts Hill
Cora Mecum...................Durham
H. Paul Strickland.............Dunn
Lucie Thompson.............Creedmoor
Margaret Royal.............New Bern
J. Sidney Shaw........Orlando, Fla.
R. C. Hatley................Oakboro
Mary Hix............Roanoke Rapids
LeGrand Elliott.............Millbrook
Reba Cousins.................Durham
Julian C. Connally.....New York City
Mrs. J. O. Long.........Rocky Mount
Patsy McKay.................Durham
Pauline Tilley...............Durham
Elizabeth Carlton............Durham
Ola Simpson..................Durham
Clyde Allison.............Yanceyville
Alyse Smith...............Burlington
Irene Pool...................Durham
Thomas S. Hill..............Newport
Vertie Moore.................Roxboro
Catherine Keever..........Linwood
Dayton Dean.................Durham
J. Ben Stalvey................Tabor
Marjorie Peoples.............Durham
H. Gilmer Howie...........Charlotte
Fred J. Walston...............Johns
Horace Fowler...............Durham
Elizabeth McFadyen..........Durham
Alma Wyche..................Durham
Don Burch...................Durham
Esther Booth................Durham
Doris Reagen................Durham
Evelyn Hancock..............Durham
Grace Harris................Durham
Katherine Hampton..........Durham
Susie Pearl Moore...........Durham
Clyde Allison...............Parkton
H. Gilmer Howie...........Charlotte

Ellwood to Lecture in Canadian School

Dr. Charles A. Ellwood, head of the sociology department of Duke University, is to give a series of ten lectures, from July 27 to August 7, at Macdonald College, a division of McGill University, in the province of Quebec, Canada, it is announced by the Canadian college. The series theme will be "The Christian Reconstruction of our Civilization," and will be discussed before an assembly of clergymen and others interested in rural welfare.

Dr. Ellwood's topics will be: "Menacing Tendencies of the Present," "The Social Gospel Christ's Gospel,"

"Christianizing Our Business Life," "Christianizing Our Political Life," "Christianizing Our International Life," "Christianizing Our Race Relations," "Christianizing Our Education," "Christianizing Our Home and Family Life," and "Christianizing Our Religion."

Dr. Ellwood is a recognized authority in the sociological field. He has written many books on sociology which have been translated in various languages, and he has lectured throughout the United States. He came to Duke last fall from University of Missouri.

R. C. Kelly and Mrs. Augusta Kramer Walker are Elected

Chosen New Presidents of Alumni and Alumnae Associations at Record-Breaking Luncheon Attended by 720 Alumni and Alumnae—Luncheon Program Notably Interesting—Council Meetings Are Held

RICHARD C. KELLY, of Greensboro, '07, and Mrs. Augusta Kramer Walker, of Elizabeth City, '04, were chosen presidents for the ensuing year of the General Alumni and Alumnae Associations respectively of Duke University, at the Alumni-Alumnae Luncheon held on Tuesday, June 9, Alumni Day of the 1931 Commencement.

Other officers were elected as follows: Alumni: Edgar S. Bowling, '99, of New York, first vice-president; W. Grady Gaston, Gastonia, '11, second vice-president; Willis Smith, Raleigh, '10, third vice-president; Alumnae: Mrs. Mabel Chadwick Stephens, '01, Augusta, Ga., vice-president; Miss Elizabeth Aldridge, '24, Durham, secretary.

These officers were elected, following the report of the nominating committees, at the most largely attended luncheon of alumni and alumnae in the history of Duke University. This being the first Commencement on the new campus, the alumni invited the alumnae to join with them in the luncheon, this resulting in the merging of the programs that had been arranged by each of the two groups. The occasion was an outstanding success, the luncheon being held in the large dining room of the University Union and bringing together 720 alumni, alumnae, faculty members and visitors. From the first minute to the last there was in evidence good fellowship, affection for Alma Mater and a spirit of determination to go out from the luncheon to work

RICHARD C. KELLY   MRS. AUGUSTA KRAMER WALKER

harder than ever before in an endeavor to interpret Duke University, its aims and ideals to community, state and nation.

J. Gilmer Korner, president of the General Alumni Association, and Mrs. Fannie Kilgo Groome, president of the Duke Alumnae Association, presided. After invocation by Rev. Mr. Vickers, of Rocky Mount, "America" and a Duke song were sung by those present, led by J. Foster Barnes. Candidates for degrees who were present in academic costume stood and were welcomed into the Association by President Korner. Dr. R. L. Flowers made a few remarks in the absence of President Few, and introduced Dr. Daniel A. Poling. He made an exceedingly forceful and inspiring talk that was heard with the greatest interest and enthusiasm by the assemblage. Mrs. Groome was called upon to preside during the alumnae part of the luncheon, this being opened with the report of the nominating committee given by Mrs. Estelle Flowers Spears, followed by an address by Mrs. Emeth Tuttle Cochran, of Daytona Beach, Fla., on "The Educated Woman in Social Service Work." Miss Baldwin spoke on "The Past Year at the Woman's College." Following a duet by Emmett McLarty and Don Correll, John A. Morgan, of Greensboro, alumni representative of the twenty-fifth year class, delivered a brief talk, "After Twenty-five Years." A resolution expressing deep regret at the absence of President Few was unanimously adopted.

The presence of a

number of distinguished guests added interest to the occasion. The service of the luncheon by the University Union staff was superb. The general opinion was that the joint alumni-alumnae luncheon was a pronounced success in every way.

ALUMNI COUNCIL MEETING

On Monday morning, June 8, the Alumni Council met at 10:30 in the University Union. Vice-Chairman Charles H. Livengood presided in the unavoidable absence of the chairman. Twenty-eight members were in attendance and there was a full discussion of the various business matters brought up.

After reading the minutes of the last meeting, the secretary submitted his report, showing accomplishments along various lines during the past year. The addition of nine new alumni groups was reported, one of these being in far-off Japan. Duke University Day was observed by thirty-six local groups. Homecoming Day in October and Alumni Month in November were generally observed. Several suggestions were made by the secretary regarding the work of the ensuing year, particular emphasis being placed on the desirability of class and local groups doing something definite during the next twelve months for the advancement of the University.

Various matters relating to the work of the Council were discussed, among others the matter of Home-

coming Day next fall. It was decided to hold the Homecoming and fall meeting of Council on different days. The date of November 21, the time of the Carolina-Duke football game next fall, was favored for Homecoming Day.

ALUMNAE COUNCIL MEETING

The Alumnae Council met at 10:30 Monday morning, June 8, in the Alumnae Room, with Miss Anne Garrard, '25, chairman, presiding. The roll was called and minutes of the fall meeting were read and approved.

Reports were heard from Mrs. W. J. Brogden, '02, chairman of the room committee; Mrs. Estelle Flowers Spears, '14, chairman of the executive committee; and from Miss Baldwin, dean of the Woman's College. The alumni secretary's report was read and the alumnae secretary reported on some matters before the Council. It was stated that the Wake County alumni group had added to its fund this year. A new room committee was elected with Mrs. Kathleen Hamlin Watkins, '18, as chairman. Mrs. Fannie Kilgo Groome was named chairman of a committee to investigate the founding of a scholarship for women.

It was decided that the Council would entertain all undergraduate women at tea next year, the occasions the past year having been notably successful and interesting.

Dr. A. M. Proctor, '10, Chairman of Research Committee

APPOINTMENT of a special research committee, a fact-finding body, charged with the duty of making a thorough survey of the educational situation in the state and reporting for public dissemination its findings in order that the people may have full information along this line, was announced recently by Dr. John H. Cook, president of the North Carolina Education association, as follows:

Dr. A. M. Proctor, of Durham, chairman; Dr. George Howard, of Chapel Hill; Dr. S. H. Hobbs, Jr., of Chapel Hill; Dr. Albert S. Keister, of Greensboro; Guy B. Phillips, of Greensboro; Major W. A. Graham, of Kinston.

The *Greensboro News* says: "The chairman of the association's research committee is professor of school administration at Duke University. He has served as superintendent of the schools at Roanoke Rapids and as county superintendent in Wayne County. Dr. Proctor has made educational surveys in two counties in North Carolina.

"Dr. Howard is professor of school administration at the University of North Carolina. He is a former county superintendent of public instruction in Edgecombe County and formerly occupied a similar position in Rowan County.

"Widely known as educator and author, Dr. Hobbs is professor of rural and social economics at the University of North Carolina. He is recognized as possessing a remarkable fund of knowledge in taxation matters.

"Dr. Keister is professor of economics at North Carolina college. He has made extended studies of public finance and for some time was an active adviser of the North Carolina Tax commission. He, too, is considered an expert on tax questions.

"Mr. Phillips is superintendent of schools in the Greater Greensboro district, a former superintendent of the schools in Oxford and Salisbury at different periods. He has made a careful statistical study of the Greensboro schools and is known as an analyst as well as school administrator.

"Major Graham is superintendent of the city

(Continued on page 206)

"Three Imperatives of Faith" Theme of Dr. Daniel A. Poling

In Commencement Sermon at Duke, Noted Preacher Emphasizes Faith in One's Self, Faith in Others and Faith in God as Essential to Really Successful Living

"THREE Imperatives of Faith" was the theme of the annual Commencement Sermon delivered on Tuesday morning, June 9, by Rev. Daniel Alfred Poling, D.D., LL.D., one of the noted preachers of America. After being introduced by Dr. R. L. Flowers, who presided at the Tuesday morning exercises, Dr. Poling spoke as follows, in part:

"In one vital matter at least, science and religion have united in a great conclusion. The answer to the riddle of the universe, the solution to the problem of being, is found not in matter but in mind. The great secret lies somewhere within the realm of the soul. The ancient text of Paul has now a significant modern application: 'Faith is the substance of things hoped for and the evidence of things not seen.'

"The three imperatives of faith are: First, faith in oneself; second, faith in one's fellows; and third, faith in God—faith in the moral integrity of the universe, faith in an ordered plan for life.

"It may be assumed that it is superfluous to suggest to the members of a graduating class faith in oneself! But this particular faith, to be valid, must have in it the element of humility. Today you who carry into the world the memories and experiences of four academic years carry too a weight of gratitude. I am sure that you are conscious of it—gratitude to parents, gratitude to members of the Faculty, gratitude to each other.

"The validated faith of a man in his ability to do the work that lies at hand, to carry the burdens of a trust that may rest upon him, and to reach the heights of character and achievement,—this faith is conscious of human limitations and has a proper regard for the necessity of constant study and preparation.

"But know at last, know always, that you are the master of your fate; that you are neither a creature of chance nor a slave of circumstance; that, in spite of handicaps and a hundred reverses, you 'can' if you 'will'! Theodore Roosevelt's great motto was 'Trust in God and take your own part.' In terms of a Christian brotherhood and within the definition of that single supreme social word 'Others,' I commend the motto to you.

"A personal faith that does not include faith in others becomes egotism. It generally issues in mediocrity. Those who succeed, whether in friendship or in business, are generally men and women who, in spite of all disillusionments, maintain their belief in the fundamental integrity of their fellows. Again and again, by believing in us, our friends make us better than we otherwise could be.

"Some of you are in this graduating class because of the vision of your parents. Today their dream for you comes true. There may have been times when your own assurance wavered or even failed. In such times there were unselfish minds and loving hearts that held you true to purposeful ambition. Now comes the hour when you are to justify this faith on wider fields, when you are to give to it an interpretation for idealism, for business, for patriotism, for international goodwill.

"Faith in terms of true patriotism dreams of a world freed from the stark terror of war. Faith in terms of true patriotism concludes that selfish nationalism is 'not enough.' The United States must find a way to distribute more widely the benefits and the economic security of her own prosperity. Unless, within her present system of government, she reorganizes industry, makes the average man secure in his savings, renounces personal license—which bears so widely the false name of personal liberty—confirms the sovereignty of law, and accepts at fair cost to herself America's mandate to help organize the world against war, disaster looms ahead.

"We do not consent to disaster! We believe in the future of American institutions and American liberty. To you is assigned a portion of the great load, a share of the challenging task. In other generations youth has accepted the mandate of great causes. Having seen the invisible with the eye of faith, let this student generation go out to do its bit and best toward accomplishing that which men of doubt have declared to be impossible.

"Faith in yourself is an imperative. Faith in your fellows is an imperative. And faith in God is an imperative. Again and again this last has lifted men and women above disaster. By it we know that life is more than a mere existence; that its successes are not measured by a physical yardstick; and that it may claim the eternities. It is in such faith that civilization sets up moral standards. It is in such faith that we assume social, as well as spiritual, obligations. It is with such faith that we declare right to be right and wrong wrong out to the last sun and to the end of time.

" 'The stars shall fade,
   The Sun himself grow dim with age,
   And nations sink in years;
   But Thou shalt flourish in immortal youth,
   Unhurt amidst the war of elements,
   The wreck of matter and the crash of worlds'.''

Reunion Class Dinners A Feature of Alumni Day

ONE of the most interesting features of Alumni Day at the recent Duke Commencement was the holding in the evening of Reunion Class dinners. Ten of these gatherings were held on the two campuses and at each of them a fine spirit of fellowship and of devotion to Alma Mater was in evidence. Reports of some of the dinners have been received and others will doubtless be available for the July REGISTER.

CLASS OF 1906

Thad G. Stem, president of the Class of 1906, welcomed the eighteen members present at the class dinner on Tuesday, June 9, at 6 o'clock in the University Union. The class stood with bowed heads while the president called the names of those who had died. Letters and telegrams from the following absent members were read: C. J. Harrell, Mary Shotwell, C. R. Pugh, Eva Branch, Thomas A. Holton, David B. Phillips, Herman Walker, R. G. Baldwin, W. M. Crook and A. G. Odell.

Short speeches were made by C. R. Warren, Maude Wilkerson Dunn and C. B. Markham.

The class approved the proposed plan of having contemporary classes meeting at the reunion period.

At the close of a most pleasant dinner, new officers were elected: Paul Barringer, president; Jim Lambeth, first vice-president; Louis Singleton, second vice-president; Kate Herring Highsmith, secretary.

CLASS OF 1921

The class dinner of the Class of 1921 was held in the student dining hall on the West Campus on Tuesday, June the ninth, at six o'clock. In the absence of the president, O. L. Richardson, who was unable to attend the dinner due to illness, Charles Bundy presided.

The minutes of the last reunion were read and approved. Various matters of interest to the class were briefly discussed.

Each member was asked to give an account of what he had been doing since the last reunion in 1926.

A motion was adopted that the secretary write letters, expressing the sympathy of the class, to Grover Mumford, who is ill at the Guilford Sanitarium in Greensboro, N. C., to Mrs. C. C. Cornwell, mother of C. C. Cornwell, who lost his life last December, and to O. L. Richardson, who has been ill for several weeks.

The class discussed the idea of having more frequent reunions and was interested in having reunions with contemporary classes of undergraduate days.

The following members were nominated for the Alumni and Alumnae Councils: Alumni Council, Dr. Robert Dunston, W. H. Humphrey; Alumnae Council, Mrs. Hubert Belvin, Mary Louise Cole.

The officers elected for the next three years are as follows: President, Charles Bundy; Vice-President, Dr. A. Rosenstein; Secretary-Treasurer, Mary Louise Cole.

CLASS OF 1926

One of the outstanding features of Alumni Day for members of the Class of 1926 was the class dinner held at six o'clock, June 9, in the Union on the West Campus. The setting was ideal, the room in which the dinner was held being one of the beautiful little rooms just off the main lobby of the Union.

Edward L. Cannon, class president, presided. The evening was informal and enjoyable. Those present discussed some important questions concerning Alma Mater and the class. The occasion was notably successful in every way.

CLASS OF 1928

The Class of 1928 held its reunion class dinner in the Woman's College Union at 6 p. m. on Alumni Day. John Burwell, president, presided, and called on each member present to give his life history since leaving college. Quartet selections were rendered by Frank Warner, John Burwell, James and Furman McLarty which were highly entertaining. There were twenty-four members of the class present for this delightful occasion.

Hon. Hustou Thompson Takes Up Present-Day Problems

Duke Commencement Speaker Discusses Forcefully a Number of Questions That Are of Vital Importance at Present Time—Strong Advocate of International Trade Tribunal

ECONOMIC disarmament as a means of bringing harmony out of the present chaotic conditions rampant in the earth was advocated at Commencement by Dr. Huston Thompson, former chairman of the United States trade commission, in addressing the 1931 graduating class of Duke University.

Such disarmament is to be affected, he advised, by a World Trade Tribunal, its representatives selected by the League of Nations. The tribunal would pass upon disputed matters of trade conditions; provide information relative to production, prices, and other economic factors, thus aiding the synchronization of supply and demand; and help break down the monstrous tariff walls that pseudo-nationalism has erected.

The battle line, represented by Chaos on one side, and a World Trade Tribunal on the other, was one of several "Battle Lines of Today and Tomorrow" suggested by the former commission head in his address to the graduates. Others were Ideas against Ideals; Politics versus Inertia; Capitalism at Bay with Communism; Rural Civilization against Urban; State versus National Government; and Nationalism opposing Internationalism.

It is to these battle lines that he summoned the graduates, of whose adventurous spirit and faith in their endeavor the older generation stood in need.

"We are in a state of shellshock and disillusionment," Dr. Thompson averred. "We have lost faith for the moment in ourselves, and fear has taken possession of us. It is for this reason we are in need of you who are about to enter upon the stage of life as no generation in the past has needed another. Opportunity for future leadership is beckoning to you beyond this campus. We need your spirit of adventure on these battlefields. We need your faith. We need your soaring imaginations that behold the heights and not the depths. With these qualities revived in us by you we will cease marking time and go forward."

The worth and significance of a World Trade Tribunal was presented by Dr. Thompson toward the conclusion of his address.

"The stage has been set for a great disarmament conference to be held under the auspices of the League at Geneva next February," he pointed out. "How are we going to disarm the nations physically until we disarm economically? Do not all present day wars come, in the last analysis, from economic pressure? There is every reasonable hope that we will adjust justiciable matters through the World Court. There is no forum, however, where the great concrete, economic problems have an opportunity of being settled. Until there is, what hope is there for a real disarmament?

"I propose that we set up a World Trade Tribunal whose representatives shall be selected, just as members of the World court, through the League of Nations. It can function in an independent way upon the world's major economic problems. I know that Woodrow Wilson had this in mind when he was fighting to put the Covenant in the Versailles treaty. If it had not been that he was struggling against such great odds to get any covenant through, I am confident that he would have inserted a paragraph providing for such a Tribunal just as he did for the International Labor office in the World Court. The need for it can be appreciated when we realize the interrelation and interdependence of nations today and the impossibility of any one nation's seeing beyond the color and circumstance of its nationalistic life.

"Few of the great economic problems can be settled simply by discussion in economic conferences of the League. We learned in the evolution of governmental affairs in America that it was necessary to set up courts and commissions that could handle concrete cases. The time has arrived for dealing with the concrete internationally. The League will always be most important in bringing about International coöperation. It will be the forum where problems will first be presented and discussed. Then they can be assigned to either the World Court, the Labor office or the World Trade Tribunal to be acted on in concrete form."

The Tribunal would not offend nations by issuing orders, the speaker went on to explain; it would hold hearings and make investigations at the instance of the League of Nations and publish the findings made. These would be sent to the offending nations and published to the world; and it would be this publicity that would bring about the agreement of the nation in the wrong to the verdict of the trade body.

"Nothing—not even a nationalistic spirit—could stand in the way," Dr. Thompson declared, "of such a searchlight of publicity as it pointed the direction for governments to take and exposed unfair trade conditions.

"Another most helpful function of such a Tribunal would be the collection of current world information on production, stocks on hand, and cost of essential commodities of life in conjunction with the several governments, and the giving out of the data monthly. In this way the warning sign of overproduction could be held high, and nations for the first time in history would have reasonably certain current information of the state of world industries.

"The blockades of the war forced on the people the idea of independence so strongly that after the war most nations surrounded themselves with tariff walls as impenetrable as if they had been made of brick and mortar. Behind these walls business, without the fear of competition, became price-made; price control was established the world over. With price control a fact, over-expansion set in; and today many parts of the world are suffering from overproduction of goods that are piled up behind these walls.

"How strange it must seem to the Master Builder of this world, as He sits in the heavens like Robin's 'Thinker', gazing down upon His people, and sees all of these nations standing still behind imaginary walls which they have constructed for themselves, and which have imprisoned them so they cannot trade with each other, while goods pile up and factories close, and starving men walk the streets of the great cities of the world. In spite of such a situation we are still possessed with the chaotic spirit of pseudo-nationalism that prevents our coöperating with our fellowmen in other nations."

In opening his address the speaker expressed his joy at escaping within cloistered walls from the world of ideas to the world of ideals. He illustrated the differences in the two worlds by the contrast of a 20-year-old, 105 pound gangster who, with a 16-year-old girl, recently held police officers at bay for a time, with another 105 pound man—not young but old—who has been holding an entire empire at bay—Mahatma Gandhi.

"Thus we have the misguided gangster fighting his way by force to the electric chair," the speaker continued, "while Gandhi, through his love for humanity, has fought his way by non-resistance to the height of the immortals. . .'. Outside these cloistered walls there is a war on between the world of ideas and the world of ideals, from which none of us can escape; and certain battles are going on in which we must take sides if we would rise above the intelligence of protoplasm."

In the battle line of Politics and Inertia, Inertia had gained the upper hand, the speaker showed, with men staying out of politics, and the intelligent voters—graduates of high schools and colleges—staying away from the polls.

"When we cease deriding politics and teach our youth the real drama and romance of politics; that politics make business and social life utterly drab by comparison, and that taking active part in citizenship is our most important public duty," the commencement speaker declared, "then education will begin to count in politics."

Another battle looming up was that of capitalism and communism. While about a year ago America and other nations were making fun of the five-year-plan of the Soviets, "Today we are not only fearful of their plan but we have adopted their nomenclature; and men and women are grouped in every city in our land planning programs for business and society and state.

"But while these plans had no coördination, those of communism were systematic, with various local communities involved, and everything being coördinated in one great group that met each month at Moscow."

Were it not for the way capitalism is acting, he would not fear Communism might submerge or control capitalistic countries, Mr. Thompson said; but with laws of economics being defied, disaster threatened. With the adoption of the shibboleth, "More business in government and less government in business," chaos has come, for such a slogan looks to the elimination of competition and free course for mergers. Communism, failing to consider the demand of human nature for individual freedom of thought and action, could not permanently succeed; but communism will certainly chastise capitalism until it changes its ways and permits freedom of thought and action among those who follow it.

In speaking of the contest between the rural communities and city dwellers—another of the modern day battle lines—the former Federal commission head analyzed what he considers the weakness of large city life.

"Human beings, when thrust close together, lean upon each other. The more they lean the less strength they have to stand straight upon their own feet and do their own thinking. Every political convention of a city today is moved and swayed by a machine which succeeds because of the very helplessness of the voters. The massing of the people and the intricacies of city life prevent them from obtaining information upon public questions or the movements of machines behind the scenes.''

There was much sophistry in America over the loss of state rights. But, in truth, it was oftentimes a surrender of rights of the state, made by its representatives, ''for a miserable mess of pottage in the form of pork barrel appropriations.'' Another reason for the government's stepping in has been the tendency of states to sleep on their rights and allow great holding companies to get beyond their control.

''We cannot overemphasize the danger of what is happening,'' Dr. Thompson declared. ''This centralization of economic power which in turn produces centralization of political power is the greatest danger that confronts our nation. But the cause lies not with the national government. It lies with the people themselves.''

Nationalism and Internationalism presented another battlefield of today; but America, once in a position to lead, has been so affected by caution and fear that she stays out of the World Court, even though the court is ''undoubtedly removing two real possibilities of war'' in the German-Austrian customs problems and the Polish-German Danzig dispute.

''The action of the nations in these two cases points the way to a settlement of disputes that gives more hope,'' the speaker averred, ''than anything that has happened in world politics up to the present hour. But international movements such as these cannot succeed so long as nations are possessed with fear and a spirit of pseudo-nationalism.''

From the heights which characterized American life during the days of the World War, its citizens had descended, Dr. Thompson pointed out, with materialism again gaining ascendency, local and national government imperilled, international ills, that might have been avoided by entrance to the League of Nations, entangling the country. It was a situation calling for new blood; and to the seniors he made the call.

Much Interest In Coaching School at Duke July 22-25

MUCH INTEREST is being shown in the four-day coaching school for high school coaches, which will be conducted at Duke beginning July 22. It will be under the direction of Wallace Wade, director of athletics, assisted by the entire Duke 'varsity staff. Planned primarily for the high school coaches, there will be full instruction in football, baseball, basketball, and other sports in which those registering are interested. No registration or tuition charges will be made, and room and board will be provided at a nominal rate.

Carl Voyles, assistant director of athletics, who arrived at the University on June 15 from University of Illinois where he has been connected for several years, will undertake his first Duke work at this time. Coach Eddie Cameron, basketball and assistant football coach, and other members of the staff will take charge of the summer registrants.

Courses will include lectures covering the science and strategy of various branches of athletics, and practical work in the fundamentals will be given on the athletic fields. Headquarters will be in the gymnasium.

Coach Wade is having a busy summer, his schedule taking him to several coaching schools and conferences. Recently he has been leading the football coaching school at the University of Utah.

Murray is Winner of Coveted Award

WILLIAM D. Murray, of Rocky Mount, football star and retiring president of the Duke University Men's Student Government Association, was announced as winner of the Robert E. Lee prize for the best all-round man in the senior class.

The prize is $100 and is the gift of Rev. A. W. Plyler, of Greensboro, a member of the Trinity class of 1892, and Mrs. Plyler. It is usually accounted as one of the most coveted awards at Duke.

Other prize winners were announced at the same time. The Robert Spencer Bell prize of $100, established by James A. Bell, of Charlotte, of the class of 1886, went to John R. Jenkins, of Parmele, adjudged the best all-round self-help student whose work in literary societies was outstanding.

The Parker cup, for excellence in physics, was awarded to Charles E. Stewart, of Rochester, N. Y. Henry Wynn, of Lykens, Pa., won the Iota Gamma Pi science fraternity award to the student adjudged a leader in scientific study.

Archive awards, each worth $25, were announced as follows: for best poetry, Edward Mylod, Glen Ridge, N. J., sonnet in February issue; short story, H. N. Douty, of Baltimore, ''Professor Collier's Room,'' in April issue; and one-act play, Oren Whitehead, of Asheville, Mrs. French's Medicine Bag,'' in May issue.

Some Alumni Personalities

M. T. PLYLER

At Commencement exercises on June 9, last, the University of North Carolina conferred the D.D. degree upon Rev. M. T. Plyler, Duke alumnus of the Class of '92. After receiving degrees from Trinity College and the University of North Carolina, he attended the University of Chicago. He is a member of Phi Beta Kappa and Omicron Delta Kappa. He has been a delegate at four annual conferences of his church, and also at the Ecumenical Conference at London in 1921. He has been for a number of years business manager and associate editor of the North Carolina Christian Advocate, being associated with his brother, Rev. A. W. Plyler. He is the author of several books. In his college days at Trinity he was a football star.

Robert Lee Durham, '91, was one of the members of the fortieth year class who attended its anniversary on June 9. Incidentally, he is usually in attendance upon Duke Commencements. As president of Southern Seminary at Buena Vista, Virginia, as lay leader of his church and chairman of the official board, as a representative of his church in the General Conference and in other ways he has taken an active part in the life of his community, state and section. He is a member of Phi Beta Kappa, and while at Duke was a three-letter man. He played on the Southern championship football team. He was captain of volunteer infantry in the Spanish-American War; author of "The Call of the South"; well known as a writer and teacher.

ROBERT LEE DURHAM

GEORGE W. H. BRITT

George W. H. Britt, of the Class of 1916, is a member of the editorial staff of the New York World-Telegram. Last year he was president of the New York Association of Duke University Alumni. On May 2, 1931, he was married to Miss Hortense Saunders, a well-known writer. Both are feature writers for the Newspaper Enterprise Association syndicate. Mr. Britt recently published, in collaboration with Heywood Broun, widely known writer, a book, "Christians Only." This was brought out just a few months ago by the Vanguard Press of New York, and has already been attracting much attention. For a long time he has conducted a column relating to books in the newspaper with which he is connected.

Duke University Architecture Discussed By President W. P. Few

In Final Statement to the 1931 Graduating Class He Points Out Significance
of Architectural Design, Stressing Its Peculiar Spirit of Unity
and Harmony—Duke's Purposes and Ideals

"THE UNITY of Architecture at Duke University and the Ideas that Underlie It" was the subject of a statement issued by President .William Preston Few as his final words to the graduates of the Class of 1931. He referred to various phases of the organization of the institution and the significance of its first year's occupancy of the new plant on the West Campus. In his statement, he stressed the architectural unity and harmony of the Duke plants, the ideas behind the physical development of the University as a place of beauty and inspiring environment, and their effect upon the lives of students and of the institution itself.

"This is the first Commencement held on this campus," said President Few, "and as such it has a special significance. Many thousands of visitors from this and other countries have observed and admired the beauty and harmony of the set of buildings now nearing completion, and often these visitors have asked for explanations concerning the building and organization of the University. I will undertake to suggest some of the underlying ideas and something of the informing spirit by which the founding of Duke University has been prompted, especially as these are illustrated in the buildings themselves.

"When I made my first address as president of Trinity College at the formal opening of the college twenty-one years ago I spoke on The College and the Symmetrical Life, and I endeavored to interpret, as I understand it, the spirit that has controlled the institution at every stage of its development. Trinity College is now an important part of Duke University and by the thread of an idea common to both I desire to link this occasion with that one twenty-one years ago.

"As I look back over the life of man in the world I think I can trace a long historic conflict that has been waged through all civilization between beauty and fullness of life without a moral meaning, on the one hand, and austerity and barrenness along with religious intensity, on the other hand. It is this, I think, that has produced that strange ebb and flow so conspicuous in all human history. It has always been difficult for human society to preserve the gains made generation after generation, and any high and .enduring civilization still awaits the synthetic power by which trained intelligence and mature religion, working together, may make steadily for progress and prosperity, for intellectual freedom and enlightenment, and for spiritual vitality and permanent values. It has long seemed clear to me that it is only through a fuller comprehension of the meaning of life that a synthesis of these two divergent elements can be effected and that the highest civilization must ever wait upon this power to combine a full and beautiful living with moral energy and enthusiasm for the causes of humanity. To produce this synthetic power is one of the missions of the highest kind of education.

"The builders of this University have sought to achieve physical beauty and unity and through these to suggest spiritual values. These buildings have been constructed with the purpose to provide a place fit in every circumstance of beauty and appropriateness to be the home of the soul of the University and in the belief that these appropriate and beautiful surroundings will have a transforming influence upon students generation after generation and even upon the character of the institution itself. The architectural harmony and strength of the plant is intended to suggest unity and fullness of life. Here stand side by side science and religion—science and scholarship completely given to the full, untrammeled pursuit of the truth and religion with its burning passion for righteousness in the world—and commit the University in its very inception alike to excellence that dwells high among the rocks and to service that goes out to the lowliest.

"This underlying conception of the mission of Duke University has affected the organization of every part of the University. For example, legal education has until very lately been less influenced by recent tendencies in education than other parts of university organization. Here we will at once try to get away from the trade-school idea and put under legal training a broader educational foundation. We shall expect the School of Law to be not just a professional training school for those who intend to practice at the bar but a school that along with professional preparation will, in close coöperation with other parts of the University also provide liberal training in the law as one of the social sciences closely allied with history, government, economics, and business administration. As I understand it, our School of Law will seek to send its graduates out as well trained lawyers, to be sure, but so imbued with the ideals of liberal education that it will be easy for them also to become enlightened public servants in one capacity or another.

"The School of Medicine profiting by all the advances in medical education that have been made in this generation will be devoted equally to science and to service.

"The primary business of the graduate School of Religion is to train ministers for service but at the same time the men on this faculty are taking, and will more and more take, their places among the foremost scholars of the University.

"The Graduate School of Arts and Sciences, the division in the University that more than any other will determine the standing of the University in the educational world, will maintain high standards and through scholarship and research will make its appropriate contributions to knowledge; but it is also making definite effort to prepare its graduates for the great business of teaching and for other professional tasks.

"This School, like every other graduate and professional school in the University, is creating for its students opportunities in their way comparable to the clinical opportunities that for so long have been provided for medical students. In this Duke, so far as I know, is unique; and I venture to mention the circumstance because it seems to me to be a good illustration of one of the essential ideas upon which the University is founded.

"Everywhere in the University, but especially in the undergraduate colleges, we are trying to break down departmentalizing walls and make the subjects exist for the student and not the student for the subjects; that is, make the student the unit. The University is built and organized with a compactness that ought to make it natural for the students and teachers to think and work more and more from a common point of view rather than from the standpoint of conflicting interests. The Union is the social centre for students and teachers alike and the dormitories have quarters for masters in residence, where we hope some of our best men will wish to live.

"I have given these illustrations of a sort of unity and common intention that I think will run through all the University. I have had, as a matter of course,

to give my own interpretation of the building and organization of the University. It may well be that everybody here will not agree with me. As we develop there will no doubt from time to time be occasion for compromise as to details, and I am certain always abundant opportunity for new and better ideas. At any rate, I think I have intimated in outlines the program for which Duke University is built and upon which it is now fairly launched. I realize that this will at times set us upon a hard road. Educational reform, like all reform, is beset with difficulties. Our program will frequently require us to row heavily against the stream.

"And if Duke University is to have this unity and all-round completeness it must ever cherish some galvanizing central principle that will hold it from disintegration. On this campus the Chapel, hard by the library and the laboratories and coöperating with the University in its every effort to promote truth and serve humanity, is not only central, but, with its stained glass, its vaulted roof and noble spire, will dominate the place. This is intended to be symbolical of the truth that the spiritual is the central and dominant thing in the life of man.

"Can this ideal be realized in our world and can religion and education in its highest forms ever engage successfully in a great formative, common undertaking to make this a better world than man has yet known? Duke University is founded in that faith; but we realize that it must be a religion that comprehends the whole of life and an education that seeks to liberate all the powers and develop all the capacities of our human nature. We are well aware that we have set up a high and difficult goal to attain; but it is a goal worth all our striving. For unless it is attained we may expect the same sort of break between enlightenment and religion, between beauty and goodness as, to a degree at least, I have always supposed came about in New England in the last century to the permanent detriment of our country and some two centuries earlier in Old England to the detriment of our race, and in so many lands and ages has kept back civilization from real greatness and permanence, and, unless we are wise enough and good enough to prevent it here, will sooner or later bring ours to ruin.

"More and more religion and education must realize and combine to teach that the advancement of mankind depends largely upon a better understanding of the laws of nature and man's relation to these laws, and that the higher life of man depends even more largely upon an understanding that we are also a part of a moral order; that morality too, is 'the nature of things' and that in our world no one of us can be safe except as he lives in loving obedience to these laws of nature and these laws of life.

"It is well known that periods of spiritual warmth

and power have always been followed by reactions into feebleness and doubt. When the forces of religion and education can heartily join in the common task not only to help the poor but to destroy the seeds of poverty; not only to provide instruction in a limited field and with limited facilities but devote themselves to painstaking and unflinching search for and defense of truth in all its relationships; not only to rescue the lost but to create an atmosphere and climate of opinion in which the truth, the beautiful, and the good can easily grow, then we may expect a steadiness in the progress of the race instead of the monotonous rise and fall in moral power, instead of the come and go in aspiration and achievement, instead of the spiritual ebb and flow that is so conspicuous in the records of mankind. Then goodness and beauty, righteousness and truth, gentleness and strength, can live together and, living together, can make a world that will sustain a really great and enduring civilization. And when that far, glad day arrives, religion and education will have a program for their combined activities in which there will never be armed neutrality or open conflicts, but the two will work together, each giving its all in whole-hearted coöperation for a completely redeemed humanity.''

Social and Human Values Discussed By John A. Morgan

IN addressing the Alumni-Alumnae Luncheon as representative of the alumni of the twenty-fifth year class, J. A. Morgan, of Greensboro, said:

"The Naughty Sixes thank the rest of you for the special recognition you give to the twenty-fifth anniversary of our graduation.

"When Trinity College sent us out commissioned to do our share of work and to bear worthily her honored name, probably most of us expected folk and things would respond more readily to our wills than they have been found to do. But against neither have we complaint to make. Instead, we look upon the intervening years as the first quarter-century of our postgraduate training. In the next quarter, we expect to be getting along somewhat; and in the third, to attain some maturity of mind and the skill so to play the game that we shall not fumble the ball.

"Notwithstanding our youthful immaturity, we of Naught Six, like the rest of you, can in no way escape the call of our generation for a more effective leadership than has yet prevailed. Just now, it is more than ordinarily evident that the world's material equipment far exceeds its power of rightful use. The present stagnation of business—with accompanying confusion of counsels, impotent leadership, and, for many, disillusionment and despair—carries both an indictment and a challenge. For the ills of which complaint is now heard on well-nigh every lip are no accident, no mere caprice of fortune. Nor are they an inevitably recurring product of impersonal so-called economic laws. The plain fact is that the disaster into which peoples, here and abroad, have plunged head-on with open but unseeing eyes, repeating a time-worn blunder, is not basically an economic one. This monstrous failure centers, rather, at the crossway where human interests find on the spiritual plane chiefly find their meeting place. And, whatever the rules of the game we may have inherited for controlling the contestants in the incidental meeting and clash of economic interests at that same crossway, and however much we may change the rules, we shall still face the inescapable, all-important truth: He who would find his life must lose it.

"In this governing principle lies the final test of the quality of our living. For, what can it profit society, with the expenditure of so much of its wealth and the lives of so many of its choicest spirits—in the opening of doors for men and women like us—if the end result is only the sending out from our colleges and universities of a few persons trained and equipped merely to be a little more clever than their fellows in snatching the prizes of a cold acquisitive game? Surely the purpose of such an investment points to a different goal. And where are to be found the capacity for sustained idealism and the costly courage which alone can carry the human enterprise on its farthest line of advance, where, if not in the sons and daughters of Duke University—you who, in your search for the essential knowledge which is one mark of educated folk, have been guided with an unfailing emphasis upon the social value of that knowledge when committed to your worthy keeping?

"In grateful and reverent appreciation of that guidance, we of the Class of 1906 happily join you in pledging afresh our loyalty to Alma Mater, always and increasingly dear to us.''

Report_of the Dean of the Woman's_College

AT THE Alumnae luncheon in June it has been the custom to have a report from the Dean of Women, telling of some of the interesting and significant happenings of the year. This year at the joint luncheon the report was brief, mentioning a few things only which it was hoped would be of interest to the men as well as the women. The report was made by Miss Baldwin, Dean of the Woman's College, as follows:

We have registered this year in all the schools 676 women. They came from Canada to Florida and from Minnesota to North Carolina, although the large majority were southerners. At the opening of the year we had 378 living on the campus while last year at the same time we had 154. Of these only 105 were old girls.

Instead of one dormitory where everyone knew everyone else there were four and instead of having all work on one campus many of the older women had to go from campus to campus. All of these new conditions and especially the small proportion of old girls created new problems, some of them difficult of solution. But gradually the girls adjusted themselves so that before the end of the year there was much greater contentment and sense of unity.

Two developments of special significance are the increasing interest in and appreciation of art and beauty. The beautiful new furniture in the Union and dormitories has been a source of great satisfaction, especially to the older women. The interest in art has centered around the Woman's Library which houses the unusually interesting collection brought to the University through the efforts of Dr. Boyd. Here several exhibitions have been held which have aroused wide interest not only among students and faculty but among Durham people and many from other parts of the country. Courses in Aesthetics have been offered for the first time this year and next year we are to begin a department of art which we believe will enrich the life of the women and the University in many ways.

In the Library also is the Booklovers' Room where the girls may see lovely things and touch and taste books outside of their usual ken. Here and in the Little Theatre some of the professors have read to small groups, poetry and plays.

In January the School of Nursing was opened with thirty-three student nurses. This offers to women the opportunity to receive after five years of study a Certificate of Nursing and a B.S. in Nursing. A number of women are hoping to become supervisors and superintendents and to enter various fields of public welfare which require such training.

A few illustrations of the varied activities of the women and a new initiative among them are the beginning, under the guarantee of the Women's Student Government Association, of a new magazine, the *Distaff*, edited and managed entirely by women; and the sending of four women, one from each class, by the Student Government Association to several colleges and universities in the south and north to study at close range the systems of student government. On their return a committee was appointed which, after hours of careful study, drew up a new constitution. Perhaps its most interesting feature is the greater opportunity it offers for coöperation between faculty and students. The Student Government Association and the Y. W. C. A. for the second time are sending a Junior to *Junior Month* in Baltimore, to which southern colleges send delegates for a month's study and work in social welfare.

Next year for the first time a Duke University student is joining one of the foreign study groups for the work of the junior year. Edith Lucas, a true Trinity College daughter, is going to France with the University of Delaware Foreign Study Group for a year of carefully supervised study at the Sorbonne and elsewhere and is to receive credit for her junior year on the satisfactory completion of the examinations. One of our recent graduates, Esther Metzenthin, who last year held a fellowship in German at Bryn Mawr, has held this year a foreign fellowship and has been studying at the University of Bonn. We hope that this is only the beginning of opportunities for foreign study for our women.

Other young alumnae have been awarded scholarships and fellowships at Duke and various other institutions in the United States.

Although we recognize that we have many problems to face before we can make the college what we want it to be we believe that we have made some progress and we hope to make yet more next year, especially in the recognition and development of what Prof. McDermott in his address to the seniors called "the enduring values."

Asheville Student Wins Appointment

Miss Evelyn Rogers, of Asheville, has been selected as the Duke University representative to study with the Baltimore Family Welfare Association during the month of June.

Miss Rogers is attending what is known as June Month, conducted each year by the Baltimore association for juniors in a number of colleges, to interest them in social welfare work.

"Enduring Values" Are Stressed By Prof. Malcolm McDermott

In Baccalaureate Address He Calls Attention to the Supremacy of Those Things Which Abide in a Constantly Changing World—Timely Advice Is Given to Candidates for Degrees

THE OPENING event of the 1931 Commencement of Duke University was the baccalaureate address delivered on the evening of Sunday, June 7, by Professor Malcolm McDermott, of the School of Law.

The speaker's subject was "Enduring Values," and he said in part:

"This is an occasion which can and must never lose its significance in the life of the nation. In days gone by we as a people have made great to do when a new army was mustered into service and sent forth to meet the enemy. At such times bands played, banners were unfurled and emotions ran high. There are few if any of us here tonight who have not experienced that peculiar sensation welling up within our breasts as we have watched American youth march forth to war.

"Today, throughout the length and breadth of the land, the nation is mustering into service a new army of citizens, recruited from her youth, intensively trained in her colleges, and now being commissioned into the great force of citizenship. Thoughtful men and women must appreciate the momentous meaning of this hour. I have no hesitancy in saying that it far surpasses in importance the day, when last we sent armed forces into the field. For mark you, my friends, our country's destiny is determined not in times of armed combat, but rather in the insidious days of peace. What these young men and women shall make of America in their every-day life, will fix her future in times of war when and if those evil days again beset us. War is but the revelation of a nation's character already formed. The preparedness that must needs engross our attention is that which produces stalwart, upright manhood and womanhood, rather than guns and battleships.

"These young graduates, will, therefore, understand just why they are the objects of our keen friendly interest and solicitude. And, they will understand, too, the spirit in which their Alma Mater celebrates this occasion as a marked day. Those of us charged with their guidance in the years past will be pardoned if now we grasp a last opportunity to speak words of final counsel unto them.

"Shortly, you will go forth from this place officially designated as 'bachelors' of the arts and of the sciences. It is interesting to know that this term 'bachelor' originally meant a youthful knight who followed the standard of another. The young knight had no retinue or following of his own; he was a novice in the field, and usually as destitute of means as he was of experience. He must therefore elect to become a follower under the banner of some older, experienced and well established leader. Such was the 'bachelor knight' of old.

"We like to think of you, young friends, as knights going forth; but, how we tremble over the choices you shall make!

"No sooner will you get located in your varied fields than will you be called upon to make one choice after another. In your business, in your profession, in the political, religious and every-day life of your community, whether you are conscious of the fact or not, you will have to choose what standard and what leader you shall follow after. This is a process that now takes place so unobserved in the life of the youth of today, that he himself is often unaware of what has been going on. He awakes to find that his choices have been made, with no clear recollection of when any such decisions were reached. This was not true with the 'bachelor knight' of ancient times; the day of decision with him was clearly defined. Before making his choice he surveyed the field; he considered carefully what the banner of each leading knight stood for, and the record behind it. He made his choice accordingly, for henceforth he was stamped with the character of his leader.

"You are aware, I take it, that never before has the world offered to youth such a variety of leadership, of schools of thought, of codes of living, and courses of action. The bars have been let down; yours is a freedom of choice such as was never made possible before. One cannot but sympathize with the youth of today who must feel fairly bewildered as he steps forth and beholds the hosts of banners beckoning him hither and yon. How shall he know which is worthy of his allegiance? How shall he know what choice to make?

"In the experience of mankind it has appeared that there is one sure test which you can safely rely upon. I have never known it to fail. The banners that meet this test are modest in appearance; they make no alluring promises; they play not upon the weaknesses of mankind. On the contrary, they make it plain to you that they will lead you over the rough pathways of endurance and sacrifice. You will recognize these banners by finding enscrolled upon them the simple phrase, 'Enduring Values.' These and only these may you safely follow. It matters not what your occupation or your station may be. By one pathway or another there is a standard bearer beckoning you on to the 'enduring values' of life. These alone are worthy of your allegiance. When fame has betrayed her devotees, when fortune has corrupted its own followers, and when indulgence has destroyed a host of fools, the 'enduring values' of life remain triumphant.

"A superficial glance at life and at history impresses one with the process of ceaseless change that appears to be going on round about us. Generations march on and then off the stage; nations come and go; time seems to take its toll of all that man deals with. Nevertheless, the educated student of history and of present-day life perceives that there are things that do endure. In the realm of science he finds the inscrutable laws of nature running true to form down through the ages. He finds, likewise, that there are laws of human life that operate in similar fashion; he finds that wickedness and corruption among men bring sorrow, destruction and death; while righteousness, decency, love and sacrifice produce happiness and life among the children of men. He finds that all that we hold worth while in this thing we call our civilization, is the stored-up, accumulated product of the lives of men and women of the past who followed after the enduring values. Until a youth can perceive these things he is not educated. The ignorant will say, 'How can I see these things since they are not perceived by the eye?' The natural laws are not thus seen with the eye nor can they be felt with the hand, but are they any the less real? My young friends, the irrefutable testimony of the experience of man upon this earth is that only by following after the enduring values of life can he find peace and happiness. In no other fashion can he link himself to the things that remain.

"I cannot let this opportunity pass without a final word of warning. One cannot deal long with youth without becoming aware of those subtle influences and temptations that destroy even the most promising

careers. The average young graduate approaches life with a pretty fair idea of relative values, with an ambition to amount to something and with a desire unselfishly to serve his fellow men. It is a real tribute to American colleges and universities that such is the characteristic spirit of the young men and women whom they send forth. I should dislike to contemplate the effect upon the nation if such were not the temper of our graduates. But unfortunately, my friends, here is what too frequently happens. This 'bachelor knight' whom I have been talking about, as he looks over the field, temporizes. He admits within his heart that he well knows the standard to which he belongs. But the lure of the blazing, enticing banner draws him on and he decides he will follow it for a while to see the world with the gay throng in unhampered fashion. He fully purposes sooner or later to return and join the force that has steadfastly refused to be drawn aside. Here is where real tragedy in life begins. There is a peculiar thing about this knighthood of life, my young friends. It will not tolerate divided allegiance. When you align yourself with the corrupt and questionable element of your community, the overwhelming odds are that you remain there. It seems that no transfer slips are provided, nor is any arrangement made for exchanges. The forces of evil are moving along at such a fast gait that the young recruit finds it well-nigh impossible to extricate himself and finally abandons the effort.

"Make no mistake, the choices you indulge in when first you begin the ordering of your life will practically settle your destiny.

> Let never man be bold enough to say,
> Thus, and no farther shall my passions stray.
> Our first sin past, compels us into more,
> And guilt grows fate which was but choice before.

"Your Alma Mater covets for you the enduring values of life."

Arkansas Student Heads Religion Group at Duke

B. T. Williams, rising senior in the Duke School of Religion, was named president of the religious group in the school's recent election. Mr. Williams' home is in Ozark, Ark., and he has been serving as student pastor for a Methodist church near Henderson.

Other officers named by the students of the School of Religion are: Raymond W. Council, Union City, Tenn., vice-president; G. R. Stafford, Abingdon, Va., secretary-treasurer.

"The Educated Woman In Social Service Work"

IN addressing the Alumni-Alumnae Luncheon on Alumni Day, Mrs. Emeth Tuttle Cochrane, '06, of Daytona Beach, Florida, said:

"One quotation I remember from college days—Dr. Few's frequent remark: 'All things excellent are as difficult as they are rare.'

"And one of these rare and excellent things, I have learned in the 25 years between then and now, is a college woman, living a so-called home life, who uses her intellect on the problems that her club, her church society, junior league or other group, elect to solve.

"In public welfare particularly, throwing aside their brains, which apparently so easily upset them, the usual run of women, college or otherwise, rush fool-like where trained social workers fear to tread and deal sentimentally with family and community difficulties that require the most careful study and delicate handling.

"One hope I have for Duke is that before many years, every student, whether embryo preacher, teacher, lawyer, doctor, business man, engineer or homemaker, will be required to take a course in family case work, in the department of sociology Dr. Ellwood is now organizing, and will elect one of Dean Miller's courses in social laws.

"These young men and women will learn from actual observation some of the basic causes of our universal need for welfare work, why we have unemployment and illness and poverty and crime and big, degenerate families; and they will be in a position when they leave college to help make democracy safe for the children-to-be.

"Of course, such knowledge and experience may reduce our Lords and Ladies Bountiful, who reside on all our Main streets, but will appreciably increase our real citizens, equipped for constructive service in the improvement of our social order.

"North Carolina for almost 15 years has been leading the south in welfare legislation and administration, largely because she has many excellent and rare women—among them Kate Herring Highsmith of the class of '06—but the tribe must increase if spiritual values are not to be swamped completely by material values.

"Public welfare work is largely preventive—not dramatic. As Dean Miller said in the May REGISTER, 'you can turn out a good crowd any time by putting in a fire alarm, but only a few insurance men and experts come to a demonstration of fire prevention methods.' You can raise money with scarcely any effort for a hurricane disaster in Florida, but when the disaster is slow starvation as a result of drought,

it is hard pulling. A whole church will flare up over the pitiable death of a woman in child-birth, leaving seven little children, and pour out old clothes and food and money, but when the shock is past they forget the day-by-day living.

"It is not enough to get the legislature to pass laws—intelligent women have a responsibility to see that laws are wisely written, are practical and enforceable, otherwise they are just duds in the legislative battlefield. The quite recent legislature passed a progressive child labor law so plainly needed and enforceable that it came near being repealed when some of its supporters were resting after the smoke of battle had cleared away.

"It is not enough to appoint committees and make resolutions—intelligent women must see that the best trained persons are appointed or elected for the administration of new agencies. A good juvenile court law is useless in the hands of a shyster lawyer, picked for judge by some political ring intent on making a 'racket' out of child welfare. The good judge is a social worker as well as a jurist. He handles his cases on an individual, not a rule-of-thumb basis.

"The woman who would meet the day-by-day challenge of preventive work must equip herself with an understanding of the history and life of the state, the workings of governmental bodies and the appreciation of practical politics. Without this knowledge she cannot make real progress in social legislation and in governmental social work; and this, it seems to me, is 'women's work,' to educate themselves and the coming generations on the social needs of the people and to see that these needs are met. To study local needs in housing, recreation, health, domestic difficulties and delinquency; to point out these needs to the community effectively through press and personality and to see them safely through a legislature that has been convinced before it gets to Raleigh.

"I do not think that when our law-makers come from the ranks of future college men and women, with knowledge and appreciation of social needs and social work, we shall have the spectacle of statesmen throwing fits over whether a couple should live apart two or three or five years, to get a divorce and then spending weeks or months debating the mysterious problem of whether cotton mill operatives should work 55 or 60 hours, or more, or whether women and children should work at night.

"In a southern state only the other day, bills were shot through the legislative hopper like bullets, creating new courts, setting up new public jobs and pro-

(Continued on page 206)

Various Records are Broken at Duke During Month of June

Record-Breaking Commencement Is Followed By Summer School Enrollment Which Establishes New High Mark; Junaluska School and Pastors' School Also Go to New Top Figures

JUNE PROVED a month for broken records at Duke University. First an unlooked-for army of alumni and other visitors made Commencement the best attended in the University annals; then followed a record-breaking summer school with more than 900 registered for the first term on the new campus; the affiliated school at Lake Junaluska registered well over 200 students; and finally the Pastors' school went over the 200 mark in its first session on the new campus.

There were many reasons to believe that the summer terms might go below par this season, but already the most successful and best attended school since the hot-weather sessions were started at Trinity in 1919 is under way, according to Dr. Holland Holton, director of the school.

Duke's fame in distant parts of the country is well illustrated by the large number of out-of-state students enrolled for the first term. They come from a score of states, and more than half of them are taking graduate work for credit toward higher degrees.

The excellent start of the summer schools continues the banner year that started with the first occupancy of the new campus last fall. All facilities of the campus were turned over to the summer students and alternating with hard classroom work are recreational and entertainment features in which all of them are participating.

Closing on July 22 the first term will be followed immediately by a second, and there is every indication that the two terms' registration will set a new high record for the thirteen years of summer school operation.

While there will not be a second term of the Junaluska school, a summer school of religion will be conducted there, with Dean Elbert Russell in charge. Professor B. G. Childs is director of the Junaluska summer school.

A capable faculty was assembled for the summer sessions. While a large part of the teaching force is composed of Duke University faculty members, a number of other institutions are represented, including the following: Dr. W. H. Callcott, University of South Carolina; Dr. O. B. Douglass, University of Texas; Dr. M. Slade Kendrick, Cornell University; Dr. J. T. Lister, College of Wooster; Dr. John Lord, Texas Christian University; Dr. Joseph C. McElhannon, dean, Sam Houston State Teachers College; Dr. T. H. Schutte, Alabama Woman's College; Dr. A. R. M. Stowe, Randolph-Macon Woman's College; Dr. D. C. Troth, Pennsylvania State College; and Dr. Douglas E. Scates, director of research and statistics in the Cincinnati public schools.

A number of education experts from various public schools are included in the school faculty.

Growth of the summer school is shown in the registration figures for the years of its operation. In 1919, the opening year, there were 88 students of college rank enrolled. Last year 826 registered for the first term in Durham and 195 for the Junaluska term. Total for all the schools during the summer of 1930 was 1,212 students.

Valuable Fellowships to Duke Economists

Trustees of the Brookings Institution at Washington in announcing the award of a number of research fellowships for next year include the name of Prof. Edward R. Gray, of the economics department of Duke University.

Professor Gray, who is a specialist in the field of financial history and public finance, has been appointed to an exchange fellowship in 1931-1932 in the Handelshochschule, Berlin, Germany. Before coming to Duke, Professor Gray was on the research staff of the United States Treasury Department. He will continue his research work in government finance while in residence in Germany.

C. B. Hagan, another member of the Duke economics department, has been appointed to hold a Carnegie fellowship in international law and will carry on research at Harvard next year.

Robert S. Smith, who is on leave of absence from the graduate school of Duke carrying on research in Spain, has received a second appointment to the Amherst memorial fellowship of $2,000.

Unique Project Being Carried Out in School of Religion

Appointment of Students to Summer Work in Rural Charges Under the Supervision of Regular Pastors Proving Decidedly Successful—Number Grows From Five the First Year to 67 This Summer

THE MOST unique project of its kind in America, and possibly in the world, is being carried out by the Duke Endowment through the Rural Life Department and the School of Religion, Duke University. The project consists of the appointment of students in the School of Religion to summer work in rural charges under the supervision of regular pastors.

Sixty-seven students went out from the University on such work at the close of the Pastors' School. Of this number, thirty-seven will serve as pastors' assistants, eighteen in religious education field work, one in colporteur work, and seventeen in evangelistic work.

The purpose of this plan is to give ministerial candidates practical training and experience in their chosen field of work while they are still engaged in their theological studies. A recent editorial in the New York *Christian Advocate* entitled "Ministerial Internes" praised the Duke project in the highest terms, pointing out that it is in line with a suggestion made several years ago by Dr. Richard Cabot. Dr. Cabot held that theological as well as medical schools should require a period of internship for their students.

Under the Duke plan, students holding scholarships from the foundation are required to do from ten to eleven weeks of supervised field work during the summer quarter. The total year's work for such students consists of the following: Regular class work during the school year; a supplementary course in the spring semester for students who have not yet spent a summer on the field; enrollment and attendance at the Pastors' School in June; ten to eleven weeks of the summer field work; and a supplementary course in the fall semester for those who have spent the summer on the field, this course dealing with practical problems met by the students in their work. The supplementary courses carry one semester hour's credit each and are taught by Professor J. M. Ormond.

As already indicated, the Duke plan has received wide notice and recognition. Directed by Professor Ormond, head of the Rural Life Department, it has grown from a small beginning, through the experimental stage, and into a permanently established policy, pioneering the way in a system of practical training that will probably be adopted in time by other schools. The advantages of the plan are immediately evident. The scholarship enables students who could not otherwise do so to take three years of graduate study in the field of religion, on the completion of which they receive the B.D. degree. The summer work enables the students to do something toward earning the generous scholarship held, rendering a practical service to rural churches which could not afford an assistant for the regular pastor, and at the same time giving the student practical experience along with his academic preparation.

The beginnings of the project were made in 1926, when five students were sent out under the supervision of Professor Ormond. The plan was formally adopted in 1927, with six students sent out that year. The number increased to twenty-one in 1928, to twenty-nine the following year, to fifty-seven in 1930, and to sixty-seven this year.

Four types of work are undertaken, as already stated. Students are sent out to work on pastoral charges only upon request of the pastor himself. The only expense for the local church is that of room, board, and transportation for the student during the summer period. The student is under the direct supervision of the pastor, to be employed in any needed work of assistance. Types of work usually undertaken are community surveys, daily vacation Bible schools, young people's work, evangelistic services in parts of the parish hitherto unreached, and regular pastoral assistance such as calling upon homes and directing groups in the local organization. For the past two years requests for student assistants have been received from more pastors than the department has been able to supply. Students are sent out only to the two North Carolina Conferences.

Students sent out on religious education field work are under the direction of the two Conference Boards of Christian Education. They work in teams of two men each and conduct five-day institutes in local

(Continued on page 205)

Herbarium Acquired By Duke; A Total of 16,000 Specimens

Schallert Collection Brings to University Many "Type" Specimens From all Parts of the
World as Well as Flowering Plants of North Carolina and the South
—Gives the Duke Collection Outstanding Rank

DUKE UNIVERSITY has recently acquired the herbarium of 16,000 specimens collected by Dr. P. O. Schallert, of Winston-Salem, N. C. This addition to the Duke herbarium, secured through the efforts of Dr. H. L. Blomquist, professor of botany at Duke, brings the Duke collection of specimens of flowering plants to outstanding rank in the South. Because the Schallert collection is the largest unit of the Duke herbarium, the entire collection in the Duke Botany Department is to be called the Schallert Herbarium. A more recent addition of another collection of 1,500 specimens, Doctor Blomquist says, continues the plan of Duke's department of botany to secure one of the outstanding herbariums of the world. Doctor Blomquist, himself, and his assistant, Mr. Harold F. Williams, are now engaged in the development of a collection of specimens and photographs of the grasses and sedges of North Carolina. This collection they hope to expand, through their own efforts and through additions from other sources, until it shall contain as nearly as possible all the sedges and grasses of eastern North America.

Dr. Schallert came to North Carolina thirty years ago from Wisconsin. He was educated at Marion College and at the University of Wisconsin, receiving his master's degree in botany. For a number of years he was a teacher in the old Salem Academy and then in Salem College. Several years ago he retired from the work of teaching, confining his work entirely to the practice of medicine and surgery. He has always been interested in botany.

In the earlier days of medicine, all physicians were botanists. They learned the value of plants as medicines and were always on the alert for new herbs which have value as healing agents. Many of them secured rare specimens and cultivated them in order always to have a supply on hand for their medicines.

Doctor Schallert began his work of collecting and preserving specimens of flowering plants more than twenty-five years ago. Many of the specimens were of strange species. These had to be analyzed to determine their names. Much of this work was done by Doctor Schallert. Often, however, he was not satisfied with his own decision. Many of the labels show that his analysis had been confirmed by officials of the United States National Museum, or by scientists of other nations to whom the specimens were sent for this purpose.

The collection contains several plants which Doctor Schallert discovered in their native habitats in Piedmont and Western North Carolina. These had never been analyzed by scientists before. Doctor Schallert analyzed them and gave some of them names.

Many "type" specimens, from all parts of the world also are found in the Schallert Herbarium. A "type" specimen is one which has been secured from the locality in which it was first discovered. Such rare specimens appear in the collection from almost every part of the world. There are preserved specimens from more than half of the United States of America; from half of the provinces of Canada; from Alaska; Labrador, Iceland, Island of Spitsbergen, located near the Arctic Circle, Mexico, Nicaragua, Guatamala, Honduras, Isthmus of Panama, British and Dutch Guiana, Brazil, Argentina, Chile, Peru, Trinidad, Porto Rico, Cuba, Jamaica, Virgin Islands, Bermuda, all parts of Africa, China, Japan, every European country, British Isles, and from India.

Outstanding are the grasses, ferns, mosses, and pod-bearing plants. There are more than 4,000 kinds of mosses represented in the collection. The specimens of grasses number over 500 with as many of the pod-bearing plants, such as beans and clover, and there are 1,000 species of ferns. Probably the most attractive group in the entire collection to the casual observer is that of the sea weeds. They represent almost every color of the rainbow. Many of these are from the North Pacific ocean.

Among the rare plants secured by Doctor Schallert, in North Carolina, are the ephebe Lesquerii Born; umbilicara Caroliniana, which are lichens; two species of hepatica, the bazarrania denudata, and bazzania nudicaulis; mosses; brothera; leana viridis; and a rediscovered specimen of campylopus Tallunensis. The campylopus Tallunensis was probably first discovered by Dr. de Schweintz, a botanist from Europe who worked in Piedmont North Carolina for several years. There seems to be only one other specimen of the ephebe in existence. This is marked "exists only in eastern North America." It was placed in a Paris herbarium by a scientist named Lesquerii, who was probably a friend of Dr. de Schweintz.

In addition to these plants there appear in the collection specimens of the famous Venus Fly Trap, which grows only in a section of about a hundred miles long and thirty miles wide, with Wilmington, North Carolina, at the center. Doctor Schallert also discovered a new pitcher plant. He is, however, most interested in mosses and lichens and is considered an authority on these. Many famous scientists have visited him for consultations concerning these types of plants.

Doctor Schallert, himself, has spent more than twenty-five years in making his herbarium. Parts of it, however, are more than a hundred years old. Rev. Mr. Denke, a Moravian minister in Salem, N. C., began an herbarium sometime between 1812 and 1824. This collection was in the possession of Salem Academy when Doctor Schallert came to North Carolina. While he was instructor in the college, he renovated the Denke Herbarium, mounting and naming many of the specimens. Duplicates were given to Doctor Schallert by Salem College to add to his own collection, which was already of considerable size.

Personal research, of course, has been responsible for much of the herbarium. Exchanging specimens with scientists in other parts of the world has added many to the collection. The Moravian Missionary System has also contributed to its success. Doctor Schallert has secured specimens from virtually every Moravian mission field in the world.

Much time and care must be given to such a collection which is virtually a small museum. It eventually grows beyond the physical ability of a practicing physician to give sufficient time to such work. But Doctor Schallert had a double interest to gratify in allowing Duke University to acquire his herbarium. In addition to his desire to place his collection where it would be well cared for he wished it to go to the institution of which his daughter is a graduate. Miss Dorothy Schallert was a member of the Class of '28. She secured a master's degree in zoölogy and is now an assistant at Cornell University, Ithaca, N. Y. His great personal friendship for Doctor Blomquist was also a factor in the transaction. The two scientists have made many trips together in their work. These reasons made possible the acquiring of the collection at a price which made it partly a gift to Duke University.

Doctor Schallert continues his interest in this field, having already started another herbarium which is growing rapidly. He hopes to be able to spend many years in this work after retiring from the active practice of medicine.

Unique Project Being Carried Out in School of Religion

(*Continued from page 203*)

churches. The institutes are known as "Cokesbury Schools" and are standardized under the system of the General Board of Christian Education at Nashville. Courses offered consist of religious education methods for the local church, training in worship, and local church evangelism. Churches make arrangements in advance with the Conference Board of Christian Education for these institutes. The students employed in this work are required to qualify with the General Board of Education as instructors before they are sent out.

The third type, that of evangelistic work, will be conducted this year in the Durham, Raleigh, New Bern, and Waynesville districts of the two Conferences, with teams consisting of two and three men each. These will conduct evangelistic services in parts of the districts difficult to reach in the regular pastoral programs. They will be under the direction of the presiding elder of the district and of the pastor of the parish in which the services are held. This work has proved to be a decided success in its results, both to the communities served and to the students in the experience of adjusting themselves to practical circumstances.

The last type of work is a new departure, an experiment in adult education. One student will be sent out this year as a colporteur, to sell and distribute literature issued from the secular and religious press. Individual qualifications of students sent out are always carefully considered in advance in order that the best results may be obtained from this plan. During the three-year course required for a degree in religion it usually happens that men are assigned to different work each summer, though in some cases their success has been so outstanding that they have been continued in the same field. The men are required to submit a written report to the Rural Life Department every two weeks, while reports are also secured from the pastors and the supervisors of teams. This year Professor Ormond plans to make a number of visits over the territory served in order to observe the work being done.

In addition to these types of work, a considerable number of students are serving as regular pastors of churches in the vicinity of the University. The University is to be congratulated upon the success of its project in this field, as are Professor Ormond and those assisting him.

Dr. A. M. Proctor Chairman of Research Committee

(Continued from page 188)

schools in Kinston and is a former president of the North Carolina Education Association.

"Dr. Cook considers the committee as a well balanced group. Jule B. Warren, of Raleigh, secretary-treasurer of the North Carolina Education Association, will serve as a member of the committee ex-officio, the same being true of Dr. Cook, who is dean of education at North Carolina college, as well as president of the association.

"The committee will obtain assistance from a number of other persons from time to time, these to include M. C. S. Noble, Jr., and L. H. Jobe, of the state department of public instruction.

"Answers to the following questions will be sought by the research committee:

"(1) What is the present standing of the public schools in North Carolina and what are their defects?

"(2) What is needed to develop the schools as they should be developed to bring them up to proper standards?

"(3) What will the cost be?

"(4) From what sources may the money be obtained?

"Findings of the committee will be made public from time to time. The final report, it is anticipated, will be made available for public consideration slightly less than one year hence, in time for its dissemination prior to the declarations of the various candidates for legislative offices."

"The Educated Woman In Social Service Work"

(Continued from page 201)

posing new projects that will take thousands of dollars in tax money to maintain, yet that legislature refused to pass a workman's compensation act, it did not provide for a state tuberculosis sanatorium so greatly needed; a probation officer was regarded as unnecessary in a county where problem children are numerous; a bill limiting the hours of labor for women was killed and one substituted that exempted practically every class of female labor in the state, and there is no specific law on the books to put an end to the activities of so-called social agencies that prey upon the charity-minded public and cripple rather than aid legitimate social welfare efforts. All this is due to the fact that men and women interested and trained in welfare enterprises were in an ineffective minority both among the legislators and the public. College women, especially, should make such things impossible at this stage of the 20th century.

"Being a social worker I cannot stop without pointing to a very obvious job for the women of this state. In 1923, by hard work, a group of rare and excellent men and women succeeded in convincing the legislature of the need of a mothers' aid law and $50,000 was appropriated by the state annually for the work, to be met by $50,000 from the counties. Four legislatures have met since then and the annual appropriation remains the same.

"There is no greater preventive work possible in the state than the preservation of its good homes. New York and Pennsylvania and other states are spending millions each year for this purpose. Florida counties, without state aid are investing about $200,-000 a year in home preservation through aid for mothers. North Carolina women should write the state board for facts on this law and stir enough interest by bombarding their county commissioners with worthy cases to get $100,000 state appropriation when another legislature meets. If the women here today would use their leisure and excess energy on this one thing between now and the 1933 session, they would be wiser women, better citizens and many a child now on the way to institutions, reform schools and prisons would enjoy the benefits of the child's Bill of Rights."

Nine Law Students Enter Legal Fraternity at Duke

Nine law students have been initiated by the Richmond Pearson chapter of Sigma Nu Phi, national legal fraternity at Duke University. They are: Henry H. Robbins, Jr., Cornelius; William C. Lassiter, Smithfield; William Franklin Howland, Jr., Henderson; James Keith Harrison, High Point; James Everett Horton, Durham; Alton J. Knight, Durham; Elliott C. Meyers, Ironton, O.; and Coy Willard, High Point.

German Fraternity Will Go to Duke

The Duke University German Club has received its charter as a member of Delta Phi Alpha, national German fraternity. The formal installation will take place in the fall.

Organized in 1929, the national fraternity will have 15 chapters when the Omicron chapter is formally established at Duke. Excellence in the German language and a better understanding of the German nation and culture is sought by the fraternity.

Officers of the Duke club are: Arthur Koffler, Stamford, Conn., president; Miss Elizabeth Powell, Warsaw, vice-president; Miss Eleanor Peek, Durham, secretary; Milton Cullen, Mattapan, Mass., treasurer; and H. A. Ellis, Asheville, program executive.

| Where They Are Located | # News of the Alumni | What They Are Doing |

Miss Elizabeth Aldridge, '24, Secretary of Alumnae Council, Editor

CLASS OF 1889

Lammie Paul Welborn taught school for about twenty years in North and South Carolina and Missouri. Since that time he has been engaged in banking and farming. He is cashier of the Houstonia Bank, Houstonia, Missouri, owner of a farm and president of the Farmers Exchange. He has three children, two daughters and a son.

CLASS OF 1897

Luther M. Carlton studied law at the University of North Carolina and received his law license from the Supreme Court of North Carolina in 1900. Since that time he has practiced law in Roxboro, being in partnership with Hon. W. W. Kitchin from 1901 to 1909. His office is in the First National Bank building. He also has a branch office in Yanceyville.

CLASS OF 1898

Silas O. Thorne has been associated with the Grinnell Company, Inc., General Fire Extinguisher Company, since 1901. He is manager of the plant at 1331 W. Morehead Street, Charlotte. He married Clarissa Abbey on July 5, 1923. They have one son, Silas O. Thorne, Jr.

John Moseley Bowden is engaged in truck and general farming at Route No. 3, Faison, N. C.

Dr. Martin L. Matthews practices medicine at Sanford, N. C. He is an eye, ear, nose and throat specialist. He received his M.D. degree from the University of North Carolina and later took graduate work at Tulane University.

CLASS OF 1899

Isabel Elias married Virgil L. Jones, who is professor of English and Dean, College of Arts and Sciences, University of Arkansas, on June 20, 1905. Their oldest daughter, Dorothy, was graduated from the University of Arkansas in 1926 and received her A.M. degree from the University of Chicago in 1927. Their second daughter, Isabel, entered University of Arkansas this year. Alice is still in high school.

Charles Gaines Montgomery, Jr., 269 Granville Road, Myers Park, Charlotte, is contact representative, U. S. Veterans' Bureau. His office is in the Johnston building.

CLASS OF 1909

Mr. and Mrs. M. A. Briggs (Frances Markham) are receiving congratulations on the birth of a son, M. Arnold Briggs, Jr., who was born in Durham on March 28.

CLASS OF 1916

Myron G. Ellis is secretary of the California Alumni Association of Duke University. He recently wrote about the gathering of a small group of Southern California Alumni and their families on Sunday, May 17, at the home of Sam J. Gantt, '13, and Mrs. Gantt (Mabel Isley, '11) at Beaumont, California. Eighteen persons were present and after a picnic dinner served in the Gantt home everyone went out to Mr. Gantt's sixty-five acre cherry ranch and helped themselves to the ripe fruit.

Mr. Ellis regretted very much his inability to attend his class reunion this year, but due to the fact that he expected to be in Juneau, Alaska, during Commencement week had to forego the pleasure.

CLASS OF 1919

Dr. John I. Gale is practicing dentistry at Rocky Mount, N. C. He was married to Miss Mary Anna Hobbs on October 9, 1930 at Emporia, Va.

The lines below in regard to Bob Bradshaw were taken from the *North Carolina Christian Advocate* for April 16, 1931.

"Robert W. Bradshaw, who for nine years has been principal of the Children's Home school system and during the past year serving as assistant superintendent in addition to his former duties, was recently recommended by the Centenary-West End quarterly conference to the Winston-Salem district conference, soon to assemble, for license to preach. It is expected that the district conference will recommend him for admission on trial into the North Carolina Conference this fall, where in all probability he will receive an appointment, thus following his distinguished father, Dr. Mike Bradshaw, '78, who last year superannuated after a most outstanding and successful period of ministry. When Mr. Bradshaw months ago informed the writer of his intention an effort was made to have him reconsider and remain with the Children's Home, where his services are so effective and he himself so highly esteemed. But when informed that a definite call, which had gone unanswered for a number of years, should no longer go unheeded, I clasped his hand with the assurance that God was having his way with one of his choice servants.

"The Children's Home will sorely miss the services of this distinguished young man. His life is closely entwined about the life of every boy and girl at the Home. We are glad that we shall have his continued services until early fall, when he will leave to join his father and mother in Durham. Mr. Bradshaw received his A.B. from Trinity College in 1921 and one year later received his A.M. from Columbia University. Sincere in soul and genuine in purpose Mr. Bradshaw will without doubt serve mighty well as a Methodist preacher."

CLASS OF 1920

S. Earl Stone has moved from Asheville to 202 Wilson Street, Lenoir.

CLASS OF 1922

Dr. Patty Groves, who is resident physician at Mount Holyoke College, South Hadley, Mass., is holding a similar position at George Peabody College, Nashville, Tennessee, during the summer term.

Irene Jeffries of Gaffney, S. C. and Mr. George D. Manning of Durham were married on Friday evening, June 12, at the home of the bride's sister in Chapel Hill, N. C. Mr. Manning is connected with the U. S. Customs Office of Durham, acting as U. S. storekeeper of government bonded warehouses of Liggett & Myers Tobacco Company. They will make their home at 108 Markham Avenue.

Rev. Martin R. Chambers is pastor at Charleston, Tennessee, in charge of three churches. He has two sons, John, age seven and Robert, age three. He says they are both looking forward to coming to Duke University as soon as they are prepared to enter the freshman class.

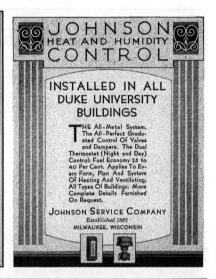

CLASS OF 1923

On April 11, at high noon, William H. Ellison was married to Miss Clara M. Sawyer of Belhaven in the Episcopal Church at Norfolk, Va. Bill is doing scientific research for the Atlantic Coast Fisheries with headquarters at New London, Conn.

At the First Presbyterian Church in Durham on April 18, Lois Claytor was married to Reverend David B. Walthall. Lois has been engaged in Christian education work in Richmond, Va. for the past few years. The Reverend Mr. Walthall is pastor of the Presbyterian church at Glade Springs, Va. He attended Davidson College and the University of Virginia, and is a graduate of the Union Theological Seminary of Richmond.

Mr. and Mrs. J. S. Babb (Lucille Massey) of Knox Circle, Durham, are receiving congratulations on the birth of a daughter, April 28.

The engagement of Gertrude Smith of Cooleemee, N. C., has been announced by her parents. She is to wed Mr. Noble Wishard Lee of Chicago, Ill., during the summer. Gertie attended the University of Chicago after leaving Duke receiving her A.M. degree in History. Mr. Lee is an alumnus of Harvard University. He was also a student of the John Marshall Law School of Chicago, where his father is dean. He is at present practicing law in Chicago and also acting instructor of law in the John Marshall Law School.

CLASS OF 1924

Mr. and Mrs. H. A. Oliver of Lumberton have a son, John Hal, who was born on Monday, April 13, 1931.

Ann Greene was born on April 16, 1931, at Wilson, N. C. She is the daughter of Mr. and Mrs. Fred Greene.

Rev. and Mrs. C. S. Green of Durham announce the arrival of Nancy Rose Green on May 29 at the Duke University Hospital. Mrs. Green will be remembered as Mary Morris, '25.

W. Leak Pegues is located at 637 Holley Avenue, Charleston, West Virginia. He is employed by the Carbide and Carbon Chemical Corporation of that city.

CLASS OF 1925

Mr. and Mrs. Jasper L. Clute have announced the arrival of Albert Leslie Clute on May 8, 1931. Jasper's address is 1802 Cervantes Street, Pensacola, Florida.

Franklin Shinn and Miss Lillie Milford, of Abbeville, S. C., were married on May 16 at the home of the bride. Mrs. Shinn has been teaching in Norwood for the past few years since graduating from Winthrop College. They will make their home in Norwood where Franklin is connected with the Norwood Manufacturing Company.

Robert Daniel Kramer, formerly of Elizabeth City, and Miss Elise Everett of Holland, Va., were married on June 16 at the home of the bride. They will make their home in Holland, Va.

Alice Dunton has received a Moore Fellowship in History at the University of Pennsylvania for next year. Alice received her A.M. from Duke University in June, 1930. She will work toward a Ph.D. degree at Pennsylvania next year.

James Rhyne Killian, Jr., editor of the *Technology Review*, one of the best publications of its kind in the country, represented Massachusetts Institute of Technology at the recent dedication of the School of Medicine of Duke University.

Nancy Louise Kirkman was married on December 24, 1930, to Mr. A. E. Poston in the Madison Avenue Church, New York City. Nancy has been with the New York Public Library for the past three years. Mr. Poston is connected with the Wachovia Bank and Trust Company in High Point.

Lillian Frost and Louise McAnally, '26, live at 110 Morningside Drive, New York City. Lillian is with the Science McCall's News Company and Louise is with the Standard Brands.

CLASS OF 1926

Gay W. Allen has accepted a position for next year in the Department of English of A. P. I., Auburn, Alabama. For the past two years he has been Assistant Professor of English at Lake Erie College, Painesville, Ohio. Gay will devote his time this summer to graduate study at the University of Wisconsin. He will live at the University Club, Madison, Wisconsin.

The marriage of Sara Winnie Jones, '26, and Byrd I. Satterfield, '22, was solemnized at the Holland Christian Church, Holland, Va., on June 11. Mr. and Mrs. Satterfield will live in Durham where he practices law.

Martin Lee Black, Jr. and Ann Biggerstaff, '31, were married at the Methodist Church in Danville, Va., on April 18. Black has been an assistant in the Department of Economics at Duke during the past year. They will reside during the summer at 902 South Brevard Street, Charlotte.

CLASS OF 1927

Esther Metzenthin has been taking graduate work at the University of Bonn, Germany, for the past year. Next year she will have a teaching scholarship at Bryn Mawr College, Bryn Mawr, Pa.

John Westbrook has accepted a call as pastor of the First Congregational Church of Cornwall, Conn. He was married on

June 20 to Miss Margaret Alice Pettigrew, daughter of Mr. and Mrs. William Pettigrew of Kangpoki, Assam, India. Frank Craven, '26, attended John as best man.

John Harry Sikes has joined the sports staff of *The Cleveland Press*. He formerly was a sports writer for *The Pittsburgh Press*.

Wilfred Turner Young, son of Mr. and Mrs. Alfred H. Young of Wilmington, was born on Friday, April 17 at Wilmington, N. C.

CLASS OF 1928

Allan D. Ivie, Jr., well known Leaksville attorney, was recently appointed solicitor of the Recorder's Court for Leaksville Township by the Board of Commissioners of Rockingham County. He was appointed for a term of two years. Allan has been practicing law in Leaksville with marked success since being admitted to the bar of North Carolina in December, 1927.

On Thursday, July 2, at the First Baptist Church in Montclair, New Jersey, Lyman H. Bishop will wed Miss Mary Chancellor Delano of that city. Lyman has been connected with the N. J. Bell Telephone Company for the past two years.

Joe Kenneth Matheson and Miss Phyllis Bryant Rogers were married in Charlotte on June 6. Mrs. Matheson graduated from N. C. C. W. and has been teaching for the past few years in Cornelius, N. C. Joe holds a position with the Mill Power Supply Company of Charlotte.

Clarence H. James has moved from 308 West 93rd. Street, New York City to 5049-48th. Street, Sunnyside, Long Island, New York.

CLASS OF 1929

J. Chesley Mathews has been awarded one of the ten University Fellowships of the University of California for the year 1931-32. He will devote his entire time to study. His address will remain Box 200, International House, Berkeley.

The wedding of Ruby Johns and H. Lynwood Elmore was solemnized on Tuesday afternoon at 4 o'clock, June 16, at the Watts Street Baptist Church, Durham. The Rev. C. S. Green, A.M. '24, officiated. Mr. and Mrs. Elmore will make their home in Rocky Mount where Lynwood is engaged in the practice of law.

The wedding of The Rev. Ernest C. Kolb, A.M. 29, and Miss Lucy Mayo Spivey took place in the First Baptist Church of Conway, S. C., on June 16 at six o'clock. After the first of July they will be at home at Windsor, N. C.

Maybeth Steidley and Mr. Emerson Clark Dillon were married on Saturday, April 25, in High Point, N. C., where they will make their home.

CLASS OF 1930

Frances Mason and Donald Hayes Clement were married on Saturday morning, June 20, at ten o'clock in Duke Memorial Church, Durham. Frances has been teaching in the Durham City Schools during the past year. She was attended by Leila Self, '30, and Priscilla Gregory, '29.

Harry Councilor was married in Winston-Salem on June 20, to Miss Mildred Fleming. Dayton Dean acted as best man. Mr. and Mrs. Councilor will spend the summer months in the mountains of Connecticut.

Charles G. Biggs was married to Miss Martha Gertrude Redfern of Lillington, N. C., on October 19, 1929. They live now at 227 Bellamy Avenue, Norfolk, Va.

Howard Reid Mobley, and Miss Sarah Johnston were married on June 9 at Halifax, Va.

Warren C. Ogden, A.M. '30, is a newspaper reporter for the Mobile *Register*, Mobile, Ala.

Harold Charles Weingarten is secretary of the Board of directors of Weingarten's Dress Company at 247 West 37th Street, New York City.

● NEW BOOKS

NORFOLK: HISTORIC SOUTHERN PORT
By THOMAS J. WERTENBAKER.
Probable price $4.00.
This history of Norfolk from the earliest settlement to the last decade is written with special attention to the effect of national events on this historic center of southern commerce. The book is a pioneer effort to link local history to national events. The method of treatment and the fascinating style make the study of value not only to the citizen of Norfolk but to the student interested in the history of the South and of the nation.

TRAILING TRADE A MILLION MILES
By JAMES A. THOMAS.
Probable price $3.50.
The personal opinions and observations of the author of *A Pioneer Tobacco Merchant in the Orient*. Between 1886 and 1923 the author travelled over a million miles as agent for tobacco companies, a pioneer missionary of trade to the Orient. Observations gleaned from the wealth of experiences and multitude of personal contacts with people of all ranks of life are set forth in this second book by Mr. Thomas.

THE COUNTRY CHURCH IN NORTH CAROLINA
By J. MARVIN ORMOND.
Probable price $4.00.
An economic and religious survey of the one hundred counties of North Carolina. A comparison of the economic resources of each county with the number of sects, value and number of church buildings, proportion of church membership to the total population, and the work of Sunday schools and other organizations is presented in a succinct manner.

THE PERIODICALS OF AMERICAN TRANSCENDENTALISM
By CLARENCE GOHDES.
Probable price $3.50.
A study of coöperative literary activity upon the part of the religious, social, and literary radicals who were called "transcendentalists." Some new Emerson material is included.

Gray Manufacturing Co.
Flint Manufacturing Co. No. 1
Flint Manufacturing Co. No. 2
Arlington Cotton Mills
Myrtle Mills, Inc.
Arkray Mills, Inc.

*Spinners and Doublers Fine Combed
and Double Carded*

LONG STAPLE PEELER and EGYPTIAN YARNS

20's to 120's.

Put up in all Descriptions for the Following Industries:

ELECTRICAL	WEAVERS
LACE	KNITTERS
MERCERIZERS	THREAD

MAIN OFFICE:	DIVISION OFFICES:	GENERAL SALES OFFICE:
Gastonia, N. C.	Boston	New York City
	Philadelphia	
	Chicago	
	Chattanooga	

FEEL *the difference* · HEAR *the difference*
TASTE THE DIFFERENCE!

Like an oasis in the dusty desert of dried tobacco, the new Camel Humidor Pack brings you the joy of fine quality cigarettes in prime mild condition.

Now, wherever you go, you can always be sure of getting a *fresh*, throat-easy cigarette when you demand Camels.

It's easy to tell the difference. Your sense of touch detects it as you roll a cigarette between your fingers. Dry tobacco is stiff and crumbly. Camels are full bodied and pliant.

Even your ear can tell the difference. For a dried out cigarette crackles when you roll it.

But the real test is taste and taste is causing a great nation-wide switch of men and women alike to Camels in the scientific new Humidor Pack.

As you draw in that fragrant, mild, cool smoke, redolent with the luxury of fine Turkish and mellow Domestic leaves, only then do you realize the full importance of this new Humidor Pack.

For scorched or dried tobacco is brash and tasteless and its smoke is unkindly hot to the tongue and throat.

If you are a Camel smoker you have already noticed the improvement the new Humidor Pack makes in this your favorite cigarette.

If you don't smoke Camels, try them for just one day to see how much you're missing. After you've known the mildness and joy of a really *fresh* cigarette, switch back if you can.

R. J. REYNOLDS TOBACCO COMPANY, *Winston-Salem, N. C.*

It is the mark of a considerate hostess, by means of the Humidor Pack, to "Serve a fresh cigarette." Buy Camels by the carton—this cigarette will remain fresh in your home and office.

CAMELS

DUKE UNIVERSITY
ALUMNI REGISTER

PHOTOGRAPHS OF NORTH CAROLINA FLOWERS
Made by Dr. H. L. Blomquist, Professor of Botany, Duke University

Duke University Alumni Register

(Member of American Alumni Council)

Published at Durham, N. C. Every Month in the Year in the Interest of the University and the Alumni

| Volume XVII | July, 1931 | Number 7 |

In This Issue

Editor and Business Manager .... HENRY R. DWIRE, '02

Assistant Editors .... ELIZABETH ALDRIDGE, '24
.... ALBERT A. WILKINSON, '26

Advertising Manager.......................... CHARLES A. DUKES, '29

TWO DOLLARS A YEAR   20 CENTS A COPY

ENTERED AS SECOND-CLASS MATTER AT THE POST-OFFICE AT
DURHAM, NORTH CAROLINA

ATTRACTED ATTENTION

The cover page on the June issue of the ALUMNI REGISTER, showing the detail of the entrance to Crowell Tower, has attracted much attention. No doubt it caused some readers of the REGISTER to realize afresh the fact that the buildings on the new Duke campus are notable, not only from the standpoint of their tremendous size and architectural excellence in their general lines, but also from the standpoint of minute detail. Many of the doors and windows on the campus are particularly beautiful, but not everyone pauses long enough to see such details.

Incidentally, there is material for a real story on the significance of the various coats-of-arms and other figures carved on the various buildings. Such a story is now being prepared, and is sure to be especially interesting to REGISTER readers.

THE JUNE ISSUE

There have been many requests for extra copies of the ALUMNI REGISTER for June, containing the various Commencement addresses. A few copies are still available for those who desire them.

NEXT MONTH

The August REGISTER, appearing about August 20, will contain much interesting information relative to plans for the opening of the new academic year at Duke. There will be some particularly good photographs.

THE EDITOR.

groups and rendering allied service of real importance; the Duke Press is rendering a service that goes far beyond the bounds of the campus by publishing books of a scholarly nature that might not be given to the world otherwise, to say nothing of the contribution rendered by its various scholarly periodicals; valuable manuscripts and documents of priceless value are being collected in the libraries, not simply for the use of Duke students but as a definite contribution to the cause of learning in a far wider sense; the university has made it possible for members of its faculty to serve on various legal, scientific, medical and other boards and commissions, and in this and other ways the state and section and nation are being served.

Many more lines of constructive effort might be mentioned in addition to those enumerated above.

Those given, however, are sufficient to indicate the ever-widening scope of influence of an institution that is not going to be content simply with offering exceptional facilities to a limited number of individuals who matriculate as students, but is going to strive constantly to be helpful to many thousands who may never see its campus at all.

AN EXPANDED PROGRAM

Coach Wallace Wade has only been at Duke a few months but he has been there long enough to make some facts regarding his policies perfectly plain.

For one thing, he has said enough and done enough since coming here to show that he thinks intercollegiate athletic contests are only one feature of a much larger athletic program and that he intends to give considerable time and attention at Duke to the development of other features.

One of them will be a comprehensive program of intra-mural sports, the purpose of this and other features being to make available to as large a group of students as possible the undeniable benefits of participation in properly conducted college sports.

One of the complaints about college athletics in the past has been that too few students have been brought into the scope of influence of such athletics.

It has been frequently said that relatively too much time and effort and money are being expended on something which at best benefits directly a very small proportion of a student body.

Coach Wade shows conclusively that it is his purpose to develop at Duke University an athletic program that will be of benefit to students generally. And in doing that he will make a real contribution to the cause of college athletics.

A DISTINCT CONTRIBUTION

A perusal of the list of eminent men in various lines who have been brought to Duke University during the past year to deliver lectures and to render service in other ways is very impressive indeed.

There is no greater source of inspiration than contact with a great man or woman and in increasing the possibility of such contacts Duke University is doing something that is decidedly worth while, not only for its students but for many outside its walls as well.

Description of Photographs on the Front Cover

THE FRONT COVER of this issue of the ALUMNI REGISTER contains some interesting photographs taken by Dr. H. L. Blomquist, of the Duke faculty, showing North Carolina wild flowers. Following is a brief description of the various flowers:

(1) Famous Venus Flytrap, Eastern North Carolina, particularly Wilmington section; (2) Lencothoe (Doghobble) Western North Carolina; (3) Flower of the Yellow Pitcher plant, commonly called "Cups and Saucers and Biscuits," Eastern North Carolina"; (4) Purple Rhododendron; (5) White-fringed Orchid, Eastern North Carolina; (6) Curious Lupine, extreme Eastern North Carolina, one of three in State; (7) Velvet Grass, a favorite of Dr. Blomquist.

Duke University Day Program At Junaluska Decided Success

Record-Breaking Attendance, Notably Good Addresses By President Few and Coach
Wade, Showing of New Duke Pictures, High-Class Musical Program and Other
Features Make Occasion One Long to Be Remembered

THE MOST successful observance of Duke University Day at Lake Junaluska in the history of these annual occasions was that of Tuesday, July 14, when alumni from all parts of Western North Carolina and other guests participated in a variety of events opening with the motorcade to the Great Smokies in the early afternoon and concluding with the public meeting at the auditorium in the evening. Coming between these two events were the water sports, the musical program at the auditorium in the afternoon and the highly successful alumni dinner at Mission Inn at 6:30 p. m.

PRESIDENT FEW'S ADDRESS

The address of President W. P. Few was the principal event of the public gathering in the evening, this being followed by the showing of the moving pictures of Duke University and preceded by a thoroughly pleasing musical program.

Speaking on the "Unity of Architecture at Duke University and the Ideas that Underlie It," President Few gave former Duke men and their friends such a picture of the new university and the future that lies ahead of it as they had not had before.

In its news report, the *Asheville Citizen* said, in part:

In Dr. Few's speech culminated the most successful reunion of Duke University alumni ever held in Western North Carolina. It was heard by hundreds of former students of Duke and many others who are friends of the institution.

COACH WADE SPEAKS

The president's address was delivered following a banquet at which the chief speaker was Wallace Wade, famous football coach of Duke University.

Dr. Few, in his address, in connection with the showing of motion pictures of the University buildings and campus, pointed out the significance of the architecture and said its peculiar spirit of unity and harmony was in keeping with the purposes and ideals of the university.

"Beyond their physical beauty and harmony," said the president, "they have a suggestive power. As they stand through the centuries the beauty of them will sensitize the soul of many a youth and lead him out into some sweet golden clime of the imagination from which he will return a transformed man as from some mount of vision.

"The architectural harmony and strength of the plant," he continued, "are intended to suggest the unity and fullness of life. Everywhere in the university we are trying to break down departmentalizing walls and make education a unified process. The university is built and organized with a compactness that ought to make it natural for students and teachers to think and work more and more from a common point of view rather than from the standpoint of conflicting interests. This underlying conception of the mission of Duke University has affected the building and organization of every part of it."

After speaking specifically of the ideals for several schools of the university, Dr. Few continued:

"These illustrations point to a unity and common intention that will run through the university. And if Duke University is to have this unity and round completeness, it must ever cherish some galvanizing central principle that will hold it from disintegration. On the campus, the chapel, hard by the library and the laboratories and coöperating with the university in its every effort to promote truth and serve humanity, is not only central, but with its stained glass, its vaulted roof and noble spire, will dominate the place. This is intended to be symbolical of the truth that the spiritual is the central and dominant thing in the life of man.

LIBERATE POWERS

"Can this ideal be realized in our world and can religion and education in its highest forms ever engage to make this a better world than man has yet known? Duke University is founded in that faith; but we realize that it must be a religion that comprehends the whole of life and an education that seeks to liberate all the powers and develop all the capacities of our human nature.

"More and more religion and education must realize and combine to teach that the advancement of mankind depends largely upon a better understanding of the laws of nature and man's relation to these laws.

"When the forces of religion and education can heartily join in the common task not only to help the poor but to destroy the seeds of poverty; not only to provide instruction in a limited field and with limited facilities but devote themselves to painstaking and unflinching search for and defense of truth in all its relationships; not only to rescue the lost but to create an atmosphere and climate of opinion in which the truth, the beautiful, and the good can grow, then we may expect a steadiness in the progress of the race instead of the monotonous rise and fall in moral power, instead of the come and go in aspiration and achievement; instead of the spiritual ebb and flow that is so conspicuous in the records of mankind. And when that glad day arrives religion and education will have a program for their combined activities in which the two will work together, each giving its all in whole hearted coöperation for a completely redeemed humanity."

At the Duke dinner, at which Henry R. Dwire presided as toastmaster, Coach Wallace Wade spoke interestingly and effectively of the athletic program for the future at Duke University.

The Duke Day events were in charge of a committee from the Junaluska Summer School, affiliated with Duke University. Quinton Holton was Chairman of the committee which worked most efficiently with Prof. B. G. Childs and the Alumni Office in the effort to make the 1931 Duke Day events at Junaluska the best ever held there.

Notable Increase In Circulation of Books In Duke University Library

Notable strides are being made in the Duke University library circulation, figures for the fiscal year ending June 30 reveal.

During the period circulation from the general library and the School of Religion library totalled 186,777, according to Benjamin E. Powell, director of circulation, while that of the Woman's College was 10,452, a total of 197,229.

These figures do not include circulation of books from the School of Law library, that of Medicine, or the sciences, biology, chemistry and physics. Much of the reading in these libraries is done in reading rooms; and records similar to those of the general library were not available from various smaller libraries.

The big gain made is shown by comparison with other years. Circulation in 1928-29 reached 128,052;

and last year there was a reading list of 154,479. The increase was 32,298, or more than 20 per cent.

The greatest number of books came out of the reserve room, the total being 110,431. Fourteen day books from the stacks came second, with a total circulation of 45,500; while volumes in the general reading room ran to a total of 14,600. The School of Religion library reported a circulation of 12,146; while the graduate reading room which, as the School of Religion, has books on open shelves, listed 3,250.

Even these circulation figures are exceeded by those of the summer school, however. The highest daily reserve book circulation prior to the summer school session was 900, Mr. Powell said; while the summer school reserve book circulation has been running between 1,000 and 1,500. The peak circulation for the summer was 1,800, or an average of two books per student a day.

Articles In South Atlantic Quarterly Attracting Attention

The South Atlantic Quarterly, published for the South Atlantic Publishing Company by the Duke University Press, is growing steadily in circulation and reader interest. The July number, just from the press, contains eight interesting feature articles in addition to many pages of book reviews and similar matter. The table of contents for the current issue is as follows:

George Washington and Entangling Alliances, J. G. Randall; God's Vagabond: St. Francis of Assisi, Gamaliel Bradford; Renouncing War and Establishing Peace, David Y. Thomas; Reid Hall: A Relic of Old Paris, Dorothy Louise Mackay; The Tall Tale in Texas, Mody C. Boatright; The Significance of the Pan-American Movement, J. Fred Rippy; The Poet Laureate of Hope End, Annette B. Hopkins; The World and Its Mail, Norman L. Hill.

During recent months a number of articles appearing in *The South Atlantic Quarterly* have attracted national attention, several being reprinted in whole or in part in widely known publications. *Current Reading* has published comprehensive digests of the articles by Dr. Alban G. Widgery on "The Motives of the Nationalist Movement in India," and by Dr. Calvin B. Hoover on "Religion in Soviet Russia"; "Unemployment and the Alien" by Harold Fields was partially reprinted in many leading newspapers; Judge Robert W. Winston's article on "A Rebel Colonel: His Strange Career" was reprinted in the Boston *Transcript*, which also reprinted extracts from the article, "The Professional Woman at Home," by Catherine Sherwood; Dean Justin Miller's discussion of "Public Opinion and Crime" was partially reprinted by *The Review of Reviews* in its department, Leading Articles of the Month.

Duke Officials Entertained By Haywood County Civic Leaders

Trustees of the Junaluska Summer School and Officers of University Honor Guests at
Dinner Characterized By Notably Fine Spirit of Fellowship and Co-operation—
President Few, in Principal Address, Discusses Duke's Ideals of Service

A NOTABLY fine occasion, characterized by a deep spirit of good fellowship and coöperation, was the dinner given by various civic bodies of Waynesville and Haywood County on Monday evening, July 13, in honor of the trustees of the Lake Junaluska Summer School, and officers of Duke University. About 100 guests were present in the dining room of Hotel Gordon for this event, which was one of real profit and pleasure to all in attendance.

In his address, the principal one of the evening, President Few discussed in an exceedingly effective way the ideals of service of Duke University. He declared that Duke is irrevocably committed to a policy of service to the people of North Carolina, of all classes and all sections, and to people everywhere whom it is in a position to serve. A front page news report in the Asheville *Citizen* the morning following the banquet had this to say, among other things:

The Duke president said that the proper coöperation, such as that which has been accorded the efforts of Duke University at Lake Junaluska by the people of all Western North Carolina, will make it possible for the university to be one of the greatest public benefactors among the institutions of the state.

Dr. Few was the principal speaker at a dinner tendered to him, the trustees of the Lake Junaluska summer school, which is affiliated with Duke University, and other guests at the Hotel Gordon, the hosts being 75 of the leading business and professional men of Haywood County, representing practically every civic organization.

President Few enunciated the simple principle of living when he declared that the highest aim of every individual should be to make the most of himself and then pass on to the public in terms of service all that he had accomplished.

The Duke University head expressed his gratitude for the splendid coöperation shown during the past six years by the people of Haywood County and Western North Carolina in the summer school activities at Lake Junaluska and assured his audience that the future held even brighter things for the summer school at the lake.

Bonner Ray, immediate past president of the Waynesville Chamber of Commerce, acted as toastmaster and introduced President Few and the other speakers. Short talks were made by Homer Henry, county superintendent of schools; Dr. W. O. Goode, Joseph E. Johnson, R. E. Nollner, Dr. B. G. Childs, H. R. Dwire, Holland Holton, Coach Wallace Wade, Josephus Daniels, Dr. C. M. Pickens, and others.

Mr. Daniels, publisher of the Raleigh *News and Observer*, who has a summer home at Lake Junaluska, painted a word picture of what Western North Carolina will be 10 or 15 years from now as a result of its educational and industrial development. He said he believed Western North Carolina will show more growth in the next 10 or 15 years than any other section of the state. He made particular reference to the Great Smoky Mountains National Park as a great factor in the future development of this mountain region, saying that the park will be of tremendous economic significance to Western North Carolina.

The Rev. Dr. C. M. Pickens, of Waynesville, spoke in glowing terms of the future of Lake Junaluska. He declared that within the next 20 years Waynesville and Lake Junaluska would have a population bigger than the present population of Asheville and that the other towns of Western North Carolina would also grow rapidly. One of the greatest factors that will aid in the development of this region, he said, is the Great Smoky Mountains National Park. It brings this section of the state before the nation, he declared.

Guests included: trustees of the Lake Junaluska summer school; Dr. Holland Holton, director of all summer school activities of Duke University; Dr. W. I. Cranford, Prof. Aldridge, and Dr. B. G. Childs, director of the Lake Junaluska summer school, all members of the Duke University faculty; Mrs. J. M. Long, Homer Henry, C. G. Plott, Hugh Sloan, J. H. Kirkpatrick, and J. R. Boyd, all of Haywood County; Josephus Daniels, the Rev. Dr. J. N. Score, of Dallas, Texas, Coach Wallace Wade, and Henry R. Dwire, director of public relations of Duke University.

Ernest L. Withers, prominent Waynesville business man, acted as chairman of the dinner committee.

Six New Books To Be Issued By Duke University Press

Three of the Works are by North Carolina Authors and a Fourth by a Former Carolinian
—More than 50 Volumes Issued Since the Duke Press
Was Organized

SIX NEW volumes will be issued by the Duke University press during the summer and early fall, three of them the work of North Carolina writers, and a fourth by a former Carolinian.

Prof. J. M. Ormond, of Duke, is the author of a work on the rural churches in North Carolina which surveys the sects, value and number of church buildings, the work of Sunday schools, and other facts about rural religious life in the state's 100 counties. Professor Ormond is associated with the rural church division of the Duke Endowment.

"Trailing Trade a Million Miles" is the title of a second Duke press book by James A. Thomas, of White Plains, N. Y., a former North Carolinian who for more than 40 years traveled throughout the Orient as an agent for tobacco companies. Observations gleaned from a wealth of experiences and a multitude of personal contacts are set forth in the book which constitutes a valuable record of early American trade expansion. Mr. Thomas' first book was "A Pioneer Tobacco Merchant in the Orient."

Floyd Stovall, of University of Texas, in a volume now in the press, "Desire and Restraint in Shelley," throws new light on both the poet's personality and his work by a study of the two conflicting forces in Shelley's life.

The history of Norfolk, Va., from the earliest settlement to the last decade is written by Thomas Wertenbaker, of Princeton University, in a volume called "Norfolk: Historic Southern Port." The author gives special attention to the effect of national events on this center of southern commerce.

Clarence Gohdes, of Duke, has prepared a study of coöperative literary activity upon the part of the religious, social, and literary radicals who were called "transcendentalists," in a book entitled "The Periodicals of American Transcendentalism."

The first monograph of the Duke University research studies in education will be issued under the title "The Effect of Unfamiliar Settings on Problem-Solving," by Prof. William A. Brownell, of the Duke faculty.

Since the organization of the Duke Press more than 50 volumes of scholarly interest have been published and distributed to all parts of the world. The press also publishes five periodicals.

Duke Professor In World Group For Narcotic Study

DR. ALLEN H. GODBEY of Duke University has been notified of his appointment to membership on the committee on law and philosophy of the International Narcotic Education association.

Dr. Godbey has been actively interested for many years in the history of the uses of narcotics and especially their ethnological aspects and associations with worship in early religions. Last year a research article by Dr. Godbey on "Incense and Poison Ordeals in the Ancient Orient" attracted wide attention after its publication in a University of Chicago journal.

In February at the meeting of the American branch of the World Conference on Narcotic Education, held in New York, Dr. Godbey made an address on "The Psychology of Narcotism Among the American Indians." Another paper by Dr. Godbey was read at Geneva.

Dr. Godbey has received cablegrams from Captain Richmond Pearson Hobson, of Santiago fame, who is now president of the American branch of the world conference, telling of the enthusiastic reception the Duke professor's paper received in Geneva, June 17, where 50 countries were represented. The conference, Captain Hobson cabled, was so successful and so much of a definite nature accomplished that plans were made to hold the international conference at Geneva every two years instead of every five.

Duke Summer School Has A Record-Breaking First Term

More Students Have Been Registered Than Ever Before—They Come From Many Different States and From Foreign Countries—Brief History of the Duke Summer Schools

DUKE UNIVERSITY Summer School, which is now closing the first term of its most successful session, has had a steady growth since its beginning in 1919. Its history reads almost like that of the University, itself. Under different names and affiliated with various other institutions, it has forged steadily forward until, today, it is a worthy daughter of a great institution.

Eighty-eight students, sixty-five of whom were teachers, came to Trinity College in the summer of 1919, to pursue professional and academic courses. The faculty had chosen a committee to conduct the summer school. This committee was composed of Dr. William K. Boyd, chairman, Dr. William H. Wannamaker, dean of Trinity College, and Dr. Robert L. Flowers, secretary to the corporation. To this committee, by faculty action, was added Prof. Holland Holton, principal of the West Durham High School, and assistant superintendent of Durham County Schools. Professor Holton was director of the County and State Summer School for Teachers. This school was operated under the direction of the School Superintendents of Durham and Person counties and of the State Board of Certification. It now became affiliated with the Trinity College Summer School. The school was operated for a period of six weeks.

No mention is made of the State and County Summer School in the 1920 summer school catalogue. Professor Holton, who by that time had become Superintendent of Schools for Durham County, was continued on the staff as "Adviser to Students in Education." Dr. Boyd was again chairman of the faculty committee in charge of the summer school.

In 1921, Professor Holton was announced as "Director of the Summer School." He was still county superintendent of schools, a position which he held for another year. The catalogue adds the name of Miss Elizabeth Fronde Hornady, as dean of women of Trinity College, and Social Director of the Summer School. Dr. Boyd was not a member of the faculty that summer as he was taking a much needed rest.

Previous to that time the school had been operated

five days a week, with a holiday on Saturday. That year the holiday was changed to Monday. Courses were offered in the subject of Educational Psychology which was rapidly becoming popular among southern teachers.

The year 1922 saw Dr. Holton a member of the Trinity College faculty and chairman of the summer school committee, as well as director of the school. The name of Dr. Bert Cunningham, professor of biology, was added to the committee that year. A teachers' appointment bureau was an added feature of the school that summer. This bureau, which has functioned successfully since that date, undertakes to secure, without charge, teaching positions for students of the institution.

In 1923, Dr. Boyd returned as a member of the summer school committee. That year a Demonstration School was added as an additional aid to the department of education. Children in elementary and high school classes were taught in this school. Teachers who were students in the summer school might observe the work of this school as a part of their summer school course. The demonstration school continued its existence during summer sessions until the present session. It has now been discontinued.

The Trinity College Summer School held its first double session of twelve weeks in the summer of 1924. This was also the last session under the name of Trinity College. Trinity became Duke University the next year. In 1924, the Seashore Summer School, at Oriental, N. C., became affiliated with Trinity. This institution remained in existence for five years, completing the work for which it was planned.

The summer of 1925 brought many changes besides that of a name. Mrs. Mary Hendren Vance was announced as dean of women and social director. Dr. William H. Glasson became chairman of the new committee on graduate instruction.

The outstanding feature of the summer of 1926, at Duke, was the establishing of the Junaluska Summer School, at Lake Junaluska in the mountains of North Carolina. That summer Duke University was operating its own school, at Durham, and affiliated schools at the seashore and in the mountains.

During Dr. Holton's absence in 1927 Dr. Arthur M. Proctor became Acting Director of the Summer School. A new name in the catalogue was that of Miss Mary Alice Baldwin, dean of women. Dr. Glasson was announced as dean of the new Graduate School of Arts and Sciences.

During that and two succeeding summers, Duke University operated a summer school for American students and teachers in France. This group was under the direction of Prof. A. M. Webb. The work was done in coöperation with the University of Dijon.

Dr. Holton returned to active work as Director of the Summer School in 1928. Dr. Proctor became Associate Director of the Summer School, which position he still holds.

The organization of the Junaluska School of Religion was announced in the catalogue for the summer of 1929. This institution is conducted under the joint management of Duke University and the Board of Christian Education, with the coöperation of the Board of Missions, and other boards, of the Methodist Episcopal Church, South.

The last session of the summer school on the old campus was held in 1930. This year witnessed much expansion and the crowded conditions necessitated the moving of the summer session to the new campus of Duke University in 1931.

The student registration in the summer of 1930 was the largest in the history of the institution, up to that time. That summer saw a total registration of 1502, for the two sessions, in all the affiliated schools.

However, the 1931 session has eclipsed all records. One hundred and six more students have registered for the first session, in the Duke school, in Durham, than were enrolled for the same period last year. The records show a total registration for the two schools of 1152 for the first term. For the Duke school, alone, there are 932 first term students. More than 500 of these are from other states and foreign countries. Never before has a summer school group at Duke been more representative of widely scattered parts of the country. Seven states have more than twenty-five students each in the school, as follows: Florida 48, Georgia 52, North Carolina 425, Pennsylvania 39, South Carolina 109, West Virginia 50, and Virginia 75. Other states represented include: Alabama 14, Arkansas 3, Colorado 2, Connecticut 1, Delaware 3, District of Columbia 2, Illinois 2, Kentucky 2, Louisiana 4, Massachusetts 2, Mississippi 12, Missouri 4, New Jersey 10, New Mexico 1, Ohio 4, Oregon 1, Tennessee 23, and Texas 5. Canada, Java, Korea, and Porto Rico, each, are represented by one student. Cuba sends two.

Student groups from various states have formed clubs for the purpose of becoming better acquainted, and to foster social and recreational programs.

(A later article, elsewhere in this issue, gives some interesting Summer School statistics, secured just as the REGISTER went to press.)

Yale Professor To Join Faculty Of Duke School

Dr. H. Shelton Smith, now professor in the divinity school of Yale University, has been elected professor of religious education in Duke University and a member of the faculty of the school of religion.

Professor Smith's services will begin at Duke in September.

The Yale professor is well known to many North Carolinians. He was born in this state and had his college education at Elon where he received the A. B. degree in 1917. Following the World War during which he served as a first lieutenant and chaplain, Professor Smith studied at Yale, receiving the degree of Ph.D. in 1923. He was conferred with the D. D. degree by Defiance College in 1928.

For five years, 1923-1928, Professor Smith was director of leadership training in the International Council of Religious Education. He began teaching in 1928 as associate professor of education in Teachers College of Columbia University, and from there went to Yale where he has been professor of religious education and director of field work.

The Duke professor-elect is a member of a number of important committees representing various educational groups.

Valuable Gift to Duke Library

A gift of over 1,000 volumes has just been received by the Duke University law library from the law firm of Lee and McCanna of Providence, R. I.

The collection donated includes volumes of statutes, reports, encyclopedias and texts and supplements texts already in the law library.

Among the books donated are a considerable number of texts, the New York court of appeals reports, volumes 1 through 215; Rhode Island manual, 57 volumes; Rhode Island reports of board of education, 10 volumes; Rhode Island school reports, 21 volumes; Providence city documents, 67 volumes; Providence city council resolutions, 47 volumes.

This gift was originally accepted on behalf of the law school by Judge William H. Sawyer, chief justice of the superior court of New Hampshire, who has frequently been of assistance to the law library in producing valuable additions.

Manuscript Department Of The Duke Library Is Very Valuable

Collection Increased During Past Year to About Four Times Its Original Size—Manuscript Department Contains Many Real Treasures, Not Only in History But in Other Fields Also

THE MANUSCRIPT Department of the Duke University Library has existed only this year, but manuscript collecting had its beginning here over thirty years ago. Dr. John Spencer Bassett, professor of history in Trinity College from 1893 to 1906, aroused an interest among faculty and students in the collection of manuscripts. There was little or no money for purchase then, so that most of the papers received were donations and loans. Dr. W. K. Boyd and Dr. Randolph G. Adams carried on the work begun by Dr. Bassett.

The old Trinity College Library had a large vault in which the treasures were kept, and two or three museum cases were used to display manuscripts and other objects of interest. Not much was done, however, to store the manuscripts in a way most conducive to their preservation, or to make them generally available for the use of students. In later years manuscript hunting was held in abeyance, and after the construction of the present Women's College Library nothing was done to increase the collection, due to the fact that there was no suitable storage space.

Since the general Library has been moved to the West Campus, the manuscripts have resumed their place of importance. There is now a room in the library assigned to manuscripts solely. It is equipped with fireproof cabinets containing 1710 steel boxes, each of which will hold about fifty manuscripts.

Within the past year extensive acquisitions have increased the collection to almost four times its original size.

Several of the Southern states are represented by various collections. Virginia provides the largest single collection in the papers of General William Mahone. These are loaned to the library. North Carolina is represented by several smaller collections, including the papers of Governor Ellis (1858-1861), of W. W. Holden of Reconstruction notoriety, and of Bryan Tyson. The Branch, Slade, and Somers family papers are also deposited here. Georgia is represented

VIEW OF MANUSCRIPT ROOM AT THE GENERAL LIBRARY

by the Harden papers, and Alabama by the Clement C. Clay collection.

Interest in manuscript hunting is not confined to the History Department. The English Department has added to its research materials by the acquisition of letters and literary manuscripts of Dr. Thomas Holly Chivers and of Paul Hamilton Hayne, both of Georgia. A smaller number of manuscripts of Dante Gabriel Rossetti make up in rarity what they lack in volume.

There is now in progress an effort to concentrate on collecting Confederate materials, with the result that there are already probably as many as two or three thousand Confederate letters and other papers, among which appear the autographs of Jefferson Davis, Robert E. Lee, and various members of the Confederate Cabinet. The most important Confederate documents

will continue to be the Register of Acts of the Confederate Congress, and 114 manuscript copies of statutes passed during the last three months of the Confederate Government's existence.

A number of faculty members are interested in locating and acquiring for the library manuscript collections of interest and importance, and the present prospect is that acquisitions will continue to be numerous in the future.

Work has been carried on in the Manuscript Room since January, 1931, with the purpose of putting the manuscripts in sufficient order to make them available for graduate students and visiting scholars. Research is already in progress on some of the collections, and will become more extensive as rapidly as the manuscripts can be made available for use.

Three Weeks of Intensive Training in Plane Surveying

THREE weeks of intensive training in plane surveying were accorded 36 students of the engineering department of Duke University during the early part of the summer, the surveying experience tying-in with theoretical instruction given during the regular school session.

The students were given instruction for nine hours a day in the use of transit and stadia, compass, level, plane table, and the setting of batter boards and grade stakes for outside work; while inside instruction was given in ordinary calculation, profile and the making of two maps of a portion of the Duke campus.

The class was considerably the largest yet conducted; the classes have previously numbered from 18 to 20. Part of the work was done on the East, or old, campus, and part on rough territory not far from the new campus. The course ended with an observation at 2 o'clock in the morning of the North Star in order to determine the true meridian.

Prof. H. C. Bird of the engineering department was in charge of the school, while taking part with him were Prof. W. H. Hall and Ralph T. Mathews, instructor.

Reading, Left to right, *back row:* J. Nutt, L. Nase, H. A. Wynn, A. Skinner, H. Hicks, W. P. Herndon, O. Southerland, S. E. Spicher, R. P. Givens, Kenneth Knight, C. A. Marckx, C. D. McQuilkin, J. R. Kornegay, J. R. Martin, and Professor H. C. Bird. *Front row:* A. W. Campbell, D. Drummond, G. M. Coffman, C. F. W. Brown, H. W. Atkinson, J. H. Sharpless, W. K. Wells, R. T. Creekmore, J. Bryce, T. J. Garrett, George Dilworth, C. K. Richardson, J. H. Armfield, J. M. Bird, A. Day, F. W. Neu, N. G. McCaleb, C. H. Kadie, Jr., S. G. Flack, L. Capling, and W. A. Batson.

An Unusual Art Exhibition; Work Of Children Is Shown

Unique Collection of Drawings and Paintings, Entirely the Product of Children's Genius,
Presented By Woman's College of Duke University—Different
Countries and Races Represented

JUST BEFORE the recent close of the academic year 1930-31, the Woman's College of Duke University held in the Chinese room of the library an unusual art exhibition, the drawings and paintings displayed being entirely the work of children.

Many different countries and races participated in the international section of the exhibit. Among them were Poland, Germany, Italy, England, China, Austria, Japan, Spain, Uruguay, and Holland; besides India, Czecho-Slovakia, and Norway, whose collections unfortunately arrived too late to be shown. Other collections contributed for the occasion were from the pre-school departments of the University of Cincinnati and the Kansas State Agricultural College; the Kate Baldwin Free Kindergarten, of Savannah, George; and the public school systems of Boston, Durham, and Atlanta.

MISS CAY WILLIAMS
Whose Oil Paintings were a feature of
the Exhibition

The purpose of the Woman's College in presenting this unique showing of children's art to the Duke University community and the public at large was to focus attention upon the deep and powerful creative undercurrent of childhood; upon the fact that even very young children find delight and stimulus in artistic expression, and that the symmetrical development of their fresh creative aptitudes during the pre-school years is vital to the emergence of any real constructive genius later in life. For progressive educators are agreed that beauty is not alone a matter of line, color, and design, but is closely related to that dynamic quality we know as a sense of values, and translates itself into conduct. The higher the taste and judgment expressed by the child in his earlier surroundings, the more probable it is that he will create for himself in the future a sane, serene, and happy existence, and be better able to take his place among the builders of the finer tomorrow.

In the American collection these educational truths were well dramatized in a comparison of the brilliant oil-paintings of Cay Williams, a child of four, and Anna Thorp, an impressionistic designer of six, with the efforts of suppressed children twice their ages.

Drawings by children as young as eighteen months, from the personality collection of Ernest Seeman, of Duke, proved also of unusual interest; as well as his collection of underprivileged Mexican and negro children's bizarre and colorful creations. As a matter of racial genius, it was noticeable and significant that the art expression of negro children revealed on the whole

"Tiger" by Japanese Child
(Shown in Exhibition)

those same mystical and sentimental religious impulses out of which have arisen the well-known "spirituals" of their race.

Inquiries concerning the exhibition have reached the Woman's College from points as far away as Boise, Idaho, and Portland, Maine; and the leaders of the North Carolina Federation of Women's Clubs, meeting in Raleigh, have expressed their intention of outlining a statewide art-and-the-child program among mothers, based on the incentive supplied in this recent exhibition at the Woman's College.

"Hansel and Gretel" Woodcut by an Austrian boy
(Shown in Exhibition)

The success of the event was in a large measure due to Mrs. Gifford Davis, herself a pre-school teacher of experience and skill, who directed its presentation, and to her committee of faculty members and their wives, who are sponsoring the opening of a pre-school on the Duke Campus in the autumn. A list of these sponsors includes: Dr. Alice M. Baldwin, Dean of the Woman's College; Doctors Holton, Davison, Brownell, Lundholm, Zener, Rhine, Collins, Easley; and Mesdames Few, Alyea, Forbus, Shands, Spears, Carty, Miles, Shryock, Seeley, Cameron, Hall, Morrell, Barnes, Ormond, Sawyer, Patton, Christian, Hollingshead, and Bryson.

Duke Hospital Wins Approval For Residences

The council on medical education of the American Medical association has informed Duke hospital of its approval for residences for graduate study, this action in effect giving the hospital recognized status as a graduate school of medicine.

Notification of the council's recent action was given to Dr. W. C. Davison, dean of the Duke school of medicine, by Homer F. Sanger, of the staff of the approving body, following a recent official visit by Dr. O. N. Anderson, of Chicago, representing the American Medical association.

Previously the association had given its approval to the Duke Hospital for the training of internes. The last action of the national medical body makes Duke hospital the first in North Carolina to secure approval for training all three classes: internes and nurses, and receiving residents for further graduate training.

Of the 101 hospitals in North Carolina, three are approved for residences, the North Carolina Sanatorium at Sanatorium, Davis hospital at Statesville, and Duke. Forty-three train nurses, and seven train internes.

Duke hospital is the 350th approved for residences in the United States from among 6,719 hospitals in this country. There are slightly more than 2,000 resident physicians in these approved institutions, all of them following specialized fields of work.

Half a century ago medical graduates were compelled to visit the greater clinics in this country and abroad to secure further training, but few were able to avail themselves of the opportunity to observe the work of the comparatively few outstanding specialists.

Later improvements in medical education and the resultant development of well qualified teachers, combined with improvements in hospital service and staffs, now makes it possible for larger numbers of medical graduates to continue in specialized fields of study. Duke Hospital now ranks with those approved for this extended service.

There are five resident physicians at Duke Hospital at the present time, 11 assistant residents, and 17 internes making a total of 33 physicians of graduate rank in addition to the permanent hospital and medical school staff. The residents are: Elbert L. Persons, internal medicine; Clarence E. Gardner, Jr., surgery; S. Leighton Avner, obstetrics and gynecology; Glenn E. Harrison, pediatrics; and Max O. Oates, pathology.

Assistant residents in internal medicine are: Royall M. Calder, Emile B. Cekada, Walter B. Mayer, and R. Eloise Smith. Walter W. Baker, Harold Finkelstein, R. Randolph Jones, Jr., and Louis B. Ziv are residents

(Continued on page 229)

Coach Wade Outlines Athletic Policies At Duke

"TO LOSE graciously and to win properly" was the goal set for the Duke University Athletic teams by Coach Wallace Wade, director of athletics, in his address at the alumni dinner held at Lake Junaluska on the evening of Tuesday, July 14.

The appearance of Coach Wade featured a most successful Duke dinner. His presence was a source of particular interest as it was his first visit to Junaluska and the first opportunity many Duke alumni had yet had to see and talk with the new athletic director, who had won such fame during his notably successful career as head coach and athletic director at the University of Alabama before coming to Duke this spring.

Following up the expression quoted above, Coach Wade outlined the policy for the Duke athletic department. He declared that the time is close at hand when the winning of athletic contests will not be the chief reason for athletic activities in colleges and universities. He declared that it is far better to lose a contest with grace and fairness than it is to win unfairly. He emphasized the statement that members of athletic teams at Duke would be instructed in the art of knowing how to lose graciously as well as how to win in a proper manner. He stressed his determination to have fair play as a guiding principle in all intercollegiate contests at Duke.

In outlining to the alumni and guests at the dinner the policies that will prevail in the athletic department he said the department would be divided into four divisions. First, there will be physical education activities of a new type for the freshman and sophomore classes. Members of these classes will be allowed, under the new policy, to choose four athletic activities for the four semesters of the two years in place of the former gymnastic exercises. One of these activities will be followed in each of the four semesters. In the second place there will be intramural athletics, with contests between different classes and groups of various kinds on the campus. A start has already been made in that direction under Coach Wade's supervision. The third feature will be instruction designed for those who intend to hold positions as coaches and athletic directors in high schools of the state. Along with the instruction in coaching they will be given such training as will enable them to pass the tests required by the state board of education as far as the holding of proper certificates is concerned. The fourth division will be that of intercollegiate activities, and in this connection Coach Wade pointed out that in the future some sports would probably be added to the list of those included in the program of intercollegiate athletics while some others might be in time eliminated.

The speaker made it plain that the alumni and other supporters of Duke University athletics would be expected to coöperate at all times in making effective the principles and policies he outlined with reference to the intercollegiate contests and other features of the athletic program. He declared that such coöperation would be decidedly important in the working out of the plans and policies outlined. The enthusiastic response by those present to his address indicated very clearly that they would gladly coöperate in every way possible.

Mrs. Wade and little daughter, Frances, were guests at the dinner.

Forest Work At Duke Is Given Recognition

Duke forest has been admitted to membership in the International Union of Forest Research Organizations —the first institution in the South to become a member of the world-wide organization, and the seventh in America.

Announcement of the selection of Duke was received by C. F. Korstian, director of Duke forest, from Sven Petrini, secretary-general of the Union, at Experimentalfaltet, Sweden. Seed service exchange, library and bibliographic material will be provided through the membership.

The other forestry institutions in the United States having membership in the Union are: the Yale School of Forestry; Harvard forest; School of Forestry and Conservation, University of Michigan; Forest Soil laboratory, Cornell University; The Forestry division, University of California; and New York State College of Forestry.

The organization was formed two years ago by the extension on the part of the International Union of Forest Experiment Stations of its field to all forest research. At the close of last year there were 54 members, and three associate, in more than 20 nations.

Some Alumni Personalities

U. B. BLALOCK ·

U. Benton Blalock, of the Class of 1896, is vice-president and general manager of the North Carolina Cotton Growers Co-operative Association. He was appointed by Governor Gardner in July, 1929, as official representative of the State to present the problems of the cotton growers to President Hoover's Farm Board at its meeting in Baton Rouge, Louisiana. Recently he was chosen president of the American Cotton Co-operative Association at a meeting of the directors in Washington, D. C. For several years he has managed the affairs of the North Carolina Cotton Growers Co-operative Association. Mr. Blalock's daughter, Monte Christian Blalock, (Mrs. R. Fred Roper) graduated at Duke University in 1929.

Kate Herring Highsmith (Mrs. J. Henry) served as Director of Publicity, North Carolina State Board of Health, for a number of years. Later she was Director of Publicity, State War Saving Campaign. She was employed by the U. S. Treasury Department to organize and direct the Thrift Campaign. Also during the war, she was chosen to represent the Southern States in a conference held to decide what to do with the war savings movement after the Armistice. The decision reached was to convert it into a Thrift Movement and work it through the schools. Miss Herring, as she was then, was made a director for organizing and carrying on the work in the Fifth Federal Reserve District with headquarters in Richmond. She later went to New York City as Director of Publicity, American Social Hygiene Society. She has met with marked success in publicity work. She is one of the most active members of the Alumnae Association and several years ago served as president of that organization.

KATE HERRING HIGHSMITH

ROBERT M. JOHNSTON

Robert M. Johnston, of the Class of 1916, is a member of the editorial department of the Chicago Tribune. Previous to going with the Tribune in 1922 he had held positions on the Chicago Herald and Examiner and the Chicago Daily News. He was managing editor of the Asheville Times, 1925-28, and in 1928 was "re-write man" on the Cleveland Press, going later to the Chicago Tribune again in the editorial department, as stated above. His first newspaper connection was as reporter and then city editor of the Daily Oklahoman, at Oklahoma City, 1918-22. He was instructor in economics at Alabama A. & M. College in 1918. He was part-time instructor in the Medill School of Journalism at Northwestern University in 1925.

Interesting Statistics Of The First Summer School Term

401 Graduate Students in Attendance; Total Enrollment of Graduate and Undergraduate
Students, 932, of These 433 Being Men and 499 Women—Two New Grad-
uate Departments, Psychology and Sociology, in Which Summer
School Students Can Work For Master's Degrees

TWO NEW graduate departments on which students can work toward master degrees, psychology
and sociology, drew 15 persons at Duke University
during the first session of summer school.
Eight of these were psychology students, six men
and two women; and seven were in sociology, three
men and four women.

Other figures relating to the studies of the 401 graduate students at Duke University during the June-
July term have been made public by Dr. Holland Holton, director of the summer school.

Education was, as might be expected, the favorite
subject of study, its pursuants numbering 166, of
whom 90 were men and 76 women. In second place
was English, with a total enrollment of 69. The figures were so tabulated as to prevent duplication; a
student taking two subjects was halved between these;
the total subject numbers are consequently the total
enrollment number.

Of 509 undergraduate students, 144 were in education, 55 in English, and 51 in economics and government.

Men outnumbered women in both graduate and
undergraduate departments, there being 208 women
graduate students as compared with 193 men; and 275
women undergraduates as compared with 234. The
total enrollment of the school was 932, of whom 433
were men, and 499 were women.

Teachers numbered 605, of whom 179 were men and
426 women; and other students, 327, with 254 men and
73 women. Of the 605 teachers 273 were North Carolinians and 332 of other states.

ENROLLMENT BY DEPARTMENTS

Enrollment in the graduate school courses, by departments, was as follows, the first item being the
subject, the second the number of men, the third the
number of women, and the last figure the total number
of students:

Education, 90, 76, 166; Zoölogy, 4, 4, 8; Economics
and government, 15, 11, 26; English, 20, 49, 69;
French, 3, 13, 16; History, 16, 18, 34; Latin, .., 8, 8;
Mathematics, 6, 20, 46; Psychology, 6, 2, 8; Religion,
10, 3, 13; Sociology, 3, 4, 7. Total, 193, 208, 401.

Undergraduate students enrolled include: Education, 23, 121, 144; Zoölogy, 33, 6, 39; Chemistry, 17,
18, 35; Economics and government, 23, 28, 51; Engineering, 35, .., 35; English, 22, 33, 55; French, 7, 7,
14; German, 18, 15, 33; Greek, 1, 4, 5; History 10, 12,
22; Mathematics, 5, 3, 8; Physics, 19, 15, 34; Psychology, 2, 2, 4; Religion, 5, 4, 9; Sociology, 1, 10, 11;
Spanish, 13, 14, 27. Total, 234, 275, 509.

Duke Hospital Wins Approval For Residences

(Continued from page 226)

in surgery; Anne L. Lawton in Pediatrics; Elbert B.
Apple in roentgenology; W. Eugene Matthews in
oto-laryngology.

The internes in internal medicine are: Earle B.
Craven, Jr., Harry C. Hudnall, Paul W. Preu, Fred-
erick M. Reese, James C. Ruegsegger, and Jerome
Syverton. Internes in surgery are: William B. Arm-
strong, James M. Hicks, Hershel C. Lennon, George
Lilly, Robert Ruark, Rowland T. Bellows, and Wel-
don N. Sanger; Ralph McC. Mugrage and B. Kenyon
Peter are internes in obstetrics and gynecology; Sarah
Vance Thompson in pediatrics; and Raymond H.
Rigdon in pathology.

Internes and residents are appointed for terms of
one year. Internes are eligible for appointment as
assistant residents. Residents may serve one hospital
for a period of years. Highly trained and skilled
specialists frequently come from the ranks of the
latter.

Books by Duke University Meu Still Attract Wide Attention

Dr. Lundholm's "The Manic-Depressive Psychosis," Recently Published By Duke Press,
Acclaimed as a Real Contribution to Literature in Its Field—New Printing of
Dr. Hoover's Book on Russia Necessitated by Prompt Demand—Duke
Press Publishes List of Rossetti Manuscripts—Book by An
Alumnus of Duke

BOOKS by members of the Duke faculty are continuing to attract the attention of a wide circle of readers in their respective fields.

Dr. Lundholm's New Work

Dr. H. Lundholm's "The Manic-Depressive Psychosis," recently appeared as Number 1 of the Duke University Psychological Monographs, published by the Duke University Press. Dr. Lundholm, who is Associate Professor of Psychology at Duke, spent nine years as Psychologist at the McLean Hospital, Waverly, Massachusetts. Much of his time was given, he says in his preface, to the study of the two great "functional" psychoses, the manic-depressive disorder and schizophrenia.

In the monograph, Dr. Lundholm sets forth the theory that manic-depressive psychosis is an acute disorder which may set in at any time of life in individuals of a certain mental constitution. He asserts that recovery from this disorder is the rule rather than the exception. The schizophrenic disorder, on the other hand, he says is mostly a chronic aberration of personality, a going astray from the very beginning of life, from normal healthy character-formation, a perversion of mental growth which is also constitutionally determined and which may blossom into an explicit disease-syndrome, whenever, before the age of about forty, an individual is confronted with some serious problem of adjustment. He hopes later to prepare a monograph on schizophrenia.

In his foreword to the monograph, Professor William McDougall has this to say about Dr. Lundholm: "I feel that I may point out here a fact which Dr. Lundholm could not well proclaim, the fact, namely, that Dr. Lundholm holds a position which, as far as my knowledge of the field goes, seems to be unique. He is neither a psychiatrist nor a psychoanalyst, but what for the purpose of promoting our knowledge of the human mind and disorders is far better, namely a well-trained and open-minded psychologist who for many years has devoted himself to pure research among patients of a large mental hospital. More-

over, he is not a psychologist of the type only too common among us, the type that dogmatically takes its stand upon the mechanistic materialism of nineteenth century science, and confidently, blindly, assumes that all the problems of human nature are in principle already solved by a mechanical reflexology. . . . That is to say that Dr. Lundholm belongs unequivocally to the school of thought which is now coming to be known as the hormic school of psychology."

Dr. Lundholm, himself, attributes his acceptance of the theory of the hormic school of psychology to the influence of his association with Professor McDougall, one of the leaders of this school. "He believes that all our intellectual structure is built upon a foundation of deepseated biological urges which while making themselves felt but obscurely or not at all in consciousness, impel us powerfully toward goals conceived, for the most part, but vaguely and inadequately; and he believes that the great functional disorders of mind are to be sought in failure of these fundamental impulses to coöperate harmoniously in the way which is of the essence of healthy personality."

Dr. Lundholm says that the manic-depressive psychosis is probably a toxic disorder produced by some kind of poison of the general nature of the depressant drug. This poison might be merely a fatigue product of metabolism but it might also be such product in conjunction with another as yet unknown chemical, developing in the body. In spite of the fact that no chemist so far has been able to demonstrate the crucial poison or poisons, there is abundant evidence in support of the toxic theory of the psychosis. Particularly strong evidence of such kind is yielded by the psychological analysis of the disease syndrom. Such analysis reveals that the major part of its symptoms can be interpreted properly as depending upon a general disintegration of personality, a condition which can be explained, in its turn, as the psychological manifestation of the general dissociation of the highest level of the nervous system by a depressant poison. During the course of the psychosis, three levels of profundity of general disintegration of personality can be distinguished, each corresponding presumably to its own level of depth of toxic influence.

He continues by saying that although a toxin is thus the cause of the disease, this toxin produces disorder only in individuals of certain characteristics. The characteristics have probably a constitutional basis, consisting in two specific inborn dispositions, the E-disposition and the Cycloid trait. The E-disposition, Dr. Lundholm says, is a peculiar inborn characteristic which promotes, all through life, the development of egotistic, and prohibits the development of altruistic, sentiments. It accounts for the enhanced egotism of the manic-depressive patient and for the fatal consequences of such enhanced egotism during the psychosis. The Cycloid trait, according to Dr. Lundholm, is a peculiar innate disposition to swing, even during normal health, between prolonged moods of elation and depression. This disposition is probably physiologically determined and can be explained hypothetically by a specific defect of the individual's vasomotorium. It accounts partly for two of the "imperial moods" of the psychosis, the feeling of omnipotency and the feeling of inadequacy. The third of the "imperial moods," the feeling of unreality, can be referred directly to the disintegrative activity of the toxin.

While the monograph may start afresh what Dr. McDougall is pleased to call "the war," it is certainly a notable contribution to the field of abnormal psychology. No student working in this field will dare ignore the trend which Dr. Lundholm's findings have set up.

More Praise for Hoover Book

The Macmillan Company, publishers of Professor Calvin B. Hoover's new book on "The Economic Life of Soviet Russia," has proceeded to still another printing of this book which has received most favorable reviews in many newspapers and periodicals.

The *New York Times* says that Dr. Hoover's book is "by all odds the best book in its field," and the *Chicago Evening Post* pronounces it "the most up-to-date picture possible of the Soviet economy." The *Christian Century* of Chicago recently published a comprehensive review that has attracted considerable attention.

Among the numerous reviews of Dr. Hoover's book, one recently appeared in the Egyptian Gazette of Alexandria, Egypt, from which the following brief excerpt is taken:

"It is no small tribute to Duke University, . . . endowed a little while ago by a tobacco manufacturer and situated in one of the most conservative sections of the United States, that it should number amongst its professors one professing a sufficiently objective

point of view to have produced a work of this character."

List of Rossetti Manuscripts

DANTE GABRIEL ROSSETTI. An Analytical List of Manuscripts in the Duke University Library, with Hitherto Unpublished Verse and Prose. Edited by Paull Franklin Baum.

A little over a year ago the Library of Duke University was so fortunate as to obtain an unusual collection of the manuscripts of Dante Gabriel Rossetti, the Pre-Raphaelite painter-poet. The manuscripts are of considerable variety, ranging on the one hand from personal memoranda of diet, a formula for his chloral, things borrowed and lent, studio accessories, addresses, and such details to finished poems which are hitherto unpublished; on the other hand they range from early poems in the author's beautiful formal script to fragments and drafts of poems in his later more careless hand. They include examples of poems in various stages of composition. There is, thus, one case of a whole stanza cancelled from one poem and used for refrain-lines of a wholly different poem. There are prose notes and metrical lines jotted down for future use, some of which we can find in his published verse and some which were never developed further. Many of the manuscripts show frequent and considerable correction, and thus enable us to follow the poet in the process of evoking the final form of a poem from its first draft. Moreover, much of Rossetti's verse is frequently considered obscure; it is, therefore, often helpful to observe the changes which a poem underwent, in order to see the ideas and phrases which he began with in relation to their later transformations. Among the most interesting are the prose outlines of poems. For a narrative poem Rossetti usually made first a "cartoon" or sketch—just as he would for a picture. One of these we have, which can be read alongside the completed poem, and thus follow him in the course of composition, noting where he expanded, where he condensed, and where he made use of the very words of his sketch. Another example is the long series of notes for a poem on the Lancelot and Guenevere subject, which he laid aside until he could see what Tennyson would do with the same subject in his *Idyls of the King*, and then never found an opportunity to rework.

These manuscripts have been analyzed by Professor Baum in the volume now issued by the Duke University Press. In the first part of the book each manuscript is listed, with annotations of variant readings and with bibliographical details. Sometimes, where the poem seemed to call for it, Professor Baum has contributed a special little study, as in comparing the two versions of the poem called *The Portrait*, or in discussing the conflicting statements concerning the manuscript copies of Rossetti's humorous ballad of

Jan Van Hunks. In the second part of the book are gathered the poems from the Duke manuscripts which were still unpublished. Some of these are perhaps not of the first quality as compared with Rossetti's standard, but others are certainly of equal merit with all but his best work. The volume will therefore be of great value for all who are interested in Rossetti. It will also be for certain poems a first edition. And perhaps chiefly it will interest those who wish to study the methods followed by a poet in the successive revisions and improvements of his verse.

Book By Duke Alumnus, '17

THE INTOLERANCE OF CHRISTIANITY. Jordan, G. Ray: New York, 1931.

The "Intolerance of Christianity" is a very appropriate title for Jordan's book. The author admits that Christianity is intolerant but clearly shows that the term when used in connection with modern Christianity does not connote bigotry, dogmatism or ecclesiasticism. The message of the book is that Christianity is intolerant of indifference to truth, of mental dishonesty, of unethical practices, of disloyalty to conscience, and disregard of human values. With that conception, "intolerance" becomes a word that has a place in Christian thought and action, "Christian Certainty," "Facing Life Squarely," "Christian Brotherhood and Industry," "The Insane Paganism of War" are a few of the suggestive chapter headings.

A large part of the material of the book has been used by the author in his weekly sermons. It is, therefore, no surprise to know that the author, although a very young man, preaches to large congregations. Jordan's sermons and writings are representative of that group of young ministers who are no longer preaching and penning platitudes but who because of technical training in universities and theological seminaries, are proclaiming a spiritual message that has a vital connection with modern conditions.

Class Of 1916 Takes Action On John T. Ring Memorial Fund At Reunion Dinner

The REGISTER last month contained reports of some of the class dinners held at the Commencement in June. Reports of some have not yet been received. It is not too late to send them in.

The REGISTER is indebted to Lucile Bullard Belk (Mrs. Henry) of Goldsboro, N. C., for the following interesting official report of the dinner held by the Class of 1916:

Members of the Class of 1916 numbering 18, count-ing wives and husbands, gathered in one of the private dining-rooms of the University Union on Tuesday, June 9, at six o'clock for their reunion dinner. L. C. Allen presided in the absence of R. M. Johnston, president, who was unable to be present.

The members elected as their representatives on the Alumni and Alumnae Councils Benjamin L. Smith, of Shelby, and Laura Mae Bivins Britt (Mrs. J. H.) of Greenville, S. C.

The representatives of '16 present instructed W. L. Ferrell, of Winston-Salem, to confer with Dr. R. L. Flowers as to the form the John T. Ring memorial fund contributed by the class should take, and gave them power to act.

The class elected as officers until the next reunion five years hence: W. L. Ferrell, president; J. H. Grigg, vice-president; L. C. Allen, secretary; and J. H. Coman, treasurer.

The class sent a message of sympathy in his illness to President W. P. Few.

During the informal good fellowship of the dinner "Ike" Coman expressed fear and trembling when "Cake" Allen took out his black book for fear that some memoranda of other days against him might appear therein; "Skin" Ferrell owned up to some of the pranks everybody had long thought he was guilty of; Ben Smith expressed as his chief pride in having been elected to the Alumni Council the fact that his young son would now think his daddy a "bigger" man; Laura Mae Bivins Britt owned up to a woman-size job in managing "Joe" and three little masculine Britts; Lucile Bullard Belk confessed to a real job in helping her husband on a daily newspaper and bringing up their six-year-old daughter; Roby Adams told of what a good time he and his family had at Como last year, where he taught school and fished; Adrian E. Brown, who received the B.D. degree in the Duke School of Religion at commencement, of preaching; J. H. Taylor of school work in a consolidated school in Cumberland County; B. D. Hathcock invited the members to visit him at his home in Washington, D. C., where he holds a responsible (not that he said this) government position; Rufus Dalton that he is with the Wachovia Bank and Trust Co. in Winston-Salem; Harry Lee Dalton that he has business headquarters in Charlotte; for "Brack" Jones, of Kinston, who also did some talking of his own, "Skin" Ferrell said that he was one of the leading lawyers in Eastern North Carolina; and Vann Secrest told of operating a drug store in Monroe. A letter was read from J. C. Gaither, of Richmond, Va., expressing his regret at his inability to be present at the dinner.

The class adjourned to meet again in 1936.

LUCILE BULLARD BELK (MRS. HENRY),
Goldsboro, N. C.

Where Aviation and Surgery Meet

TO THE cripple whose weakened limbs must support cumbersome metal braces, the subtraction of several pounds of their weight is a heaven-sent blessing, and in this particular the "heavenly" origin is not far wrong. From man's desire to fly has come a remarkably light metal which has proved a boon to orthopedics.

At the brace shop of Duke University Hospital, a division of the orthopedic section, this metal, duralumin, which has the strength of mild steel but only one-third its weight, is used whenever practicable for body and limb braces. Little did the metallurgists of Germany, seeking a light, strong metal for use in airplanes, realize their product would benefit thousands with broken and misshapen human bodies.

The new metal not only enables a patient to leave his bed or rolling chair earlier, because there is no need of waiting for a weakened limb to become strong enough to support a three-pound brace when a one-pound brace is available, but it makes recovery more rapid.

One of the best equipped brace shops in this part of the country, the Duke shop from the beginning made use of the new metal, and Duke Hospital patients and others have already benefited from its unusual qualities. The dull, silvery metal, however, requires great skill on the part of the brace-maker, for it cannot withstand great heat. It must be fashioned by an operator with a knowledge of its peculiar properties.

The Duke shop is under the charge of C. A. Letzing, who has made braces for twenty years at the Children's Hospital and the Massachusetts General Hospital, both in Boston. This work requires skill in several branches of mechanics, a broad knowledge of anatomy and orthopedics, and the ability to produce one of the best examples of shop craftsmanship.

Duke's brace shop occupies quarters on the bottom

Brace and Instrument Shop in the Orthopedic Department of Duke Hospital

Duke Summer Coaching School Is Largely Attended

Sixty high school, preparatory school, and college coaches from several states attended the Duke summer school for coaches, July 22-25, and took courses in football, track, and basketball coaching. Operated under the direction of Wallace Wade, director of athletics, the first school under the new Duke mentor proved successful in every way. Among those registering were former Duke, Carolina, Davidson, State, and Wake Forest athletes now coaching; and there were a number of coaches whose experience extends over a period of many years.

Football under Coach Wade was a feature of the brief but intensive session. Mornings were taken up with instruction in the theory and fundamentals of the gridiron sport, while track was taught in the afternoons by Carl Voyles, assistant Duke athletic director. Eddie Cameron was in charge of the basketball group.

Coach Wade was a leader in two previous warm weather schools, one at University of Utah where coaches from all parts of the country gathered to study under the famous Duke mentor, and the other at Southwestern.

Brownlee Close Third

John Brownlee, Duke's sophomore dash star, who set a new Southern time of 24 seconds flat for the 220-yard low hurdles at Birmingham, successfully represented the University early in June at the national track and field meet in Chicago. Racing with the fastest field of collegians in the country, Brownlee qualified the first day and in the finals came in a close third behind the winning time of 23.8 for the 220 low hurdles.

floor of the medical school and hospital building, and is divided into two compartments, the metal shop and the leather shop. In the metal shop are lathes, mechanical drills, a forge, and various pieces of special machinery. As all braces are made to measure, painstaking care must be taken with each brace, for alterations are more difficult than the tailor finds in working over a coat.

The leather shop adjoins the metal shop, and it is here that the braces get their adjusting straps, soft padding, and other parts intended to make them as comfortable and neat as they are strong and durable. Finest, softest leathers are used on the braces so that both clothing and wearers are protected.

This shop is the only one in this region fitted to turn out "made to order" braces. It will continue indefinitely to make them in this way, and will order ready-made parts only when there is an unprecedented demand for rush work.

Orthopedics at Duke Hospital has a broad scope of work and its physical facilities here are extensive. It is a division of surgery under the direction of Dr. A. R. Shands, Jr., a graduate of Johns Hopkins who spent three years under Dr. W. S. Baer. After practicing in Washington, D. C., Dr. Shands spent six months visiting the larger American and European clinics, and then joined the Duke staff.

Duke Visitor Tells of the Building of a New Nation

A MAN who is taking a part in the upbuilding of a new nation that is rising in southeastern Europe was a visitor to Duke University during the spring term and lectured to women students concerning his work there.

The man was Dr. C. Telford Erickson, and his work that of directing two schools, one for boys in agriculture, and the other for girls in home art and crafts, situated near Durazzo, the chief city and seaport of this new nation. The schools are partly supported by the Albanian government, which provides the land for their settlement, farm land also being allowed, and into whose control the schools are to be eventually placed.

Slides of the school were shown by Dr. Erickson during his visit at Duke. Under him there are some 16 American teachers, three of whom, Miss Emily Camp, Miss Margaret Evans and Miss Meverette Smith, went to Albania from this State.

The experiences of the founder of the institutions have been trying. When he first went into Albania in 1908 as a representative of the American Board of Missions (largely Congregational in influence) the country was a part of Turkey. The teaching of the Albanian language, which is akin to the old Sanskrit, according to Dr. Erickson, was forbidden; Dr. Erickson disregarded the restriction and suffered imprisonment and—with his wife and three children—was exiled therefor.

In 1913 Albania became, as the result of the Second Balkan war, an independent nation. Troublous days were ahead, however, including those of the World War.

As an inducement to Italy to enter on the side of the Allies France and Great Britain offered her Albania, according to the school head. In 1919 at Versailles Dr. Erickson represented the Albanian Federation of America at Paris to protest any such ac-

tion. "Thanks to President Wilson"—who was such a great champion of the nationalistic rights of smaller states—Albania gained her independence, Dr. Erickson said.

The little southeastern country, whose area is about 20,000 square miles, and population 1,250,000—these were each about cut in half after the World War, Yugo-Slavia and Greece being the benefitters by the slicing—has shown remarkable progress during the last decade.

At its opening the country was without roads, railroads or schools, Dr. Erickson said. Unlike other nations gaining autonomy following the war, as Poland, Czecho-Slovakia, or Hungary, Albania had no modern civilization to build upon. The people are of ancient Aryan stock; they are largely of the peasant, farming type.

With their own hands they built 1,800 miles of road; 600 schools now are found; exports, which were formerly outweighed by exports about nine to one, are now on about a parity.

Exported products include: skins, hides, grains, poultry, eggs, cheese, olive and olive oil. Textile goods and machinery are included among the imports,

At the schools are about 200 boys and girls receiving training. The agricultural school has about 1,500 acres under cultivation. This area serves as a demonstration farm from which knowledge of new methods in agriculture and stock breeding may be disseminated over the country.

The Albanian government provides the students with tuition; they in turn promise to give three years of service to the nation. The Near East Relief foundation has given its endorsement to the schools also.

Dr. Erickson was on the way up the coast from Florida when he dropped in to visit Duke and see the much-talked-of plant. While here he took occasion to put in a few words for the country of his adoption.

Where They Are Located	News of the Alumni	What They Are Doing

Miss Elizabeth Aldridge, '24, Secretary of Alumnae Council, Editor

CLASS OF 1872

C. B. Townsend of Lumberton, N. C., has been prominent in the life of his community for a number of years. He was among those present at Commencement.

CLASS OF 1880

James Shepherd Oliver died at his home, Marietta, N. C., on June 11. For more than half a century, Mr. Oliver was a leading farmer and merchant of Robeson County. He, with a brother, introduced tobacco-growing in his section and lived to see the wisdom of that venture proved by the fact that it has become the leading money crop of Robeson. He took an interest in public affairs, serving as commissioner, and as member of the General Assembly six terms. He enjoyed the confidence and respect of the people of his community throughout his life.

CLASS OF 1890

George K. West, who was greatly loved by his associates at Old Trinity, died at his home in Norfolk, Va., on April 16. He was formerly from Kinston but had lived in Norfolk for the past twelve years.

CLASS OF 1895

Rev. J. H. Fitzgerald is a retired missionary and makes his home at 2716 Flower street, Huntington Park, California. After graduation he served two years as pastor in Western N. C. Conference, then thirty consecutive years in Mexico and on the border as pastor, presiding elder and evangelist.

CLASS OF 1897

Ben Harrison, state budget officer, lays claim to holding public office in Oklahoma longer than any other man except one, Judge Robert L. Williams. Harrison has been in public office since 1906 with the exception of two years. He was a member of the constitutional convention in 1906 and served in the first and second sessions of the legislature. Upon completion of his second term, he was elected secretary of state, holding the office from 1911 to 1915. In the latter year he was returned to the legislature. Defeat by Campbell Russell in the race for corporation commissioner in 1915 retired Harrison to private life until 1918, when he again was

BEN HARRISON

elected to the legislature, serving in the 1919 and 1921 sessions.

At the conclusion of the 1921 term he was named state budget officer in 1923 and has held that position under Governors Trapp, Johnston, Holloway and Murray.

Ottis Green was elected mayor of Asheville, N. C. in May 1931. His son, Ottis Green, Jr., is a member of the junior class at Duke.

CLASS OF 1904

Henry B. Adams practices law at Waxhaw, N. C. He was married on April 27, 1922 to Miss Mabel Cooper. They have a son, Henry B. Adams, Jr.

CLASS OF 1908

A. W. Horton is a member of the firm of Horton Oil Company at Oklahoma City. His address is Box 277.

CLASS OF 1913

Robert Leslie Towe has been elected chairman of the Board of Education of Halifax County. He makes his home in Roanoke Rapids where he is prominently connected with the Rosemary Manufacturing Company.

CLASS OF 1914

Dr. Charles W. Davis, formerly of Zebulon, died in the Mount Wilson Hospital, Baltimore, Maryland, on July 2. After graduating at Trinity in 1914, he taught for a few years in High Point and then attended the School of Medicine at the University of Maryland. He graduated with honors and led a class of 75 in taking the medical examinations of Maryland. He was in the Medical Reserve Corps during the World War and later served on the staff of the Maryland State Sanitarium. He then became superintendent of the tubercular hospital at Olean, N. Y. It was here that his health broke down.

CLASS OF 1916

Rev. and Mrs. J. E. B. Houser of Jefferson, N. C. announce the birth of a son, Roland, March 11.

John Kilgo Gibson is general manager of the Hanaburgh farms at Rhinebeck, New York.

CLASS OF 1917

Richard H. Bennett, Jr., has been connected with the electrical operating department of the Tennessee Electric Power Company for the past six years. In the March 14, 1931 issue of the "Electrical World" there appeared an article about him which stated that he had been promoted to superintendent of the production department in charge of operating and maintenance of all company hydro and steam generating developments. He is located at Chattanooga, Tennessee.

CLASS OF 1918

Robert Webb Sanders is bookkeeper and office manager for the S. E. Massengill Company at 55 Vandam Street, New York, New York.

News has been received that Benjamin H. Muse was assigned first secretary of the American Legation at Montevideo, Uruguay. He was formerly located at Bogota, Colombia. He recently made a visit to the States and returned to Duke for a few days.

CLASS OF 1921

Samuel M. Holton has been a member of the Farmville, Virginia, State Teachers College faculty for the past three years. He was married on June 6 to Miss Mary Goldsmith Little of Simpsonville, S. C. The bride is a graduate of Winthrop College, Rock Hill, S. C., and since graduating has taught in the city schools at Lexington, Va.

C. E. Buckner has been named principal of the High School at Burlington, N. C. He has taught for the past eight years at the Durham High School where he has made an enviable record.

Announcement has been made by the Wire Reinforcement Institute, Washington, D. C., of the appointment of James S. Burch to the position of Research Engineer. James was formerly connected with technical staff of the American Road Builders' Association as investigator for the Association's special committee on subgrades and pavement bases. He possesses a background of practical and theoretical training and experience in pavement design and construction which is most valuable in his new duties as Research Engineer for the Wire Reinforcement Institute.

George D. Harmon, who has been an assistant professor in the History Department at Lehigh University, Bethlehem, Pa., has been made an associate professor of history.

CLASS OF 1924

Edwin M. Gill of Laurinburg, N. C., was recently appointed as private secretary to Governor O. Max Gardner. Edwin represented his county in the State General Assembly in 1928 and 1931. He served as chairman of the House Committee on Senatorial Districts and on other committees during the 1931 session.

CLASS OF 1926

Mr. and Mrs. Roland M. Stoneback of Elizabeth, New Jersey, are receiving congratulations on the birth of a daughter, Betty Sue, born on May 13. Mrs. Stoneback was before her marriage Elizabeth Williams of Durham.

Mr. and Mrs. H. R. Ashmore of Stedman, N. C. have announced the arrival of Ann Elliott Ashmore on March 17. Mrs. Ashmore was formerly Lalin G. Elliott, '25.

Lillian Frost and Louise McAnally have moved from Apt. 27, 110 Morningside Drive, New York City to Apt. 703 The Cloister of Tudor City, 321 East 43rd. Street, New York, N. Y.

CLASS OF 1928

Wilburt A. Jenkins and Miss Mary Morelock of Nashville, Tennessee, were married on June 9 at the home of the bride. They are living at 1006 Shepherd Street, Durham. Wilburt is a member of the faculty of Duke University.

Arthur P. Harris, Jr., was married on June 25 to Miss Joyce Rudisill of Maiden, N. C. They will make their home in Albemarle.

The announcement of the marriage of Hilda Long Burnette and Mr. James Leslie Oakley has been made. They were married in Emporia, Va., on June 18. They make their home at 2230 West Grace Street, Richmond.

Mr. and Mrs. Henry Grady McEntire live at 1040 Sheridan Road, Chicago, Ill. Mrs. McEntire was Kathryn Warlick before her marriage on June 20.

Emma Davis was married on June 11 to Mr. Edgar Milton Howell of Raleigh. Emma has taught history in the Roanoke Rapids High School since graduating from Duke. Mr. and Mrs. Howell live at 415 Morrison Avenue, Raleigh, where Mr. Howell is vice-president and secretary-treasurer of the Pike Cadillac Corporation.

Opal Winstead has had a number of her verses and stories published in current magazines. She is secretary for Henry Darling, Inc. at Augusta, Georgia. Her home address is 409 Telfair Street.

Mildred Midyette was married on June 21 to Mr. Virgil L. Turner of Rich Square, N. C. Mildred has taught in Rich Square since leaving college.

CLASS OF 1929

Jennie Campbell Greene, '29, and William Alexander Mabry, '27, were married in Trinity Methodist Church on June 30, at 8:30 o'clock in the evening. Alex. is a member of the faculty at Duke and they will make their home with Dr. and Mrs. Greene on the West Duke Campus.

William Thaddeus Rowland attended Washington and Lee after leaving Duke, receiving his B.S. degree in 1929. He is connected with the Mutual Life Insurance Company at Newark, N. J.

CLASS OF 1930

Nelle Spivey is an instructor of nurses at the Norfolk Protestant Hospital, Norfolk, Va.

Bessie Martin and Walter Eugene Johnston, Jr. were married in Hillsboro, N. C. on June 10, 1931.

Friends of Bill Werber will be interested in knowing that he has been loaned to the Newark, N. J. Bears by the New York Yankees, who signed him when he completed his collegiate career in baseball and basketball at Duke. Last year he led the Eastern League for several weeks in hitting and played earlier this season with Toledo in the Three-Eye League.

DUKE UNIVERSITY

Curricula, equipment and expense information may be
obtained from

The Catalogue on Undergraduate Instruction
The Catalogue of the Graduate School
The Bulletin of the Department of Engineering
The Bulletin of the School of Religion
The Bulletin of the School of Law
The Bulletin of the School of Medicine
The Bulletin of the School of Nursing
The Bulletin of the Summer Schools

New Academic Year Opens September 16, 1931

Address applications and inquiries to

R. L. FLOWERS, SECRETARY

DUKE UNIVERSITY   DURHAM, NORTH CAROLINA

FEEL *the difference* · HEAR *the difference*
TASTE THE DIFFERENCE!

Like an oasis in the dusty desert of dried tobacco, the new Camel Humidor Pack brings you the joy of fine quality cigarettes in prime mild condition.

Now, wherever you go, you can always be sure of getting a *fresh,* throat-easy cigarette when you demand Camels.

It's easy to tell the difference. Your sense of touch detects it as you roll a cigarette between your fingers. Dry tobacco is stiff and crumbly. Camels are full bodied and pliant.

Even your ear can tell the difference. For a dried out cigarette crackles when you roll it.

But the real test is taste and taste is causing a great nation-wide switch of men and women alike to Camels in the scientific new Humidor Pack.

As you draw in that fragrant, mild, cool smoke, redolent with the luxury of fine Turkish and mellow Domestic leaves, only then do you realize the full importance of this new Humidor Pack.

For scorched or dried tobacco is brash and tasteless and its smoke is unkindly hot to the tongue and throat.

If you are a Camel smoker you have already noticed the improvement the new Humidor Pack makes in this your favorite cigarette.

If you don't smoke Camels, try them for just one day to see how much you're missing. After you've known the mildness and joy of a really *fresh* cigarette, switch back if you can.

R. J. REYNOLDS TOBACCO COMPANY, *Winston-Salem, N. C.*

Smoke a fresh cigarette

CHOICE QUALITY

CAMEL 20's

Smoke a fresh cigarette

HUMIDOR PACK

It is the mark of a considerate hostess, by means of the Humidor Pack, to "Serve a fresh cigarette." Buy Camels by the carton—this cigarette will remain fresh in your home and office.

CAMELS

DUKE UNIVERSITY ALUMNI REGISTER

THE CROWELL DORMITORY TOWER
Crowell House at Duke was Named in Honor of the Late Dr. John Franklin Crowell, At one time President of Trinity College, An Account of Whose Recent Death Appears in this Issue.

VOLUME XVII   *August, 1931*   NUMBER 8

Duke University Alumni Register

(Member of American Alumni Council)

Published at Durham, N. C. Every Month in the Year in the Interest of the University and the Alumni

Volume XVII   *August, 1931*   Number 8

In This Issue

Editor and Business Manager ....HENRY R. DWIRE, '02

Assistant Editors ....ELIZABETH ALDRIDGE, '24
ALBERT A. WILKINSON, '26

Advertising Manager..........................CHARLES A. DUKES, '29

TWO DOLLARS A YEAR   20 CENTS A COPY

ENTERED AS SECOND-CLASS MATTER AT THE POST-OFFICE AT
DURHAM, NORTH CAROLINA

TIMELY ARTICLES

One of the interesting articles in this issue of the REGISTER is that of Prof. John S. Bradway, who comes to Duke in September, on "Law Laboratories." It is particularly timely because of the fact that this article, which first appeared in the *Survey Graphic* for June, deals with the subject of Legal Aid Clinics along the line of the one Prof. Bradway is to establish at Duke this year.

There are a number of other articles of exceptional interest in this issue.

THE COVER PAGE

The REGISTER cover pages in recent months have attracted considerable attention. The one this month presents a striking view on the Duke University campus. Dr. Blomquist's photographs of North Carolina wild flowers last month was also quite effective.

SEPTEMBER

The new session opens in September. That will make the September REGISTER especially interesting, as there will be much pertinent matter relating to the new year at Duke and its prospects. The cover page will also be particularly attractive and interesting.

THE EDITOR.

PHOTOGRAPHIC VIEW OF DUKE UNIVERSITY QUADRANGLE

PHOTOGRAPH WAS TAKEN FROM THE TOWER OF THE MEDICAL SCHOOL, LOOKING SOUTH

Duke University Alumni Register

Volume XVII   *August, 1931*   Number 8

Editorial Comment

JOHN FRANKLIN CROWELL

The recent passing of Dr. John Franklin Crowell, president of Trinity College from 1887 to 1894, brought deep grief to a host of Trinity and Duke alumni.

He presided over the destinies of the institution at a vitally significant period in its career, and his constructive, far-seeing work will not be forgotten.

Sometimes the full importance of a man's labor in a particular field does not appear until years after his work in that field has been concluded, and that was the case with respect to Dr. Crowell's pioneer work in the realm of higher education in the South.

For many years he had been a figure of national importance and following his death scores of newspaper editorials regarding his work as an educator and economist have appeared.

In one of these editorials the Baltimore *Sun* refers to Dr. Crowell "as one of the first, if not the very first, Northern man to be called to the presidency of a Southern college after the Civil War." After referring to his achievements in the upbuilding of the physical resources of the college as well as in the bringing in a new faculty of young and vigorous men, the *Sun* concludes with a reference to Dr. Crowell's later life, as follows:

"In later years Dr. Crowell turned to the field of economics. As a writer, as a member of the staff of the *Wall Street Journal* and as an economist for the Treasury Department when the war taxes were first applied, Dr. Crowell led a useful life. But it was as a new leaven in the old Southern educational lump that he achieved his greatest distinction and left his most enduring mark."

The magnificent Crowell Dormitory Tower, shown on the cover page of this issue, will be a constant reminder of the service that Dr. Crowell rendered the institution.

But there are a host of Trinity and Duke men and women who will not need such a reminder, appropriate as it is.

For, they can never think of Alma Mater without thinking of the alert, forceful, progressive man who came down from Yale in 1887 and inaugurated a new era in the career of the institution.

STILL OTHERS

We remarked in the last issue of the REGISTER that at least one president of a local Duke University Club was already planning for Duke Day on December 11, having requested a speaker for that occasion.

Since then two or three other similar requests have been made.

It is earnestly desired that the Duke Day dinners this year may be the very best and the most inspiring ever held.

If that is to be brought about, adequate preparation will be needed.

It is not too early to be thinking of the things you want to do in connection with your Duke Day dinner on December 11.

And don't forget: Call on the Alumni Office for any assistance you may desire.

ANOTHER OF THE SERIES

"I have been intensely interested in the REGISTER's series of articles on the Duke libraries," remarked an alumnus the other day. "Keep up that kind of thing. We alumni who have been away for a number of years need just the information you are giving us."

Incidentally, another story on the Library appears in this issue.

It is the intention to do something along the same line in connection with various other Duke University departments and institutions.

Not only alumni who have been away for a considerable period but others as well can derive real benefit from such articles.

"ALUMNI MONTH"

It is the intention to observe November again this year as "Duke Alumni Month."

The purpose will be, as it was last year, to turn the attention of alumni to Alma Mater with particular intensity.

It is hoped that several things will be accomplished.

First, contributions to the Alumni Fund will be in order.

It is hoped, too, that during "Alumni Month" former students will make a particular point of getting in definite touch with the Alumni Office in the rendering of some type of alumni service.

If you have not recently sent in any information about yourself, do so; if you have information about other alumni that we should have, send that in; if you have a suggestion you would be willing to make with reference to the work of the Alumni Office, and ways and means of making that work more effective, let us have it.

And send us some reminiscences of the "old days" for the REGISTER, by all means.

It is not necessary, of course, to wait until November to do these things.

As a matter of fact, every month should be "Alumni Month" for the daughters and sons of Duke.

But a little special emphasis on the obligation for service to Alma Mater during that month will not be out of place.

Let's make November, 1931, memorable in the annals of Duke University because of the success of "Alumni Month."

TWO TYPES

In looking through some files the other day, the editor ran across an address delivered several years ago at a convention of the American Alumni Association by Professor Newlin, of Amherst College. Among other things he said, in talking to alumni secretaries:

We all know there are alumni who think of college as an Amusement Park, whose idea of a campus is that of the place "where good fellows get together": whose thoughts—according to Mr. Gavit's recent book on "College"—are first, football; second, baseball; third, college pranks and scrapes; fourth, other athletics; fifth, fraternities; sixth,—there is no sixth; whose formula (the article goes on to say) is, "I know my college is the best college because I went to it"; whose philosophy is "Rah! Rah! Rah! for dear old Alma Mater!" To such alumni as these you must carry a message they will understand with great difficulty. These are they who put their education into notebooks; then laid their notebooks away with their caps and gowns; and there their education lies, motheaten, with the rest. They have not missed it much. They know that scholarship is a fine thing; they saw it once, they even had a nodding acquaintance with the lady; but they travel in another crowd now, and absent acquaintances are soon forgot. In the case of such as they, you have to sell something invisible.

Fortunately, in addition to these who suffer from the results of intellectual infantile paralysis, there is an ever increasing number who, here or there, in this course or that, with one teacher or another, actually caught a brain-fever, and have never quite recovered from it. These are and will always be your staunchest allies. These will know what you are talking about, without explanation. All alumni will give three cheers for Alma Mater; this latter group will give more; these are the ones we depend on for sturdier support than cheers. I do not know how many alumni of the former type there are in your particular group: I am sure there are some, aren't there? For them, and for these others who treat their college experience far more soberly, you are the artists who paint their picture of the college of today. What is your style in art? Are you realists? Romanticists? Impressionists? Cartoonists? Or do you furnish them with a weekly comic strip? I wonder if there is too much comic strip! It sells papers, it catches alumni. They do love a good time. "When good fellows get together" is always a drawing card.

There is little question but that the average educational institution has from time to time alumni of both types.

There is reason to feel that the number of the first type is decreasing, and of the second type increasing.

More and more college alumni are having a disposition to treat their Alma Mater seriously; not to think of "the old college" simply as a place to go for amusement but as a constant and continuing center of inspiration to which they owe a definite obligation.

We feel quite sure that this latter, and eminently proper, attitude represents the viewpoint of a vast majority of Duke alumni.

Alumni Mourn the Passing of Dr. John Franklin Crowell

Former President of Trinity College, Who Died at East Orange, N. J., August 6, Had
Vitally Important Part in Development of Institution—Estimate of His Service
to Cause of Education by Dr. W. P. Few—Duke University Represented at Funeral Service by President Few

THE DESTINIES of great institutions are inva-
riably bound up in the lives of individual leaders
who through word and action at crucial periods direct
their courses, and in consequence commit institutions
to paths which again and again call for outspoken
leadership and action on part of their successors. Institutions cannot long survive as automatons, or serve
well without dynamic human leadership, human inter-
pretations, and human purposes.

Duke University can look back over its long history
—first as Union Institute, next as Normal College,
then as Trinity College—and recognize the blessing of
continued high leadership. In lean years and in periods of plenty for nearly a century its leadership has
been of the highest order.

John Franklin Crowell, president of Trinity College from 1887 to 1894, whose death occurred on August 6 at East Orange, N. J., is representative of the
splendid leadership the institution has known from its
founding.

The history of Trinity College for the past forty
years and its rise to a place of eminence in the educational world as Duke University may have been entirely different had not President Crowell led the
administration which moved the institution from its
remote contacts in Randolph County to a place near
the heart of a new and growing industrial region.
Coming to the South in 1887 as a recent graduate of
Yale, he brought for the first time to this region something of the modern method of education widely practiced today, setting in motion influences which continue in force at the present time.

From a Late Photograph

While President of Trinity College

TELLS OF COLLEGE'S REMOVAL

President Crowell had not long been at Old Trinity before he recognized the handicap of limited service the College would continue to face so long as it remained at its ancient seat. The story of the uprooting of the College from its traditional location and transplanting to richer ground comprises one of the most important chapters in the annals of Trinity. It was a tremendously difficult task, but no institutional removal could have been more successful or its effects more far-reaching.

Dr. Crowell has written of this momentous event in the college's life: "The removal of the college grew out of this leavening purpose to infuse into the life of the state a more forceful and better balanced type of individuality, as a means of meeting the problems of the day. In the building of the character of the youth, I became convinced after a few years, that the village location was relatively a handicap rather than a help. Modern conditions of business and professional life made the readjustment necessary, and removal from isolation to contact was but an incident in the larger plan and purpose. Removal in itself was, as I saw it, an enduring endowment of resources.

"There was not meal enough in the quiet little village of Randolph for the leaven of the larger college ideal to work upon; nor could the college, including students, and faculty and their families, get the needed advantage of contact with the larger municipality with a life of its own—a life that took pride in the work of the college and must in due time see the growing need of transmuting wealth into wisdom and learning. In short, the rural village, with all its merits, was not wide enough a basis on which to work out Trinity's destiny. Only by coupling up this institutional heart of spiritual power and service with the great arteries and veins of modern life could its actual mission be made good."

HERE AT 1917 COMMENCEMENT

Best remembered by the older members of the University administration and faculty, by hundreds of alumni who were students during the last days at Old Trinity and the early days in Durham, and by other persons throughout the state, he is also remembered by later alumni who were present at commencement in 1917 when the College conferred upon him the LL.D. degree, and in 1927 when he delivered the annual 9019 Society address at Duke. Through all the years since his administration he kept in close contact with the forward movement of the institution.

BECAME PRESIDENT WHEN UNDER 30

He was under 30 years of age when he became Trinity's president, young, efficient, and possessing a great variety of interests. His affection for the stu-

dents around him was clearly demonstrated in many ways, and he participated in and encouraged many of their activities. It was Dr. Crowell who introduced football to Trinity students in 1888, and he is accredited with being the first coach to introduce the oval ball in practices held in a field near the college. For several years Trinity teams coached by their president were outstanding in competition with Southern teams. This is but illustrative of Dr. Crowell's versatility.

TAUGHT VARIOUS SUBJECTS

President Crowell taught in addition to attending to his administrative duties, beginning as Winston professor of history, political economy, and international law, and in his later administration teaching sociology. It was as head of the department of economics and sociology that he went to Smith College after leaving the college. Among those on the faculty during President Crowell's first year were Prof. William T. Gannaway, professor of Latin; Prof. William H. Pegram, professor of natural science; Prof. John F. Heitman, professor of metaphysics and Greek; Prof. James M. Bandy, professor of mathematics and engineering; Prof. N. E. English, professor of history, civil law, and oratory; Prof. Joseph L. Armstrong, professor of English; and Prof. William Price, professor of French and German.

MOMENTOUS YEARS FOR TRINITY

This was the beginning of momentous years for Trinity. Dr. Crowell was president of the College for seven years. With all its noble traditions, excellent record of service, and strength of faculty, opportunity to widen its scope of service was limited. Proposal was made to move the College to a more populous center, and this was agreed upon. A generous offer was made by citizens of Raleigh; but when Washington Duke, of Durham, extended an offer of $85,000 for buildings and endowment, and Gen. Julian S. Carr offered Blackwell's Park, a tract consisting of more than sixty-six acres, as a site, this offer was accepted. This was in the very late 80's, and plans were immediately begun to arrange for the removal.

OCCUPIED IN 1892

After a year's unexpected delay, the new plant consisting of several buildings and faculty homes was occupied in the fall of 1892. Enrollment increased steadily, and when President Crowell resigned in 1894 the College was well situated in its new environment and fully committed to a definite program of progress. The part President Crowell played in directing the College to its greater destinity has not been underestimated. He contributed a human influence that has lasted, and the development of the College in the new environment in which he played a definite part in establishing its testimony of the wisdom of his leadership.

ECONOMIST, AUTHOR AND LECTURER

While Dr. Crowell's leadership in the field of education gives him lasting fame in North Carolina, it was as an economist, author, and lecturer that he won international distinction in the maturer years of his life. When president of Trinity he was keenly interested in the development of North Carolina's resources. This was at a period when the South was still recovering from the trying years of civil war and reconstruction. In 1891 he published in a pamphlet form an open letter to the general assembly entitled a "Program of Progress." In it Dr. Crowell urged increased appropriations for education, improvement of highways, the building of seaports and railroads across the state from east to west; the making of a thorough economic survey, and lending definite aid to the farmers. This unusual and far-sighted document is preserved by the Duke library.

MANY CONTACTS

Dr. Crowell's life was an interesting one and his contacts were many. Engaging in extensive research in economic, social, and political sciences, he made valuable contributions to the development of modern government and business. As director of the World Market Institute he was in close touch with the trend of international as well as national affairs. His opinions were frequently sought by this and other governments.

BORN IN PENNSYLVANIA

Born in York, Pa., on November 1, 1857, John Franklin Crowell passed on in his seventy-fourth year. He received his A.B. degree at Yale in 1883. 1885-'86 he was Larned Scholar in Philosophy, and received his Ph.D. degree from Columbia in 1887, after spending some time traveling in Germany and studying at University of Berlin. It was at this time that he attracted the attention of the Trinity trustees, and his election to the College presidency followed. He had previously taught for a year at Schuykill Seminary, at Fredericksburg, Pa.

After leaving Trinity he taught at Smith College for two years. Then he gave up active teaching for a time and became associated with the treasury department at Washington. There he served with the United States Industrial Commission and as an expert on internal commerce for the bureau of statistics. Then for two years he was educational director of international correspondence at the University of Washington. From that position he went to New York in 1906 as a member of the editorial staff of *The Wall Street Journal*. For nine years he wrote articles and editorials on economic and commercial

problems. He was a frequent lecturer in the metropolitan universities.

WITH NEW YORK CHAMBER OF COMMERCE

From 1915 to 1917 Dr. Crowell held an executive position with the New York Chamber of Commerce. From that time until his retirement he devoted the greater part of his time to lecturing and writing. He was meanwhile identified with important organizations and movements which grew out of the war and the prospects for great economic changes after that conflict. For a time he was financial statistician in the Internal Revenue office in Washington when Daniel C. Roper was in charge of that branch. In addition to serving as director of the World Market Institute, he was director of research in government war contracts for the Carnegie Endowment. Dr. Crowell was president of the American Civic Alliance from 1910 through 1913.

WROTE NUMBER OF BOOKS

Among the books written by Dr. Crowell are "True Foundation of the American College," "Taxation in American Colonies," "The Logical Process of Social Development," "Iron and Steel Trade in the United States," "The Shipbuilding and Shipping Policy of the United States," and "Internal Commerce of the United States."

PRESIDENT FEW AT FUNERAL

Dr. Crowell was married twice. His first wife, who was Miss Laura K. Getz, of Reading, Pa., died in 1888, a year after the wedding. In 1891 he married Miss Carrie H. Pascoe, of Philadelphia, who survives. Two brothers, Davis Crowell and Halleck Crowell, and a sister, Mrs. Katherine Sniter, of York, Pa., also survive. The funeral services were conducted on Saturday, August 8, in York. President William P. Few represented the University at the final rites.

ESTIMATE OF DR. CROWELL'S SERVICES

It was President Few who in 1917, reporting the first twenty-five years progress of the College to the Board of Trustees, made a signal estimate of Dr. Crowell's services to the institution. The words of President Few, which can be even better understood today in light of the College's more recent development into a great University, are as follows:

"Before coming to Durham, Trinity College had already achieved a long and honored history at its ancient seat in Randolph County. The college had taken deep root there, and the removal from the quiet village of Trinity to a new and growing industrial center like Durham was one of the most difficult and important achievements in all the history of the college. For this and other distinguished services the College is indebted to President John Franklin

Crowell, whose administration began with the session of 1887-1888. Dr. Crowell was by temperament and training well fitted for the task which the conditions of the College and the state called upon him for at the time when he came into the place of leadership. Educated at Yale and informed with the spirit and methods of scholarship as we know it today, he was the first modern university-trained man to become president of a college in the south. In the eighties North Carolina had not recovered· from the long tedious years of convalescence that followed the Civil War and reconstruction; and it is the sober truth to say that Dr. Crowell was the very first man to bring in from the outside the real breath of progress. Directly or indirectly, education in all its grades and all phases of the life of the state were touched and inspired by his influence and by his ideas.

"The College was well settled in its new home and definitely committed to a program of progress when Dr. John C. Kilgo came to the presidency at the opening session of 1894-1895."

NAME PERMANENTLY ASSOCIATED

The name of Dr. Crowell is permanently associated with the new Duke campus in the designating of one of the new dormitory houses by his name. An important collection of economic pamphlets in the general library comprises a part of the Crowell collection. Dr. Crowell at one time donated seven thousand valuable pamphlets to the library.

William N. Reynolds Trustee of Duke Endowment

WILLIAM N. Reynolds of Winston-Salem, alumnus and trustee of Duke University and widely known business man, was recently elected a member of the board of trustees of the Duke Endowment at a meeting held in New York. Mr. Reynolds has accepted membership on the board and has already begun his duties in that connection. The announcement of his election has been received most enthusiastically by alumni of the institution and by other friends of the University and of the Duke Endowment.

Mr. Reynolds was born in Patrick County, Virginia. His early life was spent with his father on the farm and in the factory. He received an elementary education in neighboring schools. In 1882 he went to Trinity College in Randolph County, entering the freshman class and remaining through the session of 1884.

This was a notable period in the career of Trinity. Dr. Braxton Craven, that pioneer educator who was the first president of the institution, died while he was a student there, President Wood being elected as his successor. Among the members of the faculty at that time were Professors Johnson and Gannaway; Professor Heitman came to the college at this period. When Mr. Reynolds is in a reminiscent mood it is exceedingly interesting to hear him relate his experiences at "Old Trinity."

From college Mr. Reynolds went to Winston-Salem

(Copyright Ben F. Matthews)
WILLIAM N. REYNOLDS

and began his career in the tobacco business, forming a partnership with his brother, Mr. R. J. Reynolds. This continued for a few years when the corporation known as the R. J. Reynolds Tobacco Company was organized. He was vice-president of the corporation from its beginning until he became president on the death of his brother. A few years ago he resigned the presidency and became chairman of the board of directors. Upon the recent resignation of Mr. Bowman Gray from the presidency Mr. Reynolds retired as chairman of the board of directors and became chairman of the executive committee, Mr. Gray succeeding him as chairman of the board and Mr. S. Clay Williams being president of the company, with its capitalization of $100,000,000.

Mr. Reynolds was married to Miss Kate Bitting of Winston-Salem, a charming woman who has long been prominent in the National Society, Daughters of the American Revolution, and other outstanding women's organizations of the state and nation.

In addition to his connection with the R. J. Reynolds Tobacco Company, Mr. Reynolds has been prominently identified with other business organizations and with many civic enterprises. He is an outstanding citizen of his home community whose advice is always eagerly sought in community matters of large importance. He is widely known in business circles throughout the state and nation.

Law Laboratories; How Legal Aid Clinic Trains Budding Lawyers

By JOHN S. BRADWAY in *Survey Graphic* for June

PROFESSOR JOHN S. BRADWAY, now a member of the law faculty of the University of Southern California, will come to the Duke University Law School in September as professor of law. One of Professor Bradway's chief fields of. work at Duke will be the establishment of a legal aid clinic similar to the one he has been conducting in the University of Southern California. In view. of that fact the following extract from an article by him in the June *Graphic Survey* will doubtless be interesting to readers of the REGISTER.—Editor.

* : :

YEARS ago the writer, a few days after being admitted to the bar, interviewed his first client. As soon as the office door opened, a sort of stage fright gripped me. The visitor wanted a will drawn. I strained my memory for anything relevant to the subject of wills. There had been a course in law school on the law of wills, but nothing the client said had any reference to the cases studied there. Apparently the applicant had seen a will. I had not. The client seemed to know how a lawyer should act, and was obviously disconcerted by my helpless condition. The client suggested that the lawyer take notes, and practically dictated a will. This I took down in a dazed fashion without the slightest idea of what it was all about. At last the interview was at an end and I set myself actually to draw a will.

I believed that a lawyer would lose caste if he disclosed his ignorance by asking advice. I recalled the case-book method of study at law school and with what then seemed a stroke of genius, I began to review the complete case law of wills in my state as represented by the reported court decisions from 1700 down. At the end of the week when the client returned, the net result of hours of labor was a pile of notes digesting the judge-made law of wills. The client went elsewhere. I sat amid the ruins trying to find out what was wrong and why three years in a leading law school had not prepared me for a situation which reason told me must be quite simple. Why had I never seen a will? Why had I no knowledge of how to meet a client? Where did one go for these practical details of my profession?

In due course other clients came, wills were drawn correctly, the sense of stage fright was overcome, and ineffectiveness was succeeded by greater efficiency. Fellow members of the bar confessed similar experiences. Here was a difficulty of adjustment which all young lawyers, in greater or less degree had to meet —a gap to be crossed by those entering the legal profession. Social engineers build bridges across such gulfs for the convenience of the next comers. Wasn't there a chance here to do some pioneering?

As so often happens, this idea arrived at through personal experience was not entirely new. Others had realized the need and had made experiments, many of which were highly successful. The ambition to be a pioneer was modified into a desire to coöperate with those already at work on the problems. As a first step a study of the existing machinery was undertaken.

The first connecting link I found between the law school and the bar was the legal aid society. Since 1876 organized legal aid work had begun to grow nationally, and even fifteen years ago, when I first came in contact with it, it was giving annually legal advice and assistance to many thousands of poor persons. Law students and newly-admitted lawyers were occasionally taken on the legal aid society staff. In the rush of legal aid business, with no time to become morbid over mistakes, the student learned rapidly. Here was a real chance to divert to the channels of law students enough of the currents of the social and economic life of the community to start the inevitable seasoning process and so, mixing the metaphors, to bridge the gulf from theoretical training to legal practice by means of a conditional experience in dealing with law and human beings.

About 1913 the law schools began to establish legal aid clinics offering opportunities analogous to internship in medical education. In some instances this was done coöperatively by a local legal aid society and the law school. In some instances the law school set up its own organization. At present, legal aid clinics exist in one form or another at the law schools of Harvard, Cincinnati, Northwestern, Minnesota, California and Southern California. Elsewhere the plan is under way.

Let me draw on a two-year association with the legal aid clinic at the University of Southern California to show how the work goes on in one of these law school laboratories and something of its usefulness to student, client, and the community. In Los Angeles the Legal Aid Society is housed in the Law School building on the campus of the University of Southern California. Duly qualified lawyers familiar with practice are in charge of it. Legal aid clinic work is required of all senior law students. These students have had at least two years' legal training and expect the year following to be earning their living at the law.

Only persons unable to pay a fee are accepted at the clinic. The applicant presents himself at the office in person, and the student interviews him to secure the facts. Then the budding lawyer retires to the back office to confer with an attorney who helps plan the campaign and passes upon questions of law and jurisdiction. The student returns to the client in the interviewing room and the case proceeds. Most cases are disposed of by advice, or by looking up points of law, drafting legal documents, or adjusting controversies. In all this the student participates. If court action is necessary, the student prepares the papers, gathers witnesses and other evidence, briefs the law and does all the work that a junior in a large law office expects as part of his daily routine. In the clinic the student is under constant supervision. In court he listens to the attorney try the case. He goes through the motions of practicing law with someone to protect the client from his inexperience.

The client secures a high grade of legal assistance, which the enthusiasm of the student, access to an adequate law library, constant supervision by members of the bar and advice from other members of the law faculty make possible. Further, the work educates a large section of the public to rely upon the law in an era when disrespect for law is only too prevalent.

* * *

But what is the real gain to the student? Does the clinic bridge the gap between law school and law practice? The clinic sets out to teach the student five distinct things.

1. A practical view of law practice as distinguished from a theoretical view.
2. A synthesis of law school work, grouping the rules of law with reference to a client, and in action, rather than according to the formal, theoretical divisions of the law, such as contracts, torts, crimes.
3. A social viewpoint, considering the client as a whole—his individual as well as his legal needs.
4. A practical view of legal ethics and etiquette.
5. The ability to see a law case as a whole, to plan a

legal campaign, to think in terms of "What shall I do?" and not merely, "What is the law?" With these go self-confidence and a realization that justice is often eminently practical and not necessarily an insistence on abstract rights.

* * *

Perhaps the clearest picture of the range of experience open to the students in these law laboratories can be shown by an analysis of the first 1,000 cases handled by the Southern California Legal Aid Clinic:

NUMBER	CASES INVOLVING
248	Contracts, such as wage claims and small money collections
241	Relations between husband and wife
235	Real estate or personal property including landlord-and-tenant disputes
114	Tort liability, such as workmen's compensation problems, complaints against professional people, neighborhood quarrels
69	Relations between parent and child
58	Estates of deceased persons, minors, feeble-minded persons, and bankrupts
35	Criminal matters, miscellaneous

A second table indicates how these one thousand cases were handled by the clinic:

477 Advice and referred cases
    244 Advice given
    186 Referred to private attorney
133 Investigated and advice given
 95 Refused at first interview
 91 Cases terminated by client
 60 Disposed after litigation
    32 Won
     8 Discontinued litigation
     6 Lost
     6 Ex parte proceedings
     5 Settlement after litigation
     5 Purpose secured
     3 Case technically won but no practical benefit
 49 Adjusted
    28 Satisfactorily adjusted
    17 Adjusted without counsel
     4 Partial settlement
 31 Information secured and documents drawn
 30 Investigated and refused
 21 Investigated and referred to
    13 Private attorney
     5 Special agency
     3 Special court
 13 Client unable to advance costs

We have described a gulf to be crossed. Dependability and high ethical standards in the practice of the law are the goals. The legal clinic is no short-cut. But experiment proves that it does do for the law student what the hospital internship does for the student of medicine or the surveying trip for the young engineer. And beyond this the ethical idealism and practical efficiency carried over by the clinic from the classroom and library to every-day human problems should give results of real value to future leaders of the legal profession, and through them to the community.

Duke Alumnus Writes About Some Experiences in Japan

Rev. I. L. Shaver, of Class of 1919, Says That President Hoover's Moratorium Plan Is Being Highly Praised in Japan—Revision of American Immigration Law of 1924 Still Hoped for in That Country—Some Personal Experiences Related by Duke Graduate, Now in Mission Field

(REV. I. L. SHAVER, of the Class of 1919, has spent a number of years in Japan in connection with the Japan Mission of the Methodist Episcopal Church, South. He has had some decidedly interesting experiences along various lines and some time ago the REGISTER asked him for a letter for publication telling something of his work overseas. Although he has not had opportunity yet to write a formal article recently he did find time, in the midst of a busy summer's work, to write a personal letter to the editor, from which certain extracts are being published.—Editor.)

*   *   *

FOR some time I have been thinking of writing, but a thousand and one other things have prevented my doing so. This morning, however, I am going to take the time to write a few lines.

This spring weather puts me in a reminiscent mood, which brings back memories of the days spent down on an old Carolina farm. While there the only books I had to read were the Bible, the Life of Wesley, and stories of the Dark Continent. Then I dreamed of

Duke Alumnus Selling Ice Cream Cones at Japanese Bazaar

becoming a Livingstone or a Wesley. It was also while there in the country following the old Dixie plow down by the "slash" in the shade of the maples and willow oaks that my soul communed with God and dreamed dreams of the invisible.

Again, just twenty years ago this month, while harvesting wheat with my father, and while looking out over the field of golden grain, a voice within my soul urged me to look out upon other fields white unto the harvest, but where the laborers were few. That afternoon when I told my father of my decision he said, "Son, a call to service is a call to preparation. I am just a poor farmer, and haven't much money, but always remember that 'where there is a will there is a way'." Two months later I entered school at Rutherford College, and after finishing there entered Trinity College, where I graduated four years later.

I have always found the old proverb true—even to the extent of winning a pretty trained nurse from Watts Hospital, who became my bride on the day of my graduation in June, 1919.

The photograph above was taken at a workers' meeting in Oita. The man in kimono standing beside Rev. Mr. Shaver is Rev. T. Kugimiya, Duke alumnus. On the extreme right of the picture is T. Tanaka, brother of I. Tanaka, and a graduate of Vanderbilt. On the left, front row, is Rev. R. Sawada, who will enter Duke this fall.

After spending five years in Japan, we returned to America, and to Duke University, where in 1925 I received the M.A. degree.

This is our twelfth year in Japan. During this time five little Shavers have arrived to say "Ohayo" to Japan, but two of them have passed on to say "Good morning" to dear ones on the "other side." The three left are jolly kids—aged one, five, and ten. Eleanor, ten years old, has been attending school at the Canadian Academy, Kobe. Some day I expect to send all the children to Duke.

We are happy in Japan. We like the people and the country. I have not yet become a Livingstone or a Wesley, but am beginning to appreciate Paul's experiences—"In labours more abundant, in journeys often, in perils in the sea, in hunger and thirst," and "Beside those things that are without, that which cometh upon me daily, the care of all the churches," for in addition to my own charge, which is composed of three circuits, and duties as missionary superintendent of the Matsuyama district, I have the work of two other missionaries who are now in America, and am also acting presiding elder of the district in the place of a National.

My work takes me away from home often, and across the Inland Sea many times. Often I have to sit on the floor, eat on the floor, sleep on the floor, and sometimes preach on the floor—that is preach while sitting on the floor. I enjoy the work immensely. Besides this I am teaching in a commercial school here in Oita, and have many opportunities of speaking to students in the schools and here in our home.

The financial depression has hit Japan rather hard, but the number of unemployed in this country is not so great as in America. However, some of those employed receive only five or ten dollars per month. Mr. Hoover's proposed moratorium is being highly praised in Japan, and will in due time be approved. This will mean a great deal for international goodwill. Now, if the American government will just do one more thing—revise the Immigration Law of 1924 so as to admit Orientals on the quota basis—we shall be happy, and a great deal will have been done toward peace and good will in the Orient.

I have many more things of which I would like to write, but I fear that I have already written too much for one time. I am sending a fine young Japanese over to Duke this fall, Mr. Ryosuke Sawada.

Congratulations on the REGISTER.

"Yoroshiku" to all our friends.

Sincerely yours,

I. L. SHAVER.

Yale Professor Coming To Duke Next September

Announcement was recently made by President W. P. Few of Duke University of the election of Dr. H. Shelton Smith, professor in the divinity school of Yale University, as professor of religious education in Duke University and a member of the faculty of the School of Religion. The services of Professor Smith will begin at Duke in September.

Born in North Carolina and a graduate of Elon College, Professor Smith is well known to many persons in this state. After receiving his A.B. degree in 1917 he served as first lieutenant and chaplain in the army during the World War. He continued his studies at Yale University and was granted by Yale the Ph.D. degree in 1923. In 1928 he received the D.D. degree from Defiance College.

For five years following his graduation from Yale Professor Smith was director of leadership training for the International Council of Religious Education. In 1928 he was elected associate professor of education in Teachers College of Columbia University, and a year later professor of religious education in Yale University. While at Yale Professor Smith has been director of field work in religious education.

As a member of many important committees, Professor Smith is actively engaged in the work of various national education groups.

Duke Alumnus Visits France and England With Party of Twelve American Lawyers

B. S. Womble, a member of the Class of 1903 and of the Board of Trustees of Duke University, was recently a member of a party of American lawyers who visited England and France with a view to making a study of the court, and judicial systems of the two countries. In a letter received by the editor from Mr. Womble, while making the return trip, he stated that the whole journey had been most interesting and instructive, and that those in the party received much in the way of helpful information. There were about twelve members of the party who, in addition to securing facts and figures on the judicial systems of England and France, were entertained socially in a very delightful way by members of the bar in London and Paris.

Mr. Womble says that he found considerable interest among members of the bar that he met in England and France in Duke University and its work in various fields, particularly in the realm of law instruction.

J. L. Horne, Jr., New President of State Press Association

Duke Alumnus, Prominent For Years in North Carolina Newspaper Circles, Given Further Recognition—Member Alumni Council and Closely Identified in Various Ways With Duke

J. L. HORNE, JR.

JOSHUA Lawrence Horne, Jr., '09, editor and publisher of the *Evening Telegram*, Rocky Mount, N. C., was recently elected president of the North Carolina Press Association for the ensuing year, succeeding J. W. Noell, of the Roxboro *Courier*. I. S. London, of the Rockingham *Post-Dispatch*, was elected vice-president, and Miss Beatrice Cobb, of the Morganton *News-Herald*, was chosen secretary-treasurer for the eleventh consecutive time: B. A. Lowrance, of the Mecklenburg *Times*, Charlotte, was elected historian.

The new president of the Press Association has been active in North Carolina since 1909 when he left Trinity College to enter the employ of the *Daily Record* of Rocky Mount.

In 1911 he founded the Rocky Mount *Morning Telegram* and published the first edition of this newspaper on October 27 of that year. The name of the newspaper was changed to the *Evening Telegram* three months later and since that time Mr. Horne has been its publisher. In 1916 he became publisher of the Rocky Mount *Weekly News* and in 1921 acquired an interest in and acted as publisher of the Wilmington *News-Dispatch*, although he later sold this newspaper.

In 1920 he was vice-president of the Associated Press of the United States and for several years was a member of the advisory board of the press organization. He served three years as president of the North Carolina Association of Afternoon Newspapers, one year as president of the North Carolina Association of Daily Papers, and since 1924 has been president of the Associated Press Club of North Carolina.

He was chairman of the powerful legislative committee of the North Carolina Press Association during the past year prior to his election to the association presidency.

The new president of the North Carolina Press Association is a member of the Alumni Council of Duke University, and of the executive committee of the Council. He has always been deeply interested in his alma mater and her achievements and ever ready to aid in advancing her interests. For many years he has been prominent in the newspaper circles of North Carolina. He has built the Rocky Mount *Telegram* into one of the best afternoon newspapers in the state, and one that has been of great assistance in the upbuilding of its home community.

Besides his newspaper interests, Mr. Horne has been active in other things looking to the upbuilding of Rocky Mount, being prominent in the Y. M. C. A. work and in other local community endeavors. For the past two years he has been president of the Duke University Club of Nash and Edgecombe counties. He is a past president of the Rocky Mount Kiwanis Club and of the Chamber of Commerce.

Mr. Horne has a daughter in the Woman's College.

Duke Hospital Is Given Rank

Further recognition has been given Duke hospital with the announcement by the American College of Surgeons that the local institution would be placed on the next approved list of hospitals issued by the national organization in October.

Already this year the hospital has been given several distinctions. First it was given approval of the American Medical Association for the training of internes, and more recently was approved by the same association for receiving residents for graduate work.

Duke Hospital completed its first year of operation on July 20.

Some Alumni Personalities

Rev. Jesse Homer Barnhardt, D.D., of the Class of 1899, is pastor of the First M. E. Church, South, of Salisbury, and member of the Board of Trustees of Duke University. Two of his children have attended Duke, Max L. Barnhardt, of the Class of 1927, and Margaret R. Barnhardt, of the Class of 1929. Dr. Barnhardt has just issued from the Stratford Press, Boston, Mass., a new book entitled, "Looking Them Over." It is an attractive volume of over 200 pages, and contains a variety of matter of considerable human interest value. The book is divided into fifteen chapters and they are filled with genuine humor, pathos and common sense. Before assuming his present pastorate, Dr. Barnhardt served a number of the leading charges of the Western North Carolina Conference, and has been several times presiding elder.

Lila Markham (Mrs. W. J.) Brogden, of the Class of 1902, is one of the outstanding women graduates of Duke University. She takes an active part in all alumnae activities, having served as president of the Alumnae Association, chairman of the Alumnae Council and chairman of its Executive Committee. After graduating from college, she taught in the Durham high school for a number of years. In January 1917, she married Willis J. Brogden, now an associate justice of the North Carolina Supreme Court. They have two sons. Mrs. Brogden is president of the Durham Woman's Club, second vice-president of the N. C. Federation of Woman's Clubs, past director of the Chamber of Commerce and the Community Chest Board, and a trustee of the King's Daughters Home.

Nathan Carter Newbold, Class of 1898, has been in the State Department of Education for eighteen years, being Director of the Division of Negro Education. Before assuming this position, he was teacher for several years in Asheboro, Roxboro, and Washington, N. C. He is a member of Phi Beta Kappa, and Omicron Delta Kappa. He has been chairman of the committee of the National Education Association to coöperate with the National Association of Teachers in Colored Schools; chairman of the sub-committee on the negro school child of the White House Conference on Child Health and Protection, being appointed by Secretary Wilbur. He has directed studies in teacher-training programs for negroes in several states, and has served on bodies interested in inter-racial matters.

Cataloguing Work at Duke Libraries Efficiently Done

Excellence of System Used Wins High Praise—Staff of Full-Time Cataloguers Includes Nineteen, All College and University Graduates—Present Year Unusually Difficult One in This Position

THE Cataloguing Division of the Duke University Libraries is one of the most efficient library cataloguing departments in the entire nation. Miss Eva Earnshaw Malone, A.B., B.S., Duke Assistant Librarian in charge of cataloguing, is justly proud of the achievements of her staff and enthusiastic over the work which has been done during the past year.

The staff of full time cataloguers includes fourteen in the University Library; three in the Woman's College Library; one in the Law Library; and one in the Duke Hospital Library, a total of nineteen. All of the cataloguers are graduates of colleges and universities. Of the total number, twelve are graduates of first class Schools of Library Science—Simmons College, Boston; Columbia University; Drexel Institute, and the Atlanta Library School, now a part of Emory University. Of the remaining seven cataloguers, four are doing independent classifying and cataloguing, having been taught cataloguing technique by Miss Malone and Miss Wescott, first assistant cataloguer. The three junior assistants work with the senior cataloguers, typing, ordering Library of Congress cards and performing various duties that save the time of the experienced cataloguers.

This percentage of trained, experienced workers is above the average and has enabled the Duke Library to maintain for years the highest number of books per cataloguer among the best college libraries in America. Much of this success is due to the original methods of Miss Malone, who has been assistant librarian in the institution since 1914, when Duke University was Trinity College.

The cards are of the same form as the printed Library of Congress cards. The printed cards are used whenever they are available. When necessary the cards are typed. All of the books shelved in the library are fully analyzed. A separate card is made for each of the subjects which the book treats. A card is made listing the author's name and another card carries the title of the book. Throughout the division the highest standards and most excellent workmanship are observed.

The present year has been an interesting one but also a very hard one for the cataloguers. The Library was moved to the University campus during August and September. Since that time the workers have rejoiced in their new and beautiful quarters. New equipment, especially designed for cataloguers has been installed in this division. The furniture provides every convenience for speed and comfort in the work. All this has meant readjustment, training new assistants, and naturally some confusion. However, the officials are very proud of the year's work.

Accurate statistics are kept by each cataloguer, the totals tabulated each month and complete records kept by the head cataloguer. A careful record is kept of the number of cards typed and filed, and the number of books accessioned, classified, and catalogued for the month and for the year. During the current year, 133,204 cards were made and filed in the various card catalogues. For the same period, 55,380 books and pamphlets were catalogued. Of this number 9,108 were in foreign languages.

This cataloguing department is a pioneer in requiring specially trained people for special subjects. For a number of years cataloguers have been selected as carefully for their college majors as for their library training. When Miss Malone began this phase of the work, the general custom was to catalogue books by the date they were received in the library. For example, any cataloguer would have in the lot of books she was working on, books on a number of different subjects. Now a cataloguer is trained not only in Library Science, but also in the subject of the books which she is to catalogue. A different cataloguer is responsible for the cataloguing of each of the subjects of history, economics, sociology, philosophy, religion, biology, chemistry, engineering, forestry, and physics. The literatures are handled in the same way. For example, the cataloguer responsible for the cataloguing of books bought by the German department, Miss Ethel Abernathy, is a graduate of Duke, has had a number of graduate courses in German here, and is studying in a German university for the year of 1931-32.

To find trained cataloguers who knew much about the sciences was most difficult. Finally, two of Duke's own graduates, Miss Kate Israel, in chemistry, and Miss Eva Candler Malone, in biology, were interested in the library side of their subjects and were persuaded to enter the department. Now they are experts in cataloguing and in the reference work of these departmental libraries. Efforts are being made to provide the other science libraries with the same type of workers. Complete dictionary card catalogues are furnished the departmental libraries.

Departmental libraries of the University Library now are those of Biology, Chemistry, Engineering, Forestry, Physics, and School of Religion. The Woman's College Library, the Law Library, and Duke Hospital Library have their own staff and accession their books as separate units. The departmental libraries, however, work in the closest and most cordial coöperation with the University Library.

The Cataloguing Department of the University Library is a regular contributor to the Union Catalogue of the Library of Congress. A main entry card is sent to the Congressional Library for all rare or unusual books and pamphlets—titles which they do not have in their own library or of books so rare that they cannot be loaned. The chief of this division has been very appreciative and enthusiastic about the Duke contributions. A recent letter received from him by Miss Malone, says: "Your contribution is a splendid example of coöperation, both in the make-up of the cards as well as in the selection. . . . The cards covering the first hundred titles of the Lanson collection have just come in. These as well as the eighteenth century periodicals and the Peruvian collection will be a valuable addition to Union Catalogue. The workmanship deserves the highest praise. If every contributor sent such entries, the Union Catalogue would be a work of art."

From time to time the Library of Congress asks for copy so that they may print cards for unusual books in the Duke Libraries, copies of which they do not have. They present the Duke Libraries with two complete sets of the printed cards. These cards carry the printed note "Title from Duke University Library, printed by Library of Congress."

The public catalogue in the University Library may now better be called the "Union Catalogue." This catalogue contains, of course, cards for all books shelved in the main library and complete sets of cards for all other libraries of the system. There are two exceptions to this rule. The Duke Hospital Library furnishes a main entry card for all its titles. At present, these cards are filed in trays of the public catalogue labeled Duke Hospital Library. If it be-

comes necessary, subject cards will be made for them later. Later, cards for all books in the Woman's College Library may be added to the "Union Catalogue." The catalogue department of the Woman's College Library this year has accessioned 7,110 books and catalogued 6,162 books. This library is unique in having started life in the hands of trained and experienced workers.

The correct filing of so large a number of cards is a real task. In the main library, eight cataloguers file from one to two hours per day. The task is not continued long at a time because it is very exhaustive of nerve energy. Mistakes are very easily made during periods of fatigue.

As a sub-department of the cataloguing work, a group of student assistants, working ten hours a week, under the direction of an experienced assistant, prepare the books for the shelves after the cataloguers have finished with them. This work consists of typing book cards and pockets, from information on slips furnished by the cataloguer, pasting in the book plates and pockets, embossing, cutting leaves, and marking the call number on the back of the book.

Oxford Student Visiting Duke

Grady Frank, of Mt. Airy, former junior at Duke University who went to England last October as a Rhodes scholar representing North Carolina, is back at Duke for several weeks after concluding his first session at Oxford.

While at Duke Frank is dividing his time between the general library and the tennis courts. He was an exceptional student at Duke, having one of the highest academic averages in mathematics ever recorded at Duke. One of the most consistently good players in tennis at Duke in several years, he was one of the ranking varsity men for two years.

Returning to England in several weeks, Frank will continue his studies at Oxford.

European Masons Invite Ellwood To Paris Meet

Prof. Charles A. Ellwood, head of the Duke University department of sociology, has been invited by the Universal League of Freemasons to speak at the international congress to be held in Paris on September 8 to September 13. The invitation was extended by Paul Reck, secretary of the board of directors, at Basel, Switzerland.

Professor Ellwood, in the event he accepts the invitation, will speak on "The Social Surrender of Freemasonry." The Duke professor is prominently identified with Masonic affairs, being one of the four Americans on the administrative council of the International League of Freemasons.

Duke Professor Doing Much Work in Narcotics Field

Dr. Godbey, Member of International Committee on the Subject, Feels that Widespread Campaign of Education, Including Instruction in High Schools, is Needed—Dr. Godbey's Work Attracting Much Attention

DR. ALLEN H. Godbey, Professor of Old Testament in the Duke University School of Religion, recently was appointed a member of the Committee on Law and Philosophy of the International Conference on Narcotism. The chairman of this committee is former Governor Charles S. Whitman, of New York. Captain Richmond Pearson Hobson, of Spanish American War fame, is the presiding officer of the conference which was held in Switzerland during the month of June.

Asked regarding his work in this position, Dr. Godbey became reminiscent concerning the manner in which he became interested in the subject. He had been making some research in Hebrew history on the subject of blood and its part in the rites and ceremonies of that people. In 1923, he published, in the *Methodist Quarterly Review*, two articles on this subject. One of these was "Blood; Marriage Contracts," the other was "Blood; The Cult of the Dead." In the course of his investigations, he read Dr. Robertson Smith's work on "The Religion of the Semites." Dr. Smith seems to imply that the use of certain incense in odorous sacrifice was caused by the belief that this incense was formed from the "blood of an animate and divine plant." Dr. Godbey disagreed with Dr. Smith on the ground that it was not necessary to carry the blood symbol through the entire Hebrew ritualistic system. Dr. Godbey discussed this point in an article prepared for *The American Journal of Semitic Languages and Literature*, of July, 1930. In this article, he declares that the incense was used for the purpose of bringing the god under the influence of the narcotic fumes or to produce a religious frenzy in the worshipper. The article is an exhaustive study of the influence of narcotics on Hebrew worship and the war of the Hebrew prophets and Oriental leaders on the incense ritual of their time.

Dr. Godbey says that the first work of research done in this field was by Dr. John Spencer, of Cambridge, two hundred years earlier than Dr. Smith. The chief weakness of Dr. Smith's book, as pointed out by Dr.

Godbey, is in the realms of anthropology and ethnology.

Shortly after the publication of the article in the *American Journal of Semitic Languages and Literatures*, Captain Hobson wrote Dr. Godbey asking for a similar one to be read at the meeting of the World Conference on Narcotism in Geneva. After some correspondence, it was agreed that the paper should be on "The Incense and Sacrifices of the American Indian." This was necessary in order to present a compact study in the short while available before the session of the conference. The previous article had been the result of the accumulation of notes over twenty years.

Much of the material used was first hand, although an immense body of material has been prepared by the American Bureau of Ethnology. The paper goes into minute detail in discussing the psychology of narcotics among American Indians, covering more than two hundred typewritten pages.

At least a third of the article is concerned with a study of coca, the plant from which cocaine is derived. Dr. Godbey says that there are a hundred and twenty species of this plant. It grows in all parts of Mexico, Central and South America, as well as in Australia. Doctor Godbey's study says that it has ruined the Peruvian Indian. He says that the Indian who chews the leaf of this plant feels no sensation of hunger, yet he gets no nourishment from it. It paralyzes the sensory nerves.

Dr. Godbey points out the great danger to America, today, from this narcotic. He says that the habit was started in America by careless, ignorant physicians, and by dangerous patent medicines. The manufacture of the drug in America is now controlled by the Federal government. Its manufacture is restricted to the factories of two corporations. These two corporations make careful reports to the national government. Their representatives reported to the American National Conference on Narcotism in New York, that only 2 per cent of their product gets away into illicit trade.

Dr. Godbey points out the fact, however, that large quantities of the drug are being smuggled into this country and sold by "dope peddlers." He says that much of it is being sold to high school students who are unaware of its danger.

In discussing the lack of proper enlightenment of the public on the subject of narcotics, Dr. Godbey says much incomplete, and sometimes incorrect, information is found in some books of reference. Some encyclopedias he found especially correct and careful in their reports, while others were either incorrect or not complete enough to be of real use in a school library.

Dr. Godbey discusses the use by American Indians of a number of narcotics. Copal gum is secured from a large family of trees that is known throughout the world. The best known in America is the sap of the honey locust.

Saguaro is the juice of the fruit of a giant cactus. The Indians drink this at their annual fruit gathering. To fail to do so, they believe, would result in a drought and a failure of their crops for the next year. Daturos is used in all parts of the world as a powerful narcotic to produce religious frenzies. Its use is very prominent among American Indians. They make it from the "jimpson weed."

"Black drinks" is a term applied to certain powerful drinks whose purpose is to throw off all impurities. This is the origin of the expression, "Make a clean breast of it." The most common source of these drinks, in America, is the common "blue flag."

Cahoba, or parica, is a South American narcotic. Cahoba is a corruption of the name given it by the Italians. Parica is the Indian name used in Brazil and Argentine. Tesvino or Mescal is also a Spanish American product. Tesvino is a corruption of the Aztec word tehuinte, intoxicant. It is made from a number of plants. Mescal is the particular type made from the root of a century plant. Pulque is made from the juice of the plant, itself.

Chicha is the name given to Indian beers made of grain. These are powerful narcotics. Cassiri and pawarri are made all over South America from manioc, a staple food product. They are powerful intoxicants.

Peyote, Dr. Godbey says, is one of the most interesting members of this group. This is the term by which it is commercially known now. It is made of a button shaped cactus with a large bulbous root. It has peculiarly stimulating, hallucinative, intoxicating powers. It is one of the most widely spread of the Indian religious ceremonial narcotics.

Dr. Godbey does not agree with Governor Whitman that what America needs in order to correct the evil of narcotism is further governmental regulation and restriction. He is advocating a more widespread campaign of education in the subject. It is his desire to have the subject discussed widely throughout the nation, to have it taught to high school students, and to lay special stress on its being taught in the medical schools. Such a program, he believes, will accomplish more than prohibitory legislation.

Freshman Week Begins September 9th

The young men and women who are to comprise the roster of the Class of 1935 will reach the two campuses of the University on September 9 to take part in the annual Freshman Week program. A carefully planned program has been arranged for the newcomers, and in addition to the painfully necessary processes of taking placement and psychological tests, a round of get-together socials and recreational features is outlined. At assemblies talks will be made by administration leaders and student representatives of various campus organizations.

This program will open the University's second year on the new campus, while likewise the second year of the Woman's College will get under way.

Freshman instruction will begin on Monday, September 14. On the following day new students of advanced standing will be registered, and on Wednesday, September 16, the formal opening of the new academic year will be observed. On Thursday instruction for sophomores, juniors, and seniors will begin.

Graduate students will register on September 17, 18, and 19. The autumn quarter of the School of Medicine will begin on October 2.

Both administrative and faculty leaders are looking to the coming year as one that should prove successful from many points of view. With the University fully situated in its new location, the organization of departments adapted to new quarters and routine, and students orientated to various new academic features, there is every cause to believe the University is at the threshold of a successful season in every phase of its work.

Duke Hospital Clinics Doing Work of Real Importance

Not Unusual to Find Patients There From as Many as Eight Different North Carolina Counties and From Other States—Work of Clinics Promoting Feeling of Neighborliness and of Good Will

THE HEAD nurse of the Duke Hospital Clinics, Mrs. M. L. Lawler, is very enthusiastic over the work of her department. She is impressed not only with the value of the clinics as agents of medicine and surgery, but also as socializing agents in the business of promoting neighborliness.

The clinics, with their staff of physicians and surgeons who are in charge of the Duke Hospital and the various departments of the Duke University Medical School, offer, for people of moderate means, an opportunity to secure medical and surgical treatment. The head surgeon and the physician who directs the medical department of the hospital are, by virtue of their positions, heads of the clinic. Their services can be secured by the clinics whenever necessary. There are about twelve internes assisting the doctors. Four nurses take care of the patients in the process of their examinations. Two laboratory technicians furnish data for the diagnosis of the cases. An admitting officer and a stenographer take care of the office work for the fourteen clinics, which are open from 1 to 5 p. m., daily, except Saturday and Sunday. The emergency and accident departments are open all the time, day and night.

All of this is technical and part of the work of every clinic. But Mrs. Lawler calls attention to the invisible spirit of neighborliness to be found at Duke. The waiting room of the clinics now is constantly thronged with patients, their friends and relatives. It is not unusual to find patients from as many as eight different counties in North Carolina and from other states. Some of these come for social visits with the once dreaded hospital officials.

Mrs. Lawler tells the story of a young woman who for four years had been unable to walk. Treated in the Duke Orthopedic Clinic, she has learned to walk without the aid of any mechanical devices. This young woman makes periodic visits to the clinic for social calls on nurses and officials. She delights in their comments on her improvement.

Many patients come with fear in their hearts. Many who come from rural communities are unacquainted with hospital routine. The Duke Clinics officials spend much time in patient, careful explanation, allaying fears and acquainting the patients, their relatives and friends with the routine of clinics and hospital work.

A mother recently came to the clinic bringing her son. The boy was suffering with what her family physician had diagnosed as appendicitis. The clinical examination confirmed the diagnosis and preparations were made to operate immediately. The mother became alarmed and asked to speak to the head nurse and to the surgeon who was to operate.

"You all ain't hesitatin' much on the threshold, are you?" she asked. "That there's my boy, an' I love him. I want to know about this operation, first."

Realizing the situation and the feelings of the mother, the operation was delayed for an hour while the doctor and the nurse explained kindly and simply the whole problem. With grateful heart, the mother then begged them to proceed with the operation.

Two weeks later she came through the main waiting room waving good bye to the nurses as the boy was taken to a waiting car. "We're takin' him home. He's well." That two weeks had made another neighbor for Duke.

The Duke community isn't just the city of Durham, nor Durham county. It covers more than one of the southern states. It is the community of the individual patients. Hospital officials have noted with particular pleasure the success of northern specialists in the rapidity with which they have become acquainted with and adapted themselves to the conditions and customs of this widespread community.

Very cordial relations exist between the Duke Clinics and the physicians of all the territory served by the institution. No externe service is offered by the clinics. Family physicians send their patients to the clinics for a more thorough and a more technical diagnosis than can be made in the home. Usually the examination is made and the patient returned to the family physician for treatment. If hospitalization is

(Continued on page 264)

Dr. Lanning Studies History of Old Spanish Universities

Back at Duke After Year's Study in Mexico, Central and South America, He Talks Interestingly of Colonial Educational Institutions—He Also Relates Some of His Experiences as Guggenheim Fellow

DR. JOHN Tate·Lanning, Instructor in History, has returned to Duke after a year's study in Mexico, Central and South America. Doctor Lanning, during his leave of absence, was a Fellow of the John Simon Guggenheim Foundation. He visited every South American nation, except Paraguay and Venezuela.

Dr. Lanning was particularly interested in the history of the Spanish colonial universities. He studied, also, the cultural and political development of the Spanish-American countries. His work carried him to the seats of the old universities at Mexico City; Lima, Peru; Sucre, Bolivia; Santiago, Chile; Cordoba and Buenos Aires, Argentine.

Prof. Lanning says that the modern universities occupy the seats of the colonial universities, which were called royal, if they belonged to the king, or pontifical, if they were the property of the church. They are now all called national universities.

It was necessary for Dr. Lanning to visit all the modern centers of learning because all the records of the old universities in existence are stored there. Many of these, however, are missing, he says. They were used as fuel for the fires of rebel troops. · This he found to be true especially in Bolivia.

Prof. Lanning found that the first of these universities is a hundred years older than Harvard, America's first university. The records show a dozen universities in Spanish American countries by the end of the eighteenth century. Dr. Lanning says he found evidence to show that they were as politically active as today. In fact, he said, student agitation led directly to the wars of independence with Spain.

These universities appear to have had 132 holidays during each academic year. These were celebrations of Christian ceremonials, saints' days, and every type of "fiesta." The university curriculum was a very stilted one. Five faculties were required for a university but students seldom studied any courses except those of law, theology, or medicine. They did have chairs of "modern" languages, teaching the Indian

languages of the Aztecs, and the Incas. Most of the literary and scientific productions were direct products of the university faculties.

Dr. Lanning was much amused at the great display attendant on the conferring of the doctor's degree in the old universities. The expense of the ceremony often amounted to more than $10,000. This cost included the doctor's ring for the candidate; his cap and gown; the banquet for all the visiting doctors; a bull fight in the main square for the town people; fees for all the university officials; six fat hens for the university larder; and various other items of expense. Occasionally a university sold a degree outright at a much cheaper rate. The candidate usually selected some wealthy man as god father, who paid the expenses for the honor it would bring to him. Often, however, the number of visiting doctors made the cost of the banquet prohibitive, in which case the godfather asked many of them to stay away. ·

Dr. Lanning was invited to deliver an address at nearly every university he visited. At the University of Cordoba, he addressed the entire university on the history of their own institution. He wrote an article entitled "A Study of the Spanish American Colonial Universities and the Evolution of Cultural and Political Development of the New World," which recently appeared in the *Review* of the National University of Cordoba. He is now preparing an article on the formation of the mentalities which promoted the independence movement against Spain, for the Annals of the University of Chile. This article is partly psychological and partly historical.

Dr. Lanning declares, however, that he is much more interested in what the modern professors and students are doing and thinking in Spanish American countries. Everywhere, he says, he found unrest and the inclination to revolt against the government. Student agitations have overthrown governments in Chile, Peru, Argentine, and Bolivia, during the two years just passed. Prof. Lanning left Argentine in May. He says that at that time students and government employes told him of the impending revolution, which occurred recently. Everybody seemed to know that it was coming. The students already had been clubbed into submission, once.

The Peruvian revolution began in Lima, while Dr. Lanning was there. He says that this revolution was precipitated by the arrival of the Prince of Wales. Many signs ridiculing the government and university authorities had appeared on the campus of the university. These went unmolested until it was learned that Britain's Crown Prince was planning a visit to the city. The government felt that such publicity of the attitude of the students would be humiliating. Government officials proceeded to take down the signs. The students resented this action and resisted it with force. The government then sent several hundred soldiers to enforce its order. In the disturbance which followed about twelve were killed and the students were forced to submit. The students, however, claimed that the government, itself, had violated its own constitution. They insisted that the constitution provides that no campus of a university shall ever be invaded by government troops. The action of the government led to a military revolt and the overthrow of the government before the end of the month.

Dr. Lanning points out that when the students in Spanish American countries begin fighting against the government, they lead the working men. But instead of one student leading two or three hundred working men, the workers and students all march side by side. He found that in the student revolts soldiers are often ordered to fire on the students. The rushing through the streets of the gayly uniformed troops and the rattle of artillery, he believes, makes heroes of the students in the eyes of the people. It is his opinion that if the authorities would send the fire departments to turn a hose on the mob of students the revolting university men might be made to appear ridiculous and would be laughed at by the people instead of praised.

Prof. Lanning found that the students in Spanish American universities are radical, while the professors are conservative. This he believes to be caused by the fact that teachers are very poorly paid and must gain a livelihood in some other manner. Many of them have other professions or are engaged in commercial pursuits. This prevents their taking part in radical movements. The students, he says, are the only group free to do as they choose. They are ever ready, he reports, to quarrel with the capitalists and with the church. The fight in Lima originated in the desire of the students to choose their own professors.

Dr. Lanning says that sometimes the conservative professors have a following among the students. This he found to be especially true at Cordoba. But whenever a professor is found who is in sympathy with his students, the other professors whisper "Bolshevik."

Prof. Lanning found the Latin American universities very proud of the fact that the universities of our country are studying their history. He regrets the fact, however, that they have only a superficial knowledge of the United States of America. They seem to have little sense of proportion in ranking historical and literary leaders in this country. Everywhere he met the question, "What about American imperialism?" He always replied with another question, "Is there such a thing?"

Dr. Lanning is very enthusiastic over the results of his trip but declares that he is glad to be at home again.

Duke Professor Heads Engineering Groups

Prof. H. C. Bird, of the Duke University department of engineering, has been notified of his appointment as chairman of the nominating committee of the surveying and mapping division of the American Society of Civil Engineers. Other members of the committee are: Lieut. Comdr. Frank S. Borden, Washington, D. C.; W. S. Ruland, Cobleskill, N. Y.; Prof. C. O. Carey, University of Michigan; and F. W. Hough, Beaumont, Calif.

The surveying and mapping division is the largest division of the national society.

George F. Syme, president of the North Carolina Society of Engineers, has advised Professor Bird of his appointment as chairman of the professional practice committee of the state organization.

Duke History Teachers Have Part In New Book

Members of the Duke University history department are prominently identified with a significant volume just published by the MacMillan Company. The volume, "A Guide to Historical Literature," is a work of more than 1,200 pages edited by William H. Allison, Sidney B. Fay, Augustus H. Shearer, and Henry R. Shipman, and is the culmination of action taken in 1919 by the American Historical Association in appointing a committee to coöperate with the American Library Association in the preparation of a manual of historical literature.

The editors acknowledge indebtedness to Dr. Alice M. Baldwin, of Duke, and others who coöperated in making the manual possible. Professors W. T. Laprade and J. Fred Rippy of Duke wrote portions of the book. Prof. J. A. Robertson, editor of the *Hispanic American Review*, published at Duke, and others connected with the university are among those whose writings are cited.

MRS. MARY JANE EDWARDS PASSES AT THE AGE OF 91

Another Living Link Between Duke University and
Old Trinity in Randolph County is Broken by
Death of the Mother of Prof. C. W. Ed-
wards and Mrs. W. I. Cranford

WITH the passing of Mrs. Mary Jane Edwards on
July 29 at the summer home of her daughter,
Mrs. W. I. Cranford, at Lake Junaluska, another living link between Duke University and Old Trinity
was broken.
Her exemplary
life of more
than ninety-
one years was
almost parallel
with that of the
institution to
which she was
bound by
strong ties.
Born on a farm
near Trinity
and taken to
the village it-
self when a
girl, Mary Jane
White was
never far re-
moved from
the college, and
when it was
moved to Dur-
ham she fol-
lowed to re-
sume her asso-
ciations with
its faculty and
students.

MRS. MARY JANE EDWARDS

The mother of Dr. Charles W. Edwards and the
mother-in-law of Dr. William I. Cranford, both of
them long-established members of the Duke University faculty, Mrs. Edwards was not only known and
loved by older members of the community, but held
the love and admiration of many young people. Her
genuine Christian life, her devotion to her family and
church, and her motherly interest in the welfare of
others endeared her to a host of persons.

Mary Jane White was born on August 20, 1840, the
daughter of Thomas and Susan White, of Randolph
County. She spent her entire girlhood near and in
the village of Trinity, but as the college was not co-
educational at that time, she studied at Thomasville
College and Greensboro College, graduating at the latter institution in 1861. She was one of the oldest
alumnae of the college. After graduation from
Greensboro, she taught in Raleigh. Later she taught
in Greene County and there married Daniel W. Edwards. Moving to Arkansas with her husband, her
educational work was continued. Three children were
born there: Daniel Thomas, Nellie, and Charles W.
Edwards, all of whom survive.

To give her children advantages of the superior
educational contacts in the East, she returned to
North Carolina and opened a private school in High
Point. After several years she became a member of
the faculty of the High Point Academy, where she
taught for some time. When her oldest son was ready
for college, she moved back to Trinity and taught
school there.

News of her death cast a shadow of sadness over the
University campus. The funeral services were con-
ducted at Old Trinity, with Dr. W. A. Stanbury, of
Durham, in charge of the burial rites, on Thursday,
July 30. She was laid to rest in the historic cemetery
whose enduring headstones are marked by the names
of illustrious personalities in the history of Trinity
College.

Summer School Students Use Library Freely

Those who think that summer school students attend the warm weather sessions to catch up on sleep
during lectures or idle away their time in the shade of
campus trees should make inquiry at the Duke University Library.

For if use of books is any criterion, the 926 students
enrolled in the university summer school during the
first term engaged in other activities than those social
and somnolent. During the session reserved books
were circulated at a rate of 1,000 and more a day,
according to Ben E. Powell, in charge of the library
circulation, while a peak mark, reached the third day
of summer, was 1,800. This is approximately two
books to each student.

Although enrollment of students is considerably less
than half that of the regular session, the highest number of books taken from the reserve shelves during the
regular session is only half this figure. Summer students are forced to accomplish in six weeks what requires 12 at other times.

Coach Wade Faces Problems in His First Year at Duke

Has Powerful and Experienced Line, But End and Backfield Positions Present Some Real Difficulties—Season Opens on September 27 at Columbia, S. C., With University of South Carolina

ONE redeeming feature—a powerful and experienced line from tackle to tackle—is expected to pull Coach Wallace Wade's first edition of Blue Devils through the 1931 grid season with fairly good success.

Bryan and Harton, tackles; Werner and Taylor, guards; and Adkins, center, are veterans of many battles and can be depended upon. Daugherty, guard; Carpenter, tackle, and Hamrick, center, are 1930 reserve men who will be bidding for a regular berth.

On the flanks, however, things are different. Rosky, regular end, and Hayes, No. 1 substitute, have graduated, leaving one letterman, Hyatt, to return. Two promising sophomore candidates, James and Crawford, and a couple of backs who have been shifted to ends, Sink and Rogers, may prove a cure for this ailment.

The backfield appears to be the weakest spot. Bill Murray, the star halfback, who did the major portion of the ball carrying and all of the punting, has finished. Rosky called signals from his end post.

Consequently, there are no dependable ball carriers except the fullback, Captain Pierce Brewer; there is no experienced punter and no man on the squad who has called signals in a varsity game.

James, sophomore end, is a very good punter and was a star member of the freshman team last year,

but his chances of winning a berth are hard since he is a candidate for one of the most hotly contested positions on the Duke eleven.

Don Hyatt, the all-state end of last year, seems sure to win his post again which eliminates one of the two flank jobs. Sink, reserve varsity back last year, Rogers, freshman back in 1930, and Crawford, hard-hitting freshman tackle, all were shifted to end in spring maneuvers and will make the going hard for James.

Should Sophomore James come through despite the opposition, that would give Coach Wade a punter on end and enable him to have a veteran backfield combination in case some of the vets show ball-carrying ability.

In addition to Captain Brewer, veteran backs returning are Mason, who figured in several of Duke's wins last year; Brownlee, star track man who was the shining light of spring practice; Abbott, handicapped by size but a scrapper; Lemons, one of the most promising prospects last fall until he was injured; Mullen, veteran blocking back and interference man, and Ershler, part time fullback last year, who has been shifted and will be a candidate for Mullen's post this fall.

One of the most promising sophomore candidates, Rossiter, who can pass and punt excellently, is lacking in the running and defensive departments, according to his

"KID" BREWER
Captain of the 1931 Football Team of Duke University

showing in spring work, but may come through this fall.

Other backfield candidates coming up from the freshman squad are Laney and Edwards, able punters, who showed well in spring practice; Cavish, fast and heavy, who will make the blocking back post a three-cornered fight between Mullen, Ershler and himself; and Cook and Hendrickson, promising ball carriers.

Thus it appears that the coaches are faced with a colossal task. Reserve linemen, a regular end to pair with Hyatt, and some reserve flankmen must be developed; and a combination of backs which will number among those present a field general, a punter, a passer and some able ball carriers to assist Brewer, must be selected.

The following schedule shows no let-up from the opener with South Carolina on September 27 to the final game with Washington and Lee on November 28.

The card:

September 26, Univ. of S. C. at Columbia, S. C.

October 3, V. M. I. at Durham.

October 10, Villanova at Durham.

October 17, Davidson at Davidson.

October 24, Wake Forest at Durham.

October 31, Tennessee at Knoxville, Tenn.

November 7, Kentucky at Lexington, Ky.

November 14, N. C. State at Durham.

November 21, Carolina at Durham.

November 28, Washington and Lee at Lexington, Va.

The Alumni Office is always glad to give information regarding football games or other university events and to secure tickets for alumni when that is desired.

Duke Hospital Clinics Doing Work of Real Importance

(Continued from page 259)

necessary, the patients are cared for in the wards of Duke Hospital. Most of these wards are filled with cases from the clinics.

Poverty is no bar to treatment at Duke. Of course, the facilities are not unlimited. As far as possible, however, aid is given to those whose physicians apply for it. Some of the patients are really destitute. Recently a colored woman, in a critical condition, begged rides from Morehead City, N. C., to Duke. On her arrival, she was admitted to the clinic and given every care and attention as well as the treatment needed. Ambulance cases from a distance sent by welfare agencies are not uncommon.

Duke University has much to be proud of. Hospital authorities believe, however, that there is nothing greater than this spirit of neighborliness which is being developed in the community which Duke serves.

News of the Alumni

Where They Are Located

What They Are Doing

Miss Elizabeth Aldridge, '24, Secretary of Alumnae Council, Editor

CLASS OF 1911

Friends of Mabel Bruce will be grieved to hear of her sudden death in New York City on July 18. Her death was attributed to a malignant type of throat infection. She was until about three years ago, a teacher in Randolph-Macon Institute at Danville, Va., now known as Stratford College. For the past few years she has owned a tea shop in New York City where she made a specialty of Southern foods.

CLASS OF 1917

Henry E. Newbury is located at 610 Morgan Street, Tampa, Florida, where he is assistant manager of the Metropolitan Life Insurance Company. He was married on July 7, 1920 to Miss Almeyda Davis. They have one daughter, Almeyda Davis Newbury.

CLASS OF 1919

Dr. and Mrs. Fred C. Aldridge of 123 Midland Avenue, Wayne, Pa., are receiving congratulations on the birth of a daughter, Cornelia Boardman, on June 23.

CLASS OF 1922

On Saturday evening, July 4, T. C. Kirkman was married to Miss Harriette Jones at the home of the bride in St. Augustine, Florida. W. M. Marr, '10 of Jacksonville, Fla., attended "Kirk" as best man. Mrs. Kirkman is a member of an old and well-known St. Augustine family. They will make their home in Lakeland, Fla.

T. Reuben Waggoner has moved from Savannah, Ga. to Atlanta. He is still connected with the First National Company.

Blanche Barringer has been employed by the North Carolina Conference Board of Christian Education of the M. E. Church, South, as director of young people's work and extension secretary. Her duties will begin September 1. Blanche will devote most of her time to the development of the church's unified program of work for young people. She is well fitted for her work, having served seven or eight years as secretary of the North Carolina Conference Epworth League Assembly and as church secretary of both Edenton Street, Raleigh, and Duke Memorial, Durham.

Dr. J. Holt McCracken, Jr., received an M.D. from School of Medicine, Johns Hopkins University, after leaving Duke and took his interne work at Henry Ford Hospital. He is now located at 620 South Pacific Avenue, San Pedro, California. A second daughter was born at his home on July 25. Her name is Molly McCracken.

CLASS OF 1924

On July 17, Rev. and Mrs. J. G. Barden (Gene Barrett) sailed from New York to Belgium in order to take the steamer on August 10 for Wembo Nyama, Congo Belge. Mr. and Mrs. Barden have been studying for the past year at Columbia University, where they both received degrees. Gene received an A.M. and Mr. Barden a Ph.D. They will be located at the largest Methodist mission station, Wembo, Nyama, about four degrees south of the equator.

Frances John has joined the staff of the Virginia State Library, Richmond, Va. Her address is 2012 Grove Avenue. Frances was formerly working in the library at her home, Laurinburg, N. C.

Dr. John Tate Lanning has returned to Duke University after spending the past year traveling in South America on a Guggenheim Fellowship. He visited many Latin-American countries and made a special study of the early history of long-founded universities for higher education in South America.

CLASS OF 1925

W. Speight Barnes practices law in Los Angeles, Cal., with offices at 1204 Loew's State Building. He is also a part time instructor in the Law School of Southwestern University.

CLASS OF 1926

Frances and George Holmes graduated from Duke University in 1926. They both attended medical schools, Frances at the University of New York and George at the Richmond Medical College, receiving their M.D. degrees this June.

Frances has been attending physician at Camp Arden, a camp for girls in Oakland, Maine, this summer. On January 1, she will enter Bellevue Hospital, New York City, as one of the house doctors.

George is serving as physician at the Kiwanian Camp at Wallingford, Vermont, during the summer. On September 1 he will begin his internship in the Richmond Hospital. They are the children of Rev. ('92) and Mrs. Parker Holmes of Winston-Salem.

DRS. FRANCES AND GEORGE HOLMES

Dr. Walter B. Mayer of Charlotte was married on July 14 to Miss Helen Anne Dainis. They will make their home in Durham where Walter is an interne at Duke Hospital.

Bertha Mae Poe became the bride of Leslie J. Montague of Portsmouth, Va., on July 1. They live in Park View, Portsmouth, Va.

John P. Clendenin attended Georgia School of Technology, receiving a B.S. degree in civil engineering in 1926. He is an engineer and estimator for the John W. Cowper Company, Inc.,

general contractors, at 849 National Press Building, Washington, D. C.

Mr. and Mrs. W. P. Kellam (Mary Umstead, '27) live at 304 Hillsboro Street, Chapel Hill, N. C. Porter will be connected with the University of North Carolina library next year. For the past year he has been studying library work at Emory University.

Augusta C. Land teaches in the Fayetteville Street School, Hamlet, N. C. Virginia Land is a buyer for the W. R. Land Company department store, in Hamlet.

CLASS OF 1927

Doris Christie and S. J. McCoy, A.M. '29, were married in Washington, D. C. on June 23. They will make their home next year at the University of North Carolina. Doris has been teaching in Wilson for the past few years.

Friends of McPherson Beall will be interested in learning of his promotion from district manager for the Colgate-Palm-Olive Company with headquarters in Cleveland, Ohio, to general sales manager for the company with headquarters in Jersey City, N. J.

CLASS OF 1928

Bob Hatcher has been with Harris Forbes & Company of Atlanta, Ga., since leaving college. On July 1 Harris Forbes & Company and Chase Securities Corporation merged, forming a new organization known as the Chase Harris Forbes Corporation. Bob has been sent to the New Orleans office of this new corporation but his duties for the most part will be in the state of Texas.

Dr. Robert Ruark completed his four years at the School of Medicine, University of Pennsylvania, in June. He is now an interne at Duke Hospital, Durham.

CLASS OF 1929

Samuel S. McNinch, Jr. and Miss Eleanor Dockery Williams were married on July 15 at Charlotte, N. C.

William H. Covington, Jr. and Dorothy White were married in Baltimore, Maryland, on July 18. They live at 407 North Gregson Street, Durham.

CLASS OF 1930

Invitations have been received to the wedding of Nelle Z. Spivey and Lieutenant James Elmer Totten. They will be married at high noon in the Methodist Episcopal Church, South, Hertford, N. C., on Monday, August 24. Mr. and Mrs. Totten will be at home after September 15 at Fort Wadsworth, New York. For the past year, Nell has been an instructor of nursing at the Protestant Hospital in Norfolk, Va.

William Bruce Alexander is a traveling representative for the Baltimore Clipper Importing Company, 109 East Saratoga Street, Baltimore, Maryland.

Hibernia Seay, A.M. '30, was an honor graduate from Randolph-Macon Woman's College, Lynchburg, Va. She spent several years in France, studying part of the time at the Sorbonne, and later studied German at the University of Munich. She received her A.M. from Duke in 1930 and next year will teach French at Ward-Belmont College, Nashville, Tennessee.

Girard Bliss Ruddick, A.M. '30, graduated at Swarthmore before coming to Duke. He is connected with the Guaranty Company of New York, 31 Nassau Street, New York City.

Archibald Thomas Robertson, Jr., A.M. '30, is editor of *Pinehurst Outlook*, a weekly resort magazine, at Pinehurst, N. C. Mr. Robertson received his A.B. degree from Harvard University in 1928.

Floyd L. Riddle is at present connected with the North Carolina Compensation Rating Bureau at Raleigh.

CLASS OF 1931

Mary Helen Daniel, '29, and Rev. E. R. Shuler of Ozark, Arkansas, were married at the Hillsboro Methodist Church on June 30. Clarice Bowman, '31; C. D. Brown, '29; and Catherine Crews, '29 took part in the wedding. Rev. and Mrs. Shuler live in Kenly, N. C. where he is connected with the Methodist church.

Gray Manufacturing Co.
Flint Manufacturing Co. No. 1
Flint Manufacturing Co. No. 2
Arlington Cotton Mills
Myrtle Mills, Inc.
Arkray Mills, Inc.

*Spinners and Doublers Fine Combed
and Double Carded*

LONG STAPLE PEELER and EGYPTIAN YARNS

20's to 120's

Put up in all Descriptions for the Following Industries:

ELECTRICAL	WEAVERS
LACE	KNITTERS
MERCERIZERS	THREAD

MAIN OFFICE:	DIVISION OFFICES:	GENERAL SALES OFFICE:
Gastonia, N. C.	Boston	New York City
	Philadelphia	
	Chicago	
	Chattanooga	

Of course CAMELS are milder
THEY'RE FRESH!

HAVE you noticed how women everywhere are switching to the fresh mildness of Camels? Always a great favorite with the ladies, this famous blend is more popular now than ever, since the introduction of the new Humidor Pack.

If you need to be convinced, make this simple test yourself between a humidor fresh Camel and any other cigarette:

First, inhale the cool fragrant smoke of a perfectly conditioned Camel and note how easy it is to the throat.

Next, inhale the hot, brackish smoke of a parched dry cigarette and feel that sharp stinging sensation on the membrane.

The air-sealed Humidor Pack keeps all the rare flavor and aroma in and prevents the precious natural tobacco moisture from drying out. Important too, it protects the cigarette from dust and germs.

Switch to Camel freshness and mildness for one whole day, then leave them — if you can.

It is the mark of a considerate hostess, by means of the Humidor Pack, to "Serve a fresh cigarette." Buy Camels by the carton — this cigarette will remain fresh in your home and office

DUKE UNIVERSITY
ALUMNI REGISTER

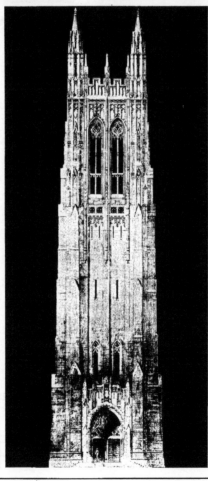

University Chapel

The Duke University Chapel, a front view of which is shown in the accompanying cut from the architect's drawing, is going forward rapidly. The tower is now over 160 feet above ground. The exterior work will doubtless be completed by the first of the new year. The handsome structure, built of the native stone out of which the other University buildings on the West Campus are being erected, and trimmed with limestone, is a most impressive one and is being greatly admired by visitors to the Duke campus from all parts of the country. A feature of the building which is attracting much interest is the Duke Memorial Chapel.

Alumni Events

Three outstanding alumni events are scheduled for fall and early winter. First, there is Home Coming Day on Saturday, October 3, the football game with V. M. I. that day being Coach Wallace Wade's first gridiron contest at the Duke stadium. Then, the entire month of November will be observed as "Duke Alumni Month" when various contacts of the alumni and the University will be emphasized. On Friday, December 11, Duke University Day will be observed, this being the seventh anniversary of the signing of the Indenture of Trust by which the late James B. Duke made possible Duke University.

Service Plus
To Our Clients

The Seeman Printery, Inc. never
leaves its selling job for you only
partly finished. Your printing when
done by this modern plant is backed up with a comprehensive merchandising service—one that doubly
strengthens its effectiveness.

THE SEEMAN PRINTERY, INC.
PRINTERS IN DURHAM, N. C., SINCE 1885

MODERN EQUIPMENT—SERVICE THAT SATISFIES

Duke University Alumni Register

(*Member of American Alumni Council*)

Published at Durham, N. C. Every Month in the Year in the Interest of the University and the Alumni

| Volume XVII | September, 1931 | Number 9 |

In This Issue

Editor and Business Manager ....HENRY R. DWIRE, '02

Assistant Editors ....ELIZABETH ALDRIDGE, '24
ALBERT A. WILKINSON, '26

Advertising Manager...........................CHARLES A. DUKES, '29

TWO DOLLARS A YEAR   20 CENTS A COPY

ENTERED AS SECOND-CLASS MATTER AT THE POST-OFFICE AT
DURHAM, NORTH CAROLINA

SEPTEMBER

This September issue of the REGISTER naturally contains quite a bit of matter relating to the opening of the new session, the second in the magnificent new Duke University plant. We feel sure that alumni will find themselves in even closer touch with Alma Mater as they read of the activities incident to the opening of the new academic year, and have their minds revert to the time, perhaps years ago, when they entered Duke University or Trinity College.

NEW FACES

The REGISTER is privileged to publish this month photographs of a number of new members of the faculty. More will appear in the next issue and thereafter. The REGISTER desires to acquaint the alumni, wherever they may be located, with the men and women who are coming here from time to time as members of the faculty of the institution.

REMINISCENCES

The REGISTER is publishing next month some letters from alumni on the Editor's Mail Bag page. We feel sure that these letters will be interesting to readers of the publication. We want even more of them. Will you not take the time to write something for the REGISTER?

THE EDITOR.

A NEW PHOTOGRAPH OF SCENE ON UNIVERSITY CAMPUS

THE MAIN QUADRANGLE OF DUKE UNIVERSITY, LOOKING NORTH BY KILGO HOUSE

Duke University Alumni Register

Volume XVII   September, 1931   Number 9

Editorial Comment

DON'T FAIL TO COME IN

"I was on the Duke University campus the other day for a few hours," remarked an alumnus in a North Carolina city in talking to the Editor recently; "but I didn't call by the Alumni Office because I knew you people were having a busy time and I didn't want to bother you, but I want you to know how much I enjoy the REGISTER."

It is always good to hear Duke alumni say that they enjoy the REGISTER, but we hope that others have not felt a similar hesitancy in calling at the Alumni Office while in Durham.

As a matter of fact, this is one of the reasons for maintaining the Alumni Office.

Certainly those composing the staff of the office are never too busy to talk to our alumni. The work in the office never gets to that point of pressure where a visit from an alumnus or alumna is not eagerly welcomed.

And it is exceedingly gratifying that more and more visits from alumni are being made and that letters from former students of the institution to the office asking for information and for other purposes are becoming more numerous all the while.

One of the most encouraging things in connection with the work of the office these days is the frequency with which alumni come in to talk for a few minutes either on business or just to pay a social call, and the number of those who are looking upon this office as a kind of clearing house for alumni information and service is constantly growing.

May we make these two very positive requests:

If you are ever in Durham, don't leave without calling at the Alumni Office if it is possible to drop in.

If there is any information you want about the institution and what it is doing, or about any other alumni or any related subject, feel perfectly free to ask for it.

As stated above, that is one of the main reasons for the maintenance of the Duke University Alumni Office.

A FRIENDLY CAMPUS

Along with its service in other lines, the Alumni Office is constantly striving to aid in the further stimulation of a friendly feeling on the Duke University campus.

Not only is it glad to welcome alumni who come to the campus from time to time, but faculty and students and visitors are always welcome.

A particular effort is made to make visitors feel perfectly at home in every possible way.

If an alumnus or alumna knows of visitors who are coming to Duke it will be a great favor to the Alumni Office if he or she will suggest that such visitors come to the office in the Union, on the new University campus, visit the Information Office conducted in connection with the Alumni Headquarters, write their names in the Visitors' Register and secure any information or assistance desired.

If they want to be shown over the campus, someone is always at hand and readily available for that service, which is gladly extended to alumni and other visitors as well.

FALL ALUMNI EVENTS

Particular attention is directed to the matter in this issue of the REGISTER relating to the three outstanding alumni occasions of the fall season.

Keep these occasions and the time of their coming definitely in mind. It is the hope and desire of those connected with the alumni work to make this fall program the most complete and far-reaching and beneficial in the entire history of the institution.

First, there is Alumni Homecoming on Saturday, October 3. There is every reason to expect hundreds of alumni to return to the campus for that occasion. The Homecoming Day last year was notably successful, but even more interest is already being manifested in the October 3 event.

Last year November was observed as Alumni Month, the particular idea in view being to encourage local groups and individual alumni to think especially of Alma Máter and its interests during that period and to strive to do something, no matter how small it might seem, to serve the institution in some definite way. One of the main purposes of Alumni Month is to make possible even more complete preparation than usual for Duke University Day.

The climax of the fall alumni activities will be the observance on December 11 of Duke University Day, this being the seventh anniversary of the signing by the late James B. Duke of the Indenture of Trust making possible Duke University. Already inquiries are coming from many sources relating to this year's observance of Duke University Day. It is confidently expected that its celebration will be more widespread than ever before.

All these alumni occasions of the fall of 1931 can be made notably successful if one thing is in evidence.

That is the wholesouled and cordial and complete support of alumni of Duke University.

We know enough of the spirit of the Duke alumni to have the confident belief that such support will be in evidence and that every member of every alumni group will do his part towards making the fall of 1931 a season long to be remembered in the annals of the Alumni Association.

AN EXPANDING MOVEMENT

A great deal is being said nowadays about adult education.

Newspapers and magazines have articles on the subject from time to time; associations of men and women interested in various phases of educational endeavor are studying the subject; bulletins on the whys and wherefores of adult education are being issued at intervals.

"The whole of life is learning,—education can have no ending," is literally true, and its truth is being more generally recognized today than ever before.

Not only is this true of the United States. We are told that there has been a great revival of adult education in Great Britain in recent years; even Turkey initiated a program of adult education two or three years ago, while in other countries the same thing is true.

A particular feature of adult education to which the ALUMNI REGISTER has referred from time to time is instruction for college graduates.

It seems that there has been for a long time a settled conviction that college men and women too often have acted as if they thought educational processes naturally ended as far as they were concerned when they graduated.

The fallacy of that assumption was readily apparent, and yet until comparatively recent years nothing in particular was done about it.

Now, however, it is a very live topic in many colleges and universities; alumni groups are discussing it in an earnest way.

Some really worth-while experiments with "Alumni Weeks" of intensive training, usually after the college commencement, and with reading courses have been tried, and some of them have passed well beyond the experimental stage.

That many alumni need something of the kind, and that a goodly number of them realize it and are willing to act upon that realization, has been definitely established.

The only problem in most cases is to find just which of the many plans of alumni education is best adapted to a particular situation.

One of the best ways of approaching the problem is through a sane and sound system of reading courses especially designed for alumni.

In more than one case an alumni publication has rendered a definite service by fostering, with the assistance of faculty members, such courses of reading.

The ALUMNI REGISTER hopes to launch something definite in that direction in the near future.

Have you any suggestions?

Duke Opens New Session With Record Enrollment of Students

After Week Devoted to Freshman Orientation, University Starts Another Academic Year September 16—President W. P. Few's Address to the Faculty and Student Body Features Opening Exercises in Page Auditorium

DUKE UNIVERSITY opened the new academic year on Wednesday, September 16, with a record enrollment. Already over 800 freshmen had registered on the two campuses during Freshman Week, this being considerably more than enrolled last year, and the registration of upper classmen and professional students brings the total registration to a new high point in the history of Duke University. Present indications are that the total enrollment will reach at least 2,600, about ten per cent increase over the enrollment of last year, which held the record up to that time.

PRESIDENT FEW'S ADDRESS

The opening of a new academic year was signalized by special exercises for faculty and student body in Page Auditorium on the University campus and in the auditorium on the Woman's College campus. In speaking at the exercises on the University campus, President W. P. Few said in part:

We are here today for the formal opening of Duke University in the beginning of its second year on this campus. Considerable progress has been made since we gathered here one year ago. The buildings in the present building program are all ready for use, except the Chapel and the Nurses' Home, and on the Woman's College campus all the buildings are in use. The Graduate Schools of Arts and Sciences, Medicine, Law, and Theology have been launched. Our program is going on schedule time.

Every now and then I hear it said, or see it written, as a comment on the developments here in the last seven years, that "a strange thing has happened to a little college"; and this always reminds me of a recent paradoxical saying of a well known English educator that "nothing is quite so stupid as a very clever young man writing about education." As a matter of fact, nothing has "happened" here. Our development has all come to pass in accordance with a well defined

and well understood plan. The ground work for it all goes many years further back and a good many people have contributed to the final result, but I have personally been working definitely on this plan since 1916, and have had a complete plan since the spring of 1921. This is precisely the plan for which the University is built. It was good enough to bring to its support a large amount of money, and in a few years has raised us to a place of considerable importance in the educational world. If now it is wrecked here and yonder I cannot be responsible for the consequences. But if it can be kept intact I am sure it will bring the University to its destined goal. There has been a lot of impatience and much pressure brought to bear, from the inside and the outside, to modify the plan for which the University has been built; and the strain has had its effects. But so far as I can see, the plan must go through as a whole, or parts will inevitably suffer. Let us all more than ever this year try to see our University development as a whole and each make his contribution towards carrying on the program without a break.

The Graduate School of Arts and Sciences with its objective pursuit of knowledge and devotion to truth, and other Graduate Schools, particularly the Medical School, will, like American higher education in general, show the influence of German universities. The Colleges—the one for men and the other for women—with the emphasis on character and on training for service to country, to causes, and to humanity, will be in the English tradition of education; and this will explain the architecture here. These buildings tie us to the historic traditions of learning in the English speaking race. The colleges, essentially in the English tradition of education, and graduate and professional schools, affected by German and other influences, are to be welded into an American university that will seek to know and use the best that has been achieved elsewhere, but that will at the same time seek to make its own contribution to the cause of education.

Louis Pasteur, who has been called the most perfect man that ever entered the Kingdom of Science, in speaking to a large number of students a short while before his death, used these memorable words: "Young men, live in the serene peace of laboratories and libraries. Say to yourselves, first of all, 'What have I done for my instructors?' and as you go on further, 'What have I done for my country?' until the time comes when you may have the happiness of thinking that you have contributed in some way to the progress and to the welfare of humanity." The words of Pasteur seem to me to give at once admirable expression for the ideals both of the College and of the University. Let's all make them our own this year and every year, and both for ourselves and for the institution as a whole.

The hard times that confront us will help us all here to learn, and I hope help us to teach to others, that while we at Duke University have a great opportunity and a great work to do, we here do not live, and have never lived, on Easy Street. Living on that street has brought America to the brink of disaster and would be equally disastrous to us. Our scientists and scholars can make their best contributions to society, even in times like these, by continuing their research, teachers by continuing to teach, and students by attending to their life and work. All of us should make every cent go as far as it will and there should be no waste anywhere. These are the times that try the qualities of our civilization and the mettle of our people. "Storms are the test of seamanship." In times like these secure foundations may be laid for future progress and for personal careers. Let the people sacrifice and do everything possible for the education of their children; and let the teachers understand that they now have the chance to show that they are not mere pedagogues and school keepers, but are real builders of civilization. There is today a rare opportunity for teachers to win the lasting admiration and gratitude of the people. It is never the material but the ideal which abides and commands.

Medical School At Duke Enrolls 145 In Four Classes

The Duke University School of Medicine, which began operation in the fall of 1930 with 70 students, will open on October 1 to begin its second year with an enrollment of at least 145 students. For the first time students will be admitted to four classes. Last year only first and third year students were accepted.

Of the 145 students already accepted for the school, the class limit of 60 will comprise the first year class. There will be 49 in the second year class, 18 in the junior class and 18 in the senior class. The first students to receive the M.D. degree will graduate at commencement next June.

Seventy-eight new medical students are being admitted this fall. These represent 53 colleges and universities in all parts of the United States. Forty-one of the new students are from North Carolina, and the remainder represent 22 other states.

Several additions to the medical school faculty have been made during the past several months.

Duke Freshmen Arrive Early For Full Week

New Students Learn All About Campus Life Before Upperclassmen Return

Faced with a full week of special activity designed to acquaint them with campus life before the arrival of upperclassmen, members of the new Duke University freshman class put in an early appearance Tuesday, September 8, in order to be ready for their first formal assembly Wednesday.

The new students came from all parts of this state and from many other states. First assembly for the men was held at 9 o'clock Wednesday morning in Page auditorium, while the first women's meeting was at 2 o'clock in the afternoon at the Woman's College auditorium.

A busy round of placement tests, physical examinations, photographing, psychological tests, library tours, socials, entertainments, matriculation, and assemblies awaited the new students. When their classes began Monday, September 14, they had become familiar with many more aspects of campus life than they would have known had the special Freshman Week not been held.

With the arrival of the new students the influx of mail at the two University branch postoffices increased greatly. In a number of instances relatives have accompanied the new students in order to see the new University campus, which is more and more becoming known as one of the most beautiful spots in the South.

Duke University's law library contains a collection of more than 30,000 volumes.

Duke University students have 100 clubs, societies, fraternity chapters, and other organizations representing many academic and social activities.

Alumni To Gather From Far And Near For Homecoming

Annual Event, Scheduled For Saturday, October 3, Is Expected to Attract Throng of Alumni From This and Other States—V. M. I. Football Game, First Home Contest Under Coach Wallace Wade, To Be An Outstanding Feature

ALL ROADS for alumni of Duke University will lead straight to the University campus on Saturday, October 3, when the annual Homecoming will be observed. Already preparations are being made in the Alumni Office to receive the greatest number of former students of Alma Mater ever to assemble at Duke on one of these annual occasions.

And unless all signs fail a larger area of territory will be represented among those who come back for the homecoming event than ever before. Letters have been received from alumni in a number of distant states, and even one from a country overseas, stating the definite intention of the writers to return to Duke for the 1931 Homecoming. An extract from one of these letters follows:

"I realize that business conditions are not as good as they might be and that it will involve quite a little expense to get there, but you can count on me for Homecoming Day. I have read so much in the papers about the new Duke University plant and about Coach Wallace Wade that I am determined to see both of them without further delay. And I am hoping to bring the members of my family with me."

There are a great many other alumni in North Carolina and other states who, while they have not yet written to that effect, feel much the same way about the matter. They have not yet seen the new Duke University plant in full working order and they desire to see the transformation that has been wrought. And they also realize that this is the first home football game under the mentorship of Coach Wallace Wade, widely known Duke director of athletics. The homecoming occasion is sure to prove a notable demonstration of welcome by the alumni to Coach Wade, who has undertaken his first year's work at Duke with 100 per cent coöperation of faculty, alumni and student body.

But to get back to the Homecoming Day features. First, alumni are expected to arrive early on the morning of October 3 and register in Alumni Headquarters, University Union. The Union lobby and reception room on the second floor will be thrown open for the entertainment of the alumni who are expected to gather in small groups and talk about the old days at college. There will be some alumni committee and group gatherings and music and other features will be enjoyed.

Many of the "homecomers" who have not yet had an opportunity to go through the new campus will doubtless appreciate the opportunity afforded to visit the different buildings, accompanied by student guides who know every nook and corner of the campus.

There will be quite a number of informal luncheon groups in the Coffee Shop of the Union, after which the alumni will turn toward the Duke stadium, where the first home game of the 1931 football season will be played, Duke's antagonist being the strong Virginia Military Institute aggregation. There will be thousands of spectators, the Duke and V. M. I. bands will be out in full force, and in other respects the game will have all the aspects of a real honest-to-goodness gala occasion. It is hoped during the day to get motion pictures of the alumni groups as well as of the game itself.

After the football contest there will be more alumni groups scattered through the Union and around the campus. Quite a number of the visitors will doubtless remain until after dinner.

Fraternity and other groups will keep open house for alumni during the day and in every possible way the entire University community will coöperate to make the Homecoming of 1931 an outstanding event, long to be remembered by those participating in it.

COUNCIL MEETINGS LATER

The meeting of the Alumni and Alumnae Councils will not be held on Homecoming Day this year, but at a date later in the month, that date yet to be selected. In addition to the election of officers at the Council meetings ways and means of observing "Alumni Month" in November in the most effective manner possible will be discussed. "Alumni Month" last year was quite a success, but the observance this time is expected to be on a considerably larger scale.

Dr. Amoss Visiting Professor in Peiping Medical School

During His Absence in China Dr. Frederic M. Hanes Will Be Acting Professor of Medicine at Duke and Head of Medical Service in Hospital—Two New Medical School Professors at Duke

DR. FREDERIC M. Hanes, widely known physician of Winston-Salem, who has been associated with the Duke University School of Medicine since its opening last year as Associate Professor of Medicine, will come to Duke about September 23 as Acting Professor of Medicine. He will serve in that capacity during the absence of Dr. Harold L. Amoss who sailed August 28 for China, where he is visiting professor of medicine in the Peiping Union Medical School. He will return to Duke about February 1.

As acting professor of medicine, Dr. Hanes will be head of the medical service of the Duke Hospital during Dr. Amoss' absence. He will be accompanied to Durham by Mrs. Hanes and they will occupy the Amoss residence in Hope Valley.

After his graduation at the University of North Carolina, Dr. Hanes studied at Harvard and took his medical work at Johns Hopkins, later studying for two years in Europe. For some time he was associated with the Rockefeller Institute for Medical Research in New York. After practicing in Richmond, Va., for some years he returned to his home city of Winston-Salem, where he has specialized in internal medicine and neurology. Dr. Hanes is active in civic affairs in Winston-Salem and in the state as well as in professional circles.

Two New Medical School Professors

Dr. Bayard Carter has recently been appointed Professor of Obstetrics and Gynecology in the Duke Medical School. Prof. Carter comes to Duke with a well established record and reputation as a teacher and surgeon. He received his A.B. degree from the University of Delaware in 1920. While a student in that institution, he was chosen as a Rhodes Scholar from Delaware and was a medical student at Oxford from 1920 to 1923. Doctor Carter received his M.D. degree from Johns Hopkins in 1925.

Dr. Carter's experience, since receiving his degree, has been that of a university man. He was appointed to the staff of the New Haven Hospital and Yale Medical School, immediately upon his graduation from Johns Hopkins. After four years in that institution he was given the appointment as Assistant Professor of Obstetrics and Gynecology at the University of Virginia School of Medicine, where he remained until his appointment to Duke.

With Prof. Carter comes Dr. Edwin B. Hamblen, as Associate Professor of Obstetrics and Gynecology. Doctor Hamblen received the degree of Bachelor of Science from Baylor University in 1921. In 1928, he received the degree of Doctor of Medicine from the University of Virginia Medical School. Since his graduation from that institution, he has been associated with Dr. Carter on the staff of the University of Virginia Medical School.

Medical School and Hospital Notes

Members of the Duke Hospital staff are constantly in demand as speakers and for conducting clinics throughout the state. At a recent meeting of the Gaston County Medical Association, in Gastonia, Dr. Christopher Johnston read a paper on "The Complications of Diabetes." Dr. Alfred B. Shands, Duke's orthopedic specialist, in August, opened the Rotary Crippled Children's Clinic of Rocky Mount, N. C. Dr. Shands conducted the initial examinations and gave advice for treatment.

In October, for the first time, the Duke Medical School will enroll members of all four classes. Registrations already made include sixty students in the first class, forty-nine in the second class, sixteen in the junior year, and fifteen seniors. In 1931, seventy-six students were in attendance in the school. These came from fifty-three different colleges. Forty-one of the students came from North Carolina colleges. The others were from twenty-two different states. The first graduating class will be given their diplomas in June, 1932.

The Duke Chapter of Alpha Omega Alpha, national medical fraternity, was established on April 29, 1931. This is the first chapter of this fraternity to be established south of the University of Virginia.

Duke Alumni Will Meet at Columbia Luncheon September 26

South Carolina Association of Duke Alumni and Alumni Office Co-operating in Arrangements For What Promises To Be Notably Successful Occasion on Day of Game With University of South Carolina

DUKE'S first football game of the 1931 season, to be played with the University of South Carolina in Columbia on Saturday, September 26, will not only be an outstanding event in the realm of intercollegiate sports but will furnish an opportunity for a Duke alumni gathering that promises to be unique and outstanding. For at twelve o'clock noon, on that day, Duke alumni of South Carolina, and neighboring sections of North Carolina, (in fact all Duke alumni who are in Columbia that day) will gather at a luncheon at Hotel Jefferson. It is expected to be one of the most significant Duke alumni events of the year.

This occasion will be in direct charge of the South Carolina Association of Duke University Alumni, of which S. B. Moyle, of Columbia, is president. Mr. Moyle is being assisted in the local arrangements for the occasion by Professor Ernest Green, of Columbia College, and other Duke alumni. It is expected that at least 150 or 200 Duke men and women will gather at this banquet. The luncheon will start two and a half hours ahead of the game so there will be no trouble about the lack of time.

The Alumni Office is coöperating in every possible way in arrangements for what is expected to be a most enjoyable and successful event. Several members of the faculty will attend the luncheon and game and altogether the day is expected to be a notable occasion from the standpoint of the University and its alumni.

Eleven hundred letters to alumni and alumnae have been sent out from the offices of the South Carolina Association and from the Duke University Alumni Office. Those receiving the letters have been asked to make reservations of plates and to secure their tickets on the day of the luncheon from the cashier's desk of the hotel. Tickets to the game may be ordered for $2.20 each from Dr. Ralph K. Foster, Director of Student Activities, University of South Carolina, Columbia, S. C., or from the Duke University Alumni Office. Good seats will be reserved for the Duke alumni at the game, which will be played at the South Carolina fairground. The fairground field has been secured because it was not felt that Melton field would be ad-

equate for the thousands who are expected to attend the game.

Already many alumni have signified their intention of attending the game and the luncheon. Those who are contemplating attending are asked to make their reservations at once. The price of the luncheon tickets will be $1.00.

Any further information regarding the events of the day can be secured from the Alumni Office, or from President S. B. Moyle, South Carolina Alumni Association, 905 Central Union Building, Columbia, S. C. Mr. Moyle, who is district manager for the Liggett & Myers Tobacco Company, with headquarters at Columbia, is doing everything possible to make this an occasion that will be long remembered by Duke alumni, and he is being ably assisted by other Duke alumni of the South Carolina capital.

Information For Duke Alumni As To Tickets For South Carolina Game

Tickets for the football game at Columbia, S. C., on Saturday, September 26, between Duke and the University of South Carolina, may be obtained now from the Duke University Alumni Office. The price of tickets is $2.20 each, and in the case of mail orders 25 cents extra should be added for postage and registration.

The tickets will be in the Duke section in the stands of the South Carolina fairgrounds where the game will be played, and assurance is given that the location of the seats is excellent. Orders should be sent in as early as possible as a rapid sale of the tickets is expected.

The fact that this is not only the first Duke game of the season but the first to be played by a Duke team coached by Wallace Wade gives added interest to the contest, which will be played at 2:30 P. M. at the South Carolina fairgrounds.

Modernly Equipped Chemistry Building Is Now Occupied

Structure Contains Four Floors Which Are Provided With Complete Facilities For the Study of Chemistry and For Research Work in That Field—Brief Description of the Arrangement of the Various Floors of the Building

WITH the completion and occupancy of the Chemistry building during the summer months, the Duke University science group on the north side of the Quadrangle, dominated by the Medical building tower, has been completed.

The latest addition harmonizes, of course, with its neighbors and provides Duke with an outstanding hall for the study of chemistry and allied branches. There are four floors in all; and these are largely equipped and ready for use.

The Chemistry building faces eastward toward the Biology building; to the left are the Medical building and the hospital; and to the right, the law library.

In the basement are found the general supply room, where most of the equipment and material for use in chemistry laboratories is stored; opening room, with facilities so as to permit the ready unloading of goods from truck; stock rooms, for the preparation of demonstration material; and the research laboratories. In these laboratories intensive studies are made of various chemical processes, and interesting problems are worked out.

In the basement are also found a storage battery room, which enables the department to have two types of current, direct and alternating, available at all times; a refrigeration room, glassblowing quarters, and a machine shop. Elevators and dumb waiters run the entire range of floors, making rapid service possible.

Back of the lobby at the main entrance on the first floor is the main lecture room, capable of seating approximately 275 students. The room is arranged so as to enable the student readily to see a demonstration set up in the front; and at the same time it is of such size and accessibility as to make it a desirable meeting place for night gatherings of the University of various sorts. This provides Duke with one of its choice small auditoriums.

The room, as well as classrooms and laboratories on the floor, is to be used by freshmen students.

There are four laboratories on the main floor for

New Chemistry Building at Duke

freshmen work; and these are so arranged as to care for five students to a desk by alternate sections, 120 being thus accommodated in each "lab." All these rooms, as well as those on other floors, have cream walls and ceilings, which factor, together with good window and electric light provisions, makes for a notably well-illuminated building. On this floor also is a laboratory equipped for bio-chemistry, and another for advanced work in organic chemistry.

The second floor houses the analytic and physical chemistry divisions, offices and research rooms; and in the front center a spacious and inviting library. Arrangement of the room and the reading material found therein are such as to induce the beginning student to read about his subjects—perhaps in popular fashion, but to read something. The library, which can care for a goodly number of students, will be open during certain evenings in the week.

While the Chemistry library is not as yet complete, books from other science departments nearby—biology and physics, and the Medical school—are available to chemistry students; and they may, therefore, make use of these facilities.

Adjoining each of the laboratories are balance rooms; and experiment preparation rooms are easily available. The laboratories on the second and third floors are well-equipped, with air, vacuum, hot and cold water, direct and alternating current, steam and gas service at the desk. Alberene stone, a hard resistant to heat and the corroding effects of acids, is used for desk tops in these laboratories.

Organic chemistry quarters are found on the third floor. The laboratories are equipped to meet the danger of explosions, hoods being provided with screen wire glass coverings, and a shower being at hand, should a student, despite other precautions, catch afire.

Research rooms and offices, a small stock room and a room to be equipped for first-aid purposes are likewise found on this floor.

The lobby at the entrance of the building presents at present a rather empty appearance, but in the course of time exhibits in cases will be placed here, and the lobby may become something of a show place.

Special features of the building include a roof over the main auditorium, and a bay window effect in the Gothic manner at the left front corner—the only such design on the quadrangle.

The building has a floor area of 57,000 square feet, and contains among other large and small laboratories, 25 double research rooms.

Much of the building is available for research and advanced teaching. While all of the laboratories are completely equipped with the usual services, there are other specially designed rooms for present or future research including a low temperature room, a photographic room, a constant temperature room, a gas analysis room, a combustion room, a bomb room, an animal room, and rooms equipped for high vacuum, X-ray, and photochemical investigations.

A glassblowing room and a well-equipped shop operated by a skilled mechanic will provide facilities for the construction of special apparatus and for the repair and maintenance of instruments.

Throughout the building intricate electrical equipment has been installed. Each room is mechanically ventilated so that chemical fumes can be quickly removed and replaced with pure air.

There are four full-time professors in the chemistry department, four instructors and various laboratory assistants. Chemistry professors are: Dr. Paul M. Gross, head of the department; Dr. R. N. Wilson, Dr. Warren C. Vosburgh, and Dr. L. A. Bigelow, while instructors are: Messrs. C. R. Hauser, J. H. Saylor, Felix Keffer and Miss Frances Brown.

Ground Is Cleared For Nurses' Home

New Structure Will Be Typical of Gothic Buildings on Duke's West Campus

First steps in the construction of a modern home for nurses at Duke University have been taken with the clearing of ground at the site of the new structure. Actual construction is expected to be started within the next few weeks.

The three-story Gothic structure will have a capacity of 225 beds and will correspond in material and architecture with other buildings on the University west campus. It will be the thirty-second building on the new campus erected under the present building program. Plans were drawn by Horace Trumbauer of Philadelphia. The construction will be done by the regular University building organization under the personal direction of A. C. Lee, chief engineer.

Instructor Added To Religion Unit

Dr. Kenneth W. Clark, of Chicago, to Teach New Testament in Duke School of Religion

Dr. Kenneth W. Clark, for the past two years a fellow in the faculty at University of Chicago, has been elected instructor in New Testament language and literature of the Duke University School of Religion.

The new teacher began his services at Duke last week. He is a native of New York City, and a graduate of Peddie School, Yale University, Colgate-Rochester Divinity School, and University of Chicago, holding the degrees of B.A., B.D., and Ph.D.

Sigma Nu Will Place Frat Chapter At Duke

Charter Is Granted Goblins Club and Installation Will Be Held During Autumn

Sigma Nu national fraternity has granted a charter to the Goblins Club of Duke University, it is announced, and will install the group into the order in special exercises to be held during early fall.

At the twenty-fifth convention of the organization held recently at Lake of Bays, Ontario, Don Marion, of Harrisburg, Pa., Duke student, represented the petitioning chapter. Ben Powell, of Durham, was a delegate from the national fraternity.

Up to March 1, 1931, the Duke University libraries had received and accessioned 233,665 bound volumes and 24,399 pamphlets. Many thousands of volumes and pamphlets have not yet been accessioned, and other purchases of books, periodicals, and brochures are in Europe awaiting shipment.

Some Alumni Personalities

Dr. J. W. Roy Norton, '20, has been appointed city health commissioner of Rocky Mount, N. C. He is a member of the American Medical Association, of the North Carolina Medical Society and the Arkansas Medical Society. He was junior interne and assistant physician at the Central Station Hospital, Nashville, Tenn., for 14 months; he was first interne and then on the medical staff of the Henry Ford Hospital at Detroit for two years; head of the Department of Internal Medicine and Holt-Krock Clinic and St. John's Hospital, Fort Smith, Ark., from June 1930, to August 1931.

Edwin Maurice Gill, Law '24, is private secretary to Governor O. Max Gardner. He represented Scotland County in the North Carolina General Assembly in 1929 and 1931. He served as chairman of the House Committee on Senatorial Districts and as a member of other committees during the 1931 session. He became a member of the law firm of Gibson & Gill at Laurinburg after leaving Trinity College.

Garland B. Daniel, '20, is a well-known attorney of High Point and was recently appointed judge of the Juvenile Court of that city. Before going to High Point in 1925 he practiced law in Littleton, N. C., for a year. He is a member of the High Point Kiwanis Club and president of the Guilford County Association of Duke Alumni. He is quite active in that capacity in coöperating with the Alumni Office and the University. He was a recent visitor on the campus.

Striking Differences in Two Dictatorships Are Pointed Out

Dr. F. S. Hickman, of Duke School of Religion, Recently Back From Trip Abroad, Discusses Conditions in Italy and Turkey—Arab-Jewish Hatred in Palestine
—Zionist Movement—Economic Status of Europe

STRIKING was the difference between two dictatorships of the Mediterranean countries to Dr. Franklin S. Hickman, professor of the psychology of religion at Duke University, who, with Mrs. Hickman, toured extensively during the summer.

The two dictatorships were those of Italy and of Turkey. In Turkey, Dr. Hickman pointed out, poverty and fear—fear that the government could not stand—prevailed, and Kemal Pasha, Turkey's ruler, exercised absolute sway. Kemal himself is lacking in character, Dr. Hickman explained; the Turks, largely relegated now to western Asia, save for their great capital city, Stamboul, the former Constantinople, are leaving their old religion and outwardly adopting western customs, but they are not making much real progress.

They lack virility—an attribute contributed by the Armenians whom the Turks had driven out—and in Kemal they have no inspiring figure to lead them out of their chaotic condition.

But in Italy, another of the great peninsulas lapped by Mediterranean waters, there was a different story to relate. Here too was a dictatorship, that of the world-famed Mussolini.

Under this assertive leader, however, the Italians had made progress, and were in as good a condition as most of the countries of Europe. In spite of his domineering qualities, Mussolini is a man of character, Dr. Hickman pointed out.

And whatever the opinion of the Italian premier outside of Italy, in his native land he is increasingly loved and revered. He shares the admiration of Americans and Europeans in Italy as well as that of his fellow countrymen, Dr. Hickman asserted, because under him conditions have been far better than before his dictatorship. Italian cities are far more sanitary than formerly; and some of the vices and distressing customs, as mendicancy, have been greatly reduced.

And despite the iron hand with which the premier rules, he seems to be doing so from the viewpoint of the progress of Italy rather than from self-interest, the Duke professor thought.

IN PALESTINE

Dr. and Mrs. Hickman visited in Egypt, Palestine, Syria, Greece, Switzerland, Germany and France as well as in Turkey and Italy.

In Palestine they were impressed with the animosity between Arab and Jew, and the hatred of each for the British. The Arabs, who have long been most numerous in Palestine, are beginning to resent the influx of the Jew, Dr. Hickman said, and to realize that the purpose is eventually to push them out.

Jews from Europe and America, backed by Zionist movement funds, have come into the Holy Land, buying at high prices choice pieces of land and leaving the Arabs the bleak, arid land which characterizes a great part of the country. The Arab is not industrious like the Jew, and pressed by the need of funds the Arab parts with his land.

At the famed wailing wall in Jerusalem fighting between the two races was likely to break out at any time. Uncomfortable was the lot of the British soldiers stationed in the land; the Jews paid them no attention, Dr. Hickman was told, unless to ask protection from the Arabs.

THE ZIONIST MOVEMENT

Just how successful will be the Zionist movement to repossess Canaan for the Jews was a moot point. It is a question whether the Jews who are tilling the soil could support themselves unless they were helped by the Zion movement funds. There is some manufacturing, and there is talk of damming the Jordan in order that more fertile land may be made available for agriculture, but so far the project has ended in talk.

ECONOMIC STATUS OF EUROPE

The American visitors were impressed generally with the sad economic plight of European countries. America is more fortunate than any of them, Dr. Hickman averred. Even the more favorably situated nations, as Switzerland, are having great difficulty because they cannot market their goods.

ALEXANDER H. FREY   GEORGE E. OSBORNE   DAVID F. CAVERS

Six New Law School Faculty Members

With the appointment of Howard E. Wahren-brock, former legal assistant of the National Commission on Law Observance and Enforcement headed by George Wickersham, to the Duke law faculty as instructor of law and assistant director of legal research, there will be six new teachers joining the school at the opening of the new academic year.

Dean Justin Miller of the Law School has previously announced the appointment of the following:

John S. Bradway, professor of law and director of the legal clinic; David F. Cavers, assistant professor of law; Lon L. Fuller, professor of law; Alexander H. Frey, visiting professor of law; and George E. Osborne, visiting professor of law.

(Photographs of Messrs. Fuller and Wahrenbrock will appear in the next issue.)

There will be 12 full-time teachers in the Duke Law School beginning with the new semester, not including other administrative officers.

JOHN S. BRADWAY

Legal Aid Clinic Opens September 21

The Law School of Duke University will open to the general public on Monday afternoon, September 21st, a Legal Aid Clinic, under the direction of Prof. John S. Bradway. This organization, which is similar to Legal Aid Societies throughout the country, is established for the purpose of rendering legal advice and assistance to persons who cannot afford to pay an attorney fee. The rule is rigid that only poor persons can be received as clients but after this test is passed the Clinic aims to serve its clients in advice or in court actions as any other attorney would serve them.

The office hours of the Clinic will be week day afternoons, except Saturday, from 1:30 to 3:30. The office will be in charge of experienced attorneys, while the third year law students will be permitted to do such portions of the work as may fall within their abilities short of actually practicing law.

It is expected that a substantial number of applicants will present themselves the first afternoon. Thereafter the work will spread as widely as the facilities of the Law School permit. The Clinic is so organized that some of the attorneys connected with it will be in charge of the civil court work, others will be in charge of the criminal court work, and still others in charge of the work that is done in the Clinic office itself.

More Books By Duke Men; Several Volumes Of Note

Works By Dr. Korstian, Dr. Rippy and Dr. Carroll, of the Duke Faculty, Attracting Real Attention—Noteworthy Reviews Emphasize Value of Contributions Made by Members of Faculty

MORE books by members of the Duke University faculty have been announced by three widely known publishing firms. Already these volumes are receiving most favorable attention in book reviews and otherwise.

"Seeding and Planting in The Practice of Forestry" by James W. Toumey, professor of silviculture at Yale University, and Clarence F. Korstian, director of Duke Forest and professor of silviculture at Duke University, has just been issued from the press of John Wiley & Sons, Inc., New York. This is the second edition of the book by Dr. Toumey on this subject, revised and enlarged to a considerable extent by Dr. Korstian. It is a manual for the guidance of forestry students, foresters, nurseryman, forest owners, and farmers.

This is the first volume in the English language devoted entirely to seeding and planting in the practice of forestry. Reviews of the book are being published in England and in various countries of Europe, Australia and elsewhere. While it will be largely used in foreign countries as a reference work, the book will have general use by students in American forestry schools.

The book has peculiar interest to Southern readers because of the stress laid on the solution of forest planting problems in the South. Attention is directed to the shrinkage in forest area in the United States and the amount of standing timber, and the necessity for expert forest management is pointed out. Governmental and private responsibility is cited by the authors, especially in connection with forest planting.

Dr. Toumey and Dr. Korstian declare the real needs in the forest situation are an increase in area of public owned forest and a saner utilization and better care of large areas of privately owned forest. They contend that at least 50 percent of the forest on non-agricultural lands should be publicly owned.

The book is profusely illustrated.

FRENCH DIPLOMACY

The Portland *Oregonian* recently had the following review of a new book, entitled "French Public Opinion and Foreign Affairs," by Dr. E. Malcolm Carroll, associate professor of history in Duke University. The book is printed by the Century Company:

"This scholarly study of public opinion in France during the period between the Franco-Prussian war and the world war is the first book in any language to trace the evolution of public opinion and its relation to foreign policy in any of the great powers between 1870 and 1914. Dr. Carroll's study not only brings to light much important information regarding the reaction of public opinion in France to public affairs but also develops a number of new points of view. His book gives evidence that public opinion in France was not responsible for the Franco-Prussian war; that the effect of the Ems dispatch in Paris has been misunderstood; that Germany's Moroccan policy in 1905, interpreted in Paris as an attempt to isolate that country, brought an end to a period of good feeling, and that the Russian subsidies of the French press in 1912-13 did not have their intended effect. This is a book of great timeliness. It illuminates European diplomacy, reveals the enduring attitude of suspicion and distrust among European nations which exists even in spite of changes in government, shows how diplomats and the press are able to arouse public sentiment and indicates how easily another great conflict might be launched. E. Malcolm Carroll, associate professor of history at Duke University, is a graduate of the University of Michigan, receiving his master's and doctor's degrees also from that university. He has traveled extensively in Europe, served in the ambulance service during the world war and in 1927 and 1928 held a Guggenheim fellowship, which enabled him to carry on extensive research in France, Germany and England in preparation for writing this book."

BOOK BY DR. RIPPY

A new book in the series of "Studies in American Imperialism" has just been issued by the Vanguard Press of New York. It is "The Capitalists and Colombia," by Dr. J. Fred Rippy, professor of history at Duke. It is a thoughtful volume that bids fair to have a very wide reading.

"WE SEE BY THE PAPERS—

REV. S. F. NICKS, of the Class of 1903, was recently elected head of the Junior Order United American Mechanics in North Carolina for the next year. He was unanimously chosen for that position by representatives of the State Council in the opening session of the forty-first annual convention in Charlotte last month.

Rev. Mr. Nicks, who is a Methodist minister of Roxboro, has been prominent in the affairs of the Junior Order for a number of years, and is held in high esteem in Junior Order and other circles. Four hundred men attended the convention at which he was chosen State Councilor.

C. B. HOUCK, of the Class of 1922, is achieving much success in the advertising agency business. His firm, Houck & Company, advertising counsellors with offices in High Point and Roanoke, has just recently been appointed to handle the entire advertising account of the Bassett Furniture Industries, Inc., of Bassett, Va. This is one of the largest furniture manufacturers in the United States, the present firm being a merger of three large companies. The firm has five plants, having recently gone into the manufacture of chairs, in addition to the manufacture of bedroom and dining room furniture. Its capital stock is nearly five million dollars.

The Houck and Company agency just a few months ago was awarded the contract for handling the entire advertising account for the Norfolk & Western Railway Company, and its other clients include some of the largest and most prosperous concerns in North Carolina and Virginia. It is steadily adding to its facilities for the handling of various kinds of advertising.

ERNEST (LEFTY) JENKINS, Class of 1931, has been receiving much publicity recently in the newspapers because of a wonderful nineteen inning 1-1 tie game that he pitched for the Springfield, Mass., Club of the Eastern League, against the Richmond, Va., Club at Springfield. The Richmond *Times Dispatch* has the following to say about the work of the young southpaw who was star pitcher at Duke during the 1928, 1929 and 1930 seasons:

"There were thrills galore in the contest that harked back to the old days of great pitching, base running and the sacrifice bunt; but the outstanding feature was the brilliant pitching of Ernest Jenkins, southpaw of the Springfield hurling staff.

"Richmond scored on the little lefthander in the opening inning, but from that point down through the gathering darkness, Jenkins turned the Colts back scoreless.

"A human pitching machine, the former Duke University star stood on the mound and mowed the Richmond team down through 18 consecutive innings. His performance must take rank as one of the best of the season and one of the best seen at League park in years."

REV. G. RAY JORDAN, Class of 1917, pastor of Wesley Memorial Church of High Point, has written a new book entitled, "Intimate Interests of Youth," which will be released by the Cokesbury Press in the near future. He has already established quite a reputation as a writer, having recently written "The Intolerance of Christianity," and "What Is Yours," two books that have attracted much attention.

P. FRANK HANES, Class of 1911, was recently elected chairman of the Board of Education of Forsyth County, to succeed G. Miller Hinshaw, deceased. Mr. Hanes has been a member of the Board for several years and has rendered substantial service to the cause of education in Forsyth County.

THOMAS B. DOWNEY, Class of 1915, holds a responsible position in an executive and research capacity with the Charles B. Knox and the Knox & Kind Gelatine Companies. After graduating at Trinity he attended classes at Columbia, and then received his Ph.D. degree in chemistry at the University of Pittsburgh. He acted as instructor in chemistry during the time he was taking his graduate work, and served in the army for two years. Mr. Downey is located at Camden, N. J.

DR. CHARLES C. WEAVER, Class of '95, who has been for several years pastor of Centenary-West End Methodist Church, of Winston-Salem, has announced the formal opening of the new Centenary M. E. Church, South, of that city on Sunday morning, September 20. The new church, which will serve the combined congregations under the name of Centenary, is a magnificent structure. The sermon on the occasion of the formal opening will be delivered by Bishop H. M. Dubose of Nashville, Tenn., who first proposed the union of Centenary and West End into one church with an outstanding house of worship.

Former Chinese Student at Trinity Won High Renown

Charles J. Soong Was One of the Strong Supporters of Dr. Sun Yat Sen—His Daughter, Also Educated in America, is Wife of President Chiang Kai-Shek, Christian Head of the Chinese Republic

(An inquiry came recently to the Department of Public Relations and Alumni Affairs asking about Chinese students who have been at Duke from time to time and particularly about Charles J. Soong, whose family has been quite prominent in Chinese affairs in recent years. From Dr. M. T. Plyler, of the North Carolina *Christian Advocate*, who recently had an article on Soong in that publication, some interesting information on the subject has been secured, as follows.—EDITOR.)

CHARLES J. Soong, a student at Trinity College in the early eighties and later, at Vanderbilt, lived a life in China characterized by noble fidelity and genuine devotion. Only the centuries can disclose the ultimate results of the Soong family. Devoted to his church and a loyal supporter of the Y. M. C. A. in Shanghai all his days, Charles J. Soong proved to be a tower of strength to a weak and struggling cause. He prospered in the printing business but most of his money went into the causes he had espoused. He was one of the strong supporters of Dr. Sun Yat Sen in the struggle for reform movements in that ancient empire. Dr. Fletcher S. Brockman, who spent more than thirty years in China, speaks in highest terms of Charles J. Soong with whom he was most intimately associated until the day of his death.

Rev. J. B. Wright of Cairo, Ga., says he first knew Charles Jonas Soon (the g was added to his name on his return to China) in Vanderbilt in September 1882. He was a good average student, with a bright mind. His work was mainly in the literary department of the University. He spoke fairly good English at that time.

"During the spring term of 1883," says Dr. Wright, "Charlie and I roomed together. We have often knelt together in our private devotions in our room.

"He was rather low of stature, probably about five feet—four or six inches—but compactly built. He was jovial in his disposition and enjoyed a laugh. He was popular with all the students. Every one knew him as Charlie Soon. I have heard him say that when he first came to America he went to Massachusetts and later to North Carolina."

Just now there is special interest in this Chinese boy whose life touched so intimately Trinity and Vanderbilt, and whose wonderful and far reaching influence in his own land furnishes such a romantic story. Dr. M. T. Plyler had an article relating to him in the North Carolina *Christian Advocate* sometime ago, from which the following extracts are taken. The title of the article was "The Debt of the President of China to America":

The press of America announced on October 23, 1930, that General Chiang Kai-shek, President of the Chinese Republic, had received Christian baptism in the home of his mother-in-law, Mrs. K. T. Soong, the minister in charge being Rev. Z. T. Kaung, D.D., pastor of the Young J. Allen Memorial church of the Methodist Episcopal Church, South, in Shanghai. It was also stated that President Chiang Kai-shek was influenced to take this step by his Christian wife and her Christian mother. The press dispatch also quoted the general as saying, "I feel the need of a God such as Jesus Christ."

This story has to do with the relation of the wife of President Chiang and her family, the Soong family of China, to America. The orient and the occident meet in this romance; eternity alone can disclose the ultimate issues.

Mei-ling (Mayling) Soong, youngest daughter of Charlie J. Soong, married President Chiang Kai-shek; Eling Soong, the eldest daughter, married Dr. H. H. Kung; and Ching-ling Soong, next eldest daughter, married Dr. Sun Yat Sen.

All three of these Soong girls attended Wesleyan College, Macon, Ga., Mrs. Chiang Kai-shek being of the class of 1916. In the Wesleyan Alumnae of February, 1930, are these words: "When Mayling first came to America, she, as the 'little sister' of Eling and Chungling, and Eloise Ainsworth, as the president's daughter, were the pets of the college; they were inseparable friends as well."

This same number of the Wesleyan Alumnae adds these significant facts: "Notable are the three Soong sisters. Chungling became the wife of the late Dr. Sun Yat Sen, who is the father of the revolution that is now bringing a new China to birth. He will go down in history as the George Washington of the Chinese Republic. In all this modern struggle she has played a vital part and thousands are looking to her yet to become a modern Joan of Arc in some crucial hour of their country's need. Mayling is the wife of General Chiang Kai-shek, present head of the government at Nanking, and known to be a most important factor in the councils of government. She is a woman of unusual brilliance and sound sense. Eling is the wife of Dr. Kung, minister of commerce and industry in the Nationalist government, and her home is a center of the most gracious hospitality."

We are told that the mother of the Soong daughters "was a student in one of the Western mission schools in Shanghai." Bishop and Mrs. Ainsworth speak of her as "a saint in Israel." Of their father, Charlie J. Soong, we have some interesting facts concerning his stay in America.

He came into Wilmington, N. C., on board the U. S. Cutter, Colfax, 1880. General J. S. Carr of Durham, N. C., became interested in him and kept him for some time in his own home in Durham. He then sent him to Trinity College (now Duke University), and later to Vanderbilt University. Fortunately certain records and the testimony of men who remember this Chinese youth are sufficient to indicate some of the forces that influenced his life and the life of his family.

Rev. D. H. Tuttle, who was pastor of Fifth Street church, Wilmington, 1885-88, gives these facts: "Fifty years ago, 1880, this Chinese boy came to Wilmington on board the U. S. Cutter, Colfax, Capt. Charles Jones, commander. Captain Jones had the best interests, temporal and spiritual, at heart for he sought advice of Christian friends in an effort to find a good home environment for his young friend. He was told by a Christian lady worker, a Mrs. Chadwick, to bring him up to Fifth Street (now Fifth Avenue) Methodist Episcopal Church, South. Captain Jones did this, and not long thereafter young Soong was led to know our Lord as a personal Saviour by Rev. T. Page Ricaud, a saintly man of God, who was then pastor of Fifth Avenue church, by whom he was also baptized, taking Charles Jones as his Christian name, thus honoring his friend, Capt. Charles Jones of the U. S. Cutter Colfax. No boy of any race or nation ever came into wiser, or more fatherly care than Charles Jones Soong. It was "Uncle Ricaud" who brought him to General Carr's attention. It was General Carr's big-hearted generosity that secured for him the educational training for his life work.

"For two or more years I enjoyed the pleasure of personal acquaintance with Brother Soong, having met him at Vanderbilt University in 1883. In 1885, during my first year at Fifth Avenue, he spent several weeks in my home, and the people of that church felt that he was their son in the gospel, and missionary to his native land. He preached for Fifth Avenue church two or more times during his stay with me, speaking good English, and to the spiritual edification of all who heard him."

General J. S. Carr sent Charlie Soon (Chinese Soong) to Trinity College, then located in Randolph county, N. C. The college records show that Charles J. Soon entered Trinity College as a special student in 1880—entered from Weichan, China.

A special from Trinity (the old site of the college before it was moved to Durham) says there are a dozen people living here who remember Charlie Soon and the cord hammocks he made and sold to add to the necessary expenses supplied by General Julian S. Carr. The despatch continues:

"Charlie boarded at Prof. W. T. Gannaway's and was an object of much interest to the other students, all of whom were fond of him. He made the hammocks which he said he learned about on shipboard, and sold them to nearly every householder in the community.

"On the Sunday before Christmas in 1880, he was taken into the Methodist church by Dr. Craven, who was pastor as well as college president, and the ceremony in the old college chapel which was for many years the Methodist church, is well remembered by old residents, and even the text of Doctor Craven's sermon, 'Go ye into all the world and preach the gospel to every creature'."

Dr. George B. Winton, acting dean of the school of religion, Vanderbilt University, writes: "Soong, or Soon as we called him, was here from '82 to '85. He was a harum-scarum little fellow, full of life and fun, but not a very good student. He gave no evidence of having any special interest in religion, even less in preaching. As a matter of fact, when he went back to China he soon became interested in some business enterprise. In the course of time he married a woman who must have been definitely his superior."

Though Dr. Winton says "he gave no evidence of any special interest in religion, even less in preaching" at Vanderbilt, Rev. D. H. Tuttle testifies that in 1885 "he spent several weeks in my home . . . and preached for Fifth Avenue church two or more times during his stay with me, speaking good English, and to the spiritual edification of all who heard him."

Dr. Winton adds: "Dr. Tillett tells me that one of his sons was in Vanderbilt a few years ago. He recalls him very clearly and said that he often had him in his home."

The records available thus indicate that in the

Soong family oriental civilization was fused with occidental culture. Charlie Soong knew something of Western schools and the mother was trained in mission schools in China. In 1906, a brother-in-law, Wan Bing Ching of Nanking was sent to Washington at the head of a commission to investigate the American educational system. Eling Soong was then a student at Wesleyan. She visited her uncle in Washington at that time. He was described as "a man of superior mentality, of polished manners, and of interesting personality."

Speaking of the present, some one will be interested in the experience of Bishop and Mrs. Ainsworth last year while superintending the Southern Methodist work in China:

"Bishop and Mrs. Ainsworth spent the night in China's 'White House,' but Mrs. Ainsworth confessed she didn't rest well in such distinguished surroundings for she heard the tramping of soldiers' feet all night long, guarding the president and his wife."

May Ling and General Chiang live very simply, Mrs. Ainsworth said, because of the unsettled conditions in China. Their "White House" is a public hall that has been converted into a home for the president and their country home is a barn on the edge of Nanking that has been remodeled into a house.

Mrs. Ainsworth declared there was nothing in the States that could touch the magnificence of the tomb of Sun Yat Sen, with its 400 steps leading up to it. She said it was a gorgeous sight to behold.

Just what the conversion to Christianity of the President of Nationalist China is ultimately to signify no one can know. The testimony of Stanley High, editor of the *Christian Herald*, is interesting.

Dr. High, both in the *Herald* and in a letter to the *Christian Science Monitor*, writes at length regarding the matter. Dr. High, who has been much in China and knows President Chiang, says in the *Monitor:*

"It was my privilege to interview President Chiang in 1927 for the *Christian Science Monitor*. I knew, before that interview, a good bit about him. I knew, for example, that Dr. Sun Yat Sen, desiring capable leadership for his Nationalist campaign in 1925, selected Chiang Kaishek—then in his early thirties—to organize the army and direct its advance. I knew, too, that in 1926, on the eve of that army's departure from Canton for the campaign against the North, this same young general had put down, with an effectiveness that was startling, a Communist attempt to wrest the army from his control. And I knew that the loyalty of this young Chinese to Dr. Sun and his ideals had cost him his entire personal fortune. President Chiang granted me an interview. He talked at length of the new China that was just coming into being. He plead with me to urge Americans to have patience with China. 'One day,' he said, 'we will justify our faith'." Dr. High thinks it altogether probable that when President Chiang Kai-shek accepts Christianity, he "means business."

Dr. High further cites as proof of Chiang Kai-shek's sincerity the fact that the most influential men in the group which he has brought into the Nationalist government are Christians. They include C. T. Wang, foreign minister; H. H. Kung, minister of commerce; T. V. Soong, minister of finance.

Record Summer School Terms Closed a Notable First Year

Duke's Initial Year on Two Campuses Marked by Unusually Fine Progress—Second
Session Began on September 16 With Prospects Bright for Another
Record of Real Achievement

THE two sessions of the Duke University summer school this season continued the unusually fine progress that has marked all of the University's departments and schools since the new campus was first occupied a year ago. A record-breaking enrollment this summer has but continued record-breaking achievements evinced by various divisions during the regular academic year.

Offering every modern facility to enable students, professors and research workers to carry on the highest type of endeavor, the new campus and its facilities have made possible a type of academic work of which the University is frankly proud. Faculty excellence has matched physical completeness, and in this way Duke University in all its phases of service is making definite contributions to the total of educational advancement.

Its first year in its new home closed a few days ago and when a final review is made it will be found that notable progress has been made by Duke in many fields of educational endeavor in this period. This is proving a surprise to many who felt the first year of adjustment to the new campus surroundings would give the several departments little opportunity to show the marked development and widened scope of service they have since exhibited.

Administrative officers were dubious as to results that would follow immediately on removal to the new campus; they felt the period would be a trying one, and that various departments would be confronted with difficult situations. But results have been most heartening; the removal was quickly made; faculty and students adjusted themselves—aided perhaps by the spirit of an age that sees remarkable changes taking place on every hand—quickly to the new régime; and the first school year did not pass without the realization of thoroughgoing and even scholarly work.

During recent weeks the good order and progress has been maintained; and both sessions of the Duke summer school have been considered quite successful, the same being true at Lake Junaluska.

One feature that aided in the transfer of the Uni-

> ## Over 1,600 Summer School Students
>
> Attendance at the Duke University summer school and its allied schools at Lake Junaluska have shown an increase over the enrollments of last year, according to Dr. Holland Holton, summer school director.
>
> Last year 1,502 students were registered in all Duke summer school terms. The total this summer reaches 1,678, or just 176 over the previous summer.
>
> The enrollments this year include 932 who attended the first term in Durham, 483 who registered for the second term, 222 who attended the session at Lake Junaluska, and 41 in the Junaluska School of Religion.
>
> These figures do not include 51 medical students in their summer quarter's work or the student nurses in the school of nursing.

versity from a residential section of Durham to the campus carved from wood outside the city was the expertness and thoroughness of the physical preparations. Not in beauty and impressiveness alone are the Duke campus and its buildings noteworthy; the comfort and convenience features also add much. The buildings and classrooms are so grouped that faculty members and students are able to attend to various college duties without a great amount of excess campus trotting that can prove quite fatiguing. Faculty members familiarized themselves with the new arrangements, and were prepared when the change came. And the plant was largely complete when the University moved over, with much work done also in landscaping.

Many significant events marked the first year in the history of Duke. A year ago Tuesday, July 21, the great and impressive Duke Hospital was thrown open to the public; the day before, July 20, twenty thousand persons swarmed into the building for one of the most striking "house-warmings" known to Durham or Duke.

Already the hospital has contributed to the section —not only in the welfare and treatment of patients but also in the advancement of the cause of medical science. The close connection with the Medical School gives a rich opportunity—and a mutual one, hospital profiting from school, and school from hospital as the one pursues more closely the theories of healing and the other practices.

Other impressive factors in the opening of the thirty buildings on the West Campus were: reorganization of the School of Law; inauguration of a college for women, this on the East Campus, and the increase in faculty members, library and laboratory equipment. Library additions have not applied alone to size of volumes; rich treasures in books of various kinds have contributed to the store of the university's reading matter.

More important than the addition of books perhaps has been the search for men and the inclusion of those in the faculty, who would prove, by their erudition and sympathy, an aid and an incentive to students with whom they came in contact, and gain for Duke wider recognition as an important institution of learning. Noteworthy attention has been given to graduate students and their interests; and effort made to provide means whereby the student may effectively carry on research in sundry fields.

The undergraduate school has not been forgotten, however, and Duke awarded 348 undergraduate degrees at the June, 1931, commencement. A sweeping revision whereby honors courses are being provided for students who are interested in rather intensive study is a significant factor in the development of the undergraduate school.

Of the more than 2,300 students in the University during the 1930-31 session 1,800 were men enrolled in the West Campus undergraduate school, carrying still the cherished name of Trinity College, and graduate departments, while 500 women were enrolled in the Woman's College on the East Campus. Other students included 70 in medicine, a similar number in law, 143 in the School of Religion, and 30 in nursing.

During the second year, which began September 16, Duke will continue its development in various spheres. In book additions the institution has already been setting a rapid pace, its purchases of books last year reaching a total of $155,000, placing it in fifth place among American universities in library expenditure.

Only University-Retired Mule Is Dead

DEATH a few weeks ago ended the career of one of Duke University's oldest servants, Old Kate, a mule which first drew campus burdens in 1894 and only in recent years became incapable of work.

Kate was at least four years old when bought by Trinity College more than 37 years ago, so the venerable animal was close to 42 years old when she died several weeks ago at the Washington Duke homestead where she had been pastured since last spring.

The mule survived by three years her harness mate, Kit, who for 28 years shared her burdens. Both were relieved of work in 1925, but it was Old Kate who lasted, though she was six years older than Kit.

Several weeks ago Kate suddenly collapsed after showing up to that moment every evidence of vigor and prospects of years more of comfortable retirement. She was unable to rise after falling, so under the supervision of Samuel R. Hunt, Duke supervisor of grounds, she was carefully lifted into a strong frame, and supported on her feet by broad canvas strips. No mule could have been given more attention and care, but Old Kate was "done for."

Duke's veteran draft animal was exceptional, according to Mr. Hunt, who first became connected with Trinity College just a month before Kate was bought. She was never ill in 37 years, was a powerful worker, and never balked at any load. Of the team, Kit and Kate, the latter was by far the favorite. In 1925 when retired from service college students painted large signs and placed them on the truck which carried her to a farm some miles from the city.

Later Kate was brought back to the campus stable, and when the Washington Duke homestead passed into the hands of the University last spring she was taken there. On this historic farm pasture Kate was given exclusive grazing rights, distinguished as probably the only university-retired mule in the world.

Varsity Squad Is Working Hard In Preparing For First Contest

Team Faces Tough Assignment in the Season's Opening Game at Columbia September 26
—Forty-three Candidates for Gridiron Honors Report For Practice September 7
—Coach Wade Has Problems.

FROM all indications, Coach Wallace Wade and his Blue Devils face a tough assignment in the season's opener with the University of South Carolina, Sept. 26 at Columbia. (Tickets available now at Duke Alumni Office).

Reports from the neighboring state make much of the Gamecock team for the coming season, predicting it will be at Duke's expense that Coach Billy Laval's outfit starts its greatest season.

With the opposite in mind, Coach Wallace Wade started things slowly when practice opened September 7. He gave the candidates, 43 in all, plenty of time to condition and then in the second week of practice put in the hard work.

At the outset he stated his problems frankly, saying; "While it looks like the line will be O. K., our ends are inexperienced, our backs need developing along ball-carrying lines, we have no passer, and no quarterback."

At this stage the weak departments are getting most of the coaches' attention. It now looks as if either Jim Mullen or Lowell Mason will call the signals, and that Norman James, soph star, will pair with Hyatt on the flanks. Brownlee, track star, appears to have won a backfield berth—to do the ball-carrying.

A serious loss to the team came the first day of practice when Glenn Lemon, veteran halfback, suffered an injured ankle which will keep him out for sometime, maybe all season.

With the season about to start, Coach Wade holds no illusions about turning out a world-beating team this fall, but intends to keep the grid game in its proper place—win or lose—as part of a "man-building" program.

The list reporting:

Backs: Captain Pierce Brewer, Winston-Salem; John Brownlee, Philadelphia, Pa.; James Mullen, Dothan, Ala.; Kenneth Abbott, Monongahela, Pa.; Glenn Lemon, Roanoke, Va.; Arthur Ershler, Hudson, N. Y.; Lowell Mason, Charlotte; Walter Belue, Charlotte; Nick Laney, Charlotte; Horace Hendrickson, Beaver Falls, Pa.; Harry Rossiter, Abington, Pa.; William Hicks, Charlotte; James Raper, Lexington; Claude Cook, Winston-Salem; William Gar-

(Continued on page 295)

1931 FOOTBALL SQUAD

Where They Are Located	# News of the Alumni	What They Are Doing

Miss Elizabeth Aldridge, '24, Secretary of Alumnae Council, Editor

CLASS OF 1909

Rev. and Mrs. J. Earl Gilbreath of Cleveland, Tenn., announce the arrival of a son, J. Earl Gilbreath, Jr., on August 12.

CLASS OF 1916

Frank H. Gibbs is a member of the law firm of Polk & Gibbs, at Warrenton, N. C. He has been mayor of Warrenton since 1920.

CLASS OF 1917

Richard H. Bennett has been with the Tennessee Electric Power Company since 1924. He is at present superintendent of production. He was formerly with the General Electric Company at Schenectady, N. Y. Dick was married on April 11, 1925 to Miss Martha Chambers Boykin. They have one son, Richard Boykin Bennett.

CLASS OF 1921

Beulah Walton is living at her home, Route 2, Morrisville, N. C. She completed requirements for a Ph.D. degree in English at Cornell University last June.

Irene Pitts is teaching history in the Wakelon High School at Zebulon, N. C., for this school year.

CLASS OF 1923

Friends and classmates of Mrs. M. E. Parker, formerly Brooks Strayhorn, will be grieved to hear of her death on August 31, which came as a result of injuries sustained in an automobile accident, occurring a few hours before her death. Mrs. Parker was a prominent woman in her community and enjoyed a wide circle of friendship. She, with her husband, operated the Belmont Dairy near Durham. She was recently elected principal of the new Hillandale School, having taught in the county schools for a number of years.

CLASS OF 1924

O. F. Barnhardt with Mrs. Barnhardt and their baby daughter, Mary Jane, recently moved to Fayetteville, N. C., where Mr. Barnhardt will be coach in the high school. He moved from Wilkesboro where he has been connected with the schools since leaving college in 1924.

CLASS OF 1925

Mr. and Mrs. Foster Young of Greenville, N. C., have announced the arrival of Betty Anne on August 26. Mrs. Young was Anne Ratledge before her marriage.

Mr. and Mrs. Downey J. Booth (Ruby Vaughan) of 314 Elizabeth Street, Durham, are receiving congratulations on the birth of a son, Judson Vaughan, on August 18.

Sidney Maxwell Kale has been principal of the high school at Mineral Springs since 1926. He was married on October 5, 1929, to Miss Lois Elizabeth Walters.

CLASS OF 1926

T. A. Shaw, formerly of Corinth, Miss., is traveling for the Associated Gas and Electric System, Bowling Green, Kentucky. In a letter recently received from him, he says: ''I travel over seven states and at the present time my June bride is traveling with me.''

Robert L. Jerome has just completed his residence work at Columbia University and Union Theological Seminary for the Ph.D. degree. He is now pastor of a Methodist church at Seaford, L. I., New York, but will return to the North Carolina Conference to take a church this fall. He says it's the Old North State for him!

Irwin F. Masten was married to Miss Elizabeth McNeel, of Union, S. C., on June 8 in St. Peter's Episcopal Church at Charlotte. He is assistant to the credit manager of the McClaren Rubber Company of Charlotte. They live at 212 College Apartments.

K. Kodama has been teaching English in the Hiroshima Girls' School since returning to Japan. He is now teaching English in the college department at Kwansei Gakuin. His address is Mikage, Japan.

William Amos Abrams is a graduate student in English at Cornell University, 144 Linn Street, Ithaca, New York. He formerly taught English in the high school at Glen Alpine, N. C.

CLASS OF 1927

Receiving one of the most coveted medical appointments in the reach of a young physician, Richard L. Pearse, son of Dr. and Mrs. Pearse of the Duke faculty, will join the staff of Massachusetts General Hospital next April as House Officer in surgery. Dr. Pearse was graduated from Harvard Medical School last June and is at present connected with the staff of the Woman's Free Hospital in Boston. His appointment beginning in April will continue for twenty-six months. During October Dr. Pearse will spend his autumn vacation with his parents in Durham.

RICHARD L. PEARSE

Evans M. Gibson has a position in the postoffice at Lumberton, N. C. He was married to Miss Doris June Odom on November 9, 1925.

Hoyle Sidney Broome is principal of the high school at Biscoe, N. C.

Mr. and Mrs. James DeHart (Lois Guffy) are receiving congratulations on the birth of twins, a boy and a girl, on Saturday, August 29.

Macon M. Simon is an examiner for the Federal Trade Commission, Washington, D. C. He is also attending evening classes at George Washington University Law School.

Ralph N. Apple is an accountant on the staff of Lybrand, Ross Brothers and Montgomery at 110 William Street, New York City. He was married on May 31, 1930, to Miss Helen Ruth Teague.

CLASS OF 1928

Ruth Beatrice Davidson received an A.B. degree from Birmingham-Southern College in 1928. She is secretary for Johnston & Jennings, patent attorneys, at 808 Bankers Bond Building, Birmingham.

The marriage of Guy H. Simpson, Jr., and Miss LaVerne Ware took place at the home of the bride in Greensboro on August 15. They will be at home after September 15 at 2505 West Market Street, Greensboro, where Mr. Simpson is connected with the trust department of the North Carolina Bank and Trust Company.

Rev. and Mrs. J. W. Frank, who have been engaged in evangelistic work on Shikoku Island, have been appointed to Palmore Institute in Kobe. Their new address is 23 Kitanagasa Dori, 4 Chome, Kobe. Their son Grady, '31, who is a Rhodes Scholar at Oxford, has been spending the summer at Duke, but will return to Oxford in the fall.

Rev. Thomas Hoyle Swofford is pastor of the Smyre Methodist Church at Gastonia, N. C. He was married on February 9, 1924 to Miss Ida Anna McCurry. They have two children, Betty and Thomas Hoyle Swofford, Jr.

Annie Laurie Oliver received her A.B. degree from N. C. C. W. in Greensboro in 1928. She teaches English in the city schools at Greensboro.

CLASS OF 1929

For the past two years, Reuben Margolis has been attending Yale University. He is now at his home, 705 N. Queen Street, Durham.

Layton Malcolm Smith, office manager of the Asheville Gas Company, lives at 15 Mount Vernon Circle, Asheville.

William Harrison Covington, Jr., and Miss Dorothy Inez White were married at the home of the bride's aunt, Mrs. Albert R. Dean of Baltimore, Md., on July 18. Mrs. Covington attended Oxford High School and later N. C. C. W. in Greensboro. Mr. and Mrs. Covington make their home in Durham where William is connected with the Christian Printing Company.

Leighton Davis Capps, 2445 Walton Avenue, New York City, is auditor for the Equitable Life Assurance Society of the United States. His business address is 393-7th Avenue. On August 26, 1930 he was married to Miss Margaret Daniel Tiller.

Gertrude E. McCrary attended Augustana College after leaving Duke and received her A.B. degree in 1928. She is now teaching Social Science in the Eugene Field School at 2919-7th Avenue, Rock Island, Ill.

CLASS OF 1930

Carter Wood Farriss belongs to a Trinity family. All the male members of his family have attended Trinity College for three generations. He is a cousin of Marquis L. Wood, a former president of Trinity College. Carter is located at 295 West 11th Street, New York City.

William James Wingate teaches in the Stonewall Jackson Manual Training and Industrial School, Concord, N. C.

William Calhoun McIntire is supervisor of final accounts for the Southern Bell Telephone and Telegraph Company at Raleigh, N. C.

Esther Jane Morris lives at 606 West 116th Street, New York City. She says she is secretary and general "handy man" in the Department of Anthropology, The American Museum of Natural History.

Thomas Jefferson J. Davis, Jr., may be reached at Box 1197, Richmond, Va. He is connected with the American Supplies Inc.

William Matthew Baucom is office secretary for the Young Men's Christian Association of Durham.

Fernley Goddard Fawcett is a research specialist in the U. S. Department of Commerce, Bureau of Foreign and Domestic Commerce, Merchandising Research Division, Nineteenth and

Pennsylvania Avenue, N. W., Washington, D. C. He is also attending George Washington University.

Dorothy Fink teaches in the schools at Hopkinsville, Kentucky. She graduated at Vanderbilt University in 1930.

Reuben Lee Leonard works in the civil engineering department of the Standard Oil Company of California. He is located at Coalinga.

William W. Lewis is a student engineer for McClintic-Marshall Corporation in Pittsburgh, Pa.

Douglas C. Giles of Chatham, Va., is savings teller for the People's Wayne County Bank at 12800 Hamilton Avenue, Highland Park, Michigan.

Carroll E. Gunnin has changed his address to The Hermitage, 4458 Washington Building, St. Louis, Missouri. He was formerly located in Chicago.

Richard H. Stearns is a student engineer in the testing department of the General Electric Company at Schenectady, New York.

Since leaving Duke, Julia Clendenin has been assistant manager of the Atlanta office, L. G. Balfour Company, Fraternity Jewelers. Her home address is 22 Eighth Street, N. E.

CLASS OF 1931

Milton J. West is a merchant at Warsaw, N. C.

Helen Peacock has accepted a position next year teaching English and mathematics in the high school at Granite Quarry, N. C. She will also direct the glee club.

Elizabeth Kelly Matthews has accepted a position to teach first grade at Rutherfordton, N. C.

Shelley Hart Millican was born on August 17 at Watts Hospital in Durham. She is the daughter of Mr. and Mrs. James L. Millican (Mary Vann Hart, ex-'32) of Chapel Hill.

Mr. and Mrs. William D. Murray with their daughter, Anne Joy, have arrived at the Children's Home in Winston-Salem and have already won the admiration of the boys and girls in the home. Bill is succeeding Robert Bradshaw, '19, who will join the Western North Carolina Conference of the M. E. Church, South, this fall.

Varsity Squad Is Working Hard In Preparing For First Contest

(Continued from page 290)

ren, Asheville; James Rupert, Grayson, Ky.; and Phil Weaver, Winston-Salem.

Ends: Don Hyatt, Waynesville; Charles Short, Charlotte; Joe Sink, Lexington; Frank Carden, Signal Mt., Tenn.; Garrett Anderson, Asheville; Thomas Rogers, Hinton, W. Va.; Henry Thompson, Gastonia; Fred Crawford, Waynesville; Norman James, Hickory; and Eugene Newsom, Durham.

Tackles: William Bryan, Winston-Salem; James Harton, Durham; Don Carpenter, Maiden; and Luther Angle, Maywood, Ill.

Guards: Albert Werner, Lykens, Pa.; John Daugherty, Jeannette, Pa.; Claude Plaster, Winston-Salem; Carl Shock, New Rochelle, N. Y.; Melvin Stevens, Brockton, Mass.; Norman Rumfeldt, Quebec, Canada; O'Neill Bryant, Duncan, S. C.; Al Means, Abington, Pa.; and Sidney Bowden, Durham.

Centers: Emory Adkins, Durham; Bert Friedman, New York City; and Waite Hamrick, Gaffney, S. C.

Nature, *not parching* makes CAMELS mild

Smoke a *fresh* cigarette

CAMEL 20's

Smoke a *fresh* cigarette

HUMIDOR PACK

HARSH tobaccos require harsh measures — like parching—to make them tolerable to the throat.

But the choice Turkish and mellow Domestic tobaccos of which Camels are blended are *naturally* mild and gentle. Parching would only ruin their exquisite flavor and aroma.

No...matter where you buy Camels you will find them always in factory-fresh condition. Their rare flavor together with their natural moisture is air-sealed-in by moisture-proof Cellophane. We call it the

Humidor Pack. This protective wrapping is dust-proof, germ-proof and weather-proof. A great boon to the smoker.

No stinging particles of peppery dust to irritate the throat; no brackish smoke from stale tobacco; no burnt tongue from the hot smoke of dried-out cigarettes.

Just the cool, mild fragrance of choice tobaccos expertly blended and properly conditioned.

If you haven't tried Camels lately, switch over for just one day. Then leave them—if you can.

● *Don't remove the moisture-proof Cellophane from your package of Camels after you open it. The Humidor Pack is protection against perfume and powder odors, dust and germs. It delivers fresh Camels and keeps them right until*

DUKE UNIVERSITY
ALUMNI REGISTER

INTERIOR OF NEW DUKE UNIVERSITY CHAPEL, LOOKING TOWARD ENTRANCE

IS YOUR PRINTING EFFECTIVE?

If not—add the Seeman Printery, Inc., with its modernly equipped plant and competent staff, to your advisory board. Every job receives the most careful attention to the last minute detail. Experience has given a thorough knowledge of your individual and business requirements. Let us work with you.

THE SEEMAN PRINTERY, INC.

PRINTERS IN DURHAM, N. C., SINCE 1885

A SERVICE THAT FOLLOWS THROUGH

Duke University Alumni Register

(Member of American Alumni Council)

Published at Durham, N. C. Every Month in the Year in the Interest of the University and the Alumni

Volume XVII   October, 1931   Number 10

In This Issue

Editor and Business Manager .... HENRY R. DWIRE, '02

Assistant Editors .... ELIZABETH ALDRIDGE, '24
ALBERT A. WILKINSON, '26

Advertising Manager .... CHARLES A. DUKES, '29

TWO DOLLARS A YEAR   20 CENTS A COPY

ENTERED AS SECOND-CLASS MATTER AT THE POST-OFFICE AT
DURHAM, NORTH CAROLINA

THE COVER PAGE

The cover page of the REGISTER this month is a reproduction of a photograph of the University Chapel interior, the photograph being taken immediately upon its completion. Elsewhere in this issue is given some interesting information regarding the dimensions of the Chapel interior.

SOME IMPRESSIONS

Several members of the Duke faculty have spent quite a bit of time in recent months in countries outside the United States. In the REGISTER this month are several articles giving some very interesting impressions gained by some of these faculty members in the course of their trips. Other similar articles will appear in the November issue.

NEXT MONTH

Another in the series of articles on the Duke libraries will appear next month. Also there will be some more photographs of new members of the Duke faculty. There will be an interesting feature article on the significance of certain phases of the Duke architecture, to say nothing of other things that will make the November REGISTER of exceptional interest.

—THE EDITOR.

MEMBERS OF THE ATHLETIC COACHING STAFF OF DUKE UNIVERSITY

Back Row: E. P. HAGUE, Asst. Football Coach; W. W. CARD, Physical Education Instructor; E. M. CAMERON, Basketball Coach and Assistant Football Coach; J. W. COOMBS, Baseball Coach; WALLACE WADE, Director of Athletics and Head Football Coach; C. VOYLES, Assistant Director and Assistant Football Coach; L. D. BAKER, Trainer; F. SINGTON, Assistant Freshman Coach; A. WAFE, Physical Education Instructor and Assistant Freshman Coach. Front Row: PROF. GREGORY, Tennis Coach; R. TUTTLE, Physical Education Instructor and Cross Country Coach; H. CALDWELL, Freshman Football Coach; DAYTON DEAN, Business Manager of Athletics; J. PIERSON, Swimming Coach; M. CRICHTON, Physical Education Instructor; K. GERARD, Physical Director and Director of Intramural Athletics; R. ALLEN, Physical Education Instructor; A. WARREN, Boxing and Wrestling Coach.

Duke University Alumni Register

Volume XVII   October, 1931   Number 10

November Will Be "Duke Alumni Month"

Again this year the month of November will be observed as "Duke Alumni Month."

From the first day to the last the attention of the Alumni Office staff, and, it is hoped, of alumni and alumnae generally, will be directed to the one object in view of bringing the institution and its sons and daughters closer together in helpful coöperation.

To that end every energy will be directed to the task of presenting in an effective way Alma Mater, "the same Alma Mater in a new setting," to the alumni scattered in forty-seven states of the Union and every single county in North Carolina, and in twenty-nine countries outside the United States.

As stated above, the purpose of the movement is to bring about a closer relationship between the University and its alumni.

The entire month's activities will culminate in "Duke University Day," to be observed in probably fifty communities in this and other countries on December 11.

Much of the success of these occasions will depend upon the way in which the preliminary work is done during "Alumni Month."

The attempt is being made to do quite a few things during the month of November.

In the first place, the relation of the alumni to the institution in a financial way will be given proper emphasis.

An alumnus was saying not so long ago that every time he thought of what he had received while at this institution in exchange for the comparatively small sum he had paid in tuition fees and other expenses, he felt that he owed a definite obligation to do something more in a financial way than he had done before.

Others have expressed the same idea. An alumnus living in another state recently made a substantial donation in a letter in which he expressed his satisfaction that his condition was such that he was able to make a donation to help Duke University in its work, particularly in connection with the Alumni Office activities.

Whether the donation is made for a specific purpose or whether it goes for the general support of the alumni program, contributions will be particularly welcomed during Alumni Month.

The REGISTER has no hesitancy whatever in making this mild appeal, for it can be truthfully said that the alumni of Duke are not being constantly approached for donations, and we have enough confidence in the devotion of the alumni to the institution to believe that when an appeal is made it will be met in a sympathetic, cordial spirit.

We have heard at times of alumni of some institutions making complaint because they felt that they never received any kind of communication from the Alumni Office unless it were an appeal for funds. We are grateful that this has not been said with reference to the Alumni Office of Duke University.

But the matter of money is not the only thing, or even the principal thing, to be stressed during "Alumni Month."

In the first place, we want to "get over" as much information as possible about what Duke is accomplishing in this new stage of its development—this stage of progress and problems, following one of the most far-reaching and significant university building programs in the entire history of American education.

In addition to buildings and equipment, there is much about which alumni generally should be informed, especially those who have not had the opportunity to be on the campus much during the past few years of progressive development in various lines. Much regarding the ideals and aspirations of the institution and of what it has been doing in its various departments will be given to the alumni through letters and printed matter, and in other ways.

Another goal for "Alumni Month":

It is hoped that preliminary steps will be taken during the month for the forming of a number of new alumni groups in time for the "Duke University Day" meetings on December 11.

There are now fifty-eight alumni groups, and the number has been growing steadily during the past few years. But in the entire territory of the association there is room for quite a few more local organizations.

In any local community or county having as many as fifteen or more alumni or alumnae there is opportunity for the organization of a new local alumni club.

The Alumni Office will be glad to hear of such possibilities and will gladly coöperate in perfecting new organizations.

———

There is another way in which alumni can be of definite service during Alumni Month.

It is hoped that every single alumnus and alumna will make it his or her particular business to "put over" during that month in a definite and effective way something of Duke's aims and purposes, its plans and ideals.

Where there has been any misunderstanding of such purposes and ideals (and such misunderstandings are likely to arise in connection with the development of a growing institution) a real service can be performed by giving the proper information to those who may not be informed about the facts.

Any information needed will be gladly supplied by the Alumni Office for this purpose.

———

Another thing:

You doubtless know of young men and young women of the type which Duke University is seeking to serve through its facilities in various lines—the type of purposeful, serious-minded individual who is willing to look upon a college course as preparation for a life career of service to humanity.

When you think of such an individual whom you would like to see as a student of Duke just take a moment off from what you are doing

and give us the name and address. Some attractive literature will be promptly sent.

Incidentally, some particularly attractive publicity matter is now being prepared.

Here is a seemingly small matter in which alumni can render a real service.

Perhaps you have overlooked sending in information about yourself that has been requested by the Alumni Office.

Will you not take the time during Alumni Month to send in that information, and also while you are doing that give us any information about any other alumni with whom you feel that there is a possibility of our being out of touch?

And remember, in giving information about yourself, make it as complete as possible. If you have done something conspicuous in a particular line of service, don't leave that out for fear it will seem that you are boasting. The Alumni Office does not look on it that way at all. We are delighted to have the information.

Much information for the files has been received in recent months, making possible the filling out of many new cards, but much more is needed.

Will you not help?

———

May we suggest several goals for Alumni Month:

1. A contribution to the General Alumni Fund by every alumnus and alumna who can possibly make such a donation.

2. A determination on the part of everyone to co-operate with the Alumni Office in the effort to make its records as complete as possible.

3. A sincere effort to interpret, to those who may be interested, the ideals and purposes of Duke University, and to correct any erroneous impressions that may exist.

———

These are just a few of the many ways in which the alumni may serve the institution during "Alumni Month."

We know enough of the fine spirit of Duke alumni to feel confident that they will respond to the appeal and make "Alumni Month" notably successful in every way.

Hundreds of Alumni Return For Homecoming on October 3

Busy Day Featured by "Get-together" Conferences, Campus Tours, Barbecue Luncheon,
Duke-V. M. I. Football Game, Orchestra Concert and Informal Reception
and Other Features—Partial List of Alumni Participating in
Day's Events

SEVERAL hundred alumni of Duke University returned to Alma Mater on Saturday, October 3, for the annual Homecoming. All the morning the lobby of the University Union, alumni headquarters, was filled with returning alumni and alumnae, greeting former college mates, renewing old acquaintances and pledging anew their allegiance to the institution, while in the afternoon the Duke-V. M. I. football game was an outstanding feature.

Promptly at 9 o'clock the registration of returning alumni began, and from that hour until the close of the day's activities with the showing of the pictures at Page Auditorium in the evening with the "homecomers" as special guests, there was something "going on." A special committee of alumni members of the Duke faculty, with Prof. H. E. Spence as chairman, aided in extending the homecoming hosts a cordial welcome.

Upon registering the alumni were given Homecoming Day badges and attractive folders listing the events of the day. During the morning campus tours were arranged for those who had not yet had the opportunity to see the new plant in detail.

At noon a delightful barbecue luncheon was served under the trees behind Crowell House to the north of the dormitory section. It was a bountiful repast, served in a most efficient manner. Following this the "homecomers" saw the Duke team defeat V. M. I. on the gridiron by the score of 13 to 0. Special interest attached to this game because it was the first contest at the Duke stadium since Wallace Wade became Athletic Director and Head Coach.

Following the game an orchestra concert was given in the Union lobby in honor of the visitors. An informal "get-together" was enjoyed at this time. The visitors were guests of the management of Quadrangle Pictures in the evening.

ALUMNI REGISTERED

The alumni present for Homecoming represented a number of different states while one alumnus, William H. Lander, registered from Madrid, Spain. A most interested attendant at the football game was Dr. M. S. Bradshaw, alumnus, member of the Board of Trustees and devoted friend of everything pertaining to the best interests of Duke University, whose appearance after an illness of weeks was a source of gratification to alumni generally.

Following is a list of those registered. Many alumni arrived only a short while before the game, being unable to come earlier, and it was impossible to secure their registrations:

D. E. Kirkpatrick, '27, New York City; C. T. Thrift, '30, Durham; H. E. Spence, '07; Durham; S. F. Nicks, Jr., '29, Roxboro; T. Spruill Thornton, '29, Durham; J. M. Reams, Jr., '30, Kingsport, Tenn.; F. B. Jordan, '26, Greensboro; Charles P. Bowles, '28, Greensboro; Fletcher Nelson, '30, Greensboro; Annie Louise Caldwell, '29, Durham; Margaret Coleman, '31, Durham; T. Rupert Coleman, '28, Durham; Charles H. Miller, '28, Durham; Audrey Johnson Miller, '29, Durham; Sam B. Underwood, '31, Farmville; Blanche Barringer, '22, Durham; Ruth King, '31, Whitakers; W. M. Edwards, '93, Ayden; W. C. Dula, '25, Durham; Ed. J. Bullock, '26, Goldsboro; Claiborne C. Ross, '28, Durham; John W. Carr, Jr., '15, Durham; Charles W. Edwards, '94, Durham; W. H. Groce, '30, Asheville.

G. F. Hood, '28, Vale; M. T. Plyler, '92, Durham; O. L. Hathaway, '30, Middlesex; M. W. Maness, '28, Rowland; J. C. Harmon, Jr., '31, Gloucester; J. Elmer Vankook, '18, Richmond, Va.; T. G. Stem, '06, Oxford; J. L. Woodward, '29, Richlands; Roland Farley, '30, Danville, Va.; T. E. Summerow, Jr., '29, Gastonia; Thomas S. Hill, '30, Newport; Ralph B. Shumaker, '28, Chapel Hill; Emmett K. McLarty, Jr., '31, Durham; A. M. Proctor, '10, Durham; C. M. Kendrick, '29, Durham; R. W. Bradsher, '19, Durham; A. C. Waggoner, '27, Eldorado; Sara Powers Waggoner, '28, Eldorado; W. A. Phelps, '28, Greensboro; Cora Mecum, '30, Durham; Margaret C. Battle, '31, Raleigh; Everett Weatherspoon, '30, Durham; J. B. Sherrill, Concord; Cecil C. Rankin, '31, Mount Holly; W. M. Sherrill, '15, Concord; Robert Bruton, '28, Lexington; Ben Powell, '26, Durham; Frank R. Filex, '27, Thomasville; R. L. Crouch, '27, Thomasville.

J. Glenn Pennington, '23, Thomasville; John D. Langston, '03, Goldsboro; W. H. Langston, '95, Goldsboro; C. M. Flowers, '09, Durham; R. G. Tuttle, '94, Leaksville; Tom C. Daniels, '91, New Bern; Anita Scarboro Swaringen, '28, Greensboro; C. C. Swaringen, '28, Greensboro; Roy A. Swaringen, '25, Winston-Salem; Emma L. Chaffin, '21, High Point; Florence McDonald, '30, Lillington; C. B. Houck, '22, High Point; Mary Tapp Jenkins, '10, Kinston; May Wrenn Morgan, '08, Greensboro; J. A. Morgan, '06, Greensboro; Clara W. Becton, '26, Kinston; O. A. Robinson, '23, Charlotte; Margaret Ledbetter, '25, Durham; Elizabeth Montgomery, '29, Durham; Frank Brogden, '31, Durham; B. F. Kendall, '31, Norwood; W. C. Lassiter, '30, Smithfield; Eva C. Malone, '28, Durham; Nellie Garrard, '28, Durham; Marjorie Peoples, '30, Durham.

C. D. Brown, '29, Durham; W. M. Upchurch, Jr., '31, Raleigh; J. W. Mann, Jr., '31, Newton; T. G. Vickers, '11, Rocky Mount; L. C. Harper, '27, Charlotte; E. R. Bond, '15, Greensboro; Woodley C. Merritt, '21, Durham; C. C. Alexander, '19, Clinton; W. A. Underwood, '26, Asheboro; C. L. Ould, '31, Roanoke, Va.; Ann Courtney Sharpe, '31, Lumberton; J. A. Sharpe, '98, Lumberton; Carl H. King, '24, Lynchburg, Va.; Mary Eskridge King, '25, Lynchburg, Va.; William E. Joyner, '31, Durham; W. W. Graves, '97, Wilson; Thomas M. M. Grant, '09, Wilson; Dwight L. Fouts, '25, Wilson; James N. Truesdale, '28, Durham; W. M. Speed, '04, Durham; W. M. Speed, Jr., '28, Durham; Edwin J. Hix, '29, Durham; David W. Carpenter, '25, Durham; Edna Widenhouse Carpenter, '30, Durham; Henry L. Kendall, Jr., '29, Kipling; Harold M. Robinson, '31, Durham; Willis Smith, '10, Raleigh; Warren Sledd, '27, Durham; R. L. Fitzgerald, Jr., '30, Pine Level; A. J. Tannenbaum, '31, Durham; Harry M. Holtz, '31, Durham.

H. G. Hedrick, '11, Durham; G. W. Rees, '30, Oxford; Catherine Crews, '29, Oxford; Amos R. Kearns, '27, High Point; D. W. Horton, '06, Durham; D. W. Horton, Jr., '30, Petersburg, Va.; J. Welch Harriss, '27, High Point; George K. Massengill, Jr., '31, Raleigh; G. T. McArthur, '20, Durham; Mattie Cousins, '32, Durham; O. B. Ader, '26, Durham; Reba Cousins, '30, Durham; Violette Judd, '30, Várina; Evelyn Hancock, '30, Durham; J. H. Separk, '96, Gastonia; H. G. Howie, '30, Charlotte; Verona Blalock, '28, Willow Springs; Bessie Whitted Spence, '06, Durham; J. A. Dailey, '96, Pittsboro; Mary Johnson Livengood, '04, Durham; C. H. Livengood, '04, Durham; H. S. Broome, '27, Franklinton; Kate Lee Hundley Harris, Durham; Frances Markham Briggs, '09, Durham; M. Arnold Briggs, '09, Durham.

Charles H. Gay, '29, Durham; Chisman Hanes, '30, Durham; Harold V. Walters, '30, Durham; Hugh A. Sawyer, '31, Mount Airy; Ralph W. Fonville, '31, Mebane; C. H. Teague, '20, Greensboro; H. C. Bost, '29, Greensboro; P. W. Smith, '29; C. D. Barclift, Jr., '27, Leasburg; S. J. Starnes, '29, Yanceyville; W. H. Rousseau, Jr., '30, Durham; Marshall Pickens, '25, Charlotte; Mrs. A. J. Jenkins, '29, Goldsboro; Sam T. Carson, '21, Greenville; R. J. Tyson, '21, Greensboro; Jack L. Kirkland, '31, Durham; Lefty Jenkins, '31, Maiden; Mayre Shipp, '29, Durham; Helen Shipp, '32, Durham; T. B. Brock, '30, Mamers; H. O. Lineberger, '14, Raleigh; J. M. Templeton, Jr., Cary; Nellie Grey Wilson, '31, Oxford; Madge Colclough, '31, Durham; Jack Holt, '31, Durham; F. C. Williams, '97, Pittsboro; Ethel Merritt, '24, Albemarle; Walter Lee Lanier, '30, Durham; Ernest C. Hester, '29, Durham; W. F. Howland, Jr., '30, Durham.

E. A. Finch, '20, Greensboro; B. H. Black, '95, Scotland Neck; J. L. Horne, Jr., '09, Rocky Mount; James Simpson, '24, Rocky Mount; R. K. Shaver, '31, Gold Hill; Garland B. Daniel, '20, High Point; H. W. Fowler, '30, Durham; Blake B. Harrison, '23, Raleigh; Stuart H. Robeson, '31, Raleigh; Wharton G. Separk, Jr., '31, Raleigh; Harris Latham, Jr., '31, Washington; F. H. Brinkley, '31, Greensboro; K. C. Corbitt, '29, Kansas City, Mo.; M. I. Cline, '30, Henderson; J. Raymond Smith, '17, Mount Airy; Fred Folger, '23, Mount Airy; Spencer Bell, '27, Charlotte; William H. Lander, '23, Madrid, Spain; Glenn Mann, '31, Durham.

New Members of Alumni and Alumnae Councils

Following is a list of the new members elected by various class groups to the Alumni and Alumnae Councils. These members, along with those already on the Councils, will be called soon to the annual fall meetings to be held at the University. Notices of this meeting will be issued at an early date.

Regarding the names appearing below it may be explained that each class holding a reunion on the occasion of its fifth anniversary or a multiple thereof nominates two candidates for membership on the Alumni Council and two for the Alumnae Council. A brief record of these four persons is prepared by the Alumni Secretary and sent to all members of the class. The ballots are mailed not later than August 15 and ballots not returned by September 15 are not counted. From these nominations members of the class choose one man and one woman and return their choices marked on the ballot to the Alumni Office.

Alumni Council: Charles B. Markham, '06, Duke University; F. S. Aldridge, '96, Duke University; Robert T. Dubstan, '21, Greensboro College, Greensboro; George P. Harris, 26, Duke Endowment; H. G. Hedrick, '11, Durham; Benjamin L. Smith, '16, Shelby; Rev. W. A. Lambeth, '01, Durham.

Alumnae Council: Olive Faucette, '26, 115 Watts Street, Durham; Annie Pegram, '96, Greensboro College, Greensboro; Maude Wilkerson Dunn (Mrs. W. B.) '06, 509 Milton Ave., Durham; Laura Mae Bivins Britt (Mrs. J. H.) '16, 401 Bennett Street, Greenville, S. C.; Mary Louise Cole, '21, 603 Alston Ave., Durham; Mattie Lou Ola Tuttle (Mrs. I. C. Moser) '11, Asheboro; Elizabeth Moore, '01, Rockingham.

Statistics Compiled Regarding Students of Duke University

Out of Record-Breaking Enrollment of 2,658, Total of 1,436 Are Undergraduate Men,
North Carolina Leading With 513—Nearly 40 States Represented Among Men in
Student Body—Score of Religious Faiths Included—Freshman Statis-
tics—Every Department at University Shows Record Enrollment

AN INTERESTING tabulation by the dean's office of students of the men's college of Duke University for their geographical representation and denominational affiliations shows 40 states and foreign countries and a score of religious faiths represented in the lists. Statistics for the other departments of the university along similar lines will also be compiled.

Enrollment figures from which the tabulation was made show a new record enrollment at Duke of 2,658 students for an increase in all schools and departments, of these 1,436 being undergraduate men. Women undergraduate students number 583. The Graduate School of Arts and Sciences has 225 students, the School of Religion 145, the School of Law 75, the School of Medicine 147, and the Nurses' School 60 students.

NORTH CAROLINA LEADS

North Carolina has an easy lead over other states in the number of students, showing 513 undergraduate men enrolled. Pennsylvania has 161 men, New York 123, New Jersey 100, and Virginia 82. There are 25 from the District of Columbia, 49 from South Carolina, 50 from Maryland, and 55 from Massachusetts; while Georgia is represented by 30 men, Tennessee by 26, Ohio 23, Florida 20, Kentucky 17, Alabama 20, and West Virginia 26.

Mexico, Brazil, Japan, Canada, and the Canal Zone have their representatives. Every Southern state is well represented and western states in the list include Minnesota, Wisconsin, Texas, California, Iowa, Colorado, and Nebraska.

MANY DENOMINATIONS

Methodists, like North Carolinians in regard to states, have an ample margin over other denominations, with 577 undergraduate men of that church registered. Presbyterians are second with 193 students, Baptists third with 162, and Episcopalians a close fourth with 151. Sixty-one students report no church affiliations. Catholics number 57, Lutherans 44, Congregationalists 41, Reformed 34, Hebrew 34, Christian 19, and Christian Scientists 13.

The list also shows 18 Protestants who do not state their denomination. Eleven Unitarians are registered, six are Quakers, three Universalists, three Moravian, three United Brethren, three Evangelical, one Independent, and one Salvation Army.

FRESHMEN STATISTICS

The 697 freshmen in the undergraduate school for men provide interesting data on the younger students at Duke. It is a cosmopolitan class, with 35 states and countries represented. As of the entire body of undergraduate men, North Carolina ranks highest in numbers with 173 members of the class of 1935. New York sends 67 freshmen, New Jersey 55, Pennsylvania 73, Virginia 32, South Carolina 17, Massachusetts 20, Georgia 22, Tennessee 18, Maryland 14, and other states from California to Maine from one to 11 students each. Every Southern state has sons in the class.

Only 19 freshmen have no church affiliations, according to the records. Methodists number 210, Presbyterians 103, Baptists 70, Episcopalians 75, Catholics 27, Christians 11, Christian Scientists 8, Congregationalists 20, Evangelical 3, Hebrew 11, Lutheran 20, Moravian 2, Independent 1, and Reformed 17.

Chapel Statistics

In view of the publication of the photograph on the cover page of this issue of the REGISTER, the following statistics regarding the University Chapel may be of interest:

Outside length, 292 feet, 8 inches.
Outside width at nave, 64 feet, 6 inches.
Outside width transept, 122 feet, 4 inches.
Height of interior columns, 50 feet, 4 inches.
Highest point of groined arches from floor, 72 feet.
Great windows, 44 x 22 feet.
Akoustolith walls and ceilings (and limestone).
Flagstone floor.
Seating capacity, approximately 2,500 persons.

Studies Migration of Animals From the Ocean to the Land

Dr. A. S. Pearse, Professor of Zoölogy, Spends Summer in the Tortugas, South of Florida, Continuing Research Previously Begun in This Subject—Finds Islands Fairly Alive With Large Birds—Four Problems Studied at Experiment Station

DR. A. S. PEARSE, professor of zoölogy at Duke, during the summer continued his studies of the migration of animals from ocean to land. He had spent a year in Asia in this study, returning to Duke last fall. This summer he worked in the Tortugas, south of Florida.

Tortuga is the Spanish word for turtle. There are seven of these little keys called Tortugas—just little keys surrounded by coral reefs, seventy miles from Key West and sixty-five miles from Havana, Cuba. All the fresh water comes from the rains and must be stored in cisterns. On one of them, an island about three-fourths of a mile long and about a fourth of a mile wide, the Carnegie Institution of Washington has established an experiment station. To this station scientists are sent to carry on research work. Dr. Pearse was chosen by the Carnegie Institution as one of its representatives at this station this summer.

There is a lighthouse, also, on this island, and a fort. The lighthouse was built about 1800 and is still in use. The fort, Dr. Pearse said, is Fort Jefferson, built by the United States government in 1840 as an outpost against the Spaniards. An interesting historical fact is that a certain Dr. Mudd was imprisoned in the fort after his conspiracy against the Federal government. He was connected in some way with the Confederate

government and never became reconciled to its failure.

Fort Jefferson was used at various times up to and including the Spanish-American War. Since then it has been abandoned. It was at one time a magnificent old building. Now, however, even its windows and door frames have disappeared.

The experiment station employs nine men to care for the scientists. These include a cook and crews for the various boats. Four boats are maintained by the station. One of these is an ocean going motor boat. It makes the trip to Key West every two weeks for supplies. Another boat provides a diving outfit for those who wish to study sea plants and sea animals. Diving suits make it possible for the scientists to study at first hand conditions below the surface of the ocean. Dr. Pearse says that the fish are so tame that they swim right up to the glass in front of the diver's nose.

The islands are fairly alive with big birds. Dr. Pearse found large numbers of the noddy and sooty tern, and men o' war hawks. The ocean around teems with big fish and sea animals. One of the photographs which Dr. Pearse brought back with him is that of a shark taller than a man. In addition to a large number of photographs, he brought back with him a number of specimens. He is preserving the specimens and

SHARK AT TORTUGAS   SPONGE AT TORTUGAS

making slides of the photographs. These he will use as illustrations for the lectures he is to deliver just before Christmas at the exhibition of the Carnegie Institution in Washington.

Among the queer plants which grow on the island is one called sisal. It is a tall plant which grows high above those around it. The new little plants germinate in the flowers and fall to the ground ready to take root.

Dr. Pearse studied four problems while he was at the experiment station. First, he wished to determine the freezing point of animal's bloods. This would determine the amount of salt in the blood. He secured much better results in this work in the Tortugas than he did last year in Japan. He found land crabs which have less salt and more water in their blood than sea crabs. They are now reducing the amount of salt in their blood and becoming accustomed to the land.

His second problem was concerned with the large sponges of the Tortugas. He calls these sponges large hotels. Many of them are two and a half to three feet across. Dr. Pearse found one which was too large to put into an ordinary wash tub. A cross section of this sponge showed that it contained more than seventeen thousand little animals. These included among other shrimps and crabs and worms. Some of the crabs were in turn inhabited by parasites.

The third project was a study of the ponds on the island. In 1916 these ponds—there are two of them—were connected with the ocean. Dr. Pearse says that some storm cut them off from the sea. They have regular tides but these are not so great as those of the ocean and they are becoming less and less salty. Although only a hundred and fifty feet from the ocean, they are much less salty than it is. In these ponds, Dr. Pearse found a constant warfare between fresh water and salt water animals. In the ponds he found dragonflies whose blood is six and two-tenths salt—about twice as salty as the sea. He found water bugs and mosquito larvae, saltier than the ocean, living with fish from the ocean. The ocean fish, he found, change their type of food when they leave the ocean and live in ponds. The needle fish were eating, not smaller fish, as they do in the sea, but insects. The mullets live on in the mud, in contrast to their former salt water existence.

Dr. Pearse's fourth project dealt with parasites. He described several new species of these interesting little animals. He has already completed and sent away a paper on these parasites to be published by the National Museum. A paper on the freezing point of animal's blood is now in preparation. This paper is to be published by the Carnegie Institution. He has also been asked to write a popular paper on his work for the Carnegie Institution.

Dr. Pearse plans a trip next summer with Dr. Frank G. Hall, also a professor of zoölogy at Duke. These two scientists expect to study the fauna of the Yucatan country. The Yucatan is peculiar in that it has no rivers. The expedition is to be a coöperative one, sponsored jointly by Duke University and the Carnegie Institution.

Dean W. F. Tillett Completing Half a Century of Service

Dr. W. F. Tillett

Dr. W. F. Tillett, who was a Trinity student in "the Seventies," is rounding out this year a half century of service with Vanderbilt University. For 33 years he was dean of the School of Religion, he having resigned 17 years ago, but he continued to occupy the chair of Christian Doctrine.

Dr. Tillett received his M.A. and B.D. degrees at Princeton University, and on the completion of his studies there, he served one pastorate at Danville, Va., before going to the Nashville institution as chaplain. Subsequently he became an instructor in the School of Religion and in 1885 a professor in the chair which he holds at present.

Dean Tillett, as he is popularly known, is the author of several books, including, "Personal Salvation," which has been translated into other languages; and "Providence, Prayer and Power," published in 1926. He has also assisted in the compilation of hymnbooks, prepared an annotated hymnal, and collected about 1,000 volumes of hymnbooks, which he has given to the Vanderbilt School of Religion library.

Duke Alumni of Two States Gather In Palmetto Capital

Luncheon Held in Columbia on Saturday, Sept. 27, Proves a Most Successful and Interest-
ing Affair—Governor Blackwood and Other Distinguished South Carolinians
Present as Honor Guests—Dean Wannamaker's Address Features
Occasion Attended by 200—President S. B.
Moyle in Charge

SATURDAY, September 27, was observed as Duke Alumni Day in Columbia, South Carolina. The opening football game of the season between Duke and the University of South Carolina made this an auspicious time to have a gathering of alumni from the Palmetto state, augmented by quite a number from North Carolina, and the day was a most interesting one in various ways, though Duke lost, 7-0.

Under the direction of Samuel B. Moyle, president of the South Carolina Association of Duke alumni, assisted by Professor Ernest Green and other Duke alumni in the South Carolina capital, arrangements had been made for a get-together of Duke men and women from various parts of the two states. Secretary William Lykes, Jr., of the Chamber of Commerce, and other members of that organization assisted in making the day an exceedingly pleasant one for the "old grads" from the two states.

The luncheon, held at noon, at Hotel Jefferson, was a notably interesting and successful affair. About 200 alumni were present in the large banquet hall of the hotel. Music was furnished by "Jelly" Leftwich and his University Club Orchestra. President Moyle presided as toastmaster in a most efficient manner, and every feature of the occasion was delightful. The room had been beautifully decorated with United States flags and Duke colors.

Dr. William H. Wannamaker, vice-president and dean of Duke University, was the principal speaker at the luncheon. He called attention to the constructive work being done at Duke at the present time and combated the erroneous idea seemingly held by some that somebody at Duke University has thought that a great university might be built overnight. Even before the

S. B. MOYLE
President of the South Carolina
Alumni Association

foundations for the new plant were laid at Duke, leaders of the various schools and departments of the University had been working diligently building upon the foundations laid through many years to augment and accentuate the work being done along various lines in a way that would be worthy of the confidence placed in the University by the late James B. Duke when he signed the Indenture of Trust making possible Duke University. Dr. Wannamaker declared that the material side of the proposition involved in the erection of handsome buildings had been completed to a considerable extent and that now the University was in the stage of progress and problems involved in the building up of a great institution. He asked for the support of the alumni in making possible a development of the kind that the administration of the University has in mind. In his remarks Dean Wannamaker paid tribute to President William P. Few and Dr. Robert L. Flowers, who were unable to attend the luncheon because of engagements elsewhere, and to Mr. A. C. Lee, chief engineer.

Dr. H. N. Snyder, president of Wofford College, Spartanburg, S. C., delivered the invocation after which the Duke alumni were welcomed to Columbia by Dr. L. B. Owens, mayor, on behalf of the city, and by former State Senator Tom B. Pearce, on behalf of the Chamber of Commerce. Henry R. Dwire, Director of Public Relations and Alumni Affairs, made the response to the welcoming addresses.

Guests introduced by Chairman Moyle to those present included the following: Governor Ibra C. Blackwood of South Carolina, Dr. L. T. Baker, president of the University of South Carolina; Dr. J. P.

(Continued on page 318)

Dr. Clement Vollmer Talks of Conditions in Germany

Duke Professor, Who Spent Summer There Doing Work in Goethe and Schiller Archives, Found Country in a Well Organized Situation—Saw No Disorder of Serious Nature During His Stay—Hitlerites Cause Some Concern

DR. CLEMENT VOLLMER, professor of German at Duke, accompanied by Mrs. Vollmer, spent virtually the entire summer in Germany, paying short visits to France, Belgium, and Holland.

Dr. Vollmer's work was done in the Goethe and Schiller Archives in Weimar. Weimar, he says, is a very interesting little city. It was here that the constitution of the German republic was written and ratified, in 1919. It is called the Weimar Constitution to distinguish it from that of the empire.

Weimar, a city no larger than Durham, has, among other notable enterprises, a municipal swimming pool which would be a credit to any city much larger. Not far away from Weimar, at Jena, seat of a great university, Dr. and Mrs. Vollmer visited the plant of the great Zeiss firm. This corporation manufactures lenses for cameras, opera glasses, telescopes, and astronomical observatories. Many of the large observatories in America have been equipped from these factories. The Zeiss firm is now developing a type of illumination which they hope will light a city at midnight as it would be at noon.

The Duke visitors were much interested in the neolithic village which has been uncovered near Cologne, in Germany. This is the first complete village of that age to be unearthed, and it is one of the great archeological discoveries of modern times. Five thousand years old, it gives more completely than any other source a picture of the life of that day.

The Goethe and Schiller Archives contain a very large per cent of all the original manuscripts and documents concerning these two great writers. The Duke professor examined the original correspondence of Goethe and Schiller with Americans, with a view to finding what relationship existed between these classic leaders of Germany and the great Americans of the early part of the nineteenth century. His work is not completed, as yet, but he is satisfied that at least a cordial understanding existed between the literary lights of the two nations at that time.

Prof. Vollmer found that the German people, them-selves, feel that Goethe was by far the leading writer of all time in Germany. They are preparing to celebrate, on a very large scale, the centenary of his death next year. This celebration is taking on the proportions of America's Washington Bi-Centennial. In connection with the celebration it is desired to re-build and restore the Goethe National Museum at Weimar. This museum is at present housed in the old home of Goethe. It is the plan of those in charge of the work to restore the whole property to its orig-inal condition. There appears, however, to be serious danger that the work will not be completed in time for the celebration because of lack of funds.

He saw other evidences of poverty in Germany also. The usual summer manoeuvers of the army were cut to about one-fourth of their usual size. Germany, the home of some of the greatest of the world's X-ray specialists, sent no delegates to the International Roentgen Congress, in Paris. The Germans are de-termined, however, that if it is at all possible to secure the money, they will send a good team to the Olympics, in Los Angeles in 1932.

Dr. Vollmer says that he found Germany in a well organized condition. There was little appearance of the depression. Although Germany has an army of 5,000,000 unemployed, very little evidence of it ap-peared on the street. Unemployment Aid Insurance

AT THE UNIVERSITY OF HEIDELBERG, GERMANY

is very well organized and the government puts the unemployed to work as fast as possible.

The Duke professor saw no disorder of a serious nature during his entire stay in Germany, although he visited nearly every large city in that country. The most inconvenient days were those of the week of July 14, when all banks were closed. Election day, August 9, when the Germans expected serious riots, especially in Berlin, passed off with good order.

On August 11, Constitution Day, corresponding to our Fourth of July and the French Fourteenth of July, a monster celebration was held in the Reichstag. Through a friend in the Department of the Interior, in Berlin, Dr. and Mrs. Vollmer secured special tickets for this celebration. They sat within a few feet of the president, Von Hindenburg, who is eighty-four years old, but who still walks as straight and erect as a man of fifty and makes a very fine figure.

The Hitlerites seem to be exciting the young people of Germany, particularly, those who feel that Germany ought to recover faster than she is recovering. But at the slightest sign of disorder, on their part, the government puts a stop to it. Hitlerite newspapers are suspended the instant they suggest revolution. The same treatment is accorded the communists, who compose the lowest element of the larger cities.

Prof. Vollmer talked with several members of the German government. From each of these he received the same reply to his question as to Germany's future.

"If the Allies can see their way clear to easing up on the financial demands, Germany can keep its house in order. There is no danger of an overturn if the financial burdens are not made so great as to enslave the people."

The Germans are still very much concerned about the war guilt issue. Several modern historians, including Professor Fay, of Harvard, have shown that the Germans were not alone responsible for the war. The committee appointed by the United States Senate to investigate the question reached the same conclusion. The Versailles Treaty, which the Germans were forced to sign, however, places all the blame for the war on her shoulders. The Germans are chafing under that. This is true particularly because the huge indemnities were imposed on Germany because of this alleged guilt. They say that if the stain of guilt has been placed on six nations, instead of one, logically, one should not be asked to bear all the financial burdens. A recognition of this fact would pave the way for a reduction of the indemnities.

The Germans are concerned, also, about disarmament. The Versailles Treaty promised that the rest of the world would reduce their armaments after disarming Germany. They claim that this has not been done. They say that they are willing to give to France virtually any guarantee that she wishes, in order that France may feel secure, provided the world gives up its terrific armament expenditure and makes an honest effort to reduce its present armaments.

47 States, 30 Nations, 100 North Carolina Counties Represented In the Duke Alumni Files

Records just compiled in the Alumni Office of Duke University show that 6,544 former students of the institution are enrolled in the alumni files. One hundred counties in North Carolina are represented in the list, forty-six other states of the Union and twenty-nine countries outside the United States. Oregon is the one state not represented.

A perusal of the records reveals some interesting facts and figures, showing the steady growth of the alumni work at Duke, and the expanding circle of the University's influence. During the past year 655 names have been added to the list. For the first time every county in North Carolina is represented, and during the past year one more state and six countries overseas have been added to the alumni registration.

Alumni whose cards are now in the files number 4,988, of this total 3,495 being from North Carolina, 1,419 from other states, and 74 from foreign countries. Of the alumnae, North Carolina is represented by 1,184, other states by 349, and foreign countries by 23. The total, including both alumni and alumnae, is 4,678 for North Carolina, 1,768 for other states, and 97 for foreign countries, this giving the grand total for alumni and alumnae of 6,544, as stated above.

The 655 names added to the list during the past year represent another graduating class, and in addition several hundred names of alumni who for various reasons have not before been in the files, quite a number of them not having been located. A diligent effort is being made constantly to increase the list so that it will represent all the alumni of the institution wherever they may be located, and whatever vocation they may be pursuing.

Duke Community Honors the University's Founder

Duke University officials and representative students took part in brief exercises on Saturday, October 10, at the tomb of James B. Duke on the occasion of the sixth anniversary of the death of the philanthropist and university founder. Mr. Duke died less than a year after creating the Duke Endowment, which not only made the expansion of Duke University possible but established several philanthropies operating throughout the two Carolinas.

In the group which gathered to place a wreath at the portal of the Duke family mausoleum are, left to right: Dr. Frank C. Brown, comptroller; President W. P. Few; Dean W. H. Wannamaker; Dr. Wilburt C. Davison, dean of medicine; Dr. Justin Miller, dean of law; Dr. W. H. Glasson, graduate school dean; Dr. Elbert Russell, dean of the school of religion; Dr. M. T. Plyler, of the *Christian Advocate;* Rev. J. C. Wooten, university trustee; Henry R. Dwire, director of public relations and alumni affairs; J. Foster Barnes, director of social and religious activities; William Farthing, president of the student Y. M. C. A.; and Martin Green, president of the Men's Student Government Association.

Student Journalists Meet

More than 100 journalists gathered at Duke on October 22-24 for the fall convention of the North Carolina Collegiate Press Association. A full program of addresses, dinners, round-table discussions, and social events featured the three-day session. Edward Thomas, editor of *The Chronicle*, president of the association, presided over the meetings. J. L. Horne, Jr., of Rocky Mount, president of the North Carolina Press Association, spoke at the Thursday evening banquet. Henry R. Dwire, Duke director of public relations; Dr. J. B. Hubbell, of the Duke English department; A. L. Brandon, of Rocky Mount; Lewis Carr, of Chapel Hill; and J. P. Hardison, of Raleigh, led interesting discussion groups.

Some Alumni Personalities

Harry M. North, '99, who received the honorary degree of D.D. in 1925, is presiding elder of the Raleigh district of the Methodist Episcopal Church, South. He was at one time headmaster of the Trinity Park School and is now a trustee of Duke University. He is a member of Phi Beta Kappa. Dr. North was a member of the General Conference of his church in 1922; Christian Education Secretary of the North Carolina Conference, 1921-27. He has recently written a book, "The Harvest and the Reapers," published by the Cokesbury Press, the work containing, among other features, a most appreciative introduction by President W. P. Few, of Duke University.

HARRY M. NORTH

William Moore Speed, '04, is president and treasurer of the Austin-Heaton Company, of Durham. A recent article in the Durham *Herald-Sun* stated that it takes more than 1,000,000 bushels of wheat yearly to keep this immense flour plant busy. The company is one of the oldest, most successful and stable of Durham enterprises. The plant now has a capacity of 800 barrels of flour per day, with an annual production of about 240,000 barrels. A quantity of mill feeds is also manufactured. Mr. Speed is secretary and treasurer of the Durham County Alumni Association.

WILLIAM MOORE SPEED

Frank M. Warner, '27, was recently elected activities secretary of the Railroad Branch of the Y. M. C. A. in New York City. In his new position he will promote and supervise activities of all kinds among the young railroad men in the New York branch "Y." The building is in process of completion and when finished will represent an expenditure of about $1,600,000. After leaving college Mr. Warner became director of young people's work at West Market M. E. Church, Greensboro, and later boys' work secretary of the Y. M. C. A. of that city. He has been notably successful in his work with young men.

FRANK M. WARNER

Mussolini is Spending Much on Archaeological Projects

Duke University Visitors to Italy Are Interested in the Dictator's Policies—Dr. and Mrs. Nelson Visit Famous Monasteries—Mountain Climbing in Apennines One of Interesting Features of Their Trip

DR. E. W. NELSON, professor of European History at Duke, Mrs. Nelson and their two children, with their colored nurse, "Nanny," recently spent several months in Europe. Much of their time was spent in Italy, where Dr. Nelson was engaged in historical research.

Professor Nelson last year was invited to contribute a volume on the "Renaissance" in a series on the history of Europe. About the same time, he was appointed as a Research Fellow in Humanities by the American Council of Learned Societies, supported by the Rockefeller Foundation. He was assigned to work in Italy. With these two objectives, he and his family left Durham in June of last year. Until January, he was occupied with research in the Cornell University Library. In January, the entire family sailed for Italy. Landing at Genoa, the old home of Columbus, they proceeded immediately to Rome.

He worked at Rome in the Vatican Library. He insists, however, that just now the Vatican Library is not in Rome but in Vatican City. This is due to the fact that since the break between the pope and Mussolini, the pope declares that the Vatican City is not a part of Rome. The Nelsons remained in Rome until May. They were there during the disturbances when St. Peter's was bombed. Mrs. Nelson gives a very interesting account of those days and of her own visit to Sicily, which she considers one of the most beautiful of the places visited.

During their stay in Rome they visited a number of other cities and interesting places. Among these were Ostia, the ancient seaport of Rome; the Villa d'Este, at Tivoli, one of the old Renaissance villas; Venice; Modena, the home of the Este Library, founded by the Este family, in the fifteenth century; the villa of Horace, famous Roman poet, in the Sabine hills; and Innsbruck, in Austria.

Dr. Nelson was especially interested in two old monasteries. Both of these are Benedictine. The first is the Abbey of Monte Cassino. The family spent a night with the monks in the old Abbey, having reached there too late to return to the city. The Abbey of Monte Cassino was the first of all those founded by St. Benedict. Its fourteen hundredth anniversary was celebrated in 1929. It has been, since its founding, a center of classical learning. Whether other monastic libraries were confiscated by the state the monks of Monte Cassino were allowed to keep theirs.

The other famous monastery is Subiaco. It is much nearer Rome than Monte. Cassino. Subiaco is famous as the birthplace of printing in Italy. The books of its library, however, have been confiscated long ago by the state.

A visit to North Italy gave the Nelsons some mountain climbing in the Apennines. They visited there the city of Urbino. The home of the Duke of Urbino, one of the principal founders and patrons of libraries, during the Renaissance, remains there.

In South Italy, they travelled through the Tiulli country. Tiulli is the name given the strange cone shaped houses built by the inhabitants. Each family builds one little cone shaped room, adding others as the family increases.

Count Ginori, of Larderello, asked Professor and Mrs. Georgia Abetti to bring the Nelsons to his home for a visit. Doctor Abetti is Royal Astronomer at Arcetri, near Florence. He has made extended visits to America and is well known among scientists here.

The Nelsons were much interested in the operations of Count Ginori, at Larderello. He has harnessed steam geysers and used the force for generating electricity which furnishes much of Tuscany with power. The constant driving of new wells is a dangerous and delicate operation. By-products of the operations include boric acid, soap, baking powder, and "dry ice." The water is full of boric acid. One of the chief boric acid establishments of the world is located there. The "dry ice" is made of compressed carbon dioxide generated from the steam. Dr. Nelson says that this may have been where Dante got some of his ideas of hell. Mrs. Nelson says that it is one place where the workers can have steam heated homes free.

In May, Dr. Nelson moved to Florence, where the family lived until they returned to America in September. A beautiful Italian villa, located several miles from the city, furnished them a delightful home during their stay there. Dr. Nelson continued his work in the National Library, located there. Florence was once the capital of Italy. The National Library, established during that period, received many sets of books from the confiscated monastic libraries. In 1923, a new building for the National Library was started. The building operations, however, ceased, before its completion, because of lack of money. In Florence, also, is the Laurentian Library, founded by the Medici.

Dr. and Mrs. Nelson brought back with them many books, magazines, newspapers, and pictures. One of the books is an attack on the pope which was published just before the controversy arose over the Catholic Action societies. This book was suppressed and supposedly confiscated a few hours after its appearance. Dr. Nelson, however, managed to keep his copy. A beautiful album of red Florentine leather, lined with rich silk, hand sewed and hand tooled, cares for their camera pictures. Many of these are quite intimate pictures of the family, the children, and visitors, against a beautiful Italian background. Others are wonderful views of Italian scenery. Some show the snow of the mountain tops, others the beautiful green of the Italian hillsides. Some are of old Roman ruins, others of modern Italian buildings.

Dr. Nelson says that it is hard to speak of Italian social and political conditions. The censorship prevents the people from talking much. Mussolini, he says, appears to be popular, except with the lower classes. His cheap excursions for the public seem to be winning him some popularity even among the lower classes. These excursions are virtually given to the people by the government which commandeers the trains, paying a small amount for their use. Dr. Nelson believes that Mussolini has the good of Italy at heart. From an economic standpoint, the fascist policy seems sound. Italy, Professor Nelson says, seems to be meeting conditions better than some other nations of Europe.

Mussolini is spending a great deal of money on archaeological projects. Recently, he went to enormous expense to raise two of the old Emperor Caligula's galleys. Renaissance engineers had tried to get these up and had succeeded in securing only a few pieces of the boats. Mussolini drained the entire lake. The galleys look like the hulls of great houseboats. It is possible to study their structure and admire the workmanship. The galleys were decorated with bronze wolf heads and lion heads. The expected treasure was not found in the boats.

From some points of view, this all seems a silly waste of money. But it is all a part of a great educa-

tional scheme through which Mussolini hopes to get the average Italian to understand and appreciate Roman history.

Duke Alumni of Two States Gather In Palmetto Capital

(Continued from page 306)

Kinard, president of Winthrop college; Dr. R. H. Bennett, president of Lander college; Dr. J. C. Guilds, president of Columbia college; Dr. W. K. Greene, dean of the curriculum of Duke University, and professor of English; Dr. W. C. Davison, dean of the Duke school of medicine; A. C. Lee, chief engineer in charge of the construction of the new Duke University plant; B. A. Early, executive secretary of the Alumni association of the University of South Carolina, and J. H. Woodward.

DUKE BAND IN FRONT OF SOUTH CAROLINA STATE HOUSE

Duke alumni were greatly enthused over the success of Duke Day in Columbia and much credit was given to President S. B. Moyle, of the South Carolina Association, who handled every detail in a most effective manner. Many of those present remarked that they had never seen an alumni affair handled more efficiently by a chairman. Mr. Moyle is an exceedingly enthusiastic alumnus and under his direction the South Carolina Association is proving a real force for the promotion of the development of Duke University.

Sororities Pledge 105

The eight sororities of Duke University Woman's College have pledged 105 students principally from the Freshman class following an unusually successful rushing season. Many enjoyable social events marked the rushing period in which a large number of young women participated. Nineteen states are represented by those receiving bids from the Greek letter groups.

Some Modern Tendencies in the Institutions of Higher Learning

Dean Alice M. Baldwin, of the Woman's College of Duke University, Summarizes Number of Present-Day Movements in That Field in Address to Educators of State—
Some of the More Significant Tendencies Emphasized

The following ten-minute address on "Modern Tendencies in Institutions of Higher Learning" was delivered in July in-Gerrard Hall, at Chapel Hill, by Dean Alice Baldwin, of the Woman's College of Duke University, at one of the sessions of the Seventh Annual North Carolina Conference on Elementary Education. The REGISTER has received a number of most complimentary comments on Dean Baldwin's address, accompanied by several suggestions that it be published. This we are delighted to be able to do in this issue of the REGISTER.—Editor.

* * *

NOWHERE has this experimental age found a more fertile field for its activities than the American college and university. Faculty committees have been and are busy all over the country. Gradually new methods have been developed, some of which have been widely adopted. Some are still in the experimental stage.

To summarize within the limits of a ten-minute paper all of the present-day tendencies in this field is impossible, and I hesitate even to touch the subject superficially, for many of you know far more about it than I. All I can attempt is to mention some of the more significant tendencies and to give a few of the more interesting illustrations.

All of the new ways are intended to deepen and enrich the intellectual life and inspire respect for hard work and scholarship, to discriminate between the man who can never be more than mediocre and the potential leader, and to train the latter so that his potential power may become a reality, but this is not all. They are intended to help each young man or woman to learn the art of fine living.

In the attempt to understand and help students certain devices have been rather generally adopted. More complete information about a student before admission, psychological and college aptitude tests, personal interviews with applicants, freshman week, placement tests, fast and slow sections, orientation courses, courses in methods of study, faculty advisers, personnel bureaus, all of these are found in many institutions.

What President Lowell calls "the recognition that man is a whole . . . a complete whole, which is best guided by someone who, so far as possible, understands that whole," is bringing about other changes. There is a growing realization that many students and some of the ablest, suffer from more or less emotional disturbance brought about by family or personal problems, and that they need expert guidance to win and maintain mental and emotional health and stability. To meet this need, departments of health have been organized, correlating the work of psychologist, psychiatrist, the college physician, and the department of physical education. The work at Yale is a good example of what such a department can accomplish.

Another change is in the housing of students. Harvard, Chicago, Brown, Yale, the new college for women at Bennington, Vermont, for example, are trying to bring faculty and students into closer association in their daily living. The plans vary in details, but each house is to be a unit with library, living and dining rooms. Harvard plans to have resident masters and unmarried instructors in each house and to give married instructors the privilege of the commons. Bennington plans to build special quarters in each house for married instructors also.

But it is in the curriculum and in the attitude toward credits and methods of work that the most radical changes are being made. In general, the aim is to give a broader foundation of general knowledge and a deeper concentration in a special field, to get away from unrelated courses and course examinations and credits, to give the students greater freedom and responsibility, to stimulate every student to more work and independent thinking, and, in one way or another, to develop here also a closer, friendlier, more informal contact between faculty and student. There is still great variance in the amount of required work, from one college requiring seventy prescribed units from all students to St. Stephen's College, a part of Columbia University, which has just decided that the faculty will make a special program for each student.

declaring that "There is no such thing as an average student. Each student is an individual. We have decided to admit it and to insure our students and our staff freedom from all academic nostrums and tricks as may ignore the real problem—which is how best to train toward maturity each trainable man."

Some form of Honors work has been adopted by a large number of institutions. For the most part this is for the abler students only, beginning in the junior year, requiring independent work and frequent conferences with tutors or professors, and freeing the student from attendance on at least a part of the usual classes. In all such cases there is at the end of the senior year a comprehensive examination. In some institutions the work begins at the end of the freshman year. At Harvard, for instance, each freshman before the end of the year is assigned to a tutor who directs his work. At Princeton the preceptorial plan is used, where each class has one or two lectures and is then divided into small groups for informal discussion. Whatever the method, the purpose is to provide an opportunity for the give and take of informal argument and discussion in pleasant, informal surroundings. It seems to be the consensus of opinion that this system has raised the standard for teachers as well as for students. A man must be at his best if he is to guide a few brilliant students over a wide field and he must be very skilful to draw them into real, informal discussion rather than to answer questions or to indulge in learned monologue.

A few colleges are trying out what is known as "the reading period." Next year Yale is abolishing all mid-year examinations and half-year courses and the final examination in each course is to be more comprehensive than hitherto. There are to be two reading periods of two weeks each during the year and a final period of one week before the final examination.

In some institutions there have been experiments with new subjects or new arrangements of old subjects. There is a growing recognition of the necessity of helping students to understand family life and all kinds of human relationships if they are to live happily in this complex world. The work of Professor Groves at the University of North Carolina and the work at Goucher, Yale, and Vassar are interesting examples. At Vassar there is the unique department of Euthenics, or, as it is defined, "the science of efficient living." In the summer Vassar holds an *Institute of Euthenics* for its graduates, usually young wives and mothers, who come, sometimes with children and husbands, to find a wise answer to the problems they are facing. The various plans for alumni education, Yale's *Institute of Human Relations*, institutes and conferences held at Rollins, the University of North Carolina, the University of Virginia, and Williams College are examples of the attempts the colleges are making to help men to more intelligent living, whether in domestic, industrial, or international relationships.

The art of living demands also an appreciation of the fine arts. There are a number of colleges experimenting along such lines. To give only a few illustrations. The work of the University of North Carolina in drama is known to everyone. Smith and Cornell, among others, are doing unusual work in music; Hunter College, Vassar, Wellesley, and Sophie Newcomb in painting and other fine arts. In this field some of the smaller, less well-known colleges are doing sincere work, although some is of questionable quality.

Such experiments as these are more or less common to many colleges and universities. There are a few more radical experiments which are being watched with interest, I can mention only a few of them. First, the public Junior Colleges of California. In 1910 there was one, in 1931 thirty-seven, with an enrollment of fifteen thousand regular students and five thousand in special day and evening classes for adults. In a recent article W. C. Eells says that these colleges are decentralizing education in California. The opportunity they offer for adult education in many counties is, I think, one of their most significant features. There are also various private junior colleges of a new type, such as Sarah Lawrence in New York state, an outgrowth of the progressive education movement, interested primarily in developing appreciation, aesthetic judgment, and a cultivated taste. The rapid growth of junior colleges, especially in the north and west, and the apparent tendency to separate sharply the junior and senior colleges in some universities has been a challenge to the four-year college. At the recent conference at Rollins College, with John Dewey as presiding officer, the answer was overwhelmingly in favor of the four-year college.

Some of these smaller college are today engaged in widely different experiments. Antioch College in Ohio has worked out the unique plan of alternating regular periods of study and class-room work with equal periods of work at a trade or profession. Under this plan it takes from five to six years to complete the work required for graduation.

Whittier College in California, a Quaker institution, is attempting, in its own words, to "restate and re-align all the departments and subjects of the curriculum so they shall one and all contribute to a Christian philosophy of life. . . . It is an excursion into religious education;—not mere education in religion."

Rollins College in Florida conducts all its classes as conferences two hours in length. There are no cuts, no required outside preparation, and each student may go ahead as rapidly as he is able.

Duke Professor's Experiences in Spain During Revolution

Dr. Earl Hamilton Working in a Building Which Was Attacked on One Occasion By Anti-Clericals—New Government Has Already Reduced the Spanish Standing Army—Duke Professor Found Spaniards Very Courteous

DR. EARL J. HAMILTON, professor of economics in Duke University, has returned to the campus after an absence of eighteen months in Spain. Doctor Hamilton is the delegate for Spain on the International Scientific Committee on Price History. This committee was formed to control a grant from the Rockefeller Foundation for research in price history in Spain, France, England, Austria, Germany, and Holland.

Professor Hamilton says that the purpose of the committee is "to give us better knowledge than we now have concerning the behavior of prices over a long historical period; to detect, if possible, the existence and periodicity of business cycles before the Industrial Revolution; to determine the effects of violent price changes on the distribution of wealth as between different social classes; and to learn the influence of economic changes as evidenced by and reflected in prices in the rise and decline of nations."

As a result of his research in Spain, Dr. Hamilton is preparing for publication a four volume work on "Money, Prices and Wages in Spain from 1501 to 1800," and a two volume account of "Money, Prices, and Wages in Aragon and Navarre from 1350 to 1500." The first two volumes of this work, which deal with the period of 1501 to 1650, are to be published sometime in 1932, possibly before Dr. Hamilton returns to Spain for the completion of his work. These will discuss the greatest price changes in the history of any country that was on a "hard money" basis, because of the influx into Europe of the precious metals from the mines of Spanish-America. Presumably, those metals, being shipped in through Spain, produced more violent price changes in that country than elsewhere.

Prof. Hamilton, in his search for material in Spain, travelled throughout the entire country coming into closest contact with the Spanish people of every class. He visited nearly every town in Spain of more than a thousand population. In such small towns as Leon, Burgos, Malaga, Cadiz, Sargossa, and Barcelona, he spent only a short time. Many months, however, were spent in the larger ones like Valladolid, Madrid, Seville, Medina del Campo, and Valencia. He was much impressed with the danger of the work.

He speaks of the unheated buildings, in which one faces pneumonia in winter; of the unsanitary conditions, which endanger the health in summer; and of the food drenched in olive oil and highly spiced. All of this was much more uncomfortable for an American accustomed to modern conditions. Dr. Hamilton tells of the difficulties encountered in securing access to the records, sources of material for his work. Often, he says, after one has travelled for days to reach a given community, one arrives there only to find that the archives have been closed for no more important reason than that the keeper is going fishing.

The most serious danger, however, which Dr. Hamilton encountered was the revolution which was in progress during the last part of his stay in Spain. He speaks of one occasion when the building in which he was working was attacked by the anticlericals. He had discovered records from 1553 to 1931 without a break or a gap. These records contained much that was of scientific importance. He and his staff of seven natives began work on these records at four o'clock in the afternoon. At 8:15, they were forced to discontinue their work and leave the building, which was

STREET CLEANING IN SEVILLE

literally torn to pieces by anti-clericals at 8:30. In this attack, priceless paintings were cut to pieces, and the library ruined. The relics of St. Thomas Villanueva, founder of the institution, were destroyed and his study wrecked. All the records prior to 1680 were destroyed, except a few which Dr. Hamilton was able to rescue from the municipal incinerator.

The sources of material for Prof. Hamilton's work he found in the charity hospitals, the convents, the monasteries, and the cathedrals, and in the records of the "House of Trade." The records of the religious institutions show prices paid for food, clothing, and other articles dispensed for charity, over long periods of time. These records were carefully kept and are accurate in detail. The fact that the church practiced indiscriminate almsgiving, and gave too much care to the poor contributed to the decline of Spain, Dr. Hamilton believes. He calls attention to the fact that this was recognized by contemporaries, even high church officials. The "House of Trade" was in charge of the India trade and outfitted the treasure ships which plied between Spain and America in the sixteenth century. These records furnished information concerning prices of that period. He has been able to assemble more material concerning prices in Spain for the hundred and fifty years from 1501 to 1650 than has been found concerning the prices in any other country for that period.

Prof. Hamilton's work received very favorable recognition in Spain. He became acquainted with the Director of Customs, whose work includes much of the same field as that of a secretary of a national Chamber of Commerce. A private secretary of this man was a reporter for the paper which corresponds to the Wall Street Journal of New York. An interview of this reporter with Dr. Hamilton was published in the Spanish paper. A part of this article, translated into English, was published in the Duke University ALUMNI REGISTER last fall.

The Duke professor found it very amusing to a man brought up in sophisticated America to see the sublime faith which the average uneducated Spanish native has in the new republic. He says that it is entirely analagous to the faith which the manumitted slaves had in the "carpet-bag" governments in the South, following the Civil War. The average Spaniard, says Prof. Hamilton, feels that he has nothing to do. He simply sits still, like a great big child, and waits for the government to take care of him.

The new government has made one move toward reformation. This is in the reduction of the army. Before the revolution, the country had an unusually large standing army. There was a commissioned officer for every ten privates and a general for every three hundred privates. But the country is headed toward the nationalization of land in excess of the one family farm, with small compensation to the owners. The use of tractors and of improved agricultural implements is forbidden by law. This movement, Dr. Hamilton believes, is not for the purpose of creating a peasant proprietorship, which might have many advantages. Its purpose, he believes, is to hold the land for the government on a communal basis. There is every reason to believe, he says, that the goods of the religious orders will be confiscated, and that the religious orders, themselves, will be expelled from the country.

Dr. Hamilton, however, has very fond recollections of the people of Spain and their officials. He speaks of their unfailing courtesy and kindness, which he says exceeded even that of our own Southland. Even when he was refused access to records he received every courtesy and sincere regret was expressed by the officials.

Dr. E. G. Moore, '80, Prominent Physician, Passes

In the death of Dr. E. G. Moore, of Elm City, N. C., of Class of 1880, Duke University loses one of its most devoted alumni. At the hour of his funeral the college bell was tolled as a mark of respect to his memory.

Dr. Moore died at his home on October 6 after an illness of several months, at the age of 70 years. He had practiced medicine for more than 45 years. He is survived by the wife and two children. The Wilson correspondent of the Raleigh *News & Observer* sent that paper the following regarding Dr. Moore's death:

"The deceased was a prominent physician and an extensive farmer, and also interested in business enterprises, and was thoroughly interested in everything that affected the welfare of the county and its people. Dr. Moore was also a gifted speaker, with a command of the English language that few men possessed.

"Dr. Moore will be sorely missed by all who knew him, and by his community which has long depended on him for counsel and guidance. He enjoyed a large

(Continued on page 318)

Duke Goal Line Crossed Only Once This Season

1931 Team, Under Direction of Coach Wallace Wade, Playing Great Defensive Game and Working Hard to Improve Offensive—Victory Over Villanova "High Spot" So Far—Adkins Wins High Praise From Noted Villanova Coach —Freshmen Win

ALLOWING their goal line to be crossed only once in five games, Coach Wallace Wade's Blue Devils have shown themselves to be one of the finest defensive teams in Duke football history.

The Devils reached the halfway mark of the 1931 schedule in the Wake Forest game and scores of the first five contests reveal that they have held the little white line in a wonderful way this season, although they had the misfortune of seeing the lone touchdown against them bring their only defeat.

Duke's loss to South Carolina was not unexpected. The Gamecocks have long been known as a "first game" team and they presented a formidable attack in downing the Devils. However, it was in this game that the lack of offensive punch when in scoring distance was first noted, for the Blue Devils had two chances to score in the first quarter but were unable to push the ball over.

On the following week-end the alumni came home to see Coach Wade make his debut in Duke stadium and the Blue Devils win a 13-0 victory over V. M. I. The Cadets were outclassed in every department of the game, their running attack stopped dead by the rushing Duke linemen.

Villanova came south from Philadelphia on October 10, slated to take their annual battle from Duke easily, but when they returned that night they carried along with them an 18-0 defeat. Duke's entire team played brilliant ball that day, the linemen charging into the Villanova backfield so fast that the Wildcat ball carriers could hardly get their hands on the ball before they were stopped. The Blue Devil linemen, ever alert, recovered three fumbles which were converted into touchdowns.

But probably the Devils thought too much the following week of the great showing they had made against Villanova. At any rate, the fighting Davidson Wildcats were just as determined as the Blue Devils that they were going to win the game and they battled to a scoreless tie. Last week Duke defeated Wake Forest 28-0.

The work of Emery Adkins, Durham boy, at center has probably been the most spectacular among the linemen. The Villanova coach, Harry Stuhldreher, who as a player was All-American quarterback for the Four Horsemen of Notre Dame, paid high tribute to Adkins after the game. He frankly said that the Duke star was one of the finest centers he had ever seen. Officials, coaches, scouts and sports writers have praised his play in all Duke games this season.

Pap Harton and Bill Bryan, tackles; Bert Fried-

EMORY ADKINS

DUKE CENTER PLAYING GREAT GAME

man, Pop Werner and Carl Shock, guards; Tom Rogers, Fred Crawford and Don Hyatt, ends, the first two sophomores, have stood firm against all scoring threats.

In the backfield Captain Kid Brewer has been the mainstay. His job this season has been hard since he was the only experienced ball carrier returning from last year (it will be remembered that he and Bill Murray did all that work for Duke last season).

In yardage gained from the line of scrimmage, the Duke captain has averaged over six yards a run and is winning wide recognition for his performances in games this season.

Lowell Mason is making a great field general for the Devils and does a lot of the passing. Mullen and Ershler have done good work at the blocking back post and John Brownlee, track star, and Nick Laney, sophomore, have turned in some good performances.

FRESHMEN START FAST

The freshmen started their campaign to retain the Big Five title with a 21-6 victory over N. C. State and in the game presented a halfback, Marion Brumbach, who bids fair to make a name for himself before the season is over.

In their next game the Imps had hard going with the Oak Ridge Cadets but were finally able to win 6-0.

Some of the frosh stars are Bryan and Tarrall, ends; Porreca, guard; and Brumbach, Cornelius, Lee, and McAnich, backs.

Herschell Caldwell, mentor of the Imps last season, is back as their coach again, assisted by Freddie Sington, All-American tackle for Alabama last year, and Alex Waite, former Asheville high school coach.

HARRIERS BEAT DAVIDSON

Before the football game at Davidson, Duke's freshman and varsity cross-country teams handed the Wildcats a double defeat, the Devils winning, 26-29, and the Imps, 17-45. Jerry Bray, Duke sophomore, finished first after the three and a half mile run.

Bob Tuttle, former Duke star, is coaching the harriers and is getting fine results. A large number are out for the team and this year's freshman runners give promise of bringing much strength to the varsity next season.

Dr. E. G. Moore, '80, Prominent Physician, Passes

(Continued from page 316)

practice and was active in this up to a year or more ago.

"Funeral services will be held from the residence tomorrow afternoon at 4:30 o'clock.

"Dr. Moore was born at Williamston November 13, 1861, the son of John Edwin and Martha Jolly Moore. He was educated at the Arrington high school at Rocky Mount, Conyers high school at Elm City and Trinity College, where he graduated in June, 1880. He took his medical degree from the University of Maryland in 1883 and passed the State board the same year in Tarboro.

"He was one of the charter members of the Wilson County Medical Society, member of the Tri-State Medical Association, Seaboard Medical Association, Fourth District Medical Society and member of the State Medical Society since 1890. He was one of the surgeons of the Atlantic Coast Line and served a number of years as member of the State Board of Medical Examiners. In 1894 he delivered the annual address before the State Medical Society. He had served as county health officer, as member of the boards of directors at both the State hospital at Raleigh and that at Goldsboro. He always kept abreast of his profession, several times taking special post-graduate work."

DR. HUBERT A. ROYSTER PAYS TRIBUTE TO DECEASED

"In the death of Dr. Edwin G. Moore, of Elm City, the medical profession of North Carolina has lost one of its leading members," said Dr. Hubert A. Royster. "Having served on the Board of Examiners with Dr. Moore, I am in a position to testify to his character, his ability and his personality. He was a man of unswerving honesty, of keen insight and of friendly disposition. In addition to a large private practice in which he was successful professionally and materially, Dr. Moore found time to attend medical society meetings, to mingle genially with his associates and to develop himself becomingly in the ways of study. None surpassed him as a ready and fluent speaker. He will be missed from the assemblies of his colleagues and will be remembered by his legion of friends for his loyalty and kindness."

Accountants Meet At Duke

Members of the North Carolina Certified Public Accountants Association held a three-day meeting at Duke University on October 22-24. Dr. Earl J. Hamilton, of the department of economics, and Dean Justin Miller of the school of law, were among the principal speakers. Dr. Hamilton spoke of the economic situation in Europe and its effect on the United States. The subject of Dean Miller's address dealt with the legal status of a county facing receivership. Members of the economics department at Duke and a number of Durham accountants joined in entertaining the visitors. Approximately seventy-five accountants from all sections of the state gathered for the meeting.

<table>
| Where They
Are Located | # News of the Alumni | What They
Are Doing |
</table>

News of the Alumni

Where They Are Located   **What They Are Doing**

Miss Elizabeth Aldridge, '24, Secretary of Alumnae Council, Editor

CLASS OF 1883

Rev. John B. Hurley was a member of the North Carolina Conference from 1883 to 1930. He took superannuate relations at the last conference. He is a member of the board of trustees of Duke University and a loyal supporter of the alumni work. He has had two children to attend Duke, Maude Hurley Chadwick, '10, and Leonard B. Hurley, '13, professor of English at N. C. C. W. in Greensboro.

Dr. William H. Nicholson is a retired physician. He makes his home in Henderson, N. C. He received his M.D. degree from the University of Maryland in 1889.

CLASS OF 1888

James J. Scarborough is district manager of North Texas for the National Life Company of Des Moines, Iowa. He is located at Sherman, Texas. Mr. Scarborough has four children and all of them attended George Washington University. His oldest daughter is an interne at Gallinger Hospital, Washington, D. C.

CLASS OF 1891

Ernest Deans is in the insurance and real estate business at 111 W. Nash Street, Wilson. He is secretary of the Wilson Loan Association and Manager of the Wilson Cotton Warehouse Company, a director of the First National Bank and the Wilson Trust and Savings Bank.

Thomas C. Daniels, secretary of the Elks Lodge at New Bern, N. C., returned to the campus for Homecoming. Mr. Daniels is a former captain of the Trinity football team.

CLASS OF 1892

Walter James Gregson lives on his farm at Central Falls, N. C.

Julius Clarence Gregson has been in the cotton manufacturing business since leaving college. He is connected with the Hadley-Peoples Maufacturing Company at Siler City, N. C. He married Miss Mabel Lee Hadley and they have three daughters.

CLASS OF 1893

Dr. Samuel P. Burt is a practicing physician at Louisburg, N. C. He is president of the Kiwanis Club and takes an active part in all community undertakings. His daughter, Lucy, graduated from Duke in 1928. She is teaching this year in Whiteville.

CLASS OF 1894

Dr. Goode Cheatham is a practicing physician at Henderson. His son, Dr. Goode R. Cheatham, practices medicine in Ray, Arizona. He is a member of the class of 1922.

CLASS OF 1895

Henry Elbert Gibbons is a crosstie contractor and makes his home in Hamlet, N. C.

CLASS OF 1897

George Edward Rives is an agent for the Atlantic and Yadkin Railroad Company. His home is in Goldston. He has been in railroad work since 1908.

Stephens S. Dent is secretary and manager of Fortune's, Incorporated, manufacturers of ice cream. His office is at 1681 Union Avenue, Memphis, Tenn. He is a Rotarian and a member of the Memphis Country Club.

CLASS OF 1898

Eli Walter Hill is an attorney-at-law at Beaufort, N. C. He gave valuable service during the World War, serving in France for several months.

CLASS OF 1903

Robert R. Taylor of Elizabeth City, N. C., has a son, Rives, in the freshman class at Duke this year. Mr. Taylor is a prominent insurance man.

CLASS OF 1907

C. E. Phillips took an active part in welcoming the members of the North Carolina Association of Real Estate Boards who met in Durham on October 9 for their annual convention. Mr. Phillips is secretary-treasurer of the local board.

CLASS OF 1911

In *Sales Management* for September, 1931, there is an article on "How One Sales Executive is Putting Fight Into the Hearts of His Men." This sales executive is James H. Warburton, who is general sales manager of the Marietta Chair Company, Marietta, Ohio.

CLASS OF 1916

In the Who's Who and Why column of the *Asheville Times* a few days ago the following appeared about Coleman Zagier of the class of 1916:

"Coleman Zagier, proprietor of the Man's Store, 22 Patton Avenue, is a native of Asheville. He began selling men's clothing in the store of his brother, R. B. Zagier, when he graduated from high school here. He kept up the practice during summers while attending college—first at Trinity College, which is now a part of Duke University, then at Johns Hopkins University.

"Mr. Zagier was a student at Johns Hopkins when the United States entered the World War. He closed his textbooks and joined the navy, serving through the conflict. He won the rank of ensign before the war ended. When the armistice was signed he returned to Asheville. He worked for his brother until, in 1922 he opened the store which he now operates.

"He married Miss Helen Bremen of Atlanta in 1924. They live at 25 Maney Avenue—and 'they' includes two young daughters.

"Mr. Zagier is a Kiwanian, a Shriner, and a member of Asheville Country Club. Golfing and hiking are his favorite sports. Athletic activities of any sort are his hobbies. He played football in high school and college and was manager of the Asheville high school baseball squad one season. That interest in scholastic sports has prompted Mr. Zagier to give trophies and cash awards for the high school's best all-round athletes."

CLASS OF 1917

H. C. Kearns, Jr., has moved from 2101 New Hampshire Avenue, N. W., Washington, D. C., to Hyattsville, Maryland.

Rupert N. Caviness has just opened the Caviness Service Station on S. Magnolia Street, Ocala, Florida. It is modern in every detail and prepared to give efficient service. Mr. Caviness has made his home in Florida for several years and is well known in his community.

CLASS OF 1918

Samuel Richardson Chandler of Lake City, S. C., is at present engaged in the tobacco business. He formerly practiced law, having received his LL.B. from the University of South Carolina.

H. Yates Edgerton visited the campus during the summer months. He is located in Atlanta, Georgia, at 992 W. Peachtree Street. He manufactures highway signs under his own patent.

CLASS OF 1920

M. A. Braswell was married on September 6 to Mrs. Audree Poole of Wilkes Barre, Pa. The wedding took place in the Holy Trinity Church, Philadelphia. Mrs. Braswell is a former resident of Charlotte but during recent months has been making her home in Wilkes Barre. Mr. Braswell is in the legal department of the R. J. Reynolds Tobacco Company, Winston-Salem.

CLASS OF 1923

Mr. and Mrs. Howell J. Hatcher of Morganton, N. C., announce the arrival of Howell J. Hatcher, Jr., on October 1.

Rufus Haywood Stark was born on July 9 at Greenville, N. C. He is the son of Mr. and Mrs. Rufus W. Stark (Sara DaShiell).

CLASS OF 1924

Frances Ledbetter is teaching this year in Rocky Mount. She formerly taught English at Davenport College, Lenoir.

Dr. Allison Lee Ormond left the State Sanatorium on October 1. He has been in ill health for the past eighteen months, but is much improved. He is now living near Rockingham. His mail address is Box 294.

Nellie Ruth Brock was married in Lawrenceville, Virginia, on September 27 to Mr. Clarence D. Nabers. Nell has been teaching for the past few years in Floral Park, L. I., New York. Mr. Nabers is a resident of Durham and holds a responsible position with the C. D. Kenny Company as manager. They make their home at 2122 Englewood Avenue.

Mr. and Mrs. Edgar B. Fisher of Gibson, N. C., announce the birth of a daughter on October 2. Edgar is pastor of the Methodist church in Gibson.

W. J. Bullock has been in educational work since leaving Duke. He is principal of the Cannon High School at Kannapolis, N. C., this year. He was formerly in Franklinton.

CLASS OF 1925

Richard H. Webb is located at Kings Mountain, N. C. He is in the dye department of the Neisler Manufacturing Company. Richard is the son of A. S. Webb, '96, superintendent of the public schools at Concord, N. C.

James Dixon Roberts is located in Dixon, Illinois, where he is connected with the State Highway Commission. He was married on October 3 to Miss Mildred Marie Bowen in Orion, Ill.

CLASS OF 1927

C. A. Waggoner, better known as "Firpo," has moved from Istanbul, Turkey, to Bombay, India. He is still connected with the American Express Company.

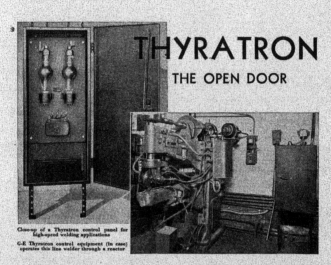

Edward H. Michaels and Miss Helen Pritchard were married at the home of the bride in Durham on September 17. Mrs. Michaels is an alumna of Peace Institute. Edward is connected with the Venable Tobacco Company in Durham. They make their home at 1011 East Trinity Avenue.

Mary Avera was married to Mr. Franklin Louis Davis on December 20, 1930, at Raleigh, N. C. She is living now at 245 E. Glenn Avenue, Auburn, Alabama. Her husband is assistant soil chemist at Alabama Polytechnic Institute.

Samuel N. Wrenn is a graduate assistant in chemistry at Pennsylvania State College this year. His address is Box 522 State College, Pa. Last year he was acting associate professor of chemistry at the Citadel in Charleston, South Carolina.

Rev. and Mrs. R. Grady Dawson announce the arrival of Mary Howland on September 19 at 332 Pacific Avenue, Jersey City, N. J.

On September 9, in Norfolk, Va., Margaret Hobgood was married to Mr. James Edward Ward, Jr. Mr. Ward is a member of the faculty at the University of Virginia and they will make their home in Charlottesville.

CLASS OF 1928

Ethel Abernethy is studying in Germany. Her address is Von der Tann, Strasse 20, Munich, Germany.

Ellen Huckabee is director of student activities at New Jersey State College for Women, located at New Brunswick. Ellen served as president of the women's student government association in her senior year. In the fall she returned and pursued graduate work in addition to serving as an assistant to the dean of women. She received her A.M. degree in English this spring. She is well fitted for her task at New Brunswick, having taken an active part in all campus activities while a student at Duke.

Verona Blalock is teaching at her home, Willow Springs, N. C. She taught for the past two years at Hickory.

Ruth Bright, '28, and Clyde Allison, '30, are teaching at Parkton, N. C., this school year.

W. W. Stanfield will complete his fourth year of medicine at the University of Richmond this year. He lives at 515 Franklin Street, Richmond.

Bob Hatcher has been connected with the Chase Harris Forbes Corporation for several months. They have recently opened an office in Houston, Texas, and Bob is in charge. His address is 2005 Second National Bank Building.

CLASS OF 1929

George Thomas Ashford is an accountant for the Pennsylvania Railroad at Philadelphia. He was married on December 22, 1929, to Miss Sarah Caroline McCormick. They live at 601 Baily Road, Yeadon, Pa.

Guy Taylor Hardee lives at the Allerton, 600 West 113th Street, New York City. He is working for the New York Life Insurance Company and at the present is being instructed by the company.

Mr. and Mrs. Matthew J. Bird announce the birth of Mary Lydè Bird on July 21, 1931, at Elm City, N. C.

Mr. and Mrs. Bernard H. Jones announce the birth of Virginia Jones on September 20 at Watts Hospital, Durham. They live at 317 West Trinity Avenue.

Mildred E. Holton is teaching mathematics in the Miami Senior High School. Her address is 1521 S. W. Second Street, Miami, Florida. She is the daughter of Thomas A. Holton, '06, who is principal of the schools in Perrine, Fla.

CLASS OF 1930

William V. Pappalardo is a law clerk for Belfatto and Belfatto, law firm, at 194 Market Street, Newark, N. J.

Frances Coleman lives at 6015 York Road, Baltimore, Maryland. She is secretary for the Connecticut General Life In-

surance Company. She was formerly secretary for the Dean of Nurses, Duke University.

Clarence Ligon Harris teaches science in the Bragtown High School, Route No. 2, Durham.

Mrs. Raymond F. Coltrane, nee Mary Elizabeth Braswell, lives at 1155 Willow Branch Avenue, Jacksonville, Fla.

Blackard H. McCaslin is managing a Chesterfield display factory at the corner of Jackson Avenue and Michigan Boulevard, Chicago, Ill. This corner is sometimes spoken of as "the busiest corner in the world."

John Paul Lucas is taking graduate work at Princeton. He traveled in Europe during the summer months. There was an interesting article in the September 20 issue of the *Charlotte Observer* telling of his trip through England and Scotland. The *North Carolina Christian Advocate* mentioned this write-up in the September 24 issue.

Horace Fowler is with the Liggett and Myers Tobacco Company in Durham. His home address is 616 West Chapel Hill Street.

C. C. Blalock of Durham is connected with the New York Telephone Company in New York City. His address is 135 Terrace-View Avenue.

Paul G. Trueblood, A.M. '30, was married on August 19 to Miss Helen Churchill. They were married in the Methodist church at Roseburg, Oregon, the home of both the bride and groom. Paul is teaching English at Friends University, Wichita, Kansas, this year.

Virginia Bowling and Russell Vernon Murray were married in Chase City, Va., on August 23. For several years Russell was connected with Hall-Wynne undertaking establishment in Durham but he is now in business in Sanford and they make their home at Chisholm Street.

CLASS OF 1931

James W. Moffitt, A.M. '31, is dean of men and assistant professor of history at the Oklahoma Baptist University at Shawnee, Oklahoma.

William Kendrick Owen is an agent for the Metropolitan Life Insurance Company with offices at 519 American Bank Building, Nashville, Tennessee.

Joseph Garland Winkler is pastor of the Methodist church at Hiddenite, N. C. He was married on June 11, 1930, to Miss Kathryn Louise Jones.

Henry Robertson Liggett is connected with the Insurance Company of North America with offices at 304 Connell Building, Scranton, Pa. He was married to Miss Elizabeth Ann Keffer on February 27, 1931.

Charles H. Livengood, Jr., has entered the law school of Harvard University. Charles made a brilliant record as an undergraduate at Duke, having been a member of Phi Beta Kappa, editor of the *Chronicle*, member of the *Archive* staff, an intercollegiate debater, a member of Red Friars, Tombs and other honor organizations. He is the son of Mr. and Mrs. Charles H. Livengood (Mary Johnson) of the class of 1904.

H. Alan Huth lives at 35 Van Reiden Avenue, Jersey City, N. J. He is employed by the William M. Mortimer Company, an insurance adjustment company of inland marine losses.

William Porter Sellers of Norfolk, Va., is studying medicine at Johns Hopkins University, Washington and Monument Streets, Baltimore.

William W. Graves, Jr., has a position in the Branch Banking and Trust Company, Fayetteville. He is the son of W. W. Graves, '97, of Wilson.

John Taggart is in the oil business at 112 Duke Street, Durham.

Lawrence T. Hoyle has charge of the stockroom of S. H. Kress and Company at Tampa, Florida. He lives at the Y. M. C. A.

Smoke a FRESH cigarette

Have you tried Camels?

THE steady increase in the sales of Camel cigarettes proves one fact beyond a doubt.

If you try Camels, the odds are very much against your ever going back to your old brand.

So great is the contrast between the delights of perfectly conditioned Camels fresh from the protection of the new Humidor Pack and the harsh, hot smoke from stale dried-out cigarettes, that your decision will be immediate.

The quality is there in the first place, for Camels are a blend of choice Turkish and mild Domestic tobaccos.

In factory-prime condition, with their rare flavor and their natural moisture still intact, they are a joy to the smoker.

Now this flavor is air-sealed-in by an outer wrapping of moisture-proof Cellophane, so that no matter where you buy Camels, in any land, in any climate, you are always certain to get fresh cigarettes in factory-prime condition.

And there are other advantages as well. For the Humidor Pack also protects the cigarettes within from dust and germs and weather conditions.

Start the day on Camels. See how much milder they are, how much more flavorful they are, how cool they are to the throat.

No peppery dust to irritate delicate membrane. No harsh, hot smoke from dried-out tobacco to burn the tongue or sear the throat.

Switch to Camels for a day, then leave them — if you can.

Tune in CAMEL QUARTER HOUR featuring Morton Downey and Tony Wons
Columbia Broadcasting System — every night except Sunday

DUKE UNIVERSITY
ALUMNI REGISTER

DUKE
UNIVERSITY
DAY

Friday, December 11, 1931

This will be the Seventh
Anniversary of the Sign-
ing of the Indenture of
Trust Making Possible
Duke University.

*At least 50 Local Meetings on that
day is the Goal!*

November, 1931

VOLUME XVII   NUMBER 11

The Sign of
Good Printing

The wise tourist plans his routes of travel from reliable road maps— then following the road directors he arrives at a definite point. This company will be glad to help you plan your special sales appeal, or help you with suggestions and direction that will bring greater profit from direct advertising. An experienced typographer will work with you in planning your illustrated catalogs or any printed materials in which you wish to bring an effective message to the buying public. Write us. Our service has steadily increased and widened since 1885.

THE SEEMAN PRINTERY, INC.
PRINTERS IN DURHAM, N. C., SINCE 1885

Good Printing is a Reliable Salesman for Your Products

Duke University Alumni Register

(Member of American Alumni Council)

Published at Durham, N. C. Every Month in the Year in the Interest of the University and the Alumni

Volume XVII   *November, 1931*   Number 11

In This Issue

Editor and Business Manager .... HENRY R. DWIRE, '02

Assistant Editors .... ELIZABETH ALDRIDGE, '24
                             ALBERT A. WILKINSON, '26

Advertising Manager .... CHARLES A. DUKES, '29

TWO DOLLARS A YEAR   20 CENTS A COPY

ENTERED AS SECOND-CLASS MATTER AT THE POST-OFFICE AT
DURHAM, NORTH CAROLINA

CIRCULATION INCREASING

The Duke University ALUMNI REGISTER now goes to every county in North Carolina, to 47 of the 48 states of the Union and to 29 other countries. Its circulation is constantly increasing. The desire is to make the REGISTER constantly more attractive to alumni and others as well, and the continued co-operation of former students of Duke to that end is solicited. One of the best ways to co-operate is to send in matter for publication, whether in the form of reminiscences or special articles.

THE COVER

By way of variety and to give special emphasis to Duke University Day, the usual picture cover on the REGISTER is eliminated this month. However, a particularly attractive cover is already being prepared for the December issue.

UNIVERSITY DEPARTMENTS

The publication from month to month of articles dealing with various departments of Duke University is being continued this month with a brief article on the department of philosophy. Another will be treated next month, and so on.

THE EDITOR.

DUKE UNIVERSITY FOOTBALL SQUAD FOR THE SEASON OF 1931

Front row (left to right): Joe Sink, Emery Adkins, Bill Bryan, Don Carpenter, Captain Kid Brewer, James Mullen, Weldon Harton, Don Hyatt, Harry Rossiter.

Middle row: Norman James, John Brownlee, Norman Remfeldt, Lowell Mason, Waite Hamrick, Horace Hendrickson, Claude Cook, Nick Laney, Walter Belue, Arthur Brehler, John Dougherty.

Back row: John Leight, student manager, Kenneth Abbott, Glenn Lemon, Henry Thompson, Melvin Stevens, Carl Shock, Al Means, Fred Crawford, Bert Friedman.

Duke University Alumni Register

Volume XVII | November, 1931 | Number 11

Editorial Comment

DECEMBER THE ELEVENTH

December the eleventh, 1924, is a date that is written large in the annals of Duke University.

On that day the late James B. Duke signed the Indenture of Trust making possible the University with its present equipment and its magnificent future prospects.

It is entirely appropriate that for the past several years the day should have been observed by Duke University groups in various parts of the country.

It is equally in order that this year, a year in which so many things have been accomplished in the furtherance of Mr. Duke's plans for the institution, the observance should be more general than ever.

For in this year the institution is establishing new records for enrollment and otherwise in all its schools and department; the magnificent new plant has been practically completed; many forward steps have been taken during 1931.

So it is peculiarly fitting that on Duke University Day this year more different groups should participate in the observance of the day, and in greater numbers, than ever before.

Then, too, there is another reason for a general observance of the day this year in a spirit of real devotion to Duke.

Progress inevitably brings problems.

One of these problems is that of correctly interpreting the institution, its purposes and ideals, to those outside its walls.

Sometimes there may be one misconception of those purposes and ideals; at another time there may be misunderstanding at a different point; misinformation may gain circulation from time to time.

Whatever may be the problem connected with the understanding of the institution and its ideals, it is important that alumni should do everything possible to aid in giving currency to a proper interpretation.

And there is no better time to gain information and inspiration for this task than at a Duke University Day dinner, when matters connected with the institution, its progress and problems, can be presented and discussed intimately and clearly and understandingly.

We do not feel that it is necessary to urge alumni and alumnae of Duke to come together on December 11 in the Duke University Day dinner and renew their allegiance to Alma Mater.

We are simply mentioning the matter in the full belief that every alumnus and alumna will make it a point to do everything possible on December 11 to aid in the furtherance of the ideals and purposes of Alma Mater.

If it is not possible for you to attend a Duke University Day dinner, there are other things that might be done in a spirit of helpfulness and coöperation.

If you can think of nothing else just simply write a letter to the Alumni Office, or to the REGISTER, giving some information that would be helpful to other alumni about yourself, about other former students of the institution, or about matters in which you think the Alumni Office should be interested.

And in doing this don't forget to pass on anything in the way of a criticism which you may have heard.

For nobody who is faithfully and intelligently attempting to do a worth-while job has any legitimate reason for objecting to constructive criticism.

So if you do not like the REGISTER, or anything the Alumni Office is, or is not doing, just let us hear about it.

We assure you that any suggestion will be received in the proper spirit.

A WORD OF APPRECIATION

Frequently there come to the ears of those in the Department of Public Relations and Alumni Affairs expressions from one source or another that are greatly appreciated.

Just the other day, for instance, an alumnus passed on to us a message of commendation from a recent visitor to Duke who lives in a far-away state.

He said that he had an idea in some way that, because Duke had a large endowment and a magnificent plant, perhaps there would be something of a rather cold, distant atmosphere on the campus; in other words, he wanted to see the institution, but he feared, as an utter stranger, that he might be given scant attention.

On the contrary, he came to Duke and was overwhelmed with kindness. He let it be known that he wanted to see something of the buildings and he was courteously turned over to an individual who seemed to think that his chief job for the day was to make him feel entirely welcome and at home.

He added that he had never enjoyed a few hours more anywhere than the time spent at Duke, nor was he ever shown greater courtesy.

Other similar remarks have been made from time to time.

Those here on the campus who know that the spirit of the institution is one of cordiality and courtesy and helpfulness wonder that anybody should expect a different attitude, for certainly the constant purpose is to make visitors feel at home.

And yet sometimes such impressions are likely to gain currency and it is gratifying to have such expressions as those quoted above from the visitor who was on the campus recently and who felt that he was treated so kindly.

The writer recently said in an Alumni Council meeting, and this is probably as good a time and place as any to reëmphasize it, that he hoped alumni and other friends of the institution would encourage other alumni and friends to visit the Duke campus whenever they happened to be in Durham, and to make it a particular point to call at the office of Public Relations and Alumni Affairs in the University Union.

Any possible help or information will be given, and courteous and competent young men are always available to show visitors things of interest on the campus and in the buildings.

PROGRESSIVE PUBLICATIONS

Alumni of Duke do not always realize just what is being done on the campus by the student publications.

Edited and managed by the students, these publications, including the weekly newspaper, the monthly literary magazine, the Annual and others, are interesting and effective and entirely deserving of the support of alumni of the institution.

Quite a considerable number of alumni subscribe to one or more of these publications. It is hoped that many others will do so.

The above is preliminary to saying that the *Chronicle,* the weekly student newspaper, is a progressive publication that has attracted and is attracting much attention, not only on the campus but on the outside as well.

Always progressive, one of its most effective recent enterprises was the publication on the evening of Friday, November 20, of an "extra" pertaining entirely to the Duke-Carolina game on Saturday.

The matter in the "extra" was timely and to the point, interesting and readable.

The spirit of the entire paper was fine.

A number of newspaper men who were here on the day of the Duke-Carolina game commented with enthusiasm upon the enterprise of the *Chronicle* staff in issuing the publication, in addition to the regular weekly number of the *Chronicle.*

THE DUKE PRESS

Speaking of publications, the REGISTER would again direct attention to a Duke University institution to which many alumni do not pay any particular attention.

In the several years of its existence the Duke University Press has published 56 volumes on various subjects, four within the past few weeks.

It is a real University asset that deserves alumni support.

Fifty Local Alumni Groups to Take Part in "Duke Day"

That Is the Goal That Has Been Set and Reports to Date Indicate That It Will Be Realized on December 11—This Will Be Seventh Anniversary of Signing by Late James B. Duke of Indenture Making Possible Duke University

REPORTS coming in daily to the Alumni Office indicate that there will be a more general observance than ever this year of Duke University Day. The time for this annual observance is December 11, the anniversary of the signing by the late James B. Duke of the Indenture of Trust making possible Duke University. The celebration will be the seventh in this series of yearly events, a series that has been regarded as vitally significant in the life of the University.

Last year there were 36 local Duke Day dinners in North Carolina and many other states, and even one in far-away Japan. This year it is expected to have at least 50 of these occasions, and instead of one gathering outside of the United States it is confidently expected to have at least two or three, perhaps more. It is quite probable that a celebration will be held in China.

The general subject for Duke University this year will be "Duke University: Its Progress and Problems." Members of the Duke faculty and administration will deliver addresses, in some cases there will be special musical programs and in various ways the Duke Day dinners will be occasions of real interest and profit. Definite assignment of speakers is now being made and complete details will be announced soon in the newspapers and otherwise.

It is estimated that several thousand people participated in one way or another in the Duke Day observance last year. Many alumni and friends of the institution who could not attend the meetings, showed, by donations made on December 11 and in other ways, that they were thinking of Alma Mater on Duke Day. This year each of the more than 6,000 Duke alumni, scattered in 100 North Carolina counties, 47 states of the Union and 29 other countries are to be asked to participate in some way in the celebration of the day.

To show the wide scope of the observance in the United States last year it is interesting to note that meetings were held as far south as Jacksonville, Florida, and as far west as Los Angeles, California.

New York, Washington, Atlanta, Richmond and other cities were included in the day's observance.

In these Duke Day dinners various matters pertaining to the interests of the University will be presented and the alumni will be drawn even closer than before, it is confidently expected, to the institution. The ties binding alumnus and Alma Mater will be accentuated and a deeper and broader relationship will be established.

Every single local alumni group is being asked to participate in Duke Alumni Day. Many are already making arrangements to that end. Others are expected to begin making plans at once. In the Alumni Office a force is working all day and sometimes into the night on the details incident to the proposition. "The best and most general observance of Duke Day in the history of the institution" is the goal that has been set. There is every reason to believe that it will be realized.

Art Exhibit Displays Negro Plantation Types In Groups of Paintings

Twenty-seven oil paintings by Mrs. Marshall McDiarmid Williams, of Faison, which portray negro plantation types, were featured in the autumn exhibition of the Art Association of Duke University beginning on Tuesday evening, Nov. 10, in the library of the Woman's College.

On the first evening of the exhibit the gallery was opened to members of the Association, and thereafter for a time the general public has been given an opportunity to view the unusual collection by one of the South's outstanding artists.

Mrs. Williams studied first under Fisher, at Washington, D. C., and afterwards under Alexander of New York. Starting her career of portrait painting, she soon achieved a state-wide reputation, and today is known as one of the South's foremost portrait painters. In the State House in Raleigh, in the Confederate museum at Richmond, and elsewhere, Mrs. Williams' portraits have been admired and will be permanently preserved.

Officers of Duke Alumni and Alumnae Councils are Named

Charles H. Livengood, of Durham, Elected Chairman of Alumni Group and Mrs. Mary Tapp Jenkins, of Kinston, of the Alumnae Body—Number of Matters of Business Considered at Fall Meeting of Two Councils

THE ANNUAL fall meetings of the Alumni and Alumnae Councils of Duke University were held on Saturday, November 14, with an attendance of more than 50 members of the two councils. Following the two council sessions in the morning, a joint luncheon was held at noon in the University Union. The entire day was a notably successful one in every respect.

ALUMNI COUNCIL

The meeting of the Alumni Council was presided over by Chairman T. G. Stem, of Oxford, Henry R. Dwire acting as secretary. The minutes of the last previous meeting were read and approved.

The secretary made a report covering the activities of the Alumni Office since the last meeting which was held on June 8. Attention was called to the record-breaking attendance of 728 on the alumni-alumnae luncheon at commencement; also to the work of the Alumni Office during the summer in compiling records and rendering other service.

The fall program for 1931 was briefly reviewed, including Homecoming Day on October 3, with its barbecue luncheon for alumni and other features; the observance of November as "Alumni Month" and the preparations already under way for "Duke University Day." Attention was called to the fact that 36 meetings were held last year, and that at least 50 this year are desired.

The matter of finances was discussed briefly, the statement being made that arrangements were under way for putting into effect the class agent plan for the raising of subscriptions to the Alumni Fund. This was recommended in a motion adopted at the June meeting.

Following the report of the secretary, there was a general and interesting discussion of various points presented, after which the following officers were elected on recommendation of the nominating committee:

Chairman—Charles H. Livengood, Durham.

Vice Chairman—T. A. Finch, Thomasville.

Secretary—Henry R. Dwire, Durham.

Executive committee—J. L. Horne, Jr., Rocky Mount, chairman; F. S. Aldridge, Durham; Dr. T. T. Spence, Raleigh; M. A. Braswell, Winston-Salem; B. L. Smith, Shelby.

Before adjournment, the members of the council heard with much interest some brief remarks by Dr. R. L. Flowers, after which a tour of the new Duke University chapel was made.

ALUMNAE COUNCIL

The Alumnae Council met in the Alumnae Room on the Woman's College campus. The roll was called and the minutes of the previous meeting were read. The new members were welcomed into the Council.

On report of the nominating committee, the following officers for the ensuing years were elected:

Chairman—Mrs. Mary Tapp Jenkins, Kinston.

Vice Chairman—Mrs. Mary Johnson Livengood, Durham.

Secretary—Miss Elizabeth Aldridge, Durham.

Executive committee—Mrs. Estelle Flowers Spears, chairman; Mrs. H. E. Spence, Mrs. Moser, Miss Mary L. Cole, Miss Mamie Jenkins.

It was decided to hold the tea for undergraduate women on February 14.

Plans for the commencement luncheon were discussed, and the council approved the idea of a joint luncheon with the men.

Miss Baldwin, dean of the Woman's College, made her report.

The secretary read the names of the council members whose terms expired with this meeting and thanked them for their loyal support and coöperation

NEXT MEETING

The next meeting of the Alumni and Alumnae Councils will be held during commencement next June.

Decorative Stone Carvings on Buildings Attract Attention

Thoroughly in Keeping With the Gothic Architecture on the West Campus of Duke University, They Are Being Generally Admired—Brief Description of the Distinctive Features of the Carvings and Their Significance

THOROUGHLY in keeping with the Gothic architecture of the University buildings on the west campus, the decorative stone traceries now in the last stage of completion have attracted wide attention. This decorative treatment, however, is on so large a scale and so minute in its details that the ALUMNI REGISTER has thought it worth while to present at least a brief survey of its main features to its readers.

One of the most interesting of these features is the use of college, university, county, municipal, and state seals and coats of arms. More than one hundred twenty-five of these have been employed on the west campus, thirty-four of which may be found on the Union alone, with American, English and European institutions represented. The campus elevation, or east side of Union, has the seals of Oxford, Geneva, Yale, Harvard, and others. Among the large number which may be identified on the library or north elevation are the Uni-

Carved Boss of Groined Arch Under Crowell Tower.

versity of Virginia, Vanderbilt, Washington and Lee, the University of North Carolina, the University of Texas, the City of Durham, and Emory and Henry College. Haverford and Millsaps colleges are on the south elevation, while the seals of many other institutions may be found in various places. The Union has, in keeping with its name, a truly cosmopolitan atmosphere.

INTERESTING ARRAY OF SEALS

Another equally interesting array of seals may be seen on the Medical School and Hospital buildings, these representing American and European medical institutions. At the top of the massive entrance to the Medical building is the device of Jefferson Medical College of Philadelphia. Beneath are two rows of seals consisting of designs that symbolize medical and scientific studies, including anatomy and surgery, with the University of Virginia and Reid Medical College given prominent places. The American College of Surgeons and the American College of Physicians are repre-

Contrasts in Facial Studies at Doorway Arches.

sented above the west or main entrance to the Hospital building.

Other famous schools represented by devices are Upsala, Leyden, Padua, Bologna, Trinity College of Dublin, Edinburgh, Gottingen, Cordova, Liege, Basle, Seville, and Christiana (Norway), and even then the list is not complete. If the visitor from another school is possessed of patience he stands a very fair chance of finding his alma mater's coat of arms carved in stone somewhere on the Duke campus. American, English, Canadian, Scotch, Irish, German, French, Belgian, Italian, Swedish, Danish, Czecho-Slovakian, Swiss, Dutch, and Austrian institutions contribute to this impressive array of educational seals.

FAMOUS PRINTING PRESSES

Famous printing presses, both modern and medieval, are represented by devices in the reference room of the Library. Among the modern presses are those of Yale and Harvard universities, Harper's, and Longmans, Green and Company. The Yale device may be recognized by its motto, *Lux et Veritas,* enclosed in an elliptic which encircles a shield upon which is carved an open Bible with Hebrew characters spelling the Biblical words, "Urim and Thummim" ("clearness and justice"). This is the third shield from the left on the west wall. Harvard Press,

Entrance to Medical School Showing Seals of Famous Universities.

with its *Veritas* upon an open book, is the third from the left on the east wall. Harper's, with its torch passed from one hand to another, is fourth from the left, east wall. Longmans, Green, represented by a swan upon the water, is also upon the east wall, seventh from the left. The device comes from the house called the "Black Swan" occupied by Thomas Longman and J. Osborn, his father-in-law, when they established the firm in 1724; it was here that they became interested in publishing the American edition of Dr. Johnson's *Dictionary.*

The oldest press of all is the Aldine, established by Aldus Mantius in Venice in the fifteenth century,

famous for its fine printing and for its scholarly editions of classic works. The Aldine family continued in business for a century, printing 908 different works, the demand for which was so great that the printers of Lyons and Florence issued counterfeits. The distinguishing mark of this device is an anchor entwined by a dolphin, with the motto either of *Festina lente* or of *Sudavit el alsit.* The device in the reference room differs from the original Aldine in its modern adaptation but is at least descended from it. It is the sixth from the left on the west wall. Other of the older presses represented are those of Simon Voster (Paris, 1501), second from left, west wall; and Reynold Wolfe (1542), fifth from left, east wall. Eighteen seals in all are carved on shields on the east and west walls of the reference room.

SYMBOLIC AND HERALDIC DESIGNS

Symbolic and heraldic designs are prominent in the carvings over doorways and in various places on the buildings. On the facade of the Union, above the right entrance, are an ancient priest and a vestal bearing the classic Grecian lamp, and the same figures may be seen on the elevation facing the Library. Over the main entrance of the Union, east elevation, are the clasped hands, signifying friendship. Classic symbols may be seen almost everywhere. But more striking than these are the grotesque Gothic figures atop the buildings, at corners, as corbels for doorway and roof arches, and sometimes as purely decorative features in almost inconceivable places. While it is commonly thought that many of these are gargoyles, this is a mistake; the only gargoyles are at the corners of the clock tower and over a rear corner of the Union. Most of the grotesque figures are dwarfs, who in Teutonic mythology were supposed to possess great cunning, wisdom, and uncanny knowledge. Many of these dwarfs are atop the cornices in dormitory courts but one of them is likely to stare

(Continued on page 333)

"Trailing Trade a Million Miles" Title of New Book

Duke University Press Publishes Volume By James A. Thomas of New York Which Is Already Attracting Attention—Had Previously Written "A Pioneer Tobacco Merchant in the Orient"

ONE OF the most interesting volumes published recently in this state has just come from the Duke University press. Written by James A. Thomas, a native of North Carolina who spent 35 years of travel in the Orient, the book, called "Trailing Trade a Million Miles," describes the people, customs, unusual characters, economic conditions, and countless believe-it-or-not incidents in remote parts of the world.

Mr. Thomas, who was for many years chief of the British-American Tobacco Company in China, was a business associate and friend of the late James B. Duke. He has made numerous valuable gifts to Duke University, among them being rare Chinese rugs, vases, oriental art objects, and many volumes dealing with Asiatic literature, art, and history. Mr. Thomas has a gift of narration, and is the author of a volume previously published, entitled "A Pioneer Tobacco Merchant in the Orient."

TO SOUTH SEAS IN 1888

Born in North Carolina and reared in close contact with the tobacco growing industry, James A. Thomas first became a tobacco expert and then an ambassador of trade to the South Seas and all countries of the Pacific. He sailed from San Francisco in 1888 and spent the next few years in Samoa, the Fiji Islands, New Zealand, and Australia. Later he lived in India and China for many years.

When Mr. Thomas returned to his native country in 1923 he could look back upon years crowded with travel, success in the field of commerce, and the establishment of friendships with men of many races. He gained so thorough a knowledge of the Far East and its peoples that he writes with authority on their current social, economic, and political problems.

He is especially interested in China's future and believes it is secure. It will take China some years to work out all her problems, he declares, but is certain that China realizes the effort is worth while. He points to that country as a vast potential market for the world's goods and her own when China's resources are fully developed.

Experiences in Japan, India, Mongolia, Siberia, Manchuria, the Dutch East Indies, Siam, the Straits Settlements, the Philippines, and other countries are described by Mr. Thomas, and he adds the enlightening observations of an experienced trader and traveler who never ceased studying the influences and trends peculiar to the country in which he was living.

HONORED BY GOVERNMENTS

JAMES A. THOMAS

Mr. Thomas being an international merchant whose efforts were exceptionally successful, his analysis of the qualities that go into the making of a successful trader are interesting. He places adaptability among the foremost requirements of one who would go into a foreign country to transact business. Other qualities are ineffective, he declares, if the traveler and trader cannot get the native point of view and learn and accept their customs.

It is the former North Carolinian, who now lives in White Plains, N. Y., but makes frequent visits to this state, who has been given credit for the development of much American trade with the Orient, tobacco directly and many other articles indirectly. Several governments have honored him by conferring upon him orders of distinction and medals. His advice on financial and industrial problems has been sought by the leaders of several governments.

FRIEND OF UNIVERSITY

Mr. Thomas has been for years a staunch friend of Duke University and is a welcomed visitor on the campus from time to time. He is chairman of the committee which has been engaged in securing funds for the Duke Memorial.

Some Alumni Personalities

WILLIAM D. MURRAY

William D. Murray, better known to Duke alumni as "Bill" Murray, star of the 1930 Duke football team and president in 1930-31 of the men's student government association, is now head coach at the Methodist Children's Home in Winston-Salem besides having other responsible duties in connection with the institution. He is proving notably successful in his work there. Recently the Winston-Salem Journal said, in part: "Murray has certainly made a success in his first year of coaching and at the rapid pace he is making in state circles, it will not be many moons before he is recognized as one of the finest young coaches in athletics in North Carolina."

MARY G. SHOTWELL

Mary G. Shotwell worked with the N. C. State Board of Charities and Public Welfare as director of children's institutions for several years, doing a notably effective piece of work. She later went to New York City and after receiving a B.S. degree from Columbia University in Social Science, she became a counsellor for the Cardiac Vocational Guidance Committee. She has recently gone to Kansas City, Missouri, where she has accepted a position as vocational counsellor and placement secretary for the Y.W.C.A.

WESLEY FRANK CRAVEN

Wesley Frank Craven, A.B. 1926, A.M. 1927, received his Ph.D. from Cornell University in 1928 at the age of 23. He is now assistant professor of history in New York University. As an undergraduate at Duke he was outstanding, being president of the senior class, member of O. D. K., secretary-treasurer of the Men's Student Government Association, winner of the Peace Oratorical Contest in 1925 and achieving other distinctions. Mr. Craven had an article in the American Historical Review in October, 1931, on "The Dissolution of the London Company of Virginia."

American Lawyer's Visit to English and French Courts

Alumnus and Trustee of Duke University Gives Some Interesting Impressions of the Way Justice is Administered in These Two Countries—Visit to Scotland Yard Proves an Interesting Feature of Trip, Taken as Member of Small Group of American Lawyers

(Attorney B. S. Womble, of the firm of Manly, Hendren & Womble, of Winston-Salem, visited England and France some time ago with a small group of American lawyers who went to those countries primarily to gain information with respect to their legal institutions. On his return home he was invited to address civic clubs and other groups, and his talks on those occasions were so interesting and full of valuable information that the REGISTER requested permission to reprint extracts from them, as follows.—The Editor.)

DURING the past summer I was one of a small group of American lawyers who visited England and France primarily for the purpose of acquiring a knowledge of the legal institutions of those two countries, but not unmindful of the opportunity that such a trip offered for a delightful vacation. A perfect voyage of six days on the S. S. France gave full opportunity for the members of our group to become thoroughly acquainted with each other.

Through friends of some of the party among members of the Bar in London and in Paris, and with the aid of the French Line most interesting and delightful programs for our entertainment and instruction were arranged in both England and France.

LONDON COUNTY COUNCIL

Our program of entertainment by members of the London Bar began with a reception by Mr. W. W. Grantham, K. C., a member of the London County Council, Barrister and Recorder of Deal. The County Hall, in which the reception was held, is one of the handsomest of London's newer buildings. It was erected during recent years at a cost of $35,000,000. While the municipality of the City of London covers only one square mile, London County comprises most of Greater London and includes within its jurisdiction more than six million people. The London County Council is the legislative body for the County. It is composed of one hundred and twenty elected members and a small number of appointed members, and is usually in session two or three days each week. There are several women on the Council, among them being Miss Ishbell McDonald, daughter of the Prime Minister, and Lady Cadmon.

THE OLD BAILEY

A day was spent at the Old Bailey, where the London Assizes and the City Sessions are held. The Old Bailey is on the site of the old Newgate prison. Here Sir Ernest Wild, K. C., Recorder of the City of London, received us on the day of the opening of the criminal courts for the Trinity Term. A very cordial welcome extended us by Sir Ernest was responded to by Chief Justice Booth of the U. S. Court of Claims. After meeting the judges, and several of the barristers, we visited different courts where criminal cases were being tried. A judge who very naturally attracted much interest was Sir Henry Fielding Dickens, the only living son of Charles Dickens. He is a man of advanced years but is still active.

SURVIVAL OF OLD CUSTOM

On the judge's desk in each court room was a nosegay, and on the floor about the desks herbs and flower petals were scattered. In answer to questions asked it was explained that the custom began a few centuries ago when it was thought that the herbs and flowers would serve to protect the judges from disease among the prisoners who were brought into the court.

HEARD SIR JOHN SIMON

The Civil Courts were also visited, and some of us attended a session of the Judicial Committee of the Privy Council. This is the highest court of appeals for cases from the British Dominions and Colonies. Here we listened to Sir John Simon, considered by many the outstanding barrister in England at this time, argue an appeal from Canada. The court was presided over by Viscount Dunedin. The Privy Council having originally been an advisory body to the King, the judgments rendered by the Council are still in the form of recommendations to the King. There is no time limit upon the arguments of cases before the Privy Council. I was told that at the last session an appeal from India, involving one million pounds sterling, was argued for twenty-two days.

DIVISIONS OF LAWYERS

There are two general divisions of lawyers in England, the solicitors and the barristers, Kings Counsellors being a division of barristers. Only the barristers appear in the courts. There are four Inns of Court which alone possess the right of calling persons to the Bar of England. These four Inns of Court are Lincoln's Inn, Grey's Inn, the Middle Temple, and the Inner Temple.

ADMISSION TO THE BAR

One desiring to become a barrister must be admitted to membership in one of the Inns of Court, and must pursue a three years' course of study under the supervision of the officials of the Inn before taking the examinations for admission to the Bar. During his three years of study the prospective barrister spends much time about the Inn. Much of his work is done in the library of the Inn. Each Inn is provided with an adequate dining hall, and, among other requirements, the candidate must take not less than seventy-two dinners with the barristers. By constant observation of and association with the barristers, during the three years of preparation, he necessarily becomes acquainted with and absorbs much pertaining to the ethics and the ideals of the profession.

An American, who was formerly a member of the faculty of the law school of one of our leading universities but who is now a barrister in London and a member of one of the Inns of Court, stated to me that he had never associated with a more delightful group of gentlemen than the barristers in England. The training required by the Inns of Court, no doubt, accounts in large measure for the gentlemanly qualities of the barristers.

AUTHOR AND LEGAL HISTORIAN

A reception was given us at Lincoln's Inn, where Sir Thomas Hughes, K. C., Chairman of the General Council of the Bar, gave a most interesting talk on the history of the Inn. Here I had the pleasure of meeting and talking with Sir Frederick Pollock, well-known author and legal historian. He is now well advanced in years, but is mentally vigorous and alert. I was told that he and Mr. Justice Holmes of our own Supreme Court have been close friends for many years.

The property and buildings now owned by the Inner Temple and the Middle Temple, respectively, were formerly the property of the Order of Knights Templar. After the order was dissolved barristers

acquired the property, and it is now occupied by these two Inns of Court.

BUILDINGS LITTLE CHANGED

The barristers have their offices, or chambers, as they are called, in the Inns of which they are members. Here were seen the chambers once occupied by William Blackstone, Oliver Goldsmith, and many others prominent in the legal history of England. Apparently there have been few changes or improvements made in the buildings. Here in the heart of London, in the quiet of physical surroundings and under conditions that have been little changed in recent centuries, the barrister practices his profession undisturbed by the noise, and little influenced by modern business, only a few blocks away. His dress is either a morning suit and derby, or cutaway with top hat, and when he goes into court he still wears a black robe and white wig.

The admission to, and the practice of, the profession of solicitor is under the control of the Law Society which has its buildings in Chancery Lane. Mr. Phillip Martineau, President of the Law Society, gave us a reception at the Law Society's Hall, after which we were shown over the buildings in which the Society is housed.

VISIT TO SCOTLAND YARD

One of the most interesting experiences enjoyed by us was a visit to Scotland Yard where we were received by Viscount Byng, who was General Byng during the World War, and since the war has served as Governor General of Canada. New Scotland Yard, Westminster, is the headquarters of the Metropolitan Police Force, as well as the "Big Five" of the criminal investigation department. Old Scotland Yard was originally situated in the Charing Cross district, and derived its name from the fact that the kings of Scotland and their ambassadors lived there when they were in London. Mr. J. F. Moylan, Receiver of the Metropolitan Police, explained in a very interesting manner the organization of the police and detective force, showing us some of the equipment used, including automobiles equipped with radio sets.

DO NOT CARRY PISTOLS

I asked Mr. Moyland why it is that policemen in England do not carry pistols. He explained that, from a psychological standpoint, there is an advantage in that there is a natural reaction on the part of the public against an officer using arms in connection with making arrests, and then, too, he said, unless the party to be arrested is armed, the officer has no need for a pistol, and that in England criminals very seldom carry pistols. When asked for his explanation as to why this is true, he said that the usual punish-

(Continued on page 343)

Philosophy at Duke; Much Attention to this Subject

Is Being Given a Distinctive Place in University Studies—Further Expansion of the Department Seems Assured—Professors Cranford, Gilbert and Widgery Offering Courses of Study in Philosophy at Present

IN THE expansion of Trinity College into Duke University the Administration has recognized the importance of the claims of Philosophy to a distinctive place in University studies. It may be said with little fear of contradiction that the higher officers of the University have a deeply rooted conviction of the necessity of philosophical training and philosophical reflection amongst students faced with the intricate problems of modern thought and modern life. Already a good beginning has been made for the promotion of the study at Duke University.

The faculty for Philosophy consists at present of three professors. Dr. William I. Cranford has been known to more than one generation of students of the College and University. Appointed on the faculty in 1891, he has completed forty years of teaching. Graduating as A.B. at Trinity College he pursued his graduate studies at Yale where he attained his Ph.D. degree, being a student of the late George T. Ladd, a thinker who exerted a marked influence on the development of philosophical Theism in America. For a time Dr. Cranford was Dean of the College. In that position as well as in his capacity as professor of Philosophy, he aroused the respect and lasting affection of a very large number of students. His influence has been personal rather than through literary contributions.

Mrs. Katharine Gilbert was appointed to the faculty in 1930. She took her A.B. and A.M. degrees at Brown University, coming under the influence of Professors Everett and Meiklejohn, the former of whom was an outstanding writer on Ethics. At Cornell, where she took her Ph.D. degree in 1912, she worked chiefly with Professors Albee and Hammond, until she became Assistant to Professor Creighton, helping him to edit the *Philosophical Review*. Dr. Gilbert has written a large number of articles, including a contribution on Spinoza to the volume published in honor of Dr. Creighton. For a time she acted as substitute Professor of Philosophy at the University of North Carolina. Her main interest is in the field of Aesthetics, in which she has published a volume entitled: *Studies in Recent Aesthetics*. She also published a book on *Maurice Blondel's Philosophy of Action*.

Professor Widgery came to Duke after a varied experience in Europe, India, and America. He graduated at Cambridge University and pursued postgraduate studies there and in Marburg, Jena, and Paris, coming under the influence of Drs. Sorley, Ward, Rashdall, Inge, MacTaggart, Eucken, Haeckel, Seailles, and Loisy. In his earlier years as instructor he worked with Dr. Lloyd Morgan at Bristol University and Dr. A. E. Taylor at St. Andrew's University. During more than eight years in India, Professor Widgery acquired considerable knowledge of oriental thought, founding and for some years editing *The Indian Philosophical Review*. In 1922 he was elected to a position on the faculty of Cambridge University. Coming to America in 1928 as the first lecturer on the Tallman Foundation at Bowdoin College, Maine, he lectured extensively in American universities and colleges, and accepted an invitation to a chair at Cornell, which he resigned on coming to Duke in 1930. Dr. Widgery is the author of a large number of books and articles. Amongst his latest work is a contribution to the volume of essays published this year under the title of *"Religious Realism"*; and an additional chapter to a new edition of Sidgwick's *History of Ethics*.

It is always of advantage in stimulating thought amongst philosophy students if their teachers represent different types of philosophy. Professors Cranford and Gilbert lean definitely to Idealism while Professor Widgery has abandoned Idealism for a pronounced Realism. Within the last two years a graduate group of students in philosophy has been formed which gives legitimate ground for hope that in the future Duke may become known for its work and students in this subject. Professor Widgery believes that in this field Duke should endeavour to become in the South what the Sage School of Philosophy at Cornell has for so long been farther North. That School may well be taken as a model, though it will obviously need much work for many years to attain a reputation such as it has acquired. There is an opportunity for someone like the late Mr. Sage to found a number of chairs in philosophy and to give his name to a School of Philosophy at Duke. Within the limits of its resources the University is building up a collection of books on the subject, but little could aid the department more than the foundation of a philosophical library by a generous donor impressed by the importance of the function philosophy has to perform today.

No account of the opportunities of students of philosophy at Duke would be adequate which did not make reference to Dr. MacDougall. Professor Mac-Dougall may be regarded as equally profound a philosopher as he is renowned as a psychologist. Students of philosophy at Duke have the rare privilege of coming under his influence in taking the courses of psychology which are usually required of them. The University also has at the head of its Department of Sociology Dr. Ellwood, whose well known work in Sociology is marked by its keen philosophical criticism, and under his guidance students may direct their philosophical studies to the consideration of the pressing problem of society. Students of Aesthetics may work with Professor Lundholm who is an authority on the psychology of aesthetics, and with Professor Hall in the history of art.

Decorative Stone Carvings on Buildings Attract Attention

(Continued from page 332)

suddenly over his misshapen nose at the campus explorer at some unexpected turn. The most interesting collection of these, however, is in the Union dining hall, where they are perched behind shields upon corbels, supporting the overhead woodwork, some of them as merry imps, some comically wistful, some reminding the observer of elves in a Nordic myth, but all of them as grotesque as the Gothic imagination could conceive.

FACIAL STUDIES

No less interesting are the facial studies at the doorway arches. These for the most part are presented as contrasts, suggestive in general, or at least in popular convention, of campus types. On one side of a doorway may be seen the face of a scholar, deep in thought, preoccupied with some abstruse problem apparently as heavy as the corbelian-supported destiny above him; on the other side may be found the roguish face of a care-free and irrepressible sophomore. There will be the lean, ascetic face of a would-be zealot under one side of the arch, flanked by the round, jovial coun-

tenance of the would-be rake on the other, as if each would bear witness to the world that the other's extremes are not to be taken too seriously. At another doorway will be found the finely modeled and sensitive features of an aristocrat, suggesting to us a future Wilson, but opposite him, and helping support the same burden, will be found his plainer, less classic-featured, but fully as idealistic brother. There are verdant freshmen, self-assured sophomores, serene juniors, and confident seniors; there are graduate students of all types: theologues, medicos, lawyers, and teachers; there are pedants and savants. It would seem that the artist who conceived it had more than a sense of humor, combining as he has done in these facial studies a democracy in representation, in mutual goodwill, and in common purpose, withal an artistic expression far more striking and far truer to real life than any stilted classic representation could have been.

GROINED VAULTING

Beneath the clock tower in the arcade is a perfect example of groined vaulting. At the focal point of each groin is a keystone or boss carved in another expression of Gothic grotesqueness. There are figures that suggest ancient prophets of forgotten ages, with long and conventionalized beards, and grasping books and scrolls in their gnarled hands. Relieving the grotesqueness, however, are foliage designs; oak leaves, vine clusters, and branches of pine needles. The same decorative treatment in varying degrees may be seen in other arched or vaulted passage-ways. Some of the arches have an especially rich decorative treatment of conventionalized floral designs, as many as twenty-six designs in a single arch with no two alike.

STUDY AND RESEARCH

An immense amount of study and research was necessary in working out the general plan and the details of the decorative treatment of the campus buildings. The work was done under the supervision of Horace Trumbauer, of Philadelphia, the architect who drew the plans of the University campus. Dr. Frank Brown, head of the Department of English, coöperated in securing heraldic designs and copies of official institutional seals, which were secured only after months of patient correspondence and collection. The carving, now nearing completion in the Chapel, was done by a staff of over forty highly trained American and European sculptors, who have worked steadily since the buildings were sufficiently advanced to permit them to begin. John Donnelly, of New York, as contractor for the stone carving, has had charge of this work. Mr. A. C. Lee, chief engineer of the University, has had general supervision.

Study is Made of Country Church in North Carolina

Book by Professor J. M. Ormond, of the Duke University Faculty, Just Issued From the Duke Press—Volume Discusses the Country Church in Relation to Other Institutions of the State—Facts and Conclusions Stated

"THE Country Church in North Carolina," by Jesse Marvin Ormond, Professor of Practical Theology in the Duke University School of Religion, is one of the newest books issued by the Duke University Press. This book is a study of the country church in North Carolina in comparison with the material progress and condition of other social institutions of the state.

Professor Ormond is a native North Carolinian. His early life was spent on a plantation in one of the fertile cotton-tobacco counties of the coastal plans area of the state. His impressions of the country life of that period have been deep and lasting. For the first seven years of his ministerial career, he served rural churches in North Carolina. This experience has given him a very vital connection with the country church.

An alumnus of Trinity College, now Duke University, and of the School of Religion of Vanderbilt University, Professor Ormond has taught Rural Sociology at Duke since 1922. During this period he has made a state-wide investigation of country church conditions in North Carolina. His new book is the result of that research.

Professor Ormond says that the study purposes to be a sort of base line of measurement for country churches in the state. He believes that the survey on which it was based is the most complete, and that its results are the most reliable, of any survey of its kind in North Carolina. Even so, he does not assume that it is complete or final. He acknowledges indebtedness to a number of persons who assisted in various capacities in collecting the data and preparing the manuscript.

The first part of the book furnishes data on the physical, economic, social, and educational aspects of the one hundred counties of the state, together with the religious background of rural church life. In this section of the study Professor Ormond gives many interesting statements. He calls attention to the fact that the climate of North Carolina is, as a whole, mild and free from sudden changes. It ranges from sub-tropical in the southeast, to north-temperate in the higher elevations of the mountains. Because of this great range of climate, North Carolina's crops include practically all fruits, vegetables, and other produce, that can be grown outside of the tropics. North Carolina's population, says Professor Ormond, has increased more than 700,000 in fifty years. Quoting from the Thirty-fifth Report of the Department of Labor and Printing for the state, he says: "Scarcely is there a single article produced by man or machine which is not being produced in North Carolina." He attributes this fact to the "community spirit" which he says exists between capital and labor within the state.

The cotton mills and the tobacco factories of the state lead the nation in their products. Third in the rank of industries are the furniture factories. The output of all the factories of the state amounts, Professor Ormond's figures show, to a quarter of a billion dollars per year.

One of the important sources of influence in the more recent growth of industries in the state Professor Ormond believes to be that of production of electric energy. He quotes Thorndike Saville, Chief Hydraulic Engineer, as saying that "New York alone exceeds North Carolina in amount of developed water power, east of the Mississippi, and only New York, Colorado and Oregon, in the entire country, have a greater developed water power."

Consolidation of public schools throughout the state, Professor Ormond believes to be responsible for the very remarkable advance of the state school system, since the Civil War. Many institutions of higher learning, he says, are supported partly by religious denominations and partly by private benefactions.

"It is impossible," says Professor Ormond, "to estimate the value of newspapers beyond a mere material basis of investment and income. The prosperity of North Carolina has been reflected in the splendid growth of its newspapers."

The second part of the book gives a detailed account

(Continued on page 345)

Planting of Trees at Duke; Campus is Being Beautified

Total of 275 Trees Have Been Transplanted, This Being Part of an Extensive Plan of
Landscaping in Progress According to Plans of Widely Known Firm of
Experts—Many Shrubs Being Used on the Campus

TRANSPLANTING of 275 trees, sowing and cultivating seventy-five acres of lawn, establishing and maintaining a nursery, along with a great number of other details, both large and small, comprise the program of beautifying Duke University campus. Few people have more than a small idea of the large scale on which this program was planned and on which it is being carried out.

Olmsted Brothers, landscape architects, of Brookline, Massachusetts, drew the plans for the campus, and the first work of executing the design was done under the supervision of Percy Gallagher, of this firm. The design itself was drawn by Frederick L. Olmsted, internationally known as the architect of the Metropolitan Park System, Boston, and of other famous park systems and grounds. His father, also Frederick L. Olmsted, organized the firm and established its world-wide reputation with his designing of Central, Riverside, and Morningside parks in New York, of the street parkways in Washington, and of the World's Columbian Exposition grounds in Chicago.

Mr. Harkey Directing Work

When the initial stage of laying out the campus design was completed, the work was taken over by the Duke Construction Company, under the direction of R. M. Harkey, landscape gardener. Mr. Harkey was retained six months ago by the University as the head of the permanent staff for maintaining the grounds. The completion of the work, as well as the maintenance of the campus, is now under his supervision. The work is carried on under the general direction of the business office of the University. A staff ranging from fifteen to thirty men, depending on the season of the year, is kept busy on the beautifying program.

Preparation of Soil

The first step taken after the grounds were laid out was the preparation of the soil in the quadrangles, courts, and spaces to be planted. Excavation and grading had removed the topsoil here, leaving a very poor grade of clay. Topsoil from the Duke forest was hauled in and after mixing was spread upon the west campus at a thickness of from four to six inches. The employment of a large force of labor was necessary for this purpose. In order to secure uniformity of grade the soil was carefully selected, as it was impossible to secure all of it in any one locality. Over fifty tons of commercial fertilizer were used on the west campus alone to enrich and condition the soil, including thirty tons of lime, twenty tons of cotton-seed meal, and several tons of bone meal, while several tons of compost were used in the planting of the shrubs. The lime keeps the soil from hardening, the cotton-seed meal is for immediate enrichment, and the bone meal is for ultimate plant food value. Fertilization of the soil is necessary about twice yearly to insure the best results in the growing of lawn grass.

Six Varieties of Grasses

Six varieties of grasses comprise the mixture planted. These are bluegrass, redtop, Italian rye, Chewing's fescue, White Dutch clover, and Bermuda. Due to the fact that the transported soil contained the seeds of wild grasses it was necessary recently to weed out the wild varieties to keep them from choking out the planted grasses.

Keeping Grass Cut

A force of six regular mowers is kept busy a large part of the time to keep the grass cut. A total of approximately seventy acres, including both campuses, has to be mowed once a week during most of the year and twice weekly during the growing seasons. The watering of the lawn, shrubbery, and trees is a large task in itself and has to be done at nights to prevent withering. Due to the unusual heat the past summer was a very hard one on the plant work, making extra watering necessary. A manufactured soil dries out more quickly than a natural soil, a fact which further complicates the problem of keeping the campus green. Three years of careful cultivation, constant weeding, and regular watering are required to grow a good campus lawn.

One of the most persistent difficulties with which the landscape gardeners have to contend is that of keeping the grass planted and growing on the plot corners. The corners are trodden upon by the forgetful. and unthoughtful until the ground becomes so hard and packed that nothing can be grown upon it. Various means have been used, none of them with satisfactory results, to prevent people from walking on the grass, and it has been repeatedly necessary to replant the trodden-down places. Since well-kept corners are essential to the trim appearance of the campus it would be a constructive type of campus patriotism for some group to start a movement to observe the classic injunction of the parks: "Keep Off the Grass."

TRANSPLANTING OF TREES

Transplanting of the trees, as already indicated, was one of the most difficult tasks undertaken. With the exception of a small group, all of the trees in the west campus quadrangle were brought from the Duke forest, sixty-five being moved and planted there. Three varieties, willow oak, white oak, and American elm, were selected because of their longevity and general suitability for shade and decorative purposes. Only those which were well-branched, growing, and free from disease were chosen. These averaged from four to eight inches in diameter, from twenty to thirty feet in height, and about twelve years in age. They were hauled from three to five miles in a wagon especially designed for this purpose by Mr. Harkey, a vehicle which could be uncoupled into three pieces and placed in the hole dug around the tree so that it could be loaded without injury to the roots. Extreme care is necessary both in loading and planting as a slight strain cracks the clay around the roots and allows the air to reach them, causing fermentation and decay. The high percentage of successful transplantings is one of the notable features in the Duke campus project, ninety-five percent of the trees and shrubs surviving. This meant a loss of only one percent, as the mortality rate of such plants in the natural state is four percent.

In planting the trees difficulty was encountered in the strata of rock which underlies the campus. It was necessary to dig holes of sufficient depth to allow drainage for the tree roots and to prevent fermentation. Burlap was placed around the trunks during the summer to prevent the sap from being drawn upward and to preserve a requisite moisture. The care of the trees requires the regular pruning of dead branches that might house destructive insects and disease growths. Watering is an especially important item during the first two years.

NATIVE CEDARS PLANTED

Two hundred native cedars were removed from the forest and planted in various places on the campus, these averaging from six to twelve feet in height. Most of them were planted around the stadium, with quite a number around the fountain at the rear of Page Auditorium. The total of all varieties of trees removed and planted is about 275. On the east campus a high record was made by S. R. Hunt, who has charge of that division, in tree and shrubbery transplanting. The willow oaks there were transplanted by Mr. Hunt sixteen years ago, most of them at an age of from six to eight years.

SHRUBS USED ON CAMPUS

Boxwood, abelia, *ligustrum lucidum*, mountain laurel, and rhododendron are the leading shrubs used in the campus decorative scheme, with abelia leading the others. A number of mountain azaleas were also used. All of these were brought considerable distances. There are two kinds of boxwood, Japanese and Old English, both very difficult to transplant and grow, a fact which makes the one hundred percent record of the Duke gardeners in moving and growing them all the more notable. About half of the boxwood was secured at Clayton, near Raleigh, and the remaining half near Danville, Virginia. Some of the plants are seventy-five and eighty years old. Good boxwood is hard to find as it has been picked over by gardeners from wealthy estates in the north and other sections, and is for that reason always at a premium. Of the mountain shrubs, rhododendron and laurel are the leading varieties, with the laurel of two kinds, Carolina and Catawba. A few hemlocks, an ornamental mountain species, are also included. All of the mountain shrubs were secured from nurseries near Asheville.

HEDGE AT STADIUM ENTRANCE

The hedge at the entrance of the stadium is of *armoriver privet*, while the hedge lining the main driveway approach to the west campus is of abelia. Relatively few diseases attack shrubs but these are of such serious nature that it is necessary to be constantly on guard against them. The red spider, the worst enemy of shrubs, is destroyed by spraying. The boxwoods require protection from the sun during the early transplanted stage, for which purpose wooden frames were built over them as shades during the past summer.

English and Boston ivy were planted around the base of the east campus buildings two seasons ago and the vines are now beginning to be quite noticeable upon the walls. The younger ivy on the west campus, however, will not attract attention for another season or two. In time as the walls become ivy-clad the Duke campus will increasingly take on the venerable aspect that lends such peculiar charm to the campuses of the older colleges and universities.

FLOWER PLOTS HAVE PLACE

Beds of flowers have for years made the east campus a place of beauty but up to this time have not been planted on any extensive scale on the west campus. The plot of roses in front of the hospital are a pleasing exception, and the row of bulbs below the terrace in front of Crowell tower added a quite noticeable touch of color to the campus during the summer quarter. Flower plots will have a definite place as the decorative scheme is developed.

BEAUTIFYING HAS ONLY BEGUN

Further improvements to be made indicate that the beautifying of Duke campus has only begun. The banks of all the roadways are to be graded and planted as fast as the program can be carried forward. The driveway connecting the east and west campuses will be improved in this manner, with shade trees set out at intervals of one hundred feet. In order to complete and maintain the landscape design the University has established a nursery on the road back of the stadium, which will probably be permanent. About twenty-five varieties of shrubs are being grown there at present and a wide range of other plant species is to be added. Cuttings, seed, and plants will thus be made available for the program of making Duke University campus one of the beauty spots of America.

TREE PLANTING AT DUKE UNIVERSITY
(1) Tree being loaded on specially designed wagon to be hauled to the campus. (2) Tree loaded and ready for hauling; note the manner of wrapping the roots in burlap and of binding them with ropes to prevent strain and exposure. (3) Scene on main quadrangle, west campus, showing tree being placed in position for planting.

Duke Entertains Delegates From Many Universities

On Thursday, November 12, Duke University had as guests for luncheon in the Union on the West Campus the delegates to the Thirty-third Annual Conference of the Association of American Universities. This organization includes the leading universities of the United States and Canada. About sixty delegates visited Duke for the luncheon and afterwards made a tour of the campus inspecting the library, the laboratories and other buildings and equipment of the University. The visitors came from all parts of the United States and Canada. They expressed themselves as greatly impressed and interested in the large program of university development which has been carried forward at Duke in recent years.

After the luncheon and tour of the Duke campus the Association returned to Chapel Hill for the meeting scheduled at the University of North Carolina for November 12, 13 and 14. Among the notable persons who addressed the sessions at Chapel Hill were Dr. Abraham Flexner, of the Institute for Advanced Study; Dean Roscoe Pound, of the Harvard University Law School; President Robert M. Hutchins, of the University of Chicago; and President H. M. Tory, of the Canadian National Research Council. Besides the delegates present at the Conference at Chapel Hill the Association invited a number of guests representing various universities and research institutions. Included in the list of guests of the Association were President William P. Few and Dean William H. Glasson, of the Graduate School of Duke University.

American Lawyer's Visit to English and French Courts

(Continued from page 336)

ment in England for carrying a concealed weapon, unless there are extenuating circumstances, is a sentence of from twelve to fifteen years in prison. After hearing this statement it was very easy to understand why criminals in England do not carry pistols. If the same punishment could be administered in America, it would, no doubt, tend very materially to decrease crime here.

ENJOYABLE RECEPTION

One of the most enjoyable social events was a reception by the Goldsmiths Company, of which Right Honorable Lord Blanesburg is the warden, at its premises in Foster Lane. The reception was attended by several members of the House of Lords and of the Judicial Committee of the Privy Council. We saw there a collection of gold plate, said to be the finest in the world.

RECORD OFFICE

We visited the Record Office in Chancery Lane, where we met the Right Honorable Lord Hanworth, Master of the Rolls. Lord Hanworth, before he was elevated to the peerage, was Sir Ernest Pollack, which family name is well known in the legal history of England. In the Record Office are many old historical documents, such as the Doomsday Book, Pope Clement's Bull, Shakespeare's Will, and many other equally interesting documents. I understand that the permanent records of all court proceedings are kept here and may be produced on short notice when needed.

INTERESTING PLACES

While our activities in London were principally related with the courts and other institutions connected with the legal profession, we also visited many places of historical interest in and out of the city, including Oxford, Eton, Windsor, Runnymede, Kenilworth, Stratford-on-Avon, and Stoke Poges.

WELCOMED TO FRANCE

Upon our arrival at the French port Boulogne-sur-Mer, we were immediately made to feel the warmth of the friendship in sunny France by M. Decugis and M. Daumas, both prominent French lawyers, who had come from Paris to meet us. M. Decugis delivered an address before the American Bar Association at its meeting in Chicago last year. Upon our arrival in Paris some of us went to the home of M. Daumas where we spent a delightful evening. On the following morning M. Fernand Payen, Battonier de l'Ordre des Avocats a la Cour d'Apel, together with other prominent members of the French bar, received us at the Palais de Justice, and afterward we were shown over the building, in which the principal courts of Paris are now held, and in the basement of which thousands of prominent Frenchmen were imprisoned during the French Revolution. It was here that Louis XVI and Marie Antoinette were kept in prison until they were taken to the guillotine.

INSTRUCTIVE LECTURES

On two mornings we listened to instructive lectures in English at the Palais de Justice by Mr. Daumas on the "History of the Paris Bar"; M. Decugis, "International Industrial Understandings"; M. de Gallaix, "Comparison of the Methods of American and French Legal Education"; M. Le Paule, "Sources of Civil and Commercial Law in France"; M. De Pachman, "Methods of Proof before the French Courts";

and Mme. Simon-Bidaux, "The Entry of Women to the Profession of Barrister." Members of the French bar accompanied us on a visit to the Courts of Justice and to the Court of Cassation, the highest court of appeals in France.

Two Groups

The legal profession in France is divided into two general groups, the Avocats and Avoues, corresponding in many respects to the Barristers and Solicitors, respectively, in England. The right to appear before the Court of Cassations, which is the highest Court of Appeals is limited to sixty persons, and this right is sold or otherwise transferred, as property. The transferee must, however, possess the required qualifications. The avocat does not have an office in the business section of the city. In France the legal profession is still a profession. It is not a business. The avocat receives his client in his library at his home. Among other requirements for admission, he must present a deed or lease for an apartment or house.

Admission to practice as an avocat, as well as continuation in the profession, is controlled by the Order of Avocats of the Court of Appeals, of which the Batonnier is the head. I was told that the Batonnier is the only dictator in France. He, with the members of the Council, exercises very extensive authority over the profession. I understand that about thirty members have been dismissed during the past year. The office of Batonnier is the highest honor that the profession can bestow.

Interesting Man

Maitre Fernand Payen, who was nearing the close of his two-year term as Batonnier when we were in Paris, is a very interesting man. He has been closely associated with Poincare and others prominent in the political life of France in recent years, but he has devoted his energies exclusively to matters relating to the legal profession, and he has made a notable record, not only as an active practitioner, but also as an author of legal publications. At the invitation of the American Bar Association, he recently attended the meeting of the Association in Atlantic City, where he appeared on the program. His term as Batonnier expired in October, when he was succeeded by M. Raymond Poincare. We enjoyed a delightful reception given us by the Batonnier in his home. Other receptions were given by President Doumer at the Elysee Palace, by Ambassador and Mrs. Edge at the American Embassy, and by the Marshal of France at the Bagdad Restaurant in the grounds of the International Exposition.

Dinners and Luncheons

Probably the most enjoyable feature of our visit to France was the opportunity that was afforded to at-

tend dinners and luncheons in the homes of several of our newly made friends. Messieurs Daumas, Decugis, Dailly, Netter, and Md. Juliet Vellieur-Duray will be especially remembered in this respect.

French Country Estate

A few of us went on one afternoon with M. Dailly to the country estate of his mother, which is located about forty miles from Paris. The country home is a beautiful old chateau that dates back five or six hundred years. The moat surrounding it is still preserved, and the formal flower gardens stretching down to the lake provide a beautiful view from the windows of the spacious drawing room. A short distance below the chateau is a peasant village with winding lanes leading between the stone houses connected with high stone walls. In the center of the village is the church. In addition to members of the family there were several invited guests, most of whom spoke English, all of which afforded a most interesting opportunity of spending the evening with a group of highly cultured ladies and gentlemen in a palatial French country home. At the dinner table I had the pleasure of sitting at the right of Md. Dailly, our hostess. She is seventy years of age, and I was interested to find that she, like many American grandmothers, as well as some who are not grandmothers, was disturbed by the growing tendency, since the war, toward lax morality among some of the younger generation, particularly among the girls of the peasant class.

While in France we, of course, visited many places of historical interest, such as Versailles, Fontainebleau, and Malmaison, and we spent three days on a motor trip through the chateau country.

Attended Several Trials

I attended several trials in both England and France, but, because of being unable to understand the French language, I, very naturally, did not form as decided impressions with reference to the conduct of the courts in France as I did in England.

Impressions of English Courts

In England I was particularly impressed with the high regard that the parties to the litigation, as well as the witnesses, apparently had for the truth. I did not hear a witness testify who did not impress me that he was endeavoring to tell the exact truth, which is not always the case in our own courts. The primary effort of the judge and of the barristers appearing in the case, apparently, was to arrive at the truth. Neither in any of the trial courts nor in the courts of appeal did I hear any attempts at oratory or appeals to prejudice or sympathy. In the criminal courts, in each case of a submission or a conviction, an officer was called on by the judge who had, apparently as the result of thorough investigation, prepared a written record of the defendant. This record usually began with the place and date of birth of the defendant, and, among other things, covered his educational training, his family relations, the work he had been engaged in, the estimation in which he was held by his employers, and whether or not he had any criminal record. It was evident that the officer had made an entirely impartial investigation for the sole purpose of acquainting the judge with the man on whom he was called to pronounce sentence. The value of such information to the judge in aiding him to impose a just sentence is obvious. While the criminal courts in England have the reputation of giving speedy trials, I was impressed with the intelligent patience and thoroughness with which the cases were investigated.

SALARIES PAID TO JUDGES

The salaries paid to judges in England may have some relation to the type of men who hold judicial positions there. According to information given me, the salaries range from $17,500, which was the salary of the judges of the criminal courts, to $30,000, the salary of the members of the Judicial Committee of the House of Lords.

COURTS IN FRANCE

In France there are no juries in any of the trial courts, except in certain criminal courts for the trial of the more serious felonies. Civil cases are tried before courts consisting of three or more judges, which in some respects, no doubt, has advantages over our jury system.

The evidence is usually reduced to writing before the case comes into court. It is only in exceptional cases that oral evidence is admitted. It is unprofessional for a lawyer to interview a witness before the time for taking his deposition. In the ordinary case witnesses are heard by a special judge appointed for that purpose, only the parties and their attorneys being present. The judge and not the lawyer examines the witness and reduces his evidence to writing, which, after it is corrected by the witness, is signed by him. All the evidence gathered by each party is communicated to the other party before the trial. The hearing in court usually consists of the arguments of law, an outline of which has been filed in advance, and of the evidence, a copy of which has been furnished the judges. The hearing of a case seldom lasts longer than one hour.

HIGH TYPE OF LAWYERS

In both England and in France I was impressed with the high type of the members of the legal profession. This is doubtless due, in some part, to the fact that in both countries admission to the profession,

and the right to continue in the profession, is controlled by organizations of the lawyers themselves.

After three weeks in London and Paris our group separated, some returning to America and others going to other parts of Europe.

Study is Made of Country Church in North Carolina

(Continued from page 339)

of the geography, area, population, industries, and rural church data, of each county in the state, arranged alphabetically. A map of each county further helps to explain these conditions.

Professor Ormond's interpretation of the data is given in Part Three. He has endeavored, throughout his book, to answer questions so often raised in the minds of religious and social leaders: "Is the country church static or dynamic? Is it leading or lagging? Has the country church been unjustly berated or is it truly belated? Should the leaders of the country church be commended or condemned? Will tomorrow find the country church extinct or extended? Are the religious leaders facing, for the country church, a new day of enlarged opportunity, or a blue day of discouragement?" His data, he says, show an excessive number of country churches. He concludes, further, that antiquated physical equipment and inadequate financial support handicap the possible future success of the country church. He finds a great need for consolidation and relocation of the country churches of the state.

Made of the best quality book paper, bound in a handsome black cloth, the front cover decorated with the imprint of a beautiful church window, the central motif of which is a large cross, the book presents a very attractive appearance.

Rotary President is Honor Guest at Duke Luncheon

Sidney W. Pascall, of London, president of Rotary International, was the guest of honor at a luncheon given on Monday, November 23, at Duke University. President W. P. Few presided at the luncheon, which was attended by a number of distinguished Rotarians here for the inter-city dinner to Mr. Pascall in the evening, University officials and several local Rotarians who were in charge of the various arrangements connected with his visit to Durham.

In talking informally to the group of twenty-five gathered at the luncheon, the president of Rotary International referred briefly to the relationships along various lines between the nations of the world. Following this he discussed, in a most interesting way, the new government of Great Britain and the matter of England's abandonment of the gold standard.

Football Season Ends on Nov. 28 with the W. & L. Contest

1931 Duke Team Makes Notably Good Showing in Spite of One Late Season Reverse—Has Several "Shut-Out" Victories to Its Credit—Great Game With Carolina Results in 0-0 Tie Before Tremendous Crowd on November 21—Strong Defensive Record

THOUGH the Blue Devils were learning an entirely new system from the ground up, the 1931 football season has been a successful one, despite the fact that one late reverse marred a brilliant early record, this being the defeat by State College. Only one game remains, that with Washington & Lee, on November 28 at Lexington, Va.

The Blue Devils made their final home appearance of the 1931 season on November 21 and battled the Carolina Tar Heels to a scoreless tie, after having been slated to lose. A tremendous crowd saw the game.

A look at the results of games for the season reveals a record of which all Duke supporters may be proud. South Carolina won, 7-0, but then followed three shut-out victories and a tie, V. M. I. going down, 13-0; then Villanova, 18-0. Davidson fought to a scoreless tie but the Devils came back to overwhelm Wake Forest, 28-0.

Tennessee's undefeated Volunteers were next on the schedule . and, al-though the Devils lost 25-2, they marred the perfect scoring record of the Vols and put up a fight that will stand for Duke teams to shoot at in years to come.

Every inch of ground the Tennessee team gained over the Devils was fiercely contested. Each of the Vols' four touchdowns came through breaks of the game as the Devils continued until the final whistle their attempt to win the contest.

The Duke team made a great "hit" in Knoxville by their brilliant playing. Officials, scouts and sports writers were high in their praise, generally conceding that the Devils put up as great a fight as any team that ever played on the Tennessee field. One Knoxville sports editor wrote: "Graceful defeat . never harmed any enemy."

Then, on their second long trip, the Blue Devils upset pre-game dope and handed the powerful Kentucky Wildcats a 7-0 defeat in a game that saw the Duke team backed down to its goal line time and again during the first half,

(Continued on page 352)

NICK LANEY
Sophomore halfback whose punting and passing have been such a feature of the Duke team's work recently.

Trustee of the Duke Endowment Was Seventy-Five Years Old Nov. 1

J. Elwood Cox, member of the board of trustees of the Duke Endowment and a staunch friend of Duke University, recently observed his seventy-fifth birthday at his home in High Point. The occasion was celebrated with a reunion of five distinguished classmates of the old New Garden School. Attending were Dr. L. L. Hobbs, president emeritus of Guilford College; Joseph A. Hoskins, of Summerfield; R. R. King, of Greensboro; W. C. Boring, of Greensboro. Absent were the two distinguished college chums since removed by death—James B. Duke and Benjamin N. Duke.

Mr. Cox is one of North Carolina's most prominent citizens. He is the state's oldest bank president, both in years and from the standpoint of service. In addition to being a trustee of the Duke Endowment, he was for ten years a member of the State Highway Commission. He served one term as president of the national bank division of the American Bankers' Association; during the war he was a member of the war finance committee; for a number of years he has been chairman of the board of trustees of Guilford College; he has been president of the Commercial National Bank in High Point for forty years since its organization, and is director of a number of other business enterprises.

NEW DUKE BOOKS

Order Now For Christmas

NORFOLK: HISTORIC SOUTHERN PORT

By THOMAS J. WERTENBAKER.   *Price $4.00.*

This history of Norfolk from the earliest settlement to the last decade is written with special attention to the effect of national events on this historic center of southern commerce. The book is a pioneer effort to link local history to national events. The method of treatment and the fascinating style make the study of value not only to the citizen of Norfolk but to the student interested in the history of the South and of the nation.

TRAILING TRADE A MILLION MILES

By JAMES A. THOMAS.   *Price $3.50.*

The personal opinions and observations of the author of *A Pioneer Tobacco Merchant in the Orient*. Between 1886 and 1923 the author travelled over a million miles as agent for tobacco companies, a pioneer missionary of trade to the Orient. Observations gleaned from the wealth of experiences and multitude of personal contacts with people of all ranks of life are set forth in this second book by Mr. Thomas.

THE COUNTRY CHURCH IN NORTH CAROLINA

By J. MARVIN ORMOND.   *Price $4.00.*

An economic and religious survey of the one hundred counties of North Carolina. A comparison of the economic resources of each county with the number of sects, value and number of church buildings, proportion of church membership to the total population, and the work of Sunday schools and other organizations is presented in a succinct manner.

The Painless Operation

An advertisement
written for TIME by
Miss Catherine P. Harris,
Junior League of Boston.

...High up under the dome of Boston's Massachusetts General Hospital, far removed from the wards so that the screams of sufferers under the knife will not horrify the ward patients, is the Hospital's famed operating amphitheatre. Many a medical student dreads the operations he is privileged to watch, frequently faints. But one day last week Dr. John C. Warren, Boston surgeon, led a group of surgeons and students (class of 1847) up the long stairs, eager, hurrying.

For there beckoned an interesting experiment—surgery without pain. Dr. William Thomas Green Morton, 27-year old Boston dentist, thought it possible, had experimented to that end with ether, a volatile, pungent chemical compound capable of producing insensibility. He had tried it on animals, on himself, then on his patients while extracting the roots of decayed teeth. Finally he had obtained permission from Dr. Warren to let him test his drug before an audience. One Gilbert Abbott, with a tumor on his neck, was to be the first trial.

At 11 a.m. the last privileged student hurried into the amphitheatre. Experimentee Abbott, fidgeting on the operating-table, looked anxiously at the clock. Casual talk ceased, sudden silence prevailed as the minute-hand crawled past the hour, and Dr. Morton did not appear. "He and his anesthetic! Humbugs both, no doubt!" mumbled a doctor. It became five minutes past eleven, ten, then a quarter after. The patient stirred uneasily, Dr. Warren selected an instrument, advanced to the table—useless to delay proceedings any longer. As his knife poised for the incision, Dr. Morton, breathless, apologetic, rushed in. He held in one hand a curious globe-and-tube apparatus.

In eager concentration, tensely expectant, the waiting group of surgeons and students watched while the newcomer—a charlatan perhaps, a genius possibly—adjusted his peculiar inhaling apparatus to the patient's mouth and with tense composure administered his anesthetic. Veiled skepticism revealed itself when the patient reacted suddenly in wild exhilaration, but this exuberance subsided, relaxation took its place, then unconsciousness. Skepticism was routed, amazement paramount. Said Dentist Morton to Surgeon Warren: "Your patient is ready."

Dr. Warren began to operate, proceeded quickly, in five minutes had finished. From the patient came no cry of pain, no agony of distress, only slight movements, mumbled words as from one who stirs on the borderland of sleep....

"This, gentlemen," exclaimed Surgeon Warren, "is no humbug."

Awake, Gilbert Abbott said, "I felt no pain."

So, in part, had TIME been published in October, 1846, would TIME have reported the first public demonstration of ether as a surgical anesthetic. So, too, would TIME have reported how one Dr. Crawford Williamson Long, of Georgia, came forward later saying that he had used ether four years previous, had given it up as impractical....So, too, would TIME have reported the bitter persecution that came to Dentist Morton when he patented his discovery as "Letheon"; the seizure of "Letheon" by the U. S. Government for its own uses; the claims of Dr. Charles T. Jackson, the Boston chemist from whom Dentist Morton had obtained his ether; the division of the Paris Academy of Medicine's 5,000 franc Monthyon Prize for 1852 between these two, with Morton proudly refusing his share; the long Congressional investigations resulting in nothing, and Dentist Morton's death in poverty in 1865.

Cultivated Americans, impatient with cheap sensationalism and windy bias, turn increasingly to publications edited in the historical spirit. These publications, fair-dealing, vigorously impartial, devote themselves to the public weal in the sense that they report what they see, serve no masters, fear no groups.

Where They Are Located	News of the Alumni	What They Are Doing

Miss Elizabeth Aldridge, '24, Secretary of Alumnae Council, Editor

CLASS OF 1873

Friends and classmates of Dr. W. R. Snead will regret to hear of his recent death in Mariana, Florida. He was a native of Johnston County, North Carolina. After leaving Trinity he studied dentistry and practiced his profession for a number of years in Mariana, Florida. His home paper had the following to say about him: "Dr. Snead had been in ill health for sometime and lived to the ripe old age of eighty-six. He spent many active years in this community and was a man of sterling integrity and a Confederate veteran with a most creditable record. He was a prominent figure at reunions."

CLASS OF 1908

Kennon W. Parham is a certified public accountant with an office in the Masonic Temple, Raleigh. He served as vice-president of the North Carolina Association of Public Accountants from 1927 to 1931.

CLASS OF 1911

W. Grady Gaston, executive secretary of the Chamber of Commerce, Gastonia, N. C., has recently had a signal honor to come his way. In a nation-wide contest among the Chamber of Commerce secretaries of the United States he was awarded first prize, a check for $100, for distinguished community service. This award was made at the annual convention that was held in Toledo, Ohio, in October.

CLASS OF 1912

Dr. Haliburton McCoy is a physician with the Hawaiian Commercial and Sugar Company and is stationed at Puunene, Mani, T. H. He was married on October 25, 1919, to Miss Emma Louise Garnett. They have three children, two sons and one daughter.

Mrs. Anna D. Levin of New York City has announced the engagement of her daughter, Hyacinth, and E. J. Londow. Mr. Londow is with the Jewish Welfare Board at 71 West 47th Street, New York City.

CLASS OF 1913

Rev. L. C. Smart was transferred from Cheriton to 1640 Shaffer Street, Lynchburg, at the last meeting of the Virginia Conference of the M. E. Church South.

CLASS OF 1915

Thomas H. Anderson attended Leland Stanford University in California after leaving Trinity. He also studied several years in France and Spain. He now holds the chair of modern languages at Miami University, Oxford, Ohio.

CLASS OF 1917

J. W. "Wat" Smoot is located in Tarboro, N. C. He is connected with Rodgers and Company, Inc., cotton shippers and exporters of Norfolk, Va.

CLASS OF 1918

Rev. A. P. Brantley, who has been stationed at Asheboro. N. C., has been transferred to Melrose Methodist Church in Kansas City, Missouri.

CLASS OF 1920

The item that follows was taken from the *Wilmington* (N. C.) *News*, dated October 15, 1931: "Headquarters of the Methodist Episcopal Church, South, announced today that the Rev. Dr. H. K. King, Methodist pastor at Jonesboro, Arkansas, has been elected international secretary of Christian Religious Education."

Sammie T. Carson was drowned near Washington, N. C. on October 21 when his car plunged through the railing of Tanters Creek and into the deep waters of the stream. His brother, Baxter, '15, who accompanied him, escaped death when he managed to get out of the car through a partly opened window and swim to the surface of the creek. Sammie had a host of friends who will be saddened to hear of his death.

CLASS OF 1923

Nat. S. Crews, who has been associated with a law firm in Winston-Salem for the past three years, has opened offices in the Wachovia Bank building and will engage in a private general practice. Nat is at present secretary-treasurer of the Forsyth County Bar Association, and served formerly as treasurer of the Junior Bar Association.

CLASS OF 1924

Rev. and Mrs. F. B. Joyner of Cary announce the arrival of Peggy Ann on Wednesday, November 4, at Raleigh. Mrs. Joyner was Mary Wilkinson before her marriage.

Lucy Taylor has been teaching in Hertford for the past few years. She was recently married to Mr. Silas Whedbee of that city.

CLASS OF 1925

Born to Rev. and Mrs. M. C. Ellerbe, on September 25, a daughter, Judith Ann. Mr. Ellerbe is pastor of the Roberdel charge of the N. C. Conference, composed of several churches in his home county. His address is Route 5, Rockingham.

CLASS OF 1926

The wedding of T. Conn Bryan and Miss Jewell Funderburgh, of Nichols, South Carolina, took place in the First Baptist Church at Chapel Hill on October 10. The father of the bride, Rev. B. S. Funderburgh, officiated. Mr. and Mrs. Bryan live at 114 Kenan Street, Chapel Hill, while Conn is taking graduate work at the University of North Carolina.

Fulton A. Lee, who formerly represented the Burroughs Adding Machine Company in Durham, was transferred to the Raleigh officer for about a year. He has returned to Durham and will maintain headquarters here for the sale of Burroughs products.

CLASS OF 1927

Furman McLarty lives at 28 Gorham Avenue, Cambridge, Mass. He is taking graduate work in philosophy at Harvard.

A brilliant gathering of educational authorities occurred during the hundredth anniversary of the founding of LaGrange College for Women on October 9, in LaGrange, Georgia. The presidents, or their personal representatives, were present from practically every Georgia college, as were representatives of a number of Southern universities. Edyth Walker, M.E. '27,

who is teaching at LaGrange College, represented Duke University at that time.

CLASS OF 1928

Ray Carpenter is engaged in research in the field of comparative psychology. He is now located at the School of Medicine, Yale University. In a few weeks he will go to Panama where his address will be, Barro Colorado Biological Station, Barro Colorado Island. He spent last year at Stanford University in California.

Claiborne Ross owns and operates "The Tailored Man," a custom shop, at 102½ West Main Street, Durham.

Ella Zena Cartwright was married on Saturday, October 3, to Mr. Robah Fidus Baynes in Halifax, Virginia. Mr. and Mrs. Baynes are making their home in Roxboro.

CLASS OF 1929

Patricia Lee Bostick was born on October 30. She is the daughter of Mr. and Mrs. W. H. Bostick, formerly Zoa Lee Haywood, '29, of 425 Mangum Street, Durham.

Henry Folger and Miss Katherine Louise Fawcett were married in the Trinity Episcopal Church, Mount Airy, on Friday, October 30, at eight o'clock. Henry is associated with his father and brother, Fred, '23, in the law firm of Folger & Folger in Mount Airy.

Littlejohn Faulkner is working for the Roth Sign Company of Newark, New Jersey. His work consists of general maintenance on all types of electric signs. He lives at 43-33 Forty-sixth Street, Woodside, Long Island, New York. At night he works in a drug store on Lexington Avenue and Ninety-third treet in New York City.

CLASS OF 1930

Mr. and Mrs. Roland Farley of Danville, Virginia, announce the arrival of John Roland on October 12. Mrs. Farley will be remembered as Elsie Neal Gibson, '31.

Reuben H. Underwood married Miss Mary Lou Edwards on November 22, 1930. They make their home in Mount Holly, N. C., where Reuben is connected with the Carolina Dyeing and Winding Company.

Robert W. Wilson, a member of the class of 1930, died at his home in Durham on October 21. He had been ill for over a year. He was the son of Mr. and Mrs. V. E. Wilson of Chapel Hill Road. His many friends will be grieved to hear of his death.

CLASS OF 1931

Mary Elizabeth Faucette lives at her home, 610 East Trinity Avenue, Durham.

Rev. T. Herbert Minga was moved at the last meeting of the Methodist Conference in Texas from Cooper to Celeste, Texas.

Elizabeth Faye Mulholland teaches science in the high school at Creedmoor, N. C.

Donald Clay MacLaughlin is a student at the School of Medicine, University of Maryland. His address is 708 St. Paul Street, Baltimore.

Football Season Ends on Nov. 28 with the W. & L. Contest

(Continued from page 346)

there to hold and repulse Kentucky thrusts.

But the Kentucky victory was a costly one. The Devils were tired from the two consecutive hard battles and the long train trips and came back home to lose to N. C. State, 14-0. The Devils were listless on the field and only at times did they show the play that brought them victories over Villanova and Kentucky.

During the out-of-state campaign, the Devils uncovered Nick Laney, sophomore halfback, who has taken his place as a regular backfield man and is destined to be one of Duke's most brilliant performers during the next two seasons.

Laney made his debut against Wake Forest and then proceeded to turn in wonderful exhibitions of play against Tennessee, Kentucky and N. C. State. A triple-threat back, he passes and punts excellently and gives promise of developing into a great ball carrier. Some of the credit for the Devils' great showing against Tennessee and Kentucky can be attributed to the kicking of this 150-pound halfback.

Among others who have played especially well in recent games are Captain Kid Brewer, fullback; Emery Adkins, center; Lowell Mason, halfback; Artie Ershler, quarterback; Don Hyatt, Pinkie James and Fred Crawford, ends; and Joe Sink, guard.

FROSH WIN AND LOSE

After victories over N. C. State and Oak Ridge, the freshmen dropped their first game to Wake Forest, 19-0. They made a brilliant comeback, however, to defeat the Carolina Tar Babies, 12-0, in an Armistice Day battle. Duke freshmen won from Davidson, 7-0.

Several of the Duke yearlings have shown that they are to be reckoned with when varsity places are allotted next fall. Among these are Andrews, guard; Dunlap and Murphy, centers; Williams and Porreca, tackles; Bryan and Tarrall, ends; and McAnich, Brumbach, Lee, West, Cornelius and Widenburner, backs.

HARRIERS LOSE TO HEELS

The varsity cross-country runners, after defeating Davidson, lost their annual race to Carolina, but the Duke freshmen runners made it an even split by downing the Tar Babies. The yearlings also have a win over N. C. State's first year men to their credit.

Something worth cheering about

If you really want to know how hugely enjoyable a fine cigarette can be, just try Camels in the Humidor Pack!

It isn't only that Camels are made of the choicest tobaccos—fine Turkish and mild Domestic tobaccos expertly blended. . . .

It isn't only that these fine tobaccos are cleaned by a special vacuum process that whisks away all the peppery dust.

It's that *all* the goodness of these fine, clean tobaccos — *all* the rare fragrance, *all* the delightful aroma — reaches you factory-perfect — prime, mild, *fresh!*

The Humidor Pack does that — seals within germ-safe, moisture-proof Cellophane *all* the natural freshness — seals it so tightly that wet weather cannot make Camels damp, nor drought weather make them dry.

So just try Camels—fine cigarettes kept fine — as a relief from stale, parched, dried-out cigarettes.

Then you'll see why millions of folks like you are finding the cool, smooth, throat-friendly pleasure of Camels something well worth cheering about!

Tune in CAMEL QUARTER HOUR featuring Morton Downey and Tony Wons — Camel Orchestra, direction Jacques Renard — Columbia System — every night except Sunday

Smoke a FRESH cigarette

Smoke a *fresh* cigarette

HUMIDOR PACK

Don't remove the moisture-proof Cellophane from your package of Camels after you open it. The Humidor Pack is protection against perfume and powder odors, dust and germs. Even in offices and homes, in the dry atmosphere of artificial heat, the Humidor Pack delivers fresh Camels and keeps them right until the last one has been smoked

CAMELS

Mild .. NO CIGARETTY AFTER-TASTE

© 1931, R. J. Reynolds Tobacco Company, Winston-Salem, N. C.

DUKE UNIVERSITY
ALUMNI REGISTER

This photograph, showing the Chapel Tower in its relation to some of the massive construction surrounding it, was taken from the rear of Page Auditorium. The foreground of trees makes the setting most attractive.

In This Issue — Double Page Illustrations of Recent Events at Duke

VOLUME XVII   *December, 1931*   **NUMBER 12**

The Christmas Fireside

OF ALL the old festivals, that of Christmas awakens
the strongest and the most heartfelt associations *
There is a tone of solemn and sacred feeling that
blends with our conviviality, and lifts the spirit to
a state of hallowed and elevated enjoyment * It
is a beautiful arrangement, derived from the days
of yore, that this festival, which commemorates
the announcement of the religion of peace and of
love, has been made the season for gathering together of family connections and drawing closer
again those bands of kindred hearts, which the
cares and pleasures and sorrows of the world are
continually operating to cast loose; and of calling
back the children of a family who have launched
forth in life, and wandered asunder, once more to
assemble about the paternal hearth, that rallying
place of the affections, there to grow young and
loving again among the endearing mementos of
childhood *

From *Washington Irving's Sketch Book*

THE SEEMAN PRINTERY INCORPORATED
DURHAM, NORTH CAROLINA

Duke University Alumni Register

(Member of American Alumni Council)

Published at Durham, N. C. Every Month in the Year in the Interest of the University and the Alumni

Volume XVII   *December, 1931*   Number 12

In This Issue

Editor and Business Manager ....HENRY R. DWIRE, '02

Assistant Editors ....ELIZABETH ALDRIDGE, '24
                                   ALBERT A. WILKINSON, '26

Advertising Manager ....CHARLES A. DUKES, '29

TWO DOLLARS A YEAR   20 CENTS A COPY

ENTERED AS SECOND-CLASS MATTER AT THE POST-OFFICE AT
DURHAM, NORTH CAROLINA

THE COVER

The cover on this month's REGISTER shows a view of the new Chapel tower taken from behind Page Auditorium. It gives some idea of the foliage as well as of the massive character of the construction of the new Duke University plant.

UNIVERSITY VIEWS

The double page spread in this issue, giving photographs showing personages and scenes at Duke University during the past month, is sure to be of interest to REGISTER readers. Duke is having many visitors of distinction these days, and interesting events are taking place here constantly. It is the intention of the REGISTER to present them in pictorial form from time to time.

LETTERS

The REGISTER is receiving letters from readers along various lines. Some commend the REGISTER very highly; some make constructive suggestions, while occasionally there is a mild and courteous criticism. We are glad to get all these letters. It shows, for one thing, that the alumni are reading the ALUMNI REGISTER. Keep it up.

THE JANUARY ISSUE

The January issue of the REGISTER will contain detailed reports of the "Duke University Day" meetings, with the names of new officers elected and other interesting information. Don't fail to read the January issue.

THE EDITOR.

HYATT   CAPTAIN BREWER   ADKINS

Retiring Gridiron Stars Are Honored

THESE six Blue Devils who finished their careers this season were given monogramed watches by the Durham County Alumni Association at its annual Duke University Day dinner on December 10.

The players are: Captain Kid Brewer, unanimous choice for All-State fullback; Don M. Hyatt, All-State end; Emory Adkins, All-Southern third team center; Bill Bryan, All-State tackle on many selections; Bert Friedman, star guard; and Don Carpenter, who played both guard and tackle during the 1931 season.

All are North Carolina boys with the exception of Friedman, who hails from New York City. Their names have been connected with Duke gridiron activities since their freshman years.

BRYAN   BERT FRIEDMAN   CARPENTER

Duke University Alumni Register

Volume XVII   *December, 1931*   Number 12

Editorial Comment

DECIDEDLY ENCOURAGING

The interest among alumni generally in the observance of "Duke University Day" this year was decidedly encouraging.

More meetings were held than ever before, not only in North Carolina but in numerous cities in other states, and even in two countries outside the United States.

And in every one of these meetings there was a fine spirit of loyalty and coöperation and helpfulness.

One particularly encouraging thing about the meetings was the eagerness to ask questions and to get further information about the things that are happening at Duke these days.

The attitude of the alumni at all the gatherings showed a constructive interest in the growth and development of Alma Mater that is sure to be reflected in a constantly closer relationship between the two.

Of course, it is obvious that all the benefits of Duke Day will not be realized unless there is a "follow up" process.

The enthusiasm engendered on December 11 should be conserved and accentuated.

It would be a fine thing if every local group in which a meeting was held would do something definite at once in the direction of service to the institution.

Committees might be appointed by the newly elected presidents to take up activities along various lines that would be calculated to bring alumni and Alma Mater closer together.

Right now, soon after Duke University Day, 1931, would be an excellent time to do something specific and constructive.

INFORMATION FOR ALUMNI

At the various "Duke University Day" meetings this year folders of information about Duke University, its growth and progress, were distributed.

If those who could not be at the meetings desire these folders of facts and figures, they will be gladly supplied on request by the Alumni Office.

Often an alumnus who has been away from the institution for some years is asked questions regarding Duke that he finds it rather difficult to answer.

Quite a few such questions are answered in the literature distributed on Duke Day.

It would be a good idea to keep one of these folders close at hand.

For one of the best services an alumnus can render the institution in these days when things are happening so rapidly at Duke is to be ready to answer the many questions being asked by those on the outside.

A GOOD IDEA

Some of the alumni groups did something at the recent meetings on December 11 that many more might try to advantage next year.

This was the making of a special effort to have the parents of students now at Duke participate in their gatherings.

All the elements connected in any way with Duke University should be considered as parts of a unified whole.

That applies to administration, faculty, students, parents of students, and alumni.

They are not to be considered in any sense as totally separate units, but on the contrary as being closely related connecting links, and anything that brings them closer together is worth while to the institution.

Not only on "Duke University Day" but at other times during the year it might be feasible for the alumni to establish closer relationships with the families of Duke students.

WORTHY OF COMMENT

The recent Duke-Carolina football game, the annual gridiron classic in North Carolina, was notable for a number of reasons.

There was considerable editorial comment on the game and practically all of it was favorable to the institutions engaged, to their teams and alumni and to the public attending the game.

For one thing, there was considerable comment, newspaper and otherwise, on the absence of drinking.

One man from outside the state, who has attended many of the big football games in all parts of the country for the past ten years or more, said he had never seen less evidence of drinking or boisterous conduct at any big football contest during that time.

And a fine spirit of sportsmanship was displayed by the teams and their adherents.

When a good play was made the applause was not confined to one side of the stadium; when a player was injured there was seemingly more of a sympathetic attitude on the part of opposing players than sometimes seems to be in evidence.

Both teams were playing hard, but in a spirit of friendly rivalry and with real sportsmanship, and were having a great time.

The contest furthered the cause of friendly relations between the two institutions participating to a notable degree.

THE CHARITY GAME

The charity football game, played at the Duke Stadium on Saturday, December 5, was valuable because of the money realized for the relief of the unemployment situation in the state, but it served other purposes as well.

It demonstrated one or two things about which some people might have been skeptical before the game.

It proved that the players of the North Carolina "Big Five" teams could play together in harmony as members of the same team.

"I never thought I would ever live to see the day when Carolina and Duke players would be joined together in harmony against one opponent," remarked an enthusiastic alumnus of one of the institutions.

But they were, and they enjoyed it, and they felt better for having done it.

And the same applies to the members of the other teams participating in the December 5 game.

THE PAST SEASON

The football season which has just closed will go down in Duke annals as a notably successful one in which real progress was made in the development of the athletic program at this institution.

The REGISTER feels confident that alumni generally have been gratified at the results achieved.

Duke did not win all its games but the team won half of them against notably strong opponents, and only lost three contests. Two other games resulted in ties, this being true of the Duke-Carolina contest.

The team's record was almost exactly what Coach Wallace Wade predicted it would be very early in the season.

One thing caused much comment during the season, namely, Duke's notable defensive strength.

The team played seven games in which the opposing team did not cross the Duke goal line. Duke's opponents scored in only three games.

In this and other respects the foundation has been laid for a decidedly successful 1932 season.

It was Coach Wallace Wade's first season here and at the end of it Duke students, alumni, faculty and others interested in the success of the institution were stronger for the new director of athletics and head coach even than they were at the beginning.

For he had shown qualities of leadership and resourcefulness and sportsmanship entirely worthy of the man who piloted a team three times to the famous Rose Bowl gridiron classic on the Pacific coast.

Duke has absolute confidence in Wallace Wade and is one hundred per cent behind him. That fact has been, and is being, amply demonstrated.

"Duke University Day" Observed in Fifty-Two Communities

Celebrations On Anniversary of Signing of Indenture of Trust By Late James B. Duke Held In Cities In North Carolina, Several Other States of the Union and Two Countries Overseas—Observance Most Far-Reaching of Any Yet Held

Duke University, 11:40 a.m., Page Auditorium, Dean W. H. Wannamaker.
Duke University, Woman's College Auditorium, Dr. R. L. Flowers.
Durham (Dinner Meeting) (Dec. 10), Wallace Wade, Henry R. Dwire, Arnold Briggs, of Durham.
New York, President W. P. Few.
Washington, D. C., Congressman Walter Lambeth.
Richmond, Va., Dr. W. H. Glasson, Henry R. Dwire.
Nashville, Tenn., Dr. W. K. Boyd.
Roanoke, Va., Prof. J. S. Bradway.
Atlanta, Ga. (Dec. 16), Coach Wallace Wade.
Lynchburg, Va., Prof. B. G. Childs.
Columbia, S. C., (Duke luncheon held Sept. 27.)
St. Petersburg, Fla., (local speaker).
Los Angeles, Calif., (local speaker).
Japan (Hiroshima).
China (Shanghai).
Craven (New Bern) (Dec. 17), President W. P. Few.
Cabarrus (Concord), Dr. R. L. Flowers.
Wayne (Goldsboro), Dr. A. M. Proctor.
Guilford (High Point), Prof. Malcolm McDermott, Bill Murray.
Forsyth (Winston-Salem), Dr. J. F. Rippy.
Wake-Franklin (Raleigh), Dr. W. T. Laprade.
Vance-Granville (Henderson), Prof. H. E. Spence.
Wilson (Wilson), Dean Justin Miller.
Richmond (Hamlet), Dr. G. T. Rowe.
Gaston (Gastonia), Dr. Vollmer, Coach Cameron.
Mecklenburg (Charlotte), Mr. W. S. Lee, Coach Coombs, "Cap" Card, orchestra.
Stanly, Anson, Montgomery (Albemarle), Prof. F. S. Aldridge.
Cleveland, Rutherford and Lincoln (Shelby), Prof. A. M. Webb.
Cumberland (Fayetteville), Prof. J. M. Ormond.
Nash-Edgecombe (Rocky Mount), Coach Voyles, Emery Adkins.
Union (Monroe), Dr. Holland Holton.
Lee (Sanford), Dr. W. I. Cranford.
Surry (Mt. Airy), Dr. Bert Cunningham.
Pitt (Greenville), Dr. F. S. Hickman.
Rockingham (Yanceyville), Dean H. J. Herring, Capt. Lowell Mason.
Rowan (Salisbury), Judge T. D. Bryson.
Pasquotank (Elizabeth City), Prof. C. W. Edwards, Miss Elizabeth Aldridge.
Buncombe (Asheville), Dr. W. K. Greene, Capt. P. O. Brewer.
New Hanover (Wilmington) (Dec. 18), Henry R. Dwire.
Catawba (Newton) (Dec. 18), Dr. A. K. Manchester.
Halifax (Roanoke Rapids), Prof. H. E. Myers.
Baltimore, Md., (local speaker).
Birmingham, Ala., Dr. F. C. Brown.
Philadelphia, Pa., Dr. J. W. Carr, Jr.
Harnett (Erwin), Prof. W. B. Bolich.
Alamance (Burlington), Dr. R. N. Wilson.
Iredell (Statesville), Dr. P. N. Garber.
Robeson (Lumberton), Dr. W. A. Stanbury, Coach Robert Allen.
Columbus (Whiteville), Dr. J. T. Lanning, Coach Waite.
Watauga (Boone), (local speaker).
Burke (Morganton), (local speaker).
Haywood (Waynesville), (local speaker).

WITH MEETINGS and speakers scheduled as above in 52 cities in North Carolina and other states of the Union and in two countries overseas, the Duke University Day observance of 1931 proved decidedly the most far-reaching in scope and interest of any since the inauguration of these annual events six years ago.

It was the seventh anniversary of the signing by the late James B. Duke of the Indenture of Trust creating the Duke Endowment and making possible Duke University. The speakers at the various meetings paid tribute to Mr. Duke and to other benefactors of the institution, notably his father, the late Washington Duke, and his brother, the late B. N. Duke. Information was given as to the progress of the institution along various lines, and its future as a great educational agency was pictured. Certain misunderstandings as to Duke University's aims and purposes were corrected by some of the speakers in a most effective way.

"Duke University: Its Progress and Problems" was the general theme for Duke University Day this year and the addresses on that subject were informative and inspiring. Music was a part of the dinner program in a number of cities, while in some cases the addresses were broadcast by radio.

At practically all the meetings officers were elected for the ensuing year. A fine spirit of harmony and good fellowship prevailed, and it was the general opinion of those participating in the meetings that Duke University and its alumni were brought closer together because of them.

At all the Duke Day dinners menu card folders giving much information about Duke University and its notable progress were distributed. In addition to this, the speakers answered many questions showing deep interest on the part of the alumni in the continued achievements of the institution.

Last year 36 "Duke University Day" dinners were held.

President W. P. Few Addresses New York Alumni Gathering

Speaks to the Metropolitan Group In a "Duke University Day" Dinner At Hotel St. Regis of Certain Phases of University's Progress and Problems—Significance of the Duke Architecture Is Pointed Out In a Forceful Way

PRESIDENT W. P. Few delivered the principal address on the evening of Friday, December 11, at the "Duke University Day" dinner at the Hotel St. Regis in New York. He spoke of some of the points of recent progress and some of the problems of the institution. Among other things, he gave a forceful interpretation of the significance of the University architecture.

Following the program there was dancing, the music being furnished by the famous Vincent Lopez orchestra.

Harden F. Taylor has been president of the New York alumni group during the past year.

President Few said, in part:

This is the seventh anniversary of the signing by the late James B. Duke of the Indenture of Trust that made Duke University possible. In recognition of this event December 11 has been widely accepted as Duke University Day. Meetings like this are being held today in centers of population throughout this country and in some foreign countries. The Alumni Office suggests that this year we focus attention of graduates upon "Duke University: Its Progress and Problems."

The University as now organized includes seven units: Trinity College, the Woman's College, the graduate and professional schools of Arts and Sciences, Medicine, Law, Theology, and the Duke Forest.

I prefer to talk to you about the things you are most interested in and I am going to ask you for suggestions. While you are turning this over in your mind I will give you my ideal for this our University now in the making. Briefly put, it is this: The Graduate School of Arts and Sciences with its objective pursuit of knowledge and devotion to truth, and other Graduate Schools, particularly the Medical School, will, like American higher education in general, show the influence of German universities. The Colleges—the one for men and the other for women—with the emphasis on culture and character, and on training for service to country, to causes, and to humanity, will be in the English tradition of education. The Colleges,

essentially in the English tradition of education, and graduate and professional schools, affected by German and other influences, are to be welded into an American university that will seek to know and use the best that has been achieved elsewhere, but that will at the same time seek to make its own contribution to the cause of education.

Louis Pasteur, who has been called the most perfect man that ever entered the Kingdom of Science, in speaking to a large number of students a short while before his death, used these memorable words: "Young men, live in the serene peace of laboratories and libraries. Say to yourselves, first of all, 'What have I done for my instructors?' and as you go on further, 'What have I done for my country?' until the time comes when you may have the happiness of thinking that you have contributed in some way to the progress and to the welfare of humanity." The words of Pasteur seem to me to give at once admirable expression for the ideals both of the College and of the University. Let's all make them our own this year and every year, both teachers and students, graduates and supporters of the University in whatever capacity.

The conception of the University will explain the architecture. The buildings tie us to the great historic traditions of learning in the English-speaking race. The builders of this University have sought to achieve physical beauty and unity and through these to suggest spiritual values. The buildings have been constructed with the purpose to provide a place fit in every circumstance of beauty and appropriateness to be the home of the soul of the University and in the belief that these appropriate and beautiful surroundings will have a transforming influence upon students generation after generation and even upon the character of the institution itself. The architectural harmony and strength of the plant is intended to suggest unity and fullness of life. Here stand side by side science and religion—science and scholarship completely given to the full, untrammeled pursuit of the truth and religion with its burning passion for righteousness in the world—and commit the University in its very inception alike to excellence that "dwells high among the rocks" and to service that goes out to the lowliest. This underlying conception of the mission of Duke University has affected the building and organization of every part of it.

And if Duke University is to have this unity and "round completeness" it must ever cherish some galvanizing central principle that will hold it from disintegration. On this campus the Chapel, hard by the library and the laboratories and coöperating with the University in its every effort to promote the truth and serve humanity, is not only central, but, with its stained glass, its vaulted roof and lofty spire, will dominate the place. This is intended to be symbolical of the truth that the spiritual is the central and dominant thing in the life of man. Can this ideal be realized in our world and can religion and education in its highest forms ever engage successfully in a great formative, common undertaking to make this a better world than man has yet known? Duke University is founded in that faith; but we realize that it must be a religion that comprehends the whole of life and an education that seeks to liberate all the powers and develop all the capacities of our human nature.

Then goodness and beauty, righteousness and truth, gentleness and strength, can live together and, living together, can make a world that will sustain a really great and enduring civilization. And when that glad day arrives, religion and education will have a program for their combined activities in which there will never be armed neutrality or open conflicts, but the two will work together, each giving its all in wholehearted coöperation for a completely redeemed humanity. To produce this sort of synthetic power is the highest mission of Duke University.

Tablet Commemorates Event

THE tapered silver pen which James B. Duke used in signing the indenture of trust creating the Duke Endowment has been imbedded in a bronze tablet carrying the facsimile of the signature to the famous document which turned over $40,000,000 for educational and other philanthropic purposes in the two Carolinas. The indenture was signed seven years ago, and throughout North Carolina and in other parts of this country and abroad more than 50 groups of former students of Duke University, which was made possible by the indenture, have been celebrating the anniversary. The tablet, with the pen attached, is being kept temporarily in the Duke library.

Durham Alumni Hold First of "Duke Day" Observances

Over 250 In Attendance—Football Squads Entertained—Handsome Watches Presented to Seniors Playing Their Last Varsity Football—R. P. Reade Succeeds H. G. Hedrick As President—Other Officers of Alumni Group Are Named

FORERUNNER as it was of the series of 1931 Duke University Day dinners, the annual meeting of the Durham Alumni Association, held at dinner in the University Union on the evening of Thursday, December 10, was notably successful in every way. Over 250 persons participated, including the Duke varsity and freshman football squads and the State Championship squad from the Durham High School, all being guests of the Durham alumni.

A feature of the evening that created great enthusiasm was the presentation to the six seniors who played their last varsity games this year of handsome watches engraved with their initials and with an appropriate inscription. These watches were the gifts of the Durham County Association of Duke University Alumni.

Officers for the ensuing year were chosen as follows:

President, R. P. Reade.

Vice-President, W. P. Budd.

Secretary, Mrs. W. B. Umstead.

Treasurer, Leroy Graham.

Executive Committee: H. G. Hedrick, A. W. Stamey, Murray Jones, Mrs. Marshall Spears, Sterling Nicholson.

Following the presentation of Dr. R. L. Flowers, Dr. W. H. Wannamaker and Miss Alice Baldwin, dean of the Woman's College, and the announcement that President W. P. Few was absent because of having gone to New York to deliver the Duke Day address there, the first talk of the evening was made by Henry R. Dwire, Director of Public Relations and Alumni Affairs. Mr. Dwire first spoke of the close relationship between Duke University and Durham, stressing the peculiar obligation resting upon Durham alumni to aid in the proper interpretation of the institution to the outside world. He went on to talk of the significance of Duke University Day, then touching briefly upon the progress and problems of the University and closing with an appeal to all present to aid in every way possible in making the future of Duke University

entirely worthy of its past and worthy of the benefactions that have given it such an admirable opportunity for service to humanity.

Arnold Briggs ('09), made a notably impressive talk on Duke, emphasizing particularly its future possibilities and the obligation imposed upon students, faculty and alumni by the opportunity presented them for service to humanity through the institution and its work. He spoke of the architecture of the new University Chapel and its significance as symbolic of spiritual ideals, stressing the fact that the institution stands, and will continue to stand, for the supremacy of spiritual values. The soundness of the foundation upon which the University was being built was pointed out in a most effective manner. Mr. Briggs' address was interspersed with humorous hits that delighted his hearers.

The Seniors to whom watches were presented included Captain "Kid" Brewer, Don Carpenter, Bert Friedman, Don Hyatt, Bill Bryan and Emory Adkins. The brief presentation speech by President Hedrick was quite effective.

The dinner opened with the singing of the Alma Mater song, led by Emmett McLarty; the invocation was delivered by Dr. W. A. Stanbury; following the presentation of the Varsity and freshman football squads, Bud Fisher led in singing "The Blue and White." Music was furnished during the service of the meal by the Blue Devils Orchestra.

H. G. Hedrick, the retiring president, presided at the meeting in an exceedingly happy manner. As chairman of the Athletic Council and in other ways Mr. Hedrick has been prominent for a number of years in Duke affairs and his year as head of the Durham Alumni Association has been notably successful. The innovation this year in the entertainment of the football squads and in the presentation of watches to the retiring gridiron stars has been the subject of much favorable comment. In every way the occasion was one of the very best in the entire history of alumni events.

History of Norfolk is a New Book from Duke Press

Volume by Thomas J. Wertenbaker Is Scholarly and Authoritative Work on One of America's Important Ports—Author Handles Masses of Material in Way That Evokes Praise From Reviewers of the Book

"NORFOLK: Historic Southern Port" is the title of a recent book by Thomas J. Wertenbaker, issued by the Duke University Press. It is a scholarly and authoritative work on one of America's important ports. The main emphasis falls upon the first 200 years of Norfolk's history, but the contemporary period is by no means neglected.

The following is from an extended review of the book in the Norfolk *Virginian Pilot:*

"The port's part in the early tobacco trade, in the West Indian trade, in the Revolutionary War, in the creation of the constitution, in the imbroglios with France and England during the Napoleonic wars, and its tragic days of struggle and subjection during the Civil War are treated at graphic length. Also lengthy . . . are the chapters dealing with the modern period compressed between the years 1880-1930. . . .

"Richly pictorial the past unfolds; and we visualize not only the development of an historic port, but follow its story as a significant chapter in the rise of the American nation. For Thomas J. Wertenbaker is the modern historian, projecting civic history against the larger background of national expansion. In this, as in his tracing of economic trends, he exceeds the scope of his predecessors, Burton and Forrest—both of them primarily local recorders."

Regarding this volume, W. L. Oliver says in the Richmond *News Leader* of November 13:

"Conceived in the brain of a covetous king, born on the shores of a disdainful colony, Norfolk found herself an infant Ishmael among her sister towns in colonial Virginia. That was in 1682. By 1931 she has become one of the great ports of the Atlantic seaboard, a definite rival of Boston, Philadelphia and Baltimore. With age has come wisdom. Norfolk is eyeing the manufacturing honors of her neighbors, determining to give shipping a rival within her own household. The future will learn of her progress in new realms.

"Thomas Wertenbaker, in his 'Norfolk: Historic Southern Port,' has compiled a fascinating record of early colonial communal life which even the most in-different Virginian will find it hard to lay aside. Facts are allowed to speak for themselves with just enough interpretation to give the reader confidence in the historian's intelligence in handling his subject, with not enough to make him scornful of the historian's views and, ergo, doubtful of the fair presentation of data.

"In the seventeenth century, plantation owners along the James wanted no seaport. Their ports were at their front doors. Ships from foreign lands docked at plantation wharves, unloaded household goods, farm implements, weapons, dainties for milady and sports wear for milord. Tobacco was taken aboard for the return voyage. Trading was haphazard and delightful. But happiness in the colonies could not be converted into pounds sterling. So the British crown ordered a seacoast town to be built. In 1662 the Virginia assembly passed an act (under orders of Charles II) creating a town to store and export tobacco.

"Norfolk's hectic history in the years that followed is presented in minute detail, always with citations from the records. From 1880 to the present there is less detail, the author explaining that lack of historical perspective, scarcity of private letters and impropriety of writing critically of the living made this too difficult.

"In his estimate of the future, the author returns to the past and treats Norfolk's history under eight divisions: first, Colonial period; second, Revolutionary period; third, post-Revolution prosperity; fourth, hard times of trade restriction era; fifth, period immediately preceding the War Between the States when internal improvements were vainly sought; sixth, war and Reconstruction days; seventh, deep-water transportation era from the seventies to 1914; eighth, the World War inflation. And it is a future ninth manufacturing period to which reference was made earlier in this review.

"Norfolk has done an exceptionally fine job of self-building in spite of over-lapping handicaps. And it would also appear that the author has acquitted himself well in his handling of masses of tedious material."

Some Alumni Personalities

David A. Houston, '91, recently delivered one of the principal addresses at the convention in Dallas, Texas, of the Mortgage Bankers' Association of America. He has won real distinction in this branch of finance, having been treasurer and later president of the Federal Farm Land Bank at Columbia, S. C., and since 1925 president of the Carolina Mortgage Company of Raleigh. After graduating at Trinity College, Mr. Houston took post-graduate work under Dr. John F. Crowell in political science in the fall of 1891. He continued this work in '92, also teaching the business course and assisting as instructor in political science.

Charles H. Livengood, of the Class of 1904, was recently elected chairman of the Alumni Council of Duke University. He served last year as vice-chairman of the council, having been an active and useful member of the body for the past several years. He is prominent in the Kiwanis club and in other civic circles. One of his sons graduated at Duke in June, 1931, and one is now a freshman. Mr. Livengood is superintendent of the Durham branch of the Liggett & Myers Tobacco Company.

Andrew Jarvis Hobbs, Jr., of the Class of 1919 at Duke, received his M.A. from Emory in 1920 and his B.D. from Yale in 1925. He has been for a number of years a member of the North Carolina Conference of the M.E. Church, South, being stationed now at New Bern. He is an active alumnus of Duke, being president now of the Craven County Alumni Association. For a number of years he has been prominent in Rotary circles, having been president of the Red Springs club before going to New Bern.

Duke University Owns Notably Valuable Newspaper Collection

Some Six Thousand Volumes, Including Files of Newspapers From 42 States and District of Columbia—457 Cities In United States Represented—Thirty-Three Countries Have Part In Foreign Section, Bulk of Foreign Papers Coming from England, France and Germany

THE NEWSPAPER Room of the Duke University Libraries is one of the most valuable of the library divisions. Miss Allene Ramage and her assistant, N. M. Blake, who have charge of the division, are justly proud of the splendid collection of newspapers on file there.

This department furnishes a fertile field for research work for graduate students. The papers have been used, primarily, by history students. English students, however, are now beginning to use them in locating and studying contributions of minor writers.

The collection, which is composed of some six thousand volumes, is quite general in origin. In it are files of newspapers from forty-two states and from the District of Columbia. All six of the states missing from the catalogue are west of the Mississippi River. Four hundred and fifty-seven cities in the United States are represented in the files. In the foreign section, thirty-three countries are represented. These include Canada, many countries of South America, Japan, Spain, Italy, Belgium, Switzerland, Austria, Holland, and a number of smaller principalities. The bulk of the foreign papers, in the collection, come from England, France and Germany.

The first interest in a newspaper section for the library appeared when Dr. W. K. Boyd was a student in Trinity College. Dr. Boyd was a member of the Hesperian Literary Society. Because of his interest in this field, the society secured two volumes of old North Carolina newspapers. These formed the nucleus of the present collection.

Dr. Boyd's interest in North Carolina papers continued after he became a member of the history faculty of Trinity, now Duke University. He continued making additions to the original volumes, finally being fortunate enough to secure files of some Virginia and South Carolina papers.

Duplicates of newspaper files, discarded by the Library of Congress and by the American Antiquarian Society, of Worcester, Massachusetts, later found their way into the Duke collection. These were mainly northern and New England papers. Doctor E. M. Carroll, Professor of History at Duke, has assisted in securing files of a number of foreign papers. Thus has the collection grown from local to world-wide interest.

One of the valuable collections of files, in the Newspaper Room, is that of old colonial papers. Most of these were published in New England, but there are many, also, from North Carolina and Virginia. There is also a large group of ante-bellum and Confederate War newspapers, published in the South during those periods of American history. These papers are more generally used by Doctor Boyd's students because of their interest in Southern history. A number of papers, published in the South, during the reconstruction period, also form an interesting collection.

Files of current papers begin around the year 1900. The library subscribes to forty newspapers, twenty of which are bound. Many of these files are complete.

A fifth collection contains German, Austrian, and French papers published during the World War period. These are all complete, as is the file for the *London Times*, for the same period. These, together, give an excellent history of the World War as it was seen by contemporary writers both in Allied and Central Power countries.

Large files of individual newspapers in the collection include the *London Times*, 1810-1846, 1857-1859, and 1870 to date; the *New York Herald*, 1860 to 1919; and the *New York Times* from 1890 to date.

Miss Ramage employs an excellent system of indexing. First, she has a check list of all papers, geographically. This list is arranged alphabetically by states. Then the cities of each state are arranged alphabetically. Under each city, titles of papers published there, which are represented in the collection, are listed alphabetically. A short historical sketch of each newspaper is given under its title. Dates of issues in the Duke files are given with this historical sketch. There is also a complete index of the newspapers, by

(Continued on page 370)

Program of the Legislative Research Department Grows

This Branch of the Duke School of Law Is Now Engaged In Six Lines of Active Research—Reports Already Made of Department's Findings In Three Particular Subjects—Although Only In Operation Short Time, Department Is Doing Valuable Work

AFTER two months of operation the legislative drafting and research department of the Duke University School of Law has rapidly increased its work and is now engaged in six lines of active research.

Three particular subjects have already been investigated and reports made of the department's findings. These written reports dealt with receiverships for counties in North Carolina; the rights of holders of repudiated state bonds with respect to property pledged to secure such bonds; and local government under the present state constitution.

All of these studies were undertaken on behalf of parties interested in these subjects. In particular, the study of local government was carried on for the constitutional revision commission of North Carolina. A thorough investigation was made of the actual workings of county and city government with relation to the provisions of the present state constitution.

An interesting phase of this study was the conferences held by the department at the law school with leading men of the state. One group consisted of the leaders in the affairs of county government, while the other group included a large number of mayors and others interested in city government.

A number of matters now holds the attention of the legislative research and drafting department. Among these are: (1) A proposed statute for the consolidation of the governments of Durham county and city, undertaken at the request of the local chamber of commerce. This project is one carried over from the preceding year and calls for exhaustive research and careful attention. Another year will be required for its completion. (2) A bill to be introduced at the forthcoming session of Congress embodying the recommendations of the Wickersham commission for the handling of juvenile offenders in federal courts. This project was undertaken at the request of parties connected with the Wickersham commission.

(3) Legislation to be introduced at the forthcoming session of Congress designed to curb the evils of "short selling." (4) A proposed statute to be introduced at the next session of the New York Legislature designed to revise the lien laws of that state. Assistance in this matter was requested by the chairman of the joint committee of the New York legislature appointed to investigate the lien laws of that state.

(5) The matter of proposed legislation in North Carolina, designed to protect more fully the rights of mortgagors in foreclosure proceedings. This is a subject of considerable importance under existing conditions which are likely to continue for some time to come. (6) Further studies and reports for the constitutional revision commission of North Carolina.

Law and Public Welfare Are Closely Allied Forces, Declares Mrs. W. T. Bost

Lawyers and leaders in the field of public welfare have a common project in regard to social legislation, Mrs. W. T. Bost, director of public welfare in North Carolina, told third-year law students in an address delivered in connection with the Duke University Law School's senior course in Legal Aid clinic work.

The course followed by the students is designed, among other things, to bring to their attention various activities in the community related to the general field of law practice.

Mrs. Bost outlined the general history of social legislation in North Carolina, contrasting its conditions one hundred years ago with conditions today, and spoke of the present organization of the state welfare department. She characterized its work as preventive as well as remedial, and emphasized the importance, particularly at this time, of keeping in mind the well-rounded program that includes other activities than supplying material relief.

Prior to the lecture at the law school, Mrs. Bost was the guest of the law faculty at a luncheon at the Union. Dean Justin Miller, Prof. Howard Jensen, sociologist, and W. T. Towe, attorney, were present at the lecture, in addition to members of the class.

Effective Work Being Done By Dramatic Arts Department

Stagecraft, History of the Theater and Playwriting Classes Are Creating Much Interest
—Successful Season For the Duke Players Is Assured—To Enter District
Dramatic Contest In a Number of Events—Good Results Being
Achieved In Scenic Design Work

PROFESSOR A. T. West's Dramatic Arts Department of Duke University is a bee-hive of energy at this time of the year. With classes filled with industrious, enthusiastic students, Professor West may justly point with pride to the growth of his work.

Mr. West is teaching three courses and directing the work of the one-time Taurian Players, now called the Duke Players. He enrolled in his stagecraft class last year eight students. This year the same class has twenty-seven members. Professor West says that the very first work of this group was better than the final work of the class last year.

In the "History of the Theatre" class, there are now enrolled fifty students. Last year this class had only twelve members. Fourteen students took the voice course last year, while thirty-five are enrolled in the course for this year. The playwriting class, which is very restricted and is limited to what Mr. West calls "handpicked" students, has only ten members, as last year.

Students in these courses are required to act in three plays, act as technical director for one play, and really direct one play, each year. These are largely one-act plays, written by the students themselves, and are studio, rather than public, productions. However, many of them are to be given in the Little Theatre, in the basement of West Duke, on the East Campus.

Professor West feels very keenly the need of a real "Little Theater" on the campus for his work. He speaks enthusiastically of other institutions which have just completed such buildings.

In discussing the plans of the department for the present school year Professor West spoke of much expansion. Three major productions by the Duke Players are planned for the year. The first of these, Shaw's "Arms and the Man," has already been presented. It was a real success. Early in the spring, the Players will give either Phillip Barry's "Hotel Universe," or George Kelly's "Craig's Wife." During the commencement season they will present a Shakespearian play. Professor West is, as yet, unde-cided whether this will be "The Merchant of Venice," or "Twelfth Night."

Last year, Professor West wrote a modern version of Shakespeare's "Taming of the Shrew," for the Taurians' final play. This year, however, the play will be given in Shakespearian style.

Work has already begun on the preparation for Duke's part in the District Dramatic Contest among colleges. A number of one act plays are to be tried out from which Mr. West will select one for use in the contest. These will be cast and ready for rehearsal before Christmas. Some of those already chosen for the preliminaries are amateur plays written by Duke students. Others are from the pens of professionals.

Last year Duke entered only one event in the contest, that of Play Production. In this contest, the Taurians won first place. At the meeting of the association Mr. West was elected state president. This year, Professor West plans to enter a number of events. These will include Play Production, Costume Designing, Makeup, Scenic Designing, and Original Play Writing.

His students are now busily engaged in stagecraft and scenic design work and in directing their one act plays. In addition, a number of students are writing scripts from which is to be selected a play for the Birthday party of the Quadrangle Pictures in February. The department is to present this play. It will take the form of a travesty on the old melodrama of the villain who holds a mortgage on the old farm, and the widow who is saved, at the last moment, by the long lost son.

Tour of Musical Clubs

The December tour of the Duke University Musical clubs was terminated on Saturday evening, December 12, in a concert given at North Carolina College for Women. During the previous week the clubs gave concerts in Lumberton, Chadbourn, Wadesboro, Charlotte, Wingate, Monroe, and Concord. Fifty-eight students made the trip, and the group were greeted by large and appreciative audiences in each community.

Observations Made During a Trip Through the Duke Forest

Dry Weather of the Fall Seems Not to Have Affected the Trees Except the Dogwood—
Forest Fires Have Caused Forest Management Considerable Concern But
So Far Have Damaged Only Comparatively Small Number of
Acres of the Duke University Property

STRANGE days have come to the silence of the thousands of acres in the Duke Forest. For years the old trees have stood amid the wild life about them, taking on new growth, annually, budding in the spring, and spreading their beautiful leaves to the sun—the sun which has watched their changing colors through the seasons. This year seasons have been different. The two droughts, the long continued high temperatures of the summer, and the extended delay of frost this fall, have changed conditions. The high temperature has changed the period of growth. There has, too, been the constant movement of men through the forest in a final effort to clear up the work of compiling the timber inventory and the completion of the great timber map. Besides all this, there has been the crackle of flames, and the hurried, tramping, feet of many men, as the forest fires have crept in to some portions of the great area controlled by Duke University.

In late October, the fall colors began to appear. The leaves of the great white oaks became a reddish brown tinged with lavender. Nearby were the bright scarlet leaves of those beauties, the scarlet oaks. The swamp chestnut or cow oaks, as they are sometimes called, were bright with their conspicuous coloring.

As the days passed by, the colors changed again and again. There appeared the yellow, and, later, the light brown, of the hickories. The red of the sourwood was as beautiful as ever. Late in November, the evergreens began their annual change. The dark blue berries of the red cedar appeared against a background of green tinged with gold. Blue and olive tints began to appear among the other evergreens. The ailanthus, or "tree of heaven," planted near one of the old homesteads, in the depths of the forest, had shed its javelin head leaves and its flowers. Stark and cold it stood there with its dried seed pods rattling in the wind and falling off to leave the bare tree stripped of all its glory—a fitting companion to the empty, forgotten fireside of the old house.

The dry weather of the fall seems not to have affected the trees of the forest except the dogwood. Its leaves were seared in the heat, browned, and released, long before their natural time.

Now the forest waits, its floor covered with its beautiful colored patch-work quilt, for the night of winter, with its extraordinarily late frost and its covering of snow.

Dr. C. F. Korstian, head of Duke's Forestry Department, reports only two little showers in October and less than that in September. He believes, however, little damage was done to the trees, except to terminate their growth a little earlier. The disastrous forest fires which recently have visited Durham and Orange counties have been a source of uneasiness and of loss of sleep for the entire department. Fortunately, at the cost of much real labor on the part of the entire forestry force, the fires have only damaged twenty-seven acres of Duke property, at the time of this writing. The fires have originated in other property and, in most cases, have been extinguished before reaching the Duke Forest.

No plans have been made, as yet, by Dr. Korstian's department for cutting any timber in the forest, beyond the taking out of about a hundred cords of fuel wood this winter. Dr. Korstian says he is waiting for the timber and pulp wood market to improve before beginning any additional cutting.

In the meantime, the work of reforestation and of caring for the agricultural sections of the forest goes on rapidly. Of the young trees planted last spring, 80% to 90% of the pines, and virtually 90% of the hardwoods, have survived, despite the dry weather.

"It is interesting to note," says Dr. Korstian, "that the dry weather, in June and July, was more critical in the lives of these young trees than was that of the early fall. This was because it came in the midst of the growing season and because it was accompanied by such a season of long continued, high temperatures." Stock has already been ordered for the planting of approximately one hundred acres of young trees this

(Continued on page 370)

Circulation Department of the General Library is Interesting

This Sixth Article in Series Relating to Duke Libraries Deals With Way in Which Thousands of Books Are Made Available For Readers—Inter-Library Circulation Plan Provides For Exchange With Other Institutions

THE CIRCULATION department of the Duke University General Library is a much more interesting organization than might seem possible at first thought. Much of its work is routine but to those who love books the very association with thousands of them becomes a never-ceasing joy.

Mr. Ben E. Powell, the head of the department, speaks of his organization with pride. Composed of six full-time workers and twenty-seven student assistants, it makes of this division of the library a veritable bee hive of industry. From Mr. Powell's office on the second floor of the library one watches students and faculty members coming and going in their search for just the right books for their work.

The main circulation desk receives from each applicant a card containing the catalogue number and the call number of the book desired. This card is prepared by the applicant after consulting the catalogue in the general card catalogue room. The card is sent through the pneumatic tube to the particular stack level where this book is shelved. The book is located by the student assistant on that stack level and returned to the main desk by way of an electric elevator which connects all stack levels with the delivery desk.

Sometimes the book desired is not on its shelf. This may be true for any one of several reasons. It may have been borrowed from the library by some other applicant. It may have been placed on reserve in either the graduate or the undergraduate reading rooms. It may be on a particular reserve at the main desk. It may be in a graduate student's carrel. Or it may have been loaned to the library of some other educational institution. In either case, the stack assistant can return the card with a note by way of the pneumatic tube, or he may discuss the situation over the telephone with the assistant in charge of the main desk. These telephones connect every stack level and every department of the library not only with the librarian's office, but also with every department of the University.

As far as possible, duplicate copies of all books in constant use eliminate the necessity of saying to an applicant; "That book is not available at present."

If the book is found on its shelf it is delivered to the applicant after two cards have been filed. These cards serve as a double check on books taken from the library. One shows the call number of the book. It is filed in order with other call number cards. The second card shows the date on which the book is due to be returned. It is filed in order by the calendar. The assistants at the main delivery desk keep these records. They also mail notices concerning books which are overdue and collect fines on them when returned. The work of the main delivery desk is in charge of a full time, experienced man, assisted by a varying number of students who have had at least one year of experience.

The assistants in the stacks check the shelves regularly keeping the books in order. They assist members of the faculty and graduate students who have stack permits to find books in which they are interested. They take care of the individual reserves in the students' carrels, returning the books to the shelves at the proper time. Permits allowing personal access to the stacks are issued to members of the faculty and to graduate students on the approval of major professors.

Each semester hundreds of books are taken from the stacks at the request of various members of the faculty and placed in the reserve reading rooms. These books may not be taken from the building except during the night. Occasionally a professor asks for a special reserve of a certain number of books to be kept at the main desk. This reserve is marked with the professor's name. Graduate students in his classes may take these books into their carrels for a limited period, returning them to the reserve when through with them.

The carrels are nooks among the shelves throughout all the stack levels. Each of these is at the end of the shelves. Each carrel has at least one window for

DUKE UNIVERSITY DURING THE PAST MONTH

The Bands: Charity Game 12-5-31

immediately after Duke-Carolina game.
Davison; Mrs. E. C. Marshall; E. C.
wment; Mrs. W. P. Few; Dr. Frederic
P. Few; Mrs. E. C. Brooks; Mrs. J. W.
Max Gardner; Mrs. O. Max Gardner;
wright; Mrs. Laurence Stallings; Mrs.
President of the University of North
the Duke Endowment.

7. The combined bands of Carolina,
Duke, State, and Wake Forest made
up the 250-piece band which played
at the Charity game on December 5
in Duke Stadium.

8. Part of the crowd in the Duke
stadium at the Duke-Carolina game.

9. Mr. and Mrs. W. N. Reynolds, of Winston-Salem, were among
the distinguished guests attending the Duke-Carolina game. Mr.
Reynolds is a member of the class of 1886, and is a member of
the Board of Trustees of the Duke Endowment and of the University Board of Trustees.

10. Dr. Frank Kingdon, of East Orange, N. J., led the religious
emphasis week services at the University early in December. He
is shown here with Dr. R. L. Flowers.

light and ventilation. It is furnished with a desk and a chair. Electric lights allow the students to work in their carrels at night. Any graduate student who is actually writing a thesis or a doctor's dissertation may have one of these carrels reserved for him by the head of the circulation department, without further cost than the regular library fee.

A student who has a carrel assigned to him may take into his carrel such books as he needs for his work. These are reserved for him there at his request. When he indicates that he has no further need for them, the stack assistant returns them to their shelves. If during the time they are on reserve in a carrel, books are urgently needed elsewhere, they may be borrowed temporarily, a note being left by the stack assistant to explain their absence.

An inter-library circulation plan provides for the exchange of books with other libraries. In this way books have been both borrowed and loaned by the Duke library in very cordial relations with a number of other libraries, including those of the University of North Carolina, Princeton, Harvard, Yale, and Columbia.

Mr. Powell's work also includes the supervision of the reference department of the library. The main reference room opens from the delivery desk. This room is under the care of one or more assistants during library hours. Encyclopedias and other reference works to which all students are allowed access are kept in this room. None of these books, however, may ever be taken from the room. Every facility is offered for research there.

Thousands of different faces, the undertone of soft voices, the tiptoeing of many feet, the flashing colors of many books, and the varied personalities of all the applicants, combine to make this one of the very pleasant departments of the great library.

Duke University Owns Notably Valuable Newspaper Collection

(Continued from page 363)

title, alphabetically; a Chronological Index, by decades; and an Editor's and Publisher's Index, listing, alphabetically, all persons who worked on the papers.

One of the most valuable bits of service given by this division to Duke students is the securing of check lists of other newspaper files. These inform students engaged in research work where they may find old files of newspapers not included in the Duke collection. Miss Ramage has secured check lists from the University of North Carolina, from the North Carolina Historical Commission, in Raleigh, and from Richmond, Virginia. The Richmond list includes those papers on file in the Virginia State Library, the Confederate Museum, and the Valentine Museum. All of these, being easy of access, are often used by Duke students. In addition, Miss Ramage has secured check lists from the Library of Congress, Washington, D. C.; and from Yale and Wisconsin Universities.

The Duke collection of newspapers is growing to such an extent that 1,439 volumes were added to it last year, to say nothing of a number of unbound copies, not yet listed.

Observations Made During a Trip Through the Duke Forest

(Continued from page 366)

winter. About twenty-five acres will be stocked with hardwoods, the remainder will be planted in pines. The young hardwoods ordered include yellow poplar, or tulip, black locust, and walnut. Open land which is least useful for agricultural purposes is being used for this reforestation.

Agricultural products of the forest, this year, in addition to the usual crop of tobacco, included small quantities of molasses, sweet potatoes, corn, and cotton. These products are marketed and the proceeds used for reforestation.

Lecture and Clinic By Dr. C. H. Mayo at the Duke Hospital

Dr. Charles H. Mayo, noted physician of Rochester, Minn., lectured at Duke Hospital on December 12 before a large group of students, members of the Hospital staff, and representatives of the medical profession of North Carolina. The distinguished surgeon spoke of the unlimited fields of scientific research that lie ahead and of the possibilities of great discoveries yet to be made in the realm of medicine for human good.

Glands and their effect on the body was the subject of Dr. Mayo's clinic. He showed numerous stereopticon slides illustrating by chart and photograph the effect of glands and their response to treatment. Dr. Mayo indicated that the study of glands holds vast possibilities for research. Many ailments, he said, which have been difficult if not impossible to diagnose have their origin in the mysterious functions of numerous glands in the body.

Following the clinic Dr. Mayo was honor guest at a luncheon given by Alpha Kappa Kappa medical fraternity, of which he is a member, held in the University Union. While in North Carolina Dr. Mayo spoke at Wake Forest College and in Raleigh.

Program of College Education To Meet This State's Needs*

Dr. W. K. Greene, of Duke Faculty, Presents Matter in Interesting and Forceful Manner
—Declares That "This Is a Day of Upheaval in the Undergraduate Curric-
ulum—A Spirit of Self-Consciousness Has Been Developed and
Experimentation Has Begun"

TOO often the message and life of a college are simply mirrors that reflect the contemporary spirit of its environment. They are not moulders but reflectors of civilization and mere reflection of a condition never changes it.

Recently, in Chicago, a conference of the representatives of 278 liberal arts colleges was held "to consider the relation of the college of liberal arts to higher education in the United States."

This is a day of upheaval in the undergraduate curriculum. A spirit of self-consciousness has been developed and experimentation has begun. As was to be expected, the experimentation is confined to a comparatively few colleges and universities. The majority are doing nothing, merely waiting for evidences of strength or weakness in the experiments. A few, fast in the shackles of tradition, are positively hostile to any change.

Within the present century the number of liberal arts colleges, we are told, has increased 40 per cent; the number of students, 600 per cent; and the amount of productive funds, 500 per cent. Two things are worthy of remembrance concerning this vast body of college students: first, no student has a right to a college education. It is his privilege if he has the ability and the industry to make the proper use of his opportunity; second, there are not too many young men and young women in college, but there are too many of them in college who ought not to be there. There are three kinds of students in our colleges and universities: first, those who have entered simply to have a good time; second, those who hope to acquire a veneer of culture; third, those who come in the spirit of a great adventure, earnestly seeking preparation for some worth-while life-work.

For some time, critics of methods and practices in higher education have felt that something was wrong with our system of college instruction. They have not been timid in pointing out the defects. These I shall attempt to summarize.

1. *There is a vagueness of aim* as evidenced by the following declarations of the purpose of a college education:

(a) "To give some measure of significant and ordered knowledge in the main fields of human interest and a large measure in one field."
(b) "To fit men and women to be useful members of society."
(c) "To prepare students for life."
(d) "To develop the intellectual life of students." (This is explained as a "Process not only intellectual in the narrow sense of learning to think, but also aesthetic, moral, social, and religious in the sense that the end sought is the finest possible texture of a student's mind.")
(e) "To make good men and women, i.e., good for something."
(f) "To train men and women in intellectual methods."
(g) "To develop the mental ability of students."
(h) "To prepare students for leadership in business, professional, and public life."
(i) "To prepare men and women for a vocation."
(j) "To train men and women in representative modes of thought."

2. *Colleges are measuring achievement by the time element.* The University of Chicago and Rollins College are boldly initiating educational processes that subordinate the element of time.

3. *Undue stress is laid upon the machinery of grades, credits, groups, and sequences.* This has given birth to the fallacy that the earning of 120 semester-hour credits makes a student an educated man. The University of Wisconsin, the University of Chicago, Emory University, Reed College, and Rollins College have laid the axe at the root of this tree.

4. *Excessive vocational pressure is brought to bear upon the shaping of the present normal curriculum.*

---

* This paper was read by Dr. W. K. Greene, Dean of Undergraduate Instruction at Duke University, before the college section of the North Carolina Educational Association. No attempt is made to treat the subject quantitatively.

There is an overwhelming preponderance of students in the "Business Administration" course. Almost every group leading to a degree is a "pre"- something and little emphasis is placed upon the group as being something within itself. The average college is thought of largely as a preparatory school for business or profession. This should not constitute the sum total of its usefulness. Professional schools are preparatory schools also but no one of them divides its curriculum into groups of "pre-this" and "pre-that."

5. *The college is too departmentalized.* The college has suffered disintegration into conglomerates of departments. There is a decided movement among the stronger institutions to do away with a water-tight departmental system in favor of divisional groups. This is one of the most urgently needed of all educational reforms, yet it is exceedingly difficult to bring many of the most prominent members of the instructional staff out of the great tradition.

6. *The dominant aim on the intellectual side is the impartation of facts rather than the development of intelligence.* This is a crushing criticism and not wholly unwarranted.

7. *The program of the college is generally lacking in individualization (departmental and instructional).* Many colleges are endeavoring to remedy this defect by the introduction of "Honors Courses," by the sectioning of students according to ability, by the earning of college credit, on entrance, by examinations, by frequent conferences of students with instructors, by the cultivation of faculty-student relationships, and by the adoption of the "House Plan." Harvard, St. Stephens, Bennington, Wisconsin, Swarthmore, Rollins, and Chicago are especially worthy of mention in connection with a program of individualization.

8. *The educational system is poorly adapted to the whole need of the individual.* The adaptation is not being made by the giving of elementary courses in the fields of human interest and by the opportunity for mastery in one field.

9. *The multi-course curriculum is non-integrated and confused.* The increase of scientific knowledge and the application of scientific methods have enlarged the field of specialization and multiplied the courses of instruction. This has produced confusion in the mind of the student when he should be encouraged to look on his work as forming one unified course of study. To accomplish this desirable end, therefore, something must be offered to replace the aggregate of dissociated elementary courses—something that will "subserve the synthetic idea of an interrelated and integrated curriculum."

It is worth while to note upon what bases the selection of curriculum courses has been commonly made in our colleges. While these bases may be perfectly valid, it may occur to some of us that the methods predicated upon these bases have not been and are not now satisfactory.

(1) *Interest of the student.* On this basis the elective system was adopted. It began at the University of Virginia and was enlarged at Harvard. The aim of the college was supposed to be the development of mental ability. It was soon found, in the first place, that students did not necessarily select the studies they needed and, in the second place, scientific studies confirmed the suspicion that ability in one field of interest could not necessarily be transferred to another field.

(2) *Need of the student.* It was felt that the curriculum should be based upon the student's need of certain constants—of certain fundamentals of human civilization with which each student should be acquainted. Therefore, he was required to sample all the main fields of knowledge (English, the natural sciences, philosophy, history, the social sciences, mathematics, and the foreign languages).

Now we are beginning to realize that it is not possible to provide students with a basis of common knowledge as in the preceding two centuries. It is equally true that a beginning course seldom gives a comprehensive view of a single field. We might just as well expect to get a comprehensive view of the State of North Carolina by a survey of Chatham County. Survey courses are largely misnomers.

(3) *Need for a comprehensive view of human civilization through other means than that of elementary departmental courses.* To this end several colleges have adopted "Orientation Courses" designed to give this comprehensive picture of human civilization. Such courses have been arranged in the physical sciences, biological sciences, social sciences, aesthetics, English history and literature, philosophy, economics and political theory. There are also general courses in mathematics and the art of thinking. The manager of an important university press told me he was a firm believer in the value of the orientation courses given in the university he represented.

The problem involved in the teaching of these courses is a difficult one. It is practically impossible for one man alone to give the course efficiently. If several men give it, there is usually a lack of proper orientation among the instructors themselves and the material of the course is therefore not properly integrated. All seem to agree that the orientation course is a failure if it is given according to the lecture system. In addition, if the endeavor to recover the common bases of knowledge is futile, then this conclusion involves the rejection of the idea of general orientation courses.

The University of Wisconsin has proceeded on this assumption in the reorganization of its curriculum.

Furthermore, the three methods deal explicitly with the subject-matter of the fields of knowledge and only implicitly with life. Thus many colleges are endeavoring to select curriculum constants on the basis of an analysis of life's activities—mental, moral, social, physical, emotional, aesthetic, religious, economic. and political activities.

10. Finally, as if to plant one death-dealing blow, critics tell us that our colleges and universities lack good teachers in the first place and are failing, in the second place, to train good high school and college teachers. So far as secondary school teachers are concerned, it must be kept in mind that they are, in general, immature, that they average less than thirty, and that 25 to 33 per cent of them change positions every year. Economic considerations, over which the colleges have no control, largely determine this condition. It is customary to point to about one really great teacher in each of our higher institutions of learning, particularly the larger ones. I think the matter of a dearth of good teachers has been exaggerated. For such dearth as exists, the administration is largely to blame. Even college presidents may be infected with the German idea. Whenever a college president actually brings it to pass that good teachers in his institution are rewarded with respect both to rank and salary equally with men engaged in research, I am confident that something will happen. Teachers should not be censured for striving after the thing that seems most eminently worth-while to their employers. Presidents themselves must demonstrate their belief in the worth-whileness of good teaching by making substantial recognition of it. It isn't altogether the young teacher's fault that the only apparent avenue to promotion lies in the pathway of research. There is a belief in some universities that the present requirements for the master's and particularly for the doctor's degree should be changed in the case of prospective teachers. This has met with much opposition in the citadels of tradition and nothing definite has as yet been accomplished. The fact, however, that national associations are giving so much time and thought to this business of teaching precludes the dismissal of the charge of ineffective teaching as a mental figment.

It was necessary to give this background before attempting to suggest a program of college education to meet the needs of North Carolina. These needs include, as a matter of course, an adequate program of teacher-training. I cannot see that there should be any essential differentiation in the training of teachers, whether it be done in a teacher's college, or in a college of liberal arts, or in the undergraduate college of a university. Here we meet with the permanently recurrent and perplexing problem of the balance between method and subject-matter. Some

teachers' colleges apparently reveal a hostility and indifference to subject-matter and some liberal arts colleges reveal a like hostility and indifference to method. Both are equally reprehensible. Some liberal arts colleges need to clip their shaggy locks of tradition and come out of their medievalism. Of what value to a teacher is learning, if it cannot be presented? Some teachers' colleges need to inform their curricula with more subject-matter. Their multi-course program of methods presents one long thin line. Of what value is training in the art of presentation if one has nothing to present? A few years ago, when dean of a college in Georgia, I examined the transcript of a transfer from a teachers' college and found a credit of twenty-four hours in methods and six hours in pure subject-matter. Such a course of study is a travesty upon the royal nature of learning. It took the Southern Association quite a long time to learn the necessity for specialization in the training of secondary school teachers. On the other hand, there is no greater fallacy than the assertion that mere knowledge of subject-matter will make a person a good teacher.

Especially does it seem to me that we should not send out, to the secondary schools of North Carolina, teachers who are totally ignorant of the history and resources of our state. The result of such a practice is that this younger generation is getting out into life completely ignorant of the greatness of their own state.

It is quite possible that we are sending out secondary school teachers who do not know what a high school is for. They are expounders of subjects. They are not "instruments to activate people but mechanisms to broadcast learning."

One of the most significant of comparatively recent developments in secondary schools is character-education—yet how few of our colleges are giving any specific training in this field!

The teachers we send out should be trained to get the concept of the unity of knowledge. The first requisite is a liberal education. The trouble with so many teachers is that they are shaped like an obelisk instead of a pyramid. The pyramid can be just as high and has a better foundation. The second requisite is mastery of a field or group of related subjects in which one's highest mastery is ultimately to fall. The third requisite is mastery of a subject and the fourth is professional in character and comprehends a knowledge of the secondary school system, a broad social outlook, the method of presenting a subject, and the knowledge of the psychology of learning and teaching as applied to the subject-matter of one's special field.

In the light of the situation I described at the beginning, it seems that we need several junior colleges to take care of that large body of college students who want a sort of general education and then a taste of life or who are seeking a two-year preparation for the work of the professional school. In saying this I am motivated by the desire to see the four-year liberal arts college and the undergraduate college of the university unhampered in the operation of a unified program. I disclaim any intention of reflecting upon the usefulness of the junior college. It possesses unity within itself but the presence in great numbers of the type of student I have described in the four-year college is bringing about a disintegration of the college and an organic separation of it into what we know as junior and senior college divisions. If this organic separation becomes general in our colleges, that will be another argument for the increase of junior colleges; for graduates of junior colleges can transfer with little inconvenience to institutions having separate junior and senior divisions. But the transfer could not be made so easily to a college where the work of the college, contrary to being organically separated, is more closely integrated than ever. I think we are being swept off our feet in this matter of organic division.

With respect to the four-year liberal arts college and the undergraduate college of the university I would like to suggest a program of education that produces a closer integration of the work of the four years. The philosophical basis of this program is the integration of the needs and interests of students, the problems of present-day civilization, and the fields of human knowledge. Such integration comprehends practically all the aims of college education and gives unity to the student's entire work. We have the fields of human knowledge. If we can correlate them with the needs and interests of students and the problems of civilization, it is my judgment that we shall be able to evolve a program of college education that will meet the needs of our state and any other state.

According to Matthew Arnold the things that go to the building of human life are (1) power of conduct, (2) power of social life and manners, (3) power of intellect and knowledge and (4) power of beauty.

In the next place we know that men must live in the world of nature; men must live with others; men must think; and men must work.

A program of education that comprehends these things would provide:

(1) A knowledge of the world in which we live.
(2) A knowledge of the literary and artistic products of our civilization.
(3) A training in communication.
(4) A familiarity with the major processes of intellectual attack upon life:
    (a) Habit of careful and accurate observation of facts.

(b) Familiarity with the methods of human development.
    (c) Capacity to use the mind abstractly.*
(5) A special skill or interest.
(6) A foundation for vocational or professional study.
(7) A preparation for social, economic and political activity.

These are the things that are more or less pertinent to the needs and interests of all students and should be the basis of any attempt at establishing a uniformity of requirements.

The fields of human knowledge may be conveniently classified in three divisions:

(1) Philosophy, Languages and Literature, Art.
(2) Mathematics and the Natural Sciences.
(3) History, the Social Sciences, Religion.

This classification provides the opportunity for cutting across departmental lines and prevents isolated departments, with their imperious or characteristic demands, from dictating the substance of the curriculum.

The basal uniform requirements in a well-integrated program will be chosen from these three divisions in the light of the provisions comprehended above. There should be a sound reason for every choice and that choice should not be made with the view of producing any artificial departmental stimulus. The greater part of this work will be completed in the freshman year and the student should be taught to see the relation between it and the three general divisions of human knowledge, for in one of these he will later seek to develop his special skill or interest. He should be encouraged early to choose a course other than his general requirement in the division where he feels that his main interest will lie.

Instead of selecting a departmental major he should select a divisional major which comprehends 48 to 54 hours divided between concentration in a specific subject and related work in the division. This will give him a conception of the essential unity of knowledge and enable him to attain a mastery in a field of knowledge rather than in an isolated department. Representatives chosen from the related departments in the divisions would act as counselors to the students in planning their divisional work. The remainder of the student's work would be chosen from the other divisions and restricted in a manner to prevent an accumulation of credits in elementary courses.

A system of examination should be arranged having for their object the attainment of a definite goal and not merely the arbitrary determination of course credit. Students upon entrance should be allowed to take examinations upon any required work in which they are prepared and should be excused from that

* From the program of the University of Wisconsin.

requirement if the examination is passed. Examinations for purposes of sectioning students should be given and general examinations, covering the field of divisional interest and achievement, should be given at the close of the senior year.

Spontaneous intellectual activity should be encouraged by giving to students special departmental reading courses which they are expected to pursue independently and in which they will be examined and given credit.

Honors Courses should be provided for able students. Every institution has a large number of students who have revealed their desire and demonstrated their ability to do a higher type of intellectual work than that ordinarily required for the degree; and in recognition of this fact the institution should offer to these students a program of Honors Courses adapted to their needs and suited to their interests. This recognition of the difference in the possibilities of intellectual achievement among college students should make a special appeal to the abler and more ambitious among them. The introduction of Honors Courses into the curriculum means the breaking-down of lock-step methods of education. It provides the student with the opportunity to attain greater mastery of a field of knowledge and its related work under conditions most stimulating to individual initiative and independence. Its primary object is the individualization of instruction on the basis of ability in the student. The granting of this opportunity to the able student for the realization of his highest intellectual possibilities is in keeping with the soundest principles of democracy wherein individual initiative and ability have a distinct and permanent value.

The University of Chicago is making a noble experiment. Grave doubt of its success has been expressed by several educators, although the university paper and educational journals, in general, discuss it with enthusiasm. The most debatable point in the new plan is the provision made for the work of the first two years. It seems that its success depends largely upon the new "housing" plan whereby faculty members and students in small groups are brought into closer relationship.

A program of college education suitable for North Carolina, after all, must be determined by the needs and conditions we face about us. The crowding of the profession of teaching may ultimately bring the teacher to the necessity of obtaining a graduate degree as a requirement for a position in our secondary schools. This is taking place probably more rapidly than we realize. This would alter the character of teachers' colleges as well as the undergraduate professional course in the universities.

The development of the idea of organic separation of the four-year college into junior and senior divisions may ultimately lead to the complete disintegration of the traditional college and the establishment of a system of separate junior and senior colleges with the latter offering a year of graduate work. In my judgment such a system is preferable to the loose-jointed tendency toward cleavage in what should represent a closely-knit unit. A house divided against itself will not long stand. In undertaking a program of competition with the junior college idea, the four-year college stands in danger of becoming neither fish nor fowl nor good red herring.

Duke Professors In Attendance On Educational Meetings At Atlanta

On the Friday and Saturday following Thanksgiving the Fifth Annual Conference of the Deans of Southern Graduate Schools was held at the Hotel Ansley at Atlanta, Georgia. Dean W. H. Glasson, of the Graduate School of Arts and Sciences, attended the Conference representing Duke. Among those who delivered the principal addresses was Dean C. W. Pipkin, of Louisiana State University, who is this year Visiting Professor of Social Legislation at Columbia University, New York. Other addresses were delivered by Dean J. C. Metcalf, of the University of Virginia, and Dean Reed Smith, of the University of South Carolina. The Conference includes representatives of seventeen universities in southern states which have organized graduate schools.

Dean Glasson also attended some of the sessions of the Southern Political Science Association which were held in Atlanta on the same days as the Graduate School Conference. This year Professor R. S. Rankin, of Duke University, was President of the Southern Political Science Association. He had arranged for the meeting an excellent program of addresses and round table conferences. The principal address of the occasion was by Professor E. S. Corwin, of Princeton University, who spoke on the subject "The Anti-Trust Acts and the Constitution." Professor Rankin presented a paper at one of the dinner meetings of the Association on the very timely subject "Interstate Agreements as a Means of Dealing with Economic Problems." Dr. L. E. Pfankuchen of Duke University discussed problems of legislative and congressional representation in North Carolina. The meeting of political scientists was well attended, and for the coming year Professor George Sherrill, of Clemson College, was elected president of the association.

Mr. Hedrick Speaks

Various phases of the legal practice before the North Carolina Industrial Commission was the subject of a lecture delivered on December 14 at the Duke School of Law by H. G. Hedrick, '11, prominent Durham attorney.

Football Team Closes Season with Notable 6-0 Victory

Washington & Lee Defeated At Lexington, Va., Nov. 28—Coach Wade's First Duke Team Makes Great Defensive Record, Scores Against Duke Being Recorded In Only Three Out of Ten Games—Basketball and Other Winter Sports to Start Now

WHILE the Blue Devils did not win any championship titles during the past season, they turned in the best record of defensive football in the annals of Duke gridiron history. Seven of the ten teams played were held scoreless by Wallace Wade's eleven in his first year at Duke.

That brilliant record of blanking opponents was completed at Lexington, Va., Nov. 28, when the Devils closed the season by defeating the Generals, 6-0, in the mud.

Lowell Mason, Duke halfback, provided the Devils' margin of victory when he ran the opening kick-off of the second half 88 yards through the entire Washington and Lee team. He was aided on the touchdown trip by the excellent blocking of his teammates.

The three teams that scored on the Blue Devils were the teams that defeated them—South Carolina, Tennessee and N. C. State. Duke's scoring totaled 74 points against 46 for opponents. Two games, the annual battles with Davidson and Carolina, were scoreless ties. Duke defeated V. M. I., Villanova, Wake Forest, Kentucky and Washington and Lee.

BASKETEERS START WORK

Basketball Coach Eddie Cameron has a job on his hands this season in moulding a team to defend the North Carolina Big Five titles that Blue Devil quints have won for the past two years.

Out of last year's squad of ten, only three returned this year. George Rogers, forward, and Joe Croson, center, the 1931 Co-Captains, have finished their careers. Burt Hill, second string center, and Don Robertshaw, guard, did not return due to scholastic difficulties. Ted Capelli, forward, and Nelson Colley, guard, are not in school.

For a nucleus around which to build a team this season, Coach Cameron has Johnny Shaw, guard; Pete Carter, sub-forward last season; and Wendell Horne, sub-forward last year who has been shifted to center this season.

In regard to prospects for the season, Coach Cameron said, "We have never had such a lack of experienced material. If we get anywhere we will have to depend on speed for we have no tall men."

Likely candidates are Johnny Shaw, Phil Weaver, Fred Lewis and Herb Thompson, guards; Wendell Horne, Roy Alpert and Charles Burnham, centers; Jim Thompson, Ted Lewis, Pete Carter and Charles Hayes, forwards.

A large squad reported for first practice, 22 in all, and from the list Coach Cameron will probably be able to form a fairly good team.

Twenty-two games are on the schedule, 11 of which are with Southern Conference teams. The Devils will take a three-day northern trip before the Christmas vacation, playing Baltimore, Georgetown and Catholic University.

THE SCHEDULE

Dec. 17—U. of Baltimore at Baltimore.
Dec. 18—Georgetown at Washington, D. C.
Dec. 19—Catholic U. at Washington, D. C.
Jan. 8—Wake Forest at Durham.
Jan. 9—William and Mary at Durham.
Jan. 13—Army at West Point, N. Y.
Jan. 14—Crescent A. C. at Brooklyn, N. Y.
Jan. 16—Navy at Annapolis, Md.
Jan. 23—N. C. State at Durham.
Jan. 29—Davidson at Durham.
Jan. 30—U. N. C. at Chapel Hill.
Feb. 1—Davidson at Charlotte.
Feb. 4—Washington & Lee at Lexington, Va.
Feb. 5—V. M. I. at Lexington, Va.
Feb. 6—Kentucky at Lexington, Ky.
Feb. 8—Tennessee at Knoxville, Tenn.
Feb. 11—Wake Forest at Raleigh.
Feb. 13—U. N. C. at Durham.
Feb. 16—N. C. State at Raleigh.
Feb. 18—Washington and Lee at Durham.
Feb. 19—V. M. I. at Durham.
Feb. 20—Maryland at Durham.

EDDIE CAMERON
Duke Basketball Coach

BOXERS, WRESTLERS WORKING

Duke's new boxing and wrestling coach, Add Warren, former North Carolina heavyweight champion, has two large squads, working daily in the gym, getting ready for the 1932 season.

Lettermen are back to fill four of the eight weights on the wrestling team, but only one veteran boxer is back- and Coach Warren must select performers from the large list of candidates.

Captain Phil Bolich of the boxers, who has never been defeated in a dual meet in high school or college, has moved up a weight this year and will fight as a light heavy. He is the lone veteran ring man back.

In wrestling, Emery Adkins, star football player, will be ending his career on the mat; Pinkie Plaster, letterman last year, is the best

PHIL BOLICH
Duke Boxing Star

candidate for the 155-pound class; Claburn Hurst, another letterman, is expected to be the 135-pounder; and Captain John Gamble will be in the 126-pound - class this year, moving up from the 118-pound weight.

Many freshman boxers and wrestlers are out, and there is some promising material on hand for the two first year teams.

THE SCHEDULE (BOXING)

Jan. 16—Virginia at Durham.
Jan. 19—U. N. C. at Chapel Hill.
Jan. 29—N. C. State at Raleigh.
Feb. 8—Tulane at Durham.
Feb. 26—Maryland at College Park (pending).

THE SCHEDULE (WRESTLING)

Jan. 11—U. N. C. at Chapel Hill.
Jan. 23—V. M. I. at Durham.
Jan. 30—V. P. I. at Blackburg, Va.
Feb. 6—Davidson at Durham.
Feb. 13—Washington and Lee at Lexington, Va.

Mason Elected Captain of 1932 Football Team

With the election of Lowell Mason, of Charlotte, as captain of the 1932 Duke football team, the captaincy remains in the backfield. Mason succeeds P. O. "Kidd" Brewer, of Winston-Salem. Mason's record as quarterback during the past season was brilliant. Not only was his running and interference creditable, but his judgment in calling signals attracted much favorable comment. His 80-yard run for a touchdown was the margin which gave Duke a victory over Washington and Lee.

MASON

Unit of International Legal Fraternity Installed At Duke

Installation of the Charles E. Hughes Law Club of Duke University School of Law as a unit of Phi Delta Phi international legal fraternity was effected a short while ago. Members of the fraternity from University of North Carolina and Emory University took the lead in the installation ceremonies.

Associate Justice George W. Connor of the state supreme court, Dean Justin Miller of the Duke Law School, and Prof. Albert Coates of the Carolina Law School were among the speakers on the banquet program held following the carrying out of the ritual.

The Duke group will be known as the Hughes Inn of Phi Delta Phi. Four members of the Duke law faculty are members, and nine student members of the local group comprised those entering the national organization. Dean Miller, Prof. Douglas Maggs, Prof. H. C. Horack, and Assistant Dean Gordon Dean are the faculty members of the Inn.

Clare Clairbert at Duke

Clare Clairbert, talented Belgian soprano, assisted by Charles Achatz, Swedish flutist, and Erno Balogh, pianist, rendered a delightful program at Page auditorium on the evening of December 14, in the third of the season's concert series at Duke University. Mary Garden, Doris Kenyon, and San-Malo are among the artists previously appearing in the concert series.

The Editor's Mail Bag

Reminiscences Of "Old Trinity"

Editor THE ALUMNI REGISTER:

I am writing in response to your request for some reminiscences of Trinity College.

When I was a boy, there was only one man in Pamlico County who was a graduate of Trinity College, and that was R. D. McCotter. He was born in Craven County in 1826, and settled in that part of Craven, now known as Pamlico County. He entered Trinity College in 1858, and would have graduated in 1862, but the War Between the States broke out in 1861, and, like most of the gifted sons of the South, he entered the Confederate Army, and for three years fought for what the people of the South still think was right.

After he returned home he became one of the closest students of his day. Although he was a farmer, he could read Greek as well at 60, as he could when he left school. I do not know when, but Trinity College gave him his Master's degree. He usually taught a school somewhere in his county within the year. Some of the bright young lawyers, doctors, preachers and business men from Pamlico County were taught by him.

His career was somewhat checkered. He was once a preacher. When I was on the Onslow circuit, they told me he was a Junior preacher on that circuit about 1867. He was a politician, or statesman, of ability. He represented his county in the legislature several times. One of the first ballots I ever cast was for him. He was one of the finest speakers in the state. He was a staunch Democrat. In 1876, the Republicans raised a Hayes and Settle flag pole, and invited Judge Clarke and his son from New Berne to make the speeches. They knew nothing about Mc-Cotter, and said a great many things they might not have said, had they known he would reply. A great many Democrats were present; and as soon as the Republicans were through, the Democrats called for McCotter and he was at his best. I need not say he put his opponents to flight that day.

I was working at a sawmill, and would go to his school when the mill did not work. He said to me one day, "You have a bright mind and you ought not to think of remaining where you are," and from that time I began to go to school. And if I have accomplished anything in life, I owe it largely to him.

But his death was a tragedy. He was a country merchant and was going one morning to his store and someone shot and killed him. He left what he had to the public schools of Pamlico County. But relatives tried to break his will, and it took what he left to settle up the estate. He sleeps in an unmarked grave in his native county. Thus ended the career of one of the brightest men that ever went out from Trinity College.

ZADOK PARIS.

Experiences In Japan

Through the kindness of an alumnus the REGISTER is privileged to publish herewith some extracts from a letter received recently from Rev. J. Doane Stott and Mrs. Flora Belle Stott, Duke alumni who are engaged in missionary work in Japan. The letter was written some time ago from Fraser Institute, Hiroshima, Japan, where they are now located:

Dear Friend:

"You will notice that the above address is not the same as it was when we wrote you from Kobe last October. We have moved to Hiroshima, and have been in our new home just one week today. It is a new home for us in two ways—the house was completed only fifteen months ago, and again it is new to us because we have been here only a short time. Mr. Cobb and his family returned to the States last week on furlough for one year, and we came here to take his place at Fraser Institute, an English night school. I (Rev. Mr. Stott) am to be principal of the school, also pastor in charge of the church on the same compound, but a native pastor will do most of the preaching and assist with the other church work during our next two years of language study. . . .

"The church, school, and residence is all on one lot (space is valuable in this city of over 200,000 people), which means that our home will be in constant use in one way or another. One of the big things in missionary life is the privilege we have of sharing a Christian home with the people among whom we live. Every week or two on Saturday nights we shall be entertaining the various classes of students who attend our school (total enrollment is about 160). We shall often have guests to share a meal or stop overnight with us, among them being many of our friends and co-workers from various countries who will pass through Hiroshima occasionally. We have a large home, too large for us (there were seven in the family that preceded us); but we shall enjoy sharing our home with other friends when they can visit us. . . .

"We have been invited to a few native homes. One, for example, just two weeks ago tonight, was the home of one of the young men in our English night school classes at Palmore Institute in Kobe, where we taught one night each week. The young man is a banker and was a member of our graduating class this year. He began to attend my Bible class this spring, and has visited in our home several times. Since his father is dead and he has no brothers—just his mother and one sister—he is head of the home. His mother is a very devout Buddhist, yet very appreciative of anything done for her son, regardless of what their religious faith may be. Although we could not speak much Japanese (the mother cannot speak any English), I don't think we ever felt more at ease in any home. It was a most pleasant visit for us. The young man interpreted for us when necessary and also instructed us in many things we shall need to know when we visit in other Japanese homes. We removed our shoes before we entered the house and sat on cushions on the floor. Japanese floors are covered with straw mats about two inches thick. Soon after we sat down the sister served us tea, and about thirty minutes later she began to bring the many kinds of food we had for supper. The mother and sister did not eat with us. It is not customary for the lady members of the family to eat with the guests. But in this case they kept themselves busy preparing the delicious dishes they served. There were not less than fifteen separate cookings necessary to prepare this feast. In preparing Japanese food practically every dish is prepared separately. We ate on a lacquer table about one foot high.

"One thing that impressed us was the little Buddhist altar in the home. Every Buddhist or Shinto home has a similar altar, sometimes called the *godshelf*, before which food is placed and prayers are said. In this instance some of the rice cooked for the meal was taken from the center of the pot of rice (this is done every time rice is cooked in this home) and placed before the idol of the Buddha, also some fresh water and other food. A small quantity of the same food was placed in front of the enlarged picture of the deceased father. This may be called ancestor worship, but to me there was something beautiful in the way the father was referred to during our conversation that night. He must have been a good father. We could not help but appreciate the way the members of the family seemed to be so devoted to each other. . . .

"We have wished many times that you people at home could visit Japan in the spring season when the cherry blossoms, wisteria, azalea, and other flowers are in their prime. During the spring holidays we spent one day on a boat traveling through the Inland Sea and making brief stops at several small ports, and at that time the scenery was beautiful—the mountains with so many ridges and intervening valleys rising from near the seashore, the terraced fields covered with such green crops of wheat and other grain, the orchards of orange trees, and beautiful flowers dotted about over the mountains and in the valleys, etc. All of these things and more are to be enjoyed in this great land of the rising sun.

"In our travels on the train between Kobe and Hiroshima, seven and a half hours on a fast train, we have seen the farmers go through each process in the growing of rice. We took this trip last November during the harvest season, after which they planted wheat on the same ground, then harvested it this spring and put out a new crop of rice. The wheat crop during the winter was grown in rows on high ridges, but before the rice plants are set out, the soil is made perfectly level in these paddy fields and covered with water. The rice plants are stuck out in squares about eight inches apart both ways. When we came down to Hiroshima last week we saw hundreds of farmers pushing a little plow through the mud between these narrow rows beneath the water. mud between these narrow rows beneath the water."

Dr. Crowell's Gift

The editor received some time since a much appreciated letter from a member of the class of '96 containing some complimentary remarks with reference to the REGISTER. He refers to the report in the REGISTER of the death of the late John Franklin Crowell, former president of Trinity College, and pays a fine tribute to Dr. Crowell. In that connection, he also mentions the fact that, while president of the college, he made a personal gift of a building to the institution. Speaking of that matter, he says:

"When we moved to Durham there were three buildings on the park, besides the faculty residences: Main Building, later named the Duke building; the Inn, later named Epworth Hall, and the science, or Crowell, building. If I have my facts right this was built by Dr. Crowell from his private funds, in honor of his first wife, and was called the Laura Getz Crowell building. Without this building it would have been impossible for the college to have functioned properly as it served to house the science departments until it was outgrown.

"I entered the college the year before the college was moved to Durham, and moved with it."

ELECTRICITY
puts the news on the street
before the fans leave the arena

As THE fight ends and final reports flash in, the last newspaper plate is made up and locked on the press cylinder. With the tiny click of a push button, the snap of contactors, the whir of motors, the roar of press units, the fight edition goes to press. Each unit automatically controlled and perfectly synchronized with Selsyn elements — each section arrives at the folder at the correct instant. Sixty thousand papers an hour. To-day the deadline is postponed — the news is red hot. The fight news is on the street before the crowd leaves the arena.

Since its beginning, the electrical industry has worked hand in hand with the newspaper industry. To-day, the high-speed, newspaper press, with maximum outputs of 50,000 and 60,000 papers per hour, owes no small portion of its success to electricity and the skill of General Electric engineers.

For the last 30 years, college graduates in the employ of the General Electric Testing Department have played an important part in the development of newspaper equipment. Here they gain experience which enables them to apply electricity to the advancement of this and countless other industries.

95-897GC

GENERAL ⟨GE⟩ ELECTRIC

SALES AND ENGINEERING SERVICE IN PRINCIPAL CITIES

Where They Are Located	News of the Alumni	What They Are Doing

Miss Elizabeth Aldridge, '24, Secretary of Alumnae Council, Editor

CLASS OF 1877

A card was recently received in the Alumni Office from Hon. John H. Small announcing his association with Lucian H. Vandoren and Joseph A. Rafferty for the general practice of law with offices in the Southern Building, Washington, D. C., on September 1.

CLASS OF 1892

Dr. Henry D. Stewart received an M.D. degree from the University of Maryland in 1898. He then located in his home town, Monroe, N. C., for the practice of medicine. He is well known as a diagnostician and therapist in chronic diseases. Dr. Stewart has been a surgeon for the Seaboard Air Line Railway since 1910. He has served as county physician for Union County; director, Monroe and Stewart Hospital; and a member of the City School Board. Dr. Stewart is also a trustee of the University of North Carolina. He has written a number of articles on medical subjects for magazines and newspapers.

CLASS OF 1893

Dr. James E. Patrick practices medicine at Bahama, N. C. His oldest son, Stuart D. Patrick, was a student at Duke two years ago.

William Crawford Stewart has been in the unlocated file in the Alumni Office for a number of years. We are glad to find that he lives in McBee, South Carolina, and is a conductor on the Seaboard Air Line Railway. He was married on December 18, 1926, to Miss Carrie Sue Fields.

CLASS OF 1894

Cullen R. Merritt is one of the charter members of the Mount Airy Furniture Company, which was founded in 1896. He has been general manager of that company for twenty-five years.

CLASS OF 1900

Rev. and Mrs. S. A. Stewart, who returned to Japan in the early spring, are located at 113 Kunitomi, Okayama, Japan. While in America Mr. Stewart studied at Duke University and also preached in some of the leading churches of Durham and neighboring cities.

CLASS OF 1903

Denison Foy Giles was in educational work for a number of years, serving as superintendent of the McDowell and Wake County schools and later with the State Department of Education. In more recent years he has practiced law in Marion, N. C. He was a member of the State Senate in 1915 and 1923. He is a prominent member of the Kiwanis Club in Marion.

CLASS OF 1906

Osborne G. Foard is a member of the firm, Lynch and Foard, architects, in Wilmington.

CLASS OF 1912

Rev. C. Excell Rozzelle completed his four years as pastor of the Methodist church at Chapel Hill, N. C., in November. He was transferred to the First Methodist church at Lenoir. Mr. Rozzelle was very active in the religious, social and civic life of Chapel Hill and it was with regret that the people of that community gave him up.

CLASS OF 1915

The wedding of Corum Dee Alexander and Miss Alice Dorothy Mann took place in Minneapolis, Minnesota, on Thursday, May 28. Since July 1, they have made their home at 660 East Monroe Street, Kirkwood, Missouri.

CLASS OF 1920

Mr. and Mrs. A. S. Trundle, Jr., of Wilmington, N. C., announce the birth of a son, Albert Sidney Trundle III, on August 30, 1931. Mrs. Trundle was, before her marriage, Gladys Price.

CLASS OF 1923

Jay L. Jackson attended the Columbia University School of Law after leaving Trinity College, receiving the degree of LL.B. in 1926 and at the same time the degree of Master of Arts in Public Law. He was awarded the E. B. Converse Legal Essay Prize for 1926 for his Master's thesis, a contest which was open only to members of the graduating class of the Law School. Dr. Charles Chaney Hyde, head of the Department of International Law, stated that the essay was the best that he had ever read in his department. This essay was later published in March and April (1928) issues of the *Virginia Law Review*.

Jay was admitted to the New York Bar in 1927. He later became associated with the law firm of Cabaniss, Johnston, Cocke & Cabaniss, of Birmingham, Ala., and more recently with the law firms of Arthur W. Eckman, and of Chandler, Wright & Ward, of Los Angeles, Cal.

In October 1931 he opened his own law office in the Taft Building in Los Angeles. He is also associated with the School of Law and the Legal Aid Clinic Association of the University of Southern California.

Mr. and Mrs. Jackson, who was before her marriage Miss Joyce Watson, of Mobile, Alabama, live at 1848 North Gramercy Place, Hollywood, Cal.

CLASS OF 1924

For the past two years, William F. Ricks has been connected with the Chilean Nitrate Sales Corporation with headquarters in Charlotte. The company has recently opened a new District Sales Office in Raleigh and Bill was moved to this point. He is in the sales division of this company and travels over the entire state.

CLASS OF 1926

On November 23, in the Watts Street Baptist Church in Durham, Evelyn Salmon was married to Mr. Carl H. Spoon of Winston-Salem. For the past few years Evelyn has been in training as a nurse at the Baptist Hospital in Winston-Salem.

CLASS OF 1927

T. A. Watson is connected with the Baton Rouge Gas and Electric Company. His address is 523 St. Hypolite Street, Baton Rouge, Louisiana.

Franklin Ray Andrews is located at 7022 Ridge Boulevard, Apartment D10, Brooklyn, New York. He is connected with the National City Bank of New York, 55 Wall Street.

Rev. and Mrs. A. C. Waggoner were moved at the last conference from Elforado to Trinity, N. C. "Jinks" says they are looking forward with great anticipation to living in the original location of Trinity College.

Mr. and Mrs. Hoyle S. Broome announce the birth of a daughter, Wilma Francis, on December 4. Mr. Broome is principal of the Wilton High School, at Franklinton.

CLASS OF 1928

Ruth Davidson was married on November 18 to Mr. Frank Lloyd Call, in Birmingham, Alabama. They make their home at 401 Monument Avenue, Richmond, Va.

The announcement of the marriage of Charles H. Litaker and Miss Eloise Greenwood of Gastonia, N. C., has been made. The wedding will take place on December 29, 1931. Miss Greenwood is chemical aid in the U. S. Bureau of Standards in Washington, D. C. Mr. Litaker is with the Woodward and Lothrop Department Store in Washington.

CLASS OF 1929

Walter Davis Merritt is an insurance investigator for the Retail Credit Company at 64 Hamilton Street, Paterson, New Jersey. He was married on December 29, 1929, to Miss Virginia Byrd Suiter. They have a small daughter, Mary Carolyn Suiter.

CLASS OF 1930

Rev. Sherwood William Funk, B.D. '30, was married on December 2 to Miss Athleene Alice Edwards in Greenville, N. C. They make their home at 519½ Wyoming Street, Charleston, W. Va., where Mr. Funk is pastor of the Methodist Church.

Henry G. Ruark is studying at Yale University and his address is 1652 Yale Station, New Haven, Conn.

CLASS OF 1931

James T. Gobbell is a salesman for the Stanback Company, Salisbury, N. C. He was a recent visitor on the campus.

William Glenn Pearson is manager of P. P. Pearson & Company at 721 West Airline Avenue, Gastonia, N. C.

Thomas Warner Bennett and Miss Lillian Mae Rogers were married in Durham on July 29. They are at present at Tom's home in Cleveland, Ohio.

Richard J. Westcott, 28 Fithian Avenue, Merchantville, N. J., is on the advertising staff of Edward J. Bailey and Son in Frankford, Pa.

Kathleen Mock is located at Route No. 3, Lexington, N. C. She is teaching English and history in the high school.

Since May 5, Roy Hunter has been solicitor for the Maryland Casualty Company with offices in the First National Bank Building, Charlotte.

Ted Mann has returned to Duke as sports writer for the Duke News Service.

Mildred Murrell lives at her home in Henderson and teaches in the high school.

There are a number of the class of 1931 that are engaged in educational work. A list of the teachers and the places that they are located follow: Hettie English, Mount Olive; Madge Colelough, Durham County Schools; Verne R. Dry, Bell's High School, Route No. 3, Apex; Bain Johnson, Rural Hall; Iva Pitt, McLeansville; Mabel Mildred Lynch, Route No. 4, Mebane; Henry Price, Jr., Route No. 2, Lexington; Zeb Glenn Barnhardt, Ansonville; Willie A. Gee, Henderson; Ruth K. Barber, Allison-James School, Santa Fe, Mexico; Nancy King, Pearisburg, Virginia; Mary Moorman, Bristol, Va.; Lacy Waverly Anderson, Kitty Hawk; Mary Lillian Blalock, Roanoke Rapids; Grace Cockerham, Taylorsville; Clara Council, Bahama; Ida Cowan, Durham; Eunice Jones, Durham; Eloise Lambert, Ironton, Ohio; Leta Mae Marr, Children's Home, Winston-Salem; Elizabeth K. Matthews, Rutherfordton; Kathleen Mock, Route No. 3, Lexington; Edith Mullen, Route No. 3, Durham; William David Murray, Children's Home, Winston-Salem; Mildred Jane Murrell, Henderson; Helen Peacock, Granite Quarry; R. E. Walston, West Durham; Elizabeth Williams, 2340 Selwyn Avenue, Charlotte; Ray Yandle, Indian Trail.

Ann Courtney Sharpe is associated with her father in newspaper work. Her father, Mr. J. A. Sharpe, '98, is editor of the *Robesonian* at Lumberton, N. C.

The names of some of the members of the class of 1931 that have returned to Duke for graduate work appear below: Earl W. Brian, Medical School; Samuel Jackson Hawkins, School of Religion; Harry M. Holtz, School of Medicine; William E. Joyner, Library work; George K. Massengill, Jr., School of Medicine; Carlton Lee Ould, School of Medicine; Jack Tannenbaum, School of Medicine; Herman Walker, Library work; Harold M. Roberson, School of Religion; Clarice Bowman, School of Religion; Clarence E. Hix, Jr., School of Religion; Henry L. Andrews, English; W. M. Upchurch, Jr., School of Law; Matilda Elizabeth Holleman, School of Nursing; Elizabeth Clark.

Francis Brinkley is connected with the Vick Chemical Corporation of Greensboro. He lives at the Y. M. C. A.

George C. Hoopy, 604 Bosler Avenue, Lemoyne, Pa., is with Henry and Rockey, Inc., bonding and insurance agents.

CLASS OF 1932

William Gurney Womble is a reporter for *The News and Observer*, Raleigh. His home address is 236 S. Boylan Avenue.

Hazel Williams, '32, and Clarence B. Utley, Jr., '31, were married in Boydton, Va., on September 17. They make their home in Oxford, N. C., where Clarence is connected with the Standard Oil Company.

After leaving Duke, Mildred Teague attended Burlington Business College. She lives at her home, 620 S. Broad Street, Burlington, and works for the Fidelity Motor Lines.

CLASS OF 1933

David J. Wilkinson was married on November 12 to Miss Harriett Gunn Hobbs in Brewster, New York. She is the daughter of the late Mr. and Mrs. C. A. Hobbs of Hendersonville and was educated at Fassifern school and St. Genevieve-of-the Pines in Hendersonville. Mr. and Mrs. Wilkinson will make their home in the Lakewood Apartments, Kenilworth, Asheville. David is manager of the Superior Cleaning Company.

Willis Roswell Stevens is studying at Emory and Henry College, Va. He is taking a ministerial course and plans to return to Duke for graduate work after two years.